SAMS Teach Yourself

Macromedia® Dreamweaver® 8 in 24 Hours

Betsy Bruce

SAMS 800 East 96th Street, Indianapolis, Indiana, 46240 USA

Sams Teach Yourself Macromedia Dreamweaver 8 in 24 Hours

International Standard Book Number: 0-672-32753-8

Library of Congress Catalog Card Number: 2004097760

Printed in the United States of America

First Printing: October 2005

08 07 06 4 3

Trademarks

Warning and Disclaimer

Bulk Sales

Sams Publishing offers excellent discounts on this book when ordered in quantity for bulk purchases or special sales. For more information, please contact

U.S. Corporate and Government Sales
1-800-382-3419
corpsales@pearsontechgroup.com

For sales outside of the U.S., please contact

International Sales
international@pearsoned.com

Acquisitions Editor
Betsy Brown

Development Editor
Jonathan A. Steever

Managing Editor
Charlotte Clapp

Project Editor
Andy Beaster

Production Editor
Heather Wilkins

Indexer
Ken Johnson

Proofreader
Juli Cook

Technical Editor
Lynn Baus

Publishing Coordinator
Vanessa Evans

Designer
Gary Adair

Page Layout
Nonie Ratcliff

Contents at a Glance

Part V: Collecting User Data by Using Forms

Part VI: Organizing and Uploading a Project

Part VII: Appendixes

Table of Contents

About the Author

Betsy Bruce is an independent developer and consultant who specializes in creating eLearning applications using Dreamweaver, Authorware, and Flash. She was lead developer at the Cobalt Group in Seattle, where her team won the 2003 Macromedia Innovation in eLearning award and was Manager of Technical Services at MediaPro, Inc., where her team won many awards for the projects they developed. She is a Macromedia certified trainer for Dreamweaver, Contribute, Flash, and Authorware. Betsy received her B.S. from the University of Iowa and her M.A. in educational technology from San Diego State University. She is frequently a speaker at conferences on creating eLearning and using Dreamweaver. She is also the author of *eLearning with Dreamweaver MX: Creating Online Learning Applications* from New Riders Publishing. Born and raised in Iowa, Betsy now lives in Seattle with her partner and two Siberian huskies. Her website is located at www.betsybruce.com.

Dedication

This book is dedicated to my father, John Bruce, who was an outstanding educator, man, and father. He touched the lives of many young people, and I was blessed to be his daughter.

Acknowledgments

I'd especially like to thank the great group at Rick Steves' Europe Through the Back Door (www.ricksteves.com) for allowing me to use examples from their website. I was lucky enough to take two of their city tours (London and Paris) with my mother during the summer of 2005 and had a wonderful time. I'd also like to thank Jennifer Henry, Eric Tremmel, and Carol Macias for their artistic contributions to this book. Thanks to the Dreamweaver development team for creating such a great product, and thanks to the wonderful crew at Sams Publishing. Special thanks to Jon Steever, my development editor; Heather Wilkins, my copy editor; and Lynn Baus, my technical editor, for their thorough and skillful editing; I appreciate you all making my text so much better.

Thanks to Dana, Shasta, and Nikko for keeping me fed and happy in Seattle. And, as always, thanks to my mom, Pat, for her consistent support and love throughout my life.

We Want to Hear from You!

As the reader of this book, *you* are our most important critic and commentator. We value your opinion and want to know what we're doing right, what we could do better, what areas you'd like to see us publish in, and any other words of wisdom you're willing to pass our way.

You can email or write me directly to let me know what you did or didn't like about this book—as well as what we can do to make our books stronger.

Please note that I cannot help you with technical problems related to the topic of this book, and that due to the high volume of mail I receive, I might not be able to reply to every message.

When you write, please be sure to include this book's title and author as well as your name and phone or email address. I will carefully review your comments and share them with the author and editors who worked on the book.

E-mail: webdev@samspublishing.com

Mail: Mark Taber
Associate Publisher
Sams Publishing
800 East 96th Street
Indianapolis, IN 46240 USA

Reader Services

For more information about this book or another Sams title, visit our website at www.samspublishing.com. Type the ISBN (excluding hyphens) or the title of a book in the Search field to find the page you're looking for.

Introduction

"Ooooooo, Dreamweaver. I believe you can get me through the night." Remember that song by Gary Wright? Okay, some of you weren't born yet. The song brought up memories of seventh-grade dances for me. I'm glad that Dreamweaver, the software, came along and replaced that vision in my head. Dreamweaver, the software, has helped me through a number of nights developing websites and web applications!

I started using Dreamweaver when it first came out. Web page–editing tools were frustrating in that pre-Dreamweaver age. Many web developers were annoyed that some tools would rewrite or even delete some of the code they had just lovingly crafted. I remember one instance where I jumped up and down, stomping in my office, for almost five minutes after one tool deleted several hundred lines of JavaScript I had just written. So, many developers at that time preferred to use a simple text editor and write HTML and JavaScript by hand. I think Macromedia web developers must have been frustrated at that time, too, because they created a tool, Dreamweaver, that had all the features a web developer could want.

And Dreamweaver has continued to be the industry standard for web development tools.

What Is Dreamweaver 8?

Dreamweaver 8 is the newest version of Macromedia Dreamweaver, an award-winning HTML editor and web application–development tool. Some people do not exploit the more powerful features of Dreamweaver because they don't know about them. You will not be one of those people with this book in your hand!

Whether you use Mac OS X or Windows, you'll get the same robust set of features from Dreamweaver 8. The interfaces for the two operating systems look slightly different but you can produce the same beautiful, functional websites with either version.

Dreamweaver is excellent at quickly creating attractive web pages that include styled text, images, forms, frames, tables, and more. But Dreamweaver really shines when you need to make your web page do something. Dreamweaver excels at Dynamic HTML (DHTML), the web functionality that enables the user to interact with your web page. Don't know how to script? No problem! Dreamweaver includes **behaviors**, scripted functionality that you simply click to add to a certain object.

Dreamweaver 8 also excels at enabling you to create and apply standard Cascading Style Sheets (CSS) to format how your web pages display in the browser. Dreamweaver 8 gives you the capability to use CSS to style your web pages. You can also use Dreamweaver tools to design your page layout using CSS.

Who Should Use Dreamweaver 8?

Whether you are creating your very first web page or have decided to try web-editing software after coding by hand for years, you are going to love Macromedia Dreamweaver 8. Dreamweaver gives you the freedom to visually design the look of a web page and the power to make it act the way you want. Dreamweaver gives you the flexibility to create your own personal web page or an entire corporate intranet site.

Who Should Use This Book?

This book is for anyone now using Dreamweaver, as well as anyone who is planning to. If you are new to web development, this book will get you up to speed creating web pages and websites. If you are already a web developer, you'll find tips, tricks, and instructions to get all you can out of Dreamweaver 8.

This book covers creating static web pages in Dreamweaver 8, including forms, images, tables, page layout, interacting with users, managing your websites and many other topics. After you have mastered the 24 hours of content covered in this book, you might want to explore the advanced capabilities of Dreamweaver 8 to create web pages that connect to databases. Even if your ultimate goal is to create dynamic web pages based on databases, you'll benefit from knowing how Dreamweaver creates and maintains static web page content.

How to Use This Book

Each hour of this book represents a lesson that should take you approximately an hour to learn. The book is designed to get you productively working in Dreamweaver 8 as quickly as possible. There are numerous figures to illustrate the lessons in the book.

Code lines, commands, statements, and any other code-related terms appear in a `monospace` typeface. Placeholders (which stand for what you should actually type) appear in *`italic monospace`*.

Each lesson begins with a list of topics and an overview. The lesson ends with a summary, questions and answers, a quiz, and some exercises you can try on your own.

Within the lessons you'll find the following elements that provide additional information:

By the Way

By the Way notes give extra information on the current topic.

Did you Know?

Did You Know? tips offer advice or describe an additional way of accomplishing something.

Watch Out!

Watch Out! cautions signal you to be careful of potential problems and give you information on how to avoid or fix them.

As you read this book and work through the examples, remember: Have fun!

Betsy Bruce

PART I

Getting Started with Dreamweaver 8

HOUR 1

A World Wide Web of Dreamweaver Possibilities

What You'll Learn in This Hour:

- Types of web pages you can create with Dreamweaver
- View examples of text, images, hyperlinks, forms, multimedia, interactivity, and page layout design created in Dreamweaver
- How Dreamweaver can create reusable, updatable web pages and web page elements
- What the built-in file transfer tool can do

Maybe you've dreamed of sharing your wedding pictures, creative writing, postcard designs, genealogical research, or a list of your CD collection with friends, family, or the entire world! Or, maybe you want to sell T-shirts, cookie mixes, books, or note cards online. You might need to create a website for your small company or the large company or public agency that employs you. These are all excellent applications for Macromedia Dreamweaver.

I've received hundreds of emails from readers around the world who, like yourself, purchased this book in order to learn Dreamweaver. Some of these readers send me links to the websites they've created using this book and I'm thrilled to view these. Other readers are students who use this book in a course on HTML and web development. Please keep those links coming!

What Can You Do With Dreamweaver?

Dreamweaver is the most popular professional web creation tool and you are in excellent company as a user of this exceptional software. Many large corporations standardize on Dreamweaver as their web development tool of choice. Dreamweaver is also a popular tool for independent web developers who work on websites for their clients. Dreamweaver appeals to a broad variety of users, including experienced and inexperienced website developers, coders (those who like to write HTML), developers who specialize in application development in languages such as ColdFusion and ASP.Net, and those who have never heard of these application languages. Dreamweaver also works similarly on Macintosh and Windows-based computers and is popular on both platforms.

Personally, I create a variety of different types of websites in Dreamweaver: my consulting business website, websites for clients, e-Learning courses, and a small e-commerce website. I can keep all these websites defined in Dreamweaver so I can quickly view and edit any of the web pages they contain. In a few hours, you will be able to do this, too.

The foundation of Dreamweaver is Hypertext Markup Language (HTML), a language used to format content to view over the World Wide Web via software called a web browser. But you don't need to know HTML to get started using Dreamweaver. I suggest to all of my students and to you, the reader of this book, that learning some HTML will help you become a more professional and flexible web page author. Hour 6, "Getting Down and Dirty with HTML," introduces you to viewing and editing HTML in Dreamweaver.

Should I Learn Dreamweaver or HTML First?

This chicken-or-the-egg-type question comes up often when I speak with people who want to learn about web design and development. I think that it's best to learn a tool such as Dreamweaver first and then expand your knowledge of HTML as you complete real-world projects. You will have more context for the HTML you are learning after you have a basic understanding of Dreamweaver.

Website Examples

If you are new to web development, you might not know some of the possibilities available to you in Dreamweaver. This hour explores examples of the types of elements you can add to your website no matter what its topic or purpose. Most people who are interested in creating web pages have spent some time looking at web pages in a browser. Now that you are learning Dreamweaver and HTML, you'll begin to look at web pages differently: Instead of reading a column of text you'll now think, "How can I create a column of text in Dreamweaver?"

One of the best ways to learn is by examining examples of web pages you find while browsing the Web. Most browser software has a Source or Page Source command (under the View menu) that enables you to view the HTML code of a web page. Even better, you can actually save a web page to your hard drive by using the Save Page As or the Save As command under the browser's File menu. After you've saved the web page, you can open the file in Dreamweaver and examine its structure. This is a great way to figure out how some other web page author created an effect. If you are a beginner, you probably won't understand everything in the web page but this is still a great way to learn by emulating others.

Watch Out!

Copyright Laws and HTML

Remember that there are copyright laws protecting the intellectual property of companies and individuals, including websites. You cannot copy the HTML or take images from other people's websites.

My friends at Rick Steves' Europe Through the Back Door, www.ricksteves.com, an international travel company located in Edmonds, Washington, have been kind enough to let me show you examples from their exceptional website. You might have seen one of Rick Steves' travel shows on your local Public Broadcasting Service (PBS) television station. Rick Steves' Europe recently revamped its website using **Cascading Style Sheets** (CSS) and modern page layout techniques enabling staff to quickly update the entire site while offering a clean, easy-to-navigate website for their users.

Basic Web Page Elements: Text, Images, and Hyperlinks

Most web pages have at least three minimal elements: text, images, and hyperlinks. Figure 1.1 shows that the Rick Steves' Europe **home page**, the web page that is the entry point for the website, contains only these elements, plus a search box in the upper-right corner of the page. These three elements are the foundation of most websites, providing information (text) along with graphical support (images), plus a method to navigate to other pages (hyperlinks).

Notice that there are several styles of text in Figure 1.1. The two columns in the middle of the page use text that is presented in a standard, highly-readable font style and size. Several words on the web page are in bold, making those words stand out on the page. The caption text under the picture of Rick on the left is a slightly smaller font size as is the text in the far right column under the "What's New" heading. There is also text at the top of the page, "Welcome to Rick Steves' Europe" that isn't text at all; it's text that is an image.

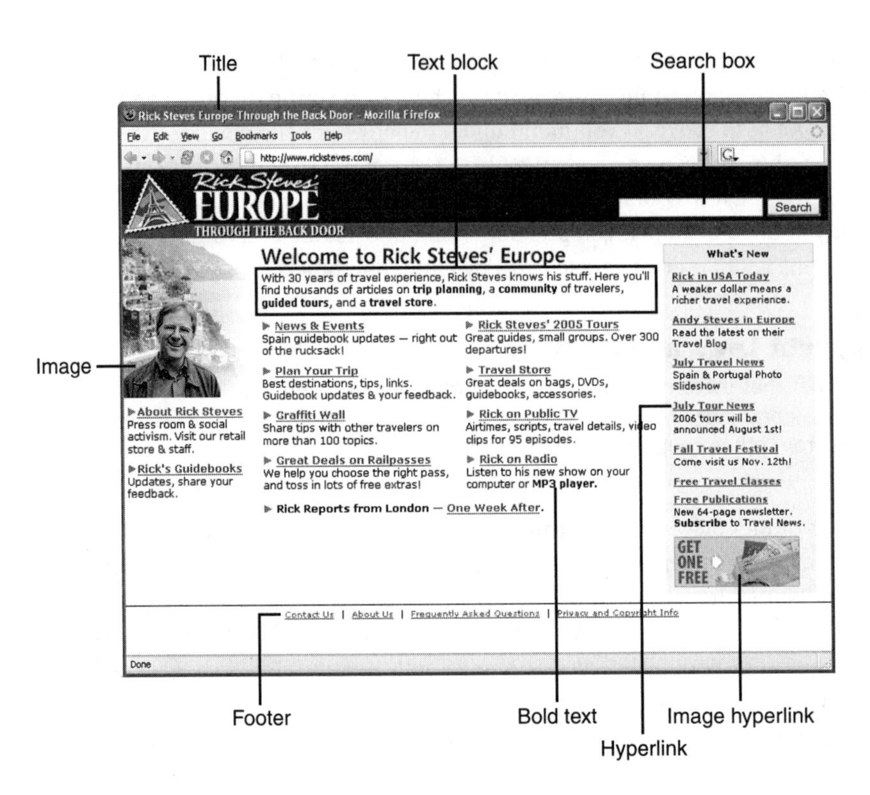

FIGURE 1.1 The Rick Steves' Europe Through the Back Door homepage contains text, images, hyperlinks, and a search box.

By the Way

About Choosing Fonts

Fonts were traditionally developed for print but several new fonts have been developed to make them easy to read on a computer screen. Verdana and Trebuchet are two popular screen fonts. You can find out more at www.microsoft.com/typography.

There are also several images displayed in Figure 1.1. In web pages, images are always external files that are incorporated into the web page by the browser. The logo in the upper-left corner of the page appears to be a single image but is actually two images in order to facilitate the design with the lighter colored line at the bottom of the logo (it's a red line when you look at the actual web page in color). Dividing an image into smaller pieces is called slicing and is discussed in Hour 8, "Optimizing and Creating Images." The two images are then butted up against one another so they appear to be a single image on the web page.

There are numerous hyperlinks in Figure 1.1. Clicking on these hyperlinks in the live website enables you to jump to different parts of the Rick Steves' Europe website. By default, hyperlinks appear in blue text and are underlined but you can change this using CSS. Rick Steves' Europe standardized on hyperlinks that are initially blue and underlined but when you roll your cursor over the link the underline disappears. All of the hyperlinks in the website have this same behavior because the CSS rule controlling this is in an external style sheet that is linked to every web page in the site. Creating types of hyperlinks is covered in Hour 5, "Setting Lots o' Links: Hyperlinks, Anchors, and Mailto Links," and formatting using CSS is covered in Hour 16, "Formatting Web Pages Using Cascading Style Sheets."

In the lower-left corner of Figure 1.1 there is an image with the text "Get a FREE DVD!" This is an image that is also a hyperlink. Dreamweaver adds the hyperlink to an image when a web address is entered into the image's properties. Dreamweaver automatically wraps the HTML tag that creates a hyperlink around the tag that displays an image. You can even define a small section of an image as a hyperlink by creating an image map. Hour 7, "Displaying Images," introduces you to image properties and the different types of images you can display in a web page. Hour 9, "Creating Image Maps and Navigation Bars," demonstrates how to add image maps to web pages.

Page Layout: Tables and Cascading Style Sheets

Page layout, the design and positioning of text and images on the web page, often requires a lot of thought, time, and experimentation. The Rick Steves' Europe website has a clean page style that makes it easy to view in browser windows of various sizes. The page layout for this website was accomplished by combining two different page layout methods: table layout, covered in Hour 13, "Designing Page Layout Using Tables," and CSS, covered in Hour 16. Figure 1.2 shows the Rick Steves' Europe home page open in Dreamweaver so that the table borders and table column values are visible. The CSS Styles panel is open on the right side of the screen displaying a list of the **CSS rules** applied to this web page.

People who are accustomed to using page layout software such as FrameMaker, InDesign, or Quark are often shocked to learn that there is no way to position an image on a web page at an exact location by simply giving the image a pixel location. This is a limitation of HTML and not of Dreamweaver itself. Dreamweaver has a special mode, covered in Hour 13, enabling you to create page designs using HTML tables so you can position elements anywhere on the web page. Most websites use tables within other tables, called **nested tables**, to create the page layout.

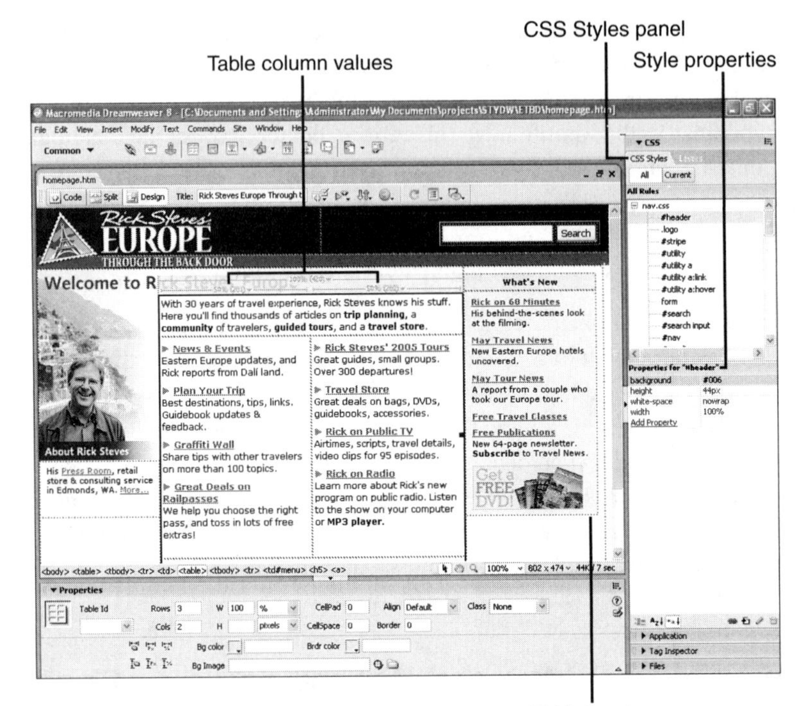

FIGURE 1.2
The Rick Steves' Europe Through the Back Door home page uses tables and CSS to design the page layout.

Did you Know?

> ### Exporting from Page Layout Software
> You can export web pages from most software programs, including Word, and then use Dreamweaver to clean up and edit the results. Do a test on a representative page first before you decide whether this method works for the content with which you are working.

CSS is the most recent method of designing page layouts for web pages and it is still an evolving technology. Although you can create complicated page layout designs entirely with CSS (see the website www.csszengarden.com for some great examples), it might be difficult for the beginning Dreamweaver user to accomplish. It is often easiest to use tables for much of the layout and then accomplish other text format and background color tasks using CSS.

CSS enables you to format the way text appears, how various HTML tags appear (such as the underlined hyperlink example earlier this hour), along with how various layout elements of a page are positioned on the web page. Figure 1.2 displays the CSS Styles panel on the right side; this is where all of the CSS rules are defined. All of the rules are listed under the external style sheet name `nav.css` showing that these rules are stored in an external style sheet that can be attached to multiple web pages. The great thing about this structure is that you can change something in the external style sheet and have that change distributed to every web page that is attached to the external style sheet.

Did you Know?

Storing Code in External Files

The great thing about storing CSS rules in external files is that you can share the rules amongst multiple web pages. This same concept is used with images, too. You only need a single image file but you can reference that same image in multiple pages. You can also store JavaScript in external files and share it with multiple web pages in a website.

As web browsers are incorporated in devices large and small, people might be viewing your web pages at various resolutions. Figure 1.3 shows a picture of a BlackBerry 7100t web-enabled wireless phone displaying a web page. Creating flexible page layouts enables viewers using different devices to have a pleasant viewing experience on your website. A savvy web developer can even use **JavaScript**, the primary scripting language for web browsers, in order to deliver different external CSS files to different types of browsers or different devices.

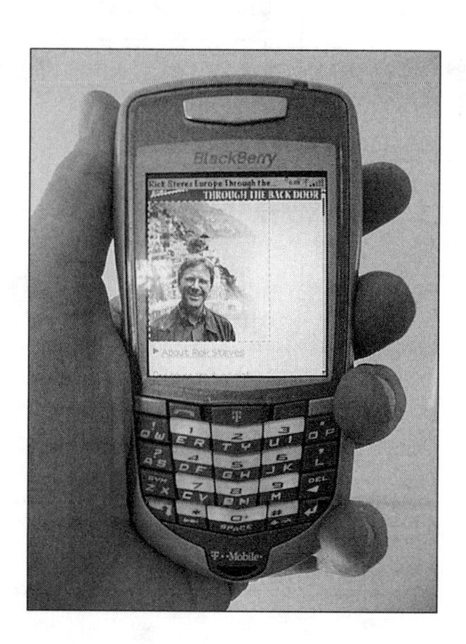

FIGURE 1.3
Small devices, such as this BlackBerry 7100t wireless phone, can display web pages.

Forms: Collecting Data for E-Commerce, Newsletters, or Anything Else

Many websites have a business purpose for exchanging information with visitors, whether it be selling automobiles (www.acura.com), auctioning off a ticket to a Neil

Diamond concert (www.ebay.com), giving people a plan for healthy diet and exercise (www.mypyramid.gov), or selling a design on a T-shirt, coffee mug, or mousepad (www.cafepress.com). All of these websites offer viewers the option of entering information into **forms** in order to purchase goods or receive information. Forms enable websites to become a two-way conduit as a viewer not only views information on the website but can also send information back.

The Rick Steves' Europe website has several web pages that use forms. The search box on the home page has already been discussed. The Search button triggers a script that exists on the **web server**, the computer where the finished website files are stored. This script searches for the words entered into the search box on all of the web pages in the site and then returns search results for the user to view. The search form shown in Figure 1.4 consists of a text field and a submit button, two of the form elements that will be discussed in Hour 18, "Creating a Form and Collecting Data."

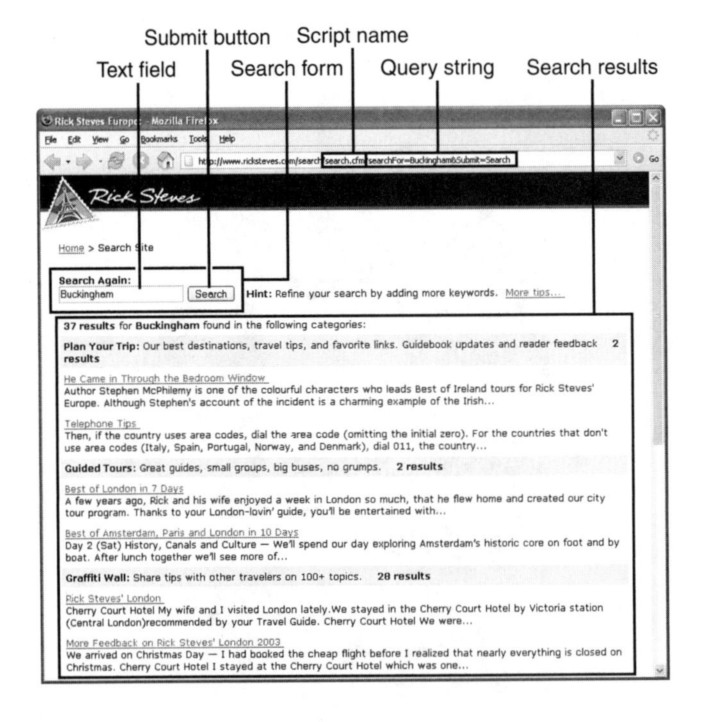

FIGURE 1.4
A search form enables the viewer to enter text and then submit it to a script which returns results.

Creating scripts is an advanced topic that is beyond the scope of this book on Dreamweaver but examples of scripting languages and locations to download scripts are discussed in Hour 19, "Introduction to Scripts: Sending and Reacting to Form Data." Rick Steves' Europe uses ColdFusion, Macromedia scripting, and application development software. You can tell that the script is written for

ColdFusion because the file extension is `.cfm`. Creating a script to search a website is the tiny tip of the iceberg of ColdFusion functionality.

Rick Steves' Europe also uses ColdFusion to dynamically display items in its travel store (travelstore.ricksteves.com). This **dynamic web page**, where items' descriptions and images are displayed based on records in a database, can also be created in Dreamweaver. After you master the 24 hours in this book, you might decide to advance to learning a server application language, such as ColdFusion. It's perfectly realistic, however, to continue creating **static web pages** (the opposite of dynamic web pages), such as the ones described in this book, and be a successful web page author.

Scripting for Forms

Although creating forms is fairly easy, creating the scripts to make those forms function is complicated.

Watch Out!

At the end of a shopping experience, such as in the Rick Steves' Europe travel store, an HTML form is used to collect information about the purchaser. Figure 1.5 displays a form that includes text fields and drop-down menus (to collect the state and country information). An asterisk (*) is a common way to signify that a text field must be filled out in order to submit the form. Dreamweaver has a Validate Form behavior, scripted in JavaScript, to provide this form validation functionality (see Hour 19).

Multimedia

Many websites include movies, audio, animations, virtual reality movies, and other **multimedia** elements. These elements require that you download and install a **player** application, such as the Flash, QuickTime, or Real players, in order to see or hear the multimedia files. Web pages created in Dreamweaver can include the web page address where the user must download a player and the browser may trigger this download automatically, making it seamless for the user. As more and more people have access to higher **bandwidth** connections, a greater number of websites include multimedia files that require more bandwidth.

Installed Player Applications

Often an operating system (such as Windows XP or Macintosh OS X) comes with several popular multimedia player applications already installed. For instance, the Macromedia Flash player comes installed on most computers. And players are also included when you install the major browsers. Sometimes, however, computers in a corporate environment have a customized version of the operating system that might have players striped out.

By the Way

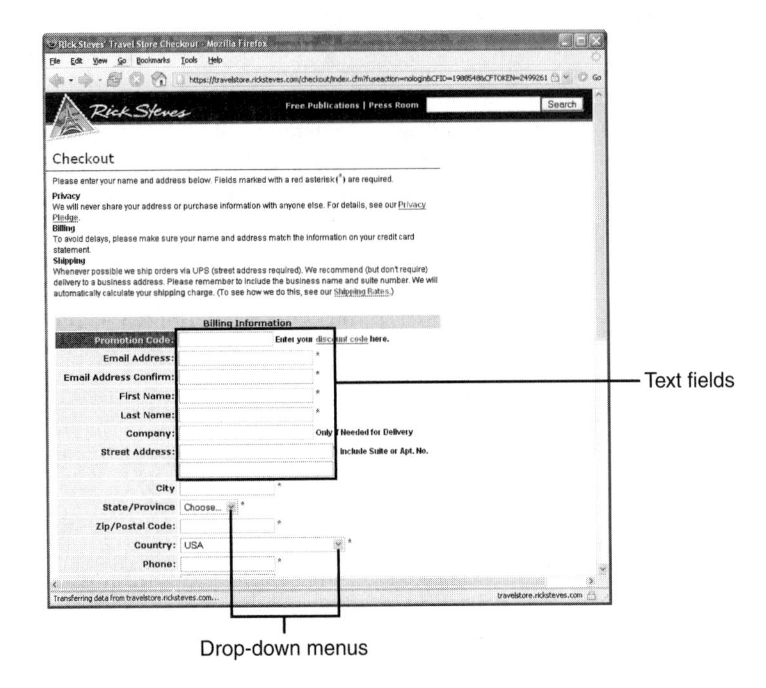

FIGURE 1.5
This form collects information about the purchaser and there is a script that validates the form, making sure that all required information is entered before the form is processed.

The Rick Steves' Europe site provides clips from Rick's travel television shows on the site, shown in Figure 1.6. These clips require that free software, either RealPlayer (www.real.com) or Windows Media Player (www.microsoft.com/windows/windowsmedia), is installed on your computer. When a viewer clicks on the link to the multimedia file, a software player opens up on top of the browser and begins playing the multimedia file.

Some web pages, such as the Macromedia home page shown in Figure 1.7, embed multimedia files right into the web page. In this case, a Macromedia Flash movie containing video, audio, and animation effects plays when you initially load the web page... if you have the Flash player installed, that is! But a large majority of computers have the ubiquitous Flash player so most viewers are capable of seeing Flash movies. Although Macromedia Flash software is required to create Flash movies, Dreamweaver is capable of inserting, configuring, and previewing Flash movies. Hour 10, "Adding Flash and Other Multimedia to a Web Page," explains how to add Flash along with other types of multimedia to a web page.

Interactivity

You can add JavaScript, called Behaviors in Dreamweaver, to a web page without knowing how to write JavaScript. Behaviors enable you to capture the user clicking on the web page, rolling the cursor over an element on the web page, or many other events that the browser can detect. I specialize in creating e-learning with Dreamweaver, and I use Dreamweaver Behaviors to walk the learner through the steps required for a specific software task. For instance, Figure 1.8 displays a tutorial on creating CSS Styles in Dreamweaver requiring the learner to click on a certain area of the screen. When they click on the correct area, or hot spot, they are automatically taken to the next page in the tutorial; if they click in an incorrect area they receive an error message.

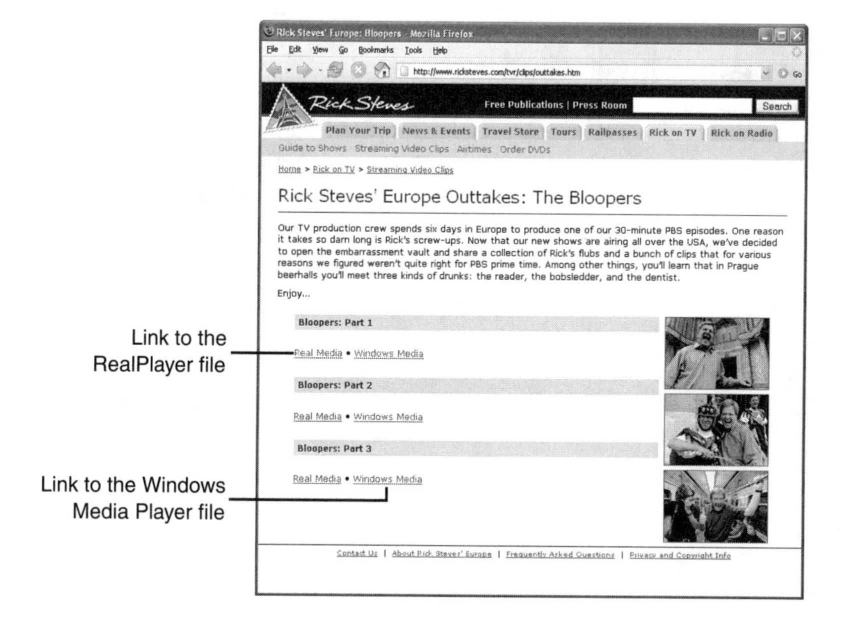

FIGURE 1.6 A web page can link to multimedia files, often offering the viewer a choice of software to view the files.

In the tutorial example in Figure 1.8, I used the Go to URL behavior triggered by the learner clicking on a **transparent image** (a GIF image that is transparent); this is a common technique for capturing a user's click on a certain region of the screen. In Hour 17, "Adding Interactivity with Behaviors," this behavior and several others are discussed and demonstrated. You might not have a need for some of the interactive capabilities of Dreamweaver, but you'll probably at least want to use the Swap Image behavior to create a rollover effect on an image, where the image changes when the user rolls his cursor over it.

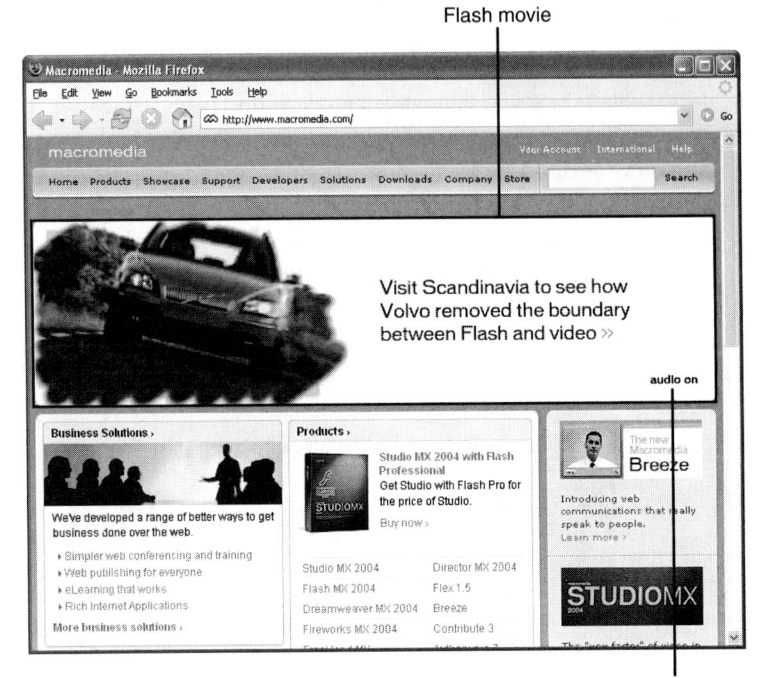

FIGURE 1.7
Flash movies, and other types of multimedia files, can be inserted into a web page.

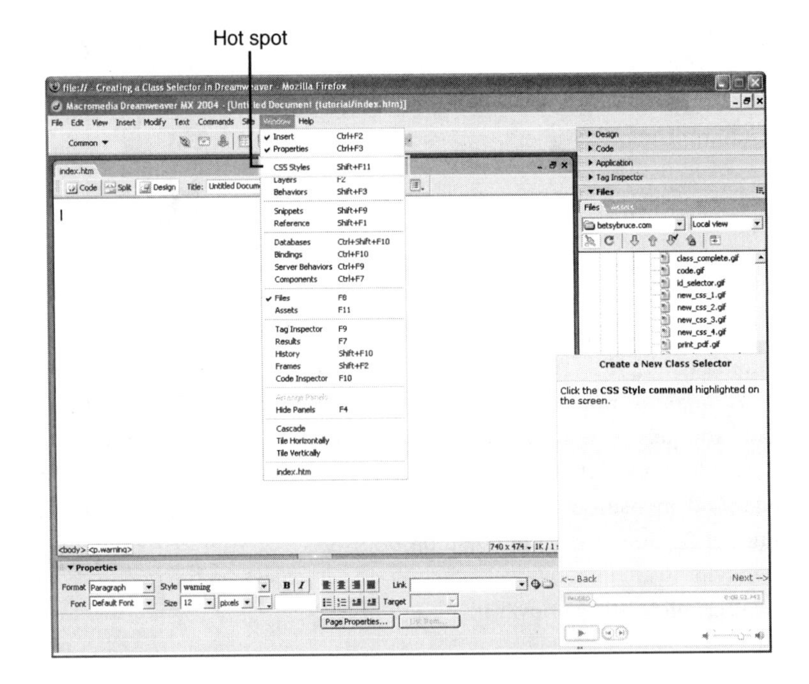

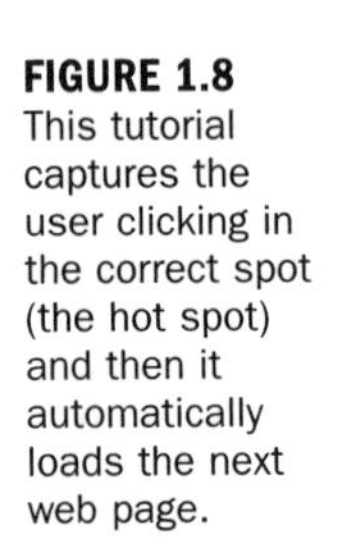

FIGURE 1.8
This tutorial captures the user clicking in the correct spot (the hot spot) and then it automatically loads the next web page.

Did you Know?

Creating Rollover Effects

Dreamweaver's Swap Image behavior can be used to create the effect where an image changes when the user rolls his mouse over the image. The behavior can also be added by using Dreamweaver's Rollover Image object—it adds the behavior for you.

The Rick Steves' Europe makes use of Dreamweaver's Open Browser Window behavior, shown in Figure 1.9, to open a custom-sized browser window. The new browser window pops up displaying a map and a hyperlink that triggers printing the map; the custom window opens without the usual browser navigation and menu toolbars. There are a number of other web pages in the Rick Steves' Europe site where this behavior is used to pop up a new browser window with additional information so the viewer can have both windows open at the same time, examining the additional information available in the new browser window.

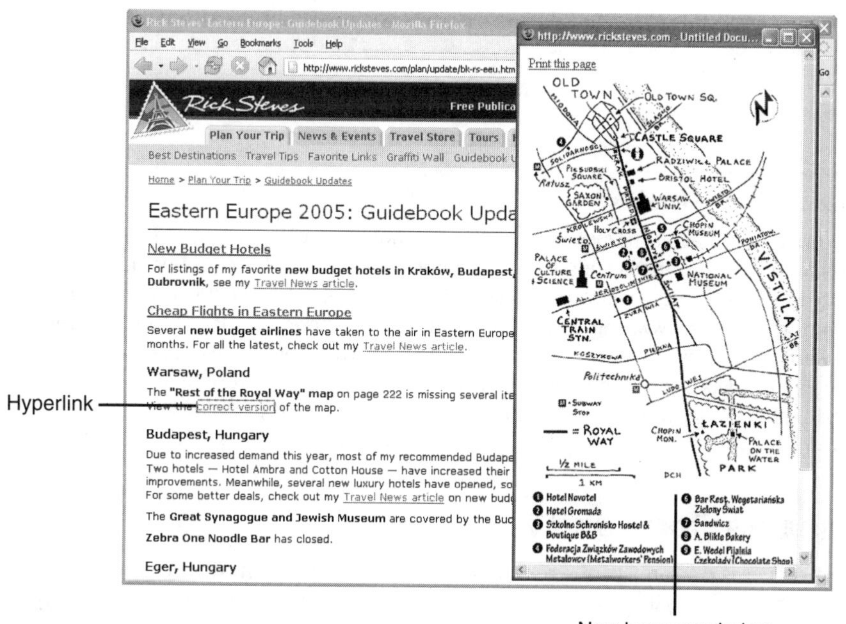

FIGURE 1.9 A hyperlink on this web page uses Dreamweaver's Open Browser Window behavior to open a new browser window in a set size.

Upload a Website to the Web

You can create web pages for days, weeks, months, or even years but eventually you'll either want or need to put them on a web server somewhere and share them with other people. You don't need another piece of software to accomplish this:

Dreamweaver has fully functional file transfer protocol (FTP) software built right in, enabling you to connect to a remote web server and upload your files from Dreamweaver. Figure 1.10 shows Dreamweaver's expanded Files panel connected to a remote web server, covered in Hour 2, "A Tour of Dreamweaver." The remote site files on the server are visible on the left and the local files are visible on the right side of the screen.

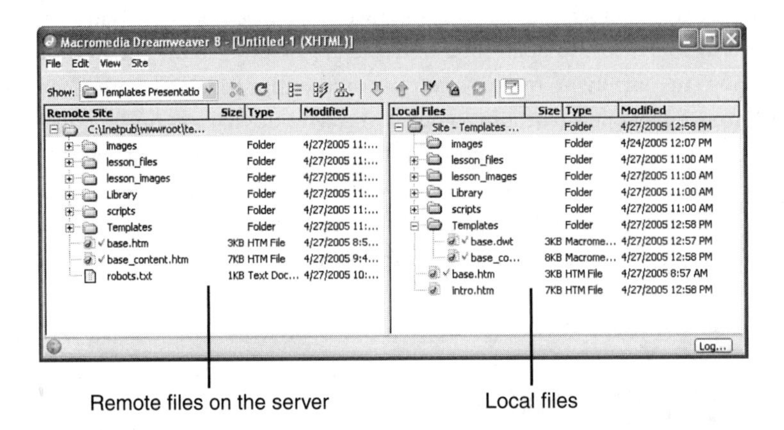

FIGURE 1.10 Dreamweaver has built-in FTP software that enables the transfer of web pages up to a web server.

Did you Know?

Finding Web Hosting

If you don't yet have a home for your remote, public website, you can find many websites rating the thousands of hosting companies vying for your business. You can type *web hosting reviews* into a search engine such as Google (www.google.com) or check out www.web-hosting-reviews.org. You need to specify the features you want on your website and what type of server you'd prefer (usually a choice of Windows or UNIX). You might want to wait to make your choice until you've finished this book so you understand more of the possibilities of the Web.

Reusable Code and Files

Dreamweaver is an industrial strength web development tool that enables you to work on individual web pages but also on very large websites. Many websites, such as the Rick Steves' Europe website, have thousands of web pages and managing all of those pages, especially when a change is required, can be a daunting task. Dreamweaver has reusable and updatable pages, called **Templates**, that can be used as a basis for a web page. Web pages created from a template maintain a link to the original template, so when the original is updated the changes can be propagated to all of the web pages based on the template. Dreamweaver Templates are covered in Hour 24, "Creating Reusable Web Pages: Using Templates."

Dreamweaver also offers another type of reusable element, called a Library Item, which inserts only a portion of a web page. Like Templates, Library Items maintain a link to the parent Library Item and can be updated throughout an entire website. In the Rick Steves' Europe website, the footer at the bottom of each page is a Library Item (shown in Figure 1.11). This enables the web developers to add additional information to the footer in the future, save the Library Item, and update every page in the website automatically without opening each web page. In the Property inspector, at the bottom of the Dreamweaver window, you can see that the properties for a Library Item are displayed.

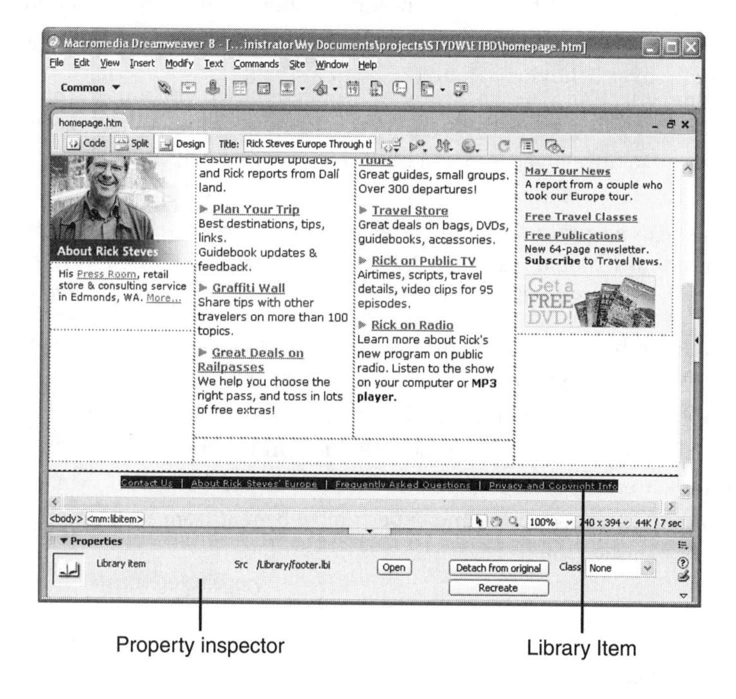

FIGURE 1.11 Dreamweaver Library Items can be inserted into web pages and then updated later without opening each web page.

Summary

In this hour, you saw examples of both basic and advanced functionalities of Dreamweaver. You examined a travel site home page, identifying blocks of text, formatted text, images, text in images, and hyperlinks. You saw examples of forms and were introduced to how scripts work in the background to process what users enter into forms. You saw examples of multimedia either launched from a hyperlink on a web page or embedded directly into the web page. Examples of interactivity, in an e-learning tutorial and on the travel site, demonstrated what you can accomplish with Dreamweaver behaviors. And you were introduced to Dreamweaver file transfer capabilities and using reusable elements to help manage large websites.

Q&A

Q. ***Do I need to understand how to accomplish everything that Dreamweaver can do before I start working on a website?***

A. You really only need to understand the basics of Dreamweaver: how to work with text, images, hyperlinks, and the Dreamweaver interface. You'll also want to understand how to design a page layout for your web pages. Then you can learn some of the specialized functions that are necessary for the website you want to create. For instance, if you are creating an e-commerce website, you'll want to learn about forms (Hours 18 and 19). If you are interested in creating an interactive website, you'll want to understand Dreamweaver Behaviors (Hour 17).

The best way to learn is by doing, so don't be afraid to dig in and create web pages in Dreamweaver. You can always improve or edit the pages later.

Q. ***I work with several programmers who say that Dreamweaver is a waste of money, that I should just learn HTML and create web pages by typing HTML tags into a text editor. Is that really a better way to create web pages?***

A. That might be the ideal way to create web pages for your programmer friends but it takes a long time to learn HTML and even longer to learn how to program and write the JavaScript that Dreamweaver Behaviors contain. I think that I can create robust and solid web pages in Dreamweaver much faster, with fewer errors, than anyone who hand codes. To each their own, of course, but I think that beginners and experts alike benefit from the built-in capabilities of Dreamweaver.

Workshop

Quiz

1. What is the name of the web page element that a user clicks to navigate to another web page?
2. What are the two major methods of designing a web page layout in Dreamweaver?
3. What is the Dreamweaver feature called that enables you to add JavaScript and interactivity to your web pages?

Quiz Answers

1. A hyperlink is the web page element that navigates the user to another web page.

2. You can use either Cascading Style Sheets, table layout, or a combination of both to design a web page layout.

3. Dreamweaver Behaviors enable you to add JavaScript and interactivity to your web pages.

Exercises

1. Go to the Macromedia website (www.macromedia.com) and search for the words *showcase* and *Dreamweaver*; a search box is in the upper-right corner of the home page. Select the result "Showcase : Showcase Finder : Dreamweaver" to display a list of case studies, interactive content, and sites of the day that are excellent examples of using Dreamweaver. Read the case studies and examine the screenshots of the websites trying to identify different web page elements and how the pages were designed.

   Macromedia occasionally redesigns the Macromedia website but these showcases should be available somewhere on the website.

2. Go to Web Pages That Suck (www.webpagesthatsuck.com) and read some of the articles and critiques of other web pages so you know what to avoid!

3. Go to CSS Zen Garden (www.csszengarden.com) and click on some of the design links on the right side of the home page. Do you notice that the content in each design's web page is exactly the same? Only the CSS changes for each design. Pretty interesting!

HOUR 2

A Tour of Dreamweaver

What You'll Learn in This Hour:

- What hardware and software you will need to run Dreamweaver
- How to install the Dreamweaver demo
- How to use the Dreamweaver user interface
- How to manage panels, inspectors, and windows

I'm sure you are itching to begin creating dazzling and fun websites, the type that you'll show off to your friends, family members, and co-workers. Or maybe you've been assigned the task of creating a website in Dreamweaver for your job. First, however, you need to understand the Dreamweaver interface and the numerous functions that are going to help you be successful as a web developer. Understanding the Dreamweaver user interface enables you to understand the instructions in the rest of this book.

If you have used other Macromedia tools, you'll recognize the standard Macromedia user interface elements, such as panel groups and inspectors. If you have used previous versions of Dreamweaver, you should quickly skim this hour to see what exciting changes and updates Macromedia has made to the new version of Dreamweaver. This hour provides an important orientation to the concepts you'll use in later hours to create web pages.

Acquainting Yourself with Dreamweaver

Dreamweaver is a complete web development environment and Hypertext Markup Language (HTML) editor, an authoring tool, a dynamic web page development tool, and a website management tool, all rolled into one. Web pages are created using HTML, but you can do many things without ever laying your eyes on any HTML. If you want to produce professional-quality web pages, including scripting, Dreamweaver makes it easy to do so.

HTML is the language of web pages. It consists mainly of paired tags contained in angle brackets (<>). The tags surround objects on a web page, such as text, or stand on their own. For instance, the HTML code to make text bold looks like this: `<strong>bold text</strong>`; notice how the tags are paired, one before and one after the text they affect. The ending tag of the paired tag always begins with a forward slash. Very few tags, such as the tag used to insert an image into a web page, are single tags: `<img src="smile.gif">`.

Dreamweaver is a WYSIWYG (what you see is what you get) web page editor that is extremely powerful while also being easy to use. You can create new websites by using Dreamweaver, and you can import and edit existing websites, too. Dreamweaver does not change or rearrange your code. One of Dreamweaver's most popular features has always been that it leaves existing sites intact; the folks at Macromedia, the company that creates Dreamweaver, call this feature **Roundtrip HTML**.

Dreamweaver is also an authoring tool. What do I mean by *authoring tool*? **Authoring tools** enable you to create a complete application that includes interactivity. Dreamweaver can be used as simply an HTML editor, and it can also be used to create multimedia applications. You can author an experience for your viewers complete with audio, animation, video, and interactions.

Installing the Software

A standard Windows or Macintosh installation program installs Dreamweaver. The installation program creates all the necessary directories and files needed to run Dreamweaver on your hard drive.

Macromedia Extension Manager

Dreamweaver also installs the Macromedia Extension Manager, a program that helps you install Dreamweaver extensions that you can download from the Internet, many of which are free. You'll learn more about Dreamweaver extensions in Hour 22, "Customizing Dreamweaver."

Hardware and Software Requirements

Table 2.1 lists the hardware and software required to run Dreamweaver.

TABLE 2.1 Hardware and Software Requirements for Dreamweaver

Windows	Macintosh
Pentium 3 (or equivalent) and later with 800 MHz or greater	G3 and later with 600 MHz or greater
Windows 2000 or Windows XP	Mac OS X 10.3 or 10.4
256 MB RAM (1 GB recommended to run more than one Studio 8 product simultaneously)	256 MB RAM (1 GB recommended to run more than one Studio 8 product simultaneously)
650MB available disk space	300MB available disk space
1024 x 768, 16-bit display (32-bit recommended)	1024 x 768, 16-bit display (32-bit recommended)

Getting the Demo Version

Macromedia offers a demo version of the software that you can evaluate before you decide to purchase Dreamweaver. You can download the time-limited demo at www.macromedia.com/software/dreamweaver/trial.

Exploring the Dreamweaver Work Area

When you first open Dreamweaver in Windows, you are given the opportunity to choose either the Designer workspace or the Coder workspace. The Coder workspace docks all of the Dreamweaver panels on the left of the screen while the Designer workspace docks all of the panels on the right of the screen. The Macintosh version of Dreamweaver automatically gives you the Designer workspace. I suggest that you pick the Designer workspace because all the figures and examples in this book refer to that workspace configuration. If you initially select the Coder workspace and then want to change to the Designer workspace, you can do so by selecting Window, Workspace Layout, Designer.

The Start Page

Prior to opening any files, Dreamweaver displays a box with a green bar across the top, called the Start page (shown in Figure 2.1). The Start page lists common Dreamweaver tasks, such as Open a Recent Item, Create New, and Create from Samples. At the bottom of the Start page are links to the Dreamweaver Quick Tour and the Dreamweaver Tutorial. Clicking the image of the Dreamweaver box takes you to the Macromedia website for up-to-date information on Dreamweaver, including tips and special offers. Whenever you don't have web pages open in Dreamweaver, you will see the Start page displayed.

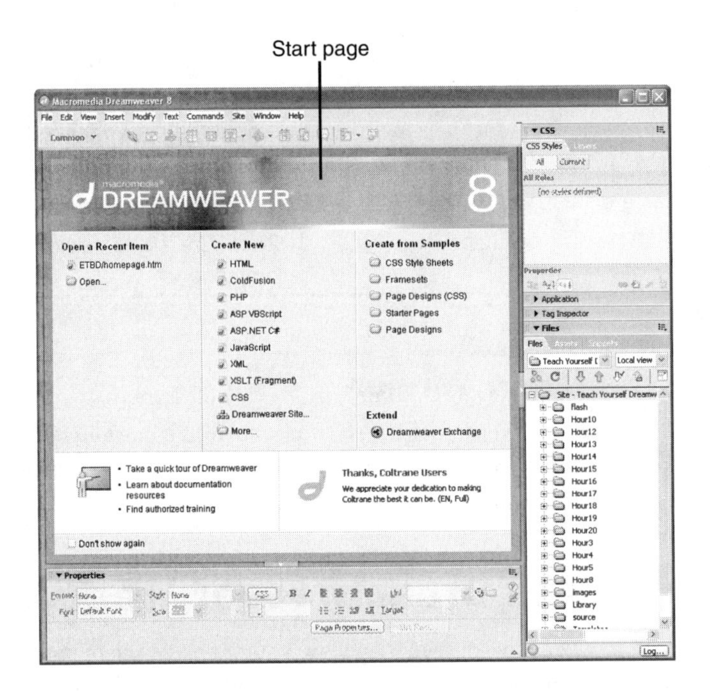

FIGURE 2.1
The Dreamweaver Start page.

You can configure Dreamweaver to not display this Start page by clicking Preferences, General, Show Start Page, as shown in Figure 2.2. You'll explore many other Dreamweaver preferences throughout this book. When you change this preference setting, you need to restart Dreamweaver in order to see the change.

By the Way

Macintosh Preferences Under the Dreamweaver Menu

Dreamweaver's Macintosh version presents the Preferences command under the Dreamweaver menu, the first menu in the Menu bar, instead of under the Edit menu.

The Start page appears in an important part of Dreamweaver called the Document window. The Document window displays a web page approximately as it will appear in a web browser. The Document window is bordered on the right by Panel groups (in the Designer workspace), as shown in Figure 2.3. These Panel groups contain the commands you use to modify and organize web pages and web page elements. The Document window, the Panel groups, and other elements, which you'll explore in a few minutes, are grouped together into an integrated interface if you are working in the Windows operating system.

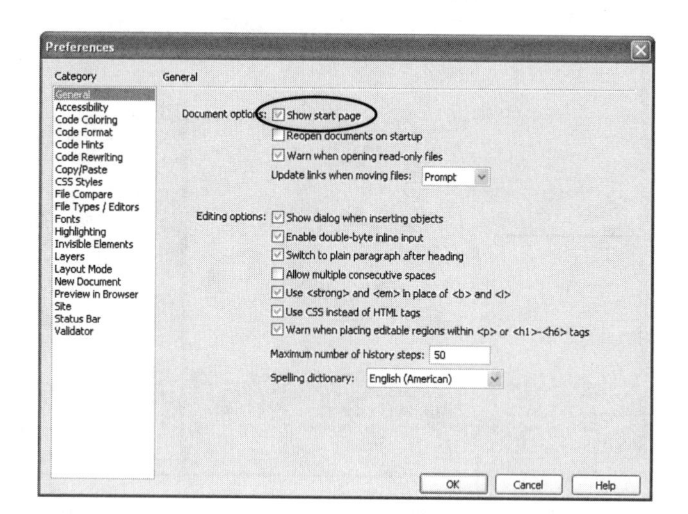

FIGURE 2.2
Turn on and off the Start page in the General category of Dreamweaver preferences.

When you open Dreamweaver 8 for Macintosh, you also see the Document window displaying the Start page, as shown in Figure 2.4. The Macintosh version of Dreamweaver 8 has panels that float on top of the Document window. The floating panels, launched from the Window menu, can be moved to any location on the desktop. The Mac and Windows versions of Dreamweaver look slightly different from each other but have the same features and functionality.

The Menu Bar

Some people prefer to use menu commands (I like keyboard shortcuts) and some people prefer to click icons. For the menu crowd, this section describes the organization of Dreamweaver's menus. The File and Edit menus (see Figure 2.5) are standard in most programs. The File menu contains commands for opening, closing, saving, importing, and exporting files. The Edit menu contains the Cut, Copy, and Paste commands, along with the Find and Replace command and the Preferences command (in Windows). Many elements of the Dreamweaver user interface and its operation can be configured with the Preferences command.

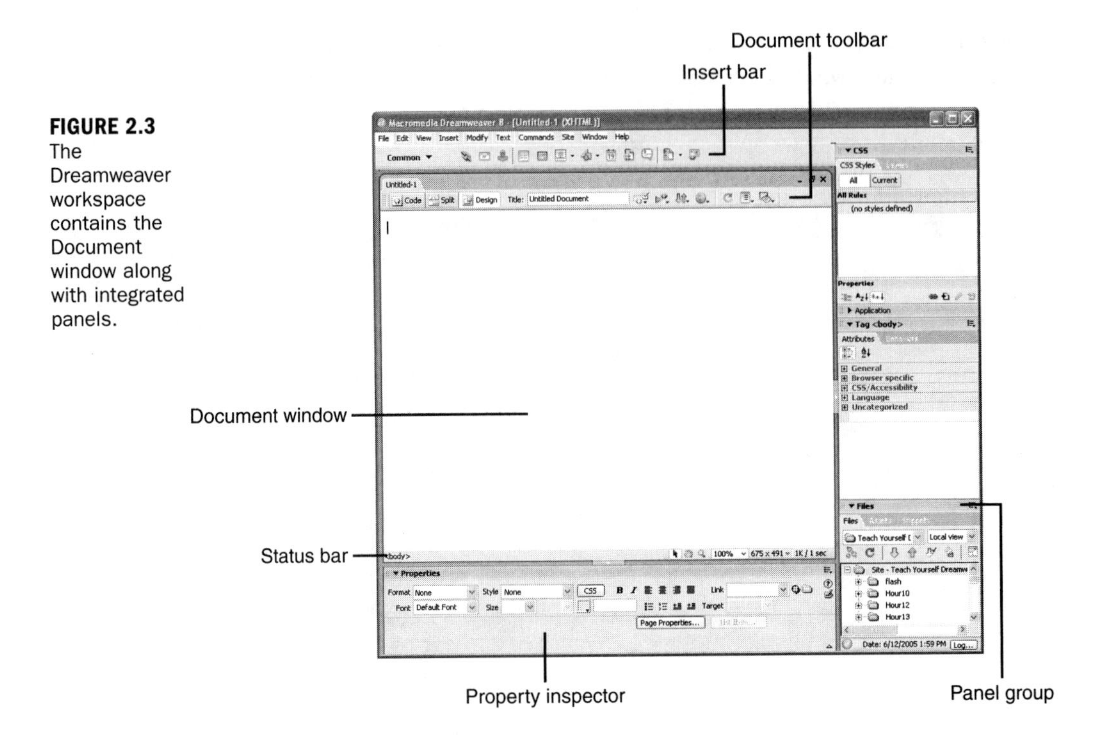

FIGURE 2.3 The Dreamweaver workspace contains the Document window along with integrated panels.

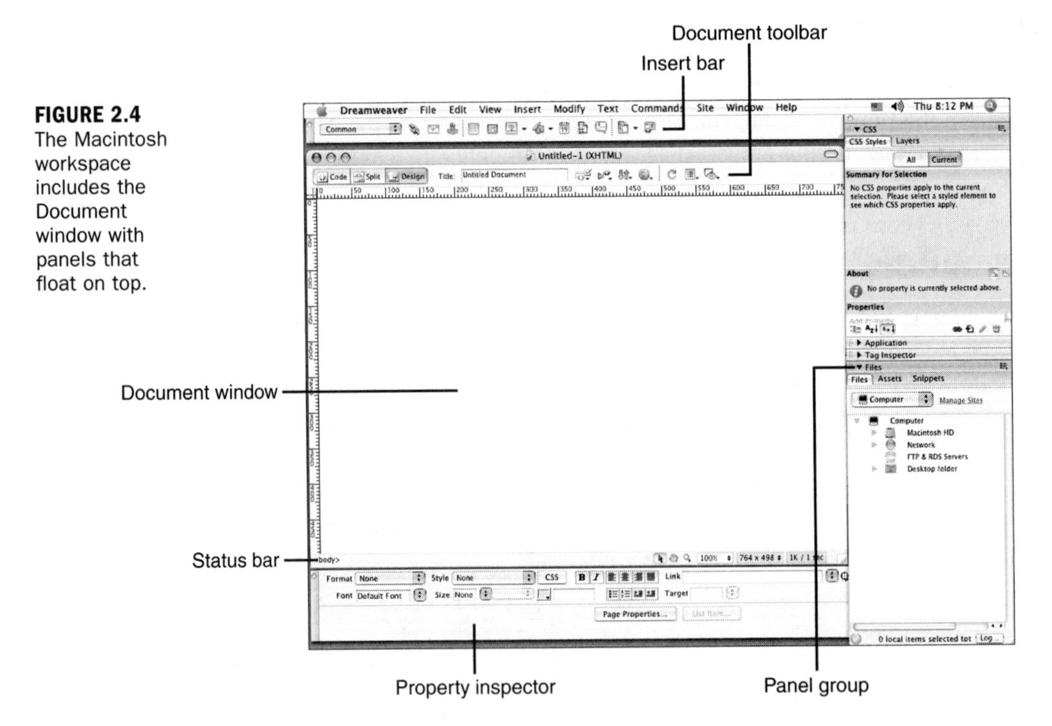

FIGURE 2.4 The Macintosh workspace includes the Document window with panels that float on top.

FIGURE 2.5 The File and Edit menus contain commands that are common to many applications, plus a few Dreamweaver-specific ones.

The View menu (see Figure 2.6) turns on and off your view of the head content; invisible elements; layer, table, and frame borders; the status bar; and image maps. You can tell whether you are currently viewing one of these elements by whether a check mark is shown beside it. The View menu also has commands to turn on the ruler, the grid, and the guides; play plug-ins; and show a tracing image. It's okay if you don't understand what these commands enable you to do because you'll learn more about them in later hours.

The Insert menu (see Figure 2.7) is roughly equivalent to the Insert bar (that you'll explore in a few minutes) because you can add all the items available on the Insert bar by using this menu. If you prefer to click icons, use the Insert bar instead of the Insert menu. The Modify menu (see Figure 2.7) enables you to modify properties of the currently selected object. After you've added an object to your web page, use the commands under the Modify menu to make it look the way you'd like.

The Text menu (see Figure 2.8) gives you access to multiple ways of fine-tuning the appearance of the text in a web page. Most important to those of you who are questionable spellers, the Text menu contains the Check Spelling command. The Text menu mirrors many of the properties available in the Property inspector when text is selected. You can use this menu to indent text, create a list, and modify font properties, as you will explore in the next hour. The Commands menu (see Figure 2.8) offers useful commands such as Clean Up HTML and Clean Up Word HTML.

You can also use this menu to record and play an animation or format and sort a table. And you can set up a color scheme and automatically jump out to Macromedia Fireworks to optimize an image.

FIGURE 2.6
The View menu houses commands to turn interface elements on and off.

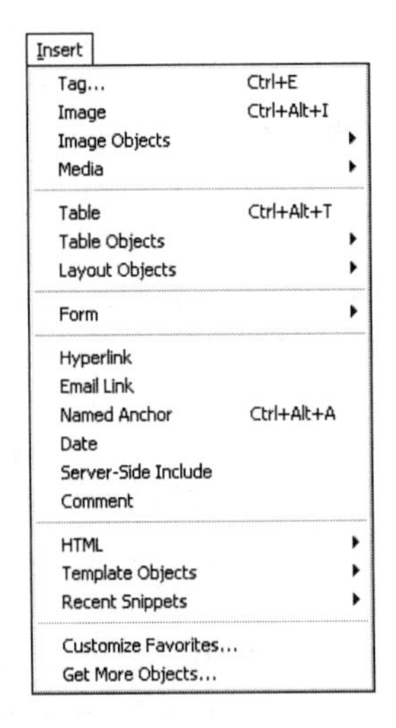

FIGURE 2.7
The Insert and Modify menus give you control over inserting and changing the attributes of objects.

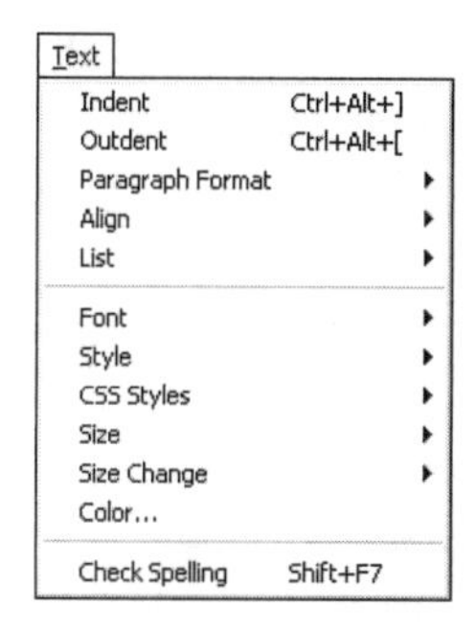

FIGURE 2.8
All the commands necessary to change text elements are in the Text menu. The Commands menu has commands to record a command, clean up HTML, and format and sort tables. Powerful stuff!

The Site menu (see Figure 2.9) presents the commands that have to do with an entire website. You will explore Dreamweaver website management in Hour 4, "Organizing: Defining and Configuring a Website," Hour 20, "Uploading and Sharing a Project to the Web," and Hour 21, "Managing and Editing a Website." The Window menu (see Figure 2.9) opens all the Dreamweaver panels and inspectors which you'll learn about later this hour. There's also a list of all the open files at the bottom of this menu.

Did you Know?

Open Panels from the Window Menu

You don't have to worry about finding a specific panel and remembering which panel group contains it because you can simply select the name of the panel from the Window menu. This Window menu enables you to quickly find and open all of Dreamweaver's panels. You'll see a check mark next to the name of the panel if it is already open. You can even open and close the Insert bar (the Insert command) and the Properties inspector (the Properties command) in the Window menu.

You'll learn about the help system in a couple of minutes. Along with providing links to the HTML-based help files, the Help menu, shown in Figure 2.10, contains the command to launch the Macromedia Extension Manager (the Manage Extensions command). There are also numerous links to Macromedia resources including the Dreamweaver Support Center on the Macromedia website. Selecting the About Dreamweaver command is useful if you need to find out which version of Dreamweaver you are running or your serial number.

The Macintosh version of Dreamweaver has the Dreamweaver menu, shown in Figure 2.11, in addition to the menus previously described. This menu contains the About command that is available from the Help menu in the Windows version.

It also gives you access to the Preferences command. The Keyboard Shortcuts command is also found in this menu instead of the Edit menu, as in the Windows version of Dreamweaver.

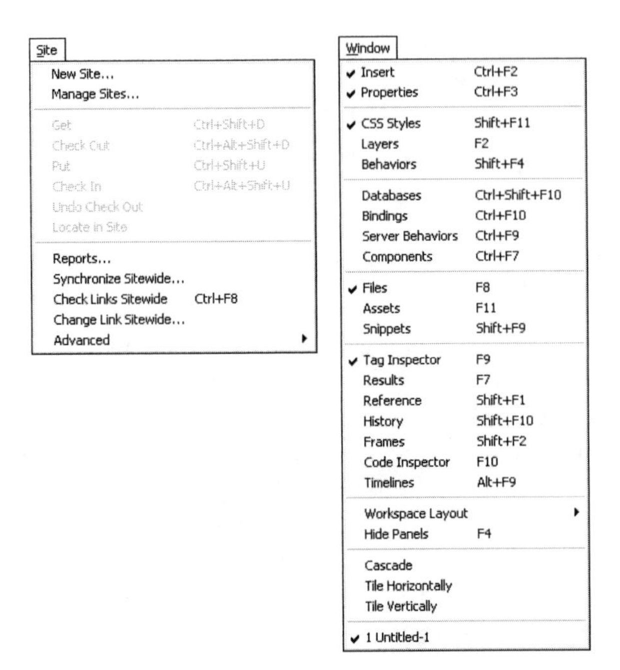

FIGURE 2.9
The Site menu commands help you manage an entire website. The Window menu commands help you manage the Dreamweaver panels and inspectors.

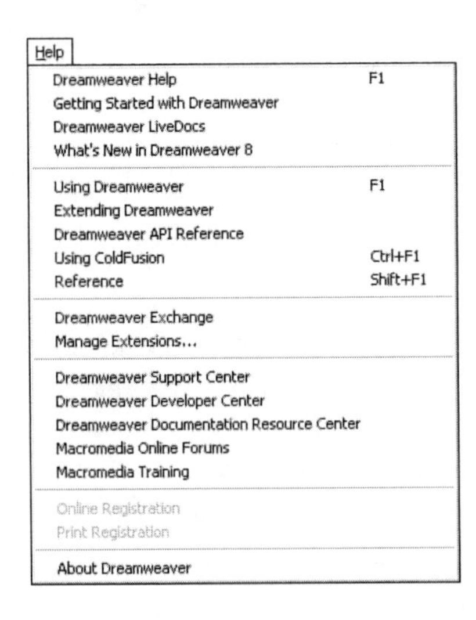

FIGURE 2.10
The Help menu gives you access to Dreamweaver's extensive help system.

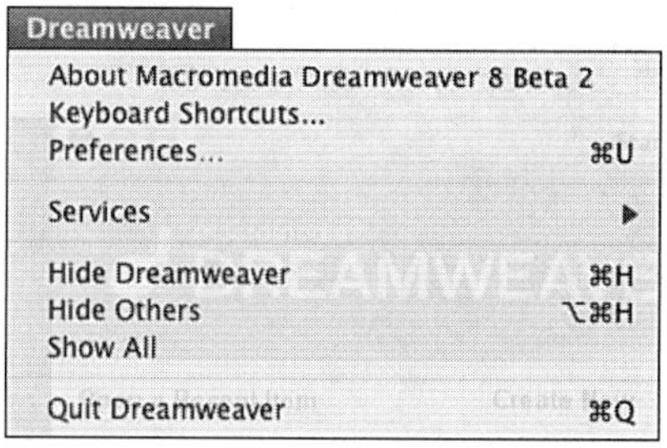

Dreamweaver
About Macromedia Dreamweaver 8 Beta 2
Keyboard Shortcuts...
Preferences... ⌘U
Services ▶
Hide Dreamweaver ⌘H
Hide Others ⌥⌘H
Show All
Quit Dreamweaver ⌘Q

FIGURE 2.11
On the Macintosh, the Dreamweaver menu gives you access to the Preferences command.

The Insert Bar

The **Insert bar** is directly beneath the menu bar in Windows and is a floating panel on the Mac. It contains buttons for inserting web page elements, such as images, tables, forms, and hyperlinks. You can either click or drag a button's icon to insert that object into a web page. All the objects in the Insert bar are also accessible from the Insert menu.

The Insert bar has a drop-down menu on its left that enables you to choose from the seven available object categories: Common, Layout, Forms, Text, HTML, Application, Flash Elements, and Favorites. To display the object in a certain category, drop down the menu and then select the category. By default, the Common category is displayed, but if you are working on forms, you might want to display the Forms category, or if you are laying out the structure of a page, you might want to display the Layout category.

Some of the objects in the Insert bar are drop-down menus that organize a group of related objects. For instance, in the Common category, the Images object drops down a menu displaying Image, Placeholder Image, Rollover Image, Fireworks HTML, Navigation Bar, Draw Rectangle Hotspot, Draw Oval Hotspot, and Draw Polygon Hotspot. All these objects have to do with images, so they are grouped together in a single drop-down menu in the Insert bar.

The Insert bar is displayed in Menu mode by default, but you can display the Insert bar in Tabs mode by selecting the last command in the drop-down menu, the Show as Tabs command, as shown in Figure 2.12. Selecting the Show as Tabs command displays the Insert bar categories as tabs across the top of the Insert bar, as shown in Figure 2.13. To return the Insert bar to Menu mode, select the Show as Menu command in the Insert bar drop-down menu.

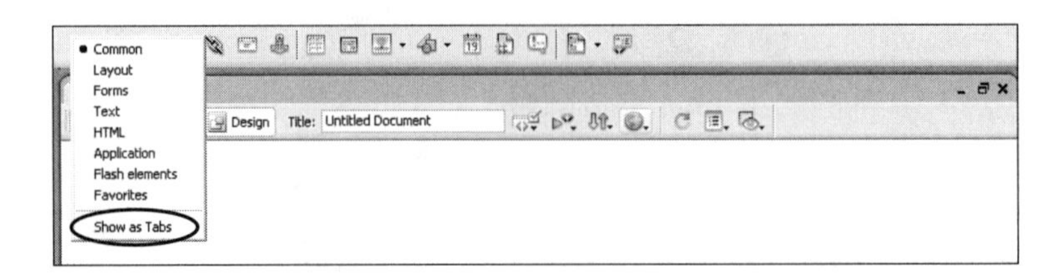

FIGURE 2.12
The Insert bar drop-down menu displays a list of the categories and the Show as Tabs command, which enables you to display a tabbed Insert bar.

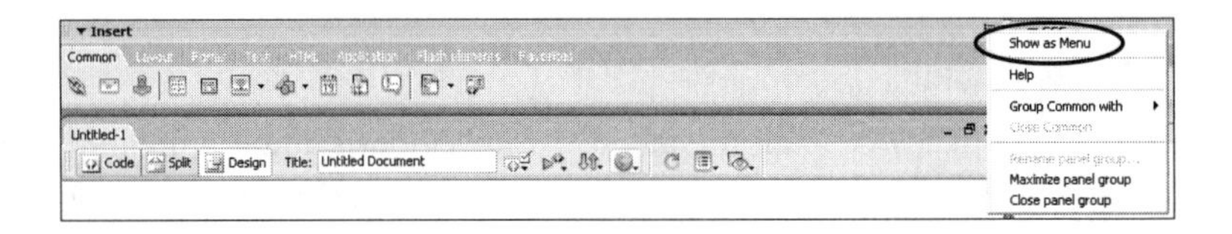

FIGURE 2.13
In Tabs mode, the Insert bar categories appear as tabs across the top of the bar.

Table 2.2 lists all the objects, with descriptions, that are available in the Insert bar. The table briefly describes each of the objects in the Insert bar except those found in the Application tab because those objects are used strictly for creating dynamic web pages. While you read through this table, familiarize yourself with the types of objects and content you can add to a web page in Dreamweaver.

TABLE 2.2 Insert Bar Objects

Icon	Icon Name	Description
Common Category		
	Hyperlink	Inserts a hyperlink, including the text and the link location.
	Email Link	Adds a hyperlink that launches an empty email message to a specific email address when clicked.
	Named Anchor	Places a named anchor at the insertion point. Named anchors are used to create hyperlinks within a file.
	Table	Creates a table at the insertion point.
	Insert Div Tag	Adds a `<div>` tag, the tag that Dreamweaver uses to create layers.
	Image	Places an image at the insertion point. (In the Images drop-down menu.)

TABLE 2.2 Continued

Icon	Icon Name	Description
Common Category		
	Image Placeholder	Inserts a placeholder for an image. (In the Images drop-down menu.)
	Rollover Image	Prompts you for two images: the regular image and the image that appears when the user puts his cursor over the image. (In the Images drop-down menu.)
	Fireworks HTML	Places HTML that has been exported from Macromedia Fireworks at the insertion point. (In the Images drop-down menu.)
	Navigation Bar	Inserts a set of button images to be used for navigating throughout the website. (In the Images drop-down menu.)
	Draw Rectangle Hotspot	Allows you to draw a rectangle over a specific region of an image and link it to a specific URL. (In the Images drop-down menu.)
	Draw Oval Hotspot	Allows you to draw a circle over a specific region of an image and link it to a specific URL. (In the Images drop-down menu.)
	Draw Polygon Hotspot	Allows you to draw a polygon over a specific region of an image and link it to a specific URL. (In the Images drop-down menu.)
	Flash	Places a Macromedia Flash movie at the insertion point. (In the Media drop-down menu.)
	Flash Button	Places one of the available prefabricated Macromedia Flash buttons at the insertion point. (In the Media drop-down menu.)
	Flash Text	Places an editable Flash Text object at the insertion point and creates a Flash file. (In the Media drop-down menu.)
	Flash Paper	Inserts a Flash Paper document into the web page. (In the Media drop-down menu.)
	Flash Video	Places and configures a Flash Video object at the insertion point. (In the Media drop-down menu.)

TABLE 2.2 Continued

Icon	Icon Name	Description
Common Category		
	Shockwave	Places a **Shockwave movie** (that is, a Macromedia Director movie prepared for the Web) at the insertion point. (In the Media drop-down menu.)
	Applet	Places a Java applet at the insertion point. (In the Media drop-down menu.)
	Param	Inserts a tag that enables you to enter parameters and their values to pass to an applet or an ActiveX control. (In the Media drop-down menu.)
	ActiveX	Places an ActiveX control at the insertion point. (In the Media drop-down menu.)
	Plugin	Places any file requiring a browser plug-in at the insertion point. (In the Media drop-down menu.)
	Date	Inserts the current date at the insertion point.
	Server-Side Include	Places a file that simulates a server-side include at the insertion point.
	Comment	Inserts a comment at the insertion point.
	Make Template	Creates a Dreamweaver template from the current web page. (In the Templates drop-down menu.)
	Make Nested Template	Creates a nested Dreamweaver template from the current template. (In the Templates drop-down menu.)
	Editable Region	Adds an editable region to a template. (In the Templates drop-down menu.)
	Optional Region	Adds an optional region to a template; this region can be set to either show or hide. (In the Templates drop-down menu.)
	Repeating Region	Adds a repeating region to a template. (In the Templates drop-down menu.)
	Editable Optional Region	Adds an editable optional region to a template. (In the Templates drop-down menu.)

TABLE 2.2 Continued

Icon	Icon Name	Description
Common Category		
	Repeating Table	Adds a repeating table to a template and defines which cells can be edited. (In the Templates drop-down menu.)
	Tag Chooser	Enables you to choose a tag to insert from a hierarchical menu of all available tags.
Layout Category		
	Table	Creates a table at the insertion point. (Also in the Common category.)
	Insert Div Tag	Adds a `<div>` tag, the tag that Dreamweaver uses to create layers. (Also in the Common category.)
	Draw Layer	Draws a layer container in a web page.
Standard	Standard mode	Turns on Dreamweaver's Standard mode, at the same time turning off either Expanded Tables mode or Layout mode.
Expanded	Expanded Tables mode	Turns on Dreamweaver's Expanded Tables mode, temporarily adding cell padding and borders to all tables.
Layout	Layout mode	Turns on Dreamweaver's Layout mode, enabling you to draw tables and table cells.
	Layout Table	Draws a table while you're in Layout view.
	Draw Layout Cell	Draws a table cell while you're in Layout view.
	Insert Row Above	Adds a row above the currently selected row of a table.
	Insert Row Below	Adds a row beneath the currently selected row of a table.
	Insert Column to the Left	Adds a column to the left of the currently selected column in a table.
	Insert Column to the Right	Adds a column to the right of a currently selected column in a table.

TABLE 2.2 Continued

Icon	Icon Name	Description
Layout Category		
	Left Frame	Creates a frame to the left of the current frame. (In the Frames drop-down menu.)
	Right Frame	Creates a frame to the right of the current frame. (In the Frames drop-down menu.)
	Top Frame	Creates a frame above the current frame. (In the Frames drop-down menu.)
	Bottom Frame	Creates a frame below the current frame. (In the Frames drop-down menu.)
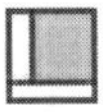	Bottom and Nested Left Frame	Creates a frame to the left of the current frame and then adds a frame below. (In the Frames drop-down menu.)
	Bottom and Nested Right Frame	Creates a frame to the right of the current frame and then adds a frame below. (In the Frames drop-down menu.)
	Left and Nested Bottom Frame	Creates a frame below the current frame and then adds a frame to the left. (In the Frames drop-down menu.)
	Right and Nested Bottom Frame	Creates a frame below the current frame and then adds a frame to the right. (In the Frames drop-down menu.)
	Top and Bottom Frame	Creates a frame below the current frame and then adds a frame above. (In the Frames drop-down menu.)
	Left and Nested Top Frame	Creates a frame above the current frame and then adds a frame to the left. (In the Frames drop-down menu.)
	Right and Nested Top Frame	Creates a frame above the current frame and then adds a frame to the right. (In the Frames drop-down menu.)
	Top and Nested Left Frame	Creates a frame to the left of the current frame and then adds a frame above. (In the Frames drop-down menu.)

ITABLE 2.2 Continued

con	Icon Name	Description
Layout Category		
	Top and Nested Right Frame	Creates a frame to the right of the current frame and then adds a frame above. (In the Frames drop-down menu.)
	Tabular Data	Creates a table at the insertion point that is populated with data from a chosen file. (In the Frames drop-down menu.)
Forms Category		
	Form	Places a form at the insertion point.
	Text Field	Inserts a text field.
	Hidden Field	Inserts a hidden field.
	Textarea	Inserts a textarea, which is a multiline text field.
	Check Box	Inserts a check box.
	Radio Button	Inserts a radio button.
	Radio Group	Inserts a group of related radio buttons.
	List/Menu	Inserts a list or a drop-down menu.
	Jump Menu	Creates a jump menu that allows users to select a website from a menu and go to that site.
	Image Field	Inserts an image field, which enables an image to act as a button.
	File Field	Inserts a file field, which enables the user to upload a file.
	Button	Inserts a button.

TABLE 2.2 Continued

Icon	Icon Name	Description
Forms Category		
	Label	Assigns a label to a form element, enabling browsers for people with visual impairments to access extra information about the form elements nested within the label.
	Fieldset	Groups related form fields together to make the form accessible to browsers for people with visual impairments. Fieldset wraps around a group of form elements and appears to sighted people as a box drawn around the group, with the fieldset title at the top.
Text Category		
	Font Tag Editor	Opens the Font Tag Editor to set up the attributes of a `font` tag.
	Bold	Makes the selected text bold by using the `b` tag. This tag has been dropped from recent versions of HTML. The approved tag for bold text is the `strong` tag.
	Italic	Makes the selected text italic by using the `i` tag. This tag has been dropped from recent versions of HTML. The approved tag for italic text is the `emphasis` tag.
	Strong	Makes the selected text bold by using the approved `strong` tag.
	Emphasis	Makes the selected text italic by using the approved `emphasis` tag.
	Paragraph	Makes the selected text into a paragraph.
	Block Quote	Makes the selected text into a block quote, indented from the right and the left by using the `blockquote` tag.
	Preformatted Text	Makes the selected text preformatted (using the `pre` tag, displaying the text in a monospaced font and with the ability to enter spaces).

TABLE 2.2 Continued

Icon	Icon Name	Description
Text Category		
h1	Heading 1	Makes the selected text a heading size 1 (largest) by using the `h1` tag.
h2	Heading 2	Makes the selected text a heading size 2 by using the `h2` tag.
h3	Heading 3	Makes the selected text a heading size 3 by using the `h3` tag.
ul	Unordered List	Makes the selected text into an unordered (bulleted) list.
ol	Ordered List	Makes the selected text into an ordered (numbered) list.
li	List Item	Makes the selected text into a list item (by using the `li` tag), a single item in an ordered or unordered list.
dl	Definition List	Creates a definition list. A **definition list** consists of definition terms and definition descriptions.
dt	Definition Term	Creates a definition term within a definition list.
dd	Definition Description	Creates a definition description within a definition list.
abbr.	Abbreviation	Wraps the `abbr` tag around text, adding a full-text definition to an abbreviation. This aids search engines in indexing a web page properly.
W3C	Acronym	Wraps the `acronym` tag around text, adding a full-text definition to an acronym. This aids search engines in indexing a web page properly.
BR	Line Break	Places a line break, the `br` tag, at the insertion point. (In the Characters drop-down menu.)
	Non-Breaking Space	Inserts a special character (` `) that creates a space. The Non-Breaking Space character also prevents a line break from occurring between two words. (In the Characters drop-down menu.)

TABLE 2.2 Continued

Icon	Icon Name	Description
Text Category		
“	Left Quote	Inserts the special character for a left quote. (In the Characters drop-down menu.)
”	Right Quote	Inserts the special character for a right quote. (In the Characters drop-down menu.)
—	Em-Dash	Inserts the special character for an em dash (—). (In the Characters drop-down menu.)
£	Pound	Inserts the special character for the pound currency symbol. (In the Characters drop-down menu.)
€	Euro	Inserts the special character for the euro currency symbol. (In the Characters drop-down menu.)
¥	Yen	Inserts the special character for the yen currency symbol. (In the Characters drop-down menu.)
©	Copyright	Inserts the special character for the copyright symbol. (In the Characters drop-down menu.)
®	Registered Trademark	Inserts the special character for the registered trademark symbol. (In the Characters drop-down menu.)
TM	Trademark	Inserts the special character for the trademark symbol. (In the Characters drop-down menu.)
	Other Characters	Opens a menu that displays many additional special characters. (In the Characters drop-down menu.)
HTML Category		
	Horizontal Rule	Inserts a horizontal rule, a simple divider line across the page.
	Meta	Inserts a `meta` tag into the `head` section of a web page. This object can insert a name type `meta` tag, aiding search engines, or an http-equiv type `meta` tag that can redirect the user to a different URL or give additional information about the web page, such as assigning parental control information to a page. (In the Head drop-down menu.)

TABLE 2.2 Continued

Icon	Icon Name	Description
HTML Category		
	Keywords	Inserts a keywords `meta` tag into the `head` section, adding keywords to the web page to help search engines properly index it. (In the Head drop-down menu.)
	Description	Inserts a description `meta` tag into the `head` section, adding a description to the web page helping search engines properly index it. (In the Head drop-down menu.)
	Refresh	Inserts a refresh `meta` tag into the `head` section. This tag sets the number of seconds before the page will automatically jump to another web page or reload itself. (In the Head drop-down menu.)
	Base	Inserts a `base` tag into the `head` section. This enables you to set a base URL or a base target window affecting all of the paths on the web page. (In the Head drop-down menu.)
	Link	Inserts the address of an external file, usually a script or style sheet file. (In the Head drop-down menu.)
table	Table Tag	Inserts a `table` tag (in Code view only). (In the Tables drop-down menu.)
tr	Table Row	Inserts a `tr` tag (in Code view only). (In the Tables drop-down menu.)
th	Table Header Cell	Inserts a `th` tag (in Code view only). (In the Tables drop-down menu.)
td	Table Data Cell	Inserts a `td` tag (in Code view only). (In the Tables drop-down menu.)
caption	Table Caption	Inserts a `caption` tag (in Code view only). (In the Tables drop-down menu.)

TABLE 2.2 Continued

Icon	Icon Name	Description
HTML Category		
frameset	Frameset	Inserts a `frameset` tag (in Code view only). (In the Frames drop-down menu.)
frame	Frame	Inserts a `frame` tag (in Code view only). (In the Frames drop-down menu.)
iframe	Floating Frame	Inserts an `iframe` tag (in Code view only). (In the Frames drop-down menu.)
frames	No Frames	Inserts a `noframes` tag to surround HTML code for browsers that cannot display frames (in Code view only). (In the Frames drop-down menu.)
	Script	Inserts scripted code at the insertion point. (In the Script drop-down menu.)
	No Script	Inserts the `noscript` tag surrounding HTML code that will be displayed by browsers that do not support scripts. (In the Script drop-down menu.)
	Server-Side Include	Places a file that simulates a server-side include at the insertion point. (In the Script drop-down menu.)
Flash Elements Category		
	Image Viewer	A Flash movie used as a slideshow viewer for a group of photos.

The Favorites category enables you to add objects that you use frequently to a single Insert bar category. You'll explore this functionality in Hour 22, when you learn how to modify Dreamweaver to your own way of working. By the end of this book you will have a better idea of the types of objects you'll want to place in the Favorites category to help you work more quickly in Dreamweaver. These are your personal favorites, the objects that you use most often, collected in one handy Insert bar category.

The Document Window

By default the Document window is maximized and its title and filename appear at the very top of the screen. You'll explore saving a file, giving it a filename, and giving it a title in Hour 3, "Getting Started: Adding Text, Lists, and Previewing in the Browser." The Document window is the part of the Dreamweaver interface that you will be using most often in your work. The Document toolbar appears at the top of the Document window.

The Document Toolbar

The Document toolbar, shown in Figure 2.14, gives you quick access to important commands. The three buttons on the left of the Document toolbar enable you to toggle between Code view, Design view, and a split view with both Code view and Design view visible. I probably use Design view 80% of the time and divide the other 20% of my Dreamweaver time between Code view and the split view. The split view showing both Design and Code views is useful when you're learning HTML because it enables you to see the tags that Dreamweaver adds while you create a web page.

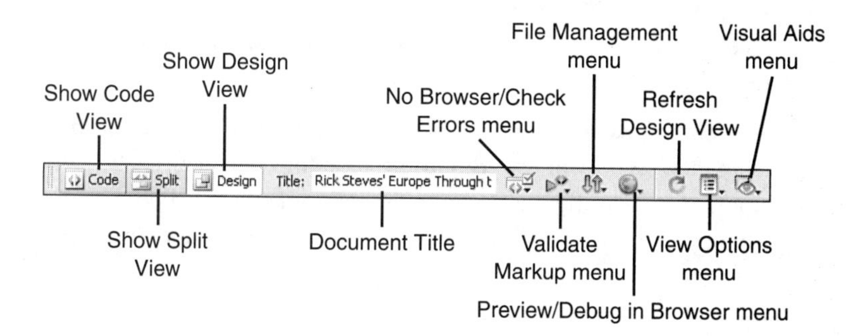

FIGURE 2.14
The Document toolbar contains commands you commonly apply to web pages when editing in Dreamweaver.

The text box in the Document toolbar is where you give a web page a title (the default title "Untitled Document" isn't very interesting!). This web page title appears in the user's browser title bar when the user views the page. It is also saved in the browser's Favorites or Bookmarks list as the name of the web page, so it needs to be meaningful.

Six drop-down menus are on the toolbar:

- The No Browser/Check Errors menu enables you to check that your web page works correctly in various browsers.
- The Validate Markup menu checks to see that the code is properly written.

- The File Management menu lists commands such as those for getting files to and from a web server. You'll explore these commands in Hours 21 and 22, when you upload and manage a website.
- The Preview/Debug in Browser menu gives you quick access to the list of browsers you'll use to preview web pages.
- The View Options menu changes, depending on whether you have Design or Code view open. While you're in Design view, this menu displays commands that are also in Dreamweaver's View menu, such as those for viewing head content or the rulers. While you're in Code view, the View Options menu contains commands that affect the way the code is displayed, such as Word Wrap and Line Numbers.
- The Visual Aids menu is only active in Design mode. The menu gives you access to turn on and off all of the visual aids that are also available in View, Visual Aids.

By the Way

Where's My Document Toolbar?

If the Document toolbar isn't visible, select View, Toolbars, Document.

The Document toolbar also contains the Refresh Design View button. This button refreshes Design view when you are editing the code (in Code view or the split screen view) so that you can instantly see the changes you make to the code. This button is only active when you are viewing the Document window in Code view or Split view.

The Status Bar

The Dreamweaver Document window has a status bar along the bottom of the page. It contains the tag selector, the Window Size drop-down menu, magnification and selection tools, and download statistics, as shown in Figure 2.15. These convenient tools are just some of the nice touches that Dreamweaver 8 offers to help you have a productive and fun experience designing for the Web.

The tag selector in the lower-left corner of the Document window provides easy access to the HTML tags that are involved in any object on the screen. If, for example, the cursor is located in a table cell, the tag selector enables selection of any of the HTML tags that control that object. The tag that is currently selected is shown in bold in the tag selector. The tags to the left of the selected tag are the tags that are wrapped around the selected tag.

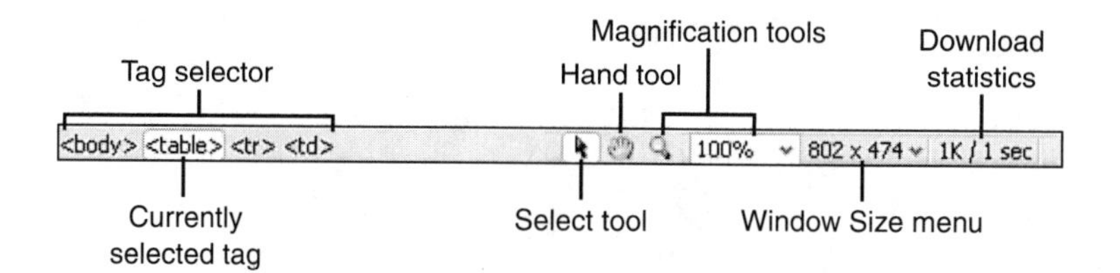

FIGURE 2.15 The status bar contains tools that help you get information about a web page.

Did you Know?

The Tag Selector Is Your Friend

The tag selector will be important later, when you start using behaviors in Hour 17, "Adding Interactivity with Behaviors." You apply behaviors to specific tags, and sometimes the tags are difficult to select, especially the <body> tag, which contains the entire web page content. The tag selector makes it very easy to select the entire body of a web page by clicking the <body> tag.

On the right side of the status bar you'll find three icons that control how the cursor appears and functions in the Document window. By default, the Select tool (arrow cursor) is selected. You can also select the Hand tool enabling you to drag the cursor to scroll across the web page in the Document window. The Zoom tool turns the cursor into a magnifying glass and enables you to zoom into the web page. Next to the Zoom tool is the Set Magnification menu where you can select a certain magnification level from 6% to 6400%.

The Window Size drop-down menu helps you re-create a target screen resolution by resizing the Document window. You will always want to make sure that your design looks good at a low (800×600) or high screen resolution. You can use the Window Size drop-down menu (see Figure 2.16) to quickly resize the Document window to view the approximate amount of screen real estate you will have at a certain resolution. The Window Size drop-down menu works only when you do not have the Document window maximized.

Notice the sizes available in the Window Size menu:

- The dimensions listed on the right (in parentheses) represent the screen resolutions.
- The numbers listed on the left are the estimated browser window dimensions. They are smaller than the screen resolutions because the browser interface (buttons and menus, for instance) takes up space. For example, when the viewer's monitor is set to 640×480, the viewable area is only 536×196 pixels.

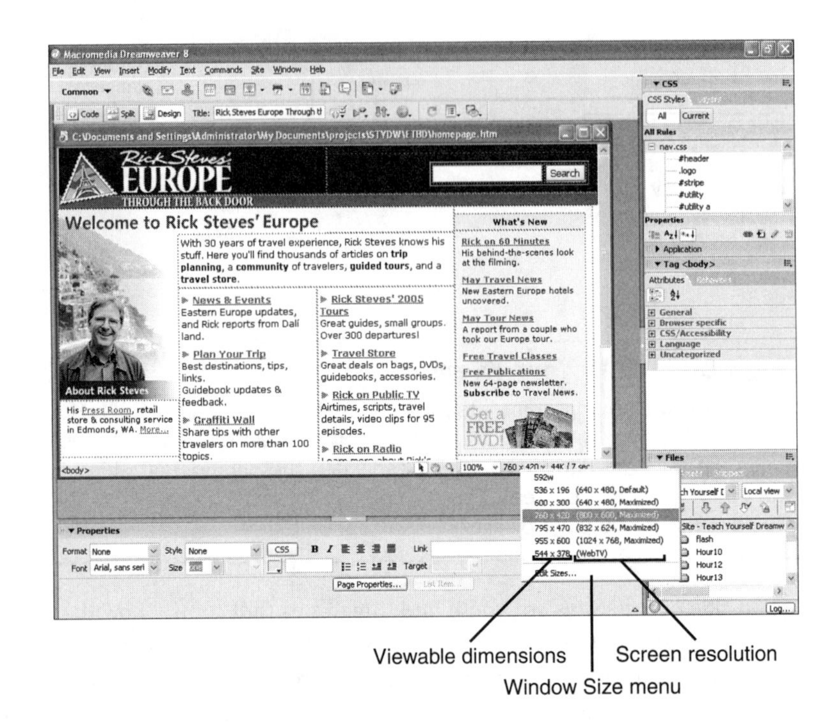

FIGURE 2.16
The Window Size menu resizes the screen, approximating how the page will look at different screen resolutions.

Did you Know?

Define Special Window Sizes

Create your own custom settings for the Window Size menu by selecting the last choice in the Window Size pop-up menu, the Edit Sizes command. This command takes you to the Status Bar category in the Dreamweaver Preferences dialog box, where you can add your custom window size. For instance, do you want to create a web page that is readable on your wireless phone? My phone has the capability to view 120×160 pixels, so I could create a custom size to create a web page for my phone.

Because bandwidth is often an issue when you're developing for the Web, it's nice to know the estimated file size and download time of a web page. The estimated download time shown in the status bar is based on the modem setting in the Status Bar category in the Dreamweaver Preferences dialog box. The default modem setting is 56Kbps; you might want to change this setting to whatever the bandwidth speed is for the targeted viewer of your web page. (Most people in the United States browse the Web at a speed of at least 56Kbps.) Dreamweaver takes into account images and other assets contained in the web page when calculating the file size and download time.

Panels and Inspectors

You set properties of objects, display panels, and add functionality to web pages through Dreamweaver's panels and inspectors. Most commands in Dreamweaver are available in several places, usually as menu commands and as panel commands. Dreamweaver's panels are grouped into tabbed panel groups beside the Document window (Windows) or floating on top (Mac).

Did you Know?

Toggle All Panels On and Off

Pressing F4 on your keyboard triggers the Hide Panels/Show Panels command (Window, Hide Panels). This command is a great way to temporarily get more screen real estate in order to see the entire web page. When the panels are visible, F4 hides them and when they are hidden, F4 shows them. This toggle button is a quick way to hide and then show the Dreamweaver panels.

You can open every panel from the Window menu and by default Dreamweaver has all the important panels and the Property inspector open. If a panel or inspector is open, its command has a check mark beside it in the Window menu. To close a panel or an inspector, deselect the command in the Window menu. The panel doesn't actually go away, but the panel group's expander arrow turns and the panel group collapses so that you don't see it anymore. Menu command names that open the panels, listed in the Window menu, might be slightly different from the names of the panels or inspectors they launch. For instance, you open the Property inspector using the Properties command and the Insert bar using the Insert command.

Panels and Panel Groups

You can expand or collapse a panel group or an inspector by clicking the expander arrow to the left of the panel title, as shown in Figure 2.17. Immediately to the left of the expander arrow is the gripper. You can undock a panel group or inspector by selecting its gripper and dragging the panel group away from where it is docked. To dock a panel group or inspector, select its gripper and drag-and-drop above or below the other panel groups or the Document window. When it is docked, you'll see an outline around the panel group. Because the Macintosh version of Dreamweaver has floating panels, you can move them wherever you want anytime!

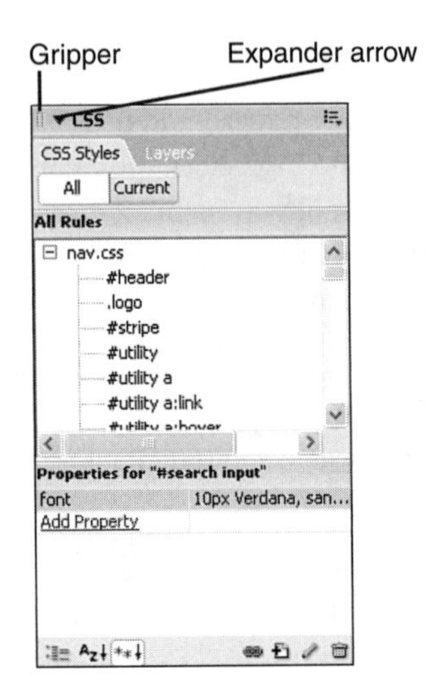

FIGURE 2.17 Expand and collapse panel groups using the expander arrow.

Did you Know?

Save Your Panel Configuration

You might have different panel configurations that are handy for different projects. Dreamweaver enables you to save individual configurations to use later by selecting Window, Workspace Layout, Save Current, and then giving the configuration a name. For instance, you might have a configuration when a site requires creating CSS that has the CSS Styles panel, the Attributes panel, and Files panel visible. You could save that with the name CSS Site.

In the Windows integrated user interface, resize the width of all the panel groups by dragging the bar that separates the panel groups and the Document window. The cursor changes to a double-arrow cursor when it is located in the correct spot. To resize the height of an individual panel group, move your cursor to the edge of the panel until it turns into a double-arrow cursor and drag the edges of the panel to the desired height. Windows users can use the Collapse button, shown in Figure 2.18, within the bars that separate the Document window from the panel groups and the Property inspector to toggle expanding and collapsing those two areas. Mac users can change the size of floating panel groups by dragging the borders of the group to the desired width and height.

Advanced Panel Maintenance

You can completely close a panel group, removing it from display on the screen, by selecting the Close Panel Group command in the panel drop-down menu located in the upper-right of each panel group. The Group With command listed in this menu enables you to group a panel with a different panel group.

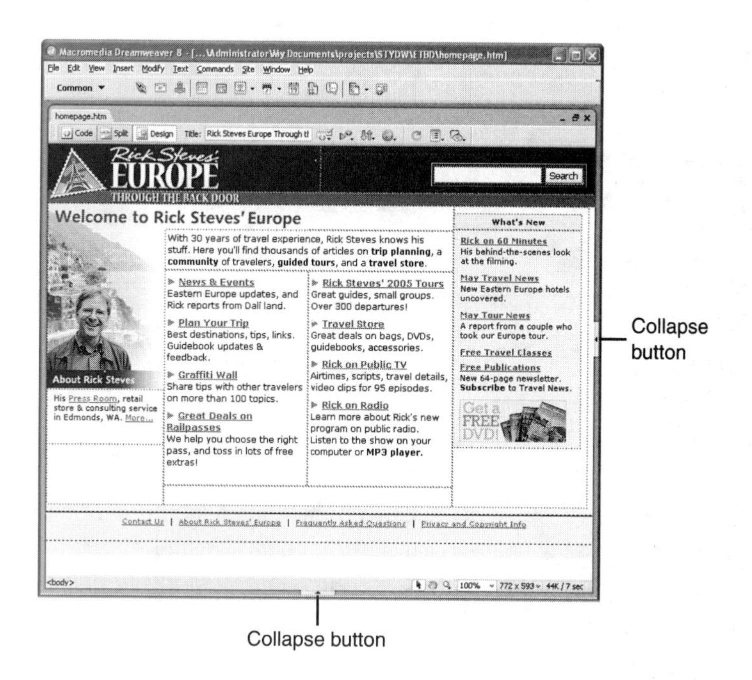

FIGURE 2.18
The Collapse buttons collapse and expand the panel group area and the Property inspector area so you have more room for the Document window.

The Property Inspector

The Property inspector displays all the properties of the currently selected object. The Property inspector is like a chameleon that changes depending on the environment; it looks different and displays appropriate properties for whichever object is selected in the Document window. For example, when text is selected, the Property inspector presents text properties, as shown in Figure 2.19. In Figure 2.20, an image is selected, and the Property inspector presents image properties.

You can expand the Property inspector by using the Expander icon so you have access to every available property. You do this by selecting the expander arrow in the lower-right corner of the Property inspector. Notice how the arrow is pointing down in Figure 2.20 and pointing up, with the Property inspector expanded, in Figure 2.19.

By the Way

Keep the Property Inspector Expanded

I think it works best to always keep the Property inspector expanded so you have access to all of the properties displayed there. If you don't have it expanded, some properties might be hidden, and you need to see all of the properties, especially while you are learning about Dreamweaver. If you need more space on the screen, either use the F4 command to hide all of the panels (and then to show them again) or use the Expander arrow button in the upper-left corner of the Property inspector to close the entire panel.

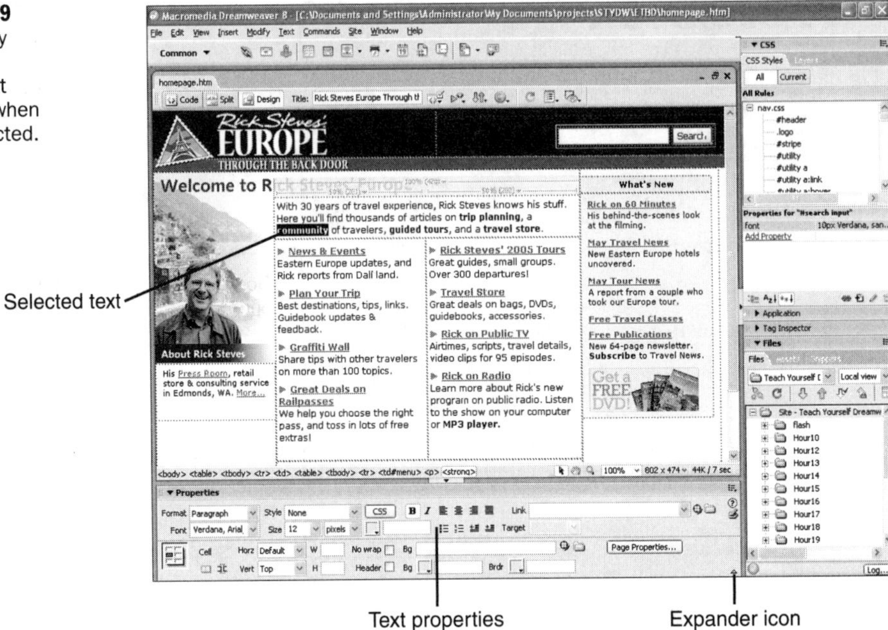

FIGURE 2.19
The Property inspector displays text properties when text is selected.

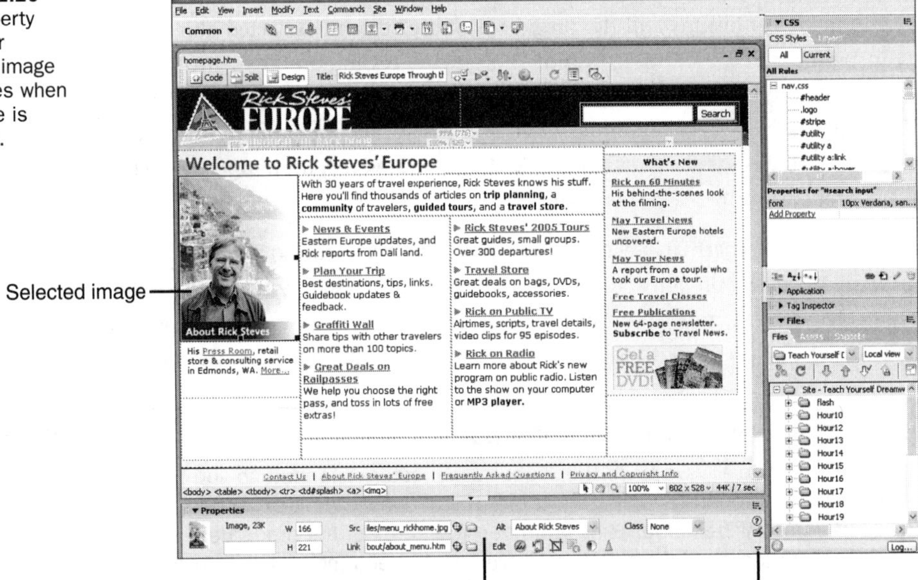

FIGURE 2.20
The Property inspector displays image properties when an image is selected.

Context Menus

You can access and modify object properties in multiple ways in Dreamweaver. I'm sure you'll find your favorite ways very quickly. Context menus are one of the choices available. These menus pop up when you right-click (Control+click on the Mac) an object in the Document window. The contents of the menu are dependent on which object you clicked. For instance, Figure 2.21 shows the context menu that pops up when you right-click a table.

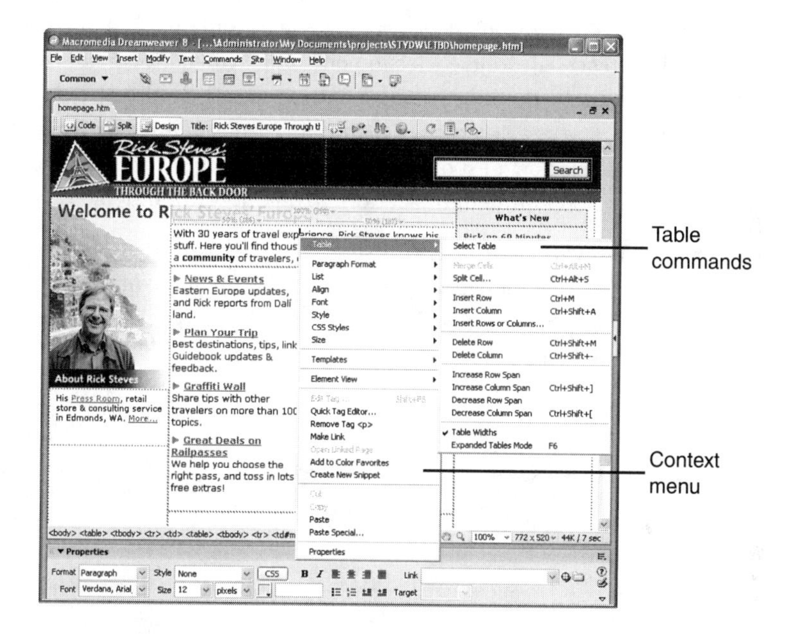

FIGURE 2.21
The context menu for tables gives you quick access to many table commands.

Getting Help

You select Help, Dreamweaver Help (or use the standard help shortcut key, F1) to launch the Dreamweaver help files. Windows users will see that the left side of the help page contains the Contents, Index, Search, and Favorites tabs. The right side of the page is where the help content files appear. The Next and Previous arrow buttons, on the far right side of the help content area, enable you to page through all the help topics.

Mac users see Dreamweaver Help displayed in the Macintosh Help Viewer application. Click on the hyperlinks to display help content. Search for specific help topics using the search box in the upper-right corner of the Help window.

Did you Know?

Using Help to Learn About Dreamweaver

While you are getting familiar with Dreamweaver, you might want to use the Next and Previous arrow buttons in the upper- and lower-right corners of the help content area to navigate through the topics. The topics are grouped, so you might get more information on your current topic on the next page. If you keep clicking either of these arrows, eventually you will go on to another topic. This is a good way to expand your knowledge on the topic you are currently researching.

In Windows, the Contents tab displays the table of contents. The table of contents is organized in subject categories. Selecting one of the categories expands the list, with subtopics under that category. The Index button shows an alphabetical index of all topics in the help system. Select the Search tab to enter a topic for which you want to search. Create your own list of favorite help topics by selecting the Favorites tab and clicking the Add button at the bottom to add the current topic.

One of the easiest ways to get help on your current task is to launch context-sensitive help. When you have an object selected (and you can see its properties in the Property inspector), click the Help icon in the Property inspector, shown in Figure 2.22, to go directly to information about that object.

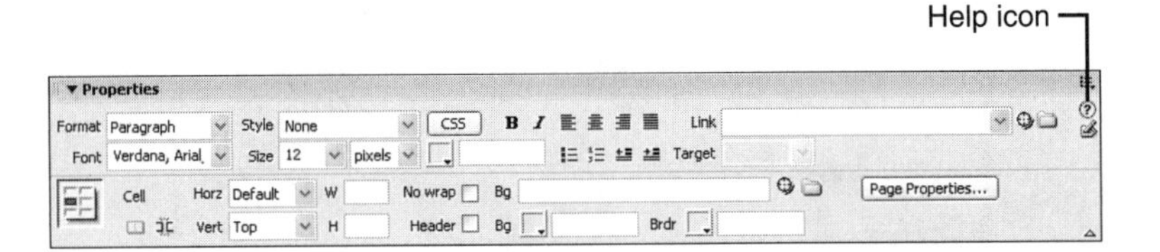

FIGURE 2.22 Clicking the Property inspector Help icon takes you directly to information about the properties of the object currently selected. In this instance, you will go directly to help on images.

Summary

In this hour, you have learned about the Dreamweaver Document window and other elements of the Dreamweaver user interface, such as the Insert bar, the menus, the status bar, and the panels. You have explored expanding panel groups. You have seen the commands available in Dreamweaver's menus, Insert bar, and the status bar. You have been introduced to the Property inspector and have learned how to access Dreamweaver help.

Q&A

Q. ***How do I get as much room in the Document window as I possibly can?***

A. First, make sure that the Document window is maximized. You can collapse the Property inspector and the panel groups by clicking the expander and the Collapse buttons. Or you can do all this much more quickly by pressing F4 (the shortcut for the Hide Panels command in the Window menu). The F4 command works in most of Macromedia's products to hide much of the user interface so you only see your project. The F4 command also toggles the panels back on.

Q. ***There's something wrong with my Dreamweaver installation because it looks very different from the examples in your book. All the panels appear on the left side of the screen, and I don't know how to move them. Help!***

A. When Dreamweaver was initially launched, someone selected the Coder workspace instead of the Designer workspace, which is used in this book. You can switch it by selecting Window, Workspace Layout, Designer.

Workshop

Quiz

1. Which menu do you use to open a Dreamweaver panel that isn't currently visible in the Panel groups?
2. What icon in the status bar enables you to magnify web pages in the Document window?
3. Is Dreamweaver an HTML editor, an authoring tool, or a website management tool?

Quiz Answers

1. The Window menu enables you to turn on and off all the panels and inspectors. There is a check mark beside a command if the panel is currently visible.
2. The Zoom tool enables you to magnify web pages in the Document window.
3. Sorry, this is a trick question! Dreamweaver is all these things.

Exercises

1. Open the Dreamweaver Preferences dialog box from the Edit menu (the Dreamweaver menu for Mac users). Select the General category and examine each of the available settings. Experiment with changing any of these settings. Click the Help button and read about each of the settings. Don't change settings randomly, especially if you don't understand what the settings accomplish.

2. Experiment with expanding and collapsing panel groups. Resize the panel groups. Explore some of the panel drop-down menus found in the upper-right corner of the panel. Use the F4 key (Hide Panels/Show Panels command) to toggle the options.

3. Launch the Quick Tour (the link that says Take a Quick Tour of Dreamweaver) from the Start page that appears when you open Dreamweaver 8. You need to be connected to the Internet to take this tour.

4. Click HTML under the Create New column in the middle of the Start page. This creates a blank HTML document in the Document window. Now you're ready for Hour 3, where you'll make your first web page!

HOUR 3

Getting Started: Adding Text, Lists, and Previewing in the Browser

What You'll Learn in This Hour:

- How to create a new web page and set up properties for the whole page
- How to use the Property inspector to change text fonts and font sizes
- How Dreamweaver creates new CSS Styles and how to rename and apply styles
- How to align text and add unordered and ordered lists
- How to preview a web page in different browsers

The most common elements in a web page are text and images, so this hour we'll start with text. You'll get started creating web pages with Dreamweaver by becoming familiar with adding text and setting text properties. You'll learn how Dreamweaver formats the appearance of text, modifying font attributes such as font face, color, and size, using Cascading Style Sheets (CSS). This hour introduces CSS while Hour 16, "Formatting Web Pages Using Cascading Style Sheets," gives more in-depth information into Dreamweaver's CSS capabilities.

Creating a New Page and Adding Text

To create a new web page, select File, New. The New Document dialog box appears, enabling you to select the type of document you want to create. Make sure that the General tab is selected in the New Document dialog box; the other tab, the Templates tab, will be discussed in Hour 24, "Creating Reusable Web Pages: Using Templates." This dialog box is organized into a Category column and a column that lists the pages in the selected category. Select the Basic Page category, and then select HTML as the Basic Page type, as shown in Figure 3.1. Click the Create button. A new document is created, and you can add text, images, and other objects to it.

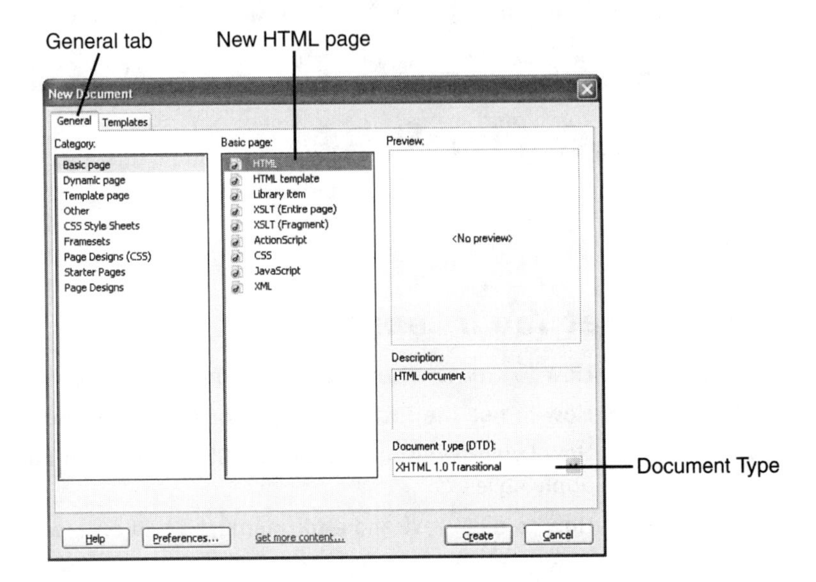

FIGURE 3.1 The New Document dialog box enables you to select the type of document you want to create.

The keyboard shortcut to open the New Document dialog box is Ctrl+N (Command+N on the Macintosh). You can also create a new page from Dreamweaver's Start Page (remember the screen that is visible in the Document Window when you first open Dreamweaver?). The middle column in the Start Page is titled Create New and you can select HTML in the middle column to quickly create a web page.

Did you Know?

What Is Document Type and XHTML?

You might have noticed the Document Type drop-down menu in the New Document dialog box. By default, Dreamweaver creates an HTML type defined using the XHTML 1.0 Transitional document type, often called doctype because it is defined using the `doctype` tag. XHTML is the most recent version of HTML, combining HTML with XML (extensible markup language). You'll explore document type more in Hour 6, "Getting Down and Dirty with HTML."

To enter text into the new web page you just created, you can simply type into the Document window. Type some text to serve as a heading at the top of the page, press the Enter key, and type a couple of sentences. This is the best way to add text to the web page if you are creating it in that moment. If the text exists elsewhere, however, such as in a Microsoft Word document, an email, or another type of text file, you'll want to look at the next section on copying and pasting text into Dreamweaver.

Did you Know?

Spelling and Grammar Are Important!

I like to create text for web pages in a robust word processing application such as Microsoft Word so I have the automatic spell check and grammar check. You can, of course, use Dreamweaver spell checker but there is no grammar checker in Dreamweaver. I can then copy and paste the text into a web page in Dreamweaver.

Copying and Pasting Text from a File

Often, you need to transfer text that exists as a word processing document into a web page. You can easily copy text from another application, such as Microsoft Word or even the spreadsheet application Microsoft Excel, and paste it into Dreamweaver. Dreamweaver can paste text two ways: with and without text formatting. Often the formatting (font, font color, and font size, for example) in the web page is different from the formatting in the original document, so I usually paste into Dreamweaver without formatting.

To copy and paste text from a word processing program or another program, follow these steps:

1. Open a Word document (`.doc`) or other word processing document.
2. Select at least a couple of paragraphs.
3. Copy the text by selecting Edit, Copy or using the keyboard command (Ctrl+C for Windows or Command+C on the Mac).
4. Go to Dreamweaver and place the insertion point where you want to paste the text.
5. Select Edit, Paste or use the keyboard shortcut (Ctrl+V in Windows or Command+V on a Mac). The text is pasted into Dreamweaver, and it retains its formatting, including fonts, paragraphs, color, and other attributes.

   If you don't want the formatting, select Edit, Undo (Ctrl+Z in Windows or Command+Z on a Mac) to remove the text you just pasted. To paste without formatting, select Edit, Page Special and one of the Paste Special options shown in Figure 3.2. This gives you finer control over what is pasted into your web page.

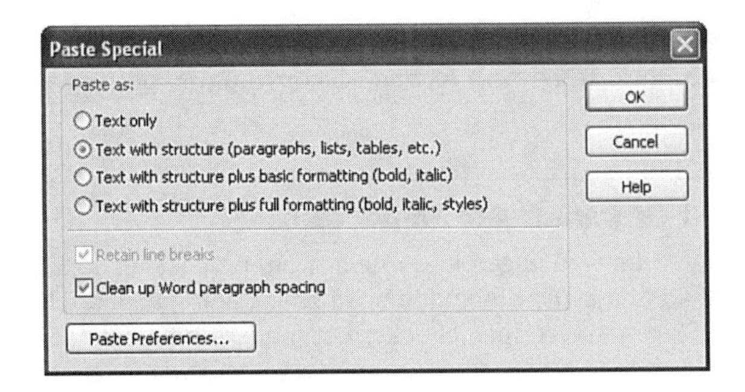

FIGURE 3.2 The Paste Special dialog box enables you to choose exactly what formatting properties get pasted along with your text into Dreamweaver.

Applying Text Formatting

The Property inspector is the panel directly beneath the Document window. You will use this panel extensively to set properties of objects on a web page. You can display the Property inspector by choosing Window, Properties. You apply standard HTML formatting to text by using the Format drop-down menu in the Property inspector. There are four basic formatting options here:

- **None**—This option removes any formatting styles currently applied to the selection.
- **Paragraph**—This option applies paragraph tags (<p></p>) to the selection. This adds two carriage returns after the selection.
- **Heading 1 through Heading 6**—These options apply heading tags to the selection. Heading 1 is the largest heading and Heading 6 is the smallest. Applying a heading tag makes everything on the line that heading size.
- **Preformatted**—This option displays text in a fixed-width, or monospaced, font (on most systems, 10-point Courier). The text resembles typewriter text. You probably won't use this format option too often.

Select the top line heading in your web page and apply Heading 1 formatting, as shown in Figure 3.3. While you are creating web pages you will use the different Heading formats and Paragraph format all of the time. These formatting options wrap the text you've selected with HTML tags. The Heading 1 format, for instance, adds the <h1> tag before the selection and the closing tag </h1> after the selection.

Understanding Paragraph and Break Tags

It's important to understand the difference between paragraph (<p>) and break (<br>) tags. Paragraph tags surround a block of text, placing two carriage returns after the block. You create a new paragraph by pressing the Enter or Return key. Think of the paragraph tags as creating a container for the block of text. This container is a square block that contains text. Later, in Hour 16, you'll understand how to modify this container with CSS.

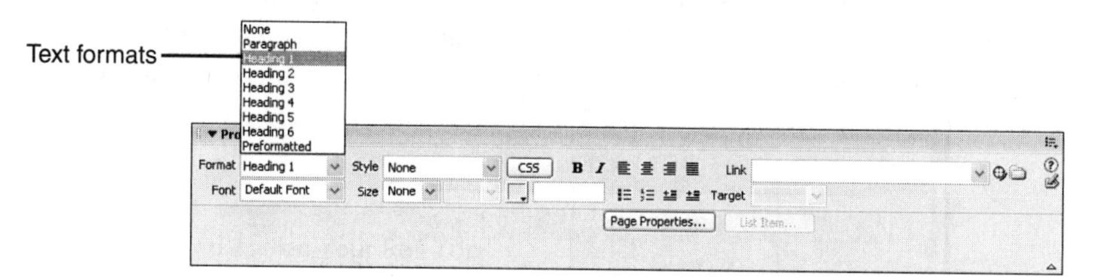

FIGURE 3.3 The Format drop-down menu in the Property inspector applies heading, paragraph, and preformatted formatting to text.

The break tag inserts a single carriage return into text. You can insert a break into a web page by using the keyboard shortcut Shift+Enter or selecting the Line Break object from the Characters drop-down menu in the Text category of the Insert bar. The break tag does not create a container as the paragraph format does. This tag is best used for creating a new line within a paragraph such as when formatting an address on different lines.

It's important to understand the difference between paragraph and break tags. Pressing Shift+Enter twice, inserting two line breaks, instead of pressing Enter to create a paragraph looks identical in a web page. However, because you haven't created a paragraph container, any formatting applied to the paragraph gets applied to the entire container. This will become more important as you begin formatting portions of web pages in different ways.

Setting Page Properties

You can also set global page properties, such as the default font and font size for all the text on the page. In addition, you can set the page title in the page properties. To get started, select Modify, Page Properties to open the Page Properties dialog box.

The Page Properties dialog box, shown in Figure 3.4, has five property categories listed in the left column: Appearance, Links, Headings, Title/Encoding, and Tracing Image. Next you'll learn about the property settings in the Appearance, Headings, and Title/Encoding categories; the Links category settings will be covered in Hour 5, "Setting Lots o' Links: Hyperlinks, Anchors, and Mailto Links," and the Tracing Image category will be covered in Hour 13, "Designing Page Layout Using Tables." You simply click on one of the categories in order to modify its property settings.

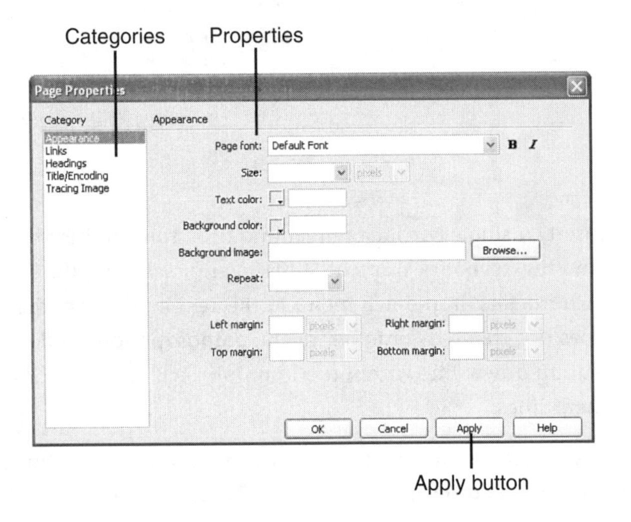

FIGURE 3.4 The Page Properties dialog box enables you to set properties for the entire web page.

Setting Global Page Appearance

You use the settings in the Appearance category of the Page Properties dialog box to set the text font, size, and color, along with several other settings, for the entire web page. For instance, the text on a web page is black by default. You can change the default text color on the web page by changing this setting in Page Properties.

Setting the Global Page Font and Size

Select the Appearance category in the Page Properties dialog box by clicking the category name on the left side of the dialog box. You can select the default Page Font for the entire page along with the default text size and color. These settings may be overridden by any local text setting, such as the settings you'll apply later this hour.

To set the default font properties, follow these steps:

1. In the Page Properties dialog box, select the font family you want from the Page Font drop-down menu.

2. You can also set the default text to be bold, italic, or both.

3. Select the font size in the Size drop-down menu. If you select a numeric font size, you also need to select a unit type, such as points or pixels.

4. Click the Apply button at the bottom of the Page Properties dialog box in order to view the font changes you've changed so far. You might have to adjust the position of the Page Properties dialog box so it isn't blocking your view. The Apply button enables you to view your changes without closing the Page Properties dialog box.

Did you Know?

Use Pixels Instead of Points

Many web designers prefer to standardize using pixels as the measurement unit of choice for font sizes (and other objects, too). Points are used for designing type for print but are often unpredictable for displaying text on a computer screen. Pixels seem to be the most predictable in various browsers and on various platforms. If you develop on Windows or on a Mac and it's important that your fonts look similar on the other operating system, use pixels as your unit of measurement for fonts.

Setting the Global Text Color

In a number of areas in Dreamweaver, you can change the color of an object or text. In HTML, colors are specified by using a hexadecimal numbering system, but if you don't know the hexadecimal translation of the color you'd like to use, you can use Dreamweaver's color picker. You access the Dreamweaver color picker by clicking on the color picker box, shown in Figure 3.5. Dreamweaver's color palette appears.

You can experiment picking a color by using the color picker in a number of ways:

- Pick one of the available color swatches by clicking it with the eyedropper.
- By default the Color Cubes palette is displayed. You can select one of the five other panels: Color cubes, Continuous tone, Windows OS, Mac OS, and Grayscale.
- Use the eyedropper to pick up any color onscreen by simply clicking the eyedropper on it. You can pick up any color on the computer screen, not just colors in Dreamweaver. Try selecting a color from one of the icons in the Insert bar. You'll need to arrange Dreamweaver so that you can see other Windows and click the eyedropper on the colors.

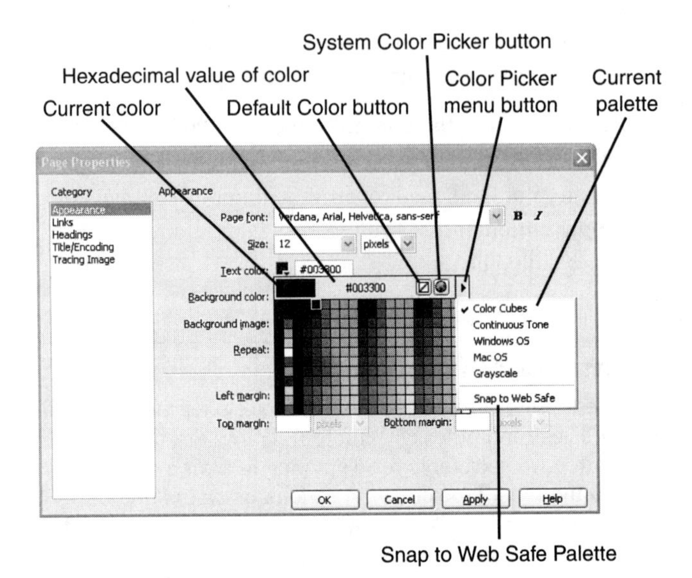

FIGURE 3.5
Select the color picker to open Dreamweaver's color palette.

- Select the System Color Picker button to create a custom color as shown in Figure 3.6. This opens the system color picker, where you can either pick one of the basic colors or click anywhere in the color spectrum to mix your own color. Click the Add to Custom Colors button and then click the OK button to use the color.

You can also type the color information directly into the color text box in the Property inspector:

- Colors are represented in HTML by three hexadecimal numbers preceded by the pound (#) sign. For instance, the hexadecimal RGB (red, green, blue) value for light blue is represented as `#0099FF`, where the value for R is `00`, the value for G is `99`, and the value for B is `FF`. If you know the hexadecimal value for a color, you can simply type it in.

- Most browsers display standard color names in addition to hexadecimal values. For instance, you could type in `red` instead of `#FF0000`.

To clear the current color without picking another color, click the Default Color button in the color picker.

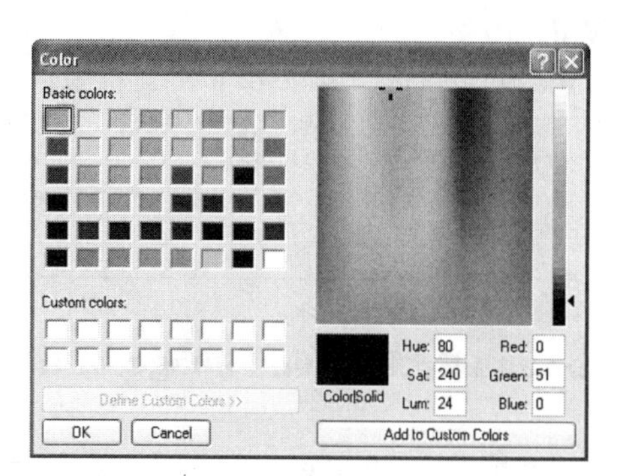

Windows System Color Picker

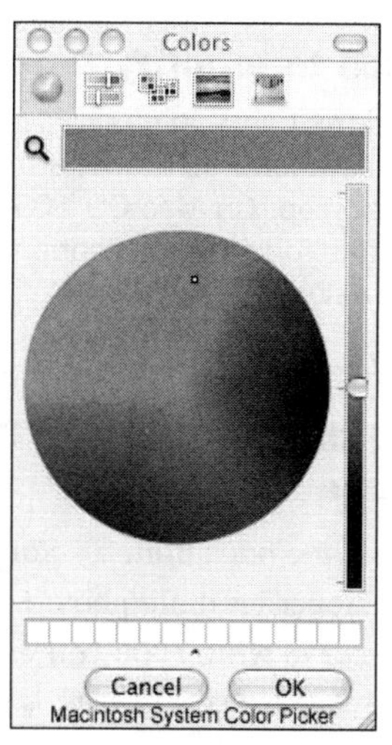

Macintosh System Color Picker

FIGURE 3.6
The System Color Picker enables you to mix your own custom colors on either a Windows (left) or Macintosh OS X (right) computer.

Watch Out!

Web-Safe Colors

The Dreamweaver **web-safe palette** (also known as a **browser-safe palette**) is made up of 212 colors that work on both Windows and Macintosh operating systems displaying 256 colors. Choosing custom colors that are not part of the panel might have an undesirable appearance in older browsers. Most newer computers automatically display more than 256 colors (either thousands or millions of colors), so some web professionals argue that the web-safe palette is no longer necessary. But if your web pages will potentially be viewed on older computers, you should be conservative and design your web pages by using the web-safe palette.

Are You Locked Into Web Safe?

If you enter a color and Dreamweaver doesn't take the value, the color you entered isn't part of the web-safe palette. If the Snap to Web Safe setting is selected in the color picker, Dreamweaver won't let you pick a non–web-safe color. You'll need to turn off the Snap to Web Safe setting before Dreamweaver will allow you to use the color. You turn off this setting in the Color Picker menu by making sure the check mark is not checked next to the Snap to Web Safe command.

Utilities to Identify Color Values

For Windows users to easily identify the hexadecimal value of a color on the screen, download ColorCop, a freeware program available at www.datastic.com/tools/colorcop. On Mac OS 10.4 (Tiger), you can select DigitalColor Meter from the Utilities folder in Applications to identify RGB values on the screen as hexadecimal values.

Setting the Background Color and Background Image of a Web Page

You can set the background color of an entire page in the Appearance category of the Page Properties dialog box. For example, if you'd like to set the web page background color to white, you can enter the hexadecimal color code (#FFFFFF) into the Background Color text box, type `white` into the box, or use the color picker. Of course, you can pick any color that you want as the background color, but make sure that the combination of the background color and the text color doesn't make your web page difficult to read. If you apply a dark background color, you need to use a light text color for contrast so the viewer can easily read the text.

You can also set a background image for a web page. This image is tiled both vertically and horizontally on the page. In order for the web page background to really look nice, you should find or create an image especially designed as a web page background. You can find these specially designed background images on the Web or in image galleries that you purchase. A background image should never interfere with the readability of a page.

To add a background image, select the Browse button and navigate to an image file saved on your hard drive. The image needs to be saved in the GIF, JPEG, or PNG formats (you'll learn more about image format in Hour 7, "Displaying Images"). Click the OK button. You might receive a message from Dreamweaver that a file:// path will be used until you save your document. Just click OK; Dreamweaver automatically corrects that path after you save the web page.

Setting the Page Margins

Margins set the amount of space between the contents of the web page and the edges of the browser window. You set the margins for a page in the Page Properties dialog box. The default setting for page margins varies from browser to browser so it's impossible to predict the amount of white space visible around the border of your web page design. You can change the page margins by entering values into the margin boxes, as shown in Figure 3.7. There are four page margin settings: Left Margin, Top Margin, Right Margin, and Bottom Margin. Many web designers set the

Left and Top Margin settings to 0 pixels so the design is snug to the upper-left corner in the browser window.

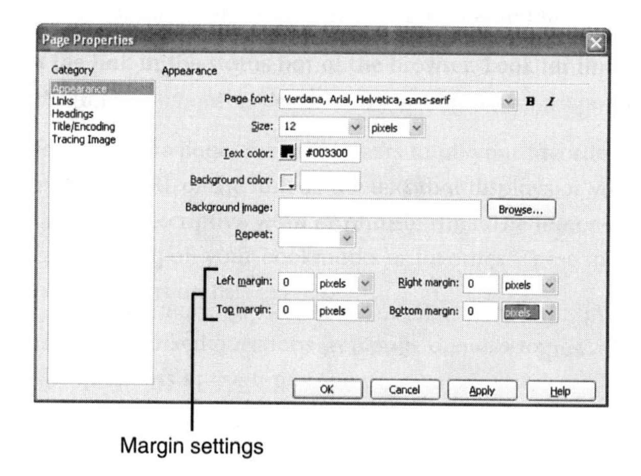

FIGURE 3.7
Set the page margins, the space between your web page design and the edge of the browser window, in the Page Properties Appearance category.

Setting Global Heading Properties

You create a Heading by selecting one of the heading formats, Heading 1 through Heading 6, in the Format drop-down menu in Dreamweaver's Property inspector. In the Headings category of the Page Properties dialog box, you can set global properties for these headings, as shown in Figure 3.8. You can select a Heading Font for all six of the sizes of headings. You can also set a unique font size and color for each of the heading sizes.

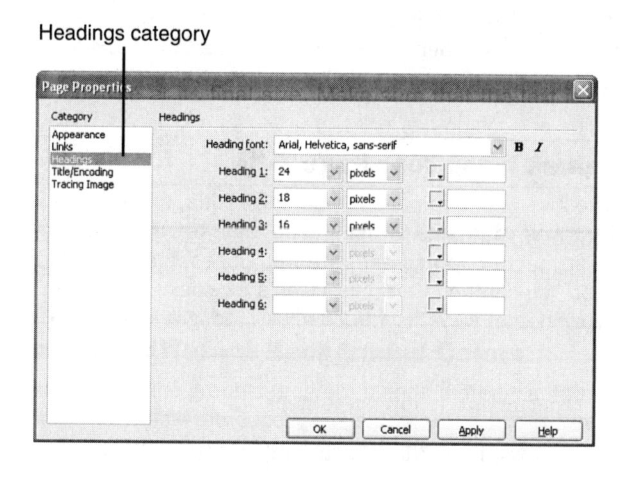

FIGURE 3.8
Set the global heading properties in the Headings category of the Page Properties dialog box. You can set a font for all of the heading sizes and then specify font sizes for each size individually.

To set how Heading 1 will appear, follow these steps:

1. Select Modify, Page Properties if you don't already have the Page Properties open. You should already have some text set to Heading 1 on the page.
2. Select a default font for all of the headings by selecting one of the fonts beside the Heading font setting. You can also select the Bold or Italic button if you'd like.
3. Select a large font size beside Heading 1. A good size to try is 36 pixels. You can also change the color by clicking on the color picker in the Heading 1 settings.
4. Click the Apply button (refer to Figure 3.4) to apply your chánges without closing the Page Properties dialog box.

Heading Sizes

Remember that the headings are meant to become smaller as the heading size number increases. So, Heading 1 is logically meant to be larger than Heading 2. You can override these sizes but it isn't a good idea to do so.

Adding a Page Title

The Title/Encoding category of the Page Properties dialog box enables you to set the document title of your web page along with the Document and Encoding Types. The title of your web page is important because it appears in the title bar of the browser when someone views your web page. This same title is also saved to a user's browser Bookmarks or Favorites list when she saves the address of your site; therefore, you should make it meaningful and memorable.

Search Engines Want Your Page Title

It's important to give your web page a meaningful title, especially if you want people to be able to find your page by using the major search engines. While search engines use many factors to find and rate web pages, the page title is often an important factor. You can find Keith Robinson's excellent discussion on writing better web page titles at www.7nights.com/dkrprod/gwt_seven.php.

To add a title to a document, follow these steps:

1. Select Modify, Page Properties if you don't already have the Page Properties dialog box open.

2. Select the Title/Encoding category.
3. Type a descriptive title in the title box at the top of the Page Properties dialog box.
4. Click the OK button to save the settings. The page title appears in the Document Title textbox in the Document toolbar, as shown in Figure 3.9. You can always add the title in this textbox instead of opening the Page Properties dialog box.

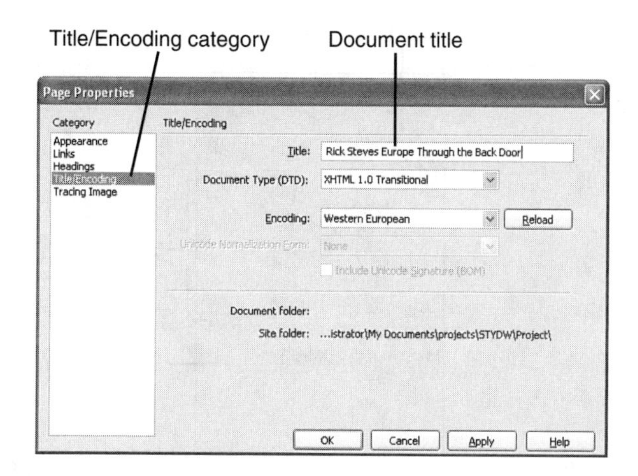

FIGURE 3.9 The document title appears in the Document Title textbox after you enter it in the Page Properties dialog box.

Dreamweaver automatically adds a tag (the <>) at the top of each web page describing the document type for the browser. This tag tells the browser the flavor of HTML that your web page is written in and helps the browser interpret the page. By default, Dreamweaver applies the XHTML 1.0 Transitional document type, which is a good choice because XHTML is an up-and-coming standard and the transitional version of XHTML enables old browsers to still view the web page. XHTML is written in XML (extensible markup language) and enables you to create web pages that are ready for the next generation of websites that are viewable in browsers and also on other devices, such as TVs or cell phones.

There are various alphabets in the world, and using the Encoding command is how you tell a web browser which one you are using for your web page. By default, Dreamweaver lists the Western European encoding type used in the United States and Europe. If you create a page using another alphabet, you need to change the Encoding setting. You can change Dreamweaver's default encoding type in the New Document category in Dreamweaver's Preferences dialog box (Edit, Preferences).

Introducing Cascading Style Sheets

You probably didn't realize it, but you were creating CSS Styles while you were modifying settings in the Page Property dialog box. Dreamweaver automatically adds CSS to your web page and the styles created are visible in the CSS Styles panel (Window, CSS Styles) as shown in Figure 3.10. To view the styles in a web page, make sure the All button is selected at the top of the CSS Styles panel and expand the list of styles by clicking on the Expand/Collapse (+) button next to `<style>`.

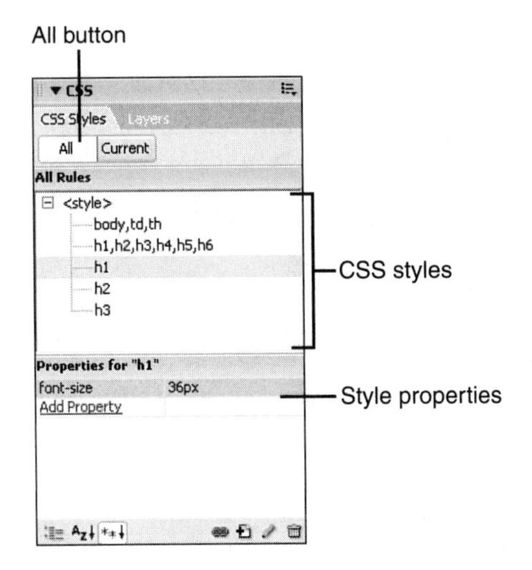

FIGURE 3.10 The CSS Styles panel displays a list of styles created by Dreamweaver when you set properties in the Page Properties dialog box.

The styles created by Dreamweaver Page Properties dialog box are Redefined Tag styles. These styles add formatting properties and alter the default appearance of various tags. For instance, when you change the background color of the page, Dreamweaver redefines the `<body>` tag, which is the tag that contains everything on the web page. These styles are defined in the web page you are working in, but in Hour 16 you'll learn how to place these styles in an external style sheet that can be shared by multiple web pages.

By the Way

Goodbye, `<font>` Tag

Note that older browsers—pre-1997 browsers older than Internet Explorer 4 or Netscape Navigator 4—don't support CSS. The older method of formatting text is to use the `<font>` tag. This tag has been deprecated by the World Wide Web Consortium (W3C), the Web standards organization. **Deprecated** means that the W3C is removing it from the approved tag list and eventually it might not be supported by browsers. Dreamweaver 8 does not insert any `<font>` tags into your code.

Changing Text Attributes in the Property Inspector

In the first part of this hour you learned about the global page settings that affect text. In the next section you'll explore setting properties of sections of text on the page using Dreamweaver's Property inspector. The Property inspector enables you to change the font, font size, and color for sections of text.

Selecting a Text Font

To apply a text font, select some text and then select the Text Font drop-down menu in the Property inspector, as shown in Figure 3.11.

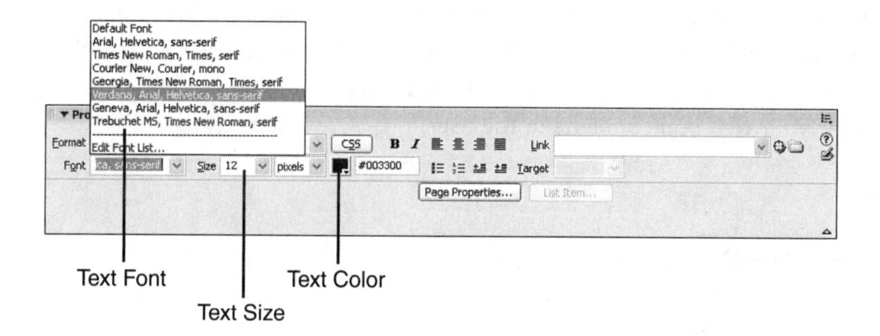

FIGURE 3.11
The Text Font drop-down menu has several font groups from which to choose.

The fonts in the Text Font drop-down menu are defined in groups. Specifying a group instead of an individual font increases the odds that your viewers will have at least one of the fonts in the group. The browser will attempt to display text with the first font listed, but if that font isn't available, the browser will continue through the list. Dreamweaver has predefined groups to choose from, and you can also create your own groups.

Remember, just because you can see the font and it looks great on your machine doesn't mean that everyone has that font. If a font isn't available, the browser will use the default font—usually Times New Roman—instead. The fonts that are in the predefined font combinations in Dreamweaver are commonly available fonts in Windows and on the Macintosh.

Changing Text Size

You change text size by selecting one of the size settings in the Property inspector Text Size drop-down menu shown in Figure 3.12, or by typing a number in the text box. If you select one of the numbers at the top of the list, the Units drop-down menu becomes active so that you can select the unit type. Point and pixel are the most common unit types. You can also select one of the relative sizes (xx-small, medium, large, and so on). These text size settings enable the text to appear relative to the size settings that the user configures in his browser. This is particularly useful for users who have vision impairment but it makes it difficult for you to strictly control how your web page appears to the user.

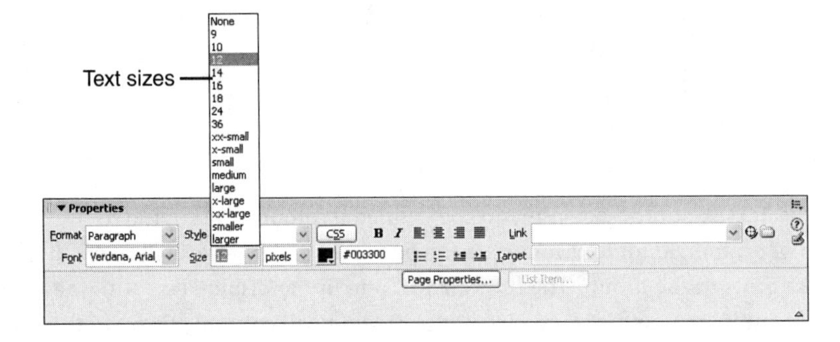

FIGURE 3.12 The Size drop-down menu in the Property inspector enables you to set the size of the selected text.

Selecting a Text Color

You change the text color by either selecting a color using the color picker or by entering a hexadecimal color value, such as #0000FF for blue, into the Text color text box.

Dreamweaver Easter Egg

By the Way

An Easter Egg is a fun bit of functionality that the programmers secretly put into software applications. It is undocumented and unsupported. If you are using Dreamweaver for Windows, there is an Easter Egg associated with text color. If you type the word *Dreamweaver* into the Text Color box in the Property inspector and then press enter, Dreamweaver displays a little game. Enjoy! Sorry, this doesn't work in the Macintosh version of Dreamweaver.

Renaming a Style that Dreamweaver Creates

When you apply text formatting in Dreamweaver's Property inspector, a CSS style is created in the code. This style defines the appearance of the text. You can see the style definition that Dreamweaver creates in the CSS Styles panel by simply clicking the CSS button in the Property inspector, shown in Figure 3.13. If the CSS Styles panel is already open, the button is dimmed. The name of the style that Dreamweaver created for you is displayed in the CSS Style drop-down menu.

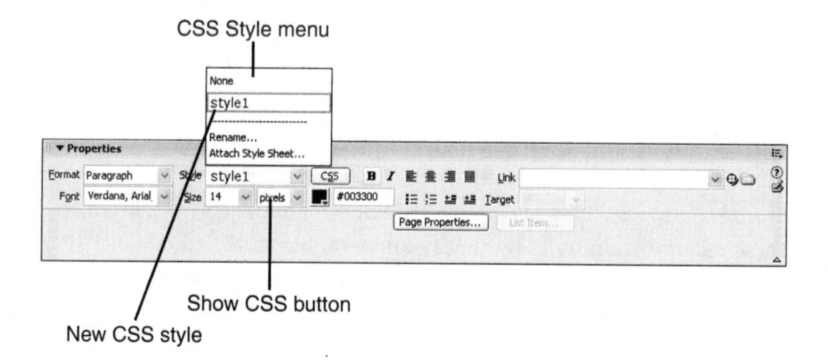

FIGURE 3.13 The name of the CSS Style that Dreamweaver created is displayed in the CSS Style drop-down menu. You can see the style in the CSS Styles panel by clicking the CSS button.

Dreamweaver gives the style a default name (`.style1`, `.style2`, `.style3`, and so on) that is visible in both the CSS Styles panel (make sure the All button is selected) and the CSS Style drop-down menu in the Property inspector. You can edit that name by selecting the style in the CSS Styles panel and right-clicking (Control+clicking on the Mac) to bring up the context menu. Select the Rename command from the menu and give the style a more meaningful name, preferably a name that describes the function of the style in the page. The Results panel might open underneath the Property inspector; you can simply close this panel by selecting the Close Panel Group command from the panel menu in the upper-right corner of the Results panel.

Instead of redefining the same formatting and the same CSS style over and over, you should re-apply an existing CSS style. First select some text on the web page and then select a style from the CSS Style drop-down menu in the Property inspector. You can repeat this process over and over. You'll learn how to edit the style definition in Hour 16.

By the Way

No Guarantees in Website Design

There is really no way to guarantee that a web page will look the same on a viewer's computer as it does on your computer. Browser preferences enable the user to override font settings, size settings, background colors, and hyperlink colors. Don't depend on the page fonts and colors to be exact. If it makes you feel better, though, keep in mind that most users don't change the browser defaults.

You might have noticed that all of the styles listed in your CSS Styles panel don't appear in the CSS Style drop-down menu in Dreamweaver's Property inspector. For instance, the `h1` style or the `body,td,th` style doesn't appear. That's because you apply these redefined tag styles by simply applying the HTML tag to text. In the case of the `h1` style, you simply select Heading 1 from the Property inspector's Format drop-down menu. The styles that Dreamweaver initially named beginning with a period, such as `.style1`, are class selectors, a special type of style that needs to be applied individually to selections of text. Again, you'll learn more about class selectors in Hour 16.

Aligning Text

You can align text to the left, center, or right side of the web page. You can also justify the text so the left and right margins are evenly set down the page. To align some text in the center of the page, follow these steps:

1. Select the text.
2. Click the Align Center icon (see Figure 3.14) in the Property inspector. These icons are very similar to icons in popular word processing programs.

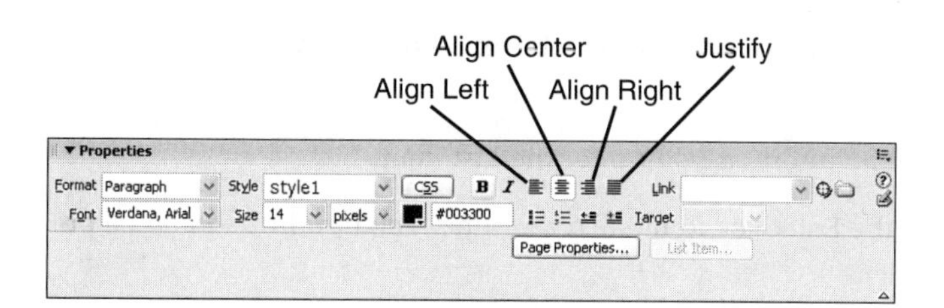

FIGURE 3.14
The alignment icons in the Property inspector look and act like the alignment commands in word processing software.

Alternatively, with the text selected, select Text, Align, Center. The Text menu also contains all the text formatting commands you have used in this hour.

Creating Lists and Indenting Text

By using Dreamweaver, you can create bulleted lists, called **unordered lists** in HTML, and numbered lists, called **ordered lists** in HTML. The Unordered List and Ordered List buttons appear in the Property inspector when you have text selected.

First, create an unordered list by following these steps:

1. Type three items for the list, pressing the Enter (or Return) key after each item so that each is on its own line.

2. Drag the cursor over all three items to select them.

3. Click the Unordered List button in the Property inspector, as shown in Figure 3.15.

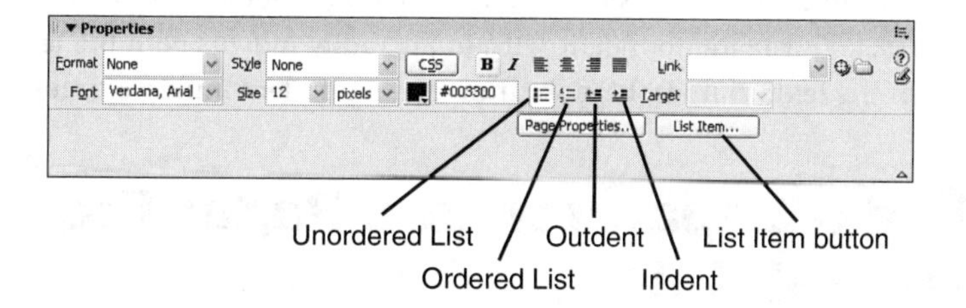

FIGURE 3.15
The Property inspector has buttons to create ordered and unordered lists. You can select the Indent and Outdent buttons to nest lists or to indent and outdent text.

Now each line is preceded by a bullet. Next, add another list that is nested in the first list:

1. Place the insertion point after the last item.
2. Press the Enter key to make a new line. The new line should be preceded by a bullet.
3. Type three items, as you did in the previous list.
4. Drag the cursor over these new items and select the Indent button in the Property inspector.

Now the second list is nested within the third item of the first list. You can tell because it is indented and preceded by a different style of bullet. Use the Outdent button to place the nested list back in line with the main list.

Did you Know?

Customize Your Bullets and Numbers

You can change the bullet or number style by clicking the List Item button in the Property inspector (refer to Figure 3.15) when your cursor is located within the list. Oddly, the List Item button does not appear if you have the entire list selected. Pick the bullet style (either bullet or square) for an unordered list or pick a number style for an ordered list. You can also start the number count at a number other than one by entering the initial number in the Start Count box.

To turn the nested unordered list into an ordered list, select the three items in the nested list again and click the Ordered List button in the Property inspector. To bring the nested list back in line with the main list, select the Outdent button.

With regular text, you use the Indent and Outdent buttons to modify the margins of a block of text. In HTML there is no easy way to tab or indent text, so Dreamweaver uses the `<blockquote>` tag to indent. This tag actually indents both the left and right sides of the text, so it might look strange if you indent multiple times.

Adding a Separator to a Page: The Horizontal Rule

A graphical item that has been around since the Web stone age (about 10 years ago!) is the horizontal rule. That little divider line is still useful. The horizontal rule creates a shaded line that divides a web page into sections. Note that you can't place anything else on the same line with a horizontal rule.

Add a horizontal rule to your web page by selecting the Horizontal Rule object from the HTML category of the Insert bar. Of course, if you're a menu kind of person, you can do this by selecting Insert, HTML, Horizontal Rule. In Figure 3.16, the Property inspector presents the properties of a horizontal rule. You can set width and height values in either pixels or percentages of the screen. You can also set the alignment and turn shading on and off.

FIGURE 3.16 Horizontal rule properties appear in the Property inspector when the rule is selected.

Many objects in HTML have width and height values either in absolute pixel values or as a percentage of the size of the container they are in. If a horizontal rule in the body of a web page is set to a percentage value and the user changes the size of the browser window, the horizontal rule resizes to the new window size. If the horizontal rule is set to an absolute pixel size, it does not resize, and the user sees horizontal scrollbars if the horizontal rule is wider than the screen.

Saving Your Work and Previewing in a Browser

Even though Dreamweaver is a WYSIWYG tool, you need to see how your page really looks in particular browsers. It's a good idea to save your work before you preview it. Saving your work lets Dreamweaver set the paths to linked files, such as images, correctly. We'll explore the concept of linked files and paths further in Hour 4, "Organizing: Defining and Configuring a Website." To save your web page, select File, Save.

Macromedia says you can define up to 20 browsers for previewing. Good luck finding 20 browsers! I generally have the following browsers installed for testing: Mozilla Firefox, Microsoft Internet Explorer, Netscape, and Opera on my Windows machine and Internet Explorer, Netscape, Safari, and sometimes Opera on my Mac. You have to have these programs installed on your computer before you can use them to preview your web pages. All the browsers mentioned have free versions and are available to download over the Internet.

Did you Know?

Get Your Browsers Here!

My favorite browser that I use on a daily basis is Mozilla Firefox and you download it at www.firefox.com. Download Netscape Navigator at browser.netscape.com/ns8 and download Microsoft Internet Explorer at www.microsoft.com/windows/ie. The most popular Mac browser, Safari, is available at www.apple.com/safari and Opera is available at www.opera.com/download.

First, set up a browser as follows:

1. Select File, Preview in Browser, Edit Browser List command. Dreamweaver's Preferences dialog box opens to the Preview in Browser category. Dreamweaver might have already located a browser and entered it here during the installation process, so the list might not be empty. My Windows installation of Dreamweaver always finds Internet Explorer and places it in this list for me.
2. Click the plus button to add a browser, as shown in Figure 3.17.

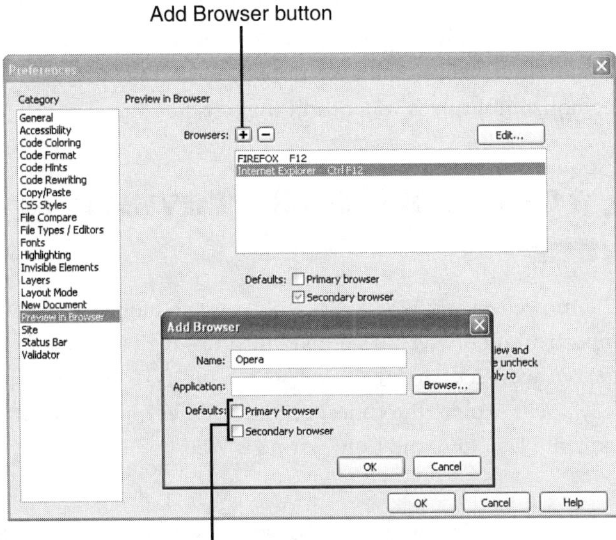

FIGURE 3.17 Set the browsers you will use to preview your web pages in the Preview in Browser category in the Preferences dialog box.

3. Leave the Name text box empty for now; Dreamweaver automatically picks up the name of the browser.
4. Click the Browse button next to the Application text box and navigate to the browser program. For computers running Windows, the default installation

location for most browsers is in the `Program Files` directory. For the Mac, look in your `Applications` folder.

5. Click either the Primary Browser check box or the Secondary Browser check box. This determines which keyboard shortcut you use to launch the browser. The keyboard shortcut for one primary browser is F12, and the shortcut for one secondary browser is Ctrl+F12.
6. Repeat steps 2–5 until all browsers have been added.
7. Make sure that the Preview Using Temporary Files is not selected. Click the OK button when you are done.

Below the browser list is a single check box option that controls whether you directly view your web page in the browser or whether you want Dreamweaver to create a temporary file to display in the browser. When the box is checked, you won't need to save your web page prior to previewing in a browser because Dreamweaver creates a temporary file for you to display in the browser. If you uncheck this box, you need to save your web page prior to previewing it in the browser. I prefer to uncheck this box and know that I'm viewing the actual web page instead of a temporary file. Even after you've saved your page in Dreamweaver and previewed it in the browser, you can still undo changes that you made prior to saving the page.

Select File, Preview in Browser or select Preview in Browser on the Document toolbar to view the current web page. Select the browser you want to use from the menu. If the browser is already open, you might have to switch to the application to see your page. If the browser isn't already open, Dreamweaver opens it and loads the requested page so you can preview it.

Dreamweaver actually checks each page you open in Dreamweaver for potential browser errors. The Check Browser menu on the Document toolbar displays whether you have any browser check errors in the target browsers selected. By default, Dreamweaver checks your page for errors in Internet Explorer 5 and Netscape 6. Modify the browsers and version in the Target Browsers dialog box, shown in Figure 3.18, by selecting Check Browser, Settings.

Congratulations! You've created your first web page in Dreamweaver and learned a lot about formatting the page and text on the page. Many of the tasks described in this hour will become habitual to you with every web page you create, and you will be able to quickly move through the steps you've practiced in this hour.

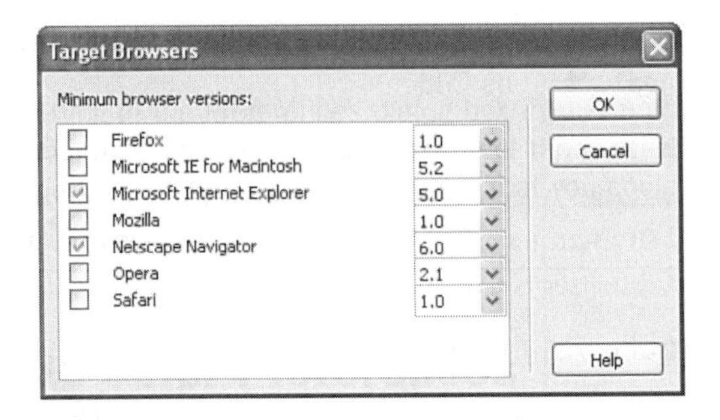

FIGURE 3.18
Select which browser definitions Dreamweaver uses to automatically check for errors.

Summary

In this hour, you have learned how to enter and import text into a web page. You have set text properties, including headings, fonts, lists, and alignment. You've been introduced to CSS, the language of presentation on the Web. You have used a horizontal rule to separate the page into sections and previewed your work in a browser.

Q&A

Q. ***Where can I learn more about CSS styles? They seem important.***

A. CSS styles are important, and they are part of the movement in web development toward separating content (the words and images on the web page) from the presentation (font size, colors, and positioning). This separation is important because it is becoming more and more common to deliver content to various devices, such as PDAs (personal digital assistants), and to people with disabilities, such as impaired sight.

You'll learn much more about CSS styles in Hour 16 and I've listed a number of books and websites in Appendix A, "Resources," that will help you learn about CSS.

Q. ***I indented a line of text by clicking the Indent button. I wanted it to act like a tab acts in my word processing program, but it seems to indent both the beginning and the end of the line. What's going on?***

A. Oddly enough, there is no way in HTML to tab as you do in your word processing program. The Indent button applies the `<blockquote>` tag to the text. This tag, as you noticed, actually indents both the left and the right of the text. The block quote tag was originally designed for quotes in research-type documents. The easiest way to indent text is to place your text in a table. You'll learn about tables in Hour 12, "Displaying Data in Tables," and Hour 13, "Designing Page Layout Using Tables."

Workshop

Quiz

1. What button in the Property inspector do you select to nest a list?
2. By default, which heading size is largest on the screen—Heading 1 or Heading 6?
3. What are the usual default font, size, and color for pages viewed in the default browser configuration?

Quiz Answers

1. The Indent button nests one list within another.
2. Heading 1 is the largest size and Heading 6 is the smallest.
3. The usual defaults for pages viewed in the default browser configuration are Times New Roman, 10 point (medium), and black text.

Exercises

1. Try changing the alignment, shading, and size of a horizontal rule. Use a pixel size value and then use a percentage size value. Test each of your experiments by previewing the page in a web browser.
2. Experiment with creating lists. Create an ordered list, an unordered list, a definition list (see the Text tab of the Insert bar), and some nested lists. As you do this, look at the tag selector in the status bar and see which HTML tags are being used. What do you think the `<li>` tag is used for?
3. Select one of the color boxes in the Page Properties dialog box and set up a custom color. Use the eyedropper to pick a color from anywhere onscreen. You can even pick a color from another application you have open.

HOUR 4

Organizing: Defining and Configuring a Website

What You'll Learn in This Hour:

- How to define a website by using the Site Definition wizard
- How to modify a website definition
- How to organize a website

You use Dreamweaver's Files panel to plan, create, and manage projects. You might have created only a single web page so far, but eventually you'll have lots of files: web pages, image files, and maybe other types of files. It's important that you define your website so Dreamweaver knows how to set links properly. Defining a new site should always be your first step when you start working on a new project.

We broke an unwritten Dreamweaver rule in Hour 3, "Getting Started: Adding Text, Lists, and Previewing in the Browser," because we neglected to define a website in Dreamweaver before we created a web page. Hopefully, that's the last time you create a web page without defining a website for it to reside within. Although you can open and edit individual web pages without a site being defined, it's always easier to manage multiple pages, links to other pages, and links to image files when a site is defined in Dreamweaver.

Defining a New Website

Every website has a root directory. The **root** of a website is the main directory that contains files and other directories. When you define a website, Dreamweaver considers that directory and all the files within it to be the entire "universe" of that particular website. If you attempt to insert an image from outside this universe, Dreamweaver prompts you to save the file inside the website.

Dreamweaver isn't overly controlling, though! The program needs to define the internal realm of your website so it knows how to reference other files. For instance, if an image is located in an images directory within the site, Dreamweaver knows how to properly reference the image within a web page. If, however, the image is somewhere outside the defined site, Dreamweaver might not be able to reference it properly, and you might end up with bad links in your website. You'll learn more about how Dreamweaver links to files in Hour 5, "Setting Lots o' Links: Hyperlinks, Anchors, and Mailto Links."

You need to define a new website for every project you create. Even when projects are related, you might decide to break them down into smaller sites so that the number of files isn't unwieldy in a single site. For instance, I create e-learning applications, courses that people can take over the Web. When I'm working on a project, I often break individual lessons of a course into separate defined sites. When I need to work on Lesson 1, I open that site, and when I need Lesson 2, I open it. You can have only a single site open in Dreamweaver at one time.

Make sure that the Files panel is visible in Dreamweaver (Window, Files). You use the Files panel to open individual web pages in Dreamweaver to work on. The file structure of a website is displayed in the Files panel, and you double-click web pages in this panel to open them to edit them in Dreamweaver. Although it's best to always define a website, if you are just making a quick change to a single web page, it'll be quicker for you to open the file without going to the effort to define a site. You open a single web page by using File, Open.

After you've defined a website, you'll see a list of the files in the website displayed in the Files panel. Prior to defining your first site, you'll simply see the files on your local drive in the Files panel. To begin defining a website, open the Manage Sites dialog box by selecting Manage Sites from the Site drop-down menu, shown in Figure 4.1. You can also open the Manage Sites dialog box from Site, Manage Sites. The Site drop-down menu is where you access the websites you have defined. If you work on multiple projects, you have multiple sites to choose from. For instance, you might have your own personal website defined, plus a site for your child's school or a site for a client whose website you are creating.

The Manage Sites dialog box, shown in Figure 4.2, is where you can create, edit, duplicate, remove, export, and import Dreamweaver site definitions. The title says it all: This is where you manage your websites! To begin defining a new site, click the New button in the Manage Sites dialog box and choose Site. The Site Definition dialog box appears.

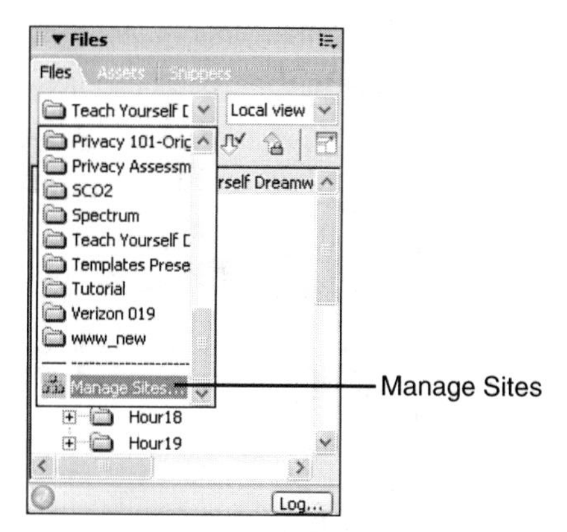

FIGURE 4.1
The Site drop-down menu lists all the defined sites along with the Manage Sites command. Selecting Manage Sites enables you to define a new site in Dreamweaver.

FIGURE 4.2
The Manage Sites dialog box lists all the websites you have defined and enables you to manage them.

The Site Definition dialog box is where you name your site and point Dreamweaver to where the files are stored on your computer. You can define a site even if you don't have any files; you simply define the site in an empty directory that is ready to hold all the web pages you create.

The Site Definition dialog box, shown in Figure 4.3, has two tabs at the top: Basic and Advanced. You'll begin by using the settings on the Basic tab, so make sure that tab is selected. The Basic tab contains the Site Definition wizard that walks you through the site definition. Later this hour you'll learn how to edit your site definition using the Advanced tab in the Site Definition dialog box.

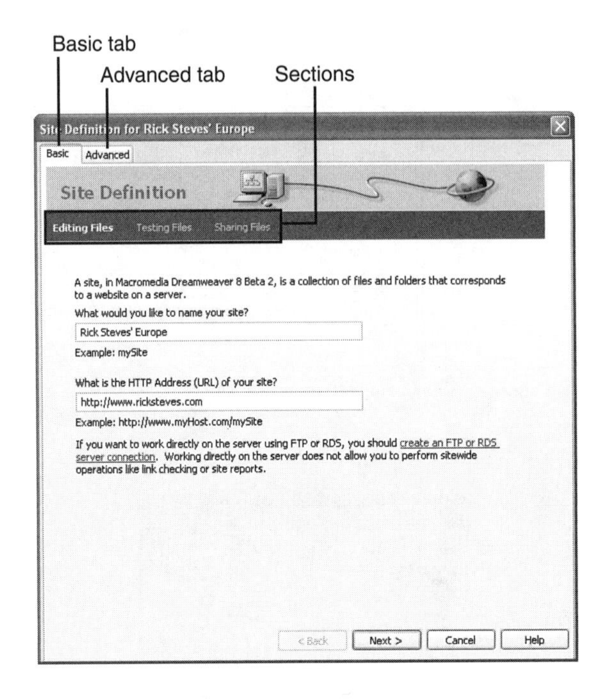

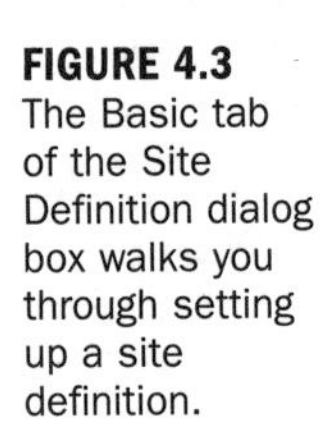

FIGURE 4.3
The Basic tab of the Site Definition dialog box walks you through setting up a site definition.

The Site Definition wizard has three main sections, shown as the section names at the top of the wizard:

- **Editing Files**—This section enables you to set up the local directory where you'll store the website. You tell the wizard whether your site uses server-side technologies. None of the sites or web pages in this book use these technologies, which connect web pages, servers, and often databases.
- **Testing Files**—This section is needed only for sites that use server-side technologies.
- **Sharing Files**—This section enables you to tell Dreamweaver how you want to transfer files to a server or another central location to share. You'll explore this functionality in Hour 20, "Uploading and Sharing a Project on the Web."

Open Manage Sites from the Site Menu

You can open the Manage Sites dialog box from the Files panel or from the Site menu. The command Site, Manage Sites opens the Manage Sites dialog box, enabling you to create a new site or manage your existing sites. Many of the commands available in the Files panel are repeated in the Site menu so you can access the commands from either location.

Using the Site Definition Wizard

Make sure you have the Basic tab selected at the top of the Site Definition dialog box. In the Site Definition wizard (refer to Figure 4.3), give your site a name. This name is used only inside Dreamweaver, so you can use spaces and characters in it if you want. The site name should be meaningful—it should identify the purpose of the website when you drop down the Site menu to change sites. My Dreamweaver installation has about 30 to 40 sites defined at times, so clear names help me quickly find the site I want to edit. If you know the final HTTP address of your site, you can enter it here on the first page of the wizard; it's also fine to leave this empty. Click the Next button.

The next page of the wizard, Editing Files, Part 2 (shown in Figure 4.4), enables you to specify whether you will be using server-side scripting to create dynamic web pages. Your web pages in this book will be regular HTML pages, so you should select the top radio button that says No, I Do Not Want to Use a Server Technology. Click the Next button.

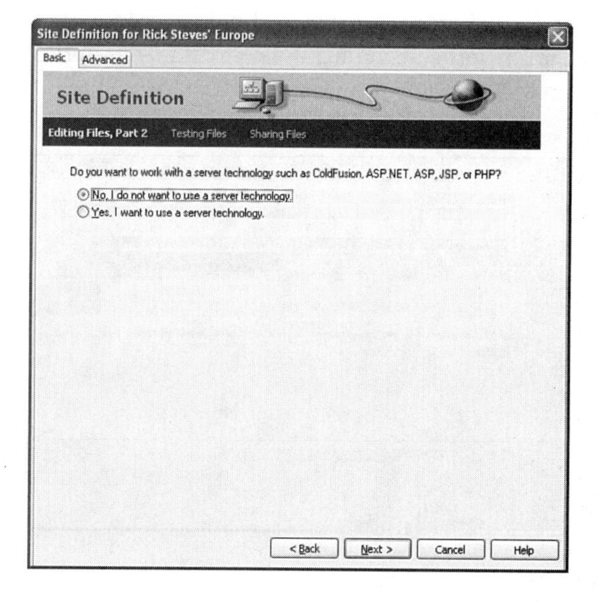

FIGURE 4.4
You tell Dreamweaver whether you will be using server-side scripting in your site.

The next page, Editing Files, Part 3, helps you specify where the files in your site are located. The site that you are creating here is your **development site**, not the final site that other people will view over the Web. You need to move the files in your development site up to a server for people to view the files over the Web (the subject of Hour 20). The website located on a web server and available to the public is called the **live site**. I always work on an up-to-date copy of a website that is located on my local hard drive.

You can store your development files in three places: on your local machine, on a network drive, or on a server somewhere. Select the top radio button to elect to store the development files on your local machine; this is where most web developers store their files. If you are working in a networked environment (at your office, for instance), you could use either of the other two choices. Right now, select the radio button next to Edit Local Copies on My Machine, Then Upload Them to the Server When Ready (Recommended).

Watch Out!

Don't Develop on the Live Site

Do not ever link to the final live site for development. You do not want to make a mistake on the real site; always make sure you are working on a copy of the site.

As shown in Figure 4.5, the text box at the bottom of the dialog box asks you to enter the location of the site directory. Click the folder icon to the right of the text box to navigate to the directory where you will store your local site, the files that you will work on in Dreamweaver. Either use an existing directory on your hard drive or create a new directory for your site. Click the Next button.

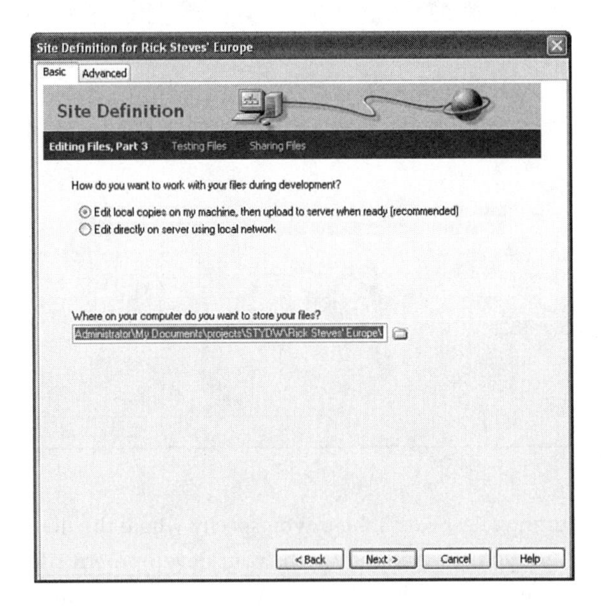

FIGURE 4.5
You enter the directory that will house your development files.

By the Way

Name Your Files Properly to Avoid Problems

Spaces, punctuation, and special characters in file and directory names might cause problems. You can use underscores or dashes instead of spaces in names. All files should be named using a combination of letters, numbers, and underscores. Don't ever begin your file names with a number because JavaScript is not able to process names that begin with numbers. You might not be using JavaScript right now, but you might in the future and it could be a lot of work to rename files.

Watch Out!

Servers Might Be Case-Sensitive

Filenames are case-sensitive on most web servers. Servers running the various flavors of the Unix operating system enable you to create files named `mydog.gif`, `Mydog.gif`, and `MYDOG.gif` all in the same directory because the capitalization differs. Microsoft operating systems, such as Windows, are not case-sensitive. So, if you are developing in Windows your links might work perfectly and then cease to work when you upload them to a case-sensitive server!

The next section in the Site Definition wizard enables you to configure how you share files. You can set up a central location where members of your team can share files. Or you can set up a location on a public web server where you share your website with the world. You'll learn how to configure this section and transfer files in Hour 20. For now, simply drop down the top menu and select None, as shown in Figure 4.6. Click the Next button.

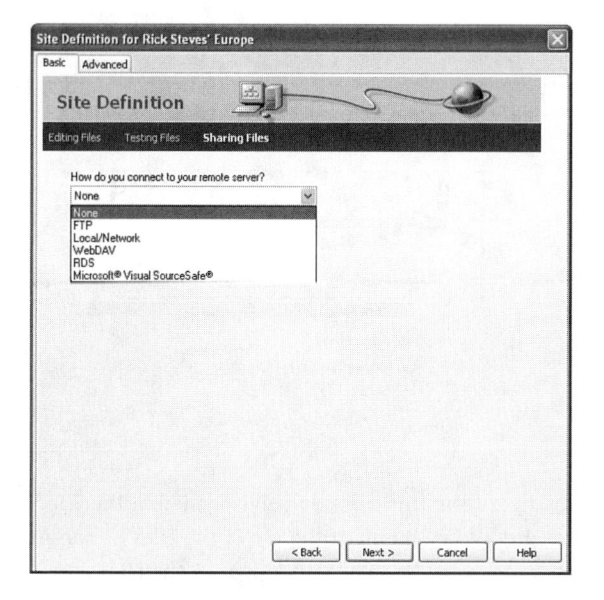

FIGURE 4.6
To set up the remote connection information later, simply select None.

The last page of the wizard displays a summary of your site, as shown in Figure 4.7. You can come back to this wizard at any time to change your site definition by selecting the Edit Sites command from the Site menu (either the one in the Files panel or the one in the Document window). Click the Done button.

After you click the Done button, Dreamweaver displays a message, telling you that it will now create the initial site cache. When you click OK, a progress bar like the one in Figure 4.8 appears (and disappears very quickly if you have nothing in your site yet). The initial site cache is created each time you create a new site. The **site cache** is used to store information about the links in your site so they can be quickly updated if they change. Dreamweaver continues to update the cache as you work.

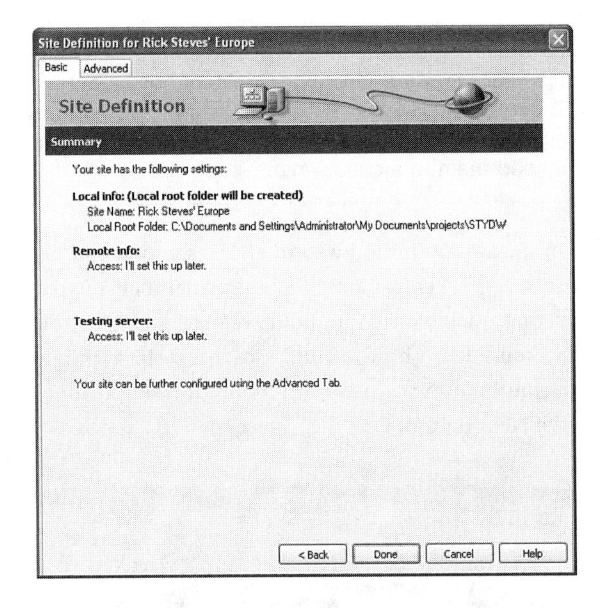

FIGURE 4.7
The Site Definition wizard displays a summary of your site definition.

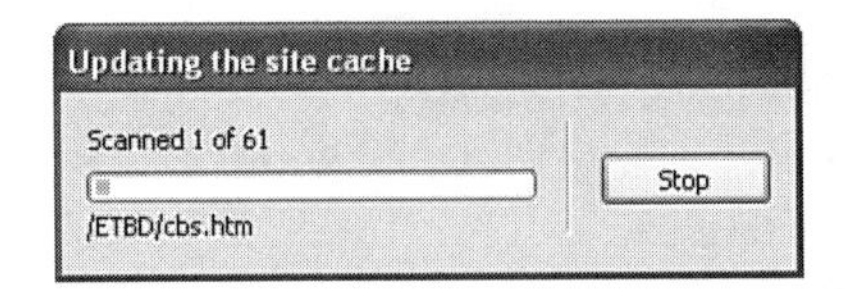

FIGURE 4.8
You might see a progress bar as Dreamweaver creates a cache for your site. This file speeds the updating of links when you move or rename a file.

After you've defined your site, the site title you specified in the Site Definition wizard appears in the Site drop-down menu at the top of the Files panel. As you create web pages and save them to your site they will appear in the Files panel. You will use the

Files panel to open web pages to edit in Dreamweaver. Right now you might not have any web pages in your site but eventually you'll want to use the Files panel to create folders to organize the many web pages you've created.

There is no special procedure for importing an existing website into Dreamweaver. While a copy of the existing website exists in a folder on your hard drive, simply define a site in Dreamweaver that points to that folder. This is all you need to do. All of the files are available to edit in Dreamweaver and you can easily modify web pages and then save them.

Using the Files Panel

You select the site you'd like to work on in the Files panel, which is shown in Figure 4.9. This is where you open web pages to edit in Dreamweaver. The Site drop-down menu gives you quick access to all your defined sites. So far you've been using the Collapsed version of the Files panel but the next section introduces the Expanded version of the Files panel.

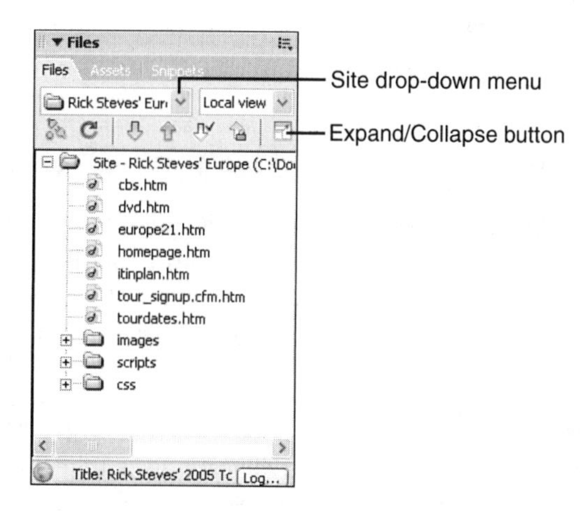

FIGURE 4.9
The Files panel enables you to change sites and open web pages.

Using the Expanded Files Panel

To get a bigger view of a site and to get access to more functionality, select the Expand/Collapse button in the Files panel to open the Expanded Files panel. The Expanded Files panel, shown in Figure 4.10, is a larger representation of the Files panel and has two panes: local files (on the right, by default) and remote site (on the left), which you will set up in Hour 20. Because you have not yet defined a remote site, you should not have any files in the remote site pane at this point.

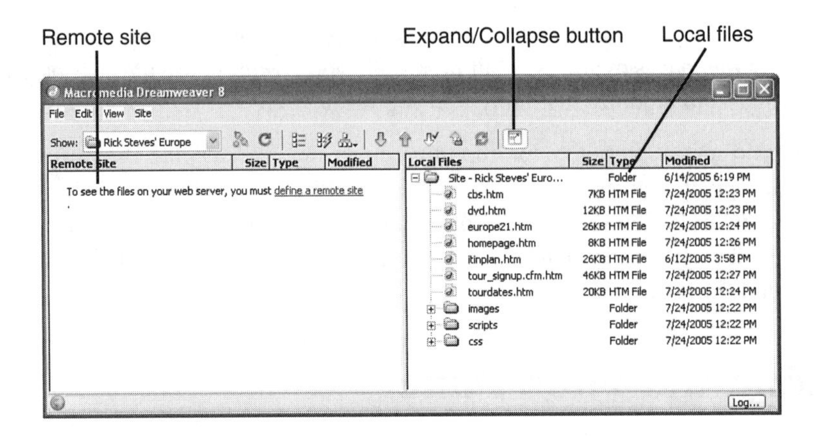

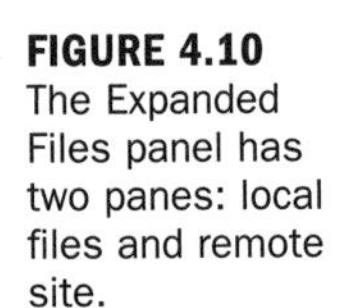
FIGURE 4.10
The Expanded Files panel has two panes: local files and remote site.

When you click the Files Expand/Collapse button on the Macintosh, the Expanded Files panel opens in a new window. On Windows, it looks like this is a new window because it looks so different from the standard Dreamweaver interface, but if you close the window by clicking the Close button in the upper-right corner, you will close Dreamweaver! In both versions of Dreamweaver, click the Expand/Collapse button again to return to the smaller version of the Files panel.

Creating New Files in the Files Panel

You can create new files and new folders right in the Dreamweaver Files panel. Right-click (Control+click on the Mac) in the Files panel to open the Files panel menu. This context menu, shown in Figure 4.11, has two commands of interest at the top: New File and New Folder. You'll use those commands to create files and folders (also called **directories**) in the Files panel.

The websites you create will need directories for organization, and probably every site will at least have an images directory for all the images in the site. Create an images directory by using the New Folder command. An untitled folder is added to your site. Give this folder the name `images`. You need to be careful about what is selected when you select the New Folder command so you do not nest the folder within another folder. To add a folder at the site root, select the top line in the Files panel, which begins with the word *Site*.

Now try adding a new file to your site. Right-click (or Control+click on the Mac) on the root folder and select the New File command. A new untitled web page is created in the website. Title the web page `index.htm`, which is one of the popular default page names for many servers. Using the **default page name** enables the user to find your page more easily by just entering a basic web page address without the specific page appended. Another common default page name is `index.html`. Both the `.htm` and the `.html` file extensions are acceptable. The `.htm` file extension became popular because the older versions of Microsoft Windows could only handle three-character file extensions; this is no longer a limitation in newer versions of Windows. After you add the new folder and a new file, the site should look as shown in Figure 4.12.

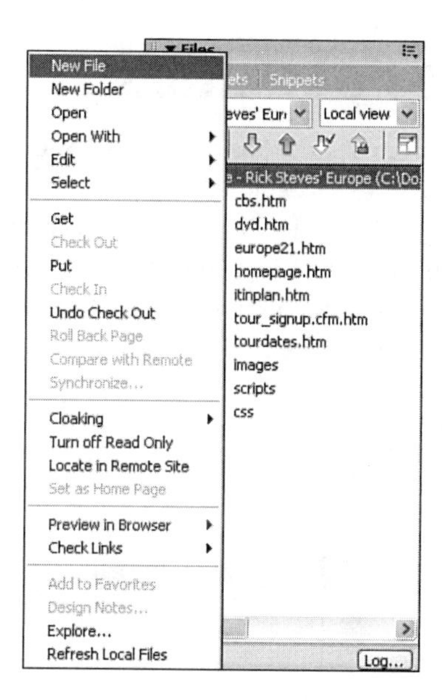

FIGURE 4.11 The Files panel context menu contains commands to create new folders and files in a website.

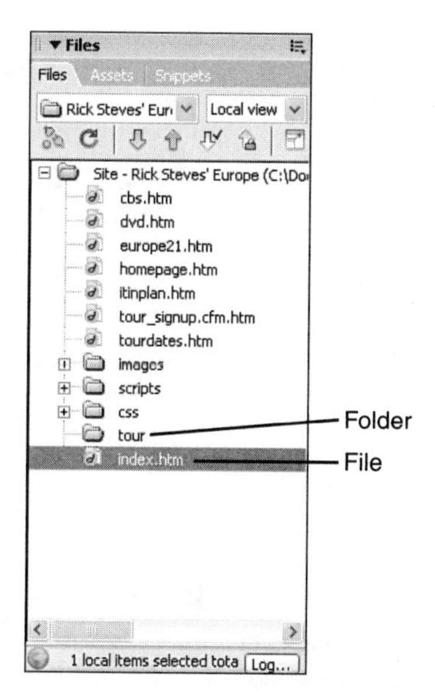

FIGURE 4.12 You can add files and folders in Dreamweaver's Files panel.

Name Files Consistently

I think it's a good idea to name everything with lowercase letters. Some servers and scripting languages are case-sensitive. When you name everything with lowercase letters, you don't need to remember whether you used uppercase letters.

Editing a Site Definition

So far in this hour, you have used the Basic tab in the Site Definition dialog box to initially define a website. Now let's explore the Advanced tab and use it to edit site settings. Open the Manage Sites dialog box again by selecting Manage Sites from the Site drop-down menu. Select the site you just created and then click the Edit button. The Site Definition dialog box opens again. Click the Advanced tab at the top of the dialog box. As shown in Figure 4.13, this is another view of the information you entered into the wizard.

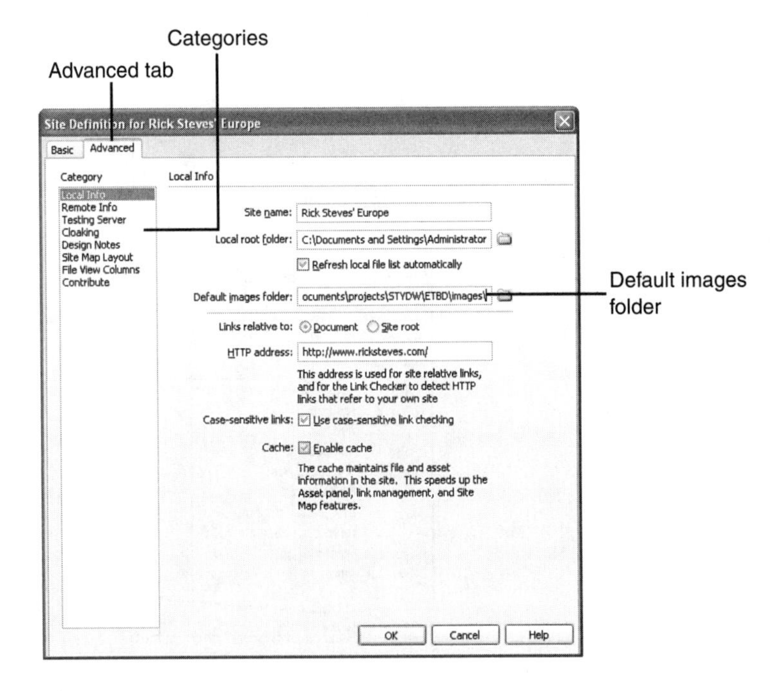

FIGURE 4.13 The Advanced tab contains all the site properties.

Did you Know?

A Quick Way to Edit Site Definitions

A fast way to open the Site Definition dialog box is to simply double-click the name of the site in the Files panel's Site drop-down menu.

The left side of the Site Definition dialog box shows categories, and the right side lists the selected category's properties. Select the Local Info category and then select the folder icon next to the Default Images Folder text box. Navigate to the images folder you just created. Now Dreamweaver knows where you'll keep your images for the site. Click the OK button to save your changes. Click the Done button to close the Edit Sites dialog box.

Did you Know?

Check Case Sensitivity

In the Advanced tab of the Site Definition dialog box, there is a check box called Use Case-Sensitive Link Checking. If you select this setting, Dreamweaver checks that the links in your site use the same case (uppercase or lowercase) as the file names. This is very useful if you are eventually uploading your website to a case-sensitive UNIX server.

You'll learn about other advanced options later in this book. In Hour 20, you'll set up the Remote Info category in order to upload your files to a remote website. In Hour 21, "Managing and Editing a Website," you'll explore the Cloaking and Design Notes categories.

Considering Site Organization

There are many opinions about the proper way to organize a website. Some people like to compartmentalize all the files into directories and subdirectories. Some people like to have a very shallow structure, with many files in a single directory. As you get more experienced at web development, you'll find your ideal method of organization. It's nice to exchange ideas with other web developers or hobbyists so you can learn from the successes and failures of others and they can learn from yours.

I have a directory on my hard drive called `Projects`, represented in Figure 4.14. The `Projects` directory contains a directory for each project on which I'm working. Within each project directory is a directory called `Web`. This is the directory where I keep all the development files for the site and the directory that I set as the root in Dreamweaver.

This directory structure enables me to put other files, such as correspondence, contracts, invoices, and spreadsheets, in the client's folder without making them part of the website. It's good practice to keep other files separate from those you plan to transfer to the Web. You might prefer to have one directory that contains all your websites. Do whatever works best for you.

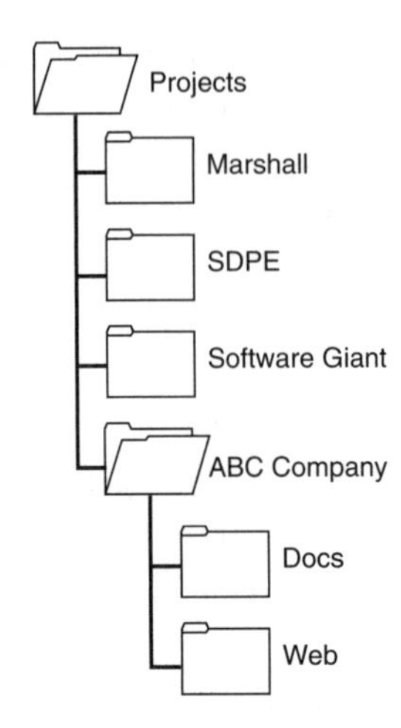

FIGURE 4.14
An example of a directory structure in which the website is housed in the `Web` directory.

Put some thought into how you'll organize the files in your website before you start a project. You will probably want to create a separate images folder to hold your images, as shown in Figure 4.15. If you have other types of assets, such as sound or video, you might want to create separate folders for those, too. I always create a scripts directory to hold external JavaScript files and external Cascading Style Sheets files; you'll explore these in the later hours of this book.

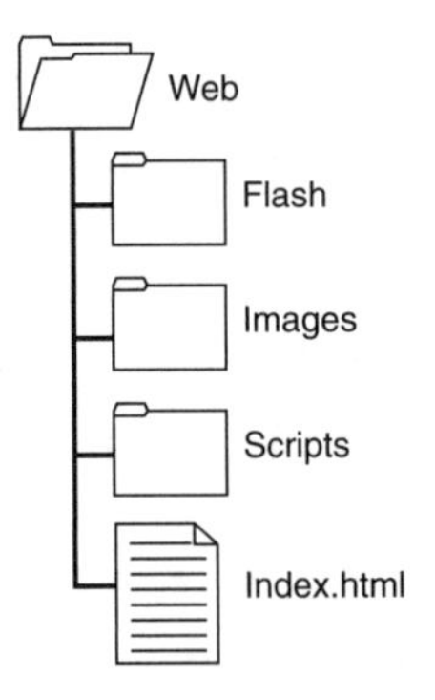

FIGURE 4.15
You can organize your website into images and other directories.

I try to logically break up sections of websites into separate directories. If your website has obvious divisions (departments, lessons, products, and so on), you can create directories to hold the web pages in each of the sections. You'll be surprised at how even a small website becomes quickly unmanageable when all the files are dumped into one directory.

Most websites use many image files. If you have different sections in your website, do you want to have separate images directories in each section? It might be a good way to organize your site. Then again, if images are used across multiple sections, it might make the images hard to find. Make sure that your organizational logic isn't going to break down as you add files to your site.

Luckily, if you do have to rearrange assets, Dreamweaver will update any links for you. When you move a file, Dreamweaver asks you if you want to search and update links to that file. That's what the site cache is created for. However, it is still best to make wise design decisions at the beginning of a big project.

Summary

In this hour, you have learned how to define a website and determine its root. You have learned how to quickly add files and folders to a site. You have learned how to use the Files panel and expand it into the Expanded Files panel. And you have explored ideas about how to organize a site.

Q&A

Q. ***How do I import a website into Dreamweaver?***

A. There is no procedure for importing a site. You simply define a site exactly as you did this hour, pointing to the root directory of the site you'd like to import. Dreamweaver presents all the files in the Files panel, enabling you to open and edit them. If the site you need to import is on a web server, you'll first need to read Hour 20 and set up remote site settings pointing to the server.

Q. ***If I need to move files within my site, is it okay to do it within Dreamweaver?***

A. If you need to do some housekeeping or rearranging, it's best to do it within Dreamweaver. Dreamweaver automatically updates links to files and warns you if deleting a file will affect other files within your site. Make sure you take care of these tasks within Dreamweaver and not elsewhere.

Workshop

Quiz

1. Why do you need to define a website?
2. What does the Dreamweaver cache do?
3. You must go through a conversion process to import an existing website into Dreamweaver. True or false?

Quiz Answers

1. You define a website so Dreamweaver knows where the root of the site is and what your site management preferences are.
2. Enabling the cache speeds up some Dreamweaver features, such as updating hyperlinks.
3. False. No conversion process is necessary to import an existing website into Dreamweaver.

Exercises

1. Try defining a new website. Add some files and folders to the new site.
2. Search for *Site Map* in Google (www.google.com) and look at the organization of other sites on the Web. The folders used to store web pages might or might not reflect the same structure outlined in the site map. Click on some of the pages and look at the folder structure in the URLs.
3. Explore the other categories in the Site Definition dialog box (Notes or Cloaking, for instance). We'll cover the other categories in upcoming hours.

HOUR 5

Setting Lots o' Links: Hyperlinks, Anchors, and Mailto Links

What You'll Learn in This Hour:

- When to use relative and absolute paths
- How to create a hyperlink to another page within a website and a hyperlink to a page outside a website
- How to create hyperlinks within a page
- How to add a link that opens a preaddressed email message

Clicking a **hyperlink** allows the viewer to jump to another web page, jump to another section of the current web page, or launch an email message. A website is made up of a group of web pages, and hyperlinks enable viewers to navigate from page to page. Hyperlinks, in the simplest form, are the familiar underlined and colored (usually blue) text that you click. You can also make an image a hyperlink.

Hyperlinks help make the Web a powerful source of information. If you've surfed the Web at all, I'm sure you've clicked many, many hyperlinks. But hyperlinks can also make the Web confusing. Sometimes it is difficult to remember the exact path you took to find information, and that can make it difficult to get back to the information when you want to see it again.

A web address is called a **uniform resource locator (URL)**. You can link many types of files over the Web, but only a few file types will actually be displayed in a browser. A browser can display the supported image formats, HTML, player applications (such as Flash), and a few other specialized types of files. If a link leads to a file that the browser can't display (a `.zip` file, for example), the browser will usually ask you if you'd like to save the file to your hard drive.

Exploring Relative and Absolute Paths

Whenever you create a hyperlink to another web page or place an image file in a web page, you need to enter a path to the file. Dreamweaver helps make sure that these paths are correct, but it's important that you understand the difference between the two main types of paths: absolute paths and document-relative paths. An **absolute path** is the full URL (more about URLs in a few minutes) to a web page. A **document-relative path** points to the location of a file in relationship to the page being viewed.

An analogy for an absolute path is a house address. If I gave the address of my house to someone who lives in another town, I would tell them, "I live at 123 Spruce, Seattle WA 98122, USA." This is all the information that anyone would need to get to my exact location or to send me a letter (this isn't my real address, so if you really want to send me a letter, send it in care of the publisher!). If I gave directions to my house to someone who lives on my street, I might tell them, "I live two doors south of you." The directions in this case are relative to my neighbor's location. This is analogous to a document-relative path.

The link to the Macromedia Dreamweaver Developer Center shown in Figure 5.1 is an absolute path. It contains the entire path to a file on the Internet. Because you have no control over this site, linking to it means that you need to check to see that the link remains valid. If the site moves in the future, you will need to update the link.

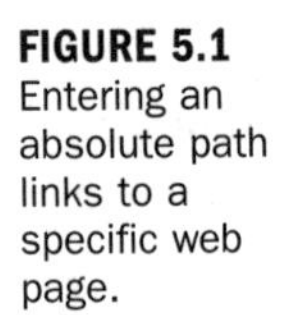
FIGURE 5.1 Entering an absolute path links to a specific web page.

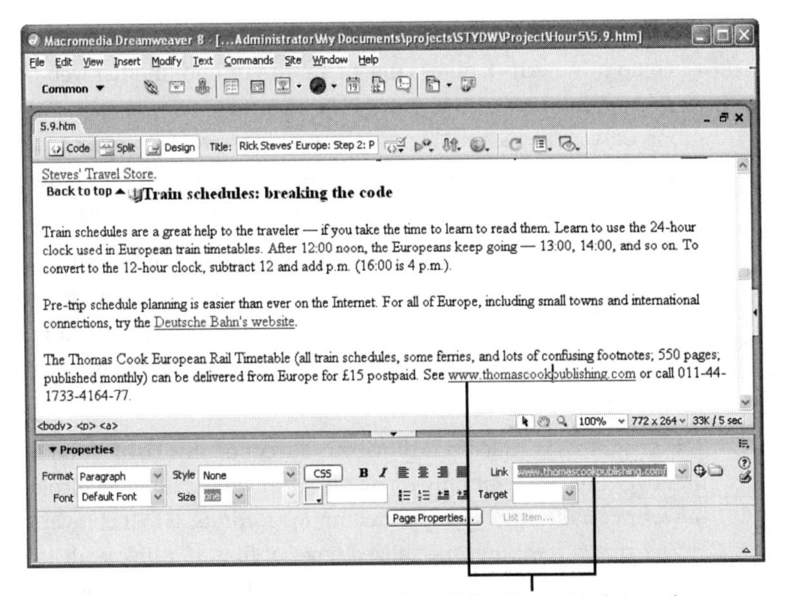

A hyperlink with an absolute path

A URL consists of up to five sections, as shown in Figure 5.2:

- **Protocol**—The first part of the URL is the protocol. It is `http` for web pages to indicate Hypertext Transfer Protocol (HTTP). Sometimes you might want to link to a file on a File Transfer Protocol (FTP) server (another method of communicating over the Internet to move files to and from a server), using `ftp` as the protocol instead of `http`.
- **Domain**—The second part of the address is the domain. This is the web server where the web page is located; for example, in Figure 5.2, the domain is www.betsybruce.com. A colon and two forward slashes (`://`) separate the protocol and the domain.
- **Port**—An optional third part of a URL is the port. The default port for a web server is port 80. When you enter `http` as the protocol, port 80 is implied and doesn't usually need to be included. You might need to enter port information when entering addresses to specialized web applications that listen on a port other than port 80.
- **Path and filename**—The fourth part of the address is the path and filename. The path includes all directories and the filename. Most web pages end in `.htm` or `.html`. Other common file endings are `.cgi`, for Common Gateway Interface; `.asp`, for Active Server Pages; `.jsp`, for JavaServer Pages; `.aspx`, for ASP.NET files; `.php`, for PHP pages; and `.cfm`, for ColdFusion Markup Language.
- **Query string**—The filenames might be followed by an optional fifth part of a URL—a query string. A query string is added to a URL to send data to a script to be processed. We'll explore query strings in Hour 19, "Introduction to Scripts: Sending and Reacting to Form Data."

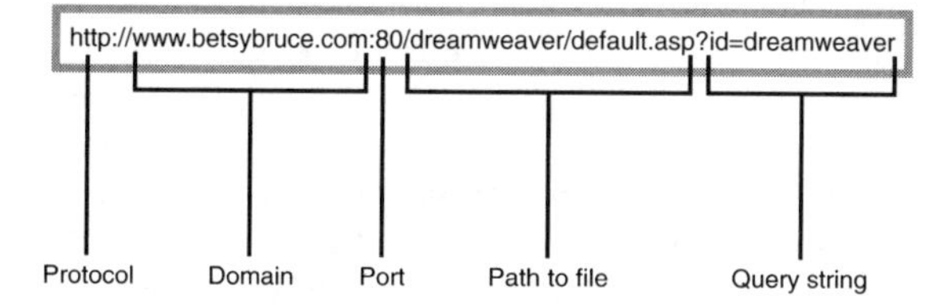

FIGURE 5.2
A URL consists of multiple sections. Every URL must contain a protocol, a domain name, and the complete path to a file.

You might see a URL that does not have a filename referenced at the end, such as http://www.macromedia.com/devnet/mx/dreamweaver. This type of address works because the web server looks for a default page in the directory. Most web servers have a default page name that doesn't need to be explicitly entered at the end of the URL. Usually the default page name is `welcome.html`, `default.htm`, `default.html`, `index.htm`, or `index.html`. On some servers, any of these names will work. This functionality can be configured in web server software.

Default pages in the root of a site are often referred to as **home pages**. To create a home page for a website, ask your webmaster or web hosting service for the default page name for your web server. If you don't have a default page on your website and a visitor doesn't enter a filename at the end of the URL, she might see all the contents of your directories instead of a web page. Or the user might get an error message!

You usually do not need to enter the protocol into the browser's address box to go to a web page. Most browsers assume that you want to use HTTP. However, if you are surfing to an FTP file, you need to enter `ftp` as the protocol at the beginning of the URL. Even though browsers assume HTTP, you still need to preface absolute links entered into Dreamweaver with `http://`.

Within your own website, you use document-relative paths so you can move your site anywhere and your links will still work. While developing in Dreamweaver, you will create a website on your local hard drive and then eventually move the site to a web server. Document-relative paths work the same in both locations.

It's important to use document-relative paths instead of absolute paths in your website. If you have an absolute path to a file on your local drive, the link will look like the following:

```
file:///C|/My Documents/first_page.html
```

This file, `first_page.html`, is on the `C:` drive in a directory called `My Documents`. If you preview this page in your browser, it works fine for you. So, what's the problem? The reason it works fine is that you have that page available on your hard drive, but other people don't have access to your hard drive and will not be able to access the page.

Document-relative paths don't require a complete URL. The path to the linked file is expressed relative to the current document. You use this type of path when inserting images into a web page. You also use a document-relative path when creating a hyperlink to a web page within your website. Luckily, Dreamweaver saves the correct document-relative path after you save a web page.

By the Way

Links Work with Other Files, Too

You don't have to limit your links to web pages. You can link to movies, word processing files (`.doc` files, for instance), PDF files, or audio files. The URLs work the same regardless of the content. Of course, the browser you are using has to recognize the content type in order to display it properly. You'll learn more about the players necessary to play audio files or view PDF documents in Hour 10, "Adding Flash and Other Multimedia to a Web Page."

The following are some examples of document-relative paths:

- When linking to a file that is in the same directory as your current file, you enter only the filename as the path. For instance, if the file `mktg.htm` in Figure 5.3 has a link to `sales.htm`, the path would simply be the filename because both files are in the same directory.

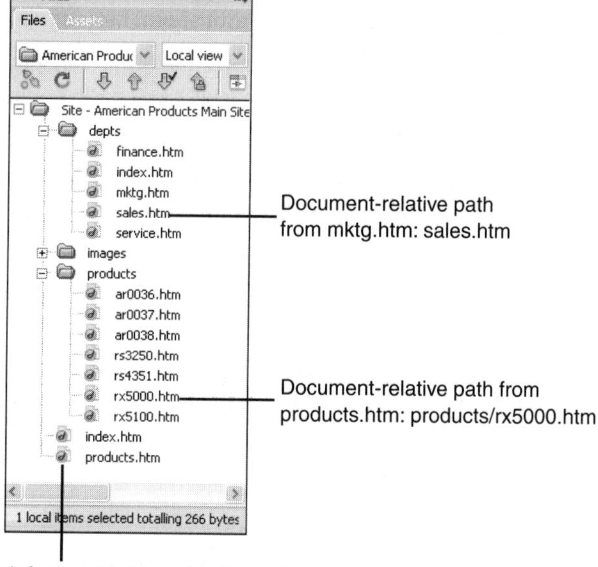

FIGURE 5.3 Document-relative paths depend on the relative position of the files in the directory structure.

- To link to a file in a directory nested within the current file's directory, you enter the directory name and the filename as a path. For instance, if the file `products.htm` in Figure 5.3 has a link to the file `rx5000.htm` in the `products` directory, the path is `products/rx5000.htm`.

- When linking to a file in a directory above the current directory (called the **parent directory**), you enter ../ plus the filename as a path. The ../ means go up to the next parent directory. For instance, if the file `sales.htm` in Figure 5.3 has a link to the file `products.htm` in the site root, the path is `../products.htm`.

Before it saves your web page, Dreamweaver inserts all links as absolute links; you might receive an error message warning you of this when you add a link. It does this because it cannot calculate a relative link until the file is saved. After the file has been saved, Dreamweaver can tell where your document is relative to all linked files and will change the links to document-relative addresses. Accidentally using absolute paths is an easy mistake to make. Dreamweaver looks out for you, however, and attempts to correct these problems for you.

There is a third type of path, called **site root–relative**. In a site root–relative link, the path is relative to the root of the entire website. The **root** of the website is defined as a certain directory of a website, usually where the site's home page is located. Site root–relative linking is used in professional environments where many different sections of the website need to access a common group of files, such as a corporate logo or common button images.

Site root–relative paths are not the best choice for beginning web development workers. The main difficulty is that you can preview pages that have site root–relative links only if they are loaded on a web server. Therefore, if you use these links, you won't be able to preview your work in a browser without loading it onto the server. Stay away from site root–relative paths until you are more experienced.

Be Careful with Your Slashes

A site root–relative path is preceded with a forward slash (/). An example of a site root–relative path is

```
/depts/products.html
```

Be careful not to enter a path this way by accident when typing in an address. The correct document-relative path would be

```
Depts/products.html
```

Adding a Hyperlink Within a Website

In this sectionyou'll create several new web pages and save them to your website. You can use these pages to practice linking by using document-relative paths, so create a couple now.

Did you Know?

Click Here...

It's generally bad form to explicitly reference a hyperlink by saying "Click here to see our statistics." It's better to incorporate a hyperlink into a natural sentence, such as, "The 2004 statistics show that sales increased by 32%." Ideally, hyperlinks are meant to seamlessly blend into the text of your documents.

Create a new page that links to an existing page:

1. Select File, New to open the New Document dialog box.
2. Select the Page Designs category in the New Document dialog box, as shown in Figure 5.4. These designs come with Dreamweaver and are a great starting place for your web page development.

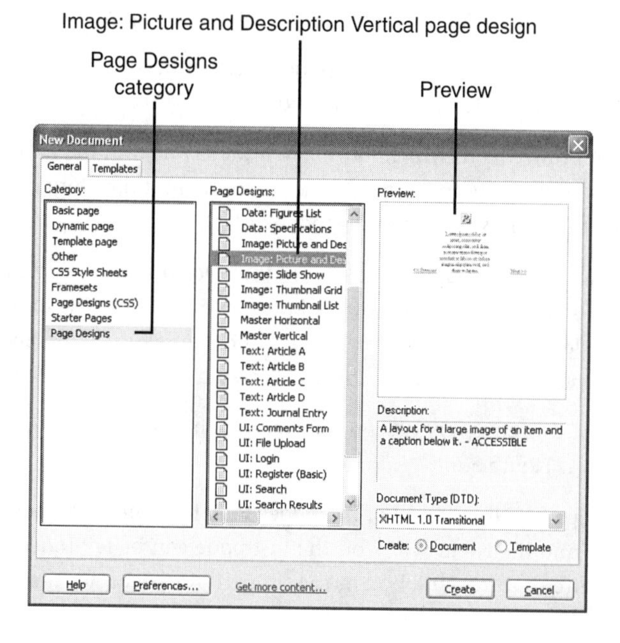

FIGURE 5.4 Using a page design gives you a head start when creating a web page.

3. Select the page design entitled Image: Picture and Description Vertical from the Page Designs list.
4. Make sure to create a document (instead of a template) by selecting the Document radio button.
5. Click the Create button.

6. You now have a web page with an image placeholder and some placeholder text. Save this document in the root of your site (File, Save). Name your pages consecutively, something like page1.htm, page2.htm, page3.htm. You'll link these pages together in a few minutes.
7. Repeat steps 1–6 to create several web pages.

You can modify the links so the pages you just created contain navigation in the form of hyperlinks. This enables the user to go forward and backward through the pages. To set up the pages and add navigation

1. Open the first page in the series (page1.htm).
2. Select and replace the placeholder text, the text beginning with *Lorum ipsum*, on one of the web pages with some text of your own. You'll learn how to replace the placeholder image in Hour 7, "Displaying Images."
3. Select the `Next>>` link on the web page by either dragging your cursor over the letters or simply clicking within the text.
4. Select the Browse icon (which looks like a folder) next to the Link drop-down menu in the Property inspector. Navigate to the root directory and select the filename that is next in the series (page2.htm).
5. In the Select File dialog box, make sure that Document is selected in the Relative To: drop-down menu at the bottom of the Select File dialog box. This creates a document-relative link instead of a site-relative link. Because the web page has been saved, Dreamweaver can create a document-relative link.
6. Click OK. Dreamweaver enters a relative URL into the Link drop-down menu, as shown in Figure 5.5.
7. Repeat steps 1–6, linking all of the pages together. The <<Previous link on the first page and the Next>> link on the last page can be left inactive by simply making sure that the Link box in the Property inspector for that text is empty.

The selected text appears as an underlined blue hyperlink in the Dreamweaver Document window. Preview the web page in the browser and click your link. You should jump to another page!

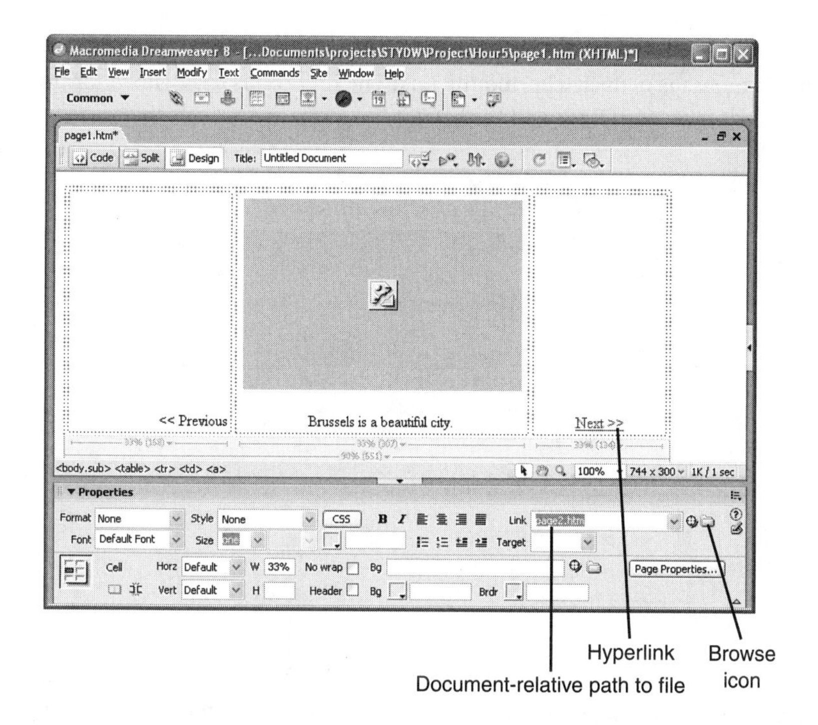

FIGURE 5.5
In the Dreamweaver Document window, you select text that you want to become a hyperlink.

Setting Link Color Preferences

You set the link colors in the Page Properties dialog box just as you set the default text color in Hour 3, "Getting Started: Adding Text, Lists, and Previewing in the Browser." Open the Page Properties dialog box (Modify, Page Properties) and select the Links category, as shown in Figure 5.6. You set the link font and font size for all the links on the page at the top of the dialog box. There are four options you can set here:

- **Link color**—The default color of all the links on the page
- **Visited link**—The color of a link after it has been visited by the browser
- **Rollover link**—The color of a link when the cursor is over the link
- **Active link**—The color of the link when the user is actively clicking the link (while the mouse button is down)

Use the color picker to add a link color, visited link color, rollover link color, and active link color. When you apply the changes to your web page, you should see all your links in the link color. When the viewer's browser has visited one of your links, the link will appear in the visited link color. The viewer sees the active link color while the mouse is actively clicking the link. The link colors are defined for the entire page, so all your links will be the color you specify.

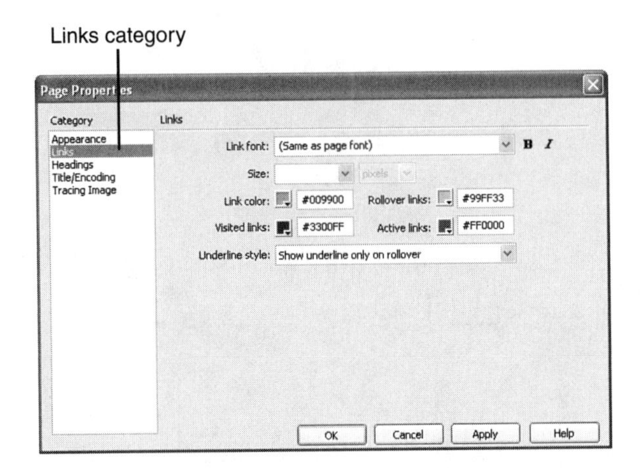

FIGURE 5.6 You set the appearance attributes of links in the Page Properties dialog box's Links category.

Dreamweaver sets the link colors by using CSS styles. You can also turn off the hyperlink underline by setting the Underline style. There are four choices here: Always Underline, Never Underline, Show Underline Only on Rollover, and Hide Underline on Rollover. Many usability experts advise against removing the underline because it makes links in the page more difficult to identify. Not using underline sure looks nice, though!

Organizing a Long Page by Using Named Anchors

Have you ever visited a web page where you click a link and it takes you to another part of the same web page? For instance, frequently asked questions (FAQ) often have hyperlinks at the top of the page listing the questions; when you click on one of the hyperlinks, you jump further down the page to the question's answer. That type of web page is created with **named anchors**. You use named anchors because sometimes it's less confusing to jump within the same web page than to jump to another web page.

To create a long page with named anchors, first add a named anchor to the location on the page where the user will jump. Then create a hyperlink that is linked to the named anchor. You can start creating a named anchor with a page that has multiple sections, such as the one shown in Figure 5.7. To create the page for this example, follow these steps:

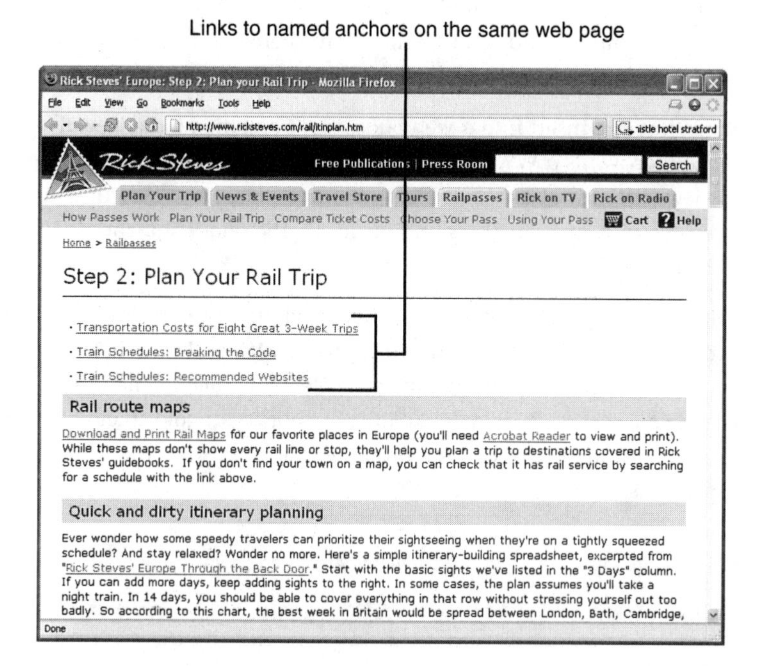

FIGURE 5.7 A website can have multiple sections, with a menu at the top of the page linking to the sections.

1. Create a new web page by selecting File, New. This time create an HTML page (under the Basic Page category). Add several headings at the top of various sections of the page. Save your page.
2. Place the insertion point where the named anchor will be located; immediately before the headings would be a good position. This is the area of the page where the user will jump when he or she clicks the link to the named anchor.
3. Select Insert, Named Anchor or select Named Anchor in the Common panel of the Insert bar. The Change Attribute dialog box, shown in Figure 5.8, appears.

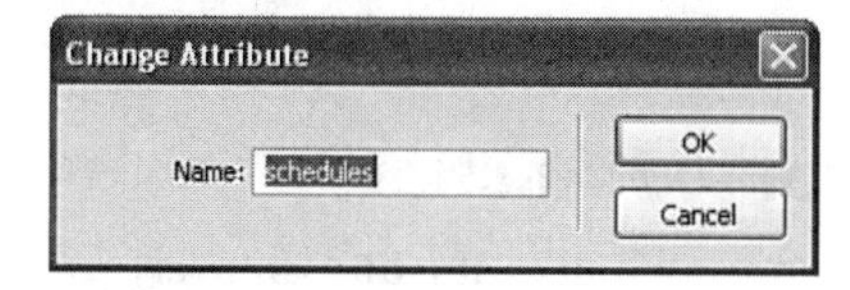

FIGURE 5.8 After you select the Named Anchor command, give the anchor a name in the Change Attribute dialog box.

4. Name the anchor and then click OK.

Understanding Invisible Elements

You might get a message saying that you will not see a named anchor because it is invisible. Or you might have a small yellow symbol, which is an invisible element, appear in the Document window at the location where you inserted the named anchor; it is the visual representation of a named anchor.

Some objects that you insert into a web page aren't designed to be viewable. Because Dreamweaver is a WYSIWYG design tool, Macromedia had to design a way for you to view objects that are invisible on the web page. So, how can you see invisible objects, such as named anchors and forms, on the page? You choose View, Invisible Elements.

You can also turn on or off Invisible Elements using the Visual Aids drop-down menu in the Document Toolbar, shown in Figure 5.9. When Invisible Elements is turned on, Dreamweaver displays the invisible elements such as the markers that represent named anchors (they look like little anchors on a gold shield). You can select the markers and view or edit the properties for the objects that they represent in the Property inspector.

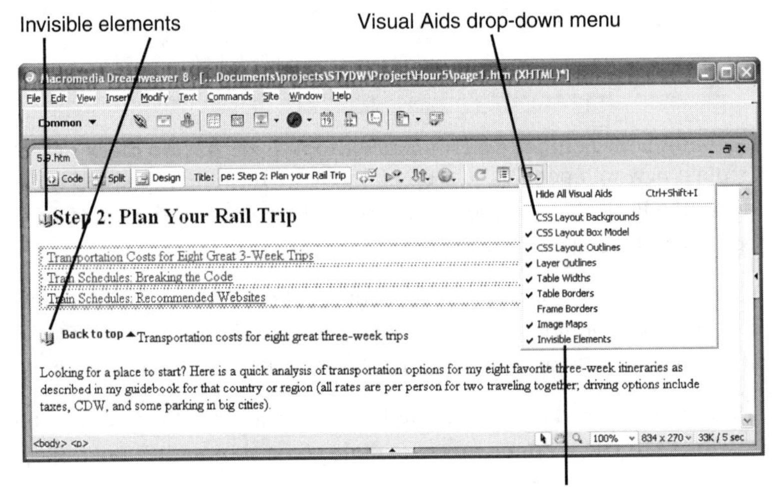

FIGURE 5.9
You can turn on and off Invisible Elements using the Visual Aids drop-down menu.

Linking to a Named Anchor

You've created a named anchor, but that really isn't very useful unless you link something to it. Add a text link at the top of the page. It might not be obvious that your web page is jumping to the named anchor location unless you have enough content to scroll in the browser, so add some extra text or simply some blank space so that you can see the jumping effect when you test your page in the browser. To link to the new named anchor, follow these steps:

1. Select the text that will link to the named anchor.
2. Enter the name of the named anchor, preceded by a pound sign (for example, `#schedules`) in the Link box, as shown in Figure 5.10.

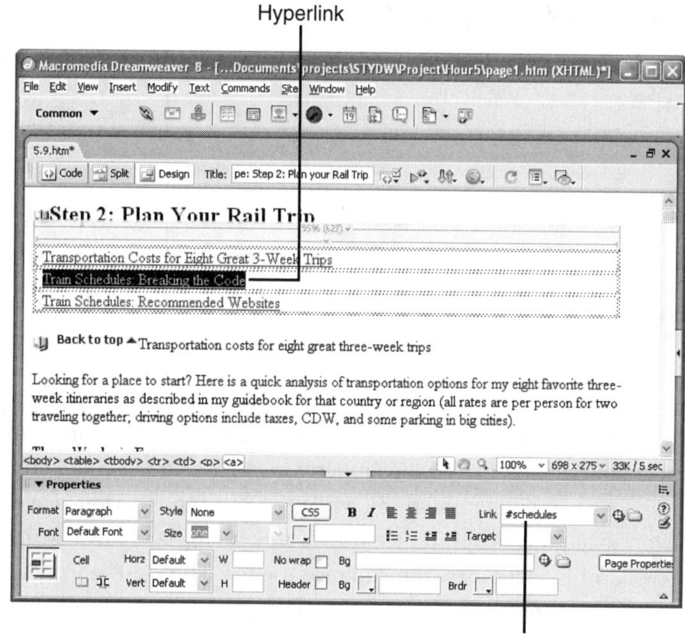

FIGURE 5.10
You enter the name of a named anchor, preceded by a pound sign, to create a link to it.

You can also link to a named anchor in another file. To do so, you simply append the name of the named anchor to the filename, as demonstrated in the following:

```
http://www.ricksteves.com/rail/itinplan.htm#schedules
```

Using the Point-to-File Icon

There's a little tool that you might have noticed on the Property inspector: the Point-to-File icon. This icon enables you to create links visually. You can drag the **Point-to-File icon**, shown in Figure 5.11, to a named anchor or a file located in the Files panel.

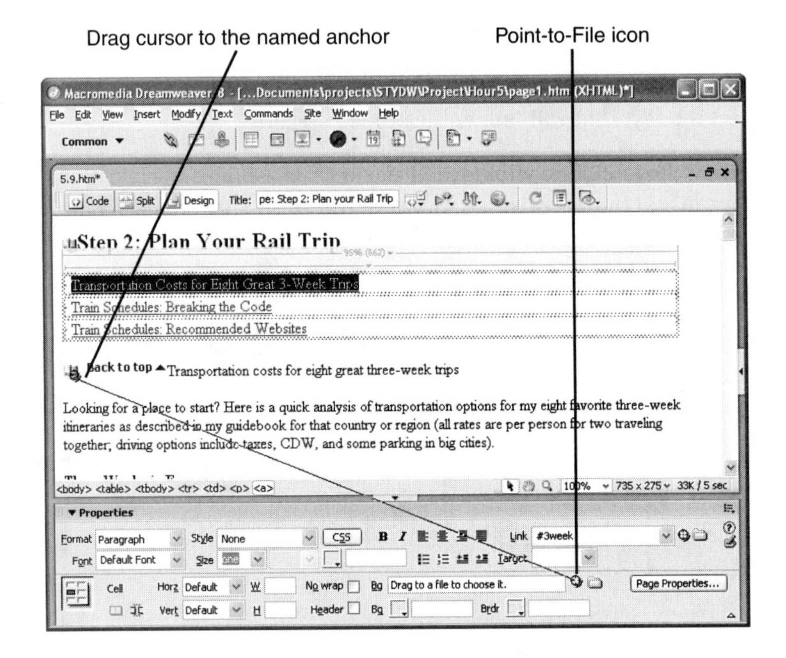

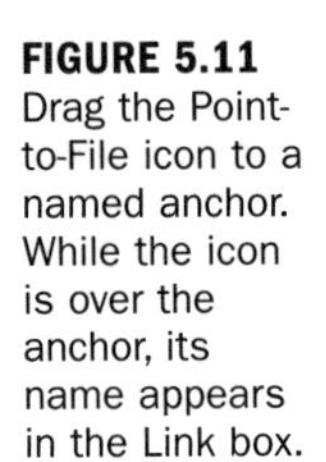

FIGURE 5.11
Drag the Point-to-File icon to a named anchor. While the icon is over the anchor, its name appears in the Link box.

When the Point-to-File icon is dragged over a named anchor, the name of the anchor appears in the Link box of the Property inspector. To select the named anchor, simply release the mouse button while the Point-to-File icon is over the named anchor. Using this icon is a nice way to link to objects or files without having to know or type in the filenames. You can also use the Point-to-File icon to link to files listed in your Files panel by dragging the icon over to the panel and highlighting a particular file.

Adding a Mailto Link

It's nice to put a link in a web page to allow a viewer to send email. This type of link is called a **mailto link**. The Dreamweaver Email Link object helps you implement a mailto link. The user must have an email application set up to work with the browser in order for these links to work.

To create a mailto link, select some text to be the link. Click the Email Link object (in the Common panel of the Insert bar), and the Email Link dialog box appears (see Figure 5.12). Enter the email address and click OK. The text looks like a hyperlink, but instead of linking to another page, it opens a preaddressed email message.

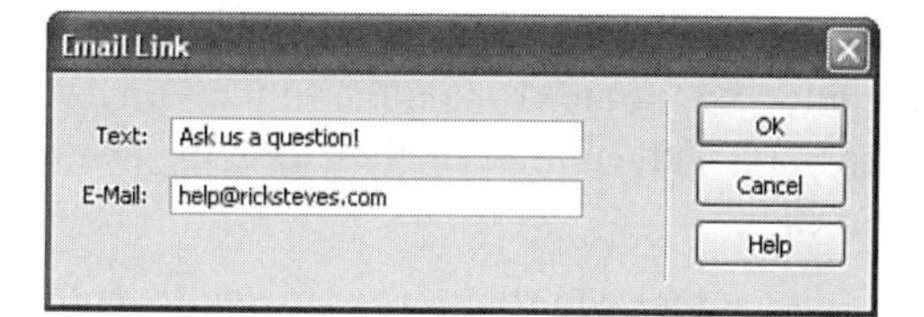

FIGURE 5.12
You create a link that creates an email message by using the Email Link object. The linked text is in the top box, and the email address is in the bottom box of the Email Link dialog box.

Watch Out!

Spammers Love Mailto Links

Spammers troll the Internet for mailto links. If you use mailto links in your web pages, expect to get a lot of **spam**, or junk email, sent to the email address used in the mailto links. Several extensions are available that can hide an email address in mailto links from spammers. Hour 22, "Customizing Dreamweaver," describes how to download Dreamweaver extensions from the Macromedia Exchange.

An **email link** is a hyperlink like any other except that it opens the user's default email application, such as Outlook or Eudora, with an email address already entered. Most users have a default email client, so these links are an easy and quick way for the user to send email. The email application has to be properly configured for the email to actually be sent.

Summary

In this hour, you have learned the difference between absolute and relative addresses. You have created links to external websites and relative links to pages within a website. You have learned how to insert a named anchor and then link to it, and you have created a mailto link to allow a viewer to launch an email message directly from a web page.

Q&A

Q. ***The named anchor that I want to link to is low enough on the page that I can't see it onscreen. How can I use the Point-to-File icon to reach it?***

A. If you drag the Point-to-File icon to either the top or the bottom of the Document window, the window scrolls. Hold the icon near the edge of the window until it has scrolled to the point where the named anchor is visible on the screen. Or first select the text that will be the hyperlink and then scroll down the page (carefully so as not to click on the window anywhere and deselect the text), and when you see the named anchor, grab the Point-to-File icon and drag it to the anchor.

Q. ***I found a page on another site that I want to link to, but the URL is really long. Do I have to retype it in Dreamweaver?***

A. The easiest way to enter a lengthy URL is to copy the URL from the browser's address text box (by pressing Ctrl+C in Windows or Command+C on the Mac). You can then paste the URL into Dreamweaver's Link drop-down menu.

Q. ***Is there any way to add a subject line into an email link?***

A. Yes! In the Dreamweaver Email Link dialog box, add a question mark immediately after the email address (no space) and then `subject=` and the subject that you want to appear. You can also add some text for the body of the email message by adding `&body=`. You can also simply edit the link in the Property inspector's Link drop-down menu. The link will look like this:

```
mailto:betsy@betsybruce.com?subject=Sams Teach Yourself
Macromedia Dreamweaver in 24 Hours&body=I'm interesting in discussing this
book.
```

Workshop

Quiz

1. How can you view a named anchor if it isn't currently visible onscreen?
2. What is the difference between a document-relative path and a site root–relative path?
3. When does a web page viewer see the active link color?

Quiz Answers

1. Select View, Visual Aids, Invisible Elements to see items that are invisible elements.
2. A site root–relative path begins with a forward slash and a document-relative path does not.
3. A web page viewer sees the active link color while he is actively clicking a hyperlink.

Exercises

1. Surf the Web for 10–15 minutes with your new awareness of the different types of links. When you place the cursor over a link, you can usually see the address of the link in the status bar of the browser. Look for links to named anchors, too.

2. Create a favorite links page, including links to all your favorite websites. You can either use the URL of the link as the text that displays or you can create a hyperlink out of a descriptive word or phrase. Hint: The major browsers have methods of exporting all your bookmarks or favorites. These methods can give you a huge head start on this exercise.

3. Create a frequently asked questions web page about a topic you understand well. List the questions at the top of the page as an unordered list. Repeat the question and put the answer at the bottom of the page and add a named anchor. Make the questions at the top of the page links to the appropriate named anchor below.

HOUR 6

Getting Down and Dirty with HTML

What You'll Learn in This Hour:

- How to structure the code in a web page
- How to use the Quick Tag Editor
- How to view and edit HTML code
- How to clean the HTML that Microsoft Word creates
- Which code reference books are available in Dreamweaver

Even though Dreamweaver handles HTML behind the scenes, you might occasionally want to look at the code. Dreamweaver also makes the transition easier for those stoic HTML hand-coders who are making a move to a visual HTML development tool such as Dreamweaver. You won't be sorry! I'm a very competent HTML hand-coder, but I can get my work done much quicker by using Dreamweaver.

Dreamweaver offers several ways to access HTML code. During this hour, you will explore the HTML-editing capabilities of Dreamweaver. You'll use Dreamweaver's capability to clean up the code produced when saving a Word document as HTML. You'll also explore the numerous reference "books" available within Dreamweaver for you to look up tags and tag attributes. If you don't already know HTML, you'll find that viewing HTML while Dreamweaver creates it for you is a great way to learn.

Exploring Code View

The Dreamweaver Document window enables you to view a web page in either Design view or Code view. You can see Design and Code views at the same time by selecting the Split View button in the Document toolbar (or choose View, Code and Design). When you do this, it's easy to pop back and forth between the views with just a click of a button. You'll probably do the majority of your web page development in Design view while occasionally looking at Code or Split view to tweak the code or troubleshoot a problem.

Toggle the Panels Off

You can toggle all the panels on and off by pressing the F4 key (or Window, Hide Panels). Pressing F4 again toggles the panels back on (or Window, Show Panels). This is especially useful for Mac users whose floating panel version of Dreamweaver might cause the panels to block the view of the web page design or code.

Create a new HTML page in Dreamweaver. Then click the Code View button in the toolbar to view the page's HTML code, as shown in Figure 6.1. The first line in the code is the **document type declaration**, which uses the `doctype` tag. In Hour 3, "Getting Started: Adding Text, Lists, and Previewing in the Browser," you selected the document type in the Page Properties (Modify, Page Properties) dialog box. The document type declaration announces which version of HTML the page uses. Dreamweaver adds this line automatically, so you shouldn't have to worry about it. After the document type declaration, the entire web page is enclosed in HTML tags.

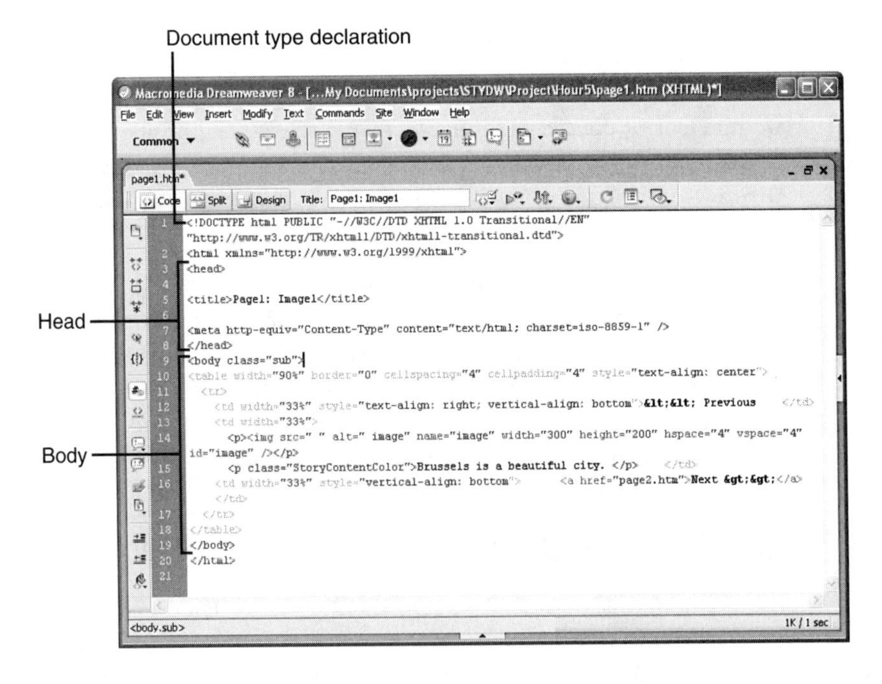

FIGURE 6.1 Code view displays the basic code of a new web page, including the document type declaration, head, and body.

By default, Dreamweaver creates web pages by adding XHTML tags (and other types of tags, such as CFML or PHP, when you get more advanced). When you select an object from Dreamweaver's Insert bar, Dreamweaver inserts the appropriate tag or tags into your web pages. Tags have properties called **attributes** that Dreamweaver uses to fine-tune the way the object displays on the page. For instance, an image tag (`<img>`) has the `src` (source) attribute, which sets the files that the image tag displays. Most image tags also have `height` and `width` attributes that tell the browser the size of the image. These are just a few of the many attributes of an image tag. Here is an example of an image tag with standard attributes:

```
<img src="market.jpg" height="156" width="124"/>
```

Exploring the Head and Body of a Web Page

There are two main sections to a web page: the head and the body. You'll see these sections in the code. The head is surrounded by head tags, and the body is surrounded by body tags. All the content visible in a web page is in the body. The head of the document contains code that supports the web page. In the head of the document, Dreamweaver automatically adds the `<title>` tag because the document title is part of the head. Right beneath the title, Dreamweaver inserts a meta tag, like this:

```
<meta http-equiv="Content-Type" content="text/html; charset=iso-8859-1"/>
```

This meta tag specifies the character set that the browser should use to display the page. The preceding example specifies the Latin character set for Western European languages. In Hour 3, you set the character set for a single web page in Page Properties (Modify, Page Properties). You can set the default character set for all web pages created in Dreamweaver in the New Document category of Preferences (Edit, Preferences), shown in Figure 6.2. You can also set the default file extension in this Preferences category.

Dreamweaver places other content into the head of the page as you author. The head is where most JavaScript and other scripting code, CSS definitions, and other code resides. While in Design mode, if you'd like to see a visual representation of the head content, select View, Head Content. You then see icons at the top of the Document window representing the elements in the head. When you select one of the icons, its properties appear in the Property inspector, as shown in Figure 6.3.

You display both Design view and Code view by selecting the middle button, the Split View button. While in Split view, place your cursor over the divider between Design and Code views to modify the window sizes. Type some text into the Design view pane. The text is inserted into the body of the document. If you select an object in the Document window, the code for that object will be highlighted in Code view. This is a quick way to get to the code of a selected object. If your web page is large, there might be a lot of HTML to go through, and it might not be easy to find the code for which you are looking. Try displaying only Design view. Highlight a single word that you typed. When you select Code view, the word is highlighted.

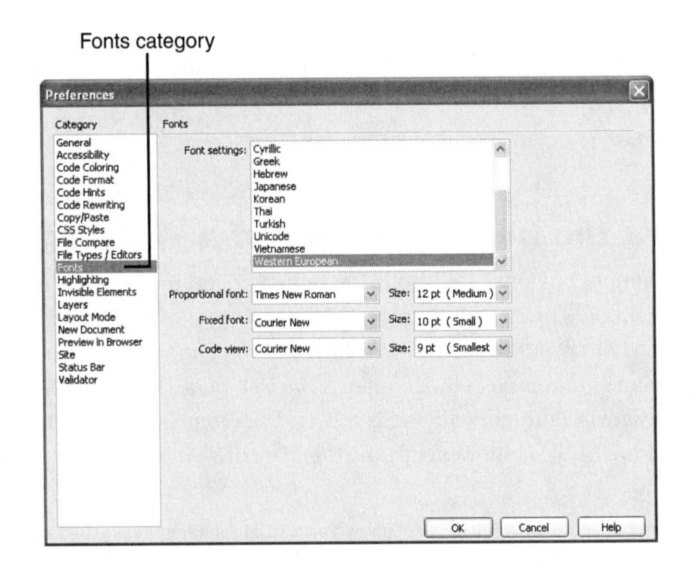

FIGURE 6.2
You set the default character set and the default file extension in the New Document category of the Dreamweaver Preferences dialog box.

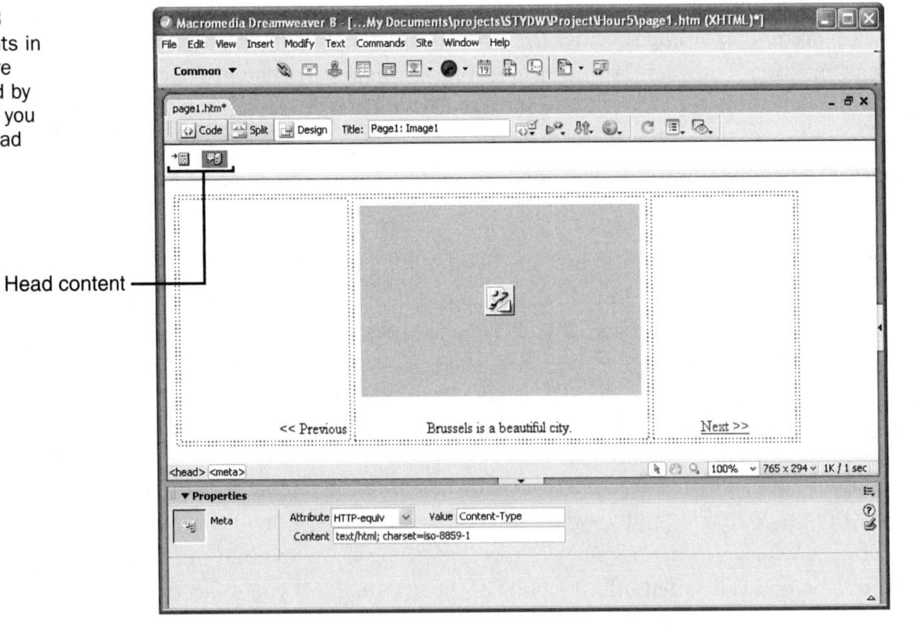

FIGURE 6.3
The elements in the head are represented by icons when you view the head content.

Discovering Code View Options

When you are in Code view, the View Options menu, shown in Figure 6.4, enables you to change the way the code is displayed. These commands are also available in View, Code View Options.

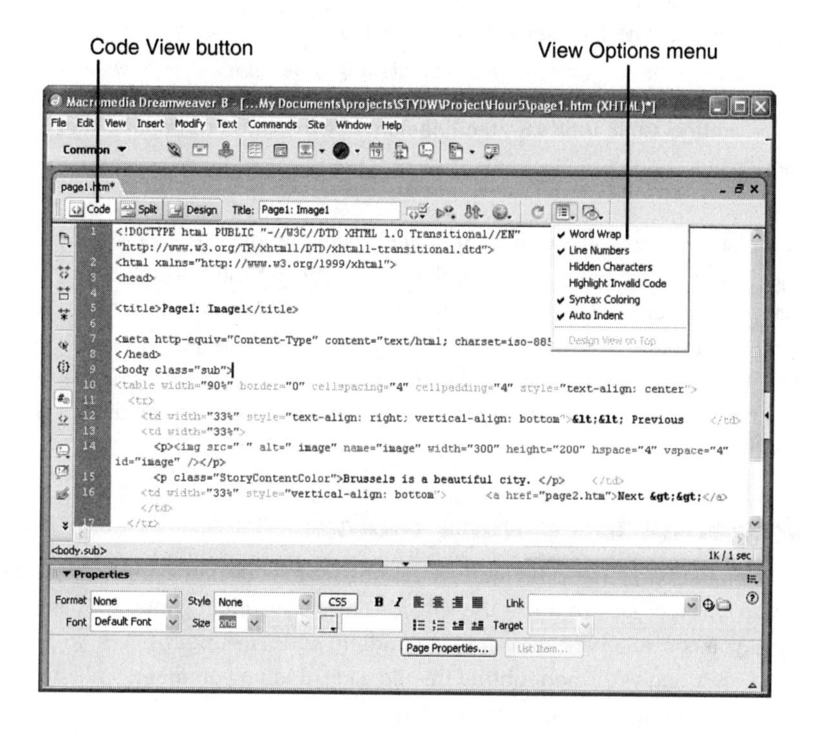

FIGURE 6.4
The View Options menu enables you to configure how code is displayed.

The following options are available in the View Options menu:

- **Word wrap**—Wraps the lines of code so that you can view it all without scrolling horizontally. This setting does not change the code; it simply displays it differently.
- **Line numbers**—Displays line numbers in the left margin.
- **Hidden characters**—Shows paragraph and space characters in the code.
- **Highlight invalid HTML**—Turns on highlighting of invalid code that Dreamweaver doesn't understand.
- **Syntax coloring**—Colors the code so elements are easier to discern. You set the colors in the Code Coloring category of the Dreamweaver Preferences dialog box.

- **Auto indent**—Adds an automatic indent so your code is more readable. The indentation size is based on the settings in the Code Format category of the Preferences dialog box.

Did you Know?

JavaScript Error? Check the Line Number

If you receive a JavaScript error when previewing a web page in a browser, the error often displays the number of the code line causing the problem. You can view the code in Code view with the line numbers displayed to troubleshoot the error.

If you make changes to the code in Split view, Dreamweaver doesn't display the changes in the Document window until you click the Refresh button in the Property inspector. If you select View Options, Highlight Invalid Code, Dreamweaver highlights all invalid tags in bright yellow in both the Code inspector and the Document window. When you select a highlighted tag, the Property inspector calls the tag invalid. It might give a reason why the tag is invalid and offer some direction on how to deal with it.

Discovering the Coding Toolbar

The Coding Toolbar, shown in Figure 6.5, is only visible in Code or Split view. The buttons in this toolbar run down the left side of the Document window. These buttons give you control over collapsing, expanding, and selecting the code within selected tags along with highlighting invalid code, adding comments, indenting, applying formatting, and other commands.

The following options are available in the Coding toolbar:

- **Open Documents**—Lists all of the documents currently open in Dreamweaver.
- **Collapse Full Tag**—Collapses all of the code within the selected tag, displaying it as a single line with a small expand button to the left of it.
- **Collapse Selection**—Collapses all of the selected code into a single line with a small expand button to the left of it.
- **Expand All**—Expands all of the currently collapsed code.
- **Select Parent Tag**—Selects the code within the parent tag of the currently selected tag. Continuing to click this button continues to move up the tag hierarchy.
- **Balance Braces**—Checks your code to make sure that all tags, brackets, braces, and parentheses are balanced with two corresponding characters.

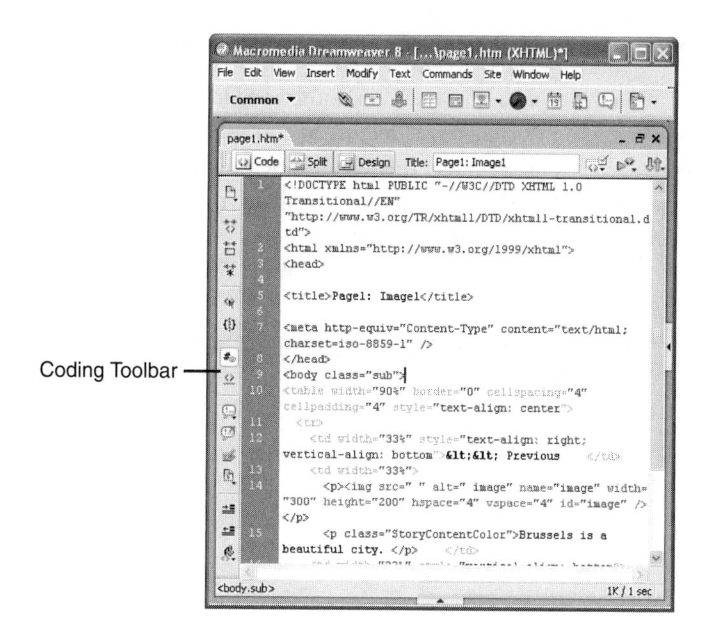

FIGURE 6.5 The Coding Toolbar is visible on the left side of the Document window when in Code view.

- **Line Numbers**—Displays line numbers in the left margin.
- **Highlight Invalid Code**—Turns on highlighting of invalid code that Dreamweaver doesn't understand.
- **Apply Comment drop-down menu**—Enables you to add various types of comments, such as HTML, CSS, or JavaScript comments, to the code. This is useful when troubleshooting problems in the code; simply comment out some code to see if it is causing the problems.
- **Remove Comment**—Removes comments from the code.
- **Wrap Tag**—Wraps a tag around the selected tag.
- **Recent Snippets drop-down menu**—Gives you a list of code snippets you've used recently along with a quick way to launch the Snippets panel. You'll learn more about Snippets in Hour 22, "Customizing Dreamweaver."
- **Indent Code**—Shifts the selected code to the right.
- **Outdent Code**—Shifts the selected code to the left.
- **Format Source Code drop-down menu**—This menu enables you to apply source formatting, which you'll learn more about later this hour. You can also edit Dreamweaver's Tag Libraries.

Using the Code Inspector

If you have a dual monitor setup, you'll prefer to see the code in a separate window so you can keep both Code and Design views open. You can use the Code inspector instead of Code view in order to accomplish this. You launch the Code inspector by selecting Window, Code Inspector. The Code inspector, shown in Figure 6.6, is similar to Code view but it launches in a separate window that you can drag to your other monitor if you are fortunate enough to work with dual monitors.

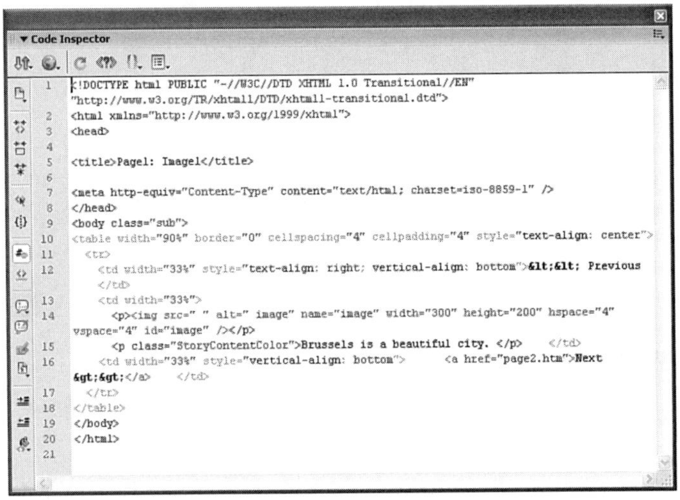

Code Inspector

```
1  <!DOCTYPE html PUBLIC "-//W3C//DTD XHTML 1.0 Transitional//EN"
   "http://www.w3.org/TR/xhtml1/DTD/xhtml1-transitional.dtd">
2  <html xmlns="http://www.w3.org/1999/xhtml">
3  <head>
4
5  <title>Page1: Image1</title>
6
7  <meta http-equiv="Content-Type" content="text/html; charset=iso-8859-1" />
8  </head>
9  <body class="sub">
10 <table width="90%" border="0" cellspacing="4" cellpadding="4" style="text-align: center">
11   <tr>
12     <td width="33%" style="text-align: right; vertical-align: bottom">&lt;&lt; Previous
       </td>
13     <td width="33%">
14       <p><img src=" " alt=" image" name="image" width="300" height="200" hspace="4"
   vspace="4" id="image" /></p>
15       <p class="StoryContentColor">Brussels is a beautiful city. </p>    </td>
16     <td width="33%" style="vertical-align: bottom">      <a href="page2.htm">Next
   &gt;&gt;</a>    </td>
17   </tr>
18 </table>
19 </body>
20 </html>
21
```

FIGURE 6.6 The Code inspector enables you to view the code in a separate window.

Viewing and Editing HTML Tags by Using the Quick Tag Editor

Using Dreamweaver's Quick Tag Editor is the quickest and easiest way to look at a single HTML tag and edit it. Remember, you can always tell which tag you have selected by looking at the Tag selector at the bottom of the Document window. You can access the Quick Tag Editor in several ways:

- Click the Quick Tag Editor icon on the Property inspector, as shown in Figure 6.7.
- Select Modify, Quick Tag Editor.
- Right-click (Control+click on the Mac) a tag in the tag selector and select the Quick Tag Editor command, as shown in Figure 6.8.

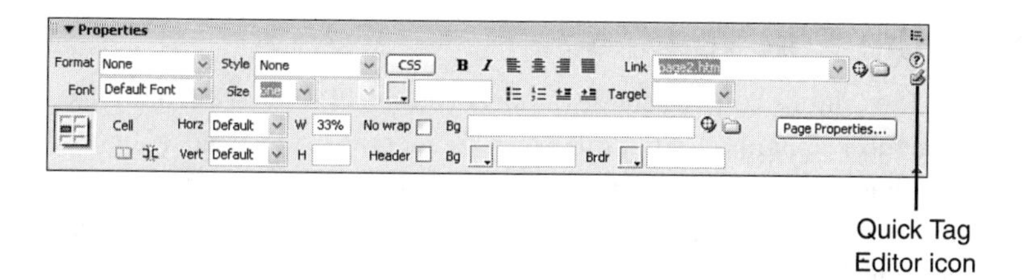

FIGURE 6.7
Click the Quick Tag Editor icon to view and edit the tag of the currently selected object.

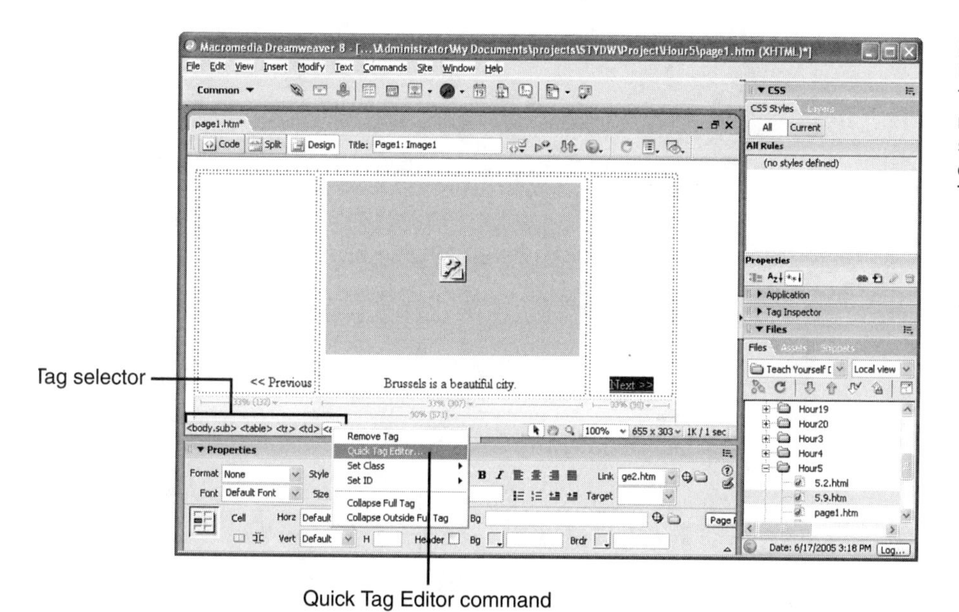

FIGURE 6.8
Using the Quick Tag Editor command in the tag selector launches the Quick Tag Editor.

When you select the Quick Tag Editor icon in the Property inspector, the tag pops up beside the Quick Tag Editor icon. When you open the Quick Tag Editor from the Modify menu, the tag pops up directly above the object in the Document window, and when you open it from the tag selector, it appears directly above the tag.

The Quick Tag Editor has three modes:

- **Edit Tag**—This mode enables you to edit the existing contents of a tag.
- **Wrap Tag**—This mode wraps another HTML tag around the selected tag.
- **Insert HTML**—This mode enables you to insert HTML in the web page.

When the Quick Tag Editor opens, you can toggle among the three modes by pressing Ctrl+T (Command+T on the Macintosh). The following sections explore each of the three modes.

Using the Edit Tag Mode

The Quick Tag Editor's Edit Tag mode enables you to edit the HTML of an existing tag and the tag's contents. To add attributes of the selected tag, place the insertion point at the end of the tag contents in the Quick Tag Editor and add a space. The Tag drop-down menu appears, as shown in Figure 6.9, with attributes appropriate for the tag. You select an attribute from the list and then type in the value.

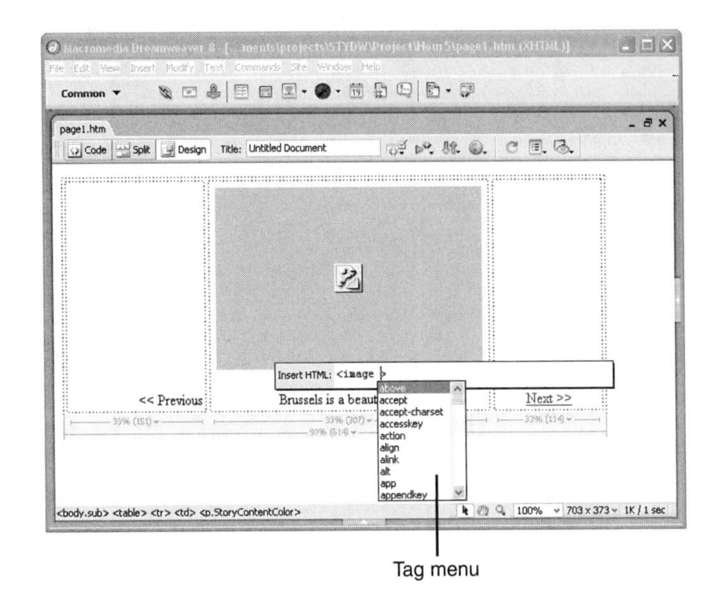

FIGURE 6.9
The Tag drop-down menu presents attributes appropriate for the current tag. It appears automatically after the delay that is set in the Preferences dialog box.

Using the Wrap Tag Mode

The Quick Tag Editor's Wrap Tag mode, shown in Figure 6.10, enables you to wrap HTML around the current selection. For instance, when you have text selected, you can wrap a hyperlink (<a href></a>) or text formatting (<h1></h1>) around the text. First select the tag you'd like to wrap by choosing it from a list. Dreamweaver adds the opening tag before the selection and the closing tag after the selection. You can also add attributes to the new tag.

Using the Insert HTML Mode

The Quick Tag Editor's Insert HTML mode, shown in Figure 6.11, shows a pair of empty tag angle brackets with the insertion point between them. You can either enter text into the brackets, select from the Tag drop-down menu, or both. Dreamweaver adds the closing tag automatically. The Quick Tag Editor starts in this mode when you do not have any object selected.

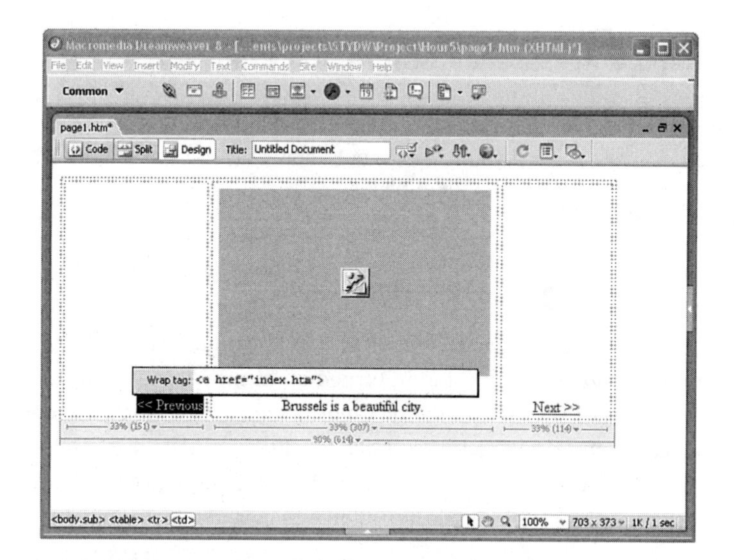

FIGURE 6.10
The Wrap Tag mode wraps an HTML tag around the current selection.

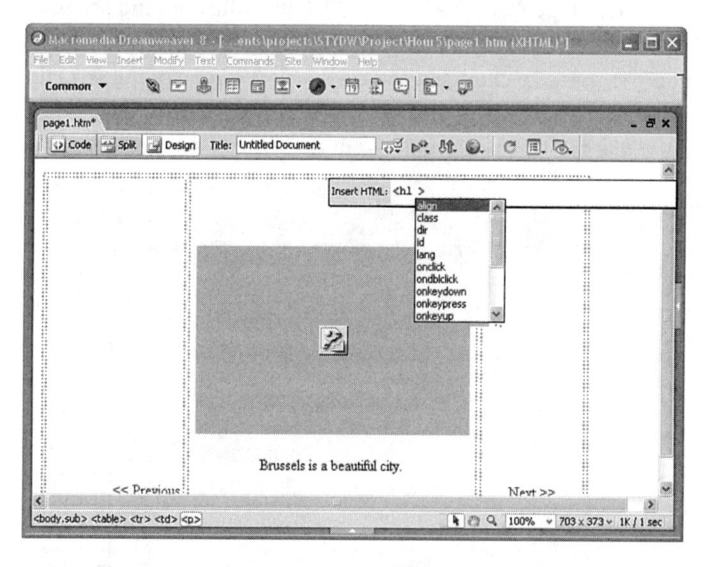

FIGURE 6.11
The Insert HTML mode in the Quick Tag Editor presents empty tag brackets. You can enter a tag name and attributes or select from the tag drop-down menu.

Setting Code Preferences

There are a number of preferences you can set for viewing and maintaining code. The four categories in Dreamweaver preferences that apply to code—Code Coloring, Code Format, Code Hints, and Code Rewriting—help control the way Dreamweaver creates and displays the code in your web pages. If you are used to hand-coding your pages a certain way, don't complain about the way Dreamweaver formats it—change it!

Watch Out!

Understand a Preference Before You Change It

Don't change a setting in the Preferences dialog box if you aren't sure what it does. Many of Dreamweaver's default settings reflect the standard way of creating web pages. Change them if you need to, but know that you could inadvertently cause a problem if you change them blindly.

Setting Code Color Preferences

Code view colors code according to the settings in the Dreamweaver Preferences dialog box. You must have syntax coloring turned on in the View Options menu in order to see colored code. Select the Code Coloring category in the Preferences dialog box. You select which type of code you'd like to edit here. Also, this category enables you to set the background color for Code view. Either enter a color in hexadecimal format or use the color picker to select a color.

Select the document type from the list and click the Edit Coloring Scheme button. The left side of the dialog box enables you to select a tag and then individually set a color for it on the right. To change a tag color, select a type of tag (HTML Image Tags are selected in Figure 6.12), and select a new text color or background color. You can also make the text bold, italic, or underlined.

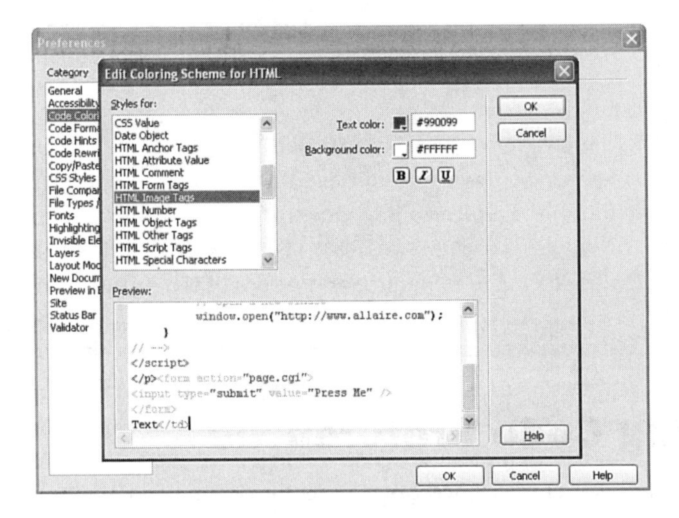

FIGURE 6.12
You set the tag colors displayed in Code view in the Dreamweaver Preferences dialog box.

Setting Code Format Preferences

In the Code Format category of the Dreamweaver Preferences dialog box, shown in Figure 6.13, you set how Dreamweaver will create code. Dreamweaver indents code to make it easier to read. You can change the size of the indent in the Preferences dialog box. You can also select whether Dreamweaver should indent the code for tables and frames.

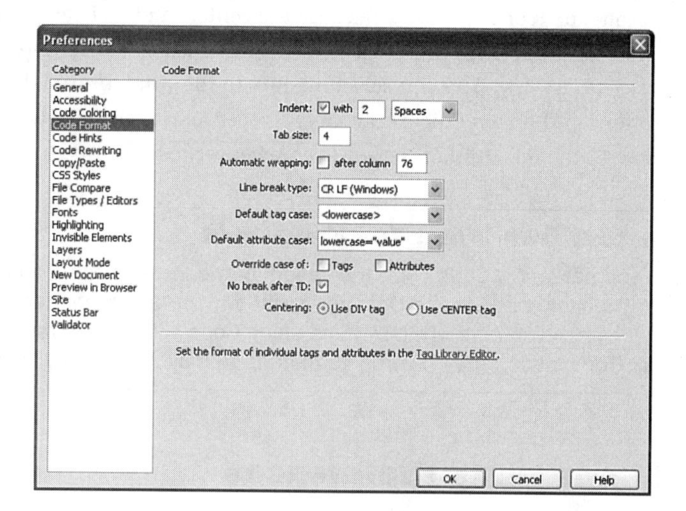

FIGURE 6.13
The Code Format category of the Dreamweaver Preferences dialog box enables you to set indentation, wrapping, and tag case.

Did you Know?

Apply Dreamweaver Formatting to Any Page

The Code Format category options apply only to new documents created in Dreamweaver. However, you can select Commands, Apply Source Formatting to apply the same formatting to an existing web page. This is an easy way to tidy up the code in a web page when it gets messy.

If automatic wrapping is selected, Dreamweaver will wrap a line that exceeds the column width entered in the After field in the Code Format category. Some lines might end up a little longer than that number because Dreamweaver does not wrap lines that will affect the appearance of the web page. You can also set the type of line break that Dreamweaver uses. This can affect the way your code looks in different operating systems.

Because the World Wide Web Consortium (W3C) standards specify lowercase tags, it's a good idea to always use lowercase tags and attributes. (W3C is the group that develops web standards. Find out more at www.w3c.org.) By default, Dreamweaver uses lowercase for tags (the Default Tag Case setting) and attributes (the Default Attribute Case setting). In limited cases, you might want to override the case for tags or attributes. For instance, if you do not want Dreamweaver to change the tag or attribute case in an existing document, check the Override Case of Tags check box and the Override Case of Attributes check box, and Dreamweaver leaves the tag or attribute case as it exists.

The last setting is whether Dreamweaver will use center tags to center objects or div tags (`<div align="center"></div>`). Because the center tag has been deprecated in recent versions of the HTML specification, you should leave this setting at the default setting, Use DIV Tag. You can select the link to the Tag Library Editor available at the bottom of the Preferences category in order to launch this editor. It enables you to edit the tags and code that Dreamweaver inserts into your page.

By the Way

You're on Your Own When You Hand-Code

The options you set in the Code Format category of the Preferences dialog box apply only to changes made in the Document window. The automatic formatting does not occur when you edit HTML by hand using Code view. Of course, you can always select Commands, Apply Source Formatting to make everything tidy.

Setting Code Hints Preferences

As you saw earlier this hour in the Quick Tag Editor examples, Dreamweaver drops down the **tag menu** displaying tag attributes for you to pick from. This is called a **code hint** in Dreamweaver. You can set which code hints Dreamweaver displays in the Code Hints category of the Preferences dialog box, as shown in Figure 6.14. Checking the Enable Auto Tag Completion setting makes Dreamweaver add a closing tag when you type the opening tag into Code view. You can also set the time delay for the tag menu by dragging the time slider bar at the top of the Code Hints dialog box. If you don't need the tag menu because you already know the name of the attribute you'd like to type, you might want to set the time delay so it doesn't continue to drop down continually while you are typing.

Setting Code Rewriting Preferences

The code rewriting preferences, shown in Figure 6.15, set what changes Dreamweaver makes when it opens a web page. Dreamweaver automatically fixes certain code problems, but only if you want it to. If you turn off the Rewrite Code options in the Code Rewriting category, Dreamweaver will still display invalid code that you can fix yourself if you need to.

Checking the Fix Invalidly Nested and Unclosed Tags check box tells Dreamweaver to rewrite tags that are invalidly nested. For instance, if you check this check box, Dreamweaver will rewrite `<strong><em>hello</strong></em>` as `<strong><em>hello</em></strong>` (which is the correct way to write it). Dreamweaver also inserts missing closing tags, quotation marks, or closing angle brackets when this setting is checked. When you select the Remove Extra Closing Tags check box, Dreamweaver removes any stray closing tags that are left in the web page.

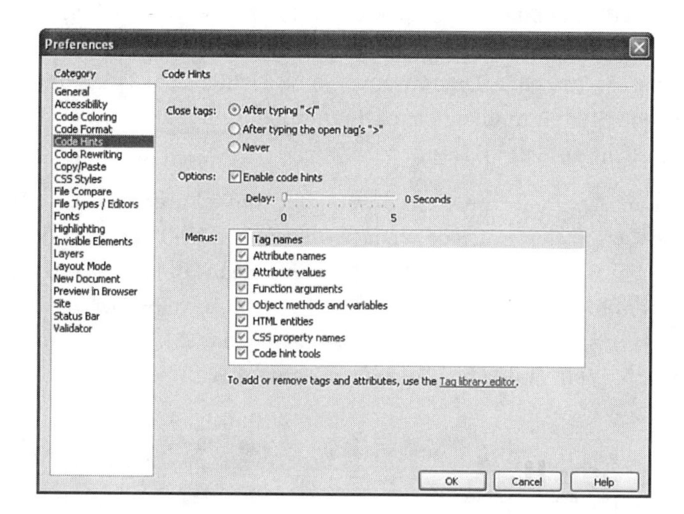

FIGURE 6.14 The Code Hints category enables you to set what Dreamweaver helps you with while you are coding.

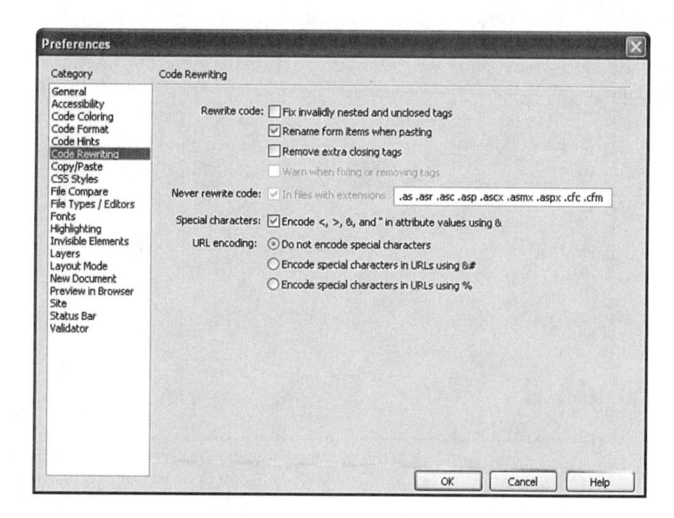

FIGURE 6.15 The Code Rewriting category of the Dreamweaver Preferences dialog box enables you to set the changes that Dreamweaver makes when it opens a web page.

Cleaning Up HTML Created with Microsoft Word

It's very convenient while working in Word to save a document as a web page. Word does a great job of creating a web page that looks very similar to the Word document and you can open and edit the web page in Word. The problem is that Word maintains a lot of extra code in the web page. If you do not need to edit the web page in Word again and you'd like to put it on the Web, you can use Dreamweaver to clean up the extra code.

To save a Word document as a web page, select File, Save as Web Page. Word prompts you to name the document and adds the `.htm` file extension. The resulting page has a lot of extra code; Dreamweaver knows which code is extraneous and can delete that code. It's fun to take note of the number of lines of code in the file before you run the Clean up Word HTML command.

When you save a Word document as a web page, make sure you close it before you work on it in Dreamweaver. Dreamweaver will not be able to open and convert an HTML document that is open in Word. Apply the Clean up Word HTML command to a web page that was created in Word and that you have opened in the Document window. To do this, select Commands, Clean up Word HTML. This launches the Clean up Word HTML dialog box, shown in Figure 6.16.

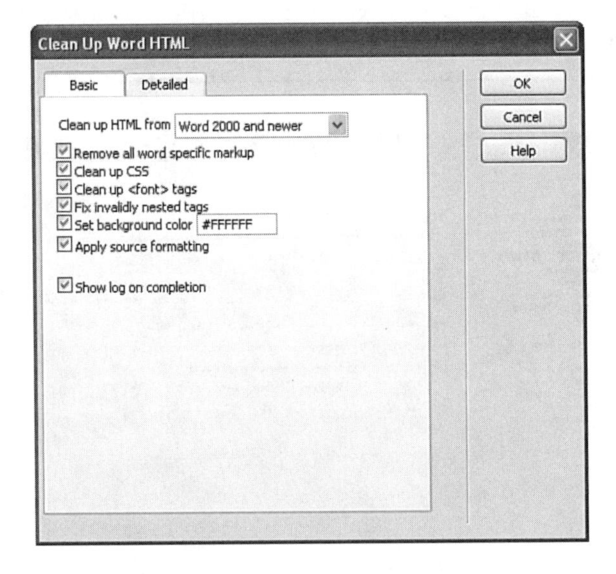

FIGURE 6.16 When you import a Word HTML document or select Clean Up Word HTML, the Clean Up Word HTML dialog box appears.

Dreamweaver should automatically detect which version of Word created the HTML file from tags that Word adds to the file. You can also choose the version manually by using the Clean up HTML From drop-down menu in the Clean up Word HTML dialog box. The Clean up Word HTML dialog box has two tabs—Basic and Detailed. The Basic tab has the following options:

- **Remove All Word Specific Markup**—Removes all the unnecessary Extensible Markup Language (XML), meta tags, and link tags from the head section; it also removes all Word XML markup, all conditional tags, all empty paragraphs, and all margins. You can select each of these options individually by using the settings on the Detailed tab.

- **Clean Up CSS**—Removes the extra CSS styles from the document. The styles removed are inline CSS styles, style attributes that begin with `mso`, non-CSS style declarations, CSS styles in table rows and cells, and unused styles. You can select these options individually by using the Detailed tab.
- **Clean Up <font> Tags**—Removes `<font>` tags.
- **Fix Invalidly Nested Tags**—Fixes the tags, particularly font markup tags, that are in an incorrect places.
- **Set Background Color**—Enables you to specify the background color of the web page. Dreamweaver's default is white, `#FFFFFF`.
- **Apply Source Formatting**—Applies the code formatting options that are set in the Code Format category in the Preferences dialog box.
- **Show Log on Completion**—Displays a dialog box with a summary of the changes that Dreamweaver made to the web page.

You can probably just accept the default options in the Basic tab of the Clean up Word HTML dialog box and then click OK. Dreamweaver then cleans up the web page. Your selected options will appear the next time you select the Clean up Word HTML command. Now your file is optimized for display on the Web. Make sure you look in Code view and see how many lines of code were removed from the original.

Exploring References

Many useful references are built right into Dreamweaver and are accessible to you via the References panel, shown in Figure 6.17. Choose Window, References to display the References panel beneath the Property inspector. The Book drop-down menu enables you to choose from numerous reference books. Of special interest to you might be the O'Reilly CSS, HTML, and JavaScript references. Who needs to buy the book when these references are included in Dreamweaver? There's also UsableNet's Accessibility reference, which helps explain how to create websites that are accessible to people who have accessibility issues, such as visual impairment.

To use the references, select tags, styles, or other objects from the drop-down menus and then read about the objects in the lower part of the panel. Notice that information on browser compatibility is located in the upper-right corner of the panel.

When not using this panel, you might want to collapse it by selecting the arrow button in the upper-left corner of the panel, or close it by selecting the Close panel group command from the menu in the upper-right corner of the panel.

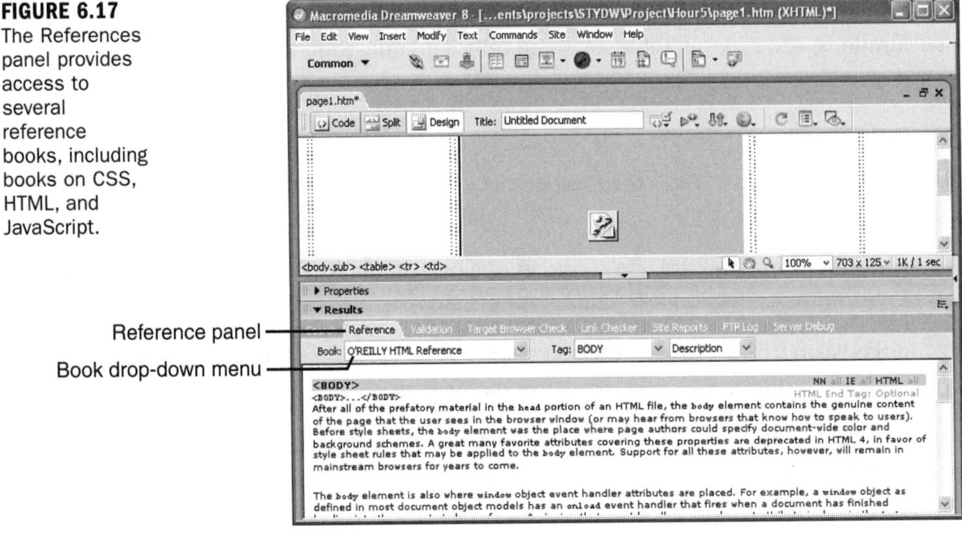

FIGURE 6.17 The References panel provides access to several reference books, including books on CSS, HTML, and JavaScript.

Summary

In this hour, you have learned how to use the Quick Tag Editor and Code view. You have learned how to set preferences for HTML tag colors, formatting, and rewriting. You have also learned how to use the Clean up Word HTML command. And you were introduced to the robust reference books that come with Dreamweaver and are available to help answer your questions about topics such as HTML, CSS, and JavaScript.

Q&A

Q. ***Which should I learn first—Dreamweaver or HTML?***

A. It's helpful to know HTML when you are developing web pages. I think the best way to learn HTML is to first learn to use a web-editing program, such as Dreamweaver. Continue to view the code as you work and use the Reference panel (by selecting Window, Reference) to look up tags or attributes that you are curious about. If you still need grounding in HTML after that, get a good HTML reference book or take a class. A good book about HTML and XHTML is *Sams Teach Yourself HTML & XHTML in 24 Hours, 6th Edition* by Dick Oliver and Michael Morrison (ISBN 0672325209).

Q. *Can I add tag attributes that don't appear in the tag drop-down menu? I saw a tag attribute listed on a website that isn't listed in Dreamweaver for that tag.*

A. Yes. Use the Tag Library Editor by selecting Edit, Tag Libraries. This editor controls the attributes that appear in the tag drop-down menu. Dreamweaver does not list every attribute that is available, so there might be one or two that you want to add.

Workshop

Quiz

1. How do you toggle through the three Quick Tag Editor modes?
2. What are the three ways to view a web page in Dreamweaver?
3. Does Dreamweaver automatically format the HTML that you type into Code view?

Quiz Answers

1. You toggle through the Quick Tag Editor's three modes by pressing Ctrl+T in Windows or Command+T on a Macintosh.
2. You can view a web page in Code view, Split view, or Design view in Dreamweaver.
3. No, Dreamweaver does not automatically format the HTML that you type into Code view. However, you can format it by using the Apply Source Formatting command on any web page.

Exercises

1. Experiment with using the Quick Tag Editor modes. Pay attention to how the Property inspector reflects selecting attributes in the Quick Tag Editor. You can select many of the same attributes by using the Property inspector's radio buttons, text boxes, and check boxes.
2. Examine the HTML of a web page in Code view. First, select an object in the Document window and then open Code view. Do you see the HTML for the selected object?

3. Create a new HTML page in Dreamweaver, open Code view, and briefly examine the general structure of the web page—head and body tags nested within HTML tags. Select and delete all the code and then re-create this general structure. What are the common tags that go into the head section of the page? Enter them. Notice that Dreamweaver enters closing tags for you if you've enabled that option in the Preferences dialog box. Press the spacebar after the tag name within any of the tags. What attributes are available for that tag? What happens when you select an attribute?

PART II

Adding Images and Multimedia

HOUR 7

Displaying Images

What You'll Learn in This Hour:

- How to insert an image into a web page and change its properties
- How to add a hyperlink to an image
- Which image formats can be used in a web page
- How to create a rollover image

As access to digital images becomes easier and Internet bandwidth increases, so does the opportunity to add images to web pages. However, much of the emphasis in web page creation remains on optimizing image file sizes to make them as small as possible so viewers are spending their time viewing your page, not waiting for it to download. Images offer a powerful way to send a message. One drawing or photograph can communicate a huge amount of information.

Adding an Image to a Page

Images are separate files that appear within a web page. Because Dreamweaver is a what-you-see-is-what-you-get (WYSIWYG) program, it enables you to see web page images right in the Dreamweaver Document window. Images are not actually part of the HTML; they remain separate files that the browser inserts when you view the web page.

Open the one of the pages based on a Dreamweaver page design you created in Hour 3, "Getting Started: Adding Text, Lists, and Previewing in the Browser," or create a new page using the page design titled Image: Picture and Description Vertical (File, New, Page Designs). Delete the placeholder image (the gray box in the middle of the page). To insert an image into the web page, follow these steps:

1. Place the cursor where you want to insert the image. You will see the insertion point blinking, as shown in Figure 7.1.

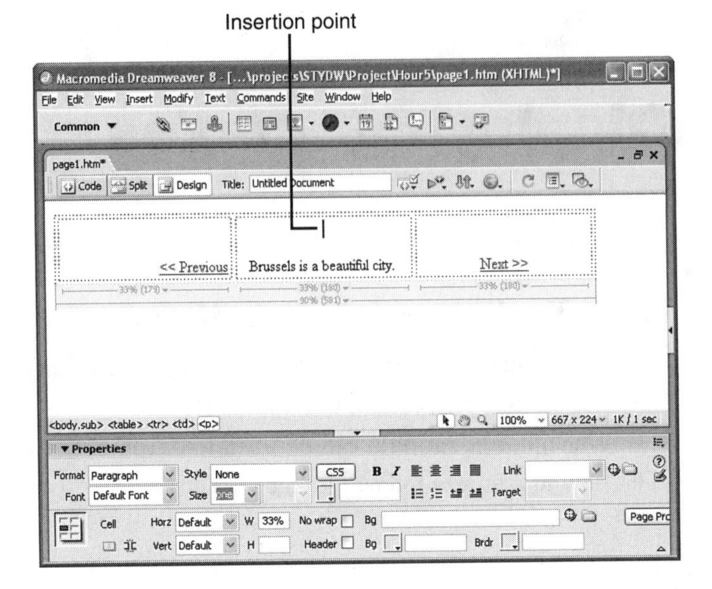

FIGURE 7.1 The insertion point signals where the image is to be inserted into the document.

2. Select the Image command from the Insert bar (or select Insert, Image).

3. Click the Browse icon (which looks like a folder) in the Property inspector to navigate to the directory where the image file resides. The Select Image Source dialog box appears.

   If you don't have any image files within the site you've defined in Dreamweaver, you can select a web image file from anywhere on your local drive and Dreamweaver will prompt you to copy it into your site. U.S. government sites, such as NASA (www.nasa.gov/multimedia/downloads), are a good source of images and movies with which to practice.

4. Select an image file (see Figure 7.2), a file that ends with `.gif` or `.jpg`. A thumbnail image is visible on the right side of the dialog box if the Preview Images check box is selected. Notice the file size, the dimensions of the image, and the download time located beneath the thumbnail (by default, at 56Kbps but this can be changed in the Status Bar category of the Dreamweaver Preferences).

   When you locate the correct image, click OK.

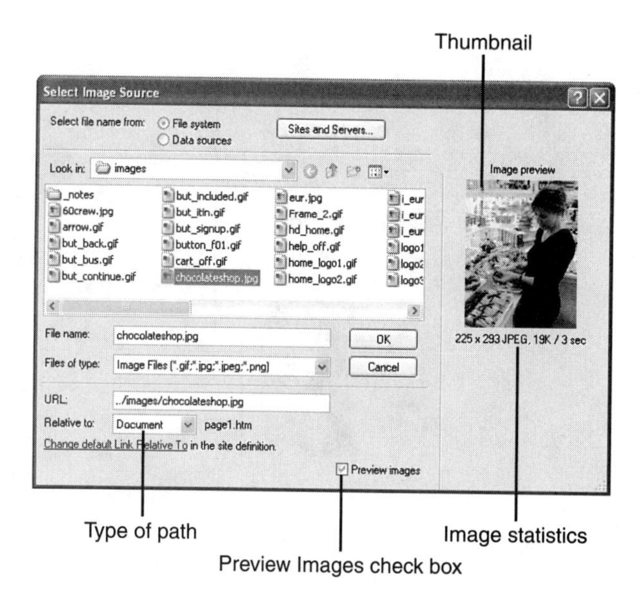

FIGURE 7.2 The Select Image Source dialog box enables you to preview an image before you select it.

By the Way

Would You Like to Copy the File?

If you select an image from outside your currently selected website, Dreamweaver asks you if you would like to copy the image to the current site. If you've added a default images folder in your site definition, Dreamweaver automatically copies the image into that directory if you agree. Otherwise, Dreamweaver asks you where you'd like to copy the image. This is an easy way to add images to your site.

As shown in Figure 7.3, the image is now visible within the web page. When the image is selected, the Property inspector displays the properties of the image. The Src (source) box displays the path to the image file. Notice that Dreamweaver automatically fills in the dimensions (width and height) of the image. Having the dimensions helps the browser by reserving the space for the image in the web page; if you don't reserve this space, the page content appears to move as the images load into it. The default unit of measure for width and height is pixels.

By the Way

Image Name Is Important for Rollover Images

Adding a name for an image will become more important later this hour, when you explore rollover images. Each rollover image must have a unique name that you add in the Property inspector. The JavaScript that facilitates the rollover requires that each image have a name.

FIGURE 7.3
The Property inspector shows the image's width, height, and other properties.

Watch Out!

Don't Resize Images in Dreamweaver

You shouldn't resize an image in Dreamweaver. It's better to resize an image in a graphics program, such as Macromedia Fireworks or Adobe Photoshop. These programs optimize the file size, whereas Dreamweaver simply stretches or shrinks the image. However, if you accidentally resize an image in Dreamweaver, it's easy to return to the actual dimensions of the image. When the image dimensions have been modified, a small Refresh icon appears next to the width and height boxes in the Property inspector. Click this button to correct the image dimensions.

Aligning an Image with Text

The Align drop-down menu in the Property inspector controls how objects that are located beside an image align with it. Align is very different from the text alignment settings you used in Hour 2, "A Tour of Dreamweaver." You use the text alignment settings to align an image in the center, to the left, or to the right of the screen. You use the Align drop-down menu to affect how *other* objects align with an image. In Figure 7.4, for instance, the image is aligned to the left of the text because Left is selected in the Align drop-down menu.

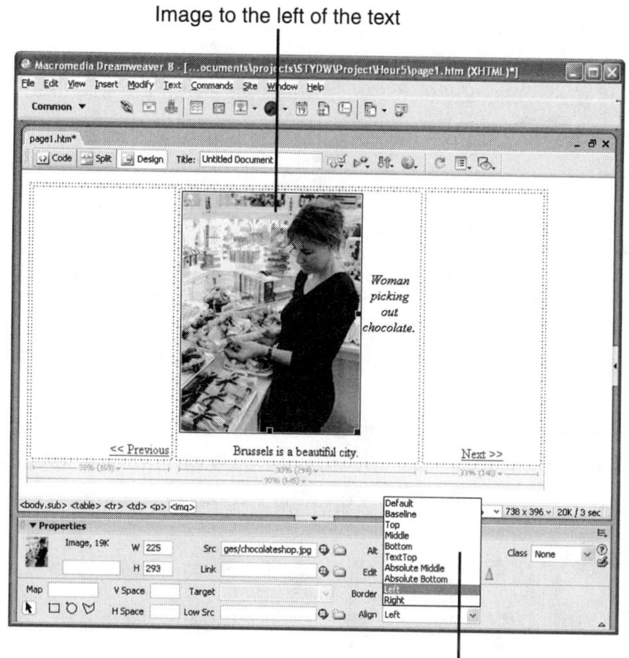

FIGURE 7.4 You can change how an image aligns with adjacent objects in the Align drop-down menu.

Change the Align setting of the image so that all the text appears to the left, beside the image. To do this, select Right from the Align drop-down menu in the Property inspector. Why select Right? The image will be on the right. Remember that the Align options apply to the image but affect other elements within its vicinity. The alignment choices are described in Table 7.1.

TABLE 7.1 Image Alignment Options in the Property Inspector

Align Option	Description
Default	Baseline-aligns the image, but this depends on the browser.
Baseline	Aligns the bottom of the image with the bottom of the element.
Top	Aligns the image with the highest element. Additional lines of text wrap beneath the image.
Middle	Aligns the baseline of the text with the middle of the image. Additional lines of text wrap beneath the image.
Bottom	Aligns the baseline of the text at the bottom of the image.
TextTop	Aligns the image with the highest text (not the highest element, as with the Top option). Additional lines of text wrap beneath the image.

TABLE 7.1 Continued

Align Option	Description
Absolute Middle	Aligns the middle of the image with the middle of the text beside it.
Absolute Bottom	Aligns the bottom of the highest element with the bottom of the image.
Left	Aligns the image to the left of other elements.
Right	Aligns the image to the right of other elements.

To increase the distance between the image and other page elements, set the V Space and H Space. *V* stands for vertical and *H* stands for horizontal. To add space to the right and left of an image, enter a value into the H Space text box, as shown in Figure 7.5. Horizontal space is added to both the right and the left of the image. Vertical space is added to both the top and the bottom of the image.

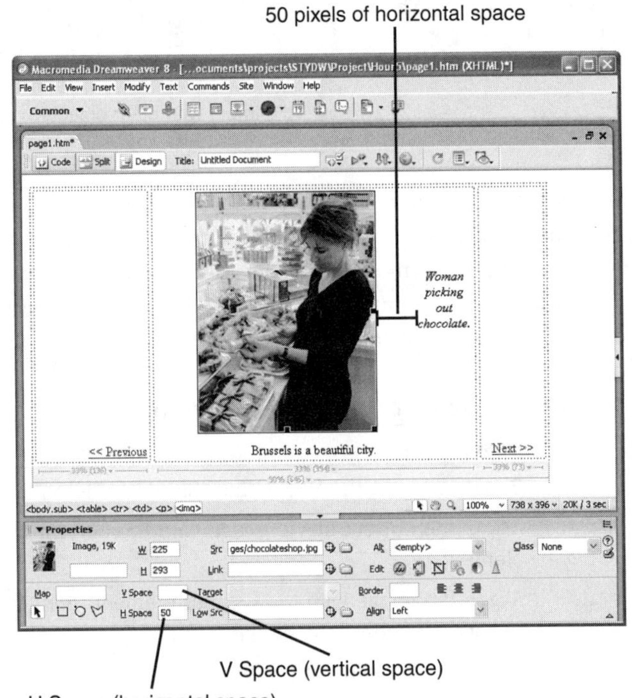

FIGURE 7.5 Put a value in the H Space text box to increase the space to the right and the left of the image. Put a value in the V Space text box to increase the space above and below the image.

Adding Alternative Text

Believe it or not, some people who might surf to your web pages are still using text-only browsers, such as Lynx. Others are stuck behind a very slow modem or Internet connection and have the images turned off in their browsers. Others are visually impaired and have text-to-speech (TTS) browsers that read the contents of web pages. For all these viewers, you should add alternative text to your images.

You enter alternative text, called **alt text**, in the Alt drop-down menu in the Property inspector, as shown in Figure 7.6. Make the text descriptive of the image that it represents. Don't enter something such as "people." A better choice would be "Rick and the 60 Minutes crew." In some browsers, the Alt text also pops up like a ToolTip when the viewer puts the cursor over an image. If the viewer has opted to turn images off in his browser, he will only see the Alt text and can then decide whether to download the images associated with the web page.

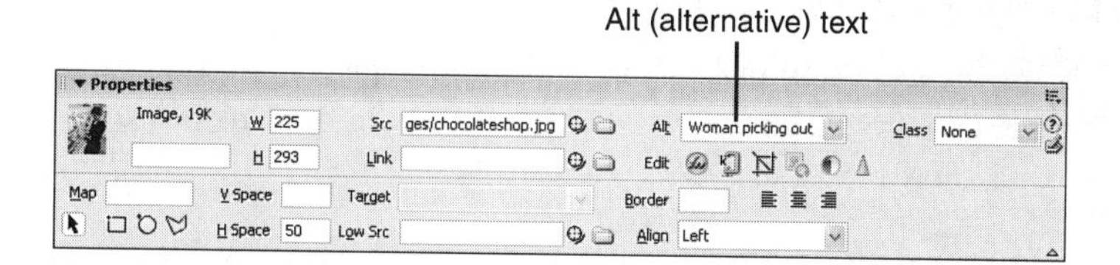

FIGURE 7.6
Alt text is useful for viewers who don't have images in their browsers or are visually impaired.

TTS browsers used by people who are visually impaired read the alt text description of an image to the user. When an image does not have the `Alt` attribute set, a TTS browser says the word *image*; listening to the browser say *image* over and over isn't very enjoyable! Some images on a web page are purely ornamental and do not add information to the page—a divider line, for instance. Select <empty> from the Alt drop-down menu in the Property inspector to add alt text with no content; this makes TTS browsers skip the image.

Did you Know?

Missing Alt Text Reporting

You can run a Missing Alt Text report by selecting Site, Reports. This report shows you all the images that are missing alt text.

You can force yourself to enter alt text and other accessibility options in Dreamweaver Preferences (Edit, Preferences). Select the Accessibility category and check the check boxes beside Form objects, Frames, Media, and/or Images in order to have Dreamweaver automatically open up a dialog box asking for the appropriate accessibility settings for each type of web page object. These settings force you to be conscious of the extra attributes required for screen readers.

Creating a Linked Image

The Link property appears in the Property inspector when you have text or an image selected. Linked images are common on the Web. When the user clicks a linked image, the browser loads the linked web page. With an image selected, you can add a hyperlink in a few ways:

- Type a URL into the Link box in the Property inspector.
- Browse for the linked page by selecting the Browse icon beside the Link box.
- Use the Point-to-File icon to link to a file. The Point-to-File icon enables you to simply drag the cursor over a file in the Files panel to create a link.

To enter a known URL as an image link, select an image on your web page and make sure the Property inspector is open. Enter a URL in the Link box underneath the Src box, as shown in Figure 7.7.

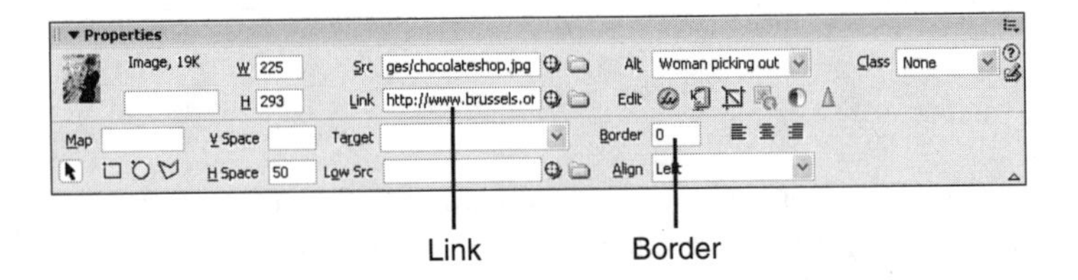

FIGURE 7.7 You set hyperlinks in the Link box in the Property inspector.

Notice that when you enter a URL in the Link box, the Border property automatically changes to 0. This is so that you do not have the hyperlink highlight as a border around the image. If you prefer to have a highlighted border, set the border to a value greater than 0. You can also set a border for an image that isn't linked to anything. The border will then appear as a black box around the image.

After you save the web page, preview it in a browser. When you click the image that has the hyperlink, your browser should go to the hyperlinked page.

Exploring Image Flavors: GIF, JPEG, and PNG

All browsers support the two standard image formats: GIF (pronounced either "gif" or "jif") and JPEG (pronounced "j-peg"). There is also a newer format, the portable network graphics (PNG—pronounced "ping") format. Here's a little more information about these three formats:

- GIF—This format is best for images that have blocks of continuous color, usually drawings.
- JPEG—This format is best for photographic images and images that do not have blocks of continuous color—for example, images that contain color gradients.
- PNG—This format is a replacement for the GIF format. It supports alpha channels that are useful for transparency. Although PNG is not as popular as the other two formats, its popularity is growing. This is the Macromedia Fireworks native file format. If you need to be compatible with all the browser versions, including old browsers, you will want to avoid using PNGs.

Did you Know?

Optimize Your Images

Image-optimization software programs can help you decide which image format is the most efficient to use for a particular image. These programs also help you reduce the number of colors in an image and improve other factors that reduce file size and download time.

If you have Fireworks, for example, in Dreamweaver you can select Command, Optimize Image in Fireworks when you have an image selected. This opens the image file in Fireworks. Another program that has image optimization is Adobe Photoshop.

The File Types/Editors category in the Preferences dialog box allows you to associate file extensions with different external programs, as shown in Figure 7.8. For example, you can associate the `.jpg`, `.gif`, and `.png` file extensions with Fireworks. When an image is selected in Dreamweaver, you can click the Edit button to open the image file in Fireworks. You make your edits and save the file. To associate an editor with a file extension, select a file extension in the File Types/Editors category, click the plus button, and browse to the image editor program.

While you're in an external image editor, you might want to create a low-resolution version of an image to link to from the Low Src box in the Property inspector. This image will appear during the initial loading of the web page and then will turn into the higher-resolution version of the image. This functionality evolved to help speed up download times. Usually the low-resolution image is grayscale or a smaller version of a color image.

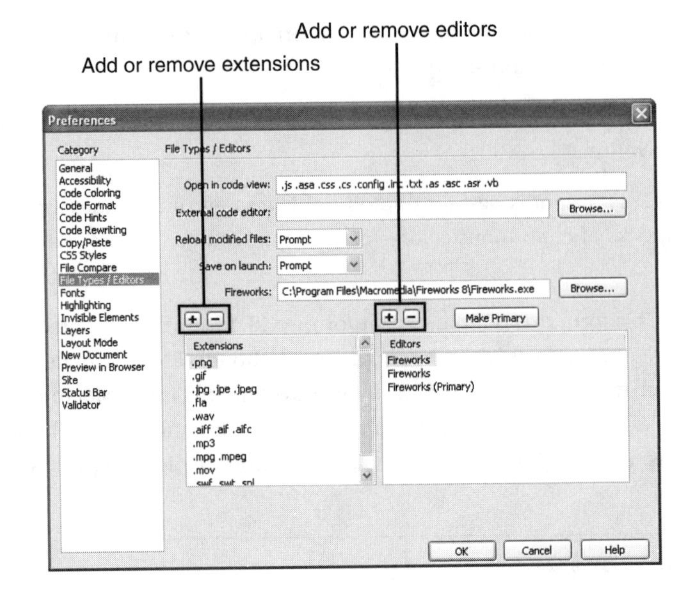

FIGURE 7.8
The File Types/Editors category in the Dreamweaver Preferences dialog box configures other applications to edit linked files.

Editing Images Within Dreamweaver

Although you will probably want to become somewhat familiar with a graphics tool to create and optimize images to put in your websites, Dreamweaver has a few basic image-editing capabilities to explore. In Hour 8, "Optimizing and Creating Images," you'll explore how to use Macromedia Fireworks for image editing. Dreamweaver has several image-editing tools built right in:

- **Edit**—Opens the selected image in Fireworks for editing (of course, you need to have Macromedia Fireworks or another image-editing program defined in the Preferences dialog box for this command to work).
- **Optimize**—Opens the selected image in the Fireworks optimization window. You'll learn more about this in Hour 8. This command requires that you have Fireworks installed.
- **Crop**—Lets you trim off unwanted portions of the image and saves the smaller file. This command works within Dreamweaver, enabling you to save the cropped image.
- **Resample**—This command becomes active after you've resized an image in Dreamweaver. It optimizes an image by adding or removing pixels in the image. This command works within Dreamweaver.

- **Brightness and Contrast**—Changes the brightness and contrast of an image to correct an image that is too bright or too dark. This command works within Dreamweaver.
- **Sharpen**—Sharpens a blurry image. This command works within Dreamweaver.

You can access all these image-editing commands from the Property inspector when you have an image selected, as shown in Figure 7.9. Make sure you have a backup copy of any images you modify because Dreamweaver changes the actual image file.

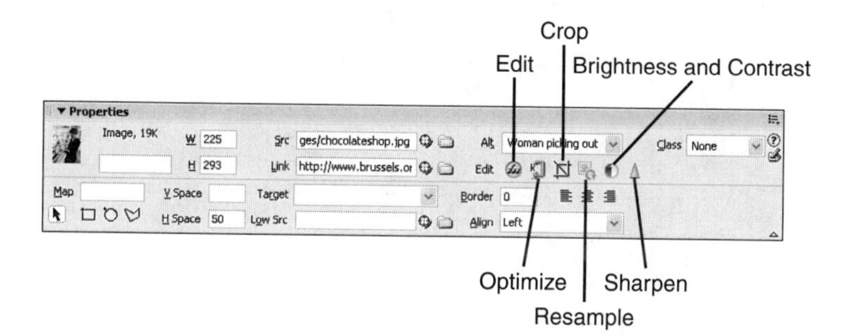

FIGURE 7.9 Dreamweaver has image-editing commands that enable you to jump out to an image-editing program or edit an image directly in Dreamweaver.

Creating a Rollover Image

Dreamweaver makes it easy to implement rollover images by using the Rollover Image object. A **rollover image** is an image that swaps to another image when the viewer's cursor is over it. You need two image files with exactly the same dimensions in order to create a rollover.

To create a rollover image, follow these steps:

1. Place the insertion point where you want the rollover image to appear.
2. Select the Rollover Image object from the Insert bar or select Insert, Interactive Images, Rollover Image. The Insert Rollover Image dialog box appears.
3. Type a name for the image in the Image Name text field.
4. Select both the original image file and the rollover image file by clicking the Browse buttons next to those options and selecting the image files.

5. Check the Preload Rollover Image check box if you'd like the rollover image downloaded into the viewer's browser cache. With a preloaded image, there is less chance that the viewer will have to wait for the rollover image to download when he or she moves the cursor over the image.

6. Add a link to the rollover image by clicking the Browse button next to When Clicked, Go to URL or type in the external URL or named anchor.

7. The Insert Rollover Image dialog box should look as shown in Figure 7.10. Click the OK button.

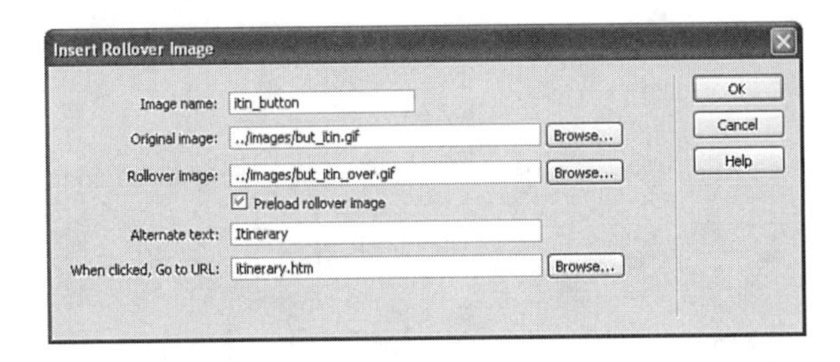

FIGURE 7.10 A rollover image swaps one image for another when the viewer's cursor is over the image. You need to enter both image paths into the Insert Rollover Image dialog box.

Summary

In this hour, you have learned how to insert an image into a web page and how to set a link, a low-resolution source, vertical and horizontal space, and alt text. You have learned how to change the size of an image border and edit the image by using an external editor. You have learned how to align an image on a page and align it in relationship to other elements beside it. You have also created a rollover image.

Q&A

Q. ***I have a lot of images from my digital camera that I'd like to display on a web page and share with other people. Can Dreamweaver help me with this?***

A. Use Dreamweaver's Web Photo Album (Command, Create Web Photo Album) if you also have Fireworks. This command automatically optimizes all of the images in a folder and displays them on a web page. You will want to read Hour 8 before trying this so you can first optimize your images. Digital cameras take high-resolution shots that appear very large on the screen. Hour 8 helps you understand how to use a program such as Fireworks to optimize your photos to display on the Web.

Q. ***I accidentally stretched an image. Help!***

A. It's easy to restore the original dimensions of an image by selecting the image and clicking the Refresh button that appears next to the width and height text fields in the Property inspector after you've resized an image.

Workshop

Quiz

1. How do you create a box around an image?
2. What are the three widely supported image formats for web pages?
3. If you want an image on the left and text beside it on the right, what Align value would you give the image?

Quiz Answers

1. Enter a value in the Border text box to create a box, or border, around an image.
2. The three widely supported image formats for web pages are GIF, JPEG, and PNG.
3. You give the image the Align value Left.

Exercises

1. Insert an image into a new page. Resize it by using the resizing handles. Click the Refresh button. Resize the image by holding down Shift while dragging the corner resizing handle. Click the Refresh button. Change the width and height dimensions by entering different values into the W and H boxes in the Property inspector.

2. Add alt text to an image. Open your browser, select the browser preferences or Internet options, and turn off viewing of images. The command for this might be called Show Pictures or Automatically Load Images. Return to Dreamweaver and preview the web page in that browser so you can see how the alt text looks.

3. Insert an image into a web page and experiment with Dreamweaver's image-editing tools. Try using sharpen, cropping, and brightness/contrast. Then resize the image and try image resampling. Does Dreamweaver actually change the original files? Be careful not to make any permanent changes to your files.

HOUR 8

Optimizing and Creating Images

What You'll Learn in This Hour:

- How to optimize images
- How to create an image in Fireworks
- How to add strokes, fills, filters, and text to an image
- How to add a rollover effect to create button states
- How to slice and export images

I know that this is a book on Dreamweaver but many readers asked for a quick introduction to creating images, so I obliged by adding this hour. Many people who purchase Dreamweaver purchase it in a software bundle that also includes Fireworks, so the examples this hour are created with Fireworks. Macromedia Fireworks is a professional image tool that could fill an entire 24-hour learning period on its own! This hour simply touches on some of the important elements and describes a few image manipulation techniques. There is so much more to learn about Fireworks than is possible in this hour.

Fireworks is an image optimization and creation tool that is an excellent addition to your web development toolbox. You will need to create and optimize the images that you use in your websites, and Fireworks enables you to quickly create images that have cool filters such as bevels and glows. If you do not have Fireworks, you can download a trial version at www.macromedia.com/software/trial_download.

Dreamweaver and Fireworks are tightly integrated. You can open Fireworks files in Dreamweaver, make changes, and see those changes in the original Fireworks file. You can also import tables, rollover images, and HTML code created in Fireworks directly into Dreamweaver.

Acquainting Yourself with Fireworks

This hour demonstrates how to accomplish image optimization and creation in Fireworks, but many of the techniques described here are achievable in other image-editing programs as well. Although the command names might differ in other image-editing programs, such as Adobe Photoshop, the techniques are still similar.

Fireworks has an integrated interface that looks very similar to Dreamweaver's interface. The Fireworks Document window, shown in Figure 8.1, contains a Tools panel on the left, a Property inspector at the bottom, and panel groups on the right. You can open an existing image in Fireworks or create a new one from scratch.

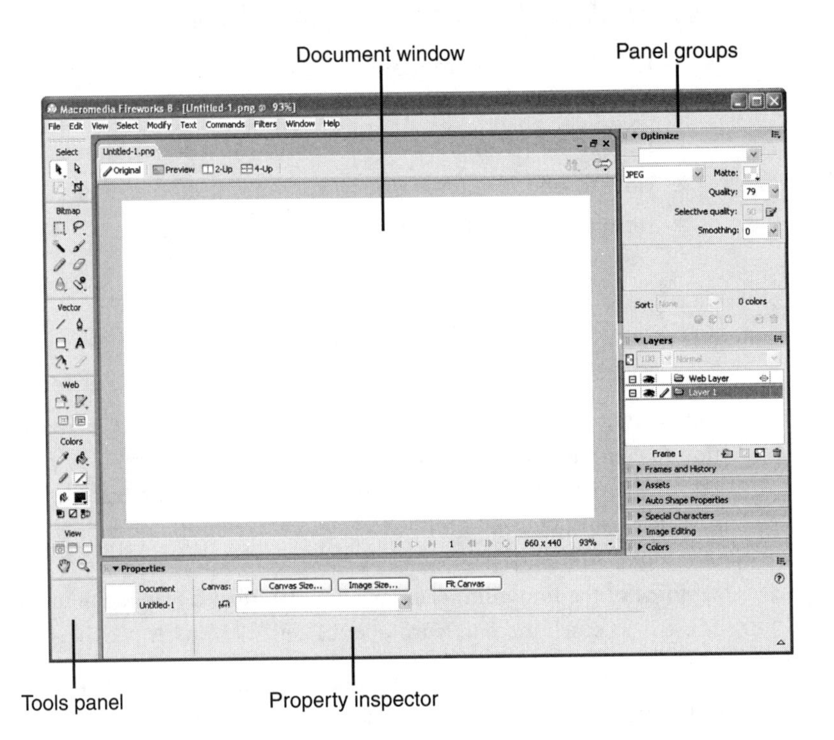

FIGURE 8.1
Fireworks has an integrated interface similar to Dreamweaver's interface.

Optimizing Images for Use in a Web Page

One of the powerful features of Fireworks is its capability to optimize an image and show you the smallest and best-looking format for the image. This is probably how I use Fireworks most frequently. To practice using this feature, open an image, preferably a photograph, in Fireworks. Because your image will be different from the one I'm working with, you will get different results than are shown here.

You can get a photo from your digital camera, from a collection of clip art, or from a free source such as NASA (www.nasa.gov/multimedia/downloads). Most of the images that you find on the Web have already been optimized so you might want to look for non-optimized file, using what is called a source file or high-resolution file. You need to optimize images to make sure that they aren't larger than they need to be because larger images mean longer downloads.

Digital cameras are often set to take pictures at a high resolution. Although a higher resolution gives excellent results for printing, these file are much too large to display on a computer screen. Have you ever had someone send you a digital photo and when you opened it on your computer, it appeared huge? That's because the photo is saved at 150 or 300 pixels per inch, but your monitor resolution is approximately 72 pixels per inch. You need to sample a photo down to the standard 72 pixels per inch before you use it in a web page. Open your selected image file in Fireworks and click the Image Size button in the Property inspector (see Figure 8.2). Or, you can select Modify, Canvas, Image Size.

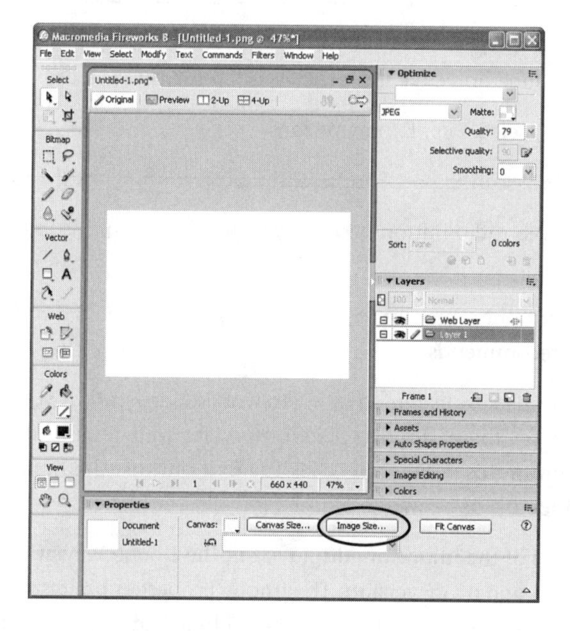

FIGURE 8.2
The Image Size button is available in the Fireworks Property inspector when nothing on the screen is selected.

The Image Size dialog box appears, enabling you to change the resolution and size of the image. First change the Resolution setting to 72 pixels per inch, as shown in Figure 8.3. Make sure that the Constrain Proportions check box is selected and then examine the pixel dimensions of the image. You can change them here by entering a new width or height, or you can change them later, during the optimization process. With the proportions constrained, you can change one of the dimensions, and Fireworks will change the other dimension proportionally for you. Because you are working with an image for a web page, you don't need to worry about the Print Size settings.

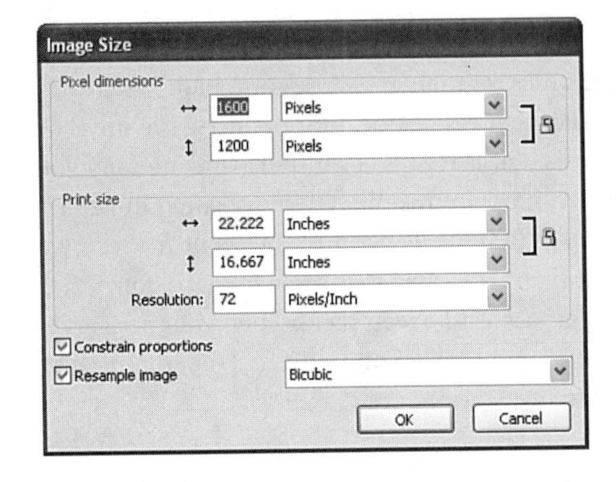

FIGURE 8.3
The Image Size dialog box enables you to change the size and resolution of an image.

To optimize the image and save it for the Web, follow these steps:

1. In Fireworks, select File, Export Wizard.
2. Select the Select an Export Format radio button and click the Continue button.
3. Select the Web radio button because you will be using this image as part of a web page.
4. Click the Exit button to display the image in the formats that Fireworks automatically recommends.
5. In the Analysis Results dialog box, Fireworks suggests that you use either a GIF or JPEG image, the major accepted formats for web pages. After you read the information in this dialog box, click the Exit button. The Image Preview dialog box appears, as shown in Figure 8.4.
6. Two versions of the image are displayed in the Image Preview dialog box: a JPEG version and a GIF version. The image properties are displayed on the left side of the box. Click the JPEG (top image) to display the JPEG properties on the left and click the GIF (bottom image) to display the GIF properties on the left.

7. Examine the image size and download time for each of the formats. Choose the format with the quickest download time. If you are optimizing a photo, the JPEG format will probably make the smallest file. Select an image file format to further optimize the file.

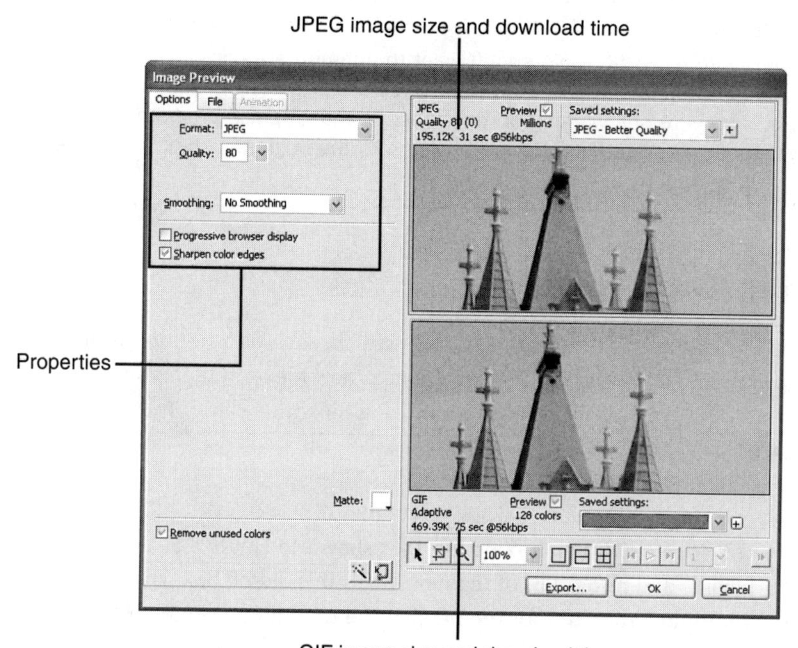

FIGURE 8.4 The Image Preview dialog box enables you to compare the file size and download time of different file formats.

8. Experiment with the image format optimization settings while examining the file size. It's safe to experiment here prior to saving the final image. Examine the preview image to make sure the quality of the image isn't degraded too much. If your image is a photo, the JPEG file format will probably be the smaller but if your image is line art, the GIF file format will be smaller.

9. Click the File tab to modify the image width and height. Decreasing the width and height of the image makes the file smaller.

10. When you are satisfied that your image is optimized, click the Export button. Give the file a name and click Save.

Your newly optimized image is now ready to be incorporated into a web page!

Did you Know?

Setting JPEG Quality

Depending on your original image, a JPEG quality setting somewhere between 50 and 80 usually works best. You need to examine the preview image while optimizing, paying attention to both the foreground and background. Check that there aren't any areas of the image that are extremely **pixilated**, where the square pixels are visible to the user, making the image appear blocky and no longer realistic.

After you've optimized a JPEG, you don't want to optimize it again. If you need to make a change to an image saved as a JPEG, open up the original source file and re-optimize. If you are still working on the image in the graphics program and you haven't yet saved it, select File, Revert to return to the original, non-optimized version of the image.

Creating an Image

In Fireworks you can create a new image from scratch, such as a button graphic that you can use in your website. First you create a new file, and then you add some color and text. Next, you apply an effect to make it look interesting. To try this, follow these steps:

1. Select File, New.
2. The New Document dialog box appears, as shown in Figure 8.5. You set the width, height, and resolution of the new file in this dialog box. Enter 70 pixels for the width and 26 pixels for the height. The resolution should be 72 because that is the standard resolution for images displayed on a computer screen.

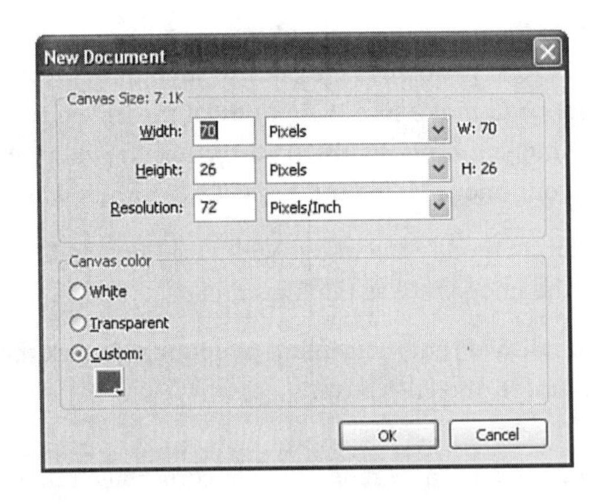

FIGURE 8.5 You set the width, height, and resolution in the New Document dialog box. You also set the canvas color here.

3. Give the button a background color by selecting the Custom radio button under Canvas Color, clicking the color picker, and then picking a color.

4. When you are done with the settings in the New Document dialog box, click OK.

5. Select 800% from the magnification drop-down menu at the bottom of the Document window, as shown in Figure 8.6. This will make it easier to see what you are working on.

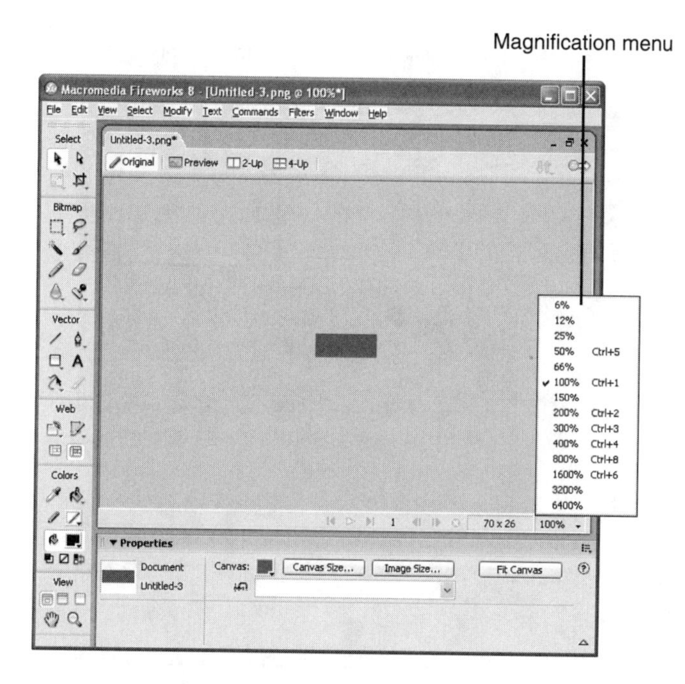

FIGURE 8.6
You can magnify the Document window by using the magnification drop-down menu. The magnification level is displayed at the bottom of the Document window.

Adding Text to an Image

You can add text to any image in Fireworks. The Text tool in Fireworks enables you to place editable text into the Document window. You should turn on guides so you can judge whether you have the text centered in the button. You can use any font on your system, and you can apply anti-aliasing and other text effects. **Anti-aliasing** is a process of blending the edges of text with its background so the letters look smoother.

Add text to your rectangle as follows:

1. Turn on the rulers by selecting View, Rulers. You need the rulers to be visible because guides are added to an image by clicking and dragging from the ruler. **Guides** are useful for lining up text and other elements within an image.

2. Click within the left ruler and drag a vertical guide to the middle of the image. Make sure that your cursor is over the image when you finish dragging the guide. Repeat by dragging a horizontal guide down from the top ruler to the middle of the image. You can open the Info panel (Window, Info) to help precisely place the guides at 13 pixels horizontally and 35 pixels vertically. The guides should look as shown in Figure 8.7.

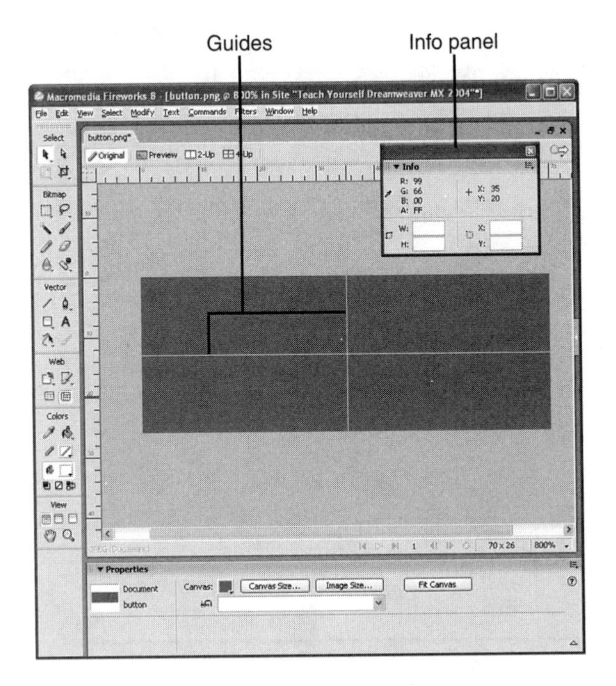

FIGURE 8.7
You can add guides to an image so you know where the middle of the image is.

By the Way

Remove or Hide the Guides

To remove the guides, simply drag them off the screen. To leave the guides in place but hide them, select View, Guides, Show Guides (Ctrl+; or Command+; on the Mac), turning off the check mark next to the command. To show the guides again, simply toggle the same command, selecting View, Guides, Show Guides to turn on the check mark next to the command.

3. Select the Text tool from the Tools panel (the button shows the letter *A*). Don't click within the Document window quite yet. First you need to set up how the text will look.

4. In the Property inspector, select a font, make the font size 14, and choose white for the color (unless white won't be visible on your canvas color).

5. Click the canvas and enter some text for a button title (try **`Next`** for a next button). Leave enough room on the right side for a small arrow.

6. Pick up and position the text object using the Pointer tool, the dark arrow button in the upper-left corner of the Toolbar, shown in Figure 8.8. After you select the text object, you can use the arrow keys on your keyboard to fine-tune the positioning. The button should look something like the one in Figure 8.8.

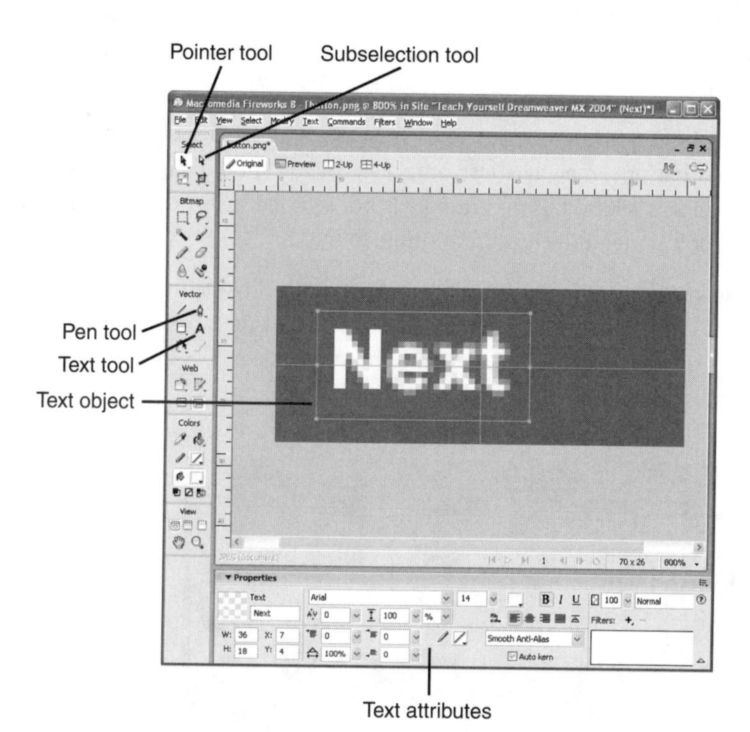

FIGURE 8.8
Create a text object and set the font, font size, and font color.

Adding a Shape to an Image

Fireworks has tools for drawing any type of shape you might want. Now you'll create a triangle shape to the right of the text on your button that looks like an arrow. After you create the triangle, you can modify the stroke (that is, the outline) and the fill. To create a triangle, follow these steps:

1. Select the Pen tool from the Tools panel. The cursor becomes an ink pen. The Pen tool adds points to create a shape. You'll create three points for a triangle.

2. Click to create one point in the triangle. Hold down the Shift key while you click to create a second triangle point. This should force the creation of a

straight line. Click one more time to create the second side of the triangle. And then click on the original point to close the shape.

3. This last line may not be perfectly straight, but you can adjust it. There are two arrow tools in Fireworks: the Pointer tool and the Subselection tool. You can use the Subselection tool (the white arrow tool) to select a single point in your triangle. Use this tool to select any of the points, and then press the arrow keys on your keyboard to fine-tune the position of the points so that the triangle is even. Use the Pointer tool to select the entire triangle and adjust its position.

4. Make sure that the triangle object that you just created is selected (in case you clicked your cursor somewhere else after step 3). You should see the three points when it is selected. If the triangle is not selected, select the Pointer tool from the Tools panel and click the triangle to select it.

5. The stroke settings are in the Property inspector. Select None from the stroke drop-down menu, as shown in Figure 8.9. Notice that the stroke color picker now has a red line through it, signifying that this object does not have any stroke attributes applied.

FIGURE 8.9
Set the stroke in the Property inspector.

Stroke drop-down menu

Stroke settings

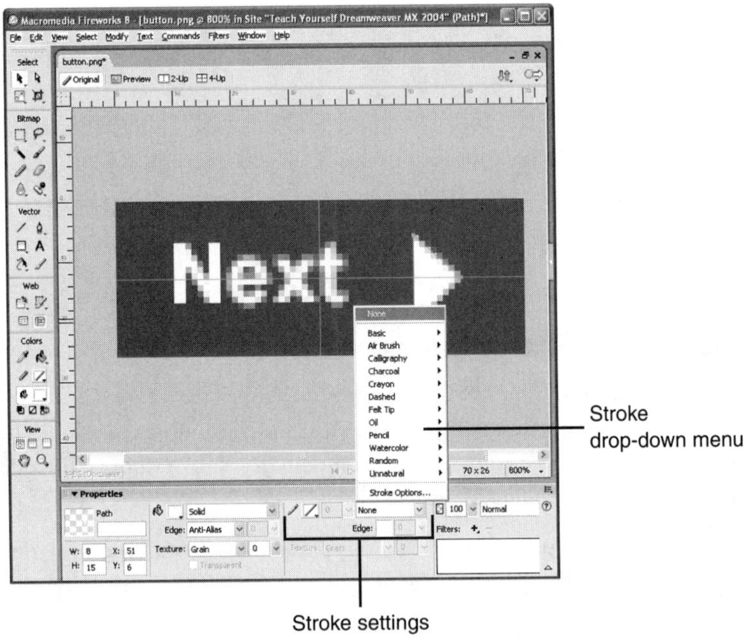

6. The fill settings are directly to the left of the stroke settings in the Property inspector. Select Solid from the fill drop-down menu, and select a color (I suggest white) from the color picker. The image should look like the one in Figure 8.10.

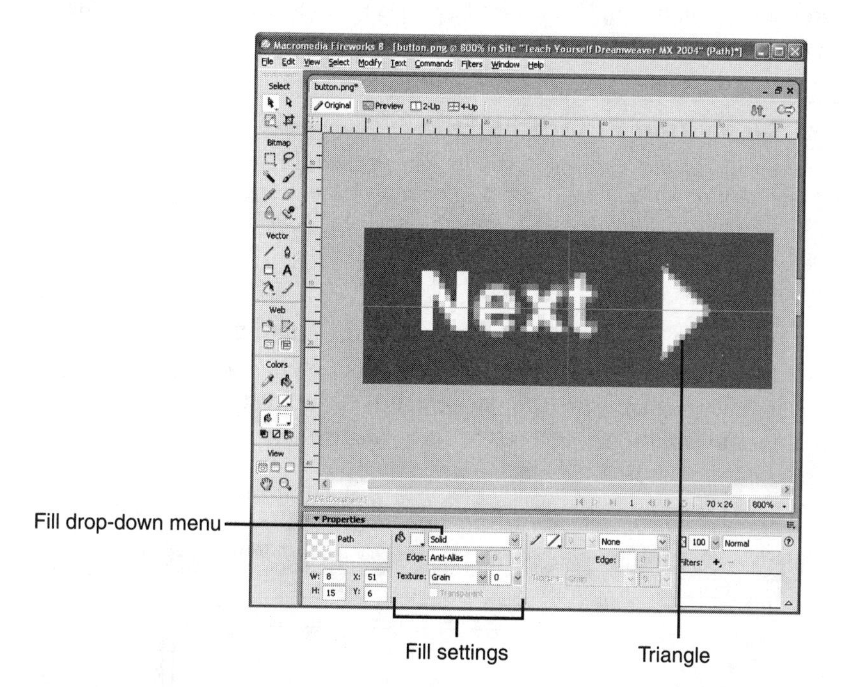

FIGURE 8.10
The triangle now has no stroke and a solid fill.

Did you Know?

Check the Final Size

You might want to reduce the magnification to 100% so that you can see what your button will look like at its final size. Make sure that the text is readable. If you need to make the font size larger, select the text object and adjust the font settings.

7. Underneath the fill settings is the Edge property. Make sure that Anti-Alias is selected so the edges of the triangle blend nicely into the background.

Watch Out!

Anti-Aliasing and Different Background Colors

When you anti-alias text, the graphic program blends the edges into the current background color. That's how the edges look smooth. But this means that you must display the image on the same background color or you will see pixels of the original background color around the text. This effect is called **ghosting**.

8. Save your file as a Fireworks PNG file. The PNG format is the native format that Fireworks uses to save files. When you do this, you save the source file, but you still need to export a file to use in your web page. Although Fireworks uses standard PNG files, these files contain a lot of extra information—information about shapes and fonts that Fireworks needs to edit the image. When you optimize, this extra information is removed.

You Can Cloak Your Fireworks Files

You can save your original Fireworks files to your website. Dreamweaver has a cloaking feature that you will learn about in Hour 21, "Managing and Editing a Website," that enables you to easily store source files in your hard drive without uploading them to your remote site.

9. Select File, Image Preview to optimize your button. Adjust the settings, as shown in Figure 8.11, to get the smallest file. Click on the Two Preview Windows button to compare two file formats (GIF and JPEG). This is the image that is inserted into your web page in Dreamweaver.

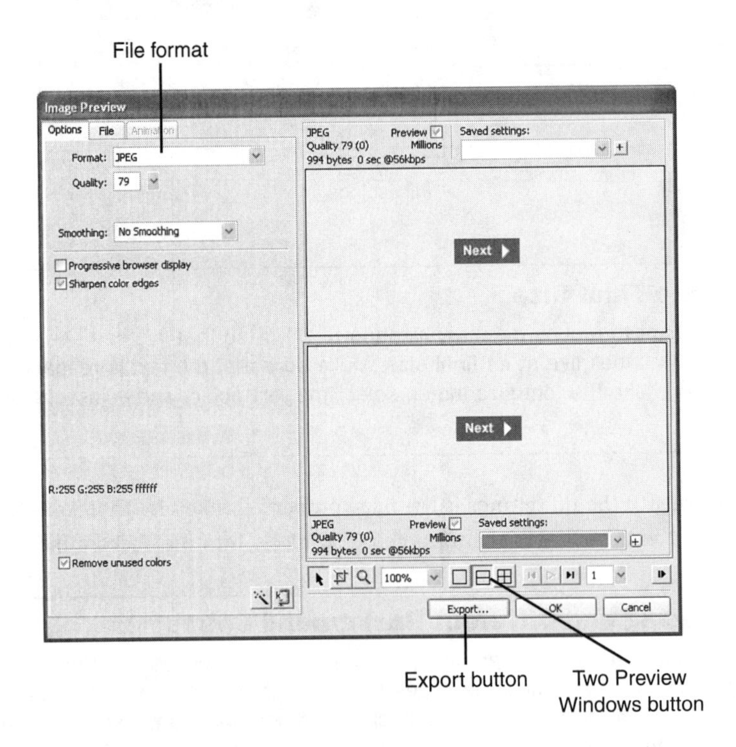

FIGURE 8.11 Use the Image Preview command to optimize a button image to use in your web page.

10. Click the Export button to save the image.

Creating a Rollover Effect

It's easy to use Fireworks to create rollover images. In this section, you'll create a rollover version of the button you just created. Remember that the trick to creating a rollover image is that the two images involved need to be exactly the same size. You'll continue using the same button file you just created. To begin creating a rollover image, follow these steps:

1. Open the Frames panel (Window, Frames). You should already have a Frame 1 which holds the button image you just created. Add a new frame, Frame 2, by clicking the New/Duplicate Frame button (the button with the plus sign) in the lower-right corner of the panel.

2. Select Frame 1 in the Frames panel and select everything in the frame by using Edit, Select All (Ctrl+A in Windows, Command+A on a Mac). Copy the contents of Frame 1 (Ctrl+C in Windows, Command+C on a Mac), click Frame 2 in the Frames panel, and paste the contents (Ctrl+V in Windows, Command+V on a Mac). Now you have an exact copy of Frame 1 in Frame 2.

3. Select the text on Frame 2 by using the Pointer tool. The text attributes appear in the Property inspector. Change the text color to a different, highlight color (try `#FFFF00`, a bright yellow color). Remember which color you use because you'll use it again in a few minutes to make the arrow glow.

Adding a Filter to a Rollover Image

Fireworks enables you to add a number of interesting filters to images to make them look unique and beautiful. Even better, they are very easy to remove if they don't turn out quite the way you'd like. Each time you add an effect to an object, it is listed in the Filters area of the Property inspector, with a check mark beside it. You simply uncheck the check box to turn off the effect for an object.

Fireworks Can Use Photoshop Plug-ins

If you have Photoshop, you can use Photoshop plug-ins in Fireworks. Point to the directory that contains the Photoshop plug-ins in the Folders category of the Fireworks Preferences dialog box (which you open by selecting Edit, Preferences). You need to restart Fireworks to load the Photoshop plug-in commands. After you restart Fireworks, it displays the Photoshop plug-in commands in the Effect Panel drop-down menu.

To add an effect to your image, follow these steps:

1. Make sure you have the triangle object on Frame 2 selected (with the Pointer tool). You'll apply the effect to this object.
2. Select the Add Filters button (the + button) to drop down the Filters menu, as shown in Figure 8.12.

FIGURE 8.12
The Filters area of the Property inspector enables you to select the effect you'd like to add.

3. From the Filters menu, select Shadow and Glow and then select Glow. The effect is applied to the triangle, and the attribute box appears.
4. Using the color picker, select the same color you applied to the text in the preceding section. If you need to edit the effect, simply double-click it in the list.

With Fireworks filters, you can add bevels, glows, and blurs to images, and you can emboss images, too. You'll probably want to experiment with the different filters. Usually you can change the colors involved, too. For instance, you can make an object glow in yellow from its center or glow from the bottom of the image as if it were on fire. Fireworks filters enable you to get professional image results without having to know all the high-end tricks of the image trade.

The image in Frame 2 will be the image the user sees when she rolls the cursor over the Frame 1 image. To simulate what the rollover effect will look like on the web page, click between Frame 1 and Frame 2. Does it look good? Now you must complete the final step to export both of the frames as separate images to use in a Dreamweaver rollover image. Fireworks uses something called **slices** to facilitate rollover images and other interactivity. To export your rollover images to Dreamweaver, follow these steps:

1. Select the Image Preview command (Image Preview, Export) to optimize your images before you export both of them (each frame).
2. Click the Export button at the bottom of the Image Preview dialog box.
3. The Export dialog box appears, as shown in Figure 8.13. Name your file `next.gif`. Select Frames to Files from the Export drop-down menu and uncheck the Trim Images check box. Save the buttons in the images directory you created in your website.

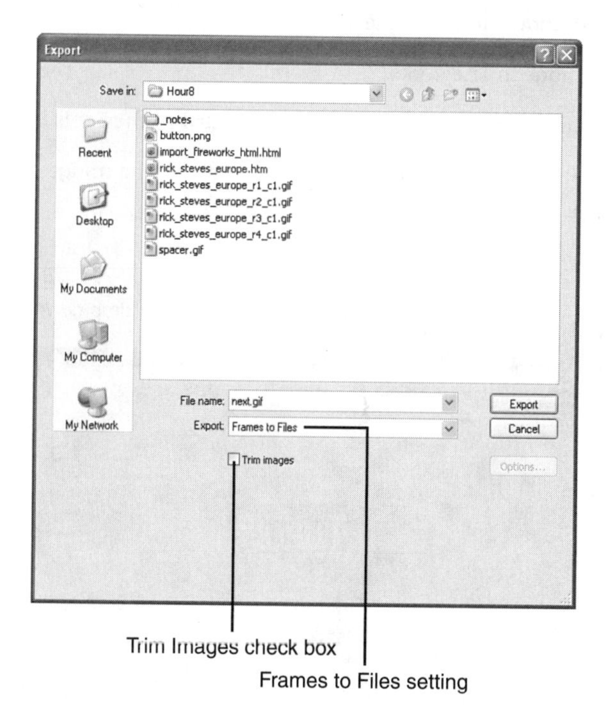

FIGURE 8.13
Use the Export dialog box to export the two frames as separate images.

4. Go to the images directory. You should see two images: `next.gif` and `Frame_2.gif`. The `Frame_2.gif` image is the content from Frame 2 of your Fireworks file.
5. Check out the Creating a Rollover Image section at the end of Hour 7, "Displaying Images," for how to add a rollover image to your web page.

So that you can make updates or changes to this button later, you should save the Fireworks file. When you reopen the file in Fireworks, you'll have access to change all the text objects, shapes, and other elements of the image. The native Fireworks PNG file can be displayed in a web page, but I don't recommend that because it isn't an optimized file format, and it is bigger than necessary for a web page.

Slicing an Image into Pieces

Fireworks enables you to slice an image into smaller pieces so you can add interactivity to the individual pieces. Slicing also facilitates creating a page layout by cutting images into pieces that will easily fit into the implementation of your page design in Dreamweaver. You can draw slice objects over an image in Fireworks and then export the slices as individual graphic files.

To create a sliced image, follow these steps:

1. Open an image in Fireworks.
2. Make sure that the Show Slices button is selected in the Tools panel.
3. Select the Slice tool and draw a rectangle on top of the image, as shown in Figure 8.14.

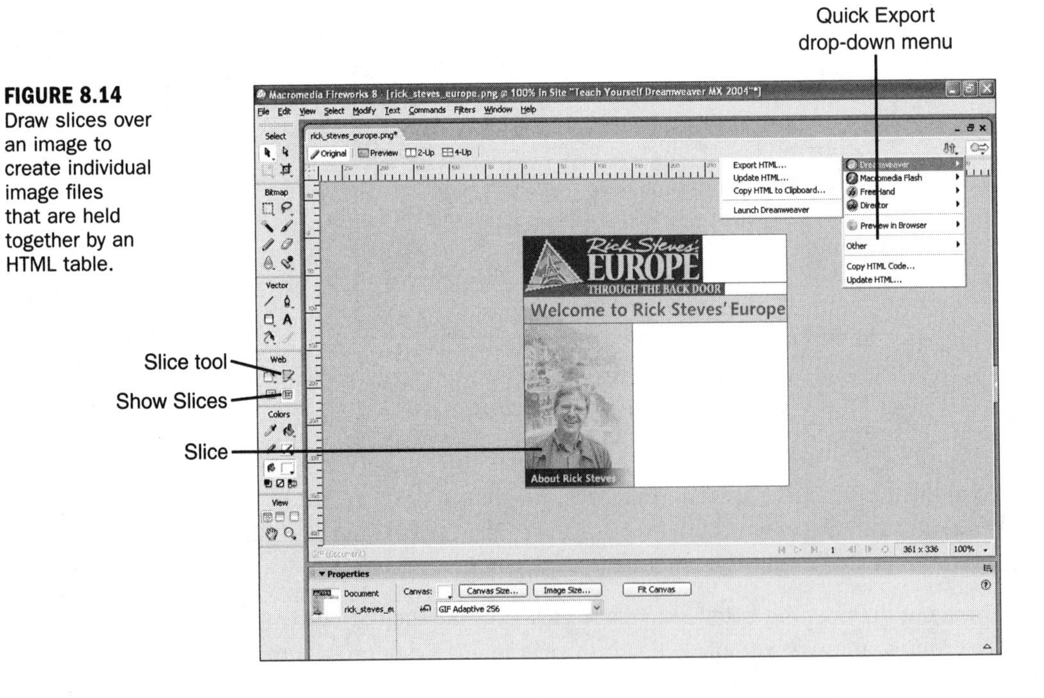

FIGURE 8.14 Draw slices over an image to create individual image files that are held together by an HTML table.

4. Slice up the entire image by repeating step 3.
5. Select the Quick Export drop-down menu in the upper-right corner of the Fireworks Document window. Select Dreamweaver, Export HTML. The Export dialog box appears.
6. Fireworks enables you to export all the slices as individual image files along with the HTML table that will display the images as if they were all one image. Make sure that Export HTML File is selected at the bottom of the Export dialog box. Uncheck the Include Areas Without Slices option.
7. Select the Save button and save the HTML file and all the sliced images into a directory.

If you open the HTML file you just created, you'll see all the slices pushed together as if they were a single image. You can open this file in Dreamweaver and edit it. In a minute, you will learn how to import the HTML into Dreamweaver.

Did you Know?

Using Slices to Optimize and Focus on What's Important

You can also use slices to both optimize and highlight a portion of an image. Create a single slice over a portion of the image that you want to be very clear because it's the portion that you want to highlight. Create slices over the remainder of the image that can be highly optimized, lowering the JPEG quality to less than 50, for instance.

Editing a Fireworks File into Dreamweaver

Dreamweaver and Fireworks are tightly integrated so you can efficiently use the two tools together. After you've imported HTML that was created in Fireworks into Dreamweaver, you can edit the HTML in Dreamweaver and update the original Fireworks files, too. Dreamweaver knows when you have inserted a Fireworks file into your web page, and it keeps track of any edits that you make to the file.

You can either open the HTML file that Fireworks created, or you can import the Fireworks HTML into an existing web page. To import the HTML and the sliced images that you created in Fireworks, follow these steps:

1. In Dreamweaver, create a new web page and then select Insert, Image Objects, Fireworks HTML. The Insert Fireworks HTML dialog box appears.

2. Click the Browse button and navigate to the HTML file that you saved in Fireworks. Select the Delete File After Insertion check box if you would like the file to be deleted after it is inserted into the web page.

3. The HTML table and images are inserted into the Dreamweaver Document window.

Now the HTML that Fireworks created is in the web page. Dreamweaver knows that the HTML originally came from Fireworks. When you select the table or the images, the Property inspector shows that the table or image originated in Fireworks, as you can see in Figure 8.15. There is also an Edit button you can click to open Fireworks and make any edits you'd like.

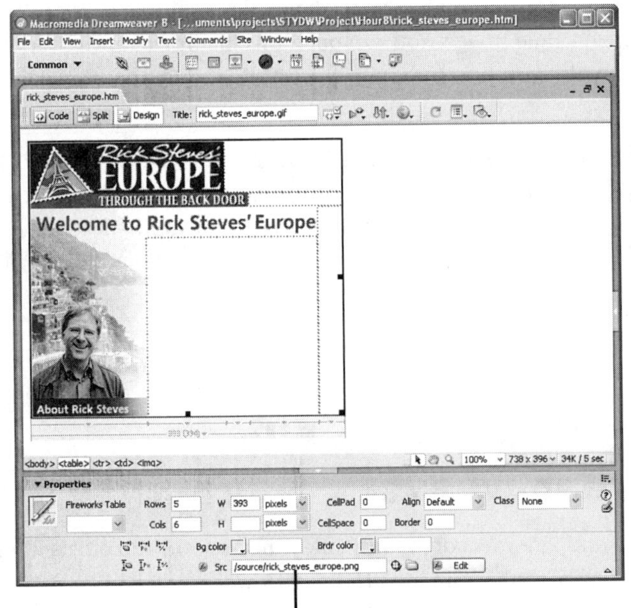

FIGURE 8.15 The Property inspector shows that the object was originally created in Fireworks, and the Edit button enables you to edit the object in Fireworks.

Summary

In this hour you have learned how to create a button image in Fireworks by using strokes, fills, and other filters. You also learned how to add text to a button. You learned how to optimize an image to make it download quickly over the Internet. You have also learned how to slice a single image into multiple images, export those images and the HTML that holds them together, and import the HTML into Dreamweaver.

Q&A

Q. ***How can I tell which file format makes the smallest file?***

A. That's what you use the optimization capabilities of Fireworks for. You don't need to know off the top of your head which format to use because you can experiment in Fireworks and find out what format creates the smallest file.

Q. ***Why would I want to use Fireworks instead of Dreamweaver to add behaviors to images?***

A. Some people, mainly graphic designers, are more comfortable working in the program they know the best. If you know Fireworks, using Fireworks to add behaviors will be easier. Macromedia has given graphic designers the power to add HTML to their graphics with Fireworks. Because you are reading this book, you probably know (or want to know) Dreamweaver. Therefore, it will probably be easier for you to apply behaviors by using Dreamweaver. Dreamweaver has many more web page–coding capabilities than Fireworks.

Workshop

Quiz

1. How do you create a guide in Fireworks?
2. What is the native file format in Fireworks?
3. Edits made in Dreamweaver will update the original Firework PNG files when you've imported from Fireworks. True or false?

Quiz Answers

1. Turn on the rulers, click within the rulers, and drag a guide into position.
2. The native file format in Fireworks is PNG.
3. True. You don't need to make changes in two places!

Exercises

1. Try applying some of the various filters available in Fireworks to an image. What does Glow do? What's the difference between Drop Shadow and Inner Shadow? Try using the Bevel and Emboss filters. What do they do? Try changing the color by using the color picker.
2. In Fireworks, select Commands, Creative, Add Picture Frame and then experiment. Export your experiment to Dreamweaver and try editing the image in Dreamweaver. What happens when you make changes in Fireworks? Are they automatically reflected in Dreamweaver?

HOUR 9

Creating Image Maps and Navigation Bars

What You'll Learn in This Hour:

- How to define an image map
- How to open a new browser window by using targeting
- How to create a navigation bar

In Hour 7, "Displaying Images," you inserted an image into a web page and created a rollover image. In this hour, you'll expand on that knowledge, creating an image map and a navigation bar. These are more complicated uses of images.

Adding Links to a Graphic by Using Image Maps

An **image map** is an image that has regions, called **hotspots**, defined as hyperlinks. When a viewer clicks a hotspot, it acts just like any other hyperlink. Instead of adding one hyperlink to an entire image, you can define a number of hotspots on different portions of an image. You can even create hotspots in different shapes.

Image maps are useful for presenting graphical menus that the viewer can click to select regions of a single image. For instance, you could create an image out of a picture of Europe. You could draw hotspots around the different countries in Europe. When the viewer clicked a country's hotspot, she could jump to a web page with information on that country.

By the Way

An Image Map Doesn't Have to Be a Map

Although creating an image map out of an image of a physical map is useful, it's not the only application of image maps. You can also create an image map from a single image that contains text which will link to the major sections of the website. Or, you could create an image map from an image with four quadrants, describing four steps in a process. Each quadrant could link to detailed information about that step in the process. There are many applications for image maps.

Creating an Image Map

When an image is selected, you see four image map tools in the lower corner of the expanded Property inspector. These four tools are used to define image map hotspots. The arrow is the Pointer Hotspot tool, which is used to select or move the hotspots. There are three image map hotspot tools: One tool draws rectangles, one draws circles, and one draws polygons.

To create an image map, follow these steps:

1. Insert an image into a web page. The image must be selected for the image map tools to appear in the Property inspector.
2. Give the map a name in the Map Name text box, as shown in Figure 9.1. The name needs to be unique from other map names in the page.

You set all the image properties for an image map just as you would an ordinary image. You can set the vertical space, horizontal space, alt text, border, and alignment.

Copying and Pasting Image Maps

If you copy and paste the image map into the same or another web page, all the image map properties come along, too.

Adding a Rectangular Hotspot to an Image Map

To add a rectangular hotspot to your image map, first select the Rectangle Hotspot tool. Click and drag the crosshair cursor to make a rectangle that is the dimensions of the hotspot you want to create. When you release the mouse, a highlighted box appears over the image, as in Figure 9.2. With the hotspot selected, enter a URL into the Link box in the Property inspector:

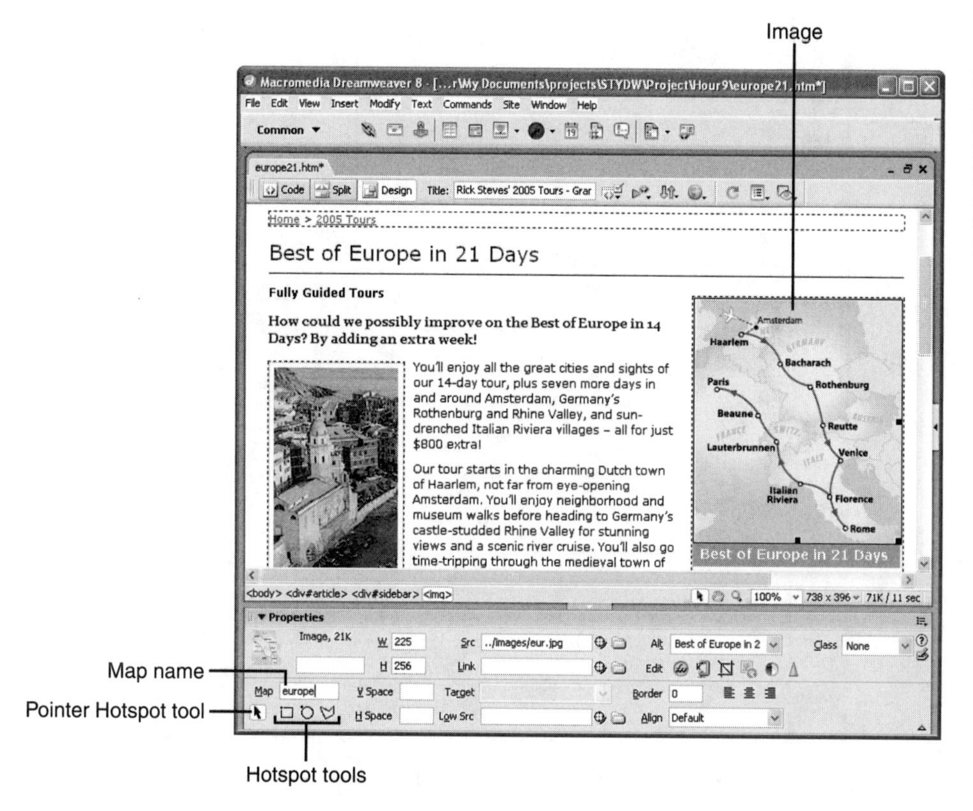

FIGURE 9.1 Give an image map a name and use the hotspot tools to draw hotspots within an image map.

1. Select one of the hotspot tools. You'll spend the next minutes exploring each of the hotspot tools in depth.

2. With a newly drawn hotspot selected, type a URL in the Link box, as shown in Figure 9.2, or click the Browse icon to browse to a local web page. You can also link a hotspot to a named anchor by entering a pound sign followed by the anchor name.

3. Enter alternative text for the hotspot in the Alt text box. As discussed in Hour 7, some browsers display this text as a ToolTip and it's necessary for visually impaired users to be able to understand your web page.

To move or adjust the size of the hotspot, you need to first select the Pointer Hotspot tool. You can't use the other hotspot tools to adjust the hotspot or you will end up creating another hotspot. Click the hotspot with the Pointer Hotspot tool and either move the hotspot to another location or resize the hotspot by using the resizing handles.

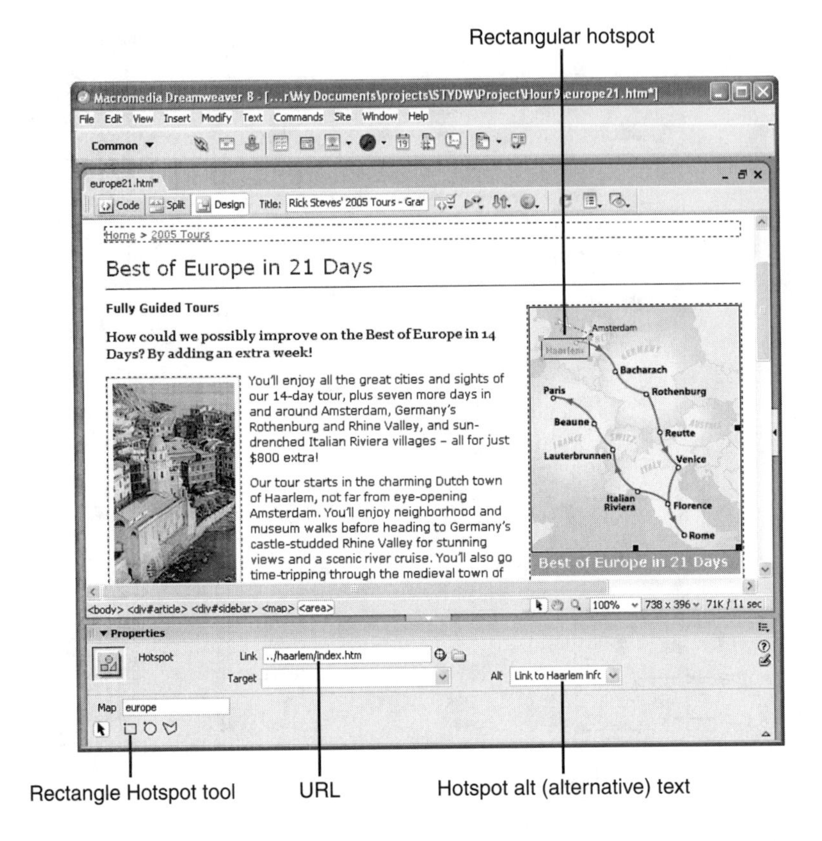

FIGURE 9.2
Enter a URL to link a hotspot with another web page or a named anchor within the current page.

In the web page HTML, the rectangular hotspot is defined by two sets of x and y coordinates. The upper-left corner of the rectangle is recorded as the first two coordinates in the code and the lower-right corner of the rectangle is recorded as the last two coordinates. The coordinates are in pixels, and they are relative to the image, not to the web page. The HTML code for a rectangular area looks like this:

```
<area shape="rect" coords="127,143,251,291" href="services.htm">
```

In this example, the upper-left corner of the rectangle is 127 pixels from the left of the image and 143 pixels from the top of the image. The bottom-right corner of the rectangle is 251 pixels from the left of the image and 291 pixels from the top. It's nice to have a visual representation in Dreamweaver and not have to figure this out yourself, isn't it?

Adding a Circular Hotspot to an Image Map

A circular area might better define some areas in your image map than a rectangular one. You create an oval hotspot just as you create a rectangular one. Select the

Oval Hotspot tool and then click and drag to create the hotspot, as shown in Figure 9.3. Reposition or resize the hotspot by using the Pointer Hotspot tool.

Watch Out!

It's a Circle, Not an Oval

The Oval Hotspot tool always creates a perfect circle. I'm not sure why it's called the Oval Hotspot tool instead of the Circle Hotspot tool! You can understand why you can have only a circle and not an oval when you see how the circular hotspot coordinates are defined.

A circle is defined by three values: The circle's radius and the x and y values that define the circle's center. The HTML code defining a circular area looks like this:

```
<area shape="circle" coords="138,186,77" href="about.htm">
```

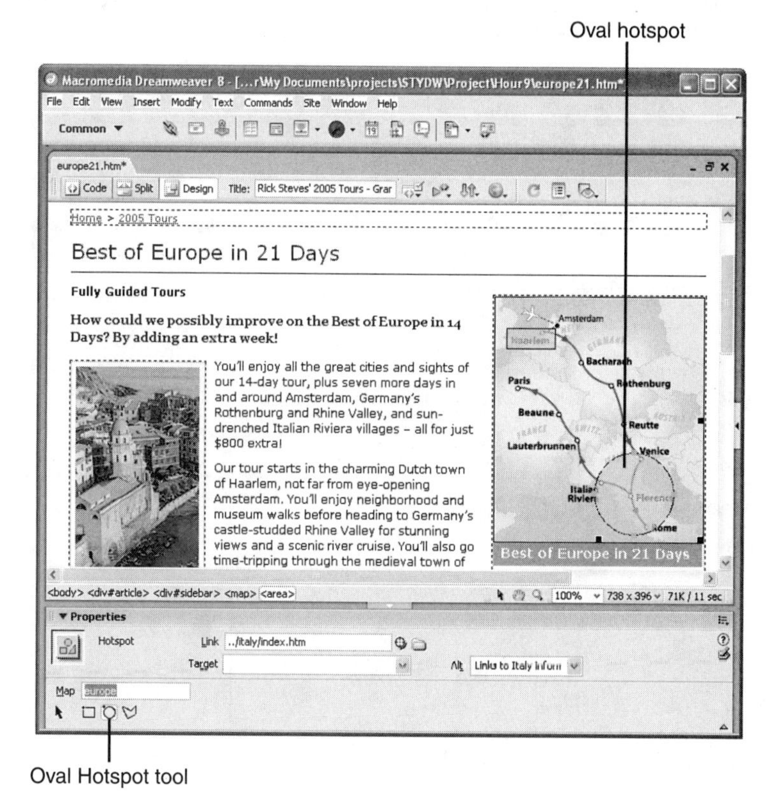

FIGURE 9.3 The Oval Hotspot tool creates hotspots that are perfectly circular.

Adding an Irregular Hotspot to an Image Map

Sometimes the area you'd like to turn into a hotspot just isn't circular or rectangular. The Polygon Hotspot tool enables you to define an irregular hotspot in any shape you want.

You use the Polygon Hotspot tool a little differently than you use the Oval or Rectangle Hotspot tools. First, select the Polygon Hotspot tool from the Property inspector. Instead of clicking and dragging to create a shape, click once for every point in the polygon, as shown in Figure 9.4. You should move around the area you want to define as a hotspot in either a clockwise or counter-clockwise manner; clicking randomly might create an odd polygon. When you are finished creating the points of the polygon, select the Pointer Hotspot tool to complete the polygon. You select the Pointer Hotspot tool in order to deselect the Polygon Hotspot tool so you don't accidentally add stray points on the screen. Or you can double-click when you are finished drawing the polygon.

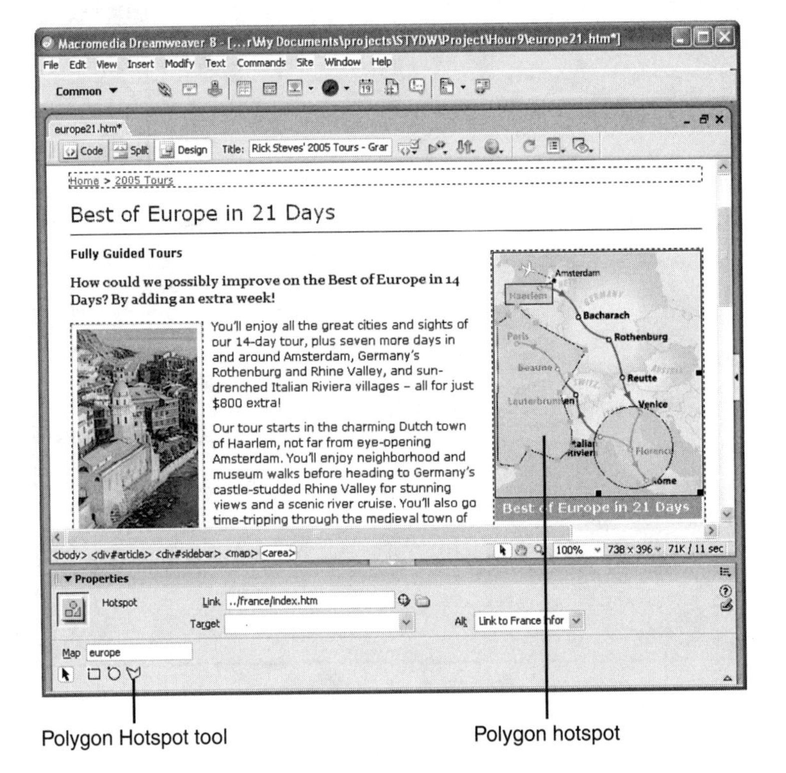

FIGURE 9.4
To create an irregular hotspot with the Polygon Hotspot tool, click once for every point and double-click to finish.

A hotspot polygon is defined by as many x and y coordinates as you need, each representing one of the corner points. The HTML code for a sample polygon hotspot looks like this:

```
<area shape="poly" coords=
"85,14,32,33,29,116,130,99,137,130,140,70,156,66,198,84" href="jobs.htm">
```

The polygon defined in this HTML is made up of eight points, so there are eight pairs of x and y coordinates.

Aligning Hotspots

Dreamweaver has built-in alignment tools that you can use to align the hotspots in an image map. First, you need to select the hotspots you want to align. To select all the hotspots in an image map, use the keyboard shortcut Ctrl+A in Windows or Command+A on the Macintosh. Or you can hold down Shift as you click hotspots to add them to the selection. You can tell when hotspots are selected because you can see the resizing handles.

Sometimes it is difficult to finely align hotspots with your mouse. You can use the arrow keys to move a hotspot or multiple hotspots one pixel at a time. The Arrange submenu under the Modify menu contains commands to align hotspots, as shown in Figure 9.5. You can align multiple hotspots on the left, right, top, or bottom. You can make multiple hotspots the same height by using the Make Same Height command or the same width by using the Make Same Width command.

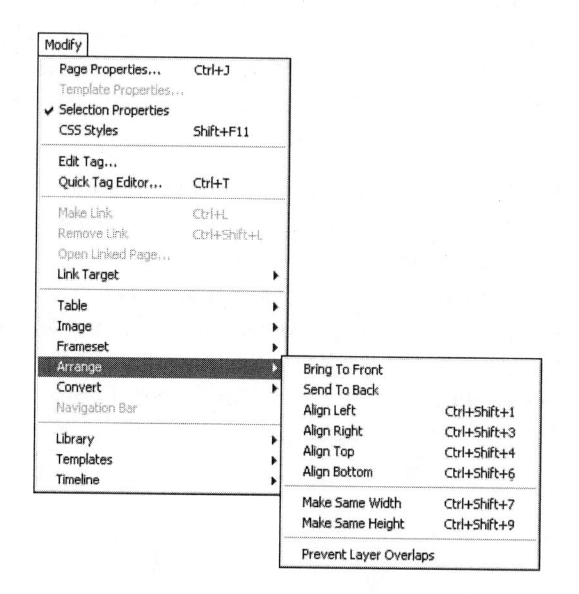

FIGURE 9.5
The Modify menu's Arrange submenu has commands for aligning hotspots.

Did you Know?

Which Hotspot Is Hot?

Hotspots can overlap each other. Whichever hotspot is on top (usually the one created first) will be the link triggered by clicking on the overlapping area. You might want to create overlapping hotspots on purpose as part of the design of an image map. For instance, you might use a circular hotspot over part of a rectangular hotspot. Alternatively, the overlapping might simply be a consequence of the limited shapes you have available to define the hotspots.

It's difficult to tell which hotspot is on top of another hotspot. If you've recently created the image map, you know which hotspot was created first and is therefore on top. You can manipulate the stacking order of the hotspots by selecting Modify, Arrange, Bring to Front or Send to Back. If a hotspot overlaps another and needs to be on top, select the Bring to Front command.

Targeting a Link to Open in a New Browser Window

When a hyperlink is selected, the Property inspector has a drop-down box called Target. Frames use the target attribute to load a page into a defined frame. Frames are covered in Hour 14, "Using Frames to Display Multiple Web Pages."

There are four reserved target names you can use with any link. Three of the four reserved target names—`_parent`, `_self`, and `_top`—are used mainly with frames. But the `_blank` reserved target name, as shown in Figure 9.6, is useful when you want to leave the current browser window open and have the link open a new browser window with the linked web page in it. To use it, select Blank from the Target drop-down menu when one of the hotspots is selected. Preview your web page in the browser and select that link. Now the original window, containing your image map, is open, and so is a new window, with the linked file in it.

Opening a new window is useful when you want to keep your original web page open but still allow the user to jump to other web pages. When the user closes the new window, the window containing your site will still be open. It's nice to warn the users about this so they will not get confused. You can add text to a link that opens a new window with a message that says something like "link opens new window" or "close new window to return." In Hour 17, "Adding Interactivity with Behaviors," you'll learn how to use a Dreamweaver behavior to open a new window. Using JavaScript enables you to set the window size.

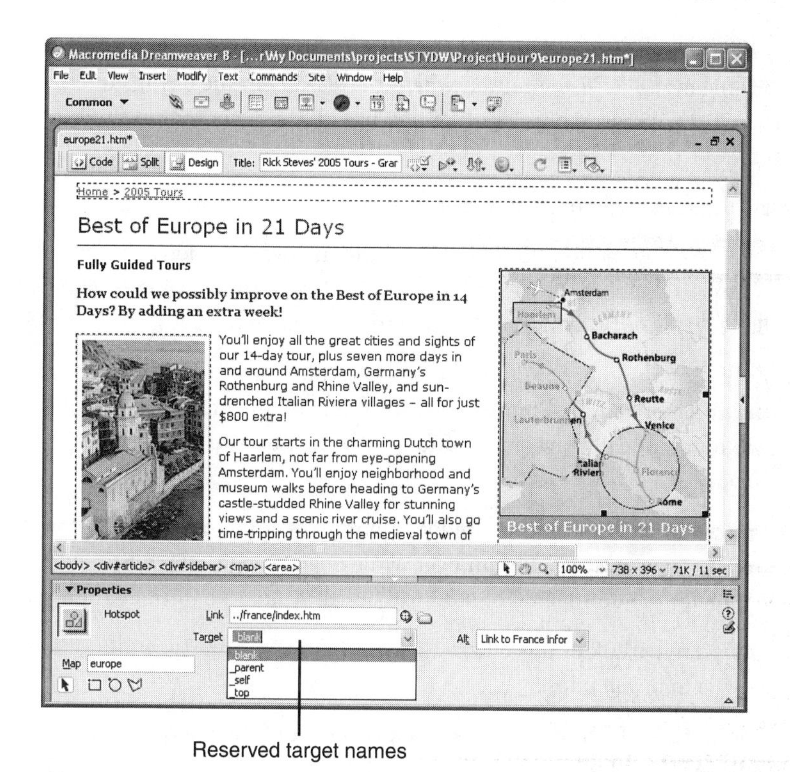

FIGURE 9.6 The `_blank` reserved target name in the Target drop-down menu in the Property inspector opens the link in a new browser window. The original document remains open.

Creating a Navigation Bar with Rollover Images and Links

What if you wanted to create a bunch of rollover images as a navigation bar? And what if you wanted each of them to have a down button state, too? You could create all these buttons individually using the Rollover Image object, or you could use the Dreamweaver Insert Navigation Bar dialog box to create all the buttons at once.

> **By the Way**
>
> **One Navigation Bar per Customer**
>
> You can have only one navigation bar per web page.

You simulate button functionality by swapping images that are the same size but look slightly different. Each image represents a **button state**. The default button state is up. The down state appears when the user clicks the mouse on the button; the down state image usually modifies the up state image so that it looks pressed down. The over state appears when the user passes his mouse over the button.

The navigation bar can also add an over when down state, which appears when the user rolls the mouse over the button when it is already in the down state. You must add an up state image to a navigation bar, but all the other button states are optional.

To create a navigation bar, follow these steps:

1. Select the Navigation Bar object from the Images drop-down menu in the Common panel of the Insert bar (or select Insert, Image Objects, Navigation Bar). The Insert Navigation Bar dialog box appears.

2. An initial, unnamed button element is visible. Change the element name to the name of your first button. (If you simply go the next step, Dreamweaver will automatically give your button the same name as the name of the image file.)

3. Browse to load a button up image, a button over image, and a button down image. You can also enter an over while down image, which is a rollover image for the down state of a button. All these images must be the same size.

4. Enter a hyperlink in the When Clicked, Go to URL box. Type in a URL or browse to a web page.

5. Check the Preload Images check box if you want the images to be automatically preloaded.

6. Add additional buttons by clicking the plus button and repeating steps 2–5. Rearrange the order of the buttons by using the arrow buttons at the top of the Insert Navigation Bar dialog box. To delete a button, click the minus button.

   If you accidentally close the Insert Navigation Bar dialog box, simply select Modify, Navigation Bar to reopen it and edit your settings.

7. At the bottom of the Insert Navigation Bar dialog box, choose to insert the navigation bar either horizontally or vertically into the web page. Select the Use Tables check box if you'd like the navigation bar to be created in a table. (Hour 13, "Designing Page Layout Using Tables," explains how to use tables for layout.) The table layout occurs here for you automatically.

8. The Insert Navigation Bar dialog box should look as shown in Figure 9.7 after you have added several elements. When you are finished adding buttons, click OK.

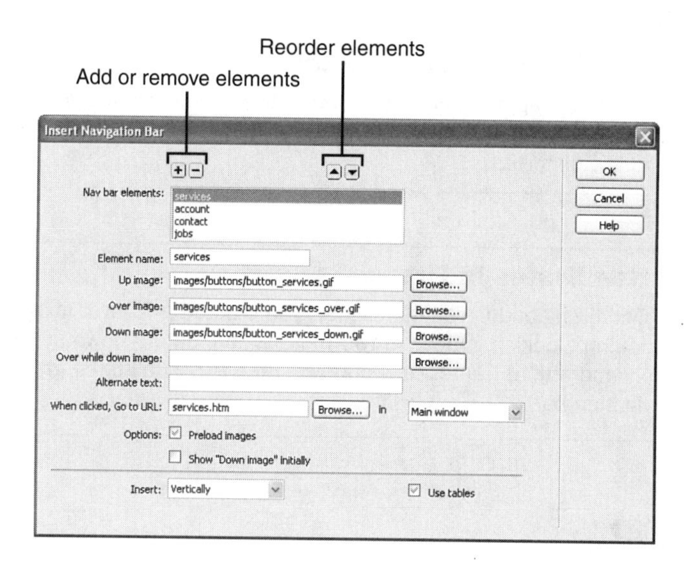

FIGURE 9.7
Each element in a navigation bar consists of multiple images linked to a URL. The navigation bar can be situated vertically or horizontally.

To test the buttons, save your file and preview it in a browser, as shown in Figure 9.8. If you've made a mistake, don't fret! You can edit the navigation bar by selecting the Navigation Bar object again.

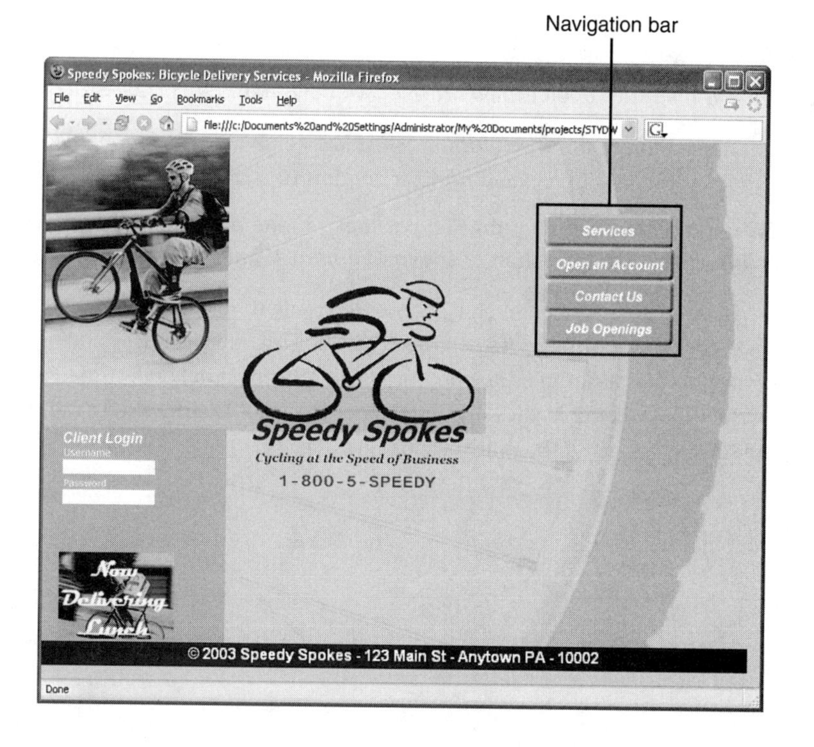

FIGURE 9.8
Test a navigation bar in a browser to make sure the elements have the proper rollover and down states and link to the correct URL.

Watch Out!

Make Button State Images the Same Size

Rollover and button images require that the up, over, and down images be all the same size. Otherwise, the over and down images stretch to the size of the original up image and are distorted.

Did you Know?

Make Button States in Fireworks

In Hour 8, "Optimizing and Creating Images," you created a rollover image by placing slightly different-looking images in two frames. To create a down state for a button, simply add a third frame. Fireworks will then export all three graphics to use in a navigation bar.

Summary

In this hour, you have learned how to create a client-side image map that includes rectangular, circular, and polygonal shapes. You have learned how to use targeting to open a new browser window. You have also created a navigation bar with various button states.

Q&A

Q. ***What if I want to open a new browser window that is a certain size?***

A. You'll need to use the Open Browser Window behavior, which you'll learn about in Hour 17, to create a browser window of a certain size.

Q. ***Every time I use the Polygon Hotspot tool, I make a mess of it. I get extra points in the wrong section of the image map. What am I doing wrong?***

A. When you use the Polygon Hotspot tool to create a hotspot, remember to click, click, click around the edges of the hotspot border. After you have defined the border, do not click the image again. Instead, immediately select the Pointer Hotspot tool or double-click on the hotspot to signal Dreamweaver that you are finished creating the polygon hotspot.

Workshop

Quiz

1. Which image map tool enables you to draw irregular shapes?
2. How many Dreamweaver navigation bars can you have per web page?
3. What's the reserved target name that opens a new browser window?

Quiz Answers

1. The Polygon Hotspot tool enables you to draw irregular shapes.
2. You can only have one Dreamweaver navigation bar per web page.
3. The `_blank` reserved target name opens a new browser window.

Exercises

1. Create several hotspots. Align the hotspots by using the alignment commands. Make one of the hotspots open a new browser window. Have one of the hotspots open up a page in a new browser window by targeting `_blank`.
2. Find images for buttons for all the states available in the navigation bar (up, down, over, over when down) or make them yourself in Fireworks (see Hour 8). Create a navigation bar.

HOUR 10

Adding Flash and Other Multimedia to a Web Page

What You'll Learn in This Hour:

- How to add Flash and Shockwave movies to a web page
- How to add Flash text and Flash buttons in Dreamweaver
- How to add multimedia files, such as sounds, movies, or PDF documents, to a web page
- How to insert and configure a Java applet in a web page

You aren't limited to displaying text and graphics in web pages. You can include movies, sounds, documents, and many other specialized types of content. This hour introduces you to some of the issues and the techniques you can use to include multimedia files in your website.

Exploring Multimedia and Bandwidth

Adding multimedia files, such as sounds, movies, and PDF documents, grows more popular as modems become faster and people browse the Web with more bandwidth. Yes, that's right: Most multimedia files take up a lot of bandwidth. **Bandwidth** is the size of the Internet "pipe" you have when you connect to the Web. Increasingly more people are accessing the Internet using a **broadband** connection: DSL or a cable modem. If you are on a cable modem, you have access to a higher Internet bandwidth than someone connecting with a 56Kbps modem.

Some formats, such as RealMedia and Shockwave files, get around the large bandwidth requirements of sound and video files by streaming content to the user. Streamed content begins to play after a short buffer period; the content continues to download in the background while previously buffered content plays. Most multimedia delivered over the Web is also compressed by using ever-improving techniques.

Some of the traditional CD-based multimedia formats, such as WAV (audio) , AVI (Windows movie), MOV (QuickTime movie), and AIFF (audio), are often too large to deliver over the Web. Some of these formats require that the user download the entire file before it will play. To deliver this type of sound and video content, you need to understand which technologies to choose; new compression and streaming tools appear all the time. The MP3 sound format is extremely popular because it can create very small files that still sound great.

Understanding Players

In order to play any multimedia file in a browser, the user needs a third-party program to play the file. These players are either plug-ins or ActiveX controls, and some are installed automatically with the browser or operating system software. Of course, you don't want to assume that a person viewing your web page has the same players installed that you have. You always want to give the viewer information on how to obtain a necessary player.

Browsers deal with multimedia files in two ways. Netscape, Opera, and Mozilla Firefox extend their capabilities with plug-ins. Each browser has a plug-ins folder where these programs are stored. A **plug-in** is a piece of additional software that adds new functionality to the browser. The user might need to restart the browser after installing a plug-in for the plug-in to work.

Microsoft Internet Explorer, on the other hand, uses its ActiveX technology to launch and run multimedia content. **ActiveX controls** are similar to plug-ins, and they are installed on the user's machine to add the ability to play different file types. Many third-party browser extensions come as both plug-ins and ActiveX controls to accommodate all browser types. An ActiveX control usually installs itself in the background and does not require the user to restart the browser after installation.

ActiveX Installation Woes

Some users have either disabled their computers' capability to install ActiveX controls or are confused and possibly suspicious when a dialog box appears, telling them they will be downloading and installing something. Also, some corporate networks block the installation of ActiveX controls. Make sure you tell users what to expect if you include content that requires them to download and install something on their computers.

It's always good form to tell a viewer where to download a required player. You can place information in your web page that includes a link to download the player. Dreamweaver adds the `pluginspace` attribute to enable the browser to automatically attempt a player download.

Adding Flash Files

Macromedia Flash has arguably become the standard for web animation. Macromedia Director, originally created for CD-ROM–based interactive programs, also has a streaming web player called Shockwave. Flash is extremely popular for creating small, interactive, web-based animations. Flash is popular because of its vector-based graphics—a graphics format that is small and scalable. Flash is fairly easy to learn and is a fun tool to create in. It has a scripting language, ActionScript, that is very similar to JavaScript, a popular scripting language for web pages.

By the Way

Don't Forget About Macromedia Authorware

Another interactive authoring tool that is available from Macromedia is the Authorware Web Player. Authorware is used to make highly interactive streaming training applications.

Flash movies usually end with the `.swf` file extension. Shockwave movies end with the `.dcr` file extension. You need to have the appropriate players installed in the browser in order to view these movies: You need the Flash player to view Flash movies and the Shockwave player to view Director Shockwave movies. To insert a Flash movie into a web page, select the Flash object in the Media menu in the Insert bar (or Insert, Media, Flash). Figure 10.1 shows the Property inspector with a Flash movie selected.

The Property inspector displays the various settings for displaying a Flash movie within a web page. There is a check box for Loop and one for Autoplay. Selecting Loop tells the Flash movie to play over and over; this functionality needs to be enabled in the Flash movie for the movie to actually loop. The Autoplay setting tells the Flash movie to play immediately when it is loaded. You can add V (vertical) space and H (horizontal) space to the Flash movie just as you can an image.

Did you Know?

Flash Movie Quality Settings

I like to set Quality to Auto High; this balances good appearance with fast loading, according to the user's connection speed. The other Quality settings enable you to balance appearance versus load time manually.

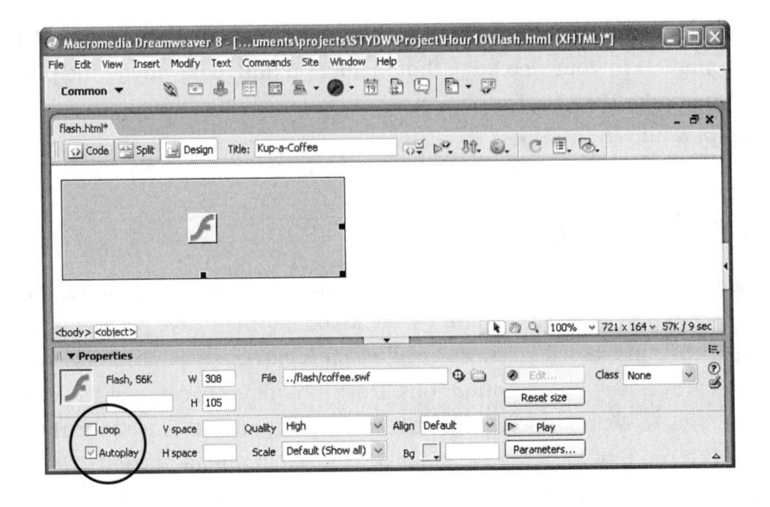

FIGURE 10.1 The Property inspector shows the properties that you can set for a Flash movie. Some are standard properties, whereas others are specific to Flash movies.

Did you Know?

Help! The Flash Movie Is the Wrong Size

If you accidentally resize a Flash movie, click the Reset Size button to return it to its original size.

Using the `<object>` and `<embed>` Tags

Two tags are used to insert multimedia content. Internet Explorer requires that the `<object>` tag is used to display Flash or Shockwave movies. But Netscape and the other browsers that use plug-ins require the `<embed>` tag. Dreamweaver automatically inserts both tags into your web page when you insert a Flash object. Using both tags enables any browser to handle the file in the optimum way. Netscape recognizes the `<embed>` tag and calls the Flash plug-in, and Internet Explorer recognizes the `<object>` tag. The `<embed>` tag is nested within the `<object>` tag, as shown in Figure 10.2.

Previewing a Movie in the Dreamweaver Document Window

You can preview Flash movies and interact with them directly within Dreamweaver. To preview a Flash movie in the Document window, select the green Play button in the Property inspector. While the movie is playing, the Play button turns into a red Stop button, as shown in Figure 10.3. Click the Stop button to stop the movie.

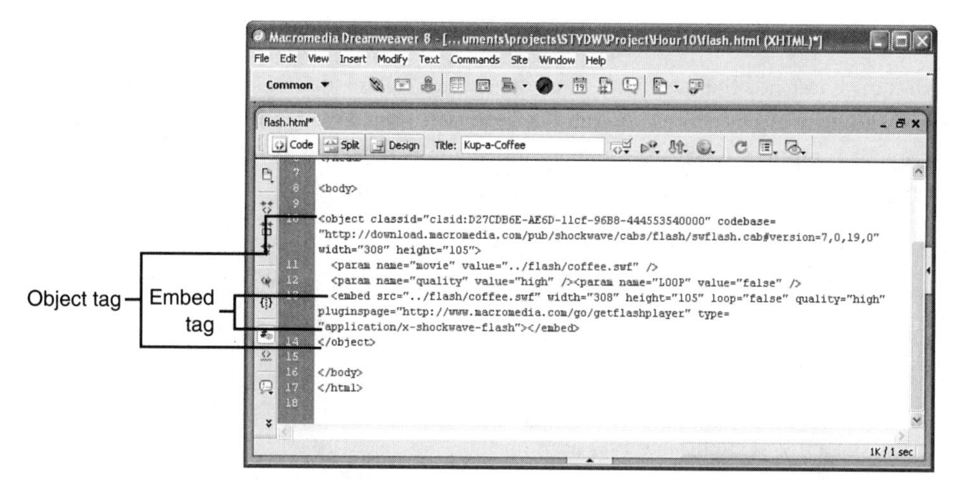

FIGURE 10.2
To insert a Flash movie, Dreamweaver inserts an `embed` tag within an `object` tag to cover all of the browser possibilities.

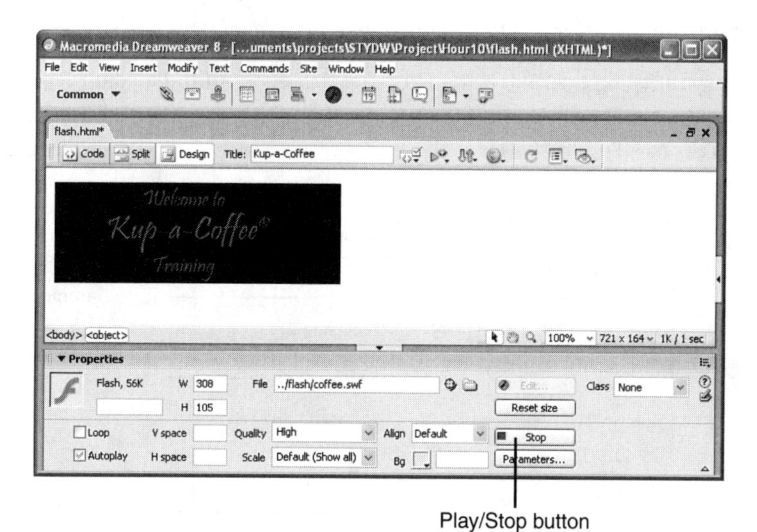

FIGURE 10.3
You can view a Flash or Shockwave movie, and other plug-in–based content, directly in the Document window.

By the Way

Learning More About Flash

Numerous websites about Flash have tutorials on using the program. Check out the Macromedia Flash Support Center, www.macromedia.com/support/flash, to find out more about Flash file formats such as Flash Paper and Flash Video. Dreamweaver can insert all these file formats into web pages.

Creating Flash Text

Dreamweaver has the capability to create special Text objects—Flash movies with text—directly in Dreamweaver. You do not need to have the Flash program installed on your computer to have this functionality. You can create Flash text and Flash buttons (you'll try this in a few minutes) right in Dreamweaver.

The Flash Text object enables you to create and insert a Flash movie consisting of text into your web page. Inserting Flash text has the following advantages:

- You can use any font available on your computer. The viewer does not need to have the font installed on her computer.
- Flash text uses vector graphics, creating a very small file size—much smaller than if you created an image.

To insert a Flash Text object into a web page, follow these steps:

1. Save your web page. Select the Flash Text object from the Media menu of the Insert bar or choose Insert, Media, Flash Text. The Insert Flash Text dialog box appears (see Figure 10.4) .

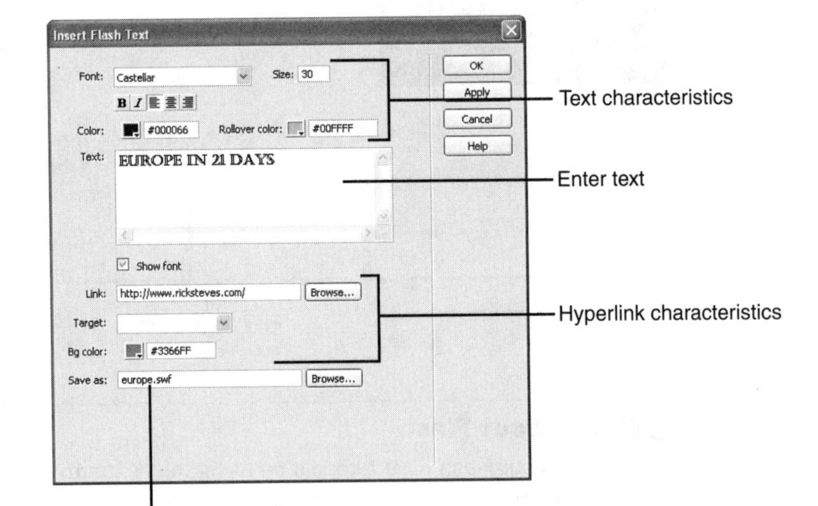

FIGURE 10.4 Set up the Flash Text object with a custom font, rollover color, and a background color.

2. Select the font, size, style (bold or italic), and alignment. Select the color, which is the initial color of the text, and the rollover color, which is the color the user will see when she places the cursor over the text.

3. Type in the Text box the text that you want to appear. Make sure the Show Font check box is selected so that you can see what the font you have selected looks like.

4. Enter a URL in the Link text box or click the Browse button to browse to a web page or enter a URL.

Watch Out!

Make Sure Flash Doesn't Prevent Search Engine Crawling

Flash might prevent search engines from crawling your website. **Crawling** is when the search engine follows the links in a site in order to index all the pages in the site. Enabling a search engine to effectively crawl a site is important for professional websites and any websites where you'd like searchers to be able to find information in the search engine. You want to make sure that important text is in regular HTML and not Flash text in order for important words to be indexed by search engines.

5. Optionally, use the Target text box to target a window for the link. You will learn more about this capability when you learn about frames in Hour 14, "Using Frames to Display Multiple Web Pages."

6. Select a background color from the Bg Color drop-down list. Simply use the eyedropper from the color picker and click your web page behind the Insert Flash Text dialog box.

Did you Know?

Setting Background Color

It's important to add a background color to the Flash movie if your web page has a background color. Flash movies are not transparent, so if the background of your web page is not white, the Flash movie will stand out as a white box. This is true for all Flash movies, including Flash Buttons that you'll learn about in a minute.

7. Enter a name for the Flash movie in the Save As box. Dreamweaver creates a separate Flash movie, with this name, for your Flash text.

8. Click OK. The text appears in the Dreamweaver Document window.

You can edit a Flash text movie after you have inserted it into a web page by clicking the Edit button (shown in Figure 10.5) in the Property inspector when the movie is selected in the Document window. You can view the changes you make without closing the Insert Flash Text dialog box by selecting the Apply button.

In the Document window, you can resize Flash text by either dragging the resizing handles or entering new values for W (width) and H (height) in the Property inspector. Click the Reset Size button to return to the original dimensions of the movie. The great thing about Flash, unlike web images such as GIFs and JPEGs, is that it resizes very well.

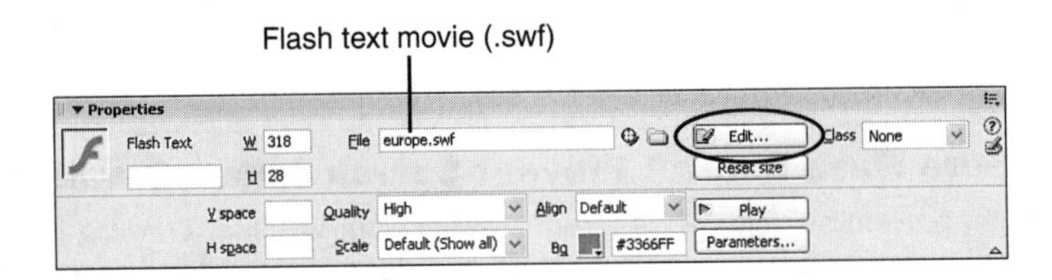

FIGURE 10.5 Click the Edit button to edit a Flash text movie after you insert it into a web page.

Creating a Flash Button

Dreamweaver comes with a number of templates for creating Flash buttons right in Dreamweaver. (You can download even more templates at the Macromedia Exchange by clicking the Get More Styles button in the Insert Flash Button dialog box; also, see Hour 22, "Customizing Dreamweaver.") As with the Flash Text object you just created, you can have Dreamweaver create Flash button movies automatically. Flash buttons use custom fonts and many have animations when the user places his mouse over the button. To insert a Flash button into a web page, follow these steps:

1. Save your web page. Select the Insert Flash Button object from the Media tab of the Insert bar or select Insert, Media, Insert Flash Button. The Insert Flash Button dialog box appears (see Figure 10.6).

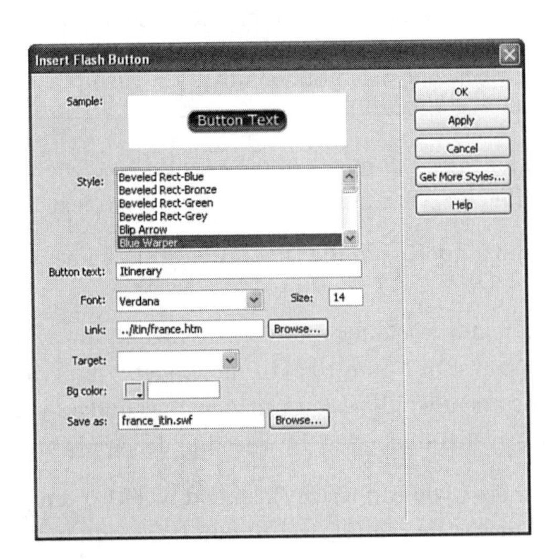

FIGURE 10.6 You select a Flash button and enter button text in the Insert Flash Button dialog box.

2. Select a button style from the Style list. A preview of the button appears in the Sample window at the top of the dialog box. You can click the preview to see what the down state of the button looks like and to see any animation effects that the button has.

3. Add text for the button in the Button Text field. Only buttons that already have the default *Button Text* text in the Sample window will display this text. You cannot add text to buttons that do not already display text.

4. Set the font and font size for the button text in the Font drop-down menu and Size text box. You can choose any font that's installed on your computer.

5. Enter a URL for a hyperlink and a target, if necessary, in the Link and Target text boxes, respectively. As when you create Flash text, you need to be careful about document-relative addressing. It's best to save the Flash movie in the same directory as the linked web page.

6. Add a background color from the Bg Color drop-down list. This color appears around the button, not within the button art. Again, be sure to complete this step if you have a background color on your web page so that there isn't any white surrounding your button.

7. Click OK. The button appears in the Dreamweaver Document window.

You can edit the Flash button as you did the Flash text earlier in this hour. Both the button and text movies are saved as Flash `.swf` files and can be edited in Flash. Some buttons can be used as groups. For instance, a number of e-commerce buttons are available to create purchasing and checkout applications.

Adding a Link to a PDF File

So far in this hour, you've been embedding multimedia content into a web page. You can also link to content that appears by itself. You link to multimedia files just as you would link to another web page. If the multimedia file is within your defined website, you can use a document-relative URL. If the multimedia file is on another site, you must use an absolute URL.

Adobe Acrobat Reader is a freely distributed player that has become the standard for viewing formatted text files over the web. Portable Document Format (PDF) files enable a viewer to see a file exactly as it was meant to be seen—fonts, page layout, and graphics appear predictably. You create PDF files by using an application called Adobe Acrobat Distiller and view them with the Acrobat Reader. An Acrobat Reader plug-in is usually installed when the Reader application is installed.

To display a PDF file, you simply create a hyperlink with the URL to a PDF file. The file will then open within the browser if the Acrobat plug-in is present, as shown in Figure 10.7. If the plug-in isn't installed but the Acrobat Reader is, Acrobat Reader will run as a standalone application and display the PDF file. You can download the Acrobat Reader at www.adobe.com/products/acrobat/readstep2.html.

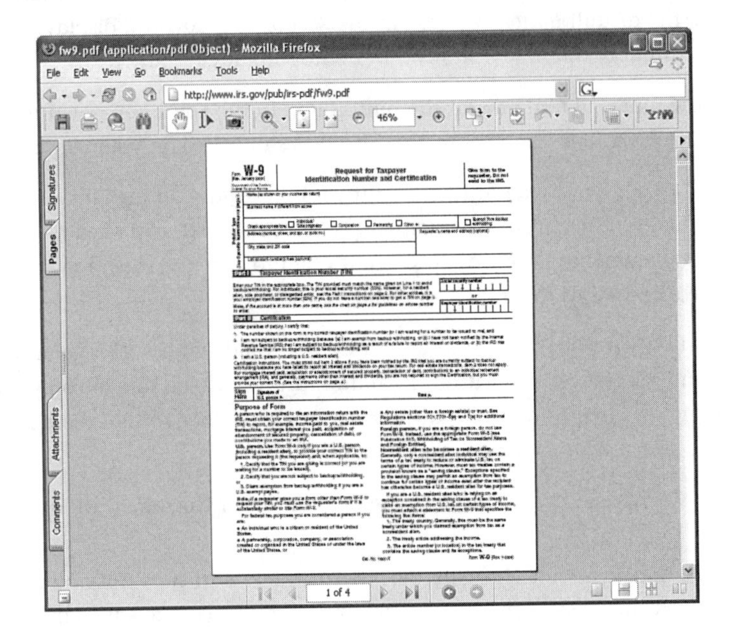

FIGURE 10.7 The PDF viewer, Acrobat Reader, loads right in the browser window, displaying the PDF document.

Adding a Sound File to a Web Page

Adding a sound file to a web page can sometimes add to the experience. And it's a good way for you to get familiar with adding multimedia files. You use the Plugin object from the Media tab of the Insert bar (or Insert, Media, Plugin) to insert a sound into a web page.

Did you Know?

Find Sounds on the Web

Your operating system should have some sound files available for you to use. To find them, search for a directory called `media` or `sounds` or `multimedia`. If you'd prefer to download audio files from the Web, check out www.archive.org/audio. Click on the Open Source Audio link at the top of the page to find open source music in numerous genres. Or, try theme songs from classic TV shows at www.tvland.com/theme_songs. I wish they had the Petticoat Junction theme song…I love that song.

To insert a Plugin object, follow these steps:

1. Position the insertion point in the Dreamweaver Document window where you would like the sound control to appear when the page is viewed in the browser.

2. Select the Plugin object from the Media tab of the Insert bar (or select Insert, Media, Plugin). The Select File dialog box appears. Navigate to a directory that contains a sound file and select a file. Select All Files from the Files of Type drop-down menu. Then click the Select button.

3. Save your changes, and then preview your web page in a browser to see what it looks and sounds like.

Notice that the Property inspector for the Plugin object has some properties that are similar to ones you have seen while working with images (see Figure 10.8). Selecting a file fills in the Src box. There is an Align drop-down menu, similar to the one for images, which affects how other objects align with the Plugin object. Other familiar properties are W (width), H (height), V (vertical) Space, and H (horizontal) Space.

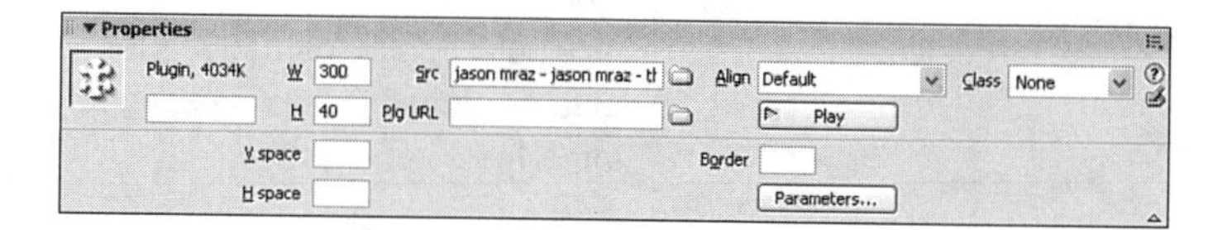

FIGURE 10.8
Some plug-in properties are similar to image properties, and some are not.

Watch Out!

Controlling Sound

It's a good idea to give your user control over whether a sound plays. Many players enable you to include playback controls. A web page that contains a sound that cannot be turned off can be an extreme annoyance. You'll need to explore the documentation, which is usually available on the website of the company that created the plug-in, to find the parameter names and how to add playback controls.

When you're delivering multimedia, much depends on which browser and plug-ins the user has. Some plug-ins and sound file formats are more popular than others. The popularity of file formats is constantly evolving. As of this writing, the RealMedia, Windows Media Player, and MP3 sound formats are popular and quite common on the Web. MIDI files are common, too. Table 10.1 lists some of the most popular sound file formats.

By the Way

What's Your Default Audio Program?

The last audio application that you installed on your computer probably set itself as the default application to play audio files. You might have different applications than are depicted in this hour.

TABLE 10.1 Common Web Sound Formats

Sound Format	Streaming?	Description
RealMedia	Yes	Real-time streaming audio and video format.
Shockwave Audio	Yes	Real-time streaming audio format.
MP3 (MPEG 3)	Yes	Compact file size with excellent sound quality. This open-standard sound format has become very popular.
Liquid Audio	Yes	Small file sizes with excellent sound quality.
Beatnik	No	Sound format that combines MIDI and digital audio.
AIFF	No	A popular Macintosh sound format. Not ideal for longer sounds because of its large file size.
WAV	No	A popular Windows sound format. Not ideal for longer sounds because of its large file size.
u-Law (.au)	No	Originally, a popular web sound format from Sun, but not very common today.
QuickTime	Yes	Apple's movie format, which can also play sounds. File sizes can be large.
MIDI	No	An open-standard sound format that uses defined MIDI sounds on the user's computer. Files are very compact.

Flash Audio

I prefer to save audio files as Flash files simply because Flash is good at compressing audio (it uses the MP3 compression algorithms) and the Flash player is available to most viewers.

Resizing a Control

The default size of the Plugin object is 32×32 pixels. That's pretty small, but you can resize a Plugin object by dragging one of the resizing handles. You can also enter a width and a height in the Property inspector with the Plugin object selected. Predicting an appropriate size for a plug-in can get tricky because you can't predict which player application the user will be displaying in their browser. If you have embedded a sound file into your web page, some viewers might use the QuickTime plug-in to play sounds in a web page. Others might use Windows Media Player or the RealMedia Player. The controls for these players are all different sizes.

Increasing the width and height of a plug-in can cause more controls to be visible. In Figure 10.9, for example, giving the plug-in a width of 300 pixels and a height of 40 pixels looks great in Internet Explorer. The height of 40 pixels in this case is necessary to display the Windows Media Player buttons. Depending on what player your browser has registered to play MP3 files, yours might or might not look the same. Figure 10.10 shows a browser, Mozilla Firefox in this case, that doesn't have a player configured to handle this type of file but the browser displays a button linking to a location to download an appropriate player.

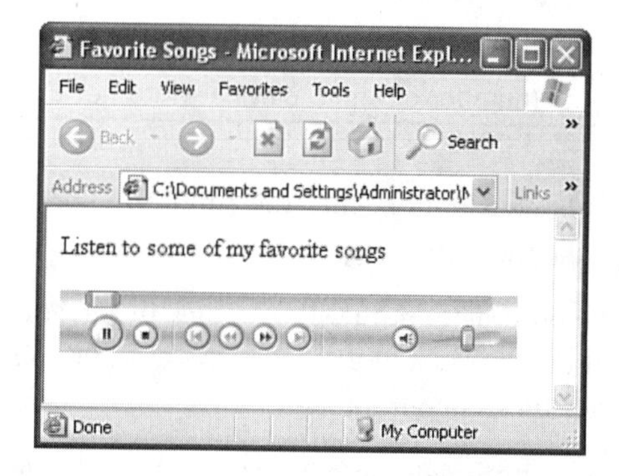

FIGURE 10.9
The Windows Media Player in Internet Explorer with a width of 300 pixels and a height of 40 pixels displays all the audio controls.

Looping the Sound

Dreamweaver offers the flexibility to deal with advanced attributes of objects—even attributes that haven't been created yet—through the Parameters dialog box. Clicking the Parameters button in the Property inspector opens the Parameters dialog box. Parameters consist of two parts: a parameter name and a value.

Different plug-ins have different parameters available. Table 10.2 lists some common sound parameters. Many plug-ins have optional or required parameters you can set in the Parameters dialog box. The parameters available for sounds, such as `loop` and `autostart`, might or might not be available for other formats.

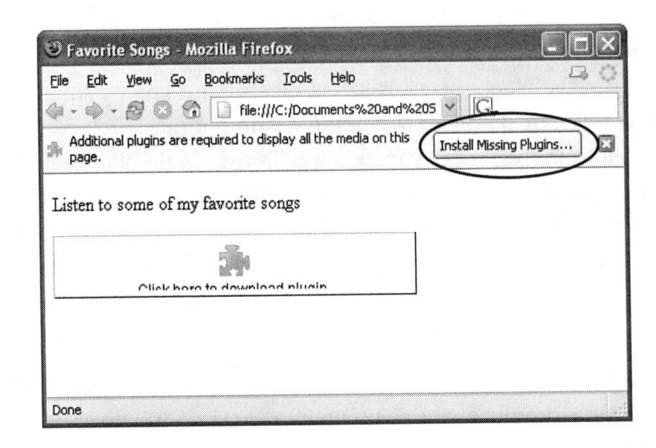

FIGURE 10.10 Mozilla Firefox doesn't have any player configured to play a MP3 file.

TABLE 10.2 Common Sound Parameters

Parameter	Values
`loop`	`true`, `false`, n (number of times playing)
`autostart`	`true`, `false`
`hidden`	`true`, `false`
`volume`	`0–100`
`playcount`	n (number of times playing—Internet Explorer only)

After you click the Parameters button, click the + button to add a parameter. Then do the following to make the sound loop:

1. Type `loop` as the parameter name. Tab or click in the Value column and type `true`. The default is `false`, so if you want the sound to play only once, you do not need to enter the `loop` parameter.
2. Add the `playcount` parameter in addition to `loop`. The default for `playcount` is for the sound to play once. Enter a number for the number of times the sound will play.

You can enter multiple parameters in the Parameters dialog box. Figure 10.11 shows the Parameters dialog box with parameters entered. You add the parameter name in the left column and then click or tab to the right column to add the parameter value. After you have finished adding parameters, click the OK button. To edit a parameter, again click the Parameter button in the Property inspector and then click in the parameter you want to change. To delete a parameter, click the – button. Use the arrow keys to rearrange the order of the parameters. Disregard the lightning bolt icons; they are involved in loading dynamic data into parameter fields when you are using server-side scripting.

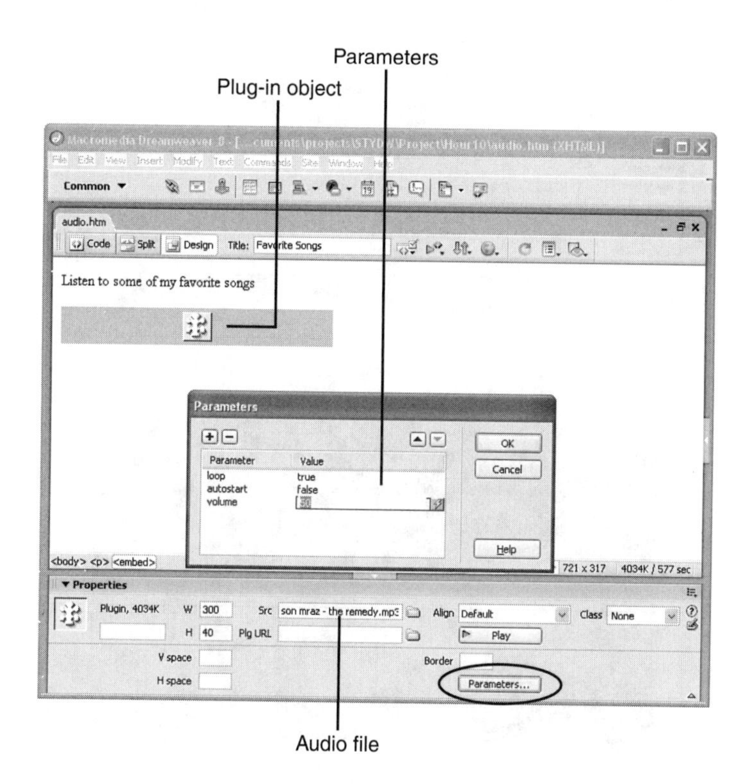

FIGURE 10.11 The Parameters dialog box can contain many parameters that affect the functionality of a plug-in.

Linking to an Audio File

So far, you have had the browsers display an **inline**, or **embedded** player, meaning that the player appears within the flow of your web page. However, if you create a hyperlink to a sound file, the user's browser launches the player controller in a separate window when the user selects the link. Figure 10.12 shows iTunes open in a separate window. Another computer configuration might launch the Windows Media Player, as shown in Figure 10.13.

FIGURE 10.12
When the link to the audio file is clicked, iTunes opens and plays the MP3.

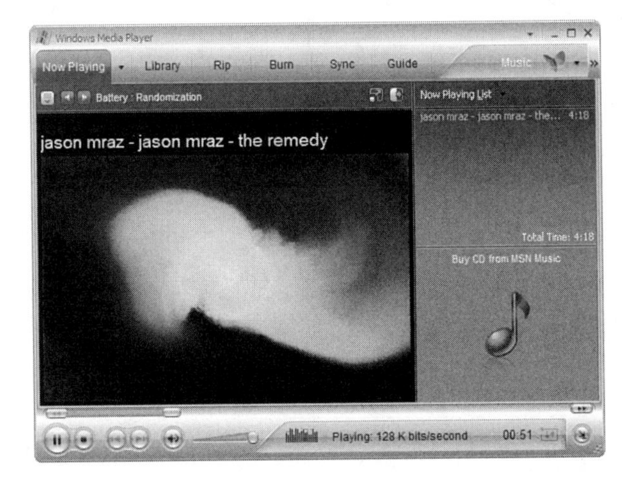

FIGURE 10.13
The Windows Media Player launches in a separate window to play an MP3 file on another person's computer.

Adding a Java Applet to a Web Page

Java is a programming language used to create self-contained programs called **applets**. Java applets run within the browser window just like the other multimedia objects you've been working with in this hour. You can put a Java applet into your page, add parameters, and add some interesting multimedia to your web page.

Watch Out!

Java Versus JavaScript

Java and JavaScript are not the same thing. Nor are they really related. **JavaScript** is a scripting language that is used in web page development to set the properties of a web page. **Java** is a compiled programming language that is used to develop applications.

To insert a Java applet into your web page, you must have all the appropriate files for the applet. The number and type of files might vary. You need to read the documentation for the applet that you are using. The example here uses a classic snow applet, available from www.pagesbyjustme.com/downloads.html. See examples of the applet in action by going to www.pagesbyjustme.com/snowthumb.html and clicking on one of the thumbnails. The snow applet simply requires the Java file that he has written, `alcsnow.class`, and a web image file to present an image that looks like snow is falling on it.

Watch Out!

Be Careful with Java Applets

Some users might have Java turned off in their browser, so you should be careful about including information that is vital to the web page in a Java applet.

Any Java applet that you intend to use in your web page should come with instructions on how to set it up. Be sure to read the instructions carefully and enter all the parameters correctly, or the applet might not work. If you do not set up the applet correctly, users will simply see an empty gray box on the page. Dreamweaver will create the HTML code for you, but you need to pay attention to the parameter values that you need to add to the Java Applet object.

To insert an applet into a web page, follow these steps:

1. Create a new HTML file and save the file. Copy an image file into the same directory as your HTML file. This is the image where the snow will appear.
2. Select the Applet object from the Media tab of the Insert bar or select Insert, Media, Applet. This opens the Select File dialog box.
3. In the Select File dialog box, navigate to the directory that contains the Java applet files. Select the appropriate file stipulated in the applet documentation. For the snow applet, for example, you select the file `alcsnow.class`.
4. Enter all the parameters that are required by the applet documentation by first clicking the Parameters button to open the Parameters dialog box.

   The snow applet requires a parameter with the address of the image file on which the snow will appear, as shown in Figure 10.14. Add a parameter called `grph` and enter the name of the image file you copied in step 1.
5. Save your web page and preview it in a web browser to make sure it looks the way you want it. The snow applet, viewed in a browser, is shown in Figure 10.15.

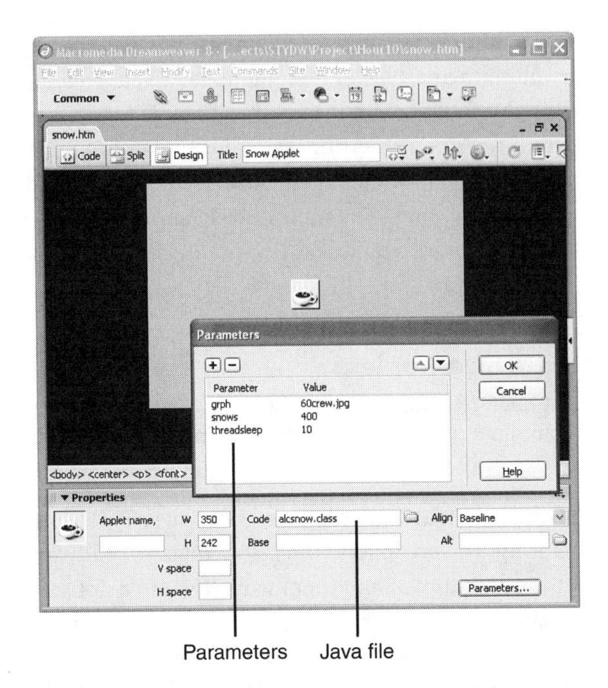

FIGURE 10.14
A Java applet requires parameters specific to the applet.

FIGURE 10.15
The snow applet animates snow falling over the picture when viewed in the browser.

Summary

In this hour, you have learned how to add multimedia files, including Flash and Shockwave movies, to your web page. You have added a URL that the browser can redirect the viewer to if she does not have the appropriate player to view your files. You've created Flash text and you've used some of the Flash buttons that come with

Dreamweaver. You have added parameters to multimedia files to change properties that weren't specifically shown in the Property inspector. And you have inserted and configured a Java applet.

Q&A

Q. ***I placed a value in the Border text box in the Property inspector when I had the Plugin object selected, but no border appeared around the plug-in. Did I do something wrong?***

A. Some plug-ins respond to the Border attribute and some plug-ins don't. The plug-in that you tried to put a border around was not capable of adding a border.

Q. ***Why do I see only a gray box when I insert a Java applet into my page?***

A. You haven't entered a required parameter or you have entered a parameter incorrectly. Go back into the Parameters dialog box and double-check that you have spelled everything correctly. If you misspell something or reference a file incorrectly, you won't receive an error message; your applet will just appear as a gray box. Also, make sure you have saved your web page so that the path to the Java applet is correct (and relative to your web page).

Java applets can be problematic because the user might not have the correct version of Java installed. Check the documentation of the applet you are using in your web page and add a link that leads to the correct Java version so the user can download it if necessary. Check the Sun website for download information: www.java.com/en/download.

Workshop

Quiz

1. Which tag contains information for a plug-in, and which tag contains information for an ActiveX control?
2. Java and JavaScript are the same thing. True or false?
3. What are the two components of a parameter?

Quiz Answers

1. The <embed> tag contains the information for a plug-in, and the <object> tag contains the information for an ActiveX control. Dreamweaver automatically configures both tags with the appropriate information for Flash and Shockwave files.
2. False. The two are unrelated. Java is a programming language and JavaScript is the language that Dreamweaver uses for behaviors, which you will learn more about in Hour 17, "Adding Interactivity with Behaviors."
3. A parameter consists of a parameter name and a value.

Exercises

1. Insert a sound or movie file into a web page. Create a hyperlink to the same file. Explore how the embedded sound or movie works differently from the linked sound or movie.
2. Insert into a web page a hyperlink to a PDF file. The Internal Revenue Service (www.irs.gov/formspubs) is a popular site to find PDF files. Don't get me wrong—I'm not saying the IRS is popular, just the PDF files! (The IRS is the national tax agency for the United States, for those of you in other countries, and nobody likes paying taxes.) You can copy the URL to a file by right-clicking the link in the browser and then selecting either the Copy Shortcut command in Internet Explorer or the Save Link As command in Netscape. Paste the link into Dreamweaver's Property inspector as a hyperlink.

HOUR 11

Managing Assets Using the Assets Panel

What You'll Learn in This Hour:

- What assets are and how to manage them in your website
- How to create favorite assets and give them a nickname
- How to create and add assets to another website

After you have designed your web page, you can populate your page with content. The elements that make up your individual web pages are likely to come from various sources and will be different types of objects. You might include Flash movies, images created in Fireworks, various colors, links, clip art, and photographs in your web pages.

You need to gather and organize these page elements before you start to create a web page. Dreamweaver's Assets panel enables you to organize the elements of a website to quickly access and reuse items. The Assets panel can help you become more efficient and better organized! Putting out a small effort to organize pays off especially well when you work on the same website all the time.

What Are Assets?

Web pages are not just made out of text and code. You use images, movies, colors, and URLs to present information in web pages. These web page elements are called **assets**.

The Assets panel organizes these elements, enabling you to quickly find an image or a color that you want to use. You can preview assets in the Assets panel. You can also create a list of favorite assets—ones that you use often.

The Library and Templates panels are part of the Assets panel. These panels are covered in Hour 12, "Displaying Data in Tables," and Hour 13, "Designing Page Layout Using Tables."

Managing Assets in the Assets Panel

Dreamweaver automatically catalogs the assets for an entire site. When you open the Assets panel, you can select one of the category buttons from along the left side of the panel to display a list of all the assets of that type in your site. The Assets panel includes the following categories:

- Images
- Colors
- URLs
- Flash movies
- Shockwave movies
- Movies
- Scripts
- Templates
- Library

You can browse an asset category to preview the assets by selecting one of the asset category buttons. The Assets panel enables you to quickly add a selected asset to your current page. Later this hour you'll learn how to set some assets as favorites so you can find them even more quickly. The Assets panel has different capabilities based on the asset category you've selected. For instance, when the Images category is selected you can view a thumbnail of each image, but when you have the Colors category selected, the hexadecimal code for the color is displayed.

Assets are specific to the current site you are working in. Often you'll use certain page elements in multiple websites. You can also copy your assets from one website to another using the Assets panel.

Listing Assets in a Site

When you open the Assets panel, Dreamweaver goes through the cache and automatically catalogs all the assets within your current site. It places the assets into the correct categories by examining the file extensions of the files in the website. The

Assets panel lists only the assets that are in the currently selected site. When you change sites, you might have a message box appear briefly while the Assets panel is being updated.

You can view all the assets in a category by selecting a category button along the left side of the Assets panel. Each of the categories, except the Library and Templates categories, has two radio buttons at the top of the panel, as shown in Figure 11.1, enabling you to select whether you want to see all the assets of that type or just your favorites. You'll learn how to create a favorite asset in a few minutes.

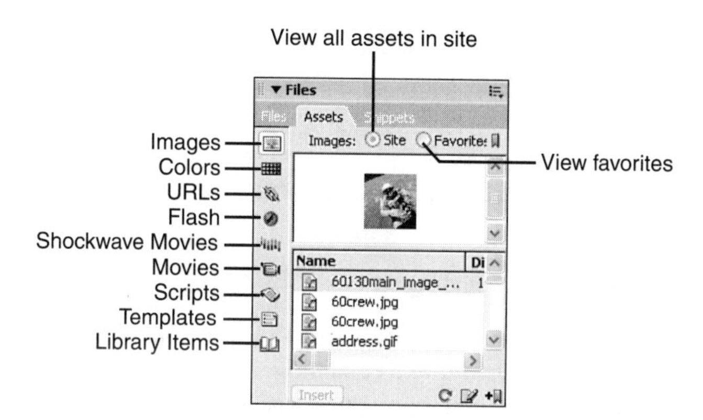

FIGURE 11.1 The Assets panel has buttons for the different categories along the left side and radio buttons at the top to select whether to view all the assets or just your favorites.

After you add an asset to your site, you might need to click the Refresh button to see it listed in the Assets panel. You can refresh the list of assets anytime.

Previewing Assets

When you select a category in the Assets panel, the first asset in the list of that category is selected in the lower half of the panel, and a preview of that asset appears in the upper half. You can preview assets by selecting them in the list, as shown in Figure 11.2.

By default, the items listed in the Assets panel are sorted alphabetically. You can sort the items by any of the available column headings by clicking a column heading. For instance, if you want to sort your image assets by file size, you click the column heading File Size.

Sometimes you might see an asset file in the Assets panel and wonder where that asset resides in the actual website structure. Highlight an item in the Assets panel and then right-click (Control+click on a Mac) to bring up the context menu. Select the Locate in Site command and Dreamweaver opens the Files panel with the same file highlighted. This works only on assets that are individual files, such as movies or images, and not on assets that are elements of web pages, such as URLs or colors.

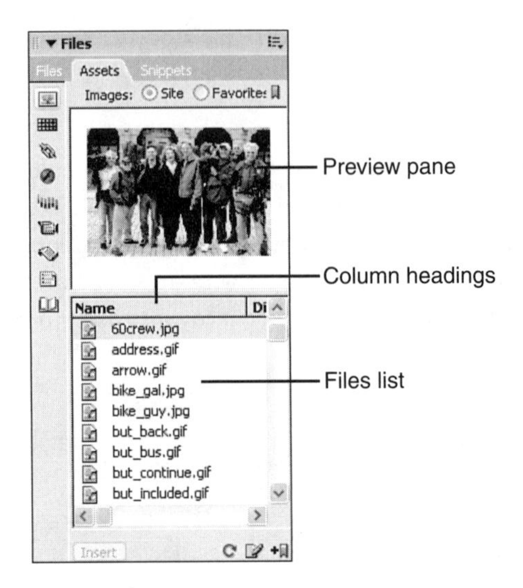

FIGURE 11.2
A preview of the asset selected in the list appears in the upper-half of the Assets panel.

Exploring Image Assets

The Images category of the Assets panel displays all the images in your defined website (refer to Figure 11.1). Dreamweaver catalogs images in GIF, JPG, or PNG format. Dreamweaver displays a preview of the selected image in the top half of the Assets panel.

The Assets panel is very useful when trying to find an image in your website. Although the Files panel displays the file name, the Assets panel displays both the file name and a thumbnail of the image. It's often easier to quickly identify an image by what it looks like rather than its file name. When I'm looking for an image file in Dreamweaver, I'll open up the Assets panel and select the first image in the list. Then I'll simply press the down arrow key while viewing the thumbnails, quickly scrolling through the image assets, until I find the image for which I'm looking.

Exploring Color Assets

The Colors category of the Assets panel, as shown in Figure 11.3, displays all the colors used in the defined website. All the colors in the website are cataloged in the Assets panel and are displayed in hexadecimal format. Dreamweaver displays a preview of the selected color, along with both its hexadecimal and RGB (red, green, blue) definition, in the top half of the Assets panel. Beside the color name, Dreamweaver displays whether the color is part of the web-safe palette.

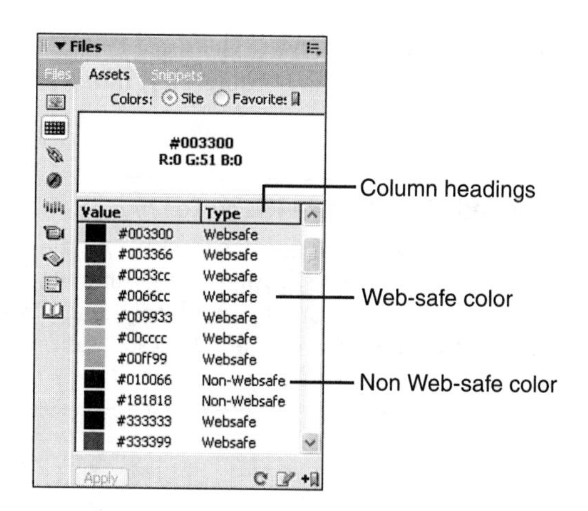

FIGURE 11.3
The Colors category shows the hexadecimal and RGB definition of the colors in the website.

By the Way

Is the Color Web-Safe?

You explored the Dreamweaver palettes when you learned about the color picker in Hour 3, "Getting Started: Adding Text, Lists, and Previewing in the Browser." One of the available palettes is the web-safe palette, which contains the 216 colors that work on all browsers on both the Windows and Mac platforms. The Assets panel tells you whether the colors listed in the Colors category are within those 216 colors by marking them as Websafe or Non-Websafe in the Type column. You might have to widen the panel in order to view this column.

You can select one of the colors in the Colors category of the Assets panel and drag and drop it onto text, a layer, a table, or other objects that accept color. Just as you created CSS styles in Hour 3, this creates new CSS styles in the web page `head`. If you do this, you'll need to go in to the CSS Styles panel and rename the styles with a name that makes sense for your site (rather than `style1`, `style2`, and so forth).

Exploring Link Assets

The URLs category of the Assets panel holds all the hyperlinks contained in the currently defined website (refer to Figure 11.2). This category lists all URLs in the site, including FTP, mailto, JavaScript, HTTP (Web), and HTTPS (secure Web). These are the absolute links in your website; the document-relative links, links to other pages in the same site, are not listed in the URLs category.

Exploring Movie Assets

The three movie asset categories are Flash Movies, Shockwave Movies, and Movies. The Movies category catalogs movie types other than Flash or Shockwave movies, such as QuickTime or MPEG movies. There is a Play/Stop button in the upper-right corner of the preview window (see Figure 11.4) that enables you to play the movie in the preview window.

Watch Out!

Links Shouldn't Begin with `file:///`

You should not use URLs that begin with `file:///` because those URLs do not work when you move your site anywhere other than on your computer. Find those locally referenced URLs in your site and change them by examining the URLs category of the Assets panel. Use Find and Replace (Edit, Find and Replace) to find the incorrect URL.

FIGURE 11.4 All the movie categories enable you to play a movie in the preview window.

Exploring Script Assets

The Scripts category is where you see some of the scripts you create with Dreamweaver. (You'll learn more about scripts in Hour 17, "Adding Interactivity with Behaviors.") The Scripts category of the Assets panel catalogs all the *external* script files in your website, as shown in Figure 11.5. External script files end with the `.js` or `.vbs` extensions. These script files contain JavaScript or VBScript functions you can call from your web pages. The preview window shows the actual code in the script.

In order to have access to the functions contained in an external script file, you reference the script in the head section of your web page. If you call a function that is contained in an external script, you need to link the external script file to your web page by dragging it from the Scripts category of the Assets panel into the Head Content (View, Head Content) section of the Dreamweaver Document window, as shown in Figure 11.6.

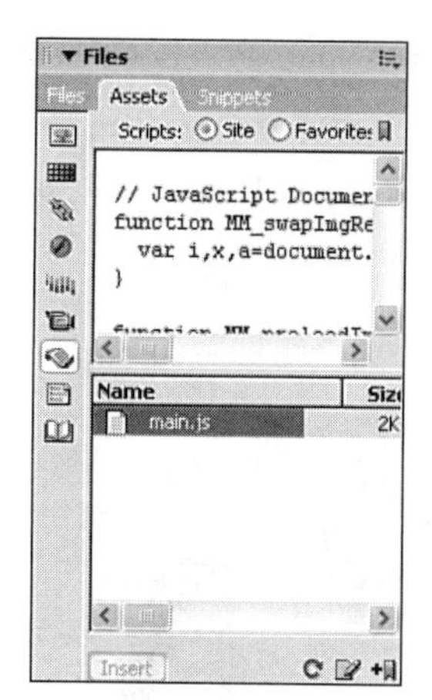

FIGURE 11.5
All the external script files are shown in the Scripts category of the Assets panel.

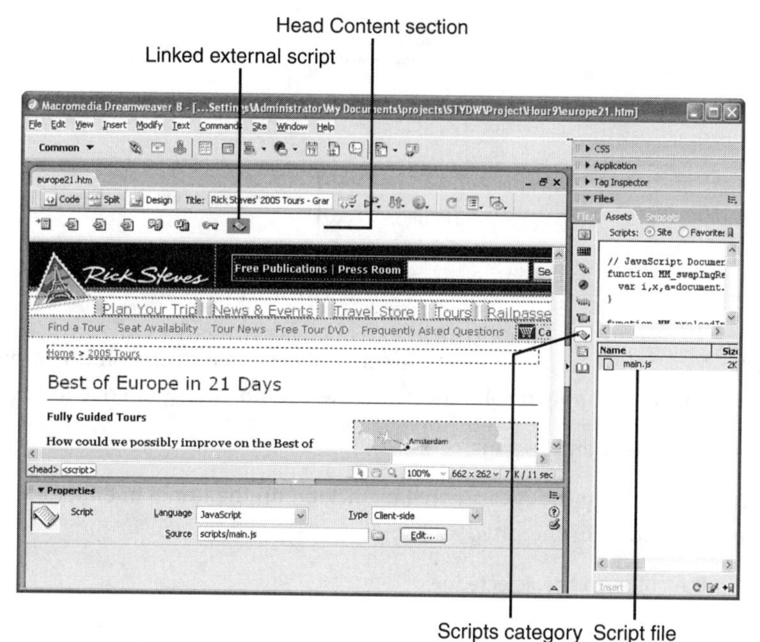

FIGURE 11.6
Drag an external script from the Scripts category of the Assets panel into the Head Content section of a web page.

Adding Assets to a Web Page

Use the Assets panel to add assets to a web page. To add an asset to your web page, follow these steps:

1. Select the category.

2. Find the asset you want to add by scrolling through the list for the name or viewing the preview in the Preview window.

3. Place the insertion point in your web page where you want the asset to be located.

4. Click the Insert button, shown in Figure 11.7, and the asset is inserted into your web page.

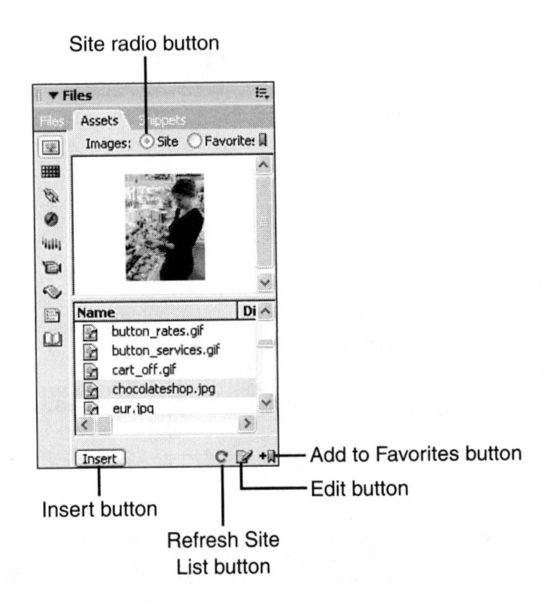

FIGURE 11.7 You insert an asset into a web page by clicking the Insert button.

You can also use assets from the Assets panel to affect other objects on a web page. For instance, you can apply a color asset to some text on your web page as follows:

1. Select some text on the page.

2. Drag a color from the Assets panel by picking up the name in either the Preview window or the category list.

3. Drop the color on the selected text.

Instead of dragging and dropping, you can simply select the text and the color and then click the Apply button to apply the color to the text.

Adding a color to text creates a CSS style that you'll see both in the Property inspector (when the text is selected) and in the CSS Styles panel. Again, you'll want to rename this style (as in Hour 3) and then continue to apply the style to other text on the page. Don't keep dragging colors from the Assets panel, creating the same type of style over and over again. CSS styles are meant to be reused!

Did you Know?

Jump Assets Alphabetically

To quickly jump to a section in the assets list, click within the assets list and then type the first letter of the name of the item for which you are looking. You will jump to the first item that begins with that letter.

Creating Favorite Assets

You often use certain assets repeatedly in your website. You can assign these assets to the favorites list so they are easy to pick out of the Assets panel. The favorites list is displayed when the Favorites radio button is selected at the top of the Assets panel.

To create a favorite asset, select the asset in the Assets panel and then select the Add to Favorites button. When you select the Favorites radio button, the favorite assets that you just added should be listed, as shown in Figure 11.8. You can give a favorite a different name by right-clicking it (Control+click on the Mac), selecting the Edit Nickname command, and typing a name that is easy to remember.

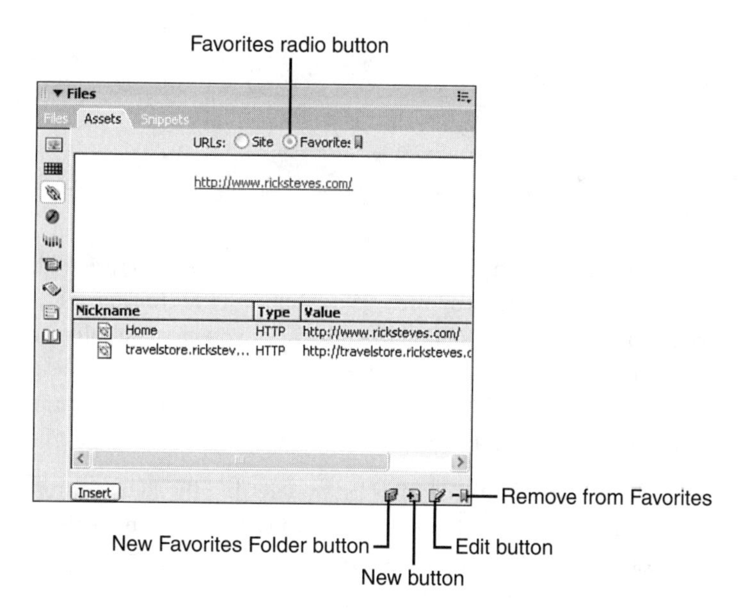

FIGURE 11.8 You can list only your favorite assets in a certain Assets panel category instead of all the assets in the site.

By the Way

No Templates or Library Favorites

Favorites are not available for the Templates and Library categories of the Assets panel.

You can also add objects as favorites in the Assets panel while you are working in Dreamweaver's Document window, adding images, colors, and movies. Right-click (Control+click on the Mac) on an image or color to bring up the context menu. Select the appropriate Add to Favorites command, as shown in Figure 11.9: Add Image to Favorites, Add Color to Favorites, or Add Flash to Favorites. This is a quick way to save a file to your favorites list in the Assets panel.

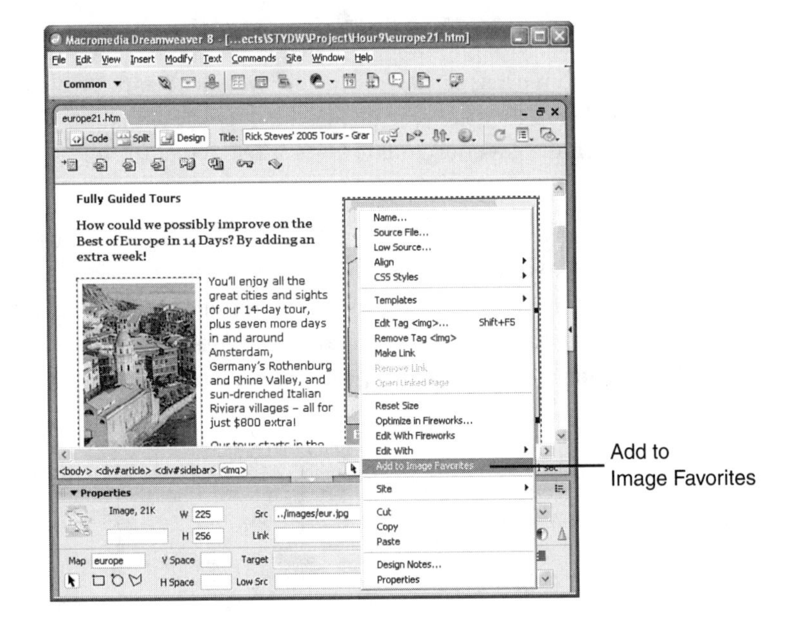

FIGURE 11.9 Add an image to the favorites in the Assets panel by selecting the Add Image to Favorites command in the context menu.

You can organize your favorites into groups by creating new folders within the favorites list. The New Favorites Folder button (refer to Figure 11.8) enables you to create a folder within the favorites list. After you create a folder, drag and drop items into the folder. Figure 11.10 shows favorite items organized into folders. Expand the folder to view the contents by selecting the + button next to the folder name. Collapse the folder view by selecting the – button next to the folder name.

Remove items from the favorites list by selecting the Remove from Favorites button. The item is removed only from the favorites list and is not deleted from the website. You can also delete an item from the list by right-clicking the item and selecting the Remove from Favorites command from the context menu.

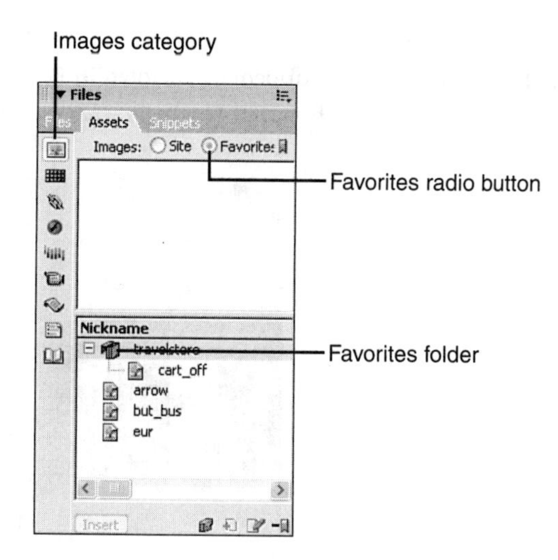

FIGURE 11.10
Organize your favorite assets by creating folders in the favorites list.

Creating New Assets in the Assets Panel

You can use the Assets panel to help design your website. Dreamweaver enables you to create new assets in certain asset categories. You can add a new color, URL, template, or library item. Hours 23, "Using the Library: Reusing Elements in a Website," and 24, "Creating Reusable Web Pages: Using Templates," describe how to create new library items and templates.

When you begin creating a website, you can organize your development effort with the help of the Assets panel. Organize your image assets into favorites so commonly used images are easy to find. Define commonly used links and colors so they can be quickly applied to web pages. When web designers work with graphic artists, the graphic artists sometimes provide a list of the colors and other specifications in the design they have created. You can use this list to add the colors to the Assets panel and then be ready to apply them when you start the project.

The Assets panel catalogs the assets that already exist in your site. When you are in the favorites list, you can also create new URLs and colors to use in your site. These new assets are then available, even though they haven't yet been used in your website.

To create a new color or link asset, follow these steps:

1. Select the Favorites radio button at the top of the Assets panel. Select either the Colors category or the URLs category.

2. Select the New Color or New URL button at the bottom of the Assets panel. Either the color picker appears, as shown in Figure 11.11, or the Add URL dialog box appears, as shown in Figure 11.12.

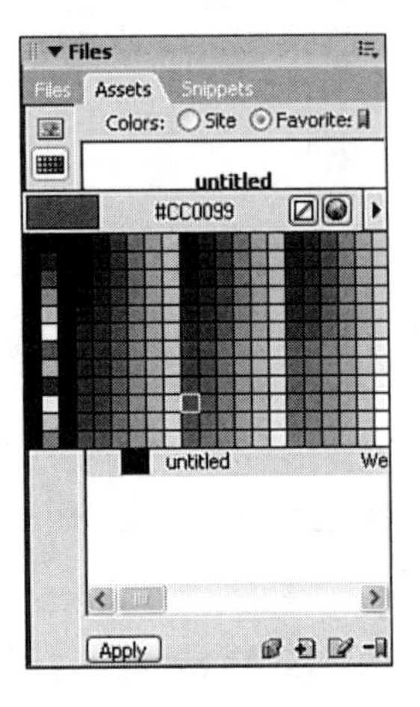

FIGURE 11.11 Use the color picker to create a new color in the favorite colors list of the Assets panel.

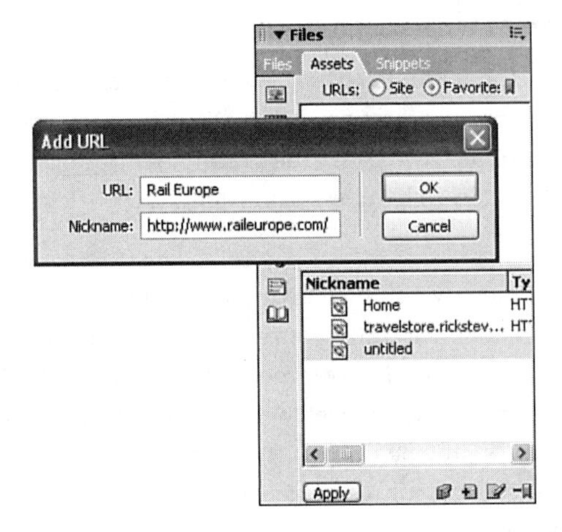

FIGURE 11.12 Create a new favorite link in the URLs category of the Assets panel.

3. Pick a color from the color picker or fill in the URL and nickname in the Add URL dialog box.

Copying Assets to Another Site

The Assets panel displays the assets of the current site. When you select a different site from the Site drop-down menu in the Files panel, the assets of the new site are displayed in the Assets panel. Sometimes you might want to copy assets to a different website. You can copy a single asset, a group of assets, or a favorites group to another site.

To copy a single asset to another site, simply right-click (Control+click on the Mac) the item name in the Assets panel and select the Copy to Site command. Select the site to which you want to copy the asset. Dreamweaver copies the exact folder structure and the file for an image or movie asset to the other site.

To copy a group of assets to another defined site, select multiple asset items by holding down the Shift key while clicking (Control+clicking on a Mac) on the item names in the Assets panel. Right-click (Control+click on a Mac) the group and select the Copy to Site command from the context menu. All the assets are then copied to the other site. You can also copy a group of favorites to another site by following these steps.

Summary

In this hour, you have learned how to use assets from the Assets panel. You have learned how to sort, add, and organize assets. You have explored the various types of assets and learned how to create favorites. You have also learned how to copy assets from site to site.

Q&A

Q. *What is the best way to organize images?*

A. Many web developers divide images into logical directory structures so they can more easily find the images they want. The Assets panel can help you organize images so you might not need to use various directories for organization. You might want to use a naming convention to help sort your images. For instance, all the images for section 1 of a website can begin with the number 1 (`1_image1`, `1_image2`, and so on). After you've sorted the images, you can create favorites and folders to organize the favorites so you can quickly find the images you need.

Q. *I have some URLs that begin with* `file:///` *listed in the Assets panel. How can I find and fix these?*

A. When you notice in the Assets panel that you have links beginning with `file:///`, you know you have a problem with your site. The way to identify the pages that contain these links is to run the Check Links report from the Site panel. Select each file that appears in the report as having a link that begins with `file:///` and change the URL to a document-relative address.

Workshop

Quiz

1. Which asset categories list individual files that are referenced (or embedded) in a web page?
2. How can you organize favorite assets?
3. When you copy assets to another site, Dreamweaver creates exactly the same folder structure in the site to which the assets are copied. True or false?

Quiz Answers

1. The Images and Flash Movies, Shockwave Movies, Movies, and Scripts categories list actual files that are referenced in web pages.
2. You create and name folders to organize your favorite assets to make them easier to find and use.
3. True. The assets are stored in exactly the same folder structure.

Exercises

1. Create some favorite assets and then create folders. Organize the favorites in the folders you created. Right-click on an image in a web page and add it to the favorites list.
2. Practice copying image assets to another site. Open the site you copied the files to in the Files panel and confirm that Dreamweaver created a new directory and copied the images to that directory.

PART III

Web Page Layout with Tables and Frames

HOUR 12

Displaying Data In Tables

What You'll Learn in This Hour:

- How to create and format a table
- How to add and sort data in a table
- How to import data to and export data from a table

Tables not only provide the ability to logically present data in columns and rows, but they also enable web page designers to control where objects appear on the page. This hour introduces you to creating tables. In Hour 13, "Designing Page Layout Using Tables," you'll explore controlling page layout with tables.

Using tables can be a powerful way to organize and display data. You use tables in HTML just as you use them in a word processing application. Tables consist of rows, columns, and cells. Dreamweaver presents many ways to format tables the way you would like them to appear to your viewer.

Creating a Table for Data

Let's begin exploring tables by adding to your web page a table that will hold some data. Examples of this type of table are a phone list of people in your company or class at school, an ocean tide table with times and tide levels, and a recipe with amounts and ingredients. This type of table usually has a border around the cells, although it doesn't have to. Generally, tables used for page layout purposes, explored next hour, have the table borders turned off.

Adding a Table to a Web Page

Dreamweaver has two modes, enabling you to create tables in two different ways. When Dreamweaver is in Standard mode, you insert a table by using the Table object and set the number of rows and columns in the Table dialog box. In Layout mode, you can draw tables and table cells by using the cursor. You set which mode you are in by clicking one of the buttons in the Layout category of the Insert bar or by selecting View, Table Mode. For this hour, make sure you are in Standard mode and not Layout mode. You should not see a colored bar with the title Layout Mode across the top of the Document window. You'll use Layout mode in Hour 13.

To insert a table into your web page, follow these steps:

1. Place the insertion point in your web page where you want the table to be inserted.
2. Select the Table icon in the Insert bar or choose Insert, Table. The Table dialog box appears, as shown in Figure 12.1.

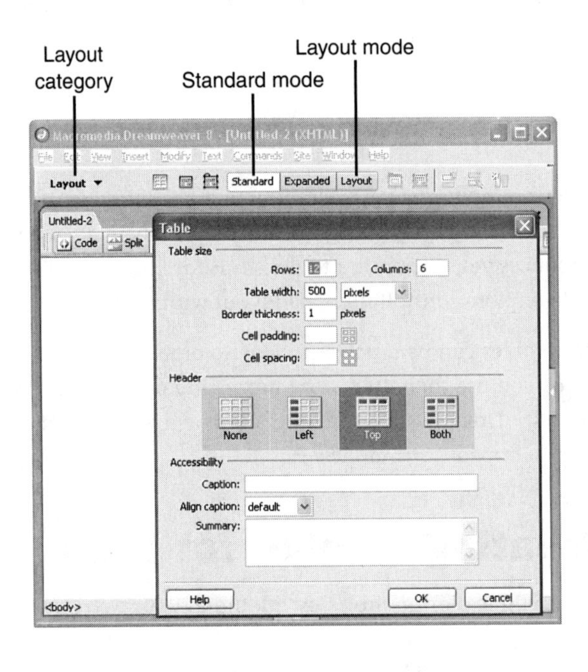

FIGURE 12.1 The Table dialog box allows you to set the initial values of the table. You can always edit these values in the Property inspector later.

3. Accept the default values or enter your own values into the Rows and Columns text boxes. You can also select the width of the table and the border size in this dialog box. You'll learn about all these parameters, including the accessibility settings at the bottom of the dialog box, later in this hour.
4. When you're done setting values in this dialog box, click OK.

Tables (`<table>` and `</table>`) are made up of table rows (`<tr>` and `</tr>`) that contain table cells (`<td>` and `</td>`). In HTML, tables are structured by their rows;

you do not need to define columns, and there isn't a tag in HTML that creates columns. In the rest of this hour and the next hour you will modify the attributes of tables, table rows, and table cells. There are also header tags (`<th>` and `</th>`) that you can optionally use to create header cells; by default, the text in header cells appears bold and centered.

When you select a table or when the insertion point is within a table, Dreamweaver displays the width of the table and the width of each of the columns in the **table header menu**, which appears either above or below the table. The Table Selector menu, shown in Figure 12.2, is the green menu that is visible only in Dreamweaver and doesn't appear in the web browser. To turn off the display of the Table Selector menu in Dreamweaver, select View, Visual Aids, Table Widths. You'll explore the Table Selector menu a bit more later this hour.

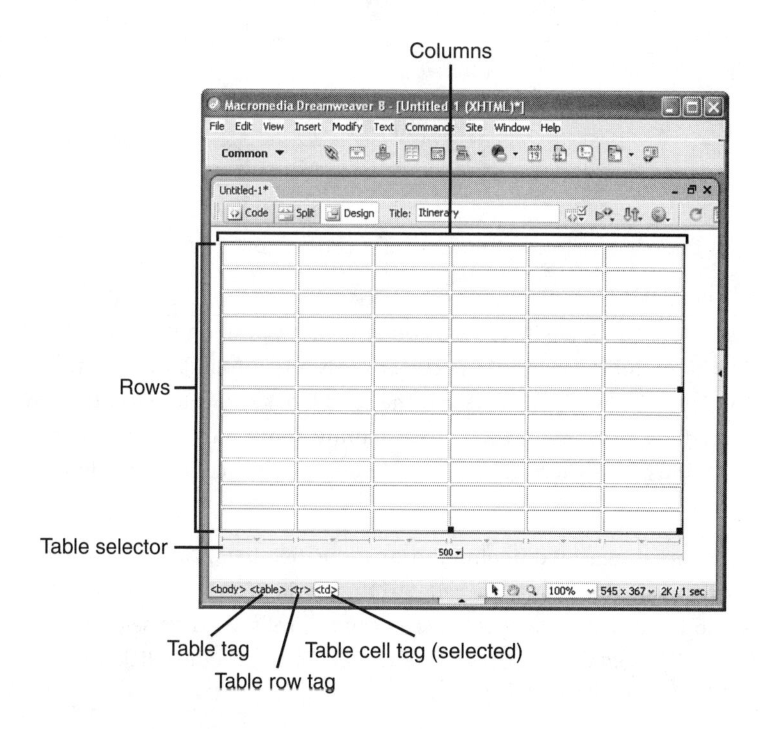

FIGURE 12.2
Dreamweaver displays the Table Selector menu below a table.

Selecting Table Elements

You can select a table in a couple ways. I think the easiest way to select the table is to click the little arrow in the Table Selector menu, shown in Figure 12.3. Choose the Select Table command from the Table Selector menu to select the table. You can also use the tag selector in Dreamweaver's status bar by clicking the table tag to select a table. Click inside one of the cells in your table. The status bar displays the tag hierarchy, including the table tag that you can click on to select the entire table.

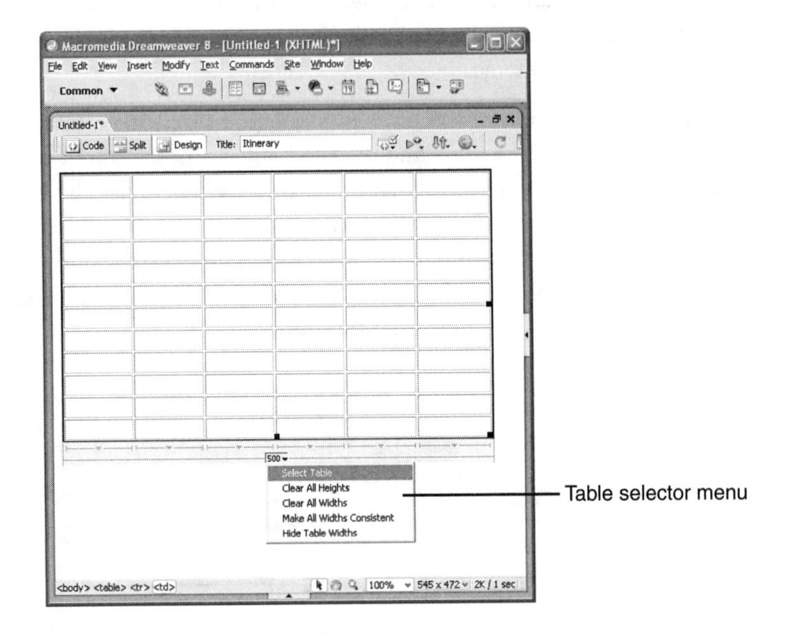

FIGURE 12.3 The Table Selector menu contains commands, including the Select Table command.

To select a cell, simply click inside it. To select an entire row, position your cursor slightly to the left of the table row until the cursor turns into a solid black arrow, as shown in Figure 12.4. Click while the cursor is the solid black arrow to select the row. Use the same procedure, positioning your cursor slightly above the column to select an entire column. Or use the Select Column command from the column header menu.

You can select a group of cells by dragging the cursor across them. Another way to select a group of cells is to first select one cell and then hold down the Shift key while you click another cell. All the cells between the two cells are then selected. To select cells individually, hold down Ctrl while you click (or Command+click on the Mac) a cell to add it to the selection.

Watch Out!

Drag over Cells Carefully

When a table is empty, it's easy to drag the cursor across the group of cells you want to select. Start dragging while your cursor is inside the first cell. When the cells contain assets, however, it's too easy to accidentally move objects from their cells when you use this procedure.

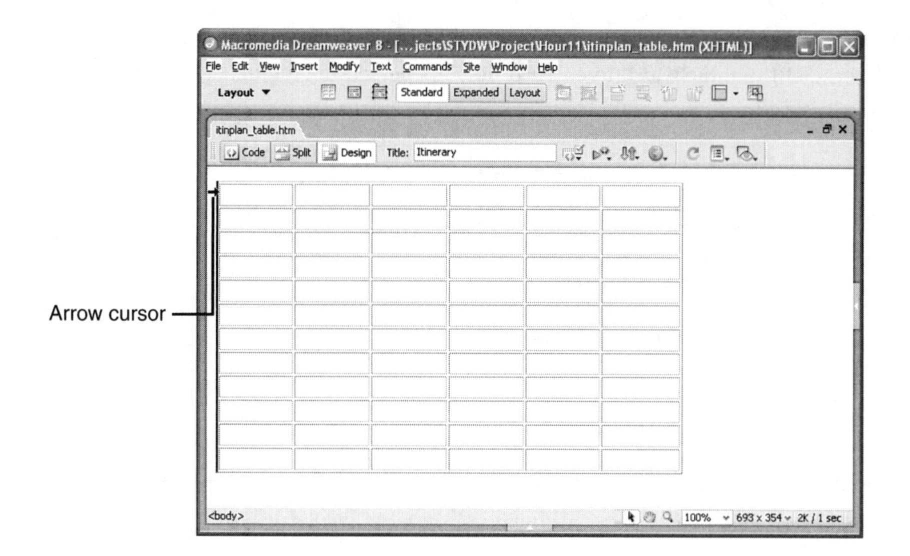

FIGURE 12.4
The cursor, positioned slightly to the left of a table row, turns into a solid black arrow. Select an entire row by clicking with this cursor.

The Property inspector shows different attributes, depending on what you currently have selected. There are two basic ways that the Property inspector appears while you're working with tables:

- When an entire table is selected, the Property inspector looks as shown in Figure 12.5, displaying properties of the entire table.

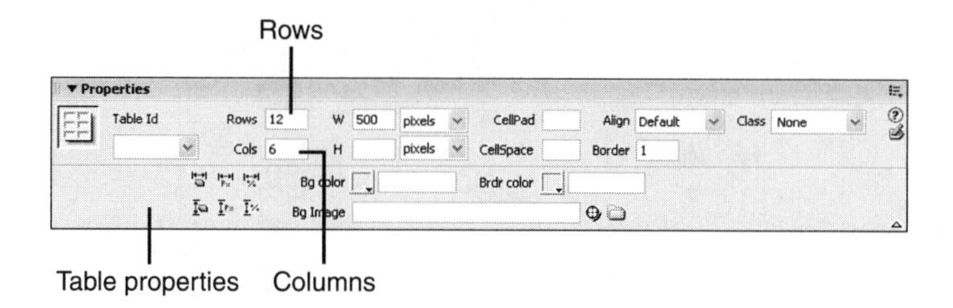

FIGURE 12.5
The Property inspector displays properties that apply to the entire table when the entire table is selected.

- When an individual cell, entire row, or entire column is selected, the Property inspector looks as shown in Figure 12.6, displaying properties that affect the selected cells.

Setting Cell Padding and Cell Spacing

Let's start over by adding a new table. Again, click the Table icon in the Common category of the Insert bar (or select Insert, Table). In the Table dialog box, set the number of rows and columns you'd like the table to have (you can always change this later). Set the table width to either a pixel or percentage value. Set the border thickness also.

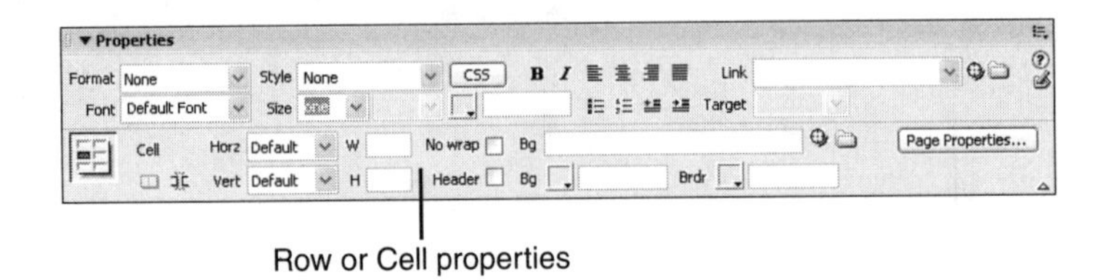

FIGURE 12.6 The Property inspector displays properties of selected cells when an individual cell, entire row, or entire column is selected.

The next settings in the Table dialog box are for **cell padding** and **cell spacing** (see Figure 12.7):

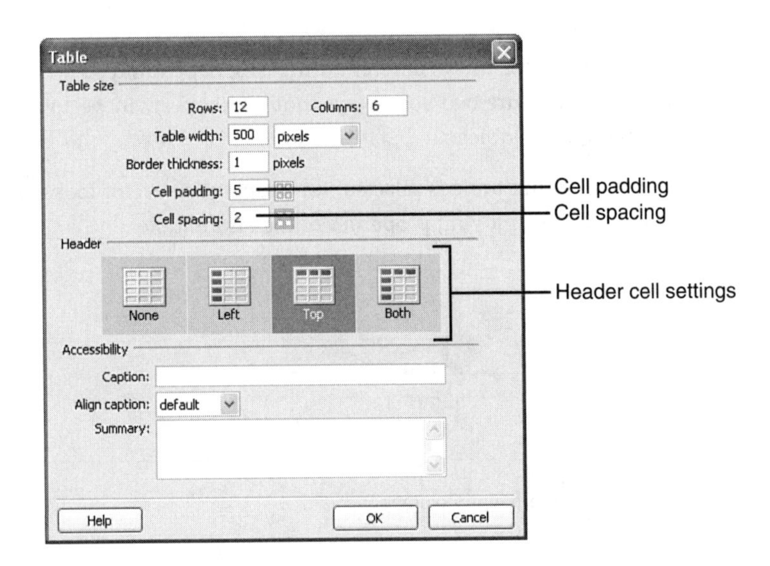

FIGURE 12.7 Set the Cell Padding and the Cell Spacing settings in the Table dialog box.

- **Cell padding**—This is where you set the amount of space between an object contained in a cell and the border of the cell. The cell padding sits between the contents of the cell and the inside cell border.
- **Cell spacing**—This is where you set the amount of space between table cells. The cell spacing sits between the outer cell borders of adjacent cells.

The Table dialog box displays illustrations next to each of these settings, highlighting the area of the cell that the setting affects.

Dreamweaver Keeps Your Table Settings

Did you notice that when you inserted another table, Dreamweaver kept the row and column settings you entered earlier? That makes it easy to create multiple tables that have similar settings.

Did you Know?

Adding Header Cells to a Table

As mentioned earlier, contents of header cells appear bold and centered. You can select which table cells in a table should be header cells by selecting one of the choices in the Table dialog box. I usually think of header cells as the top cells in table columns. But you can add header cells along the left edge of a table as headers for each row or have headers for the rows and columns, too.

Making a Table Accessible to People with Disabilities

Users who are visually impaired and using text-to-speech synthesizer software to read your web page will have the most trouble reading large tables full of data. These users will greatly appreciate your small effort to design a table that is easier for people to navigate and extract data from. Dreamweaver has made this easy for you by placing the accessibility settings at the bottom of the Table dialog box.

You can add a caption for a table that appears in the browser and is visible to everyone. You set the alignment for the caption so that it appears either above or below or to the left or right of the table. You should always add a summary for your table, as shown in Figure 12.8. The summary is read only by text-to-speech browsers and helps the user evaluate whether to progress through the table data or skip the information.

After you've entered all of the settings into the Table dialog box, click the OK button to create the table.

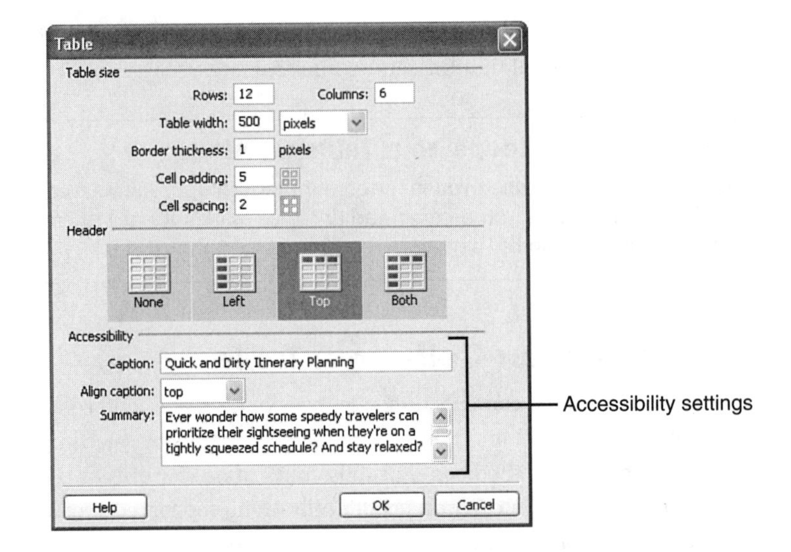

FIGURE 12.8
The Accessibility settings are important for people who have visual impairments.

Modifying a Table and Adding Content

When you have your table structure determined, you can start adding text or images to the table. You can also fine-tune the structure as you work in Dreamweaver by using the Property inspector and selecting table cells or entire tables. Later in this hour you'll use some of the built-in table color schemes available in Dreamweaver.

Adding and Sorting Data

To enter data, you click in a table cell, type, and then tab to the next cell. You can press Shift+Tab to move backward through the table cells. When you reach the rightmost cell in the bottom row, pressing Tab creates a new row. Add data to your table until you have enough data to make it interesting to sort.

Creating New Table Rows

When you press the Tab key to create a new table row, Dreamweaver gives the new row the attributes of the previous row. This might be what you want. But if you use Tab to create a new row from a header cell row, your row will be more header cells!

Dreamweaver makes it easy to sort the data in your table by using Commands, Sort Table. To sort a table by using the Sort Table command, follow these steps:

1. Select the table and then select Commands, Sort Table. The Sort Table dialog box, shown in Figure 12.9, appears. It contains a number of drop-down menus to help you sort the table.

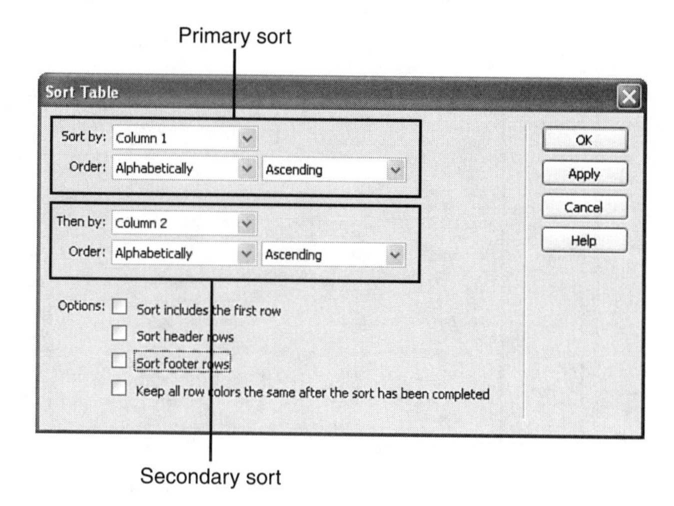

FIGURE 12.9
The Sort Table dialog box contains drop-down menus with sorting options.

2. Select the column to sort in the Sort By drop-down menu.
3. Select whether you want to sort the column alphabetically or numerically in the Order drop-down menu.
4. Select whether you want to sort in ascending or descending order in the drop-down list directly to the right of the Order drop-down menu.
5. Below this first set of sorting options you can set up a secondary search, if necessary. If you do this, Dreamweaver will first sort by the primary column and will then sort by the secondary column.
6. If the first row of the table is a header row, leave the Sort Includes the First Row box unchecked. If you don't have header cells, you should include the first row in the sort.
7. The Keep All Row Colors the Same After the Sort Has Been Completed check box allows you to keep table row attributes with the row after the sort. If you have formatted your table in a certain way, you should check this box so your formatting isn't lost.
8. Click OK to start the sort.

Figure 12.10 shows an example of a sorted table.

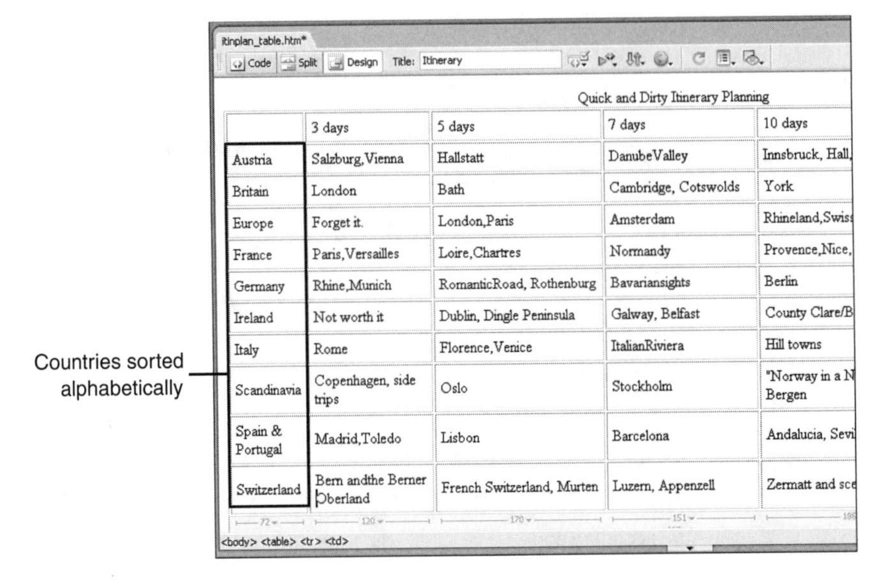

FIGURE 12.10 Data can be sorted alphabetically or numerically in either ascending or descending order by the Sort Table command.

Adding and Removing Rows and Columns

To remove a row or column from a table, use the context menu that pops up when you right-click (Control+click on the Mac) a table cell. Right-click (Control+click on the Mac) a table cell and select the Table submenu; another menu appears, with a number of commands to add and remove rows, columns, or both, as shown in Figure 12.11. Select one of these commands to make a change to the table.

Use the icons in the Layout category of the Insert bar to add rows either above or below the current row or to add columns to the left or the right of the current column. You can also add or remove rows and columns by editing the table properties in the Property inspector. Adjust the number of rows and columns in the Property inspector with an entire table selected to add or remove groups of cells.

Modifying the Number of Rows and Columns

When you use the Property inspector to adjust the number of rows and columns, Dreamweaver inserts a new column to the far right of the table. It inserts a new row at the bottom of the table. If you remove columns or rows in the Property inspector, the columns are removed from the right side and the rows are removed from the bottom. You lose any data that is in the removed columns or rows.

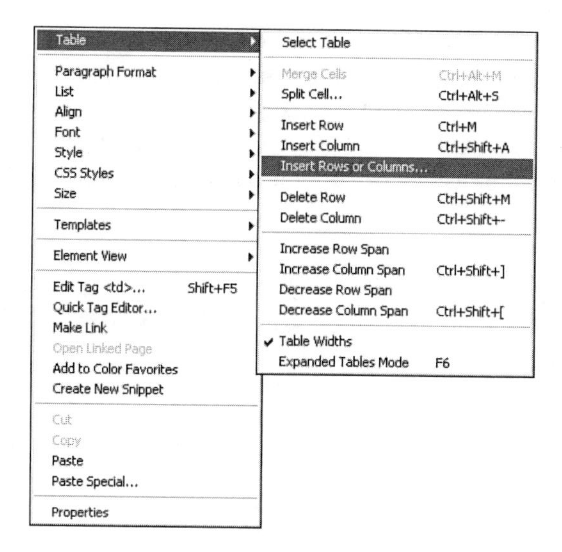

FIGURE 12.11 The context menu has a Table submenu that contains many commands to add, remove, or change the rows and columns of a table.

Changing Column Width and Row Height

You can change column width and row height by dragging the cell borders or by entering values in the Property inspector. If you prefer to eyeball the size, position the cursor over a cell border until the cursor turns into the double-line cursor. Drag the double-line cursor to change the column width or row height.

Use the W (width) and H (height) boxes in the Property inspector to give exact values to widths and heights. Values are expressed in either pixel or percentage values. As with the horizontal rule you created in Hour 3, "Getting Started: Adding Text, Lists, and Previewing in the Browser," a percentage value will change your table size as the size of the browser window changes, whereas a pixel value will always display the table at a constant size.

Resizing a Table and Changing Border Colors

Just as you can change the size of cells, rows, and columns, you can change the size of an entire table. With the entire table selected, drag the resizing handles to make the table a different size. If you have not given width and height values to cells, rows, and columns, the cells distribute themselves proportionally when the entire table size is changed. Or use the W and H boxes in the Property inspector, with the entire table selected, to give the table either pixel or percentage size values.

To clear all the width and height values from a table, select the Table Selector menu when the table is selected in the Document window. This menu contains commands to clear the cell heights and widths. It also contains commands to convert all the values to pixel or percentage values. These commands are handy if you set table attributes to pixel values and want to change them to percentage values or vice versa. Buttons for these commands are available in the lower half of the Property inspector when the table is selected, as shown in Figure 12.12.

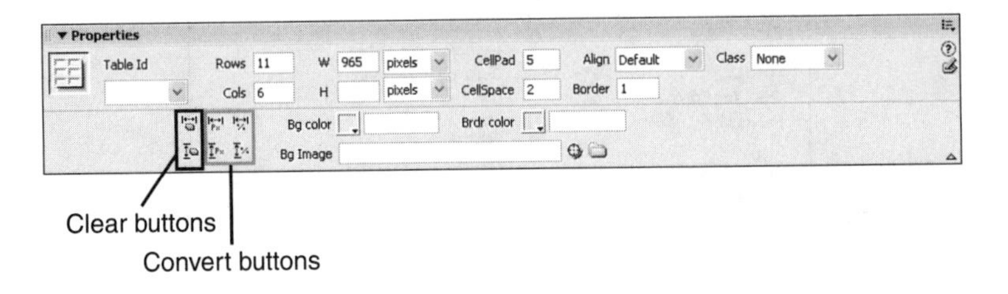

FIGURE 12.12 When an entire table is selected, the Property inspector has buttons available to clear the row height and the column width. There are also buttons available to convert dimension values to pixels or percentage.

Using a Dreamweaver Preset Table Format

Dreamweaver contains a number of preset table formats that you can apply to a table. The format affects the colors, alignment, and border size of the table. Instead of applying colors and alignment to each cell, row, or column, you can use the Format Table command to quickly format an entire table.

Watch Out!

Table Format and Captions Don't Mix

Dreamweaver is unable to use the Table Format command when a table has a caption. If you added a caption when using the Table command, you will need to remove the `<caption>` tag from inside the `<table>` tag.

To apply one of the preset formats to a table, follow these steps:

1. Select the table.
2. If you added a caption (in the accessibility settings section of the Table dialog box) while setting up the table, you need to remove it before using the Format Table command. Dreamweaver doesn't allow you to add formatting to tables that have captions. First delete the text by selecting and deleting it in the Document window. Without moving the cursor, click the `<caption>` tag in the tag selector and press the Delete key. Or, you can go in to Code view and remove the opening tag, the closing tag, and its contents.

3. Select Commands, Format Table. The Format Table dialog box appears (see Figure 12.13).

4. Select a format from the scrolling menu in the upper-left corner of the Format Table dialog box. The little demonstration table in the dialog box shows a preview of the format's appearance.

5. Click the Apply button to apply the format to your table. Change the format until you are satisfied and then click the OK button.

The Apply All Attributes to TD Tags Instead of TR Tags check box at the bottom of the Format Table dialog box enables you to apply the formatting to table cells instead of table rows. Because there are usually more cells than rows, applying the formatting to all the cells results in more HTML code in your web page. The HTML code applied to the cells, however, takes precedence over the code applied to rows.

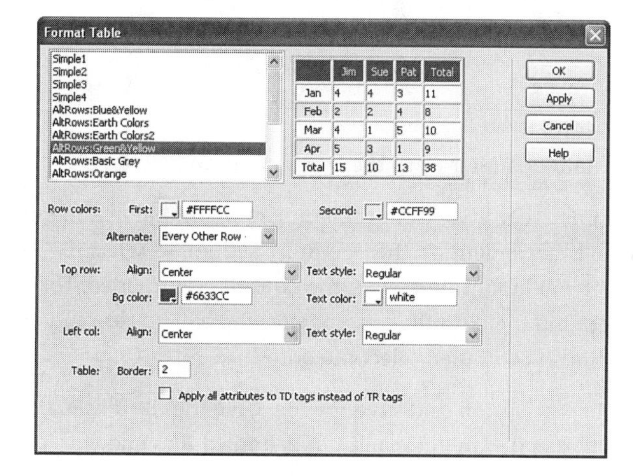

FIGURE 12.13
The Format Table dialog box contains the commands to format all the cells, rows, and columns in a table.

You can use the Format Table command even if you use a custom color scheme for your web page. Select one of the formats available but enter your own custom hexadecimal numbers for specific colors into the boxes. You can also use a custom text color and add a background color for the header row.

Exporting Data from a Table

You can export table data from an HTML table. You can then import the data into a spreadsheet, a database, or another application that has the capability to process delimited data; that is, data separated by a delimiter. A **delimiter** is the character used between the individual data fields. Commonly used delimiters are tabs, spaces, commas, semicolons, and colons. When you are exporting a data file, you need to pick a delimiter that does not appear in the data.

To export table data from Dreamweaver, follow these steps:

1. Select a table or place your cursor in any cell of a table.
2. Select File, Export, Export Table. The Export Table dialog box appears, as shown in Figure 12.14.

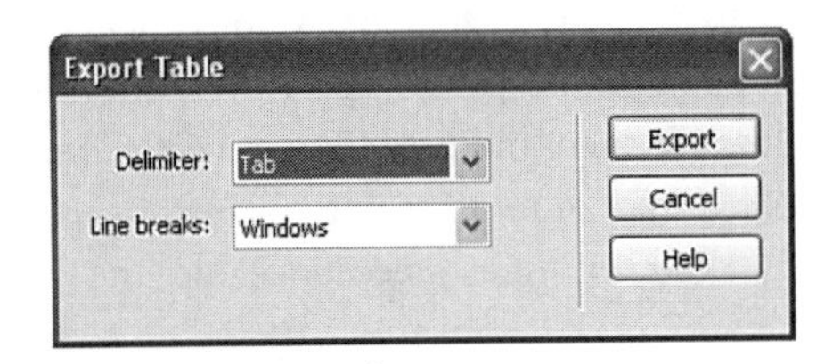

FIGURE 12.14 Open the Export Table dialog box by selecting File, Export. You use this dialog box to export delimited data that can be imported by other applications.

3. Select the data delimiter from the Delimiter drop-down menu.
4. Select the line break style from the Line Breaks drop-down menu. The line break style is dependent on the operating system, so select the operating system that will be running when the data file is imported. For example, if you are sending the data file to someone who will be running a spreadsheet on a Macintosh computer, select Macintosh.
5. Click the Export button and save the file. Give the file a title. Usually comma-delimited files end with `.csv` and tab-delimited files end with `.txt`.

Did you Know?

Get Data from Pages on the Web

Dreamweaver's Export Table command is useful to get information from any web page. You can save a web page with table data from anywhere on the Web by using the browser's Save As or Save Page As command and then open the web page in Dreamweaver. Select a table on the page and then export the data. This enables you to use the data in a spreadsheet application such as Excel or to import it into your own web page.

Importing Table Data

If you already have data in a spreadsheet or database, why retype it or paste it into Dreamweaver? You can import data exported from spreadsheet or database applications into Dreamweaver by using the Import Tabular Data command. Most spreadsheets and database applications can export data into a text file that Dreamweaver can import. You need to know what delimiter character is used in the data file before you can successfully import data into Dreamweaver.

Did you Know?

Exported Files from Excel

Microsoft Excel, a commonly used spreadsheet application, imports and exports files with the file extension `.csv` as comma delimited and files with the file extension `.prn` as space delimited.

Did you Know?

Create a Delimited Data File

Create your own data file to work with by opening a text editor, such as Notepad, and entering some data. Type some data, press the Tab key, type some more data, and then press the Enter (or Return) key; you just created a single record. Create multiple records by repeating this process on subsequent lines in the text file. Save your file and import it into Dreamweaver as a tab-delimited data file. Make sure to save your data file as plain text with the `.txt` file extension.

To import table data to Dreamweaver, follow these steps:

1. Place the insertion point in the Document window where you want the table located.

2. Select the Tabular Data object from the Common tab of the Insert bar or select Insert, Table, Tabular Data. The Import Tabular Data dialog box appears, as shown in Figure 12.15.

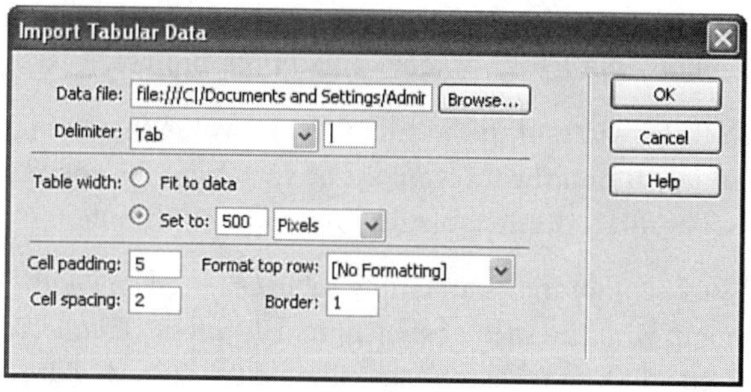

FIGURE 12.15
The Import Tabular Data dialog box enables you to import data files directly into a Dreamweaver table.

3. Select the Browse icon (which looks like a folder) to browse to the table data file to import it into Dreamweaver.
4. Dreamweaver attempts to automatically select the delimiter, or you can select the field delimiter manually from the Delimiter drop-down menu. If the delimiter isn't one of the four common delimiters listed, select Other from the Delimited drop-down menu and enter the delimiter.
5. In the boxes beside Table Width, select whether the new table should fit to the data or be a certain pixel or percentage value.
6. Enter values in the Cell Padding and Cell Spacing text boxes, if necessary. Remember, you can always change these values by editing the table later.
7. Select from the Format Top Row drop-down menu a value for the format of the first (header) row. You need to know whether the data file has column headings that will appear as header cells in your HTML table.
8. Enter a value for the table border size.
9. Click OK to import the table data.

Summary

In this hour, you have learned how to add a table to a web page. You have also learned how to add and remove table cells and rows and how to set the column width and row height of a table. You have entered data into a table and then sorted the data by using the Sort Table command. You have learned how to import data into a Dreamweaver table and how to export table data for an external application to use.

Q&A

Q. ***When I set a column width to a certain value, such as 50 pixels, why doesn't the column display at that value in the browser?***

A. Have you set the width of the entire table to a value that is the sum of all the column values? If not, the table might be stretching the columns to make up for the extra width that the table has in its width attribute.

Some browsers do not make an empty table cell a given width. Web developers came up with the trick of stretching a 1-pixel GIF, called a spacer image, to the desired width to force a table cell to be the correct width. If you use a spacer image, it will require hardly any download time and will not be seen by the viewers.

You'll learn about more about spacer images in Hour 13.

Q. ***Are pixel values or percentage values better to use with tables?***

A. It depends. If you want your table to always appear the same size, use pixel values. However, if the browser window is narrower than the table, the viewer will have to scroll horizontally to view the entire table. Horizontal scrolling is not desirable. If you use percentage values in your table, it's much harder to predict what the final table is going to look like in the viewer's browser. If you use tables with pixel values, you might need to mandate a certain screen resolution to view the table. Be aware that some people disapprove of this type of mandate on the Web.

Workshop

Quiz

1. What are the HTML tags, as displayed in the Dreamweaver tag selector, for a table, a table row, and a table cell? Extra credit: What's the tag for a table header?
2. What are two types of sorts that Dreamweaver can perform on a table?
3. What's the name of the character that separates cell data held in a data text file that can be imported into Dreamweaver?

Quiz Answers

1. The tag for a table is <table>, the tag for a table row is <tr>, and the tag for a table cell is <td>. The tag for a table header is <th>.
2. There are two answers to this question. First, you could sort alphabetically or numerically. Second, you could sort by ascending or descending order.
3. The character that separates cell data held in a text file is called a delimiter.

Exercises

1. Create a table with text in column 1 and numbers in column 2. Try both ascending and descending sorts on both the alphabetic (text) data in column 1 and the numeric data in column 2.

2. Create a table in Dreamweaver, enter some data, and export the table data by using the Table Export command. Remember where you saved the file and then open it with a text editor, such as Notepad. What does the file look like? Add another record in Notepad, making sure you use the same delimiter, and then import that data back in to Dreamweaver.

HOUR 13

Designing Page Layout Using Tables

What You'll Learn in This Hour:

- How to use Dreamweaver's Layout mode
- How to merge and split table cells
- How to align the contents of table cells
- How to nest a table within a table cell
- How to turn a table into a group of layers

In Hour 12, "Displaying Data in Tables," you explored some of the properties of tables and table cells. You used tables in web pages in the same way you might use tables in a spreadsheet or a word processing application—to present data in an organized way. In this hour, you will apply more properties and new commands, using tables to aid web page layout.

By the Way

What Is Page Layout?

Page layout refers to designing the way a page will look when viewed in a browser. When you lay out a page, you position text, menus, and other page elements in an efficient and attractive way.

Tables give web developers the ability to make page elements appear in a specific place onscreen. Dreamweaver enables you to work in Layout mode so you can draw table elements directly onto the Document window. This makes it easy to create tables for page layout.

Using Layout Mode

Traditionally, designing tables for page layout has been a complicated task. Making changes or creating the perfect number of cells has required web developers to **merge** and **split** cells (you'll learn more about these terms later in the hour) in various rows and columns to get pages to look the way they wanted. Dreamweaver includes Layout mode, which enables you to easily draw, move, and edit table cells.

To turn on Layout mode, select the Layout Mode button on the Layout tab of the Insert bar or select View, Table Mode, Layout Mode. You might see a Getting Started in Layout Mode dialog box giving you an introduction to Layout mode; read the information in this dialog box.

When you turn on Layout mode, two layout buttons in the Layout category of the Insert bar become active. One of these buttons, Layout Table, shown in Figure 13.1, draws a layout table; the other, Draw Layout Cell, draws an individual layout cell (a table cell).

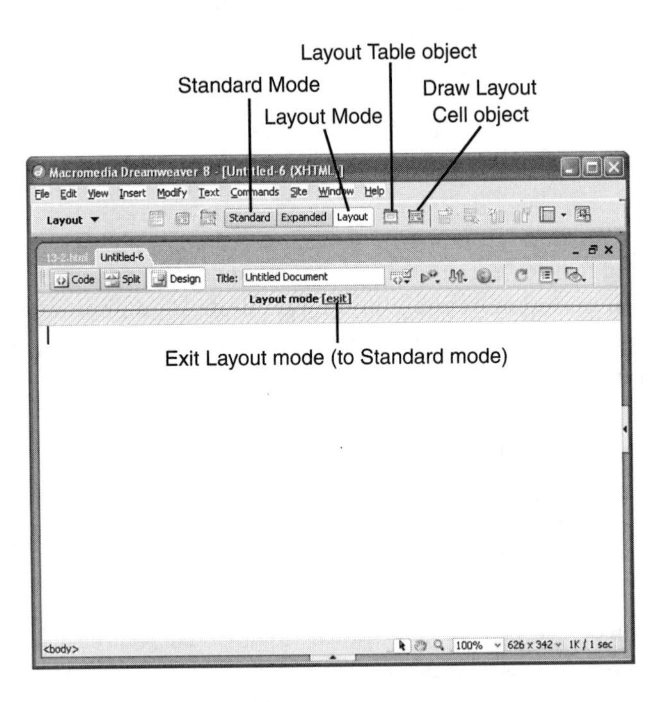

FIGURE 13.1
You select the Layout Mode button in the Layout tab of the Insert bar. You can go back and forth between the Layout and Standard modes.

A **layout table** looks just like a regular HTML table in the web browser, but it looks slightly different in Dreamweaver. In Dreamweaver, you can manipulate layout tables and layout table cells by dragging and dropping them into position on the page.

Adding a Layout Table and Layout Cells

Dreamweaver's Layout mode enables you to draw onto the Document window a design that will appear in table cells. You create areas for content, menus, and other elements of a web page by selecting the Draw Layout Cell command and drawing cells for each page element. This is a different way of creating a table than you used in Hour 12. Using Layout mode isn't appropriate for tabular data types of tables.

Did you Know?

Choose a Screen Resolution for Your Design

Design for a specific screen resolution by first selecting a resolution from the Window Size drop-down menu in Dreamweaver's status bar.

To create a page layout, follow these steps:

1. Select the Layout Mode button in the Layout category of the Insert bar.
2. Select the Draw Layout Cell button in the Insert bar.
3. Draw cells in the Document window for page elements, as shown in Figure 13.2. A layout table is automatically created to hold the layout cells.

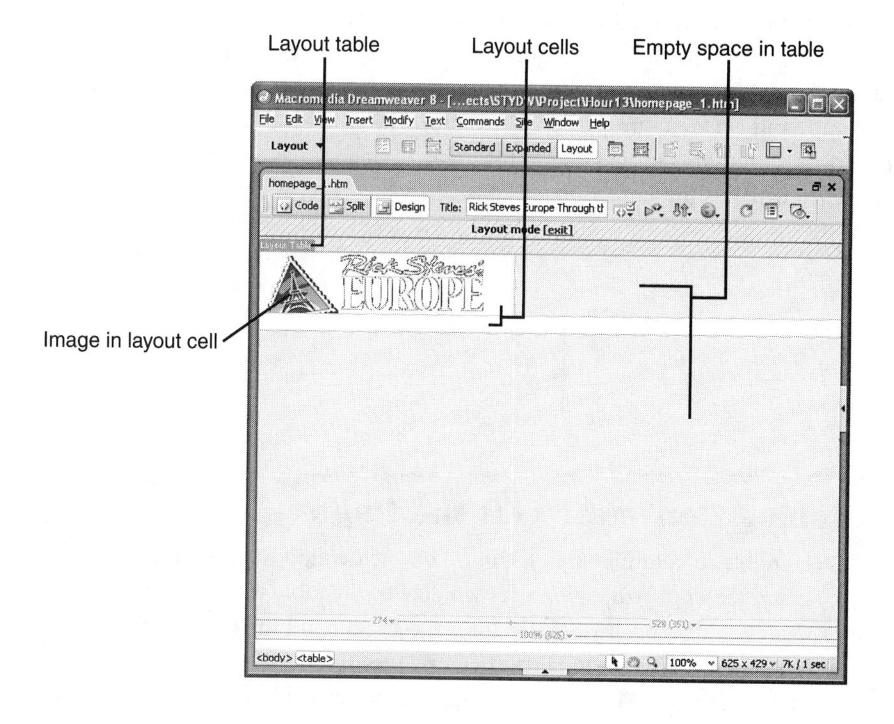

FIGURE 13.2
In Layout mode, you can draw table cells in the Document window. The cells are contained within a layout table.

4. When you place your cursor over the edges of a layout table cell that isn't currently selected, the outline of the cell changes from blue to red. When the cell is red, click the cell to select it. A selected cell appears as a darker solid blue, with resizing handles visible. Move cells by selecting and dragging them.

5. Resize cells by dragging the resizing handles at the corners and sides of the cells.

6. Resize the table that contains the cells by dragging the resizing handles at the corners and sides of the table.

Did you Know?

Draw Multiple Layout Cells

To create multiple layout cells without having to click the Draw Layout Cell button every time, select the Draw Layout Cell button, hold down the Ctrl key in Windows or the Command key on the Mac, and then draw a layout cell. As long as you hold down the Ctrl or Command key, you can continue drawing layout cells.

When you click within a table cell, you display the properties of the cell's content in the Property inspector. But what if you want to see the cell's properties? To quickly select a cell to edit its properties, hold down Ctrl and click (Command+click on the Mac) within the cell. As shown in Figure 13.3, the Property inspector presents the Width, Height, Bg (background color), Horz (horizontal alignment), Vert (vertical alignment), and No Wrap properties. These properties are exactly the same table cell properties that you learned about last hour. There's one additional property, Autostretch, which is unique to layout tables.

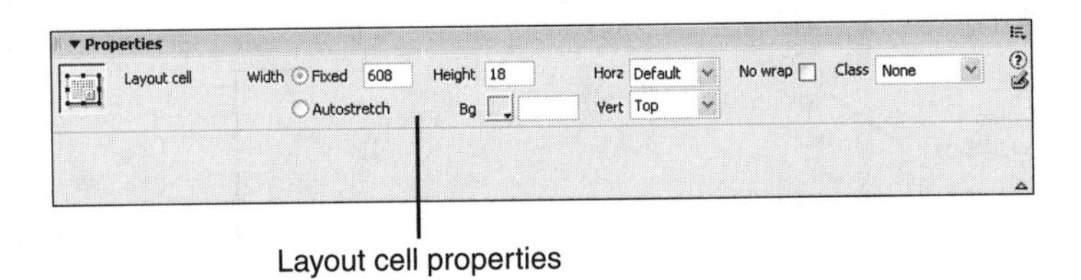

FIGURE 13.3 In Layout mode, the Property inspector displays layout cell properties.

Stretching Content to Fit the Page

Autostretch enables a column to stretch to fill all the available space in the browser window. No matter what size the browser window is, the table will span the entire window. When you turn on Autostretch for a specific cell, all the cells in that column will be stretched. This setting is particularly useful for cells that contain the main content of the page. The menus can stay the same width, but the content can stretch to take up all the available space. Or you can place a stretched cell on the right side of a table and stretch the background colors over the width of the screen, no matter what the user's resolution.

Did you Know?

Expanded Tables Mode Shows Table Borders

Sometimes it's difficult to see the edges of tables when they don't have a border. You can turn on the Expanded Tables mode, using the button directly to the left of the Layout Mode button in the Insert bar, to display borders within Dreamweaver. Or, select View, Table Mode, Expanded Tables Mode. This doesn't actually add borders to the web page. It simply displays borders and adds a little artificial space between the cells in Dreamweaver so the table is easier to see.

Dreamweaver will automatically add spacer images to table cells to make sure they remain the size that you intend in all browsers. The spacer image trick is an old trick used by web developers to ensure that table cells don't collapse when viewed in certain browsers. A transparent 1-pixel GIF is stretched to a specific width. This image is not visible in the browser. The GIF maintains the width of all the cells that are *not* in the autostretched column. If Dreamweaver did not add a spacer image, any columns without an image to hold their size might collapse.

To turn on Autostretch, follow these steps:

1. Select a cell by holding Ctrl while clicking the cell.
2. Select the Autostretch radio button in the Property inspector.
3. Now instead of the width of the column, the Table selector displays a squiggly line for the autostretched column, as shown in Figure 13.4.

You can also apply the Autostretch command by selecting the column header menu, shown in Figure 13.5. Each column heading displays the width of the column in pixels. You can also simply add a spacer image to the column or remove it by selecting the appropriate commands from this menu. When a column has a spacer image added, the line at the top of the column appears thicker.

You can set a spacer image for a site in the Dreamweaver Preferences dialog box. After you have set a spacer image for the site, Dreamweaver no longer prompts you to create or choose a spacer image; the code for the spacer image is simply added to your web page. Create or select a spacer image for an entire site by opening the Layout Mode category of the Dreamweaver Preferences dialog box, as shown in Figure 13.6. Note that you can also use this category to change the colors in which layout objects appear in Dreamweaver and whether spacer images are automatically inserted.

Autostretched column

Macromedia Dreamweaver 8 - [...ents\projects\STYDW\Project\Hour13\homepage.htm (XHTML)]
File Edit View Insert Modify Text Commands Site Window Help
Layout Standard Expanded Layout
homepage.htm
Code Split Design Title: Untitled Document
Layout mode [exit]
<body> <table> <tr> <td>
Properties
Layout cell Width Fixed Autostretch Height 96 Bg Horz Default Vert Top No wrap Class None

Autostretch setting

FIGURE 13.4
The Table selector shows that the column is autostretched instead of having an absolute width value in pixels.

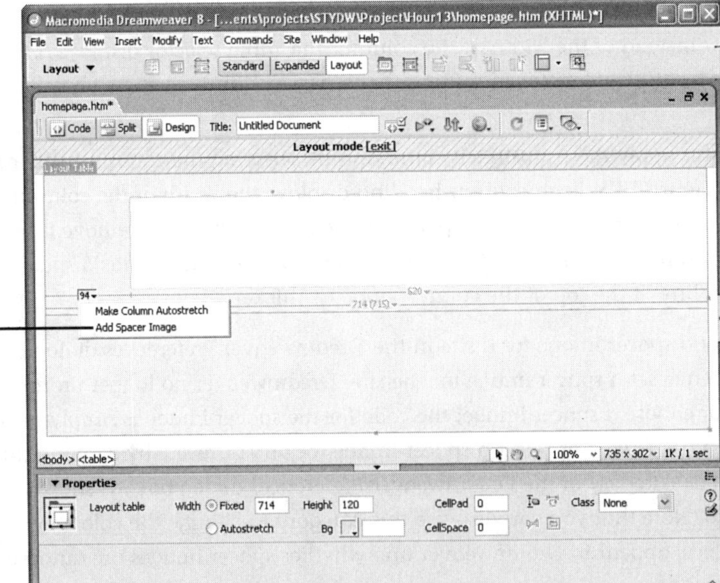

FIGURE 13.5
Use the column header menu for a layout table column to turn on Autostretch for a table column.

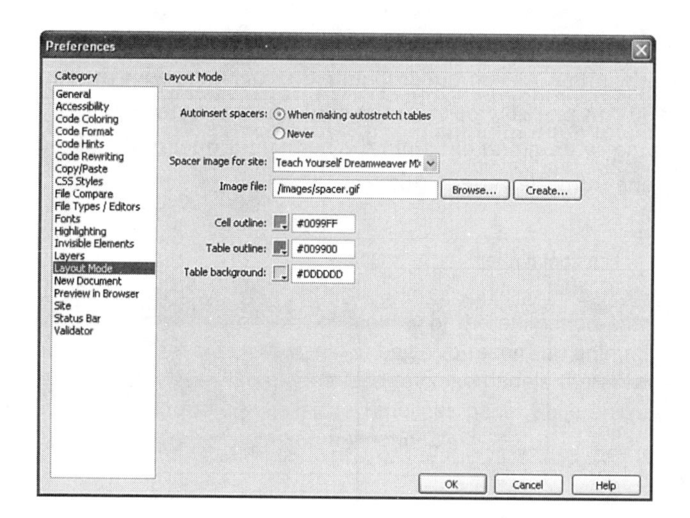

FIGURE 13.6 Set a spacer image for an entire site in the Layout Mode category of the Dreamweaver Preferences dialog box.

Watch Out!

The Spacer Images Are in the Bottom Row

Dreamweaver adds an additional row at the bottom of your table for the spacer images. Do not remove this row.

Fine-Tuning Your Design in Table Layout Mode

When working in Layout mode, I find it's easier to begin adding cells and content in the upper-left corner of the web page. Then I work down and to the right, adding cells, content, and nesting new tables (you'll explore this later this hour). You might find that as you add content and new table cells that the table changes and you have to go back and adjust the existing cells. This seems to happen less if you begin in the upper-left corner of the web page.

There are several tools in Dreamweaver that can help you create a page layout. Turning on Guides (View, Guides, Show Guides) displays lines on the screen that you can use to guide your design. For instance, select View, Guides, 1024×768, Maximized to add guides outlining the page design space you would have available for a web page displayed at that screen resolution.

You can create your own guides. First, you need to turn on the rulers by selecting View, Rulers, Show. Notice that you can also set the measurement units to pixels, inches, and centimeters under View, Rulers. I usually work in pixels.

To add a new guide on the screen, click within the ruler and drag a guide into the Document window. As you are dragging, the cursor displays the current pixel location so you can precisely position the guide, as shown in Figure 13.7. You add a horizontal guide by dragging one from the horizontal ruler and add a vertical guide by dragging one from the vertical ruler.

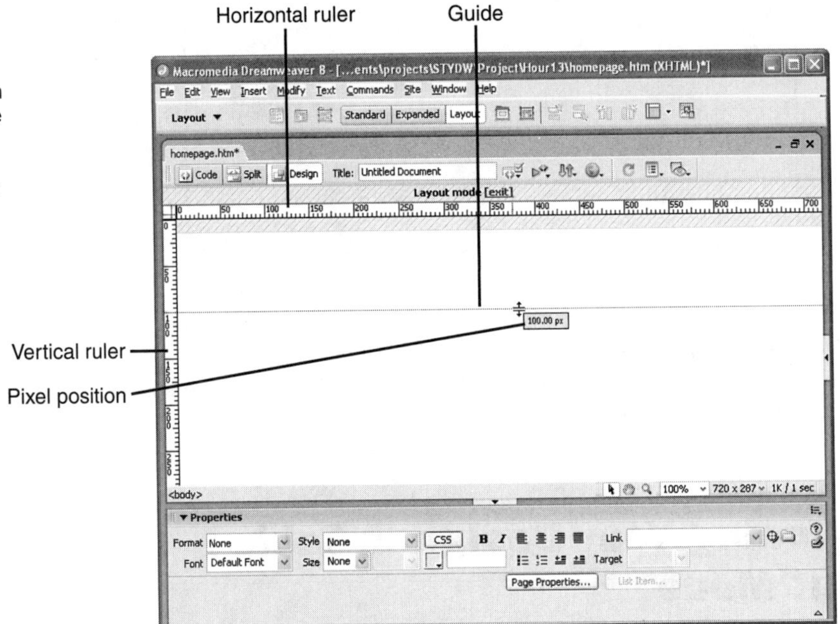

FIGURE 13.7 Drag a custom guide from the ruler and position it in the Document window.

It's easy to accidentally move a guide while working in Dreamweaver, so after you've set your guides you should lock them (View, Guides, Lock Guides). You can always unlock them by choosing this command again later. Sometimes the guides get in the way of viewing the page design so you can turn the guides off without actually removing them by selecting View, Guides, Show Guides and removing the check mark by the command in the Guides submenu.

The Zoom tool is also helpful while designing a page layout in Dreamweaver. This tool is in the status bar of the Dreamweaver Document window, next to the Select tool and the Hand tool. Select the Zoom tool and click on the Document window to zoom in on the design to fine-tune positioning, as shown in Figure 13.8. After you've zoomed in you'll need to choose the Select tool in order to select objects such as table cells or images.

To quickly return to 100%, simply double-click the Zoom tool.

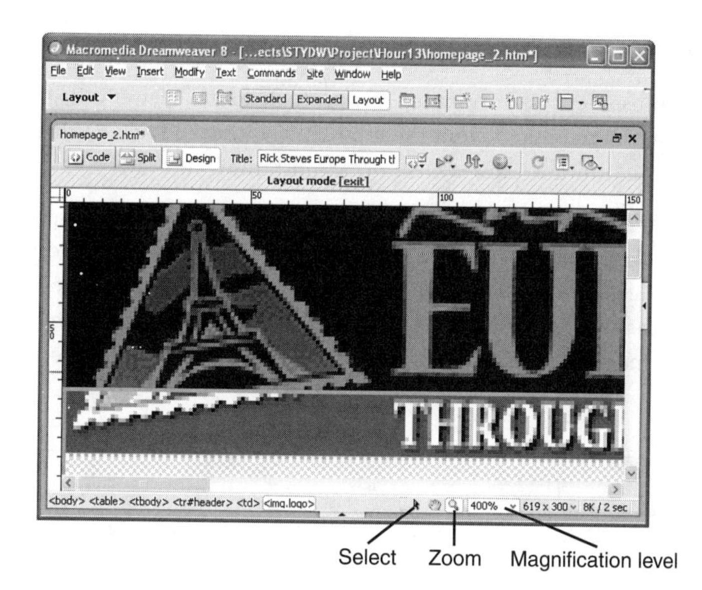

FIGURE 13.8
You can zoom in on the page design using the Zoom tool.

Watch Out!

Don't Zoom Accidentally

It's good to get into the habit of clicking on the Select tool immediately after finishing using the Zoom tool. Otherwise, you'll waste a lot of time accidentally zooming.

Editing a Table in Standard Mode

After you've designed your layout in Layout mode, you need to add content to the table. You can also edit your layout table and add content in Standard mode by changing the attributes of the table and its cells. You also need to set the alignment of the contents of the cells. The settings discussed next are available only when you are in Standard mode. You can either click the Standard Mode button in the Layout category of the Insert bar or click the [exit] link in the Layout mode bar at the top of the Document window.

Use Both Standard and Layout Modes

When I'm working on tables in Dreamweaver, I usually go back and forth multiple times between Standard and Layout modes. Some procedures are easier in Layout mode, such as sizing, moving, and drawing table cells, while I think it's easier to set various table properties in Standard mode.

Merging and Splitting Table Cells

You might want some rows or columns in your table to have fewer cells than other rows. For example, you might want the top row of a table to have a title that is centered over all the columns. How do you accomplish that?

You can increase or decrease the column span and row span by either **splitting** or **merging** cells. To merge an entire row so that it appears as one cell, select the row and click the Merge button (see Figure 13.9) or right-click (Control+click on the Mac) anywhere on the row and select the Merge Cells command from the Table submenu of the context menu. Now the content of the entire row can be positioned over all the columns.

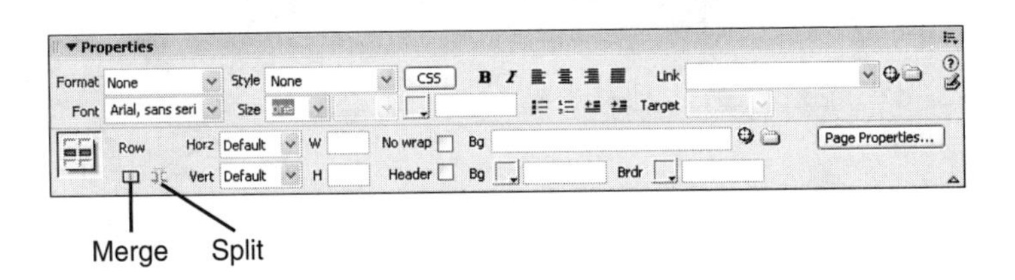

FIGURE 13.9
The Merge button appears in the Property inspector when an entire row is selected. This button causes all the selected cells to appear as one cell.

Use the Split Cell command to add additional rows or columns to a cell. The Split button is beside the Merge button in the Property inspector. Select the Split button or right-click (Control+click on the Mac) in the cell and select the Split Cell command from the Table submenu of the context menu, and the Split Cell dialog box appears, as shown in Figure 13.10. Enter the number of rows or columns you would like the cell to be split into and click OK. Now a single cell is split into multiple cells.

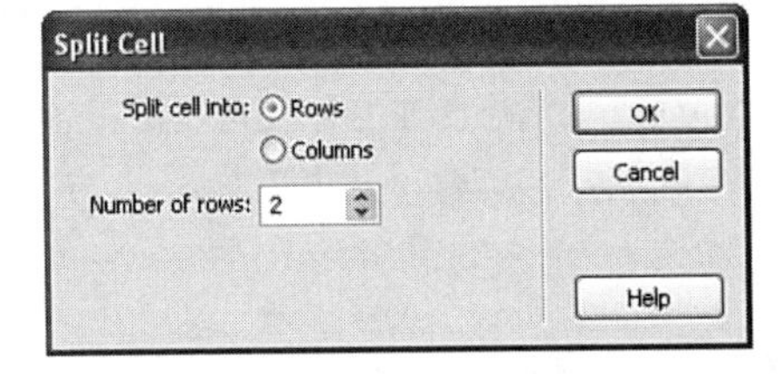

FIGURE 13.10
The Split Cell dialog box enables you to split a single cell into multiple columns or rows.

Aligning Table Cell Contents

You can align the contents of a cell or a group of cells vertically—from top to bottom. The Vertical Alignment drop-down menu (see Figure 13.11) sets the vertical alignment for the contents of an individual cell or a group of cells. When setting the vertical alignment, you have the following options:

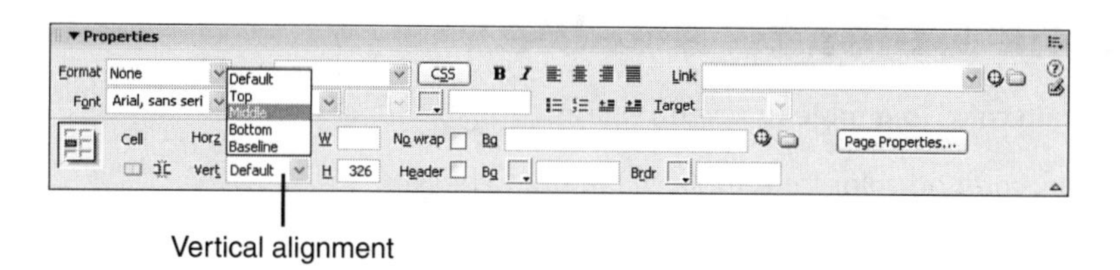

FIGURE 13.11
The Vertical Alignment drop-down menu aligns cell contents vertically from the top and bottom of the cell.

- **Default**—This is usually the same as middle alignment of the cell contents.
- **Top**—This aligns the cell contents at the top of the cell.
- **Middle**—This aligns the cell contents in the middle of the cell.
- **Bottom**—This aligns the cell contents at the bottom of the cell.
- **Baseline**—This is applied to multiple cells in a row, aligning the bottom of the objects across all cells. For instance, if you have very large text in the first cell and small text in the second cell, the bottom of each line of text will be aligned with baseline vertical alignment.

Align the contents of a cell or a group of cells horizontally—from left to right—with the Horizontal Alignment drop-down menu, shown in Figure 13.12. When setting the horizontal alignment, you have the following options:

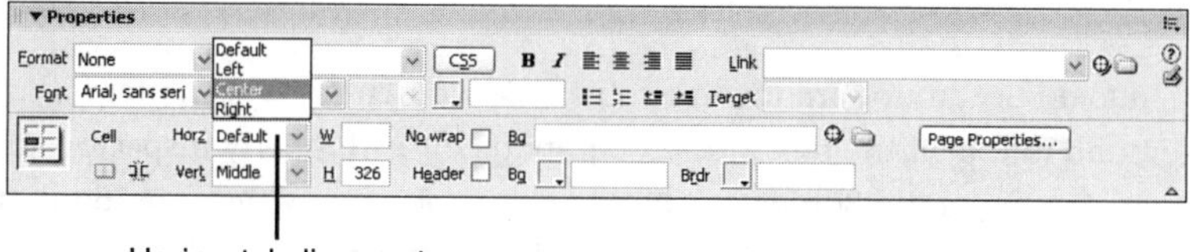

FIGURE 13.12
The Horizontal Alignment drop-down menu aligns cell contents horizontally from the left and the right sides of the cell.

- **Default**—This is usually the same as left for cell content and center for header cell content.
- **Left**—This aligns the cell contents on the left of the cell.
- **Center**—This aligns the cell contents in the center of the cell.
- **Right**—This aligns the cell contents on the right of the cell.

Adding Color to a Table

You can add color to a table in several places:

- A background color for a table cell or group of cells
- A background color for the entire table
- A border color for a table cell or group of cells
- A border color for the entire table

Figure 13.13 shows where the different color settings are located in the Property inspector. Cell properties always have priority over the same properties in the table. For instance, if you applied blue as the table background color and then applied red to an individual cell, the one cell would be red and all the other cells would be blue. Set the table background and table border in the Property inspector. The Brdr Color setting determines the border color of the entire table.

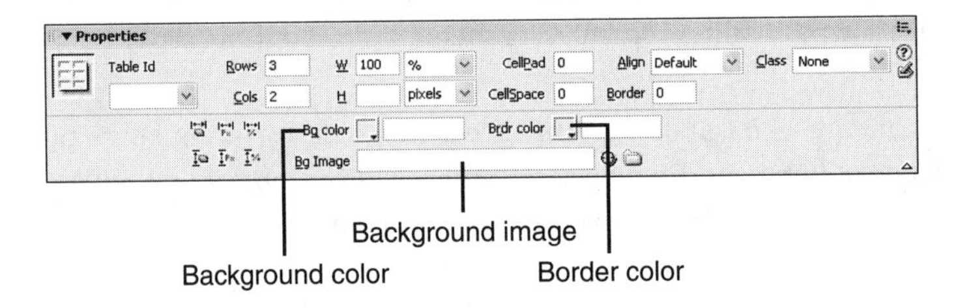

FIGURE 13.13 Adding colors in the Property inspector controls the table border and table background color attributes.

You can add a background image to a table cell or an entire table. Enter the URL for a background image in the box labeled Bg Image in the Property inspector. You can enter a pixel value in the Border text box to see a border; however, you don't usually add borders to a layout table. If you add a border color and don't see the border, you might have the border size set to zero. Set the cell background and cell border colors in the Property inspector with a cell or group of cells selected.

Nesting a Table Within a Table

Placing a table within a table cell creates a **nested** table. The dimensions of the table cell limit the nested table's width and height. To nest a table, place the insertion point inside a table cell and insert a new table (Insert, Table).

You can also draw a table when in Layout mode using the Layout table object in the Layout category of the Insert bar. Drawing a layout table by using this tool enables you to draw a table over any area in the page that doesn't already have an existing cell, as shown in Figure 13.14.

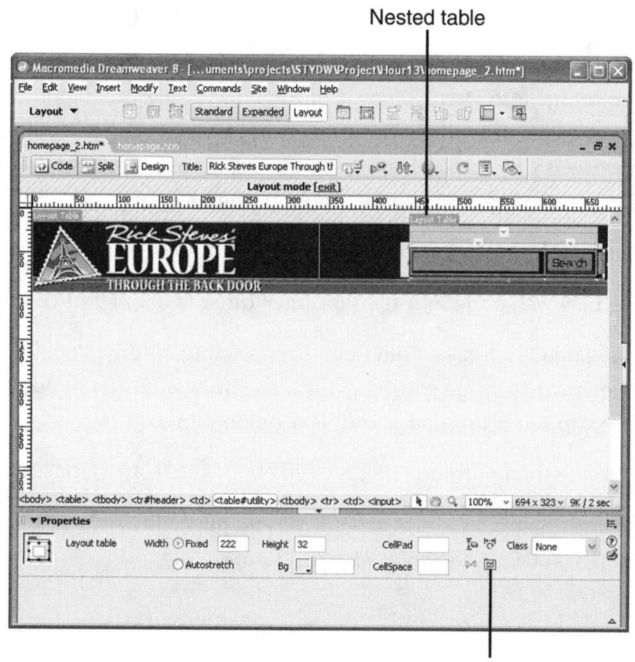

FIGURE 13.14 Draw a nested table in Layout mode in an area of a table where there isn't yet a cell drawn.

Watch Out!

Don't Use Too Many Nested Tables

It's fine to nest tables within tables within tables. But if you nest too much, the browser might display the tables slowly. Make sure that your design doesn't get too complicated.

Using a Tracing Image to Transfer a Design to a Web Page

A tracing image is useful when you are creating a page design and you have an image showing all the completed page elements. You can use this image as a **tracing image**. Instead of estimating where the elements go onscreen, you can display a tracing image and lay the individual image and text elements over the tracing image perfectly. A tracing image makes it easy to align objects.

I'm lucky enough to get to work with talented graphic designers when I work on most of my projects. They will usually design the page layout in a graphics tool such as Fireworks or Photoshop. I can ask them to give me a "flattened" version of the file, meaning a single JPG with all of the layers in the graphic merged into one. Then I can use this as a tracing image in Dreamweaver.

Load a tracing image into Dreamweaver in the Page Properties dialog box. The tracing image is visible only in Dreamweaver and is never visible in the browser. A tracing image covers any background color or background image. The background color or background image will still be visible in the browser.

To load a tracing image into Dreamweaver, follow these steps:

1. Create a new web page in a site you have already defined in Dreamweaver.
2. Open the Page Properties dialog box (by selecting Modify, Page Properties) and select the Tracing Image category. Click the Browse button beside the Tracing Image box to select the image that is a tracing image.
3. Browse to the tracing image file. It needs to be a GIF, JPEG, or PNG.
4. Drag the Transparency slider to set how opaque (solid) or transparent the tracing image will be, as shown in Figure 13.15.

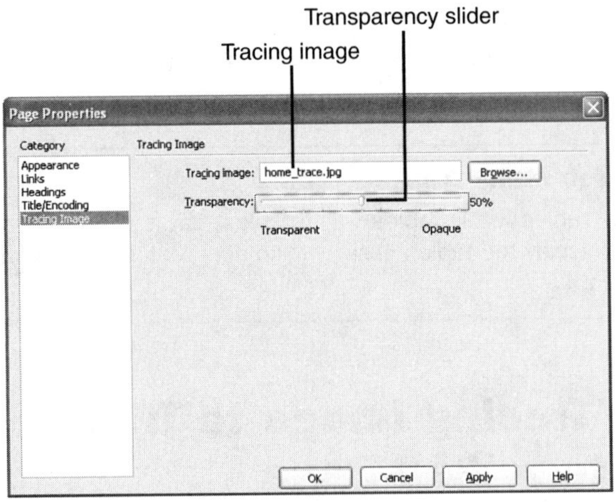

FIGURE 13.15 You can load a tracing image into the Page Properties dialog box. Set the transparency with the slider.

5. Click OK. Your tracing image appears in the background of the Document window, with the transparency setting you specified.
6. Draw the design that you see in the tracing image, as shown in Figure 13.16. You also need to look in the Assets panel to see how the images in the design have been sliced up.

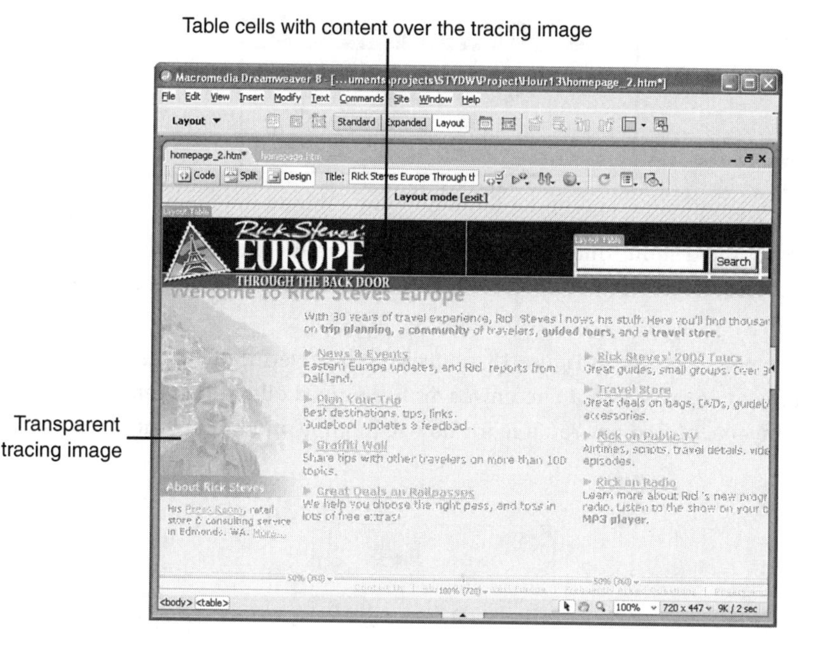

FIGURE 13.16
With a tracing image loaded, you can trace a design onto a web page.

Did you Know?

View the Entire Tracing Image

If you use a tracing image with 0-pixel margins for the page, you will lose the 10 pixels at the top of the screen when you are in Layout mode. The Layout mode banner across the top blocks some of the tracing image. You can turn off the 10 pixels of the Layout mode banner by selecting View, Visual Aids, Hide All.

Turning a Table into a Group of Layers

During Hour 15, "Using Dynamic HTML and Layers," you will use layers to position objects on a web page. **Layers** allow absolute placement of objects on the page. Whereas tables are positioned relative to the content on the page, layers can position content anywhere on the page. Using layers is another effective way to position content on the screen, and Dreamweaver can convert a table into a group of layers.

To convert a table into a group of layers, follow these steps:

1. Select the table and make sure you're in Standard mode. The Convert Tables to Layers command is unavailable while you are in Layout mode.
2. Select Modify, Convert, Convert Tables to Layers. (Did you notice that there's also a command to convert layers to a table?) The Convert Tables to Layers dialog box appears, as shown in Figure 13.17.

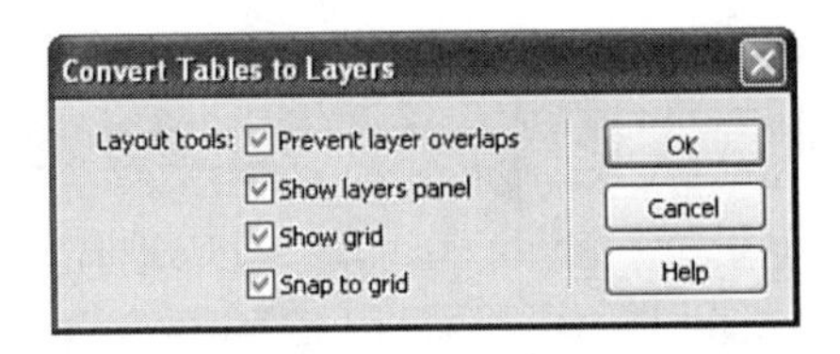

FIGURE 13.17
The Convert Tables to Layers dialog box creates a layer for every table cell.

3. Accept the defaults and click OK. (You'll explore the properties controlled by the check boxes in the Convert Tables to Layers dialog box in Hour 15.)

The Layers panel, shown in Figure 13.18, lists all the layers that Dreamweaver created from the table. Notice that Dreamweaver has named all of the layers `layer1`, `layer2`, `layer3`, and so on. You'll learn how to rename and manipulate layers in Hour 15.

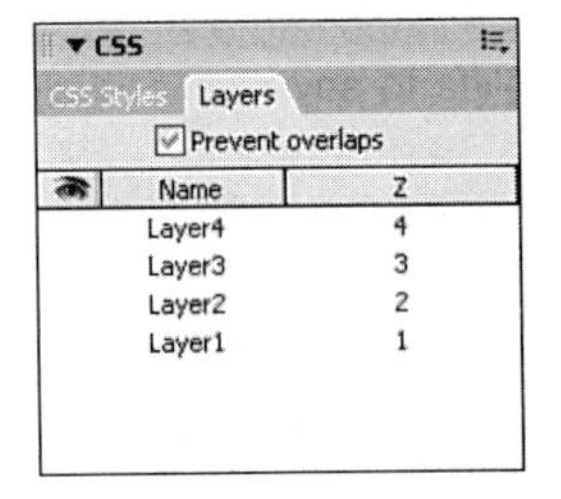

FIGURE 13.18
The Layers panel lists the layers that were created from a table.

Summary

In this hour, you have learned how to use Layout mode to draw cells and tables to create a page layout. You have used the column and row spanning properties to merge and split individual cells and groups of cells. You have also learned how to align the contents of cells both vertically and horizontally. You have learned how to apply colors to an entire table, table cells, and table borders, and you have learned how to convert a table into a group of layers.

Q&A

Q. ***Why shouldn't I center objects in a table cell by using the text alignment buttons?***

A. You can use the text alignment buttons to center an object. Doing so will add an additional tag around the selected object and then apply the Center property. Everything in the table cell might not be centered when you do this, however. Only the objects within the added tags will be centered. If you later add an object to the cell, it might or might not be centered, depending on exactly where the insertion point was when you inserted the new object. Using the alignment properties of a cell is the way to make certain all objects in the cell will have the alignment you want.

Q. ***Every time I position a table cell, everything in the table moves! How can I prevent this from happening?***

A. You can't prevent it from happening, but you can make it easier by first positioning images and text in the upper-left corner and then working to the right and down. The cells are relative to the upper-left corner of the table, so you need to solidify the positioning in that area first.

Q. ***I like fine-positioning table cells by using the arrow keys, but it takes a long time to move the cells across the screen. Any way to make it go faster?***

A. Hold down the Shift key while using the arrow keys to position table cells 10 pixels per keypress instead of a single pixel per keypress. Also, remember you can use the Zoom tool to see your design up close.

Workshop

Quiz

1. If you apply a background color to an entire table and a background color to a cell, which color shows up in the cell?
2. What's the easiest way to add a row at the bottom of a table?
3. How do you horizontally align all the objects in a cell in the center?

Quiz Answers

1. The cell attributes take precedence over the table attributes, so the color you applied to the cell will show up.
2. Put the insertion point in the last cell (the one in the lower right) and press the Tab key. Or, with the table selected, add to the number of rows in the Property inspector. It's your choice.
3. Put the insertion point in the cell and select Center from the Horz drop-down menu in the Property inspector.

Exercises

1. Surf the Web, looking for web page layouts that use tables. You might be surprised at how many websites use tables heavily. If you are not sure whether a site uses tables, select the View Source command in your browser and look for table tags in the code.

2. Insert a table and experiment with merging and splitting cells. Insert a nested table into one of the cells in Standard mode or draw a nested table in Layout mode. If you are drawing in Layout mode, make sure you are drawing on an area of the table that does not have a cell drawn in it.

3. Find a web page design that you like and take a screen capture of it (by pressing Alt+PrtScrn in Windows or Shift+Command+3 on the Mac—or use Mac OS X's Grab utility). Save this screen capture in a web image format (GIF, JPEG, or PNG) and load it in Dreamweaver as a tracing image. If you have a graphics program available, you can crop the web page design out of the browser so that you have only the web page visible in your image. Lay the page out by using layout tables and table cells.

HOUR 14

Using Frames to Display Multiple Web Pages

What You'll Learn in This Hour:

- The difference between frames and framesets
- How to target content to load in a specific frame
- How to set frame attributes such as scrolling and borders
- How to use behaviors to load content into more than one frame at a time

Love 'em or hate 'em, many people seem to have strong opinions about frames. Creating a web page with frames enables you to display multiple web pages in a single browser window. The user can select a link in one frame that loads content into another frame, enabling the user to stay in the same browser window.

Using frames can be an excellent way to present information on your website, but frames can also be a navigational nightmare for your users. Make sure that your frames are carefully created so the user can navigate to links you provide in your site without being perpetually caught in your frames.

Certain types of websites are excellent candidates for a frame structure. A good example is a site with a table of contents constantly available so the user can make multiple selections. Why make the user continually navigate back to a table of contents page? You can load the table of contents page into a frame and load the requested content into another frame so both are present onscreen.

There are several disadvantages to using frames. Because frames enable you to load web pages without changing the web page address in the browser, there is no way to bookmark the current web page. Your users might browse to a web page within your frames and bookmark it, but when they return, they return to the home page instead of the page they thought they bookmarked.

Did you Know?

> **What Frame Configurations Are Available?**
>
> To see common frame configurations, open up Dreamweaver's New Document dialog box (File, New) and select the Framesets category. As you select the various framesets available, you can see a preview of the configuration in the Preview portion of the dialog box. Each section of a frame layout represents an individual web page.

Another disadvantage is that search engines might not properly index a website that uses frames, making it difficult for users to find content within the site. Visually impaired users visiting a website using a text-to-speech browser might not be able to access framed content. Later this hour you'll use Dreamweaver accessibility settings to make it easier for these users to navigate your site.

In spite of the disadvantages, there still may be valid reasons for creating web pages that use frames. When it's necessary to view multiple web pages at the same time, using a framed web page is the only solution. It also might be advantageous to present one frame that remains visible while the user is scrolling content in another frame.

> **What Is a Web Page?**
>
> The description *web page* can get a bit confusing when you are talking about frames. A page can either represent an individual HTML file, of which there might be multiple instances in a frame layout, or it may represent a view of everything that is currently visible in a browser window.

Creating a Frameset

Frames consist of individual web pages—one for each frame—held together by a web page that contains the frameset. The **frameset** defines the size and position of the individual frames. You can either load an existing web page into a frame or create a new web page. The frameset contains the instructions that hold all the frames together. The frameset web page is only visible to the user through the content held in the frames defined by the frameset.

Figure 14.1 shows an example of a web page using frames. One web page called `banner.htm` is displayed across the top of the framed page. The lower part of the page, below the banner, is split into two frames: the table of contents, `TOC.htm`, on the left and the main display area, `main.htm`, on the right. The links in the table of contents frame load content into the main frame. The banner and the table of contents remain constant, while different web pages are loaded into the main display area.

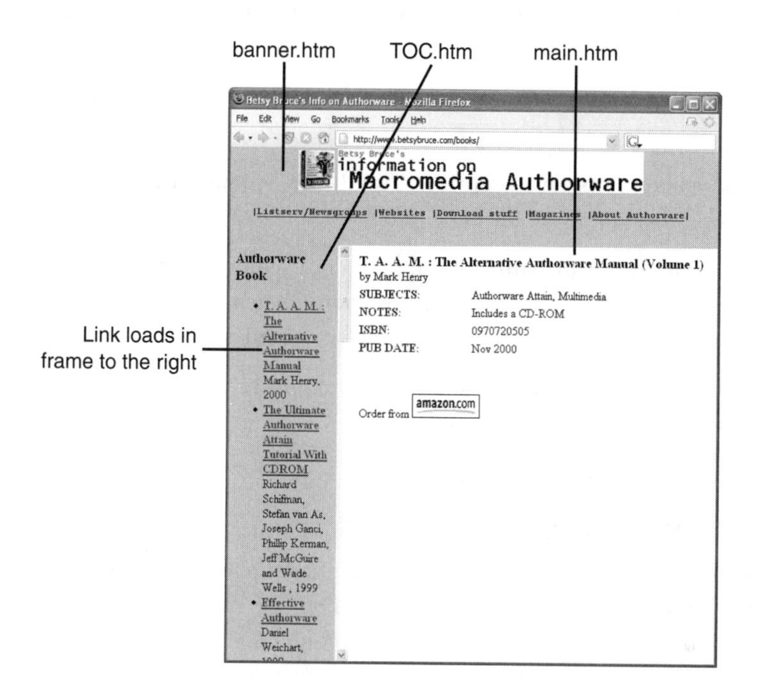

FIGURE 14.1
This web page contains three frames: one at the top, one in the lower left that contains the table of contents, and one in the lower right that displays different web pages when the links in the table of contents are selected.

Did you Know?

Frame Layouts Simplify Site Browsing

Imagine if you could have a book's table of contents visible on every page of a book. And that you could simply touch an entry in the table of contents entry to instantly turn the page to that section of the book. That is the idea behind using frames.

When you are creating projects that use frames, you might want to use the prebuilt framesets that come with Dreamweaver. A variety of configurations are available; you access them by clicking the icons in the Frames menu of the Layout category in the Insert bar (or by selecting Insert, HTML, Frames). This hour you'll begin by creating a set of frames in a frameset by hand. This will familiarize you with how frames work, how they are named, and how they are saved.

When you are working with frames, using the Save command becomes more complicated than it usually is. Are you saving the web page in a frame, or are you saving the frameset? While you are working with frames, Dreamweaver activates the

Save Frameset and the Save Frameset As commands in the File menu. You can also use the Save All command to save all the frame content and the frameset, too. There is also an additional Open command, the Open in Frame command, that appears in the File menu when you are working with frames. You can open an existing web page in a frame by using this command.

In a few minutes you'll get started creating some frames. There are three methods of creating frames:

- View the frame borders (by selecting View, Visual Aids, Frame Borders) and then drag the borders to divide the page into frames.
- Use the commands under the Frameset submenu in Dreamweaver's Modify menu. You might need to use these menu commands when the frame configuration you want to create is not possible by dragging borders.
- Use the prebuilt frame configurations that are available in the Frames menu of the Layout category in the Insert bar.

Viewing Frame Borders

You need to view the frame borders before you can drag them to create frames. Select View, Visual Aids, Frame Borders. You see a set of borders surrounding the page. These borders are visual aids within Dreamweaver and don't represent how the finished page will look in the browser. While you are working with your web pages, you can move these borders to resize your design. When you are ready to turn them off, simply select View, Visual Aids, Frame Borders again to toggle the setting off.

Splitting a Page into Frames

To begin creating frames, drag the frame borders. Create two frames, top and bottom, in an empty web page by dragging the top frame border down, as shown in Figure 14.2. You now have three web pages: the page in the top frame, the page in the bottom frame, and the web page with the frameset. When viewers enter the URL of the frameset page, the browser automatically loads the individual pages that belong in each frame.

Get Rid of a Frame

If you change your mind about a frame, just drag the border off the edge of the page, and it will be deleted.

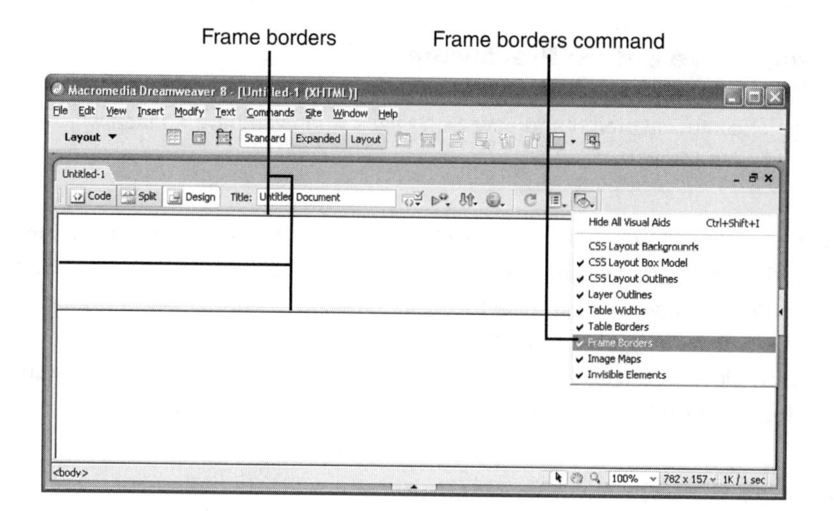

FIGURE 14.2 When you view the frame borders, you can simply drag one of the borders to create frames and a frameset.

Naming Frames

Naming and keeping track of frames can be confusing. Type the word `banner` into the top frame's web page. With the cursor in the top frame, save the web page as `banner.htm` after selecting File, Save Frame. When you are first working with frames, it's least confusing to save each frame individually. Repeat this procedure with the bottom frame: Type the word `main` in the frame and save it as `main.htm`. Your frames will look as shown in Figure 14.3.

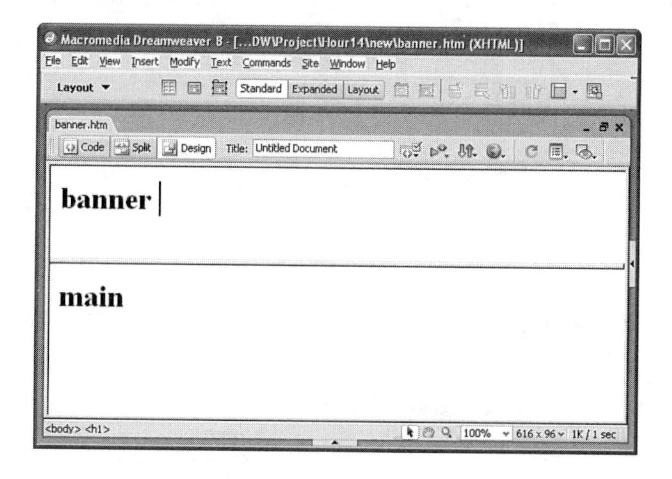

FIGURE 14.3 This web page is divided into two frames named `banner.htm` and `main.htm`.

Watch Out!

Always Save Before Previewing

Be careful not to preview the web page before you save, or you will be caught in a series of confusing prompts to save web pages when you have no idea which page you are saving!

When the Frame Borders command is not checked under the Visual Aids submenu of the View menu, the web page appears as it will in the browser, without borders. Later in this hour, you will change the actual border sizes and other attributes of frames. It can be helpful to turn off the frame borders to approximate how the frames will look in the browser. Turn off the frame borders to see what your web page looks like without them and then turn the borders on again.

By the Way

Frames Objects Prompt Naming

When you use any of the built-in frames layouts that come with Dreamweaver, you are prompted to name the frame when you insert the object.

Now you will divide the bottom frame into two frames. Don't drag the left frame border because you will end up with four frames—two on the top and two on the bottom. Instead, split the bottom frame into two frames by using the commands under Modify, Framesets. To do this, follow these steps:

1. With the cursor in the bottom frame, select Modify, Frameset, Split Frame Right, as shown in Figure 14.4. This places the existing frame on the right and adds a new frame on the left.

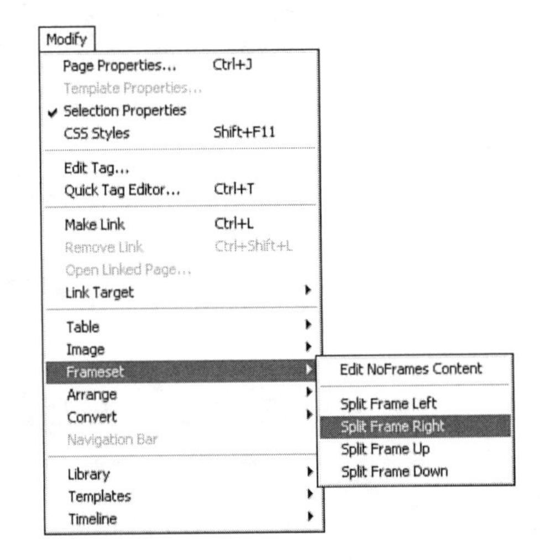

FIGURE 14.4 The Frameset submenu in the Modify menu lists a number of commands you use to split frames into multiple frames.

2. Type **`table of contents`** into the web page within the new frame (lower-left frame).

3. Save the web page where you just typed by making sure your cursor is in the frame and then selecting File, Save Frame. You can name this web page `toc.htm`.

You have created three frames and saved the web pages they contain. It's sometimes difficult to select the frameset. The easiest way is to place your cursor over one of the frame borders and click. You can tell you have the frameset selected when you see the `<frameset>` tag in the tag selector. Save the frameset web page by selecting File, Save Frameset. You can name the frameset `index.htm`. The URL of the frameset is the only address the viewer will need to view all the web pages.

While you have the frameset selected, give the web page a title in the toolbar. Because the titles of the individual frames do not appear in the browser's title bar, it isn't necessary to give a frame a title. However, it's always good practice to give web pages titles, and if you ever reference the web page outside the frames, you will be assured that each page already has a title.

You just saved each of the web pages individually. But if you hadn't already saved the web pages in the frames and the frameset web page, Dreamweaver will prompt you to save before you preview in the browser. The first time you save, it's less confusing to individually save the web pages contained in each frame and the frameset web page than to save all the files at once when Dreamweaver prompts you. Dreamweaver will prompt you to save the files every time you preview the frames.

Using the Frames Panel

The Frames panel (which you open by selecting Window, Frames), shown in Figure 14.5, enables you to select individual frames and set frame attributes. Notice that the Frames panel visually represents the configuration of the frames in a web page. Select a frame by clicking the frame's representation in the Frames panel. You can also select a frame by holding down Alt while clicking (Shift+clicking on the Macintosh) inside the frame in the Document window.

When you click the representation of a frame in the Frames panel, the properties for that frame are available in the Property inspector, as shown in Figure 14.6. The Property inspector is where you set up the frame's scrolling and border attributes. You'll explore those in a few minutes. This is also where you give each frame a unique name.

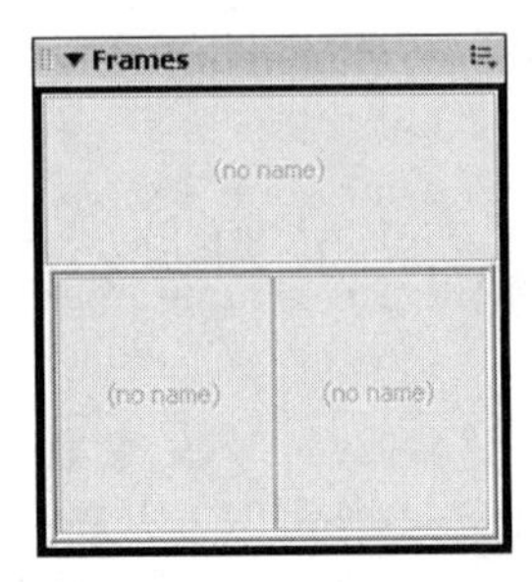

FIGURE 14.5
You select frames in the Frames panel. This panel visually represents the frame configuration in the current web page.

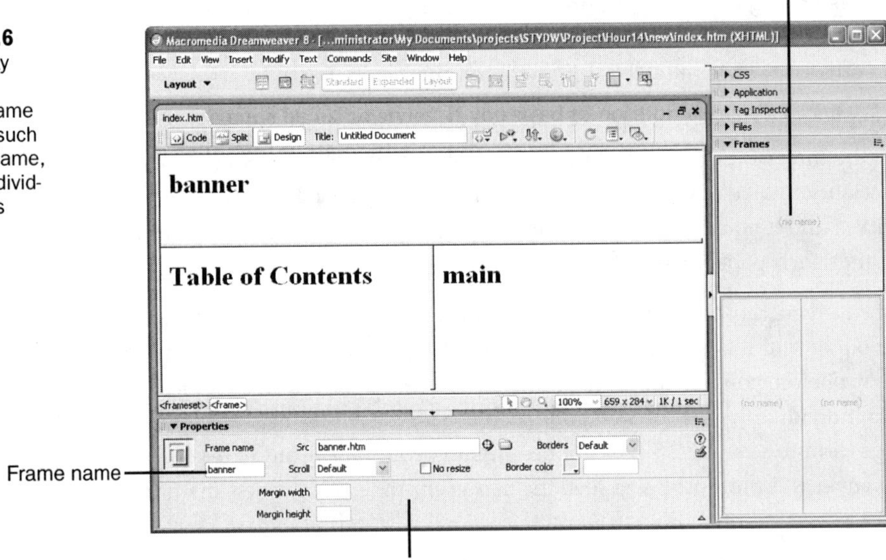

FIGURE 14.6
The Property inspector presents frame attributes, such as Frame Name, when an individual frame is selected.

It's important that each frame have a name. This is not the filename that you gave each frame a few minutes ago; this is an actual name for a frame that is stored in the frameset file. The frame name is used to target the frame, making a web page load into the frame when a link is clicked in another frame. Click on each frame in the Frames panel and type a name in the Frame Name box in the Property inspector. You can name the top frame `banner`, the left frame `toc` (for table of contents), and the right frame `main`.

By the Way

Name Your Frames Correctly

Frame names should not contain punctuation, such as periods, hyphens, or spaces. You can, however, use underscores in frame names. Also, you should not use the reserved names top, parent, self, and blank.

Nesting Frames

You can nest one frameset inside another frameset to have **nested frames**. Actually, that is what you just did! When you split the bottom frame into two frames, Dreamweaver created a frameset defining the bottom two frames. The original frameset now consists of a frame on top of the nested frameset. You nest framesets by nesting one `<frameset>` tag within another, within a single frameset web page. If you'd like to see the code, select the frameset (by clicking the frame borders) and then look at the code in Code view. It should look something like this:

```
<frameset rows="96,157" cols="*">
    <frame src="banner.htm" id="banner" />
    <frameset rows="*" cols="206,437">
        <frame src="toc.htm" id="toc" />
        <frame src="main.htm" id="main" />
    </frameset>
</frameset>
```

In Design view, click one of the lower frames in the Frames panel and look at the tag selector. You should see a `<frame>` tag inside a `<frameset>` tag inside another `<frameset>` tag, as shown in Figure 14.7. Click the top frame in the Frames panel. The tag selector shows the frame is in one frameset. The bottom two frames are in a nested frameset.

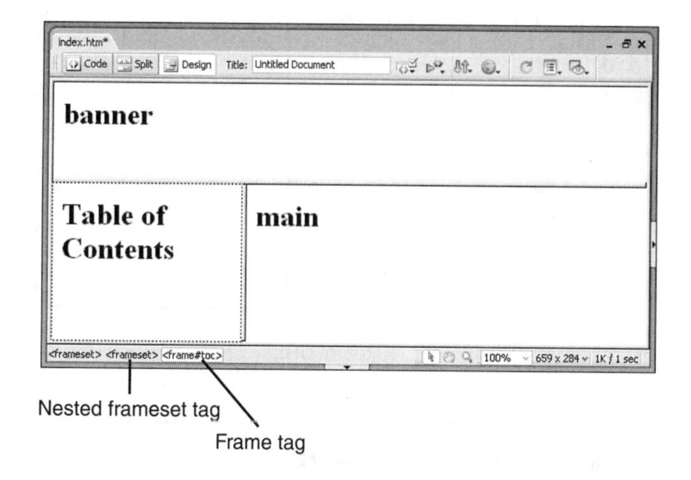

FIGURE 14.7 The tag selector shows that the currently selected frame is contained in a frameset nested within another frameset.

In order to make the type of frame design you just set up, Dreamweaver must create an additional frameset because framesets can contain either rows or columns, but not both. The first frameset you created has two rows. The second frameset you created has two columns.

Using Existing Web Pages with Frames

So far this hour, you have created new web pages in all your frames. However, you might want to load a web page that you created prior to setting up your frameset into a frame. To load an existing web page into a frame, follow these steps:

1. In the Frames panel, click a frame.
2. In the Property inspector, select the Browse icon next to the Src text box and browse to an existing web page. You should see the web page displayed. If you link to an external URL instead of your local site, Dreamweaver will display a message, as shown in Figure 14.8, saying that the frame contains a remote file and listing the URL.

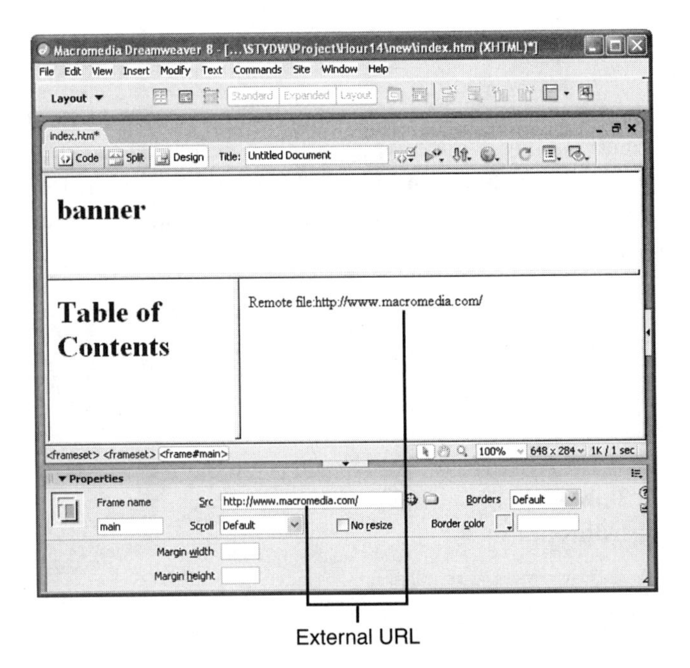

FIGURE 14.8 If a frame references an external URL, it will contain a message displaying the URL.

By the Way

Open an Existing Web Page in a Frame

You can open an existing web page in a frame where the cursor is located by selecting File, Open in Frame.

Setting Frame and Frameset Attributes

There are separate attributes for the individual frames and the frameset that holds them together. Some of the attributes exist for both frames and framesets (borders, for instance), so you must be careful what attributes you are setting and where you are setting them. You should experiment with frameset designs that come with Dreamweaver to quickly try different attributes.

Setting the Scrolling and Resize Attributes

It's important to consider whether you want the user to be able to scroll the material in a frame. Frame scrollbars can appear either horizontally or vertically in a frame. Horizontal scrollbars are not common and are not generally desirable. Vertical scrollbars are very common and appear when the material in the web page is longer than what is visible in the browser window. You can't turn on horizontal and vertical scrollbars separately; after you enable the scrollbars, you enable both horizontal and vertical scrollbars.

By the Way

Selecting a Frame

Remember, in Dreamweaver you can select the frame or the content in the frame. To select the frame, always use the Frames panel (Window, Frames).

Each frame has its own scrolling attributes displayed in the Property inspector when a frame is selected in the Frames panel. There are four settings in the Scroll drop-down menu of the Property inspector, as shown in Figure 14.9.

- **Yes**—This setting turns scrollbars on, even if the content does not require them. Both vertical and horizontal scrollbars might appear, depending on the browser.
- **No**—This setting turns scrollbars off, even if the content requires them. If viewers cannot see all the content in the frame, they have no way to scroll to see it.
- **Auto**—This setting turns the scrollbars on if the content of the frame is larger than what is visible in the browser window. If all the content is visible, the scrollbars are off. This setting turns on only the necessary scrollbars, horizontal or vertical, and is usually a better choice than the Yes setting.
- **Default**—For most browsers, this setting is the same as Auto.

Select the No Resize check box in the Property inspector if you do not want the user to be able to resize your frames. Allowing users to resize the frames can sometimes help them maintain the readability of your web page, but it also might ruin your page design. If a frame-based web page is well designed, taking into account how the page will look at various monitor resolutions, users shouldn't have to resize the frames.

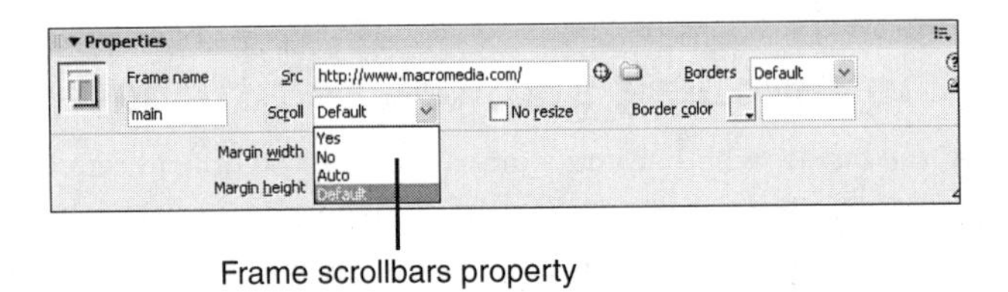

FIGURE 14.9 The Property inspector lists scroll choices when a frame is selected.

Setting Borders

The default look for frame borders a gray shaded border between the frames. You might not want your frame-based web page to be so obviously framed. While you're surfing the Web, it's sometimes difficult to identify websites that use frames because they have turned off the frame borders or colored them to blend with the site design.

In Dreamweaver, you can turn borders on and off, set the border color, and change the border width. Border attributes are a little tricky because some of them are set in the frame, some are set in the frameset, and some can be set in both places. Setting properties in an individual frame overrides the same properties set in the frameset. If you set attributes for frames but they don't seem to work, check to make sure you have set the attributes in all the framesets; you might be working with a nested frame that is affected by *two* sets of frameset attributes.

Set the border width in the frameset. The easiest way to select the frameset and display the frameset attributes in the Property inspector is to select the `<frameset>` tag in the tag selector. The tag selector displays the `<frameset>` tag when a frame within the frameset is selected. You can also click the frame borders to select the frameset, as you did earlier this hour. Remember that nested frames may be in more than one frameset.

Select a frame in the Frames panel and click the <frameset> tag farthest to the left. The frameset properties, shown in Figure 14.10, enable you to change border width and color. Give the border a width value and select a color from the Border Color box. You should see these changes immediately in the Dreamweaver Document window.

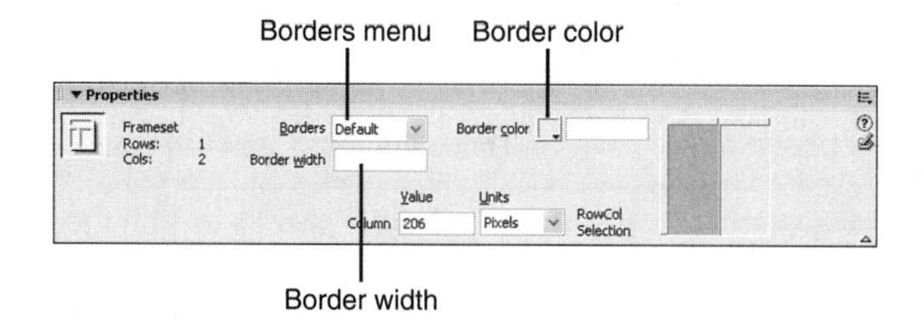

FIGURE 14.10 The Property inspector enables you to set frameset properties such as border width and border color.

To turn off the frame borders, make sure the frameset is selected and then select No from the Borders drop-down menu. You need to turn the border off in all the framesets in the page. If the borders in the individual frames are set to Yes, they override the frameset settings, and borders are visible. To turn off a border, all the adjacent frames must have borders turned off, too. If you do not want borders to appear, you should also make sure no border color is assigned.

Setting the Frame Size

You can simply drag the frame borders in Dreamweaver to resize a frame. If you want finer control over the size of a frame, you can set frame sizes in the Property inspector while the frameset is selected, as shown in Figure 14.11. You can select the rows or columns in the frameset by clicking the small representation in the Property inspector. Often, the first frame has an **absolute** value (either pixel or percentage), whereas the second frame is defined as relative. When a frame is defined as **relative**, it takes up the remaining space either horizontally or vertically.

Creating an Alternative to Frames

All modern browsers support frames, and the large majority of users have modern browsers. Lack of accessibility is one major reason some people do not like frames. Some people with disabilities, such as the visually impaired, might use software that does not easily interpret content in frames. To respect viewers who cannot view frames, you should add information to the NoFrames content, the part of a frameset that displays in browsers that cannot display frames.

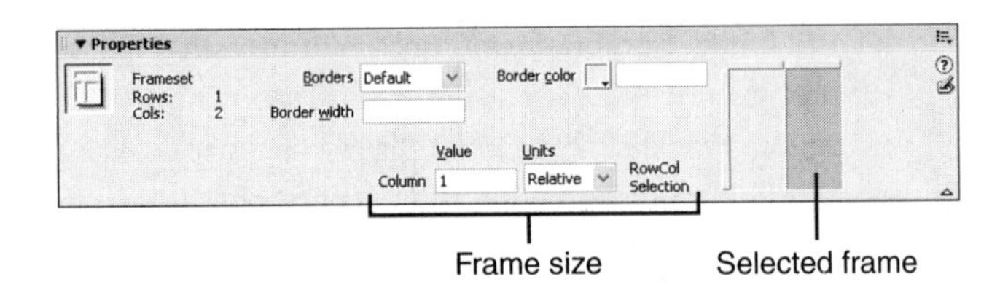

FIGURE 14.11 A frame size value can be set to relative so the frame takes up the remaining space in the browser window.

Select Modify, Frameset, Edit NoFrames Content. Note that a bar that says NoFrames Content appears across the top of the Document window, as shown in Figure 14.12. You can simply type in a disclaimer or, better yet, you can provide a non-frames version of the web page. Turn off the NoFrames Content command by deselecting it in the Frameset submenu of the Modify menu.

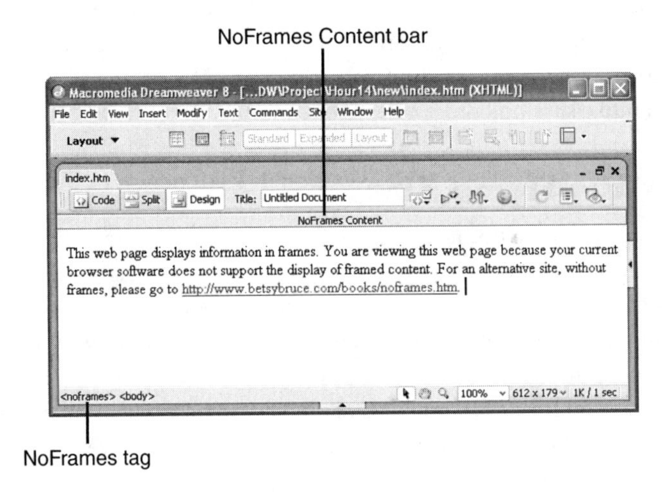

FIGURE 14.12 NoFrames content appears to viewers who have older or text-based browsers.

By the Way

No Way to Preview NoFrames Content

I don't know of any way to preview NoFrames Content in a browser other than by installing an old version of a browser on your computer. You will probably have to trust the WYSIWYG Dreamweaver display to be a true representation of what the web page will look like to those with very old browsers. When you preview the web page with a modern browser, you will see the frame content.

Dreamweaver will automatically prompt you to add the title attribute for the `<frame>` tag if you have enabled frames accessibility prompting. To turn on this feature, open the Preferences dialog box (by selecting Edit, Preferences), select the Accessibility category, and select the Frames check box. You can also turn on automatic prompting for the accessibility attributes of form objects, media, and images. When you turn on the frames' accessibility prompting, Dreamweaver asks you to give each frame a title that is read by text-to-speech browsers.

Using Frames Objects

The quickest way to create frames in Dreamweaver is to use the prebuilt frames objects that are available in the Frames menu in the Layout category of the Insert bar. The Insert bar has several common frame configurations that can quickly get you going with a set of frames. If you are not quite sure what each of the configurations looks like, look at the Framesets category in the New Document dialog box, shown in Figure 14.13. This lists the same prebuilt frames objects as the Insert bar. There is a preview of the frames object's structure on the right side of the dialog box.

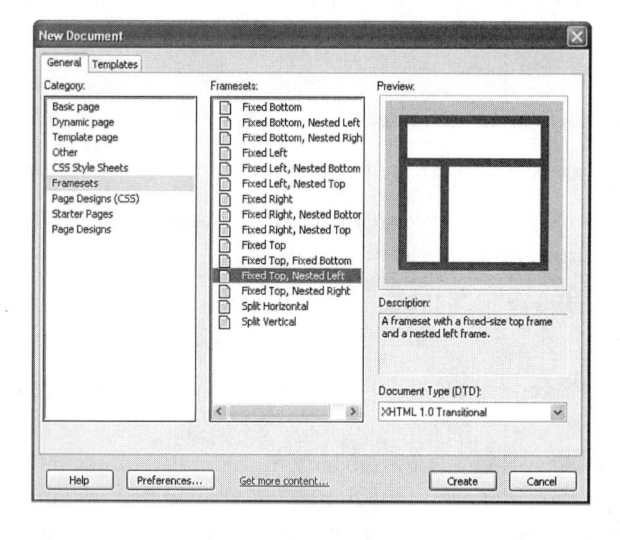

FIGURE 14.13
The Framesets category in the New Document dialog box enables you to preview what the frames will look like.

If one of these prebuilt configurations fits the way you want your frames to look, you'll have a head start by using these frames objects. You can fine-tune the frame settings by using the same methods you've used so far in this hour.

With a new web page open, add a frames object by either clicking an icon from the Frames menu in the Layout category of the Insert bar or selecting Insert, HTML, Frames. The framesets in these frames templates all have the borders turned off.

The individual frames are already named, but you need to select and save each file as you did earlier in this hour.

Watch Out!

Frames with No Borders Are Difficult to See

The frames objects that come with Dreamweaver are configured without borders, so when you add one of these objects to a web page the borders are difficult to see. Use the Frames panel to select each frame and use the same technique you used earlier this hour of typing some text into each frame so you can tell the frames apart.

Targeting Linked Pages to Open in a Specific Frame

One of the most exciting features of frames is their capability to load content in one frame after a user clicks a link in another frame. The frameset is the parent, and the frames or framesets it contains are its children. Understanding these concepts helps you understand **targeting**. You can load a web page into a frame or window by targeting it. You add the target attribute to a hyperlink to send the linked content into a specific window or frame.

There are four reserved target names:

- `_top`—This opens a linked web page in the entire browser window.
- `_self`—This opens a linked web page in the same window or frame that contains the link. This is the default setting.
- `_parent`—This opens a linked web page in the parent frameset. If the parent frameset is not nested, the linked page will fill the entire browser window.
- `_blank`—This opens a linked web page in a new browser window.

The Target drop-down menu in the Property inspector lists all the reserved target names, plus the names of any of the frames you created that are currently open in the Document window, as shown in Figure 14.14. Creating a hyperlink and selecting a frame name from the Target drop-down menu will cause the linked page to load in that window. If no target is entered, the linked page will load in the frame that contains the link.

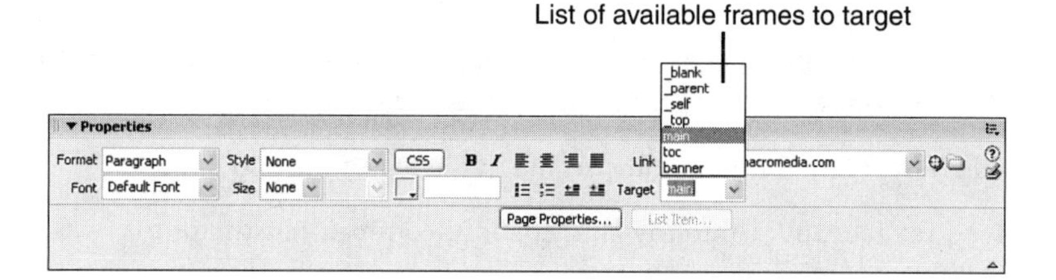

FIGURE 14.14
The Target drop-down menu lists the reserved target names, plus all the names of the frames in the current web page.

Use the original group of frames that you created at the beginning of this hour to target a hyperlink, as follows:

1. Create a hyperlink in the frame named `toc`. Add a link to an existing web page or to an external URL.
2. Select `main` from the Target drop-down menu. This loads the hyperlink into the selected frame.
3. Use the Save All command (by selecting File, Save All).
4. Preview the frames in the browser. Click the link, and the web page should load in the other frame.

Did you Know?

Set the Target for an Entire Page

If you are going to be targeting the same frame for all the links in a web page, add the `<base>` tag to the head of the web page, specifying the target once for all the links. While the insertion point is in the frame with the links, select Insert, HTML, Head Tags, Base and select a target name from the Target drop-down menu. You can leave the Href text box blank. Now you can leave off the target attribute for each individual hyperlink because the base target of the page is set.

Using the Go to URL Behavior to Load Frames

The Go to URL behavior has the capability to target frames, and using it is an easy way to get content to load into two frames at once. For instance, you might want to change both the table of contents and the main content frames when the user clicks a hyperlink in the banner frame. The user may select a different section of the content that has a different table of contents and main content web pages. Because a hyperlink can change the contents in only one frame, you have to use the Go to URL behavior. To use the Go to URL behavior, follow these steps:

1. Add a hyperlink in the banner frame at the top of the page.
2. Type `javascript:;` into the Link box in the Property inspector to create a null link.
3. Open the Behaviors panel (Window, Behaviors); make sure you don't open the Server Behaviors panel—that is a different panel. With the hyperlink selected, click the + button in the Behaviors panel and select Go to URL.
4. The Go to URL dialog box opens. Select the frame named `toc` from the Open In list box, as shown in Figure 14.15. Enter a URL in the URL box and press the Tab key to record your changes.

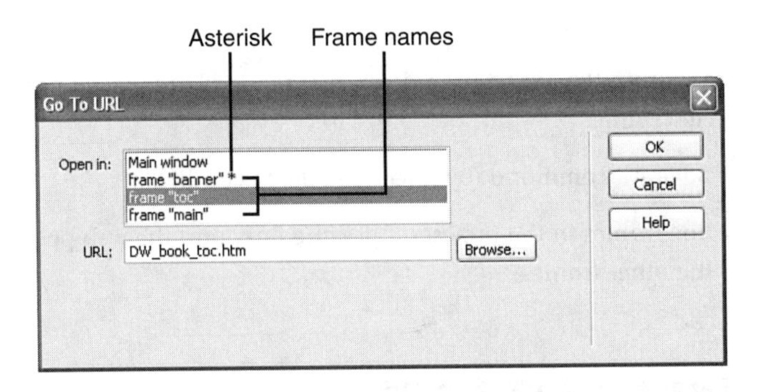

FIGURE 14.15 The Go to URL dialog box enables you to select the target frame for the URL.

5. Notice that there is an asterisk by the frame named `toc`. That means that there is a URL entered for this frame (you entered it in step 4). Add another URL to a different frame by first selecting the frame named `main` and then entering a URL in the URL box. Now both frames will load new URLs when the link is clicked. Click OK to save the behavior settings.
6. Save the frames and preview the page in a browser. Click the link in the top frame. Both lower frames should have the new URLs load.

By the Way

Set Text of Frame Behavior

There is also a Set Text of Frame behavior that enables you to modify the text in a certain frame based on some action by the user. For instance, if someone clicked on a link titled List links in French, you could change the list of links in a particular frame to French text instead of English text.

Summary

In this hour, you have learned how to create, name, and save frames and framesets. You have learned how to change the border, scrollbar, and resizing attributes. You have learned how to target content to a specific frame or browser window, and you have learned how to load two frames at once by using Dreamweaver behaviors.

Q&A

Q. ***What's the difference between the reserved target name* `top` *and the reserved target name* `parent`*?***

A. The `top` target name targets the entire window, whereas the `parent` target name targets the parent of the frame where the link resides. Sometimes these are the same. If the browser window contains several nested framesets, using the `top` target name loads the linked web page, replacing them all. Using the `parent` target name in this case, however, simply loads the linked web page in the immediate parent frameset of the frame that contains the link.

Q. ***Why do my frames look different in different browsers?***

A. Browsers can display frames with sizes defined in either pixel values or percentages. Some versions of Netscape translate pixel values to percentage values, causing some rounding to occur. You are more likely to get similar results in Internet Explorer and Netscape by actually using percentage values to define the frames. There are also differences between the ways browsers display borders.

Workshop

Quiz

1. How many files are needed for a web page that has three frames in it?
2. Can a single frameset contain rows and columns?
3. Where would linked content targeted with the reserved target name `_self` load?

Quiz Answers

1. The web page would contain four files. Three files would be loaded into frames and the fourth file would hold the frameset.
2. No. A frameset can contain either rows or columns, but not both. However, you can nest a frameset within a frame, creating the appearance of rows and columns.
3. Linked content targeted with the `_self` reserved target name would load in the same frame as the original link.

Exercises

1. Surf the Web, looking for whether some of your favorite websites use frames. Google's image search, www.google.com/images, displays images based on search parameters. When you click an individual search result, it is displayed in frames. Why is this a useful way to design this type of page? Or, when you jump out to sites that are external from the various information sites at www.about.com, there is a frame at the top of the page to help you return to the original site.
2. Use one of the prebuilt frames from the Frames menu of the Layout category in the Insert bar. Explore all the attributes of both the individual frames and the framesets.

PART IV

Dynamic HTML: Layers, Cascading Style Sheets, Behaviors, and Timelines

HOUR 15

Using Dynamic HTML and Layers

What You'll Learn in This Hour:

- What layers are, how they work, and how they are used
- How to add a layer and position it on the page
- How to set the stacking order, background color, and visibility of a layer
- How to use Dreamweaver timelines to add animation to a web page

Dynamic HTML (DHTML) provides you with the flexibility to lay out your web pages and make them interactive. Dreamweaver's layers provide a way to control where objects are placed on the page. You can place items precisely where you want them, without having to create elaborate tables. Layers are the more modern way to position content on a web page. I use them extensively in the sites I create.

You don't have to pick between tables and layers. You can use both in a web page, taking advantage of the strengths of each. Layers are not meant to stretch to fit the screen, whereas tables can be set to a percentage of the screen, allowing for stretching to different screen resolutions. Unlike a table cell, layers are autonomous and can be moved individually. You'll experiment with layers and be able to compare them to what you've learned about tables in Hour 12, "Displaying Data In Tables," and Hour 13, "Designing Page Layout Using Tables."

What Is DHTML?

DHTML enables you to create an interactive experience for the web page user. DHTML isn't an official term; it's a term used by web developers to reference a collection of technologies used together to produce a more interactive web page. The three main components of DHTML are layers, Cascading Style Sheets (CSS; see Hour 16, "Formatting Web Pages Using Cascading Style Sheets"), and JavaScript (see Hour 17, "Adding Interactivity with Behaviors").

DHTML is an extension of HTML that gives web page developers greater control over page layout and positioning. DHTML also allows greater interactivity without depending on interaction with a server. When people talk about DHTML, they usually mean the combination of HTML 4 (as defined by the W3C Web standards organization) and CSS. These elements work together through a scripting language, usually JavaScript.

Here's a short list of the types of things you can accomplish using DHTML:

- Add to your page images that are hidden from view that will appear when the user clicks a button or a hotspot.
- Create pop-up menus.
- Enable the user to drag and drop an object around the screen at will.
- Cause text to change color or size when the user rolls her mouse over it.
- Repetitively load text into an area of the screen as feedback to the user. For instance, if the user clicks the wrong answer in a quiz, you can give feedback and then replace that feedback when the user gets the answer right.

In this hour, you'll experiment with **layers**, the containers that enable you to position items on the screen wherever you want.

Adding a Layer

Layers are containers that you use to position content on a web page. The term *layers* is a Dreamweaver term, and if you speak with other web developers who aren't using Dreamweaver (what's wrong with them?!), they won't know what you mean. Those who haven't been initiated into the wonders of Dreamweaver might call layers "divs," referring to the tag that is used to implement layers. The `<div>` tag is intended to logically divide a web page into sections.

Layers have two very interesting attributes:

- **Visibility**—This property enables you to hide all the content in a layer and then trigger its appearance when the user performs an action on the screen. For instance, you can simulate a click on a menu in a software program. The layer holding the menu image is initially hidden. When the user clicks on a menu title on the screen, a script changes the visibility of the menu layer from hidden to visible.

- **Z-index**—This property controls the *stacking order* of all the layers on the page. You can stack layers on top of one another (overlapping) and control which one is on top. This gives you the power to create complicated designs.

Did you Know?

Extensions to Dreamweaver

There are many extensions to Dreamweaver (you'll learn more about extensions in Hour 22, "Customizing Dreamweaver") that enable you to accomplish cool things with Dreamweaver. There are extensions such as Slide Layer that makes a layer slide to a specified position and Persistent Layer that makes a layer that doesn't scroll with the page. There are also several extensions to create drop-down menus using layers.

You can create a layer in Dreamweaver in two ways:

- The simplest way is to select the Draw Layer object from the Layout category of the Insert bar and drag the crosshair cursor on your page to approximately the desired layer size, as shown in Figure 15.1.

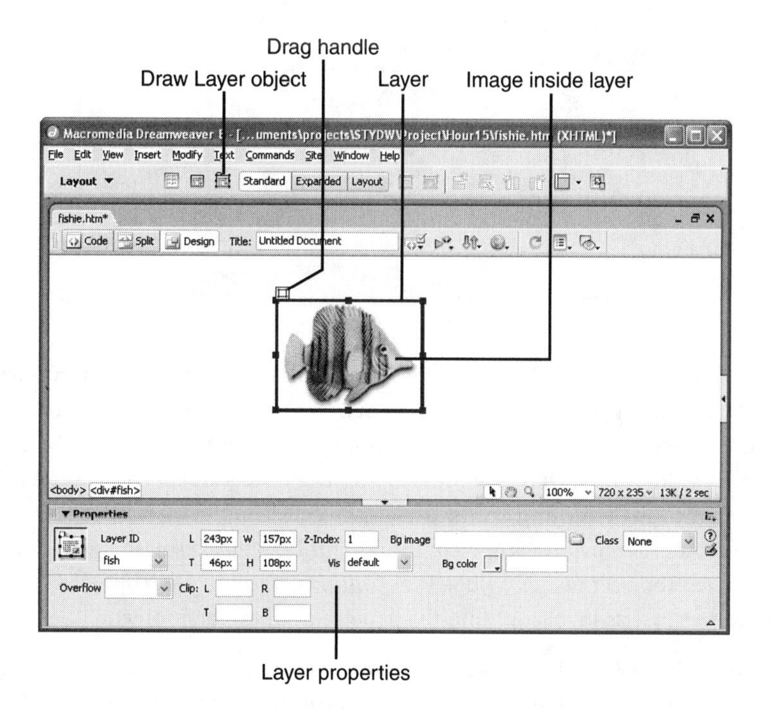

FIGURE 15.1 Selecting the Draw Layer object from the Insert bar enables you to draw a layer by dragging the crosshair cursor.

- Select Insert, Layout Objects, Layer to insert a layer.

By the Way

> **Draw Layer Doesn't Work in Layout Mode**
>
> If the Layer object is grayed out in the Insert bar, you are currently in Layout mode. Make sure that the Layout Mode button in the Layout category of the Insert bar isn't depressed and that you are in Standard mode.

The Layers category in the Dreamweaver Preferences dialog box, shown in Figure 15.2, is where you set the default layer values. You can set the default visibility, width, height, background color, and background image. If you have a standard layer size that you use often, you might want to set that size as the default in the Preferences dialog box. You can also enable nesting by checking the Nesting check box.

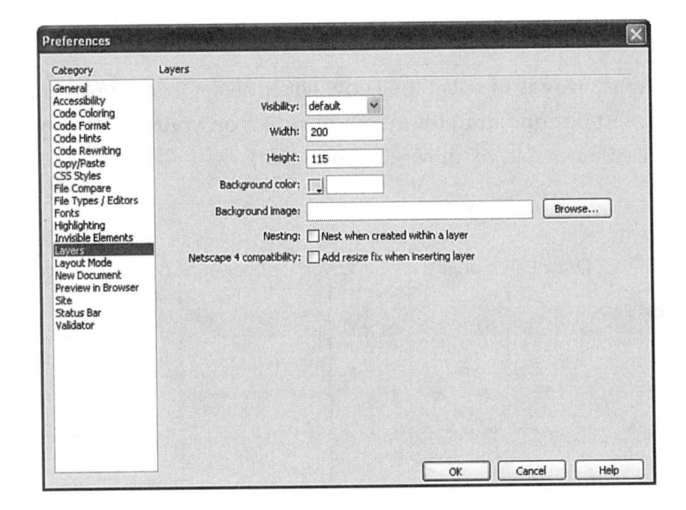

FIGURE 15.2
The Layers category in the Preferences dialog box is where you set the default values of layer attributes.

Check the Add Resize Fix When Inserting Layer check box to have Dreamweaver automatically insert the Netscape layer fix behavior whenever you insert a layer into a web page. On any page that includes layers and will be viewed in Netscape 4, a very old version of the Netscape browser, insert the Netscape layer fix. You can do this automatically by turning on the preference or manually by selecting Command, Add/Remove Netscape Layer Fix. This behavior resolves problems that happen when the user resizes a page that contains layers in Netscape 4. Dreamweaver inserts JavaScript into the page that solves the problem.

You'll notice the resizing handles on each border of your layer. You can drag these handles to make a layer bigger or smaller. You can also set the width and height of the layer in the Property inspector. The W and H properties in the Property inspector are the width and height of the layer. The default measurement unit is pixels.

Watch Out!

Use the Layer Fix Only If Necessary

Don't insert the Netscape layer fix unless it is absolutely necessary. The fix causes the page to reload and might be distracting to Netscape 4 users. And it just adds unnecessary code to web pages that will be delivered to mostly non–Netscape 4 users. Test your page by opening it in a small Netscape 4 window and then maximize the window. Do your layers stay small? If so, you need to apply the Netscape layer fix. You can download older Netscape versions at http://browser.netscape.com/ns8/download/archive.jsp.

It's a good idea to always name your layers. When you start adding behaviors, names help you identify specific layers. You can specify a name in the Layer ID box in the Property inspector, as shown in Figure 15.3.

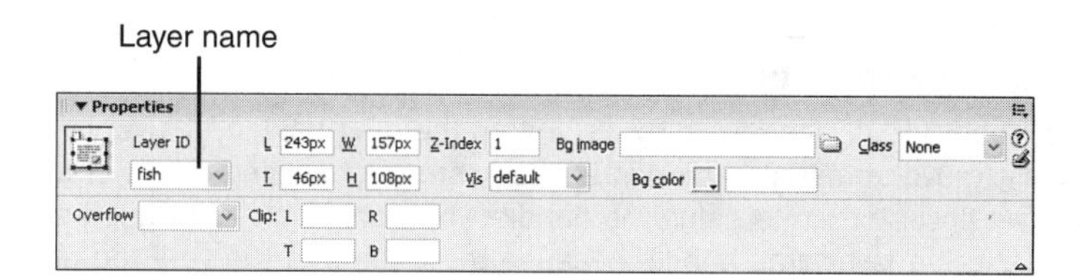

FIGURE 15.3 Change the layer name in the Layer ID box of the Property inspector. It's important to give layers meaningful names.

Did you Know?

No Punctuation in Layer Names

Don't use spaces or punctuation in layer names. If you later apply a behavior to the layer, sometimes JavaScript isn't happy with spaces or punctuation in a layer name. If you want to name your layer with multiple words, you can use capitalization or underscores to make the name readable. For instance, `CestLaVieBakery` and `Green_Grocer` are possible layer names.

You can also name Dreamweaver layers in the Layers panel. Double-click the name in the Layers panel Name column until it becomes editable and then type in a new name, as shown in Figure 15.4. Notice that when you select a layer in the Layers panel, the layer is selected in the Document window also.

Setting Layer Positioning

A layer has a drag handle in the upper-left corner. You can reposition a layer by picking it up and moving it with this handle. To select multiple layers, hold down the Shift key while clicking layers to add them to the selection. You can also use the arrow keys on your keyboard to move a selected layer.

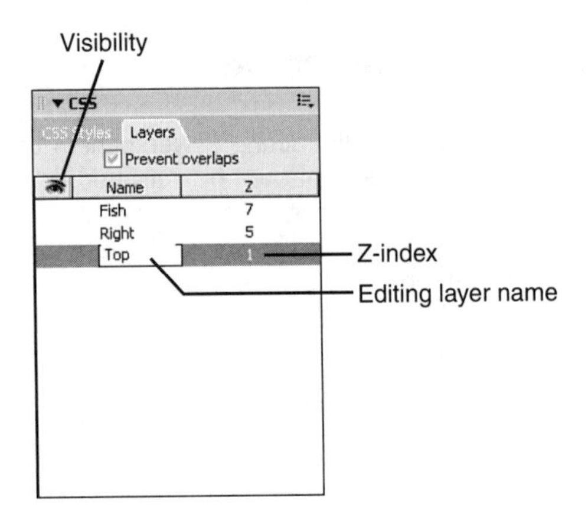

FIGURE 15.4
You can edit the name of a layer in the Layers panel by double-clicking the name and changing it.

Did you Know?

Use the Drag Handle

Get in the habit of moving layers by picking up the drag handle. It's very easy to accidentally move items contained in a layer instead of moving the layer itself. If you become accustomed to using the handle, you won't make that mistake. If you can't use the layer drag handle because the layer is at the very top of the Document window, select it in the Layers panel and use the arrow keys to move the layer. Or enter positioning values in the Property inspector.

Use the Layers panel to select one or many layers. The Layers panel enables you not only to select layers, but also to see and set some layer characteristics. You'll learn about the two characteristics that you can set—the z-index and the visibility—in a few minutes. Notice that you can select a check box at the top of the Layers panel to prevent layers from overlapping. If you notice that you cannot place your layers on top of one another, this check box is probably selected.

The main reason you would want to prevent overlaps is if you were going to eventually convert the layers into a table; a table cannot have overlapping elements. In Hour 13, you learned how to export a layout table as layers by using the Tables to Layers command (by selecting Modify, Convert, Tables to Layers). You can also use the Layers to Table command (by selecting Modify, Convert, Layers to Table) to turn the layers in your page into a layout table.

You can use the drag handle to drag a layer anywhere on the screen, or you can use the Property inspector to set the exact positioning of a layer. The L and T properties stand for the left (the offset from the left edge of the page) and top (the offset from the top edge of the page). These positions are relative to the entire browser window. You can move a layer either by dragging it (with its selection handle) or by positioning it exactly by entering values in the L and T boxes, as shown in Figure 15.5.

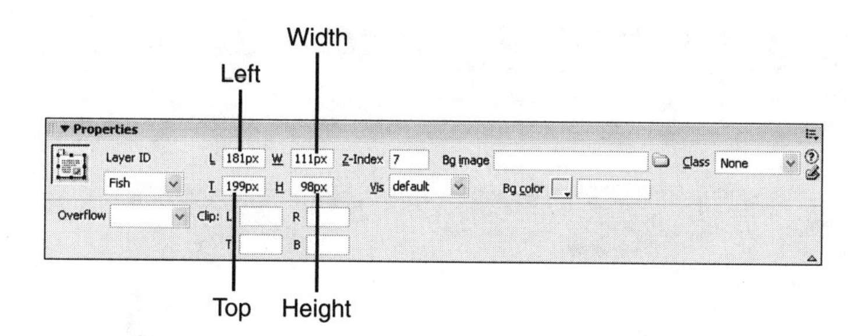

FIGURE 15.5
Position a layer exactly by entering values in the L (left) and T (top) boxes of the Property inspector.

Did you Know?

Where Did the Layer Properties Go?

If you don't see layer properties in the Property inspector, it's because you don't have a layer selected. You might have accidentally selected the contents of the layer instead of selecting the layer itself.

Adding a Background Color and Background Image

A layer can have a background color, as shown in Figure 15.6. You can use the color picker or type in a color in the standard HTML hexadecimal format, preceded by a #. Make sure you leave the Bg Color option blank if you want your layer to be transparent. If your page background is white and you make your layer background white, it will seem as if it's transparent until you position it over something else!

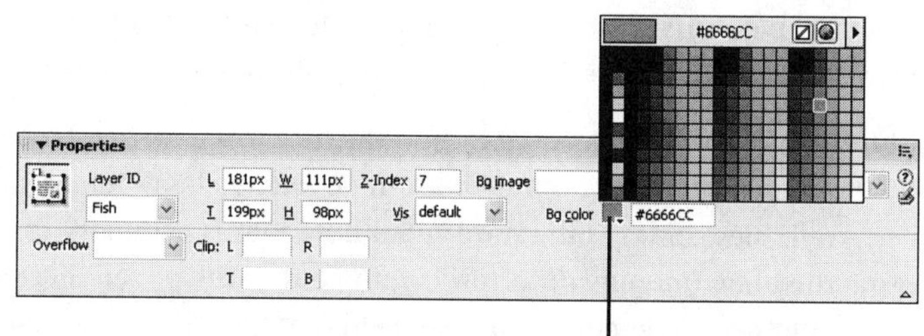

FIGURE 15.6
A layer can have a background color just as a table cell can. Enter a background color in the Property inspector.

You can also place a background image in a layer. The image repeats multiple times (called *tiling*) within the layer if the layer is larger than the image. Any objects or text that you put within the layer are on top of the background image. Select the Browse icon (the folder) beside the Bg Image box in the Property inspector and navigate to the background image file. Figure 15.7 shows the Property inspector when a layer that contains a background image is selected.

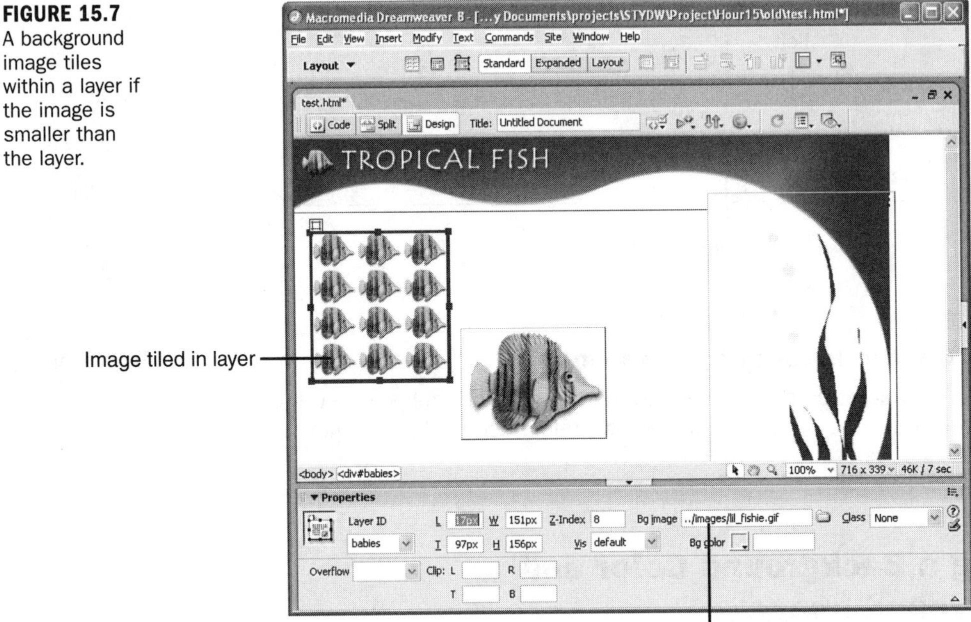

FIGURE 15.7
A background image tiles within a layer if the image is smaller than the layer.

Exploring Layer Stacking Order

Not only can you position layers in exact places on the page, you can also allow layers to overlap one another. So, which layer is on top? The stacking order decides which layer is on top of other layers. The **z-index** value, in turn, determines the stacking order. The z-index can be either a negative or a positive number.

The layer with the highest z-index is the one on the top. The term *z-index* comes from the coordinate system that you used back in geometry class—remember x and y coordinates? Well, the z-index is the third coordinate that is necessary to describe three-dimensional space. Imagine an arrow coming out of the paper or screen toward you and another going back into the screen or paper. That is the z-index.

Dreamweaver prefers to give each layer a unique z-index value. In HTML, you can legally have multiple layers that have the same z-index. Remember, though: If you reorder the layers, Dreamweaver will renumber each with a unique z-index, so why waste your time?

You can set the z-index in the Z-index box in the Property inspector, as shown in Figure 15.8. The Layers panel also displays the z-index to the right of the layer name. The Layers panel displays the layers according to z-index value, the top being the highest z-index and the bottom being the lowest. You can easily rearrange the stacking order by selecting the layer name in the Layers panel and then dragging and dropping it somewhere else.

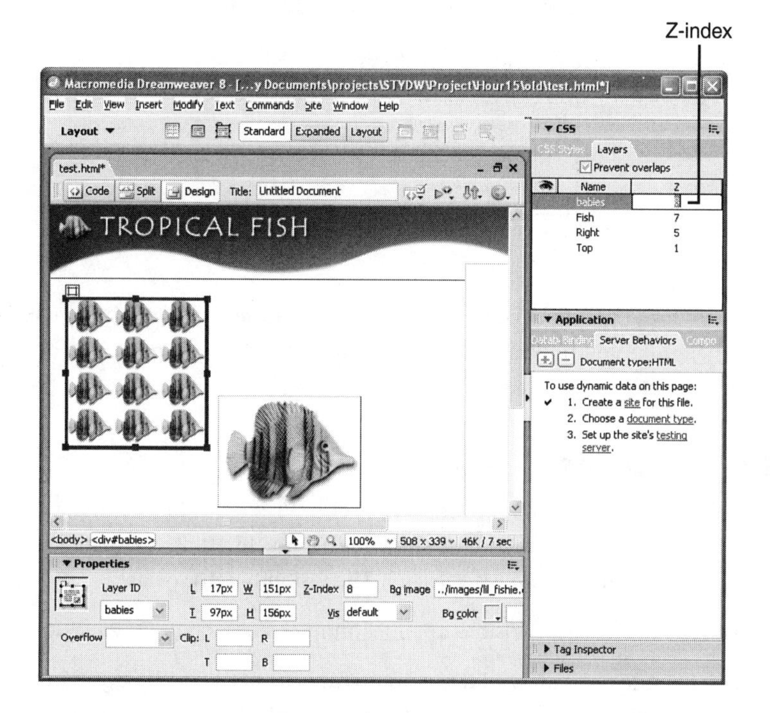

FIGURE 15.8
The z-index value represents the stacking order of layers. You can set the z-index (as either a positive or negative value) in the Property inspector.

Aligning Layers and Using the Grid

The Dreamweaver grid commands are found under View, Grid. You can show the grid, snap to the grid, and adjust the grid settings. After you show the grid by selecting the Show Grid command, you see the grid lines in the Design window. You can turn off the grid by deselecting this same command. You can also turn the grid on and off from the View Options menu in the Dreamweaver toolbar.

The grid is especially useful if you have elements in your site that must be lined up and are similar in size. You can require layers to snap to the grid by selecting the Snap To command. You can also configure the gap between the grid lines.

Open the Grid Settings dialog box, shown in Figure 15.9, by selecting the View, Grid, Grid Settings. If you need the grid to have larger or smaller increments, you can adjust its value in the Spacing box. You can also change the snapping increment. The grid can be displayed with either solid lines or dots. The dots are nice because they are lighter and less invasive on your page design. You can also select a grid color by using the color picker.

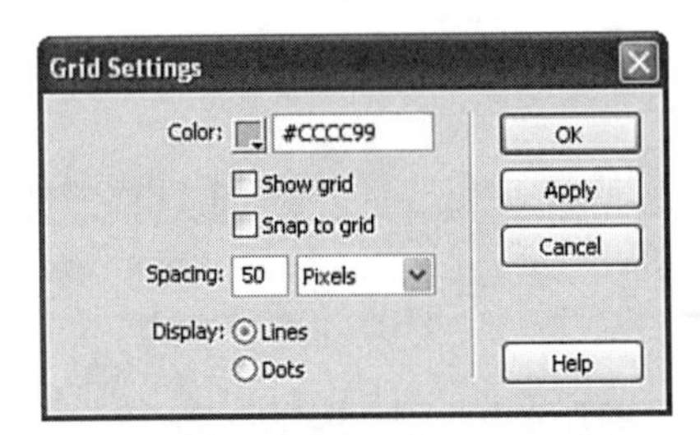

FIGURE 15.9
The grid settings enable you to change the appearance of the grid (the color and the line type) and set the snapping increment.

Hour 13 introduced you to Dreamweaver's guides feature which might be easier to use than the grid if you have specific placement needs. You use guides by dragging them from the ruler (View, Ruler).

Changing Layer Visibility

Layers have a visibility attribute that can be set to Visible, Hidden, Inherit, or Default. The Vis drop-down menu, as shown in Figure 15.10, is in the middle of the Property inspector when a layer is selected. The visibility settings are

- **Visible**—A layer set to Visible appears on the web page upon loading.
- **Hidden**—A layer set to Hidden does not appear on the web page. You can later make the layer visible by using the Show-Hide Layer behavior.
- **Inherit**—A layer set to Inherit has the same visibility as its parent. You'll learn more about nesting and parent layers in a few minutes. If the parent is set to Hidden and a layer is nested within that parent and set to Inherit, it is also hidden.
- **Default**—The Default setting is actually the same as Inherit in most browsers.

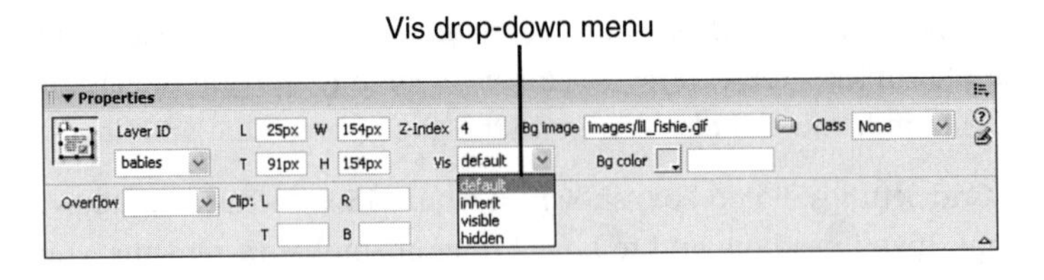

FIGURE 15.10
The Vis drop-down menu enables you to set the visibility attribute for a layer.

It's obvious why you might want layers to be visible, but why might you want them to be hidden? So that you can display them later, after something has happened! You'll learn about using the Show-Hide Layers behavior in Hour 17.

The Layers panel represents visibility with a picture of an eye. The eye beside a layer is open when the layer is set to Visible. It's closed when the layer is set to Hidden. The Inherit setting does not have an eye representation. The eye is a toggle that moves through the Default, Visible, and Hidden settings and then goes back to Default.

You can set the visibility characteristics of all the layers by selecting the eye icon in the header of the Layers panel.

Watch Out!

Don't Accidentally Click the Eye Icon Column Header

Be careful when clicking the eye icon column setting for your top layer. It's easy to accidentally click the header instead and set all the eyes in the column. You need to click in the eye column *beside* the layer of which you want to set the visibility property.

Nesting Layers

You can create a layer within another layer; the new layer is nested within its parent layer. When you move the parent layer, the new child layer moves with it. The child layer also inherits its parent's visibility attributes.

To create a nested layer, you place the cursor inside the parent layer and choose Insert, Layer. You draw a nested layer by using the Draw Layer object to draw inside an existing layer while holding down the Ctrl key (the Command key on the Mac). Also, you can place an existing layer within another layer by picking it up in the Layers panel while holding down the Ctrl key in Windows or the Command key on the Mac and then dropping it into another layer. The nested layer appears indented in the Layers panel, as shown in Figure 15.11.

The easiest way to un-nest a layer if you make a mistake or change your mind is to pick it up in the Layers panel and drop it somewhere else in the list of layers, as shown in Figure 15.12.

Did you Know?

Can't Draw? Check Prevent Overlaps

If Dreamweaver doesn't seem to be allowing you to draw a nested layer by holding down the Ctrl key, you probably have the Prevent Overlaps check box selected at the top of the Layers panel.

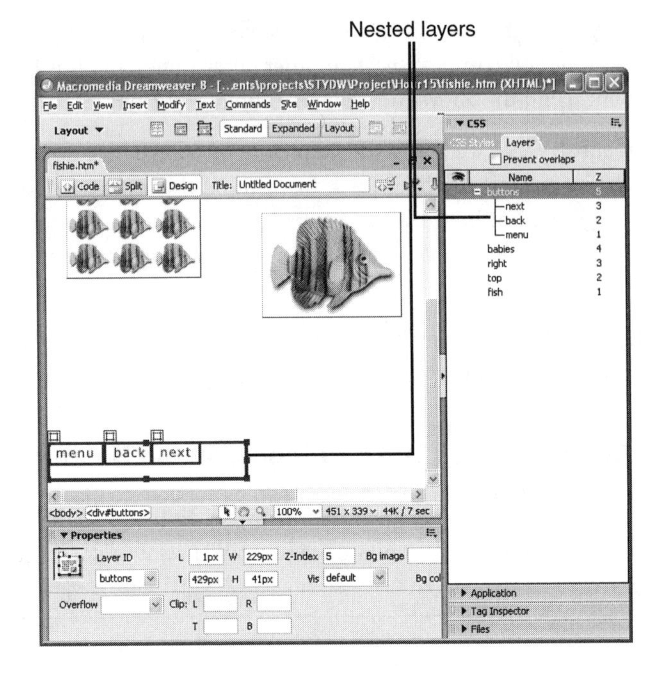

FIGURE 15.11
A layer nested within another layer appears indented in the Layers panel.

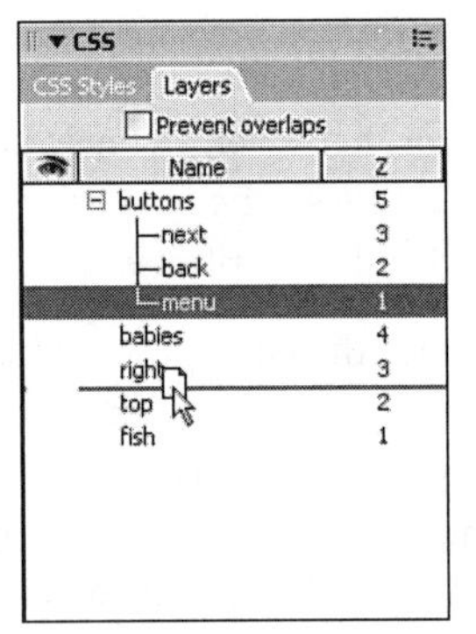

FIGURE 15.12
Pick up a nested layer and move it to another position within the Layers panel to un-nest it.

Watch Out!

Where Did the Layers Go?

Did your layer disappear from the screen when you un-nested it? When a layer is nested, its position is relative to its parent. When you un-nest the layer, its position is then relative to the page. The layer coordinates might cause the layer to be off the screen. To fix this problem, select the layer in the Layers panel and give it Left and Top attributes that place it back on the screen.

Animating with Timelines

Dreamweaver's capability to create time-based animation makes it unique as a Web-based authoring tool. Those familiar with Macromedia's animation programs, Director and Flash, will quickly feel comfortable with Dreamweaver's Timelines panel. Those not familiar with animation programs will soon be creating animations after learning a few key concepts.

Creating an Animation

Timelines change properties over time to create an animation. To make a layer move, you change the positioning properties—left and top—over time. To make objects appear or disappear, you change the visibility properties over time. To change the stacking order of objects, you change the z-index over time. You'll learn more about time-based animations in this hour.

By the Way

Changing Images

You can also place images into timelines and change the image source over time. You cannot make images move around the screen unless they are contained in a layer.

The animations that Dreamweaver creates play natively in the browser. You don't need any plug-ins to play Dreamweaver timelines. Your viewer needs to have a browser capable of viewing Dynamic HTML (either Internet Explorer or Netscape Navigator 4.0 or better) to see your timelines.

When you create a timeline, Dreamweaver inserts JavaScript into your web page. The JavaScript defines all the timeline functionality. If you edit the HTML source, be careful not to delete or move the JavaScript that creates the timeline.

Using the Timelines Panel

Open the Timelines panel (Window, Timeslines), shown in Figure 15.13; it appears beneath the Property inspector in Windows or as a floating panel on the Mac. The numbered *channels* run vertically up and down the timeline. Channels enable multiple objects to be animated in the same timeline. The numbered *frames* run horizontally from left to right along the top of the timeline. The number of frames affects the pace of the animation.

There is a special channel across the top of the timeline that is labeled with a B. You can set behaviors in this channel so behaviors execute in a certain frame. You'll learn more about behaviors in Hour 17.

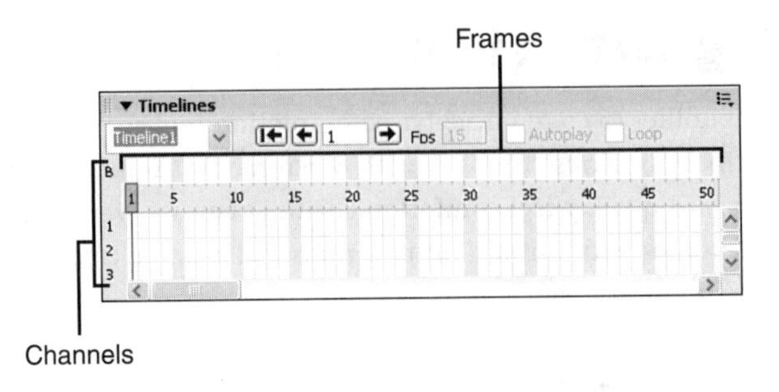

FIGURE 15.13 Use the Timeline panel to configure animations in your web page. A timeline is made up of channels (vertical axis) and frames (horizontal axis).

The red square with a line extending down is the playback head. It rests on the current frame and controls which frame is currently selected. Drag the playback head to any frame in the timeline to view a specific frame.

The playback controls at the top of the Timelines panel, shown in Figure 15.14, manage the playback head. The rewind button moves the playback head to frame one. The Back button moves the playback head back one frame. The Play button moves the playback head forward one frame. If you hold down the Back or Play buttons, you can move through all the frames. The current frame number is displayed between the Back and Play buttons.

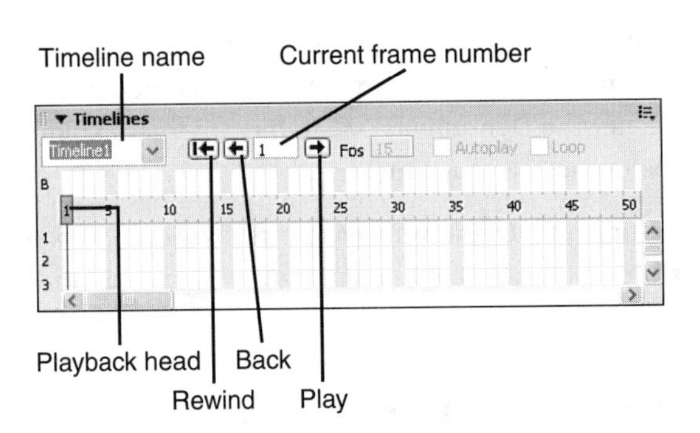

FIGURE 15.14 The playback controls, at the top of the Timeline panel, enable you to move through all the frames in the animation both backward and forward.

You set the frames per second (fps) in the Fps box beside the Play button. This sets the number of frames that occur per second in your timeline. The higher the fps, the faster the animation because more frames are crammed into one second. If you are moving an object around the screen, more frames will make the animation smoother. There is a certain point, however, where the browser just can't animate any faster even if you increase the fps.

By the Way

The default fps setting of 15 is a good place to start. This setting means that 15 frames will take one second to play.

Recording a Simple Animation

Try creating an animation. The quickest way to make something move in a timeline is to record it. First, you will need a layer with something in it (an image, some text, or a background color). Usually animated layers contain images. All the objects that you place in your timelines need to be in layers.

Did you Know?

Before you begin recording the movement of a layer, you'll want to make the Timelines panel small and place it out of the way of the animation path. Dreamweaver opens the Timelines panel when you begin to record an animation if the panel isn't open already. It's also a good idea to close panels that might be in the way. Be careful not to drop the layer in the Timelines panel while animating. This has a different effect than recording an animation.

To record an animation path, follow these steps:

1. First, make sure that Prevent Layer Overlaps is turned off in the Layers panel. Otherwise, you will not be able to move your animated layer over other layers on the screen.
2. Select the layer you want to animate. The layer is selected when you see its drag handles. A layer must be selected for the Record Path of Layer command to become active.
3. Select the Record Path of Layer command under the Timeline submenu in the Modify menu.
4. Make sure that the playback head in the Timelines panel is on frame one. If it is not, move it there.
5. Pick up the layer's move handle and drag the layer on the path that you want. A dotted line marks your path. It's best to start out making your animation short.
6. When you release the mouse button, the path becomes a solid line, as shown in Figure 15.15.

Congratulations! You've created a timeline animation in Dreamweaver. The default name for your timeline is `Timeline1`. To change the timeline name, click in the Timelines drop-down menu, change the name, and press Enter. You can select different timelines to display in the Timelines panel with this drop-down menu.

You see the name of your layer in the first channel of the Timelines panel. The line through the channel marks the duration of the animation. You can drag the playback head along the frames to see the animation in the Document window.

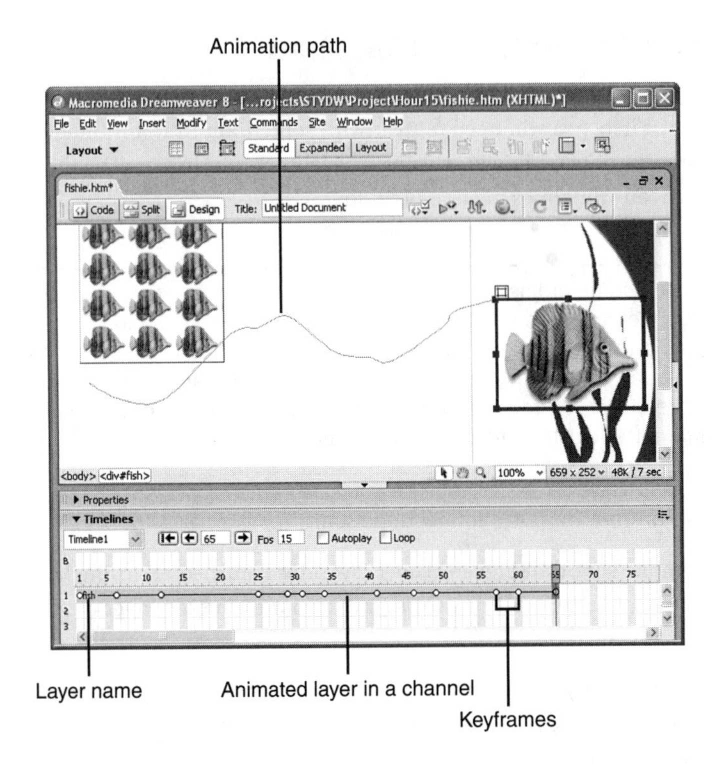

FIGURE 15.15
The path of the animation becomes a solid line after you stop dragging the layer. This is what all animation paths look like.

The solid circles in the animation bar are called **keyframes** (refer to Figure 15.15). Keyframes are an important part of timeline animations because changes can be defined *only* in keyframes. The code in Dreamweaver calculates all the intermediate steps between keyframes. You need a keyframe every time the animation changes direction or anything else new happens. You'll explore adding and editing keyframes in a few minutes. Notice that your recorded animation probably has many keyframes. Dreamweaver added one every time the direction changed when you recorded the movement of the layer.

Preview the animation in the browser. Did anything happen? Probably not. You haven't yet set anything to trigger the animation to play. You'll do that next.

Turning on Autoplay and Looping Your Animation

There are two check boxes in the Timelines panel, shown in Figure 15.16, that you haven't learned about yet: Autoplay and Loop. Check the Autoplay check box to make the timeline play when the web page loads. This setting automatically adds the Play Timeline behavior to the `<body>` tag, triggered by the `onLoad` event. After you check this setting in the Timelines panel, preview the animation in the browser. It works!

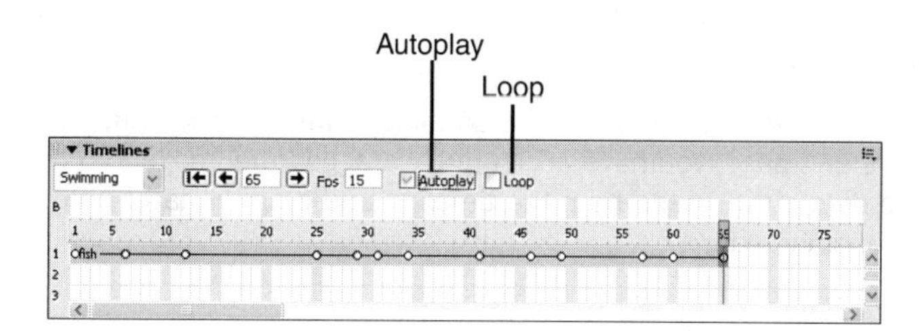

FIGURE 15.16 The Autoplay setting inserts a behavior into the <body> tag that makes the animation play when the web page is loaded. The Loop setting inserts a behavior in the B channel that sends the animation back to the first frame.

To make the animation play continually, select the Loop check box. Dreamweaver inserts the Go to Timeline Frame behavior in the B channel of the Timelines panel. Dreamweaver inserts the behavior in the last frame of the animation. What timeline frame do you think the Go to Timeline Frames behavior is set to go to? You're right if you said frame one.

Adding a Layer to the Timeline

The Record Path of Layer command is nice for capturing animations that have complex movement. But most of the time you want to set the length of a timeline and its keyframes manually. Plus, you can also add multiple layers to your animation.

Create another layer to add to the timeline that you just created. Make sure the Timelines panel is open. To add the layer to the timeline

1. Pick up a layer, drag it into the Timelines panel, and drop it in the second channel beneath the previously animated layer, as shown in Figure 15.17.

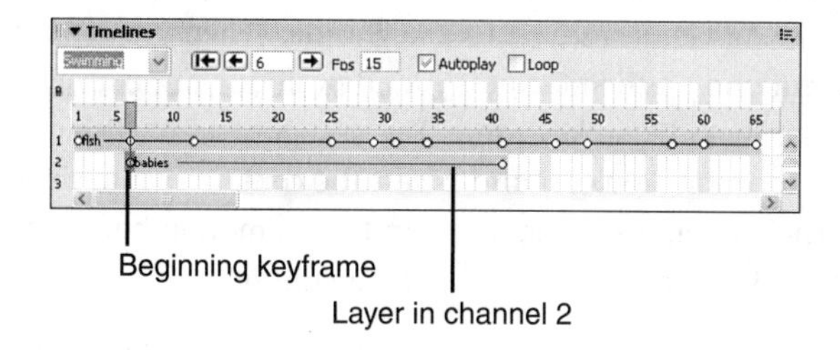

FIGURE 15.17 Another layer is dragged into the Timelines panel. The layer is placed in channel 2 beneath the other layer.

Watch Out!

Grab the Layer

If you see the name of an image in the timeline instead of the name of the layer that contains an image, you have accidentally dragged the image into the timeline. You need to delete the image from the timeline and drag the layer onto the Timelines panel instead.

2. You might receive a message box warning you about which layer attributes Netscape does not support. You won't be using any attributes that Netscape doesn't support, so you can close this box.
3. Note that the animation bar begins and ends with a keyframe. Pick up the animation bar and move it in the same channel or to a different channel if you want.
4. To increase or decrease the length of the animation, drag the end keyframe.
5. Click on the beginning keyframe. This is the position that the layer will be in at the beginning of the animation. You can adjust the beginning position *only* while you have the first keyframe selected.
6. Click on the ending keyframe. This is the position that the layer will be in at the end of the animation. Only while the ending keyframe is selected, pick up the layer and move it to its end position. When you release the mouse button you will see a line in the Document window showing the animation path, as in Figure 15.18.
7. Preview the animation in your browser. Note that the second layer moves in a line from one point, the beginning keyframe, to another point, the end keyframe.

Adding a Keyframe

To create a more complex animation or make something happen at a specific frame, you need to turn that frame into a keyframe. When you hold down the Control key (Command on the Macintosh) and position your cursor over an animation bar, the cursor looks like a keyframe. Yes, you guessed it; click and you insert a keyframe at that location. You can also access the context menu, shown in Figure 15.19, by right-clicking on a specific frame in the animation bar. It contains the Add Keyframe command that accomplishes the same thing.

With the newly created keyframe selected, move the layer. When you release the mouse button, the animation path has changed, as shown in Figure 15.20.

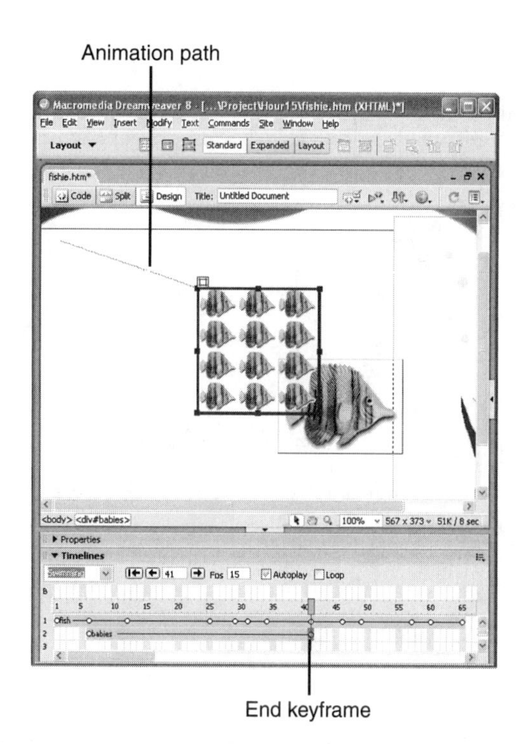

FIGURE 15.18
A line represents the animation path when you have a timeline selected in the Timelines panel.

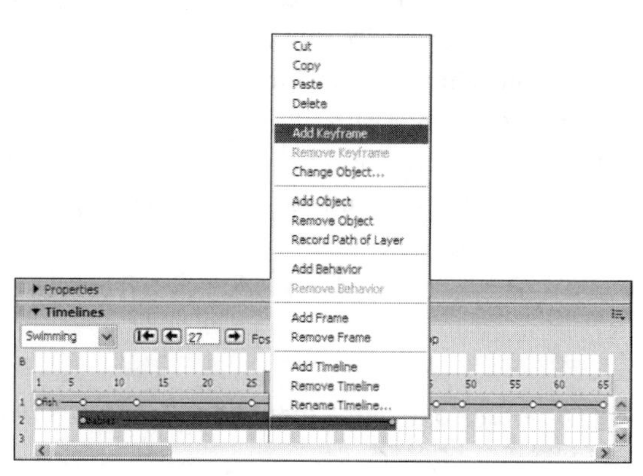

FIGURE 15.19
The context menu contains many useful commands for manipulating timelines, including the Add Keyframe command.

You can add as many keyframes as you want. If you need to adjust the position of a layer at a certain keyframe, select the keyframe and move the layer. If you need to add or remove frames, right-click on the frame in the animation bar to select either the Add Frame or the Remove Frame command. When you add or delete frames, they are added or deleted from the entire timeline, not just a single channel.

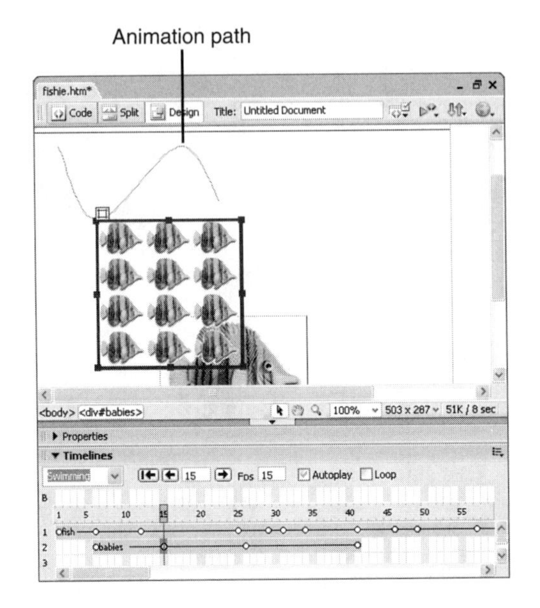

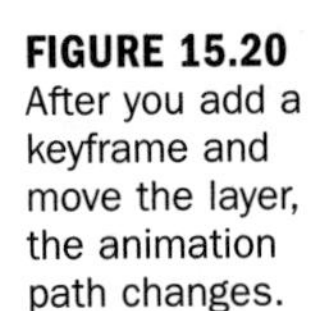

FIGURE 15.20
After you add a keyframe and move the layer, the animation path changes.

Summary

In this hour, you have learned how to insert a layer into a web page. You have learned how to change the layer's size, position, background color, and name. You have explored setting the stacking order, or z-index, of layers and setting layer visibility. You have also become familiar with the `<div>` tag. You learned how to record the movement of a layer. You learned how to add layers to a timeline and change their properties. And you added a keyframe so you could add properties to an additional frame.

Q&A

Q. ***The*** `<div>` ***tag is described as implementing CSS layers. I thought that CSS had to do with text. Am I right?***

A. The CSS standard does define many attributes for manipulating text. But it also defines *box elements*, which are what layers are. This might make more sense to you after you have completed the next hour, which is all about CSS. In that hour, you'll learn about the different attributes of layers that you will be able to set up in a style and how powerful that capability is.

Q. *Why would I want to use layers in my web pages?*

A. You might decide not to use layers and might end up using other methods—tables, for instance—to position content on your web pages. But if you'd like to have some content overlapping or sitting on top of other content, you'll need to use layers and set the layer z-index to a value higher than the underlying content's z-index. Alternatively, if you'd like to hide an image or text on the screen and then show it later by using the Show-Hide Layers behavior (see Hour 17), you'll of course need to use layers. In Hour 18, "Creating a Form and Collecting Data," you'll learn how to animate layers to move around a web page.

Q. *Help! My timeline doesn't play. What's wrong?*

A. First, check that you dragged a layer into the Timelines panel and not an image. Then make sure you have checked the Autoplay check box. Is the animation bar starting at frame one? If not, your animation might be playing empty frames before it gets to your content.

Q. *I'm right-clicking in the Timelines panel, but I don't see the Insert Keyframe command in the context menu. Where is it?*

A. You need to right-click on an individual animation bar to get the context menu to appear. You can't click on the top of the playback head or the frame numbers. If you continue to have trouble, hold down the Ctrl key (Command key on the Macintosh) and use the keyframe cursor to add keyframes.

Workshop

Quiz

1. What does a keyframe do?
2. What is the most common cross-browser tag used to implement layers?
3. The layer with the lowest z-index is the one on the top. True or false?

Quiz Answers

1. A keyframe is a frame where you can change properties.
2. The `<div>` tag is the most logical choice. It is meant to logically divide sections of the page, and it works in most version 4.0 and higher browsers.
3. False. The layer with the highest z-index is the one on top.

Exercises

1. Create a web page that has multiple layers. Experiment with inserting images and text into the layers. Change the background color of one of the layers. Be sure to make a few of the layers overlap so you can see how the z-index works.
2. Create a banner and a navigation bar for a site by placing a layer across the top of the site for the banner. Place individual layers with the text Home, Previous, and Next in them. You can make these hyperlinks if you like. Now convert these layers into a table.
3. Create an animation in which a layer moves around the screen. Add more keyframes. Do the keyframes change the way the animation runs? For instance, does the animation run more smoothly with more keyframes?

HOUR 16

Formatting Web Pages Using Cascading Style Sheets

What You'll Learn in This Hour:

- How to create each of the three style types: classes, redefined HTML tags, and advanced styles
- How to apply styles to objects
- How to create an external style sheet for an entire website

The Cascading Style Sheets (CSS) standard enables you to apply a property or group of properties to an object by applying a **style** to that object. You define and apply styles in Dreamweaver's CSS Styles panel or in the Page Properties dialog box, as you did in Hour 3, "Getting Started: Adding Text, Lists, and Previewing in the Browser." When thinking about styles, you usually think of creating and applying styles to text, which certainly is possible. However, styles can also be used for positioning objects, creating borders, and lots more.

The trend in Web standards is toward separating the presentation of a web page (the way the page is displayed visually) from the content (the words and images that make up the page). Dreamweaver has been completely re-engineered to rely on CSS styles to control the presentation of the HTML content. Separating the content from the presentation paves the way to supporting various operating systems, browsers, and devices such as personal digital devices (PDAs) and cell phones.

One of the benefits of using styles is the ability to simultaneously update every object with a certain style. If you create a style for all the paragraph text on the page, say a style defined as Arial 14-pixel text, you can later change the style's font to Times Roman, and all the paragraph text will instantly appear in the new font. You don't have to search through your entire page for updates but can simply make a change in one spot.

CSS is defined by the World Wide Web Consortium's (W3C) CSS specification (get more information at www.w3.org/Style/CSS). Your viewers will need to have a 4.0 or later browser version to view styles and, luckily, most web users do. Current browser statistics say that almost 98% of browsers are modern version, versions later than 4.0 (check out www.w3schools.com/browsers/browsers_stats.asp).

Dreamweaver displays a preview of how most styles will look in the browser. There are three types of CSS *rules*, also called CSS styles, and during this hour you will learn how to create styles that use all three: You will create a **class**, redefine the appearance of HTML tags, and use another type of style called a **CSS selector**.

Did you Know?

What Does Cascading Mean?

The topic of this hour is called Cascading Style Sheets, not just Style Sheets. That's because the cascading portion of the definition of this standard refers to which styles and attributes take precedence over other styles. The CSS standard defines a complicated hierarchy of style precedence dependent upon the style's proximity to the object it's applied to, the type of style, and when the style loads. A very rough rule of thumb is that the closer the style definition is to the object, the more heavily weighted it is. So, a style defined in a web page would override a conflicting style that is defined in an external style sheet that is in another file.

Creating and Applying a Class

The CSS Styles panel lists styles that have been defined and are ready to be applied to objects on your web page. You define a class by creating a new style and defining it in Dreamweaver. The Dreamweaver Style Definition dialog box has panels that list numerous style settings. First, you create a class and apply it to text. Then you can define the font, font size, and font color.

To create a class, follow these steps:

1. Click the New CSS Rule button from the CSS Styles panel, shown in Figure 16.1. You can also select New from the menu in the upper-right corner of the CSS Styles panel or you can select Text, CSS Styles, New.
2. The New CSS Rule dialog box appears, as shown in Figure 16.2. Select the radio button beside Class (Can Apply to Any Tag).
3. Enter a name for the style in the Name box at the top of the New CSS Rule dialog box. A class name must begin with a period. Dreamweaver enters the period for you if you forget to enter it.

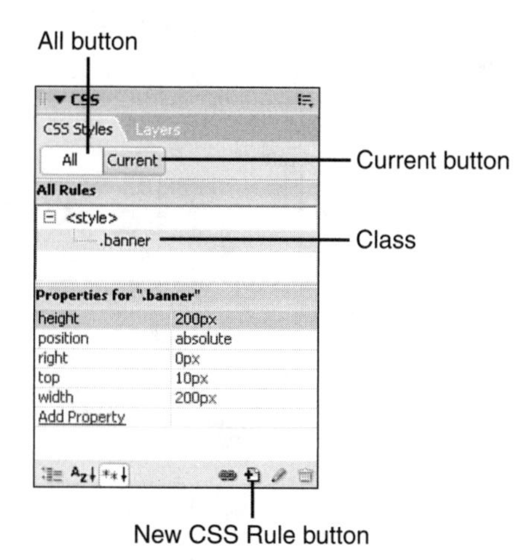

FIGURE 16.1
You create a new style with the New CSS Rule button.

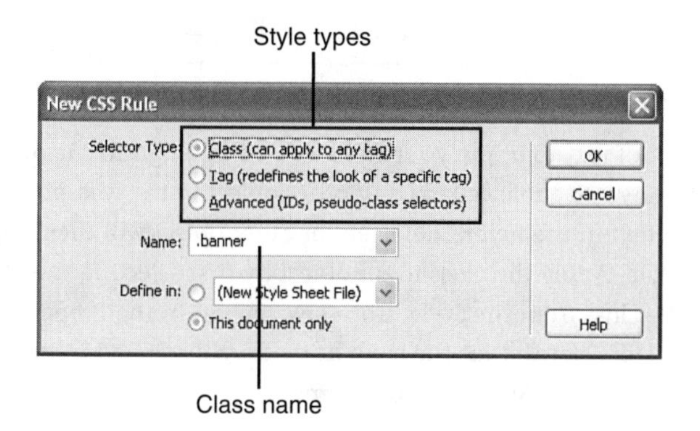

FIGURE 16.2
You select which of the three types of styles you are defining in the New CSS Rule dialog box.

Did you Know?

Naming Classes

Don't use spaces or punctuation in style names (except for the period at the beginning!), and don't begin a style name with a number.

4. Select the radio button beside This Document Only in the Define In section. This places the style definition in the head of the web page. If you forget this step, Dreamweaver prompts you to save the style as an external style sheet. We'll discuss external style sheets later this hour.

5. The CSS Rule Definition dialog box appears, as shown in Figure 16.3. The box opens with the Type category selected. In the Type category, select a font and font size from the appropriate drop-down menus. Also, select a font color by using the color picker.

6. Select OK to save the style. The CSS Styles panel lists the new class (make sure that the All button is selected at the top of the CSS Styles panel).

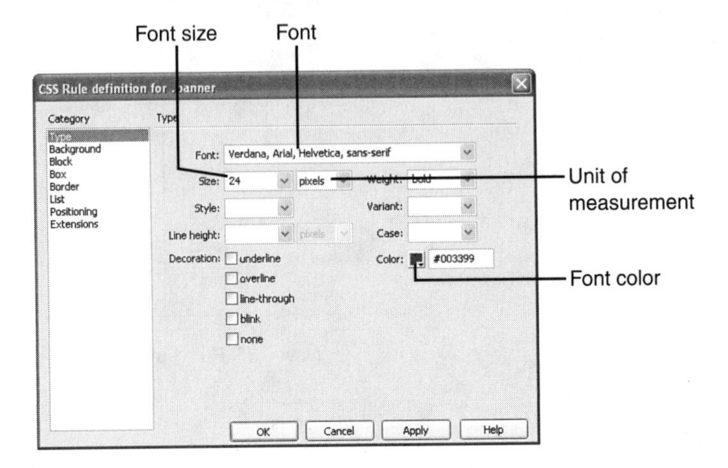

FIGURE 16.3 The CSS Rule Definition dialog box is where you set up the attributes of a style.

You select a block of text to apply your style to by dragging the cursor across it. You can also select a layer, a table cell, or any other object in the web page and apply the style. All the text in the layer, table cell, or other object will then appear as defined by the style. Apply the class to an object by first selecting the object and then selecting the class from the Style drop-down menu in the Property inspector, as shown in Figure 16.4. Notice that the style names are displayed in their respective fonts and font styles in the Style drop-down menu.

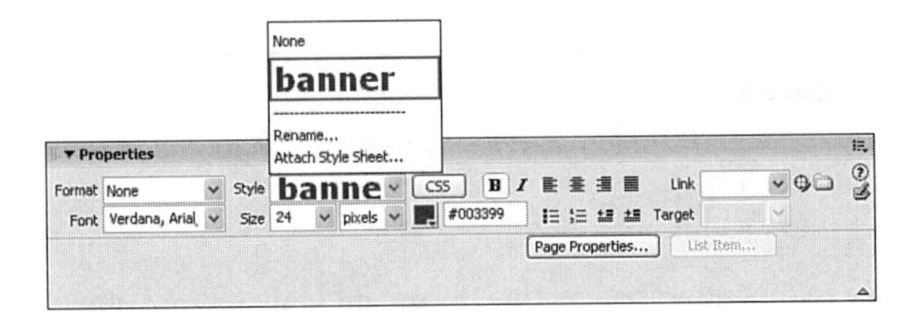

FIGURE 16.4 Select an object and then apply a class by using the Style drop-down menu in the Property inspector.

Watch Out!

Apply Styles to the Correct Tag

Some style attributes only work when applied to certain tags. For instance, a style called `bigcell` with the cell padding values set in the Box category of the CSS Rule Definition dialog box does not have any effect on text because padding is not an attribute of text. Applying this style to an appropriate object, such as a table cell, does have an effect.

Did you Know?

Remove a Style

If you accidentally apply a style to an object, you can remove it by selecting None in the Style drop-down menu in the Property inspector.

Exploring Style Settings

The CSS Rule Definition dialog box has eight categories with numerous settings you can use to define a style. As you are defining a style, select the panels to gain access to the settings for each category. Any settings that you do not need to set should be left alone. The following categories are available:

- **Type**—This category defines type attributes, such as font and font size. These style settings can be applied to text or to objects that contain text.
- **Background**—This category defines background attributes, such as color and image. These style settings can be applied to objects, such as layers and tables, where you can set a background.
- **Block**—This category defines type attributes for paragraphs.
- **Box**—This category defines attributes, such as margin size, that are applied to box objects, such as layers and tables.
- **Border**—This category defines attributes that are applied to objects that have borders, such as layers and tables.
- **List**—This category defines list attributes, such as bullet type.
- **Positioning**—This category defines layer attributes, such as visibility and z-index. See Hour 15, "Using Dynamic HTML and Layers," for an explanation of layers and layer attributes.
- **Extensions**—This category defines miscellaneous attributes that are either future enhancements or for Internet Explorer only.

Table 16.1 lists the style settings available in the various categories of the CSS Rule Definition dialog box.

TABLE 16.1 Style Settings in the CSS Rule Definition Dialog Box

Setting	Description
Type Category	
Font	Sets the font family.
Size	Sets the font size and unit of measurement.
Style	Specifies the font as normal, italic, or oblique.
Line Height	Sets the height of the line of text and the unit of measurement. This setting is traditionally called **leading**. It is added before the line.
Decoration	Adds an underline, an overline, or a line through the text. You can set the text decoration to blink, or remove the decoration by choosing None.
Weight	Adds an amount of boldface to text. Regular bold is equal to 700.
Variant	Sets the small caps variant on text.
Case	Capitalizes the first letter of each word or sets all the text to lowercase or uppercase.
Color	Sets the text color.
Background Category	
Background Color	Sets a background color for an object.
Background Image	Sets a background image for an object.
Repeat	Controls how the background image is repeated. No Repeat displays the image only once, Repeat tiles the image horizontally and vertically, Repeat-x tiles the image only horizontally, and Repeat-y tiles the image only vertically.
Attachment	Sets whether the background image scrolls with the content or is fixed in its original position.
Horizontal Position	Specifies the initial horizontal position of the background image.
Vertical Position	Specifies the initial vertical position of the background image.
Block Category	
Word Spacing	Adds space around words. Negative values reduce the space between words.
Letter Spacing	Adds space between letters. Negative values reduce the space between letters.

TABLE 16.1 Continued

Setting	Description
Block Category	
Vertical Alignment	Sets the alignment of the object relative to objects around it (for example, the Alignment settings discussed in Hour 7, "Displaying Images").
Text Align	Aligns text within an object. Choices are left, right, center, and justify.
Text Indent	Sets how far the first line is indented. Negative values set outdent.
Whitespace	Sets how whitespace will appear in an object. Normal collapses whitespace, Pre displays all the whitespace, and Nowrap sets the text to wrap only when a tag is encountered.
Display	Sets how and if an element is displayed. The None setting, for instance, hides the item on the page, the Block setting displays the element with a line break before and after, and the Inline setting displays the element with no line breaks.
Box Category	
Width	Sets the width of an object.
Height	Sets the height of an object.
Float	Sets whether text will float to the right or the left of the object. The None setting enables an object to appear where it is actually embedded in the code.
Clear	Clears floating so that objects (such as text) do not float around another object.
Padding	Sets the amount of space between the object and its border (or margin).
Margin	Sets the amount of space between the border of an object and other objects.
Border Category	
Style	Sets the style appearance of the borders. The choices are Dotted, Dashed, Solid, Double, Groove, Ridge, Inset, Outset, and None (for no border).
Width	Sets the border thickness. You can set the widths of the top, right, bottom, and left borders separately.
Color	Sets the border color. You can set the colors of the top, right, bottom, and left borders separately.

TABLE 16.1 Continued

Setting	Description
List Category	
Type	Sets the appearance of the bullets. The choices are Disc, Circle, Square, Decimal, Lower-roman, Upper-roman, Lower-alpha, Upper-alpha, and None.
Bullet Image	Sets a custom image for bullets.
Position	Sets whether the list content wraps to the indent (Outside) or to the margin (Inside).
Positioning Category	
Type	Sets how an element is positioned relative to the page. The choices are Relative (at the coordinates relative to its position on the page), Absolute (at the exact coordinates), and Static (at its place in the document flow).
Width	Sets the width of a container.
Height	Sets the height of a container.
Visibility	Sets the container's visibility. The choices are Inherit, Visible, and Hidden.
Z-Index	Sets the container's z-index (that is, stacking order).
Overflow	Sets what happens when the container's contents exceed its size. The choices are Visible, Hidden, Scroll, and Auto.
Placement	Sets the left, top, width, and height attributes for a container.
Clip	Sets the top, bottom, left, and right clipping attributes for a container. Clipping defines how much of an element is visible.
Extensions Category	
Page Break	Forces a page break during printing, either before or after the object. This style is not widely supported, but might be in the future. Be careful with this property; use it only when you absolutely need to control where the page breaks for printing.
Cursor	Changes the cursor when it is placed over the object. Supported only in Internet Explorer 4.0 or later and Netscape 6 or later.
Filter	Applies special effects, including page transitions, opacity, and blurs, to objects. The filters included with Dreamweaver are supported only in Internet Explorer 4.0 or later. See msdn.microsoft.com/workshop/Author/filter/filters.asp for more information. You can hand code filters for other browsers.

Redefining an HTML Tag

You can redefine HTML tags by using CSS styles. You apply these styles by applying the HTML tags as you normally would. For instance, you apply the <h3> tag by selecting Heading 3 from the Format drop-down menu in the Property inspector. Text formatted with the <h3> tag by default appears in a large italic font, slightly indented from the left margin, with one or two blank lines above and below. After you redefine the <h3> tag, any text with that tag applied to it immediately appears with the new CSS formatting.

Did you Know?

Use Less Classes

Web page developers who are new to CSS often use a lot of classes to apply CSS to their pages. But as you become more savvy, you'll begin to think of ways to use HTML tag CSS rules and selectors (you'll learn about those later this hour) instead.

Type some text in the Dreamweaver Document window and apply Heading 3, the <h3> tag, to it. Do this so you can see what the text looks like before you redefine the <h3> tag. Create a new style by clicking the New CSS Rule button in the CSS Styles panel. The New CSS Rule dialog box appears. Select the radio button beside Tag (Redefines the Look of a Specific Tag) and then select h3 from the Tag drop-down menu in the dialog box that appears, as shown in Figure 16.5.

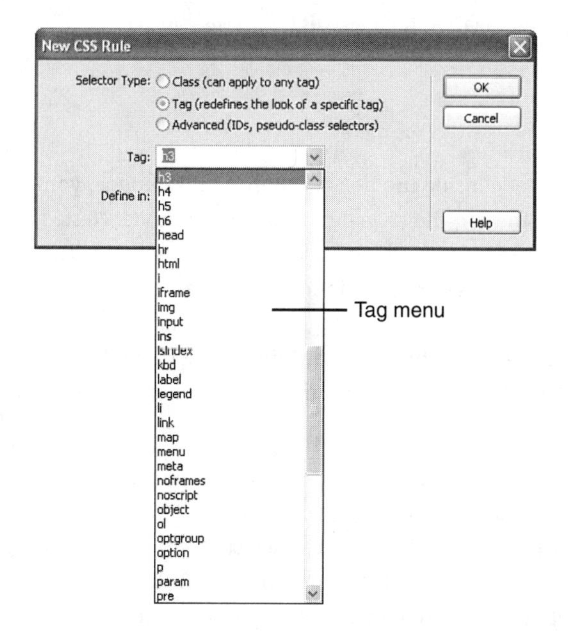

FIGURE 16.5
The Tag drop-down menu contains a list of all the HTML tags you can change by using CSS styles.

By default, the <h3> tag makes objects left justified. To use styles to center the h3 text, select the Block category. Select Center from the Text Align drop-down menu, as shown in Figure 16.6, and click the OK button. Immediately after you click OK, the h3 text in your web page should jump to center alignment. You can also apply a font in the Type category if you'd like.

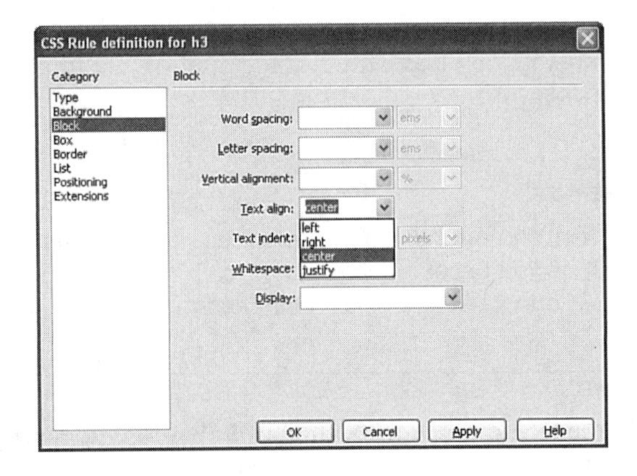

FIGURE 16.6
The Block category properties apply to blocks of text. You can change the default alignment of a text block in the Text Align drop-down menu.

Styles are defined in the head section of the web page. Dreamweaver automatically records the styles you create in the CSS Styles panel into the head of the document. An example of the code for the h3 style looks like this:

```
h3 {
    font-family: Verdana, Arial, Helvetica, sans-serif;
    font-size: 13px;
    color: #6600FF;
    text-align: center;
}
```

If you look at the code inside the head section of a web page, you'll see paired `<style>` tags surrounding the style definitions in the code. Nested within the style tags are paired comment tags (the `<!--` and the closing `-->`). The comment tags are added so that older browsers simply ignore the styles and don't cause errors. The rule for the style is between the style tags and contains the tag name, in this case, h3, followed by paired curly brackets containing the property name and the property value. Notice that a colon separates the property name and property value.

The lower half of the CSS Styles panel, the properties pane, displays information about the style that's selected in the top half of the panel. The three buttons in the lower-left corner of the panel enable you to control what is displayed in the properties pane. With the Show List View button selected, the style name appears at the top of the pane, and the style's definition appears in the list, as shown in Figure 16.7. Notice that you can also edit CSS style properties in the properties pane.

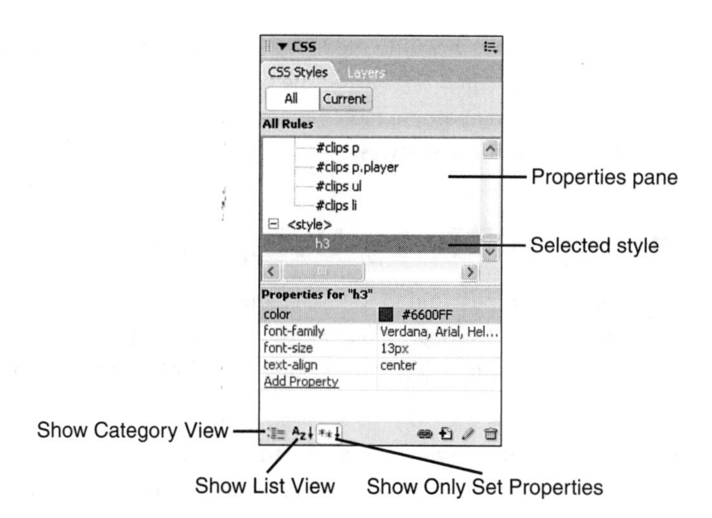

FIGURE 16.7
The CSS Styles panel enables you to view the style definition code.

Editing Styles

After you create styles, you might need to edit them. You can edit styles using the Edit Style button in the bottom-right corner of the CSS Styles panel, as shown in Figure 16.8. Select any of the styles in the CSS Styles panel and click the Edit Style button to re-open the CSS Rule Definition dialog box. Edit the style and save your changes.

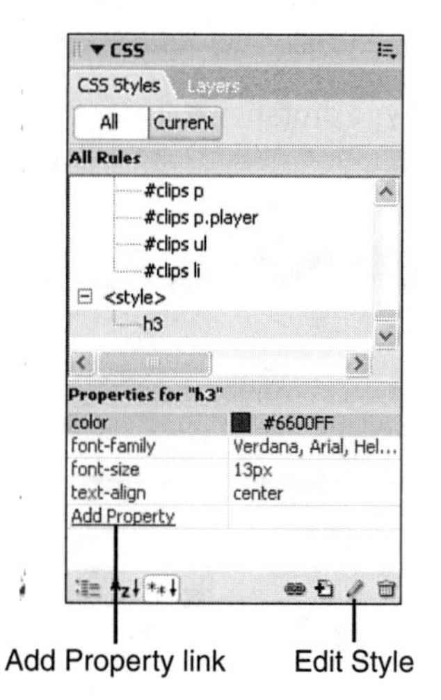

FIGURE 16.8
You can easily edit CSS styles by using the Edit Style button in the CSS Styles panel.

You can also edit CSS style properties in the properties pane in the bottom half of the CSS Styles panel. Simply click on any of the properties in any of the three views

(Category, List, or Add Property views) to modify or add the property to the style definition. It is easier for you to edit a style using the Edit Style button while you are learning Dreamweaver. As you become more advanced, you might want to use these new property views to edit CSS styles.

Positioning a Div by Using CSS

In Hour 15 you worked with positioning layers, created with `<div>` tags, in a web page. Dreamweaver automatically positioned those layers using CSS! Since you'll be using the Dreamweaver Div Tag object in this hour, I'll refer to containers as div tags instead of layers.

So far this hour, you've applied styles to text. Div tags are useful in positioning objects on the page by using styles. If you need to position content contained in div tags in a consistent place on the screen, it's an excellent idea to define a style for them. The other advantage to using styles is that if you'd like to move all the div tags at once, you can simply edit the style definition.

To define a positioning style for a div, follow these steps:

1. Create and name a new class, as you did earlier in this hour. You can call it `.banner` if you'd like.
2. Select the Positioning category in the CSS Rule Definition dialog box. Notice that the properties in this category are properties that you used in the last hour, when you created layers.
3. Select Absolute in the Type drop-down list at the top of the dialog box. Set the Left, Top, Width, and Height values as shown in Figure 16.9.

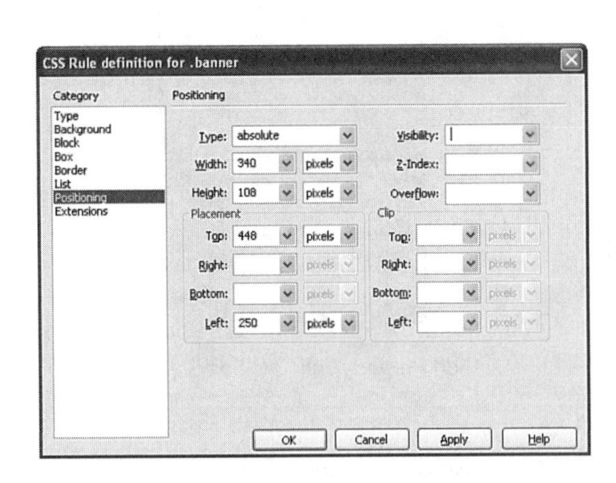

FIGURE 16.9
To create a positioning style, set the Left, Top, Width, and Height properties in the Positioning category of the CSS Rule Definition dialog box.

4. Click the OK button to save your style.
5. Now you will create the div tag to which the class is applied. Place the cursor in your web page and select Insert, Layout Objects, Div Tag.
6. Select the class you just created from the Class drop-down menu, as shown in Figure 16.10. Notice the New CSS Style button? You could have inserted the div tag and then created your style by selecting this button!

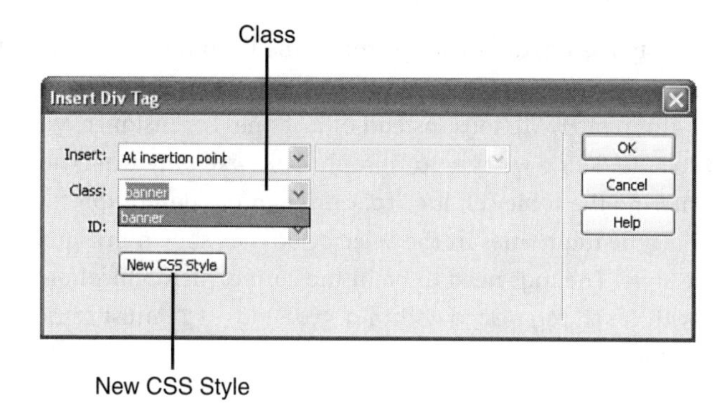

FIGURE 16.10 The Insert Div Tag dialog box enables you to insert a div tag into the web page and apply a CSS style to it.

7. Click the OK button to add the div tag to the page.

Notice that the div tag appears as `<div.banner>` in the tag selector, where banner is the name of the class applied to the div tag. You can see the style definition of the CSS that is applied to the current selected object on the web page by selecting the Current button at the top of the CSS Style panel, as shown in Figure 16.11.

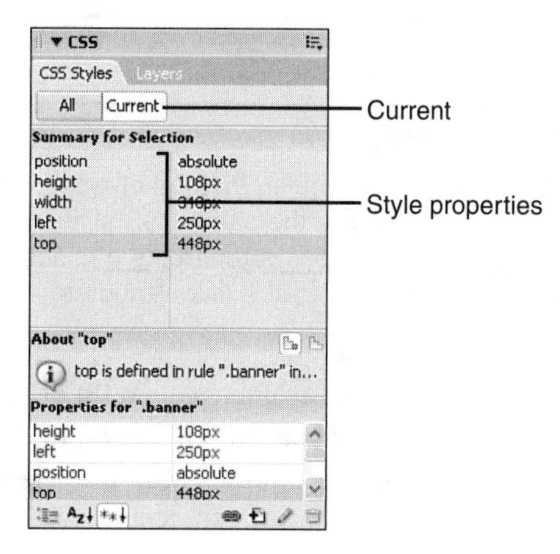

FIGURE 16.11 The Current button displays the CSS applied to the object selected in Dreamweaver's Document window.

The CSS style you just created is absolutely positioned at a certain top and left value on the web page. You can also position an object relative to the flow of the web page by choosing Relative instead of Absolute in the style definition. Using relative positioning when creating div tags for page layout enables you to easily add new div tags without having to reposition everything.

Creating Advanced CSS Styles

The third type of style is advanced styles; this is the third radio button that is available when you are creating a new CSS style with Dreamweaver. This type of style can redefine a group of HTML tags instead of just one. For instance, you could use an advanced style to define what a paragraph looks like only when nested within a table cell by entering the table cell tag, `td`, and then the paragraph tag, `p`. To do this, you enter all the tag names in the Selector box, as shown in Figure 16.12, and then define the style. The tags need to be in the correct hierarchical order, so if you create a style with a `<p>` tag nested within a `<td>` tag, `<td>` must come before `<p>` in the style selector.

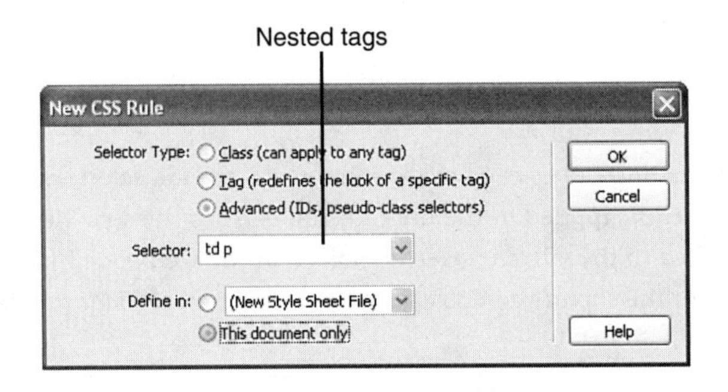

FIGURE 16.12
You can define attributes for a tag within another tag by using advanced styles in the New CSS Rule dialog box.

Did you Know?

Link Selector Styles

If you drop down the Selector menu instead of typing tags into the box, you see a list of the selectors. These are the same CSS styles you modified in the Page Properties dialog box in Hour 5, "Setting Lots o' Links: Hyperlinks, Anchors, and Mailto Links," when you changed the link attributes.

You also use the Advanced CSS style to create a list of HTML tags that you'd like to define together. For instance, if you want `h3`, `p`, `td`, and `li` tags to all share the same style definition, you'd enter `h3, p, td, li` in the Selector textbox in the New CSS rule dialog box, as shown in Figure 16.13. Notice that you enter the tags separated by commas. This is different from how you created the previous nested tag example when you entered the tags without any separator.

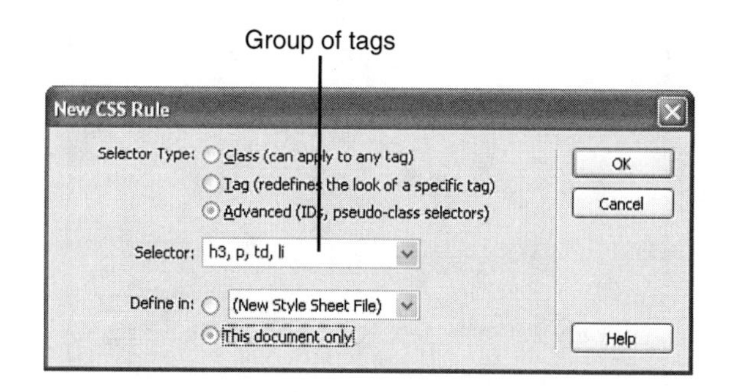

FIGURE 16.13 You can define attributes for a group of tags by using advanced styles in the New CSS Rule dialog box.

Creating an External Style Sheet

Adding styles to a single web page is nice, but wouldn't it be great to apply the same styles to a number of web pages? External style sheets allow you to do this. Instead of defining styles in the head of a web page, you define all the styles in one text file. External style sheets end with the `.css` filename extension. When you update a style in an external style sheet, the changes apply to every page that is linked to that style sheet.

To create an external style sheet, follow these steps:

1. Create a new style and then select the top radio button in the Define In section of the New CSS Rule dialog box. Select (New Style Sheet File) from the drop-down menu beside the radio button, as shown in Figure 16.14. Click the OK button.

2. The Save Style Sheet File As dialog box opens. Browse to the directory where you want to save your external style sheet. Enter a filename, as shown in Figure 16.15, and make sure it has the `.css` file extension. Click OK.

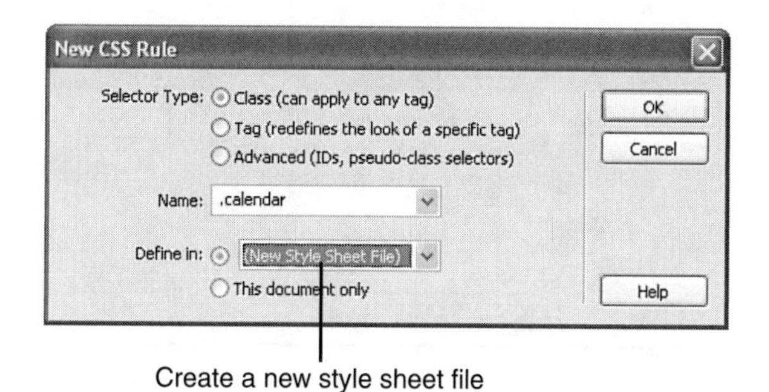

FIGURE 16.14 Select (New Style Sheet File) to define a new external style sheet.

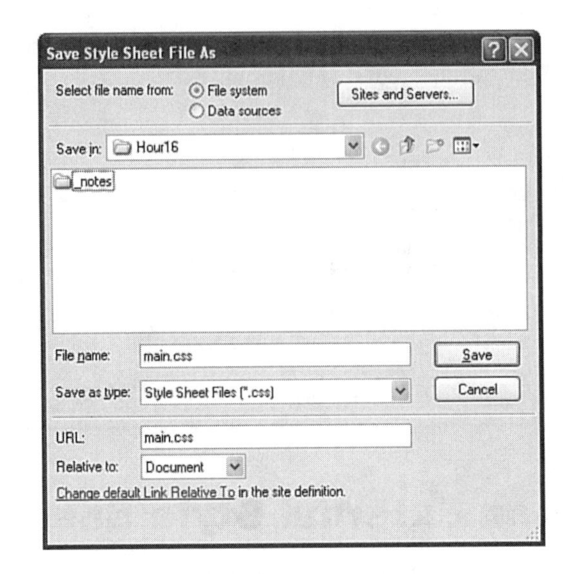

FIGURE 16.15 Create an external style sheet by browsing to the correct folder and saving a file with the filename extension `.css`.

3. The CSS Rule Definition dialog box opens. Notice that the title bar says that you are defining this style in the external style sheet you just created. Create and save your style as you did earlier this hour.

Did you Know?

Where to Store the CSS?

Many web developers store external style sheets in a directory called `CSS` or `Scripts`.

When you create an external style sheet, Dreamweaver creates a new file and places the style definitions in it. Dreamweaver also references the external style sheet in the head of your web page. To add additional styles to the external style sheet, select the name of the external style sheet from the Define In drop-down menu when you are defining a new style, as shown in Figure 16.16.

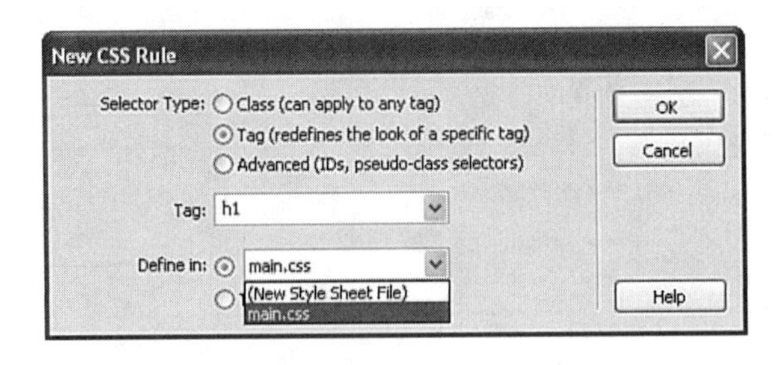

FIGURE 16.16 Select an external style sheet from the Define In drop-down menu to create a new style in the external style sheet.

CSS Style Preferences

It can be confusing when Dreamweaver automatically opens an external style sheet when you add a style to it. You can turn this option off in Preferences (Edit, Preferences) in the CSS Styles category. You can also set what Dreamweaver opens when you double-click a style name in the CSS Styles panel.

Did you Know?

Export Internal Styles

If you already created some styles in a web page and then decide to use an external style sheet, select File, Export, Export CSS Styles to export the styles defined in the web page into an external `.css` file. Link to the `.css` file by using the Attach to Style Sheet button at the bottom of the CSS Styles panel.

Did you Know?

Summary

In this hour, you have learned how to create and apply classes, redefined HTML tags, and advanced styles. You've learned how to position a div tag using CSS. You've seen how Dreamweaver can store styles internally, in the same web page. And you have also made an external style sheet that allows the same styles to be used throughout an entire website.

Q&A

Q. ***Can I link more than one style sheet to a web page?***

A. Yes. You can link as many style sheets to a web page as you'd like.

Q. ***How can I remove the underline from hyperlinks by using CSS styles?***

A. Some people might advise against doing that, but if you feel your design demands it, it's your call. To remove the underline from hyperlinks, redefine the <a> (anchor) tag in the CSS Rule Definition dialog box. Set Decoration (in the Text category) to None. All the hyperlinks on the page will no longer be underlined. You might want to define `a:hover` (select it from the Selector drop-down menu in the New CSS Rule dialog box) with an underline so the user can easily find the links when he places the cursor over them.

Q. ***I know it's important to separate presentation from content, so how can I load a unique style sheet depending on the user's browser to optimize the user's experience of my web page?***

A. In Hour 22, "Customizing Dreamweaver," you'll learn about extensions to Dreamweaver, files that you can download and install into Dreamweaver to extend its capabilities. There are a couple of extensions on the Dreamweaver Exchange, Macromedia's repository for extensions (`www.macromedia.com/exchange`), that add code to your page that loads different style sheets, depending on the user's browser and version. You can download one of these extensions, install it into Dreamweaver, and then use the extension to accomplish your goal of using different style sheets, depending on the user's browser.

Workshop

Quiz

1. What are the three types of CSS styles?
2. What should you create in order to use the same styles for all the web pages in a website?
3. If you redefine the `<h3>` tag as red in an external style sheet and then redefine the `<h3>` tag as blue in the web page, what color will h3 text be in that page?

Quiz Answers

1. The three types of CSS styles are classes, redefined HTML tags, and advanced styles (CSS selectors).
2. You need to create an external style sheet and link it to each page in your website.
3. The text will be blue because the internal style, the one defined in the page, is closer to the actual code and is dominant.

Exercises

1. Create a page as well as a class style that modifies text. Try applying this style to text in the page, table cells, layers, and other objects in the page. Save the style internally (This Document Only setting) and then export the styles to an external style sheet (File, Export, CSS styles). Delete the style from the web page by selecting <style> in the CSS Styles panel and selecting the Delete CSS Rule button (the trashcan). Use the Attach Style Sheet button to attach the external style sheet to the web page.

2. Create different definitions for the four hyperlink selectors: `a:active`, `a:hover`, `a:link`, and `a:visited`. You can find these selectors under the Selectors drop-down menu when Advanced is selected in the New CSS Rule dialog box. Create a unique style for each selector. Write down the four colors you used and then figure out when each appears by previewing a link on the page with the style definitions in the browser.

HOUR 17

Adding Interactivity with Behaviors

What You'll Learn in This Hour:

- ▶ What a Dreamweaver behavior is
- ▶ How to apply a behavior to an object in a web page
- ▶ How to use behaviors to add interactivity to a web page
- ▶ How to select events to trigger behaviors

Dreamweaver behaviors add interactivity to web pages. Interactivity usually requires coding in JavaScript, but Dreamweaver adds all the JavaScript for you, so you don't have to understand scripting to use behaviors. Behaviors enable you to make something happen when the user clicks the mouse, loads a web page, or moves the cursor. You used your first behavior, the Go to URL behavior, in Hour 14, "Using Frames to Display Multiple Web Pages."

What Is a Dreamweaver Behavior?

When you add a behavior to a web page, Dreamweaver inserts JavaScript functions and function calls, enabling users to interact with the web page or make something happen. I like to think of a **function** as a little code machine—you send it some information, it processes it, and it sends you a result or makes something happen. A **function call** is the code added to an object that triggers the function and sends it any information it needs to do its job. For instance, a popular Dreamweaver behavior is the Swap Image behavior you used in Hour 7, "Displaying Images."

When you insert a behavior, Dreamweaver writes a function in the head of the web page. The function that controls the Swap Image behavior is called `MM_swapImage()`. The code in that function isn't called until some event on the page triggers it; until it's triggered the function code just sits waiting in the head. For instance, the `MM_swapImage()` function is usually triggered by the `onMouseOver` event—the event fired when the cursor is placed over whatever object to which the function is attached. When the user rolls her mouse over an image with a behavior attached, the event triggers the function which swaps the image source with another image.

A **behavior** is an action that is triggered by an event, or you could look at it this way:

event + action = behavior

Actions are the JavaScript code that Dreamweaver inserts into a web page, the function. Browser events are user actions that are captured by the browser; for example, clicking on a button on a web page triggers the `onClick` event. Table 17.1 lists examples of common browser events. Different browsers might capture different events. Also, different objects capture different events. This is just a small sampling of the events that are available, but luckily, most of the events are named so that the functionality is fairly obvious. The `onDblClick` event, for instance, is similar to the `onClick` event, except that the user clicks twice instead of once.

TABLE 17.1 Common Browser Events

Event	Description
`onMouseOver`	Triggered when the user places the cursor over an object. This event is often captured from images or hyperlinks.
`onMouseDown`	Triggered when the user presses the mouse button. This event is often captured from images or hyperlinks.
`onMouseUp`	Triggered when the user releases the mouse button. This event is often captured from images or hyperlinks.
`onClick`	Triggered when the user presses and releases, or clicks, the mouse button. This event is often captured from images or hyperlinks.
`onLoad`	Triggered when the object or web page finishes loading. This event is often captured from the body of a web page and occasionally used with images.
`onUnload`	Triggered when the web page is unloaded from the browser—when the user goes to a new URL or the browser is closed. This event is usually captured from the body of a web page and is often responsible for triggering those annoying pop-up windows that seem impossible to close.

TABLE 17.1 Continued

Event	Description
onChange	Triggered after a user has made and committed a change to a form object, usually a text field, textarea, drop-down menu, or list. The user commits to the change by leaving the form object, usually by putting the focus elsewhere on the web page.
onSelect	Triggered when a user selects text within a form object, usually a text field or textarea.
onSubmit	Triggered when the user submits a form by using a submit button or an image button.
onBlur	Triggered when an object loses **focus**, or becomes inactive. This event is often captured from the body of a web page, when the user switches to a different web page, or from form objects, such as a text field or a check box.
onFocus	Triggered when an object receives focus, or becomes active. This event is often captured from the body of a web page, when the user switches to a different web page, or from form objects, such as a text field or a check box.

To learn more about individual events, use the Dreamweaver Reference panel (by selecting Window, Reference), shown in Figure 17.1. There are several reference books built right into Dreamweaver. To find the events, select JavaScript Reference from the Book drop-down menu and select an event name from the Object menu. The Reference panel displays a description of the event including which browsers support the event (in the upper-right corner) and typical targets for the event.

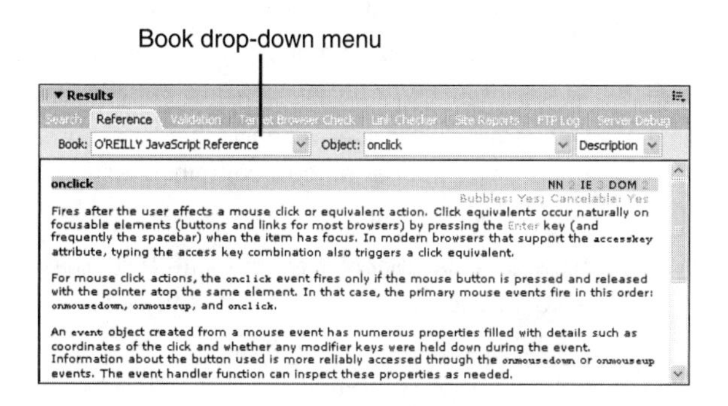

FIGURE 17.1 The Reference panel displays the JavaScript reference that includes descriptions of events.

Dreamweaver comes with many powerful behaviors. You can also download third-party behaviors, called **extensions**, that you will learn more about in Hour 22, "Customizing Dreamweaver." Table 17.2 lists the behaviors that are preinstalled in Dreamweaver.

TABLE 17.2 Dreamweaver Behaviors

Behavior	Description
Call JavaScript	Specifies custom JavaScript code. You use this behavior when you want to add custom JavaScript code to Dreamweaver.
Change Property	Changes an object's properties. This behavior enables you to change properties of layers (such as the background color or the size), form objects, and images.
Check Browser	Determines what browser the user has. This is useful when you are have authored content specific to various browser versions. This behavior can redirect the user to different web pages based on which browser she is using.
Check Plugin	Determines whether the user has a particular plug-in installed. You usually trigger this behavior by using the `onLoad` event of the `<body>` tag.
Control Shockwave or Flash	Controls Shockwave or Flash movies. Can be set to Play, Stop, Rewind, or Go to Frame.
Drag Layer	Makes a layer draggable and defines a target to which to drag it.
Go to URL	Loads a URL into the browser. This behavior also enables you to load several new URLs into frames as described in Hour 14, "Using Frames to Display Multiple Web Pages."
Hide Pop-up Menu	Hides a Dreamweaver pop-up menu (described later in this table, with the Show Pop-up Menu behavior).
Jump Menu	Edits a jump menu. You'll create a jump menu in Hour 18, "Creating a Form and Collecting Data." This is a menu that enables users to jump to various URLs.
Jump Menu Go	Adds a custom jump menu's Go button. This button is used to trigger going to the newly selected URL.
Open Browser Window	Opens a new browser window. This behavior is often used to open an additional window containing extra information.
Play Sound	Plays a sound file.
Popup Message	Pops up a JavaScript alert box with text. This box contains an OK button that the user clicks to close the message.
Preload Images	Preloads images into the browser cache in the background. This behavior is often included with the Swap Image behavior. The image to be swapped is loaded into the cache so it appears quickly.
Set Nav Bar Image	Changes the image in a navigation bar. You created a navigation bar in Hour 9, "Creating Image Maps and Navigation Bars." This behavior enables you to set a button state.

TABLE 17.2 Continued

Behavior	Description
Set Text of Frame	Puts text (or HTML) into a frame.
Set Text of Layer	Puts text (or HTML) into a layer.
Set Text of Status Bar	Puts text into the browser's status bar.
Set Text of Text Field	Puts text into a text field in a form.
Show Pop-up Menu	Shows a Dreamweaver pop-up menu with links. This menu uses CSS to present a complex menu. You use this behavior to set the color, position, text, and other attributes of the menu.
Show-Hide Layers	Shows or hides a layer or group of layers. This behavior changes the layer visibility attribute.
Swap Image	Swaps the image source for another image source.
Swap Image Restore	Restores a previous image swap.
Go to Timeline Frame	Goes to a specific frame in a timeline.
Play Timeline	Plays a timeline.
Stop Timeline	Stops a timeline.
Validate Form	Validates the data in a form, enabling you to check whether the user has entered information into certain text fields and validating whether it is the correct type of information. You'll use this behavior in Hour 19, "Introduction to Scripts: Sending and Reacting to Form Data."

You attach behaviors to objects in a web page. When you attach a behavior, Dreamweaver opens the appropriate behavior dialog box. After you've set up the behavior characteristics in the dialog box, you select the event to trigger the behavior. Dreamweaver inserts the necessary JavaScript into the head of the web page. Code is also added to the object's tag to capture the event and call the JavaScript.

By the Way

When you add a behavior to an object, Dreamweaver adds an attribute to the HTML tag, enabling the tag to respond to the event. The attribute includes a function call to the appropriate function inserted by the behavior. For instance, the code for an image tag with a Show-Hide Layers behavior attached looks like this:

```
<img src="button_up.gif" width="80" height="35"
➥onClick="MM_showHideLayers('Layer1','','hide')" />
```

When the user clicks this image, the layer named `Layer1` becomes hidden.

You need to attach behaviors to appropriate objects. Dreamweaver won't let you attach behaviors that aren't appropriate; inappropriate behaviors are grayed out. You can tell which object you have selected in the Document window because the tag name is displayed in the title bar of the Tag panel group, as shown in Figure 17.2. This is the panel group where you find the Behaviors panel.

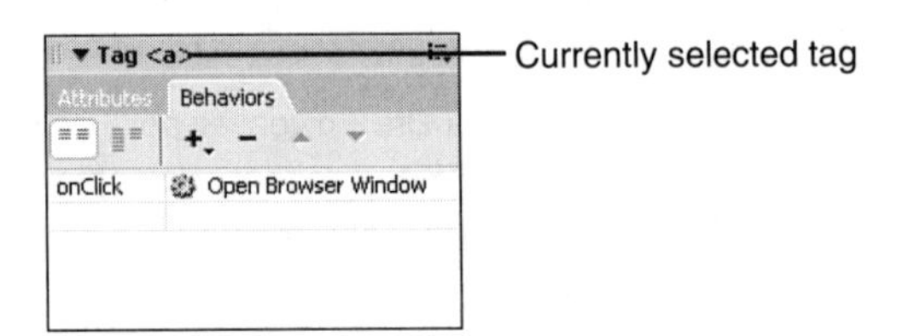

FIGURE 17.2 The tag of the object that is currently selected is displayed in the title bar of the Tag panel group.

Watch Out!

Different Behaviors

The Behaviors panel is not the same as the Server Behaviors panel. The Server Behaviors panel works with sites that use server-side scripting, such as ASP, ASP.NET, JSP, PHP, and ColdFusion. The Behaviors panel uses JavaScript, which is client-side scripting (and does not rely on a server).

You can attach multiple behaviors to an object. One event can trigger several actions. In Figure 17.3, you can see that the `onClick` event triggers a number of actions. The actions happen in the order in which they are listed. You can change the order in which the actions occur by moving the actions with the up and down arrow buttons on the Behaviors panel.

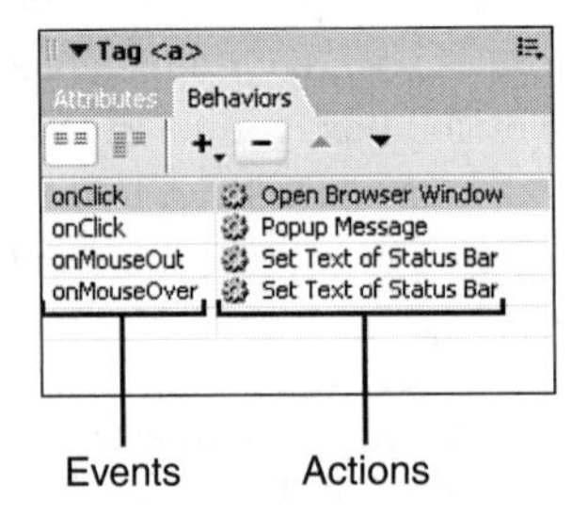

FIGURE 17.3 One event—for example, the `onClick` event shown here—can trigger multiple actions, and you can have multiple behaviors attached to a single object in a web page.

The biggest difference between the various browsers is the events they support. When you use behaviors, you need to be aware of which browsers you are going to support. If it's crucial that you support every browser available—on a government website, for instance—then you might be slightly limited in the events available to you. Dreamweaver enables you to select various versions of Netscape and Internet Explorer because these browsers sometimes capture different events.

Dreamweaver enables you to set the browser events that it presents in the Behaviors panel based on browser versions. The Show Events For drop-down menu, shown in Figure 17.4, enables you to target specific browsers and browser versions. Depending on the selection in this menu, different events will be available. You access the Show Events For drop-down menu by clicking the Add Actions (+) button in the Behaviors panel.

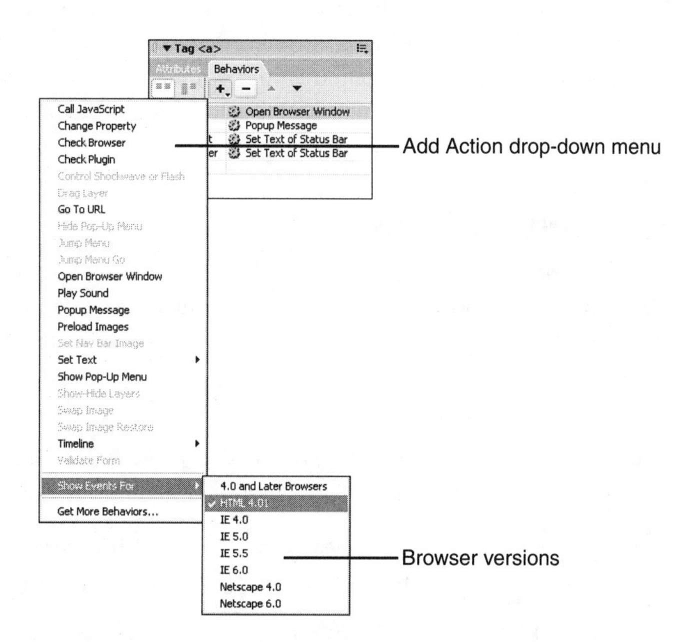

FIGURE 17.4 The Show Events For submenu enables you to choose browsers and browser versions. Only the actions and events that work with the browser and version you choose are available.

Did you Know?

Which Events Setting Is Best?

You will have access to the largest number of events by choosing IE 6.0 and the fewest number of events choosing 4.0 and Later Browsers. The HTML 4.01 events offer a good standards-based compromise between a useful number of events and compatibility with almost all browsers, so you'll generally want to choose the HTML 4.01 setting.

Watch Out!

What Happens When the Event Isn't Supported?

If you select an event that does not work in a certain browser, users using that browser will either have nothing happen or will receive a JavaScript error.

Showing and Hiding Layers

Now you're ready to add your first behavior. The Show-Hide Layers behavior has a name that pretty much says it all: You can use it to show or hide a layer on the web page. You don't usually apply a behavior to the object that it affects, so you'll need to have another object on the page that triggers the behavior. For instance, Dreamweaver won't allow you to attach the Show-Hide Layers behavior to the layer you want to hide.

To begin, you need to add an image or a hyperlink that captures the user's click and hides the layer. Dreamweaver is also smart enough to not display the Show-Hide Layers behavior in the Add Action drop-down menu if you don't actually have any layers in the web page, so you'll need to add a layer to the page before you add the behavior.

Selecting a Behavior

You will now use the Show-Hide Layers behavior. It's important to name your layers when using the Show-Hide Layers behavior. The Show-Hide Layers dialog box displays all the layers on the page by name, so it helps for the layers to have meaningful names. Type some text in the layer, insert an image into it, or give it a background color so you can see the effect in the browser.

First, define a site in Dreamweaver and create a new HTML page if you haven't done it already. To add a Show-Hide Layers behavior to a hyperlink, follow these steps:

1. Create a layer and set its visibility attribute to hidden. You learned about the visibility attribute in Hour 15, "Using Dynamic HTML and Layers."
2. Add text or an image somewhere on the web page. Add a null hyperlink to the text or image by first selecting it and then typing `javascript:;` in the link box of the Property inspector, as shown in Figure 17.5.

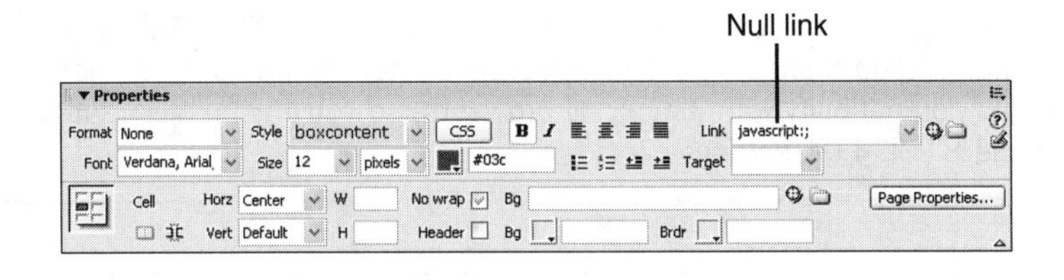

FIGURE 17.5 Create a null link that will trigger the behavior but won't load another web page.

3. Open the Behaviors panel and click somewhere within the newly created hyperlink. Make sure that <a> (the anchor tag) is visible in the title bar of the

Tag panel group. This means that you are applying the behavior to the <a> tag, the tag that implements hyperlinks.

4. Click the Add Action (+) button in the Behaviors panel, as shown in Figure 17.6. Select the Show-Hide Layers behavior. The Show-Hide Layers dialog box appears.

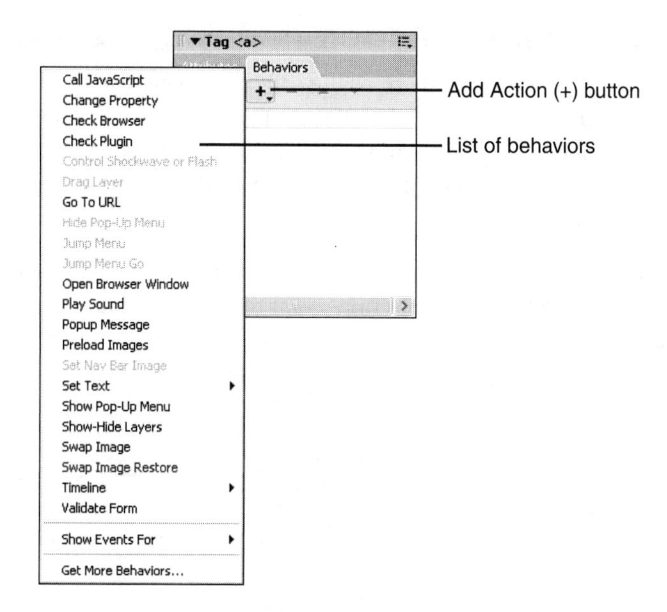

FIGURE 17.6
The Add Action (+) button drops down the Add Action drop-down menu, with all the actions available for the selected object.

5. The Show-Hide Layers dialog box, shown in Figure 17.7, lists all the layers in the page. There are three buttons: Show, Hide, and Default. Highlight the correct layer and click the Show button. The word *show* then appears in parentheses next to the layer name.

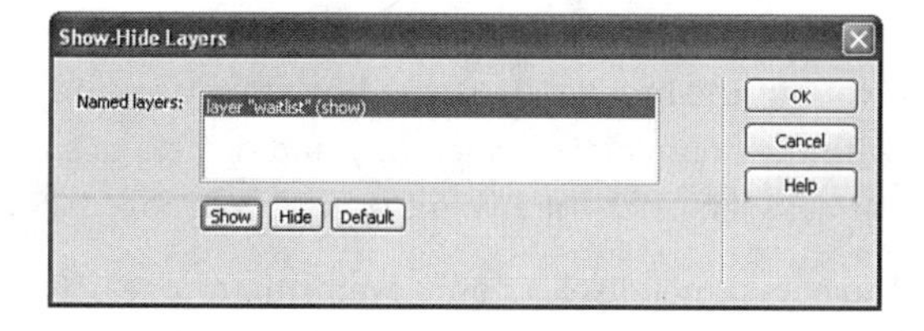

FIGURE 17.7
The Show-Hide Layers dialog box lists all the layers and enables you to change their visibility attributes.

The functions of the Show and Hide buttons in the Show-Hide Layers dialog box are obvious. You click the Show button to make a layer visible, and you click the Hide button to make a layer hidden. When a layer is set to Show, clicking the Show button again turns show off (the same goes for the other buttons). The Default button restores a layer to default visibility (which is usually visible).

6. Click the OK button to save your changes.

Selecting the Action that Triggers a Behavior

At this point, you have selected the action, but you also have to select the other half of the behavior: the event. The Behaviors panel lists the Show-Hide Layers behavior under the Action column and defaults to the `onClick` event. You could use the `onClick` event to trigger showing the layer, but that's too easy! Try using the `onMouseUp` event instead:

1. Drop down the Events menu by clicking the arrow button, as shown in Figure 17.8. You need to select the event for this button to be available.

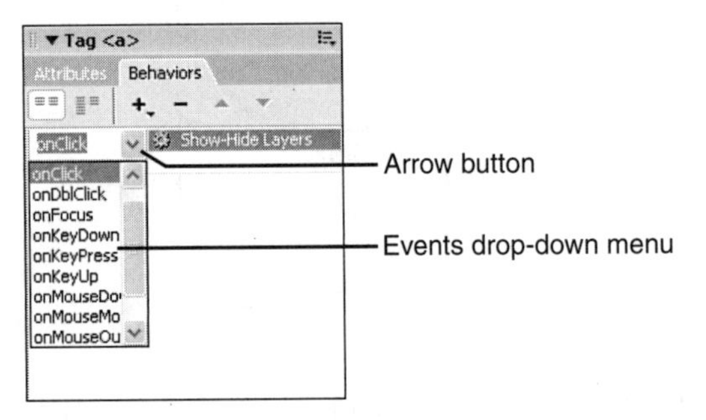

FIGURE 17.8 The arrow button beside the event drops down a menu containing the available events.

2. Select `onMouseUp` in the event drop-down menu. When the user lets up the mouse button, the Show-Hide Layers behavior is triggered.

Now that you have set up the action (Show-Hide Layers) and the event (`onMouseUp`), you can test your work in the browser. First you have to make sure the layer you have set to show with the behavior is hidden (if you didn't do this earlier). Preview the web page in the browser. Click the hyperlink, and your layer should appear!

By default, the Behaviors panel displays only events that have actions associated with them. You can set the Behaviors panel to display all the events available by clicking the Show All Events button, shown in Figure 17.9. The events list depends on the object selected on the web page and the browser(s) selected in the Show Events For drop-down menu. If any of the events have actions associated with them, you will see them displayed in the Actions column. If you want to display only events that have actions attached, click the Show Set Events button.

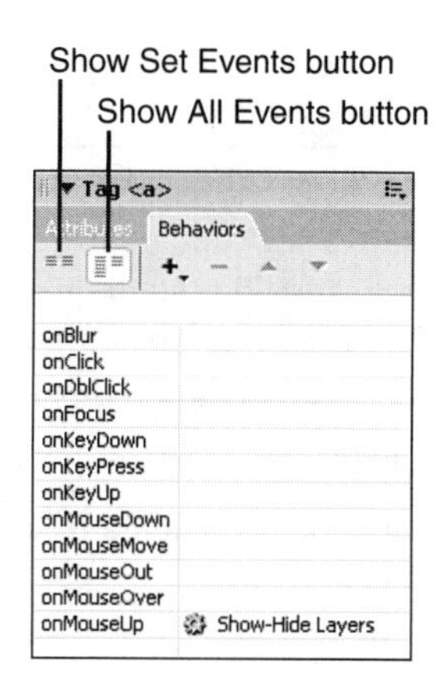

FIGURE 17.9
You can display all available events by clicking the Show All Events button in the Behaviors panel.

If you made a mistake while setting up the Show-Hide Layers behavior, simply double-click Show-Hide Layers in the Action column of the Behaviors panel. This re-opens the Show-Hide Layers dialog box where you can make changes. When you have Show or Hide selected for one of the layers, you can just click the same button again to toggle the selection off.

Opening a New Window

Use the Open Browser Window behavior to open a new browser window and display a URL. This time you will capture the user clicking an image to trigger the action. When the user clicks the image, the `onClick` event fires. This then triggers the Open Browser Window behavior that opens a new browser window.

You can open a browser window at a specific size and with specific browser attributes. Browser attributes, listed in Table 17.3, control whether the browser window has controls that enable the user to navigate out of the window. You set up the browser attributes in the Open Browser Window dialog box.

TABLE 17.3 Browser Properties for the Open Browser Window Behavior

Attribute	Description
URL	Sets the URL of the page that is opened in the new window.
Width	Controls the width (in pixels) of the window.
Height	Controls the height (in pixels) of the window.
Navigation Toolbar	Contains the Back, Next, and other navigation buttons for moving to different URLs.

TABLE 17.3 Continued

Attribute	Description
Location Toolbar	Displays the current URL.
Status Bar	Displays the status bar (the bar located at the bottom of the browser). The status bar displays the loading status of a web page as well as the URL of a moused-over link.
Menu Bar	Contains all the standard browser menus.
Scrollbars as Needed	Enables the user to scroll the browser window.
Resize Handles	Enables the user to resize the browser window.
Window Name	Specifies the optional window name. This name can be used to control the window with JavaScript, so spaces and punctuation cannot be used in the name.

To have a new browser window open when the user clicks an image, follow these steps:

1. Save the web page. The Open Browser Window behavior needs the web page to be saved so that it knows how to build the URL that it will load in the new browser window.
2. Insert an image into this web page. Select the image, and make sure the correct tag shows in the title bar of the Tag panel group (the `<img>` tag).
3. Click the + button in the Behaviors panel. Select the Open Browser Window behavior, and the Open Browser Window dialog box appears.
4. Fill in a URL that will load in the new window. You can use a web page that you created previously or load an external web page from any website.
5. Set the width and height of the window. Check the browser attributes (listed in Table 17.3) that you want the new browser window to have. Optionally, give the window a name.
6. The Open Browser Window dialog box should look something like the one shown in Figure 17.10. Click the OK button.
7. In the Behaviors panel, select the `onClick` event from the Events drop-down menu if it wasn't selected by default.

Preview the web page you created in a browser. When you click the image, your new window should appear. To edit a behavior, simply select the object where the behavior is applied. The behavior appears in the Behaviors panel. Double-click the behavior to reopen the Open Browser Window dialog box and edit the settings. You can edit the event by simply selecting a different event in the Events drop-down menu. Delete a behavior by selecting it and clicking the – button in the Behaviors panel.

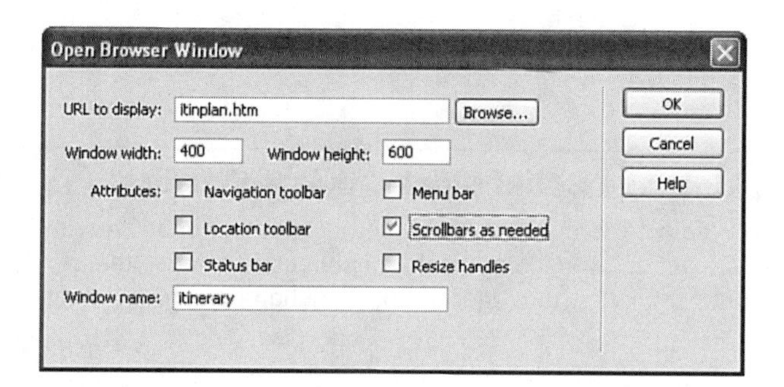

FIGURE 17.10 The Open Browser Window dialog box enables you to turn on or off various attributes of browser windows.

Watch Out!

Pop-up Blockers Might Block Opening a New Window

Be aware that many browsers and browser add-in programs (such as the Google or Yahoo! toolbars) add a pop-up blocker functionality. Although that's great for getting rid of unwanted pop-up ads, it's not good news for opening new browser windows. The better pop-up blockers only stop windows that open when triggered by the `onLoad` event of the <body> tag (you'll learn more about this later this hour). But some block all pop-up windows, even those triggered by the user.

Popping Up a Message

Next, you'll add an additional behavior, a pop-up message, to the same object you used to open a browser window. The Popup Message behavior displays a JavaScript alert box with a message.

To add the Popup Message behavior, follow these steps:

1. Select the object where you applied the behavior in the preceding section. You should see the Open Browser Window behavior listed in the Behaviors panel. Make sure the appropriate tag appears in the title bar of the Tag panel group.
2. Click the + button and select the Popup Message behavior.
3. The Popup Message dialog box includes a text box where you type your message, as shown in Figure 17.11. Click OK after typing the message.
4. Select the `onClick` event as you did in the Open Browser Window dialog box earlier.

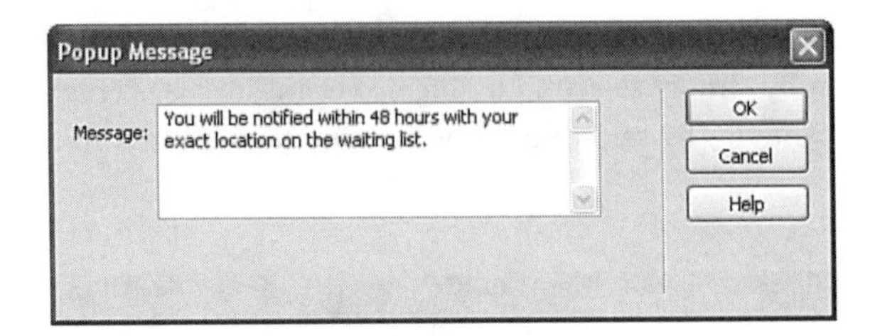

FIGURE 17.11 The Popup Message dialog box has a text box where you type the message that will pop up for the user.

Watch Out!

A Pop-up Message Could Block Other Behaviors

Make sure you select the `onClick` event and not the `onMouseOver` event. If the Popup Message action is triggered by the `onMouseOver` event, the browser never receives an `onClick` event to trigger the other actions you have attached to the object.

Preview your web page in the browser. Does it work ideally? It would probably be better if the message popped up and then the user went to the new window after he clicked the OK button in the message box. You can change the order of behaviors that are triggered by the same event.

To change the order of the behaviors, follow these steps:

1. Select the object where the behaviors are applied. You should see both behaviors listed in the Behaviors panel.
2. Select the Popup Message behavior. Click the up arrow button to move the Popup Message behavior above the Open Browser Window behavior, as shown in Figure 17.12.

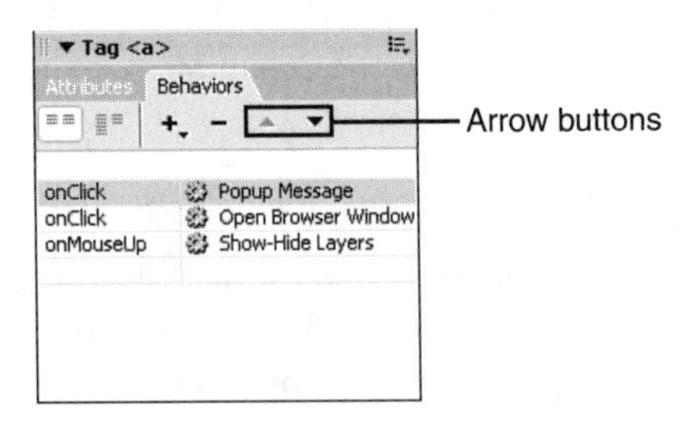

FIGURE 17.12 You can change the execution order of the behaviors by using the arrow buttons above the Actions column of the Behaviors panel.

Preview your web page in the browser. Now the pop-up message appears first. After you click the OK button on the pop-up message, the new browser window should appear.

Sending Text to a Layer

You can insert behaviors that write to various objects: frames, layers, text entry fields, and the browser status bar. To use the Set Text of Layer behavior, follow these steps:

1. Add a layer to the web page (Insert, Layout Objects, Layer) and name it `feedback`.
2. Select an object on a web page to trigger the behavior. You can add this behavior to the same object you've used earlier this hour or you can add a null link to an object on any web page.
3. Click the + button in the Behaviors panel. Choose the Set Text of Layer behavior from the Set Text submenu—the menu that appears when you place your mouse over Set Text in the Add Action drop-down menu. The Set Text of Layer dialog box appears.
4. Select the layer named `feedback` from the drop-down menu.
5. Enter some text in the New HTML text box, as shown in Figure 17.13. Click OK.

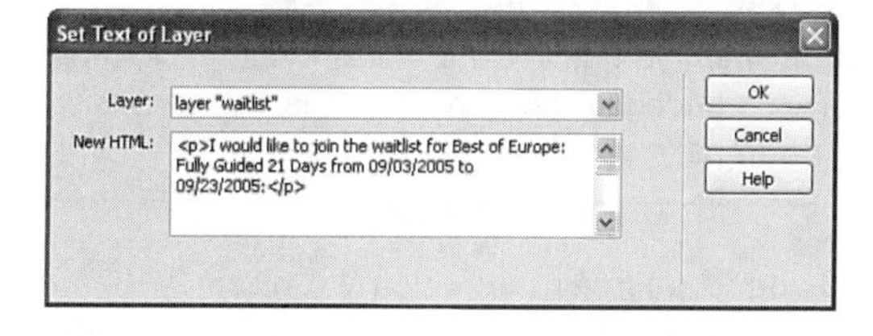

FIGURE 17.13 The Set Text of Layer dialog box enables you to enter text (and HTML) to display in the specified layer.

6. Select the `onClick` event from the Event drop-down menu in the Behaviors panel.

Preview the web page in your browser. When you trigger the action, the text you entered appears in the layer.

Adding a Draggable Layer to a Web Page

The Drag Layer behavior enables you to create layers that the user can drag around the browser window. You can even constrain the area within which the layer can be dragged. This capability is useful for creating sliders, puzzles, dialog boxes, and other interactions.

You can use the Drag Layer behavior to let users interact with objects on your web page. For instance, you might have a layer that contains a map legend. You could make that layer draggable so the user could move it out of the way if it happened to be blocking part of the map. Or you could create a blank face and let people drag different noses, ears, eyes, and so on, onto the face.

Did you Know?

Check out CourseBuilder!

If you need to create complicated drag-and-drop interactions, you should investigate the CourseBuilder extension to Dreamweaver, which is available at the Macromedia Exchange (see Hour 22 for information about extensions to Dreamweaver). The drag-and-drop interactions created by CourseBuilder have the capability to make an object return to its original position if dropped incorrectly.

The Drag Layer behavior enables a layer to be dragged. You need to turn on this behavior before the layer can be dragged. This behavior can be triggered when the web page loads by capturing the `<body>` tag's `onLoad` event. You select the `<body>` tag in Dreamweaver's tag selector. You should see `<body>` in the title of the Tag panel group.

By the Way

The `<body>` Tag Holds Everything Visible

You might notice that when you select the `<body>` tag, everything in your web page is selected. That's because the `<body>` tag is the container within which all the objects on your web page reside.

After you've created your drag layer and given it a name, you're ready to apply the Drag Layer behavior. To use the Drag Layer behavior, follow these steps:

1. Add a layer to a web page (Insert, Layout Objects, Layer) and give it a name.
2. Select the `<body>` tag from the tag selector in the Dreamweaver status bar.
3. Click the Add Action (+) button in the Behaviors panel and select Drag Layer. The Drag Layer dialog box appears, as shown in Figure 17.14.
4. Select from the Layer drop-down menu the name of a layer to be dragged.
5. Click OK to save your changes.
6. Make sure that the `onLoad` event is listed in the Behaviors panel next to the Drag Layer action. This means the Drag Layer behavior is triggered when the web page loads.

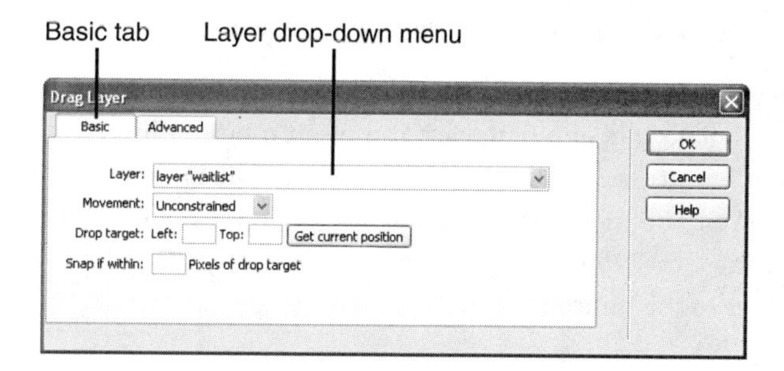

FIGURE 17.14 The Drag Layer dialog box enables you to select the layer you want to be draggable.

Check to see that the Drag Layer behavior is working the way you want it to by previewing the web page in a browser. The correct layer should be draggable.

> **Did you Know?**
>
> **Can't Find the Behavior?**
>
> If you do not see the behavior attached to the <body> tag when you select it, you've applied the behavior to the wrong tag. You need to hunt down the object to which you applied the behavior and delete the behavior in the Behaviors panel. As you click objects in the Document window, look at the Behaviors panel to see which object has the behavior attached to it.

Summary

In this hour, you have learned that a Dreamweaver behavior consists of an event that triggers an action. You have used the Show-Hide Layers behavior, the Open Browser Window behavior, the Popup Message behavior, and the Set Text in Layer behavior. You have captured events from a hyperlink and an image. And you have used the `onMouseUp`, `onClick`, and `onLoad` events as triggers for Dreamweaver actions. You have learned how to configure the Drag Layer behavior to create a draggable layer.

Q&A

Q. ***How can I apply a behavior to a layer that is hidden?***

A. You can select a hidden layer in the Layers panel. Switch to the Behaviors panel, without selecting anything else, and apply the behavior. Or you can temporarily make the layer visible, apply the behavior, and then hide the layer again.

Q. *How can I create a button that triggers a behavior?*

A. We'll cover forms and buttons in Hour 18. Basically, you place a button into the web page to trigger a behavior. You insert a button from the Forms tab of the Insert bar. If Dreamweaver asks you if you'd like to add a `<form>` tag, you can click Yes. The trick is to make sure the button is not a Submit or Reset button. Select the None radio button in the Property inspector and then apply a behavior to the button.

Q. *Where can I learn more about JavaScript?*

A. There are some excellent resources and tutorials on the Web where you can learn some JavaScript. You don't have to understand everything about JavaScript to use it. The short statements that you used during this hour should be easy to find in any JavaScript book or reference. Check out Appendix A, "Resources," for links to helpful sites. You might want to start out with *Sams Teach Yourself JavaScript in 24 Hours* by Michael Moncur.

Workshop

Quiz

1. What is the equation that connects an event, an action, and a behavior?
2. You have the most behaviors and events available when you choose 3.0 and Later Browsers from the Show Events For submenu in the Behaviors panel. True or false?
3. What two events add up to an `onClick` event?

Quiz Answers

1. The equation that connects an event, an action, and a behavior is

   event + action = behavior.

2. False. Most Dreamweaver behaviors use DHTML, which requires 4.0 or later browsers. Selecting 4.0 and Later Browsers enables you to use far more events and behaviors than does selecting 3.0 and Later Browsers. You have the most events available when you select IE 6.0 as the target browser.
3. An `onClick` event consists of the `onMouseDown` and `onMouseUp` events.

Exercises

1. Create a second hyperlink for the Show-Hide Layers example that you did earlier in the hour. Type **`Hide the Layer`**, make it a hyperlink, and make clicking this hyperlink hide the layer you created.

2. Try using some behaviors that are similar to the behaviors you have used in this hour (for example, the Set Text in Layer behavior and the Go to URL behavior). What events are available for these behaviors? What objects do you need to have on the web page for these behaviors to work?

3. Create a layer and make that layer draggable by attaching the Drag Layer behavior to the `<body>` tag. Figure out how to constrain the layer movement to only horizontal (select Constrained from the Drag Layer dialog box). Check the web page by previewing it in a browser. Then try constraining the movement to only vertical. Finally, constrain the movement to an area.

PART V

Collecting User Data by Using Forms

HOUR 18

Creating a Form and Collecting Data

What You'll Learn in This Hour:

- How to insert a form into a web page
- How to add text fields, radio buttons, and check boxes to forms
- How to add lists and drop-down menus of choices to forms
- How to add different types of buttons to forms
- How to create and edit a jump menu

In this hour, you will create a form to collect user input. Dreamweaver gives you easy access to a number of form elements, including text boxes, radio buttons, check boxes, lists, drop-down menus, and buttons to capture user choices. We'll cover how to submit form data in Hour 19, "Introduction to Scripts: Sending and Reacting to Form Data."

With forms, you can collect information, such as comments or orders, and interact with your users. In your form, you can ask for your user's name and email address, have the user sign a guestbook, or have the user purchase a product from your website. You can send this information back to the web server if you'd like. Dreamweaver enables you to validate information so you know it's in the correct format for a script that accepts the form data.

Creating a Form

A **form** is a container for other objects, as well as an invisible element. When you add a form to a web page, Dreamweaver represents it as a red, dashed-line box if you have Form Delimiter checked in the Invisible Elements category in the Preferences dialog box (Edit, Preferences), as shown in Figure 18.1. Make sure you have this option selected so you can see the outline of each form.

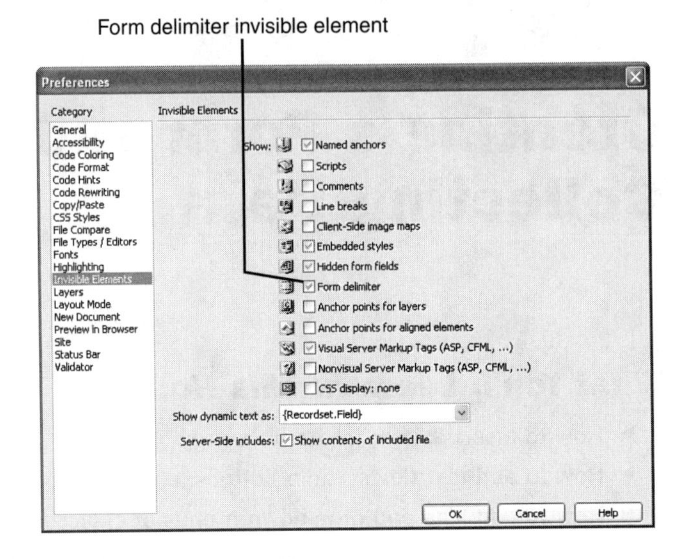

FIGURE 18.1
The Invisible Elements category in the Preferences dialog box enables you turn on and off the red, dashed-line box that represents the form outline.

While you're creating a form, it might be helpful to have the Forms category selected in the Insert bar, as shown in Figure 18.2. The first step in creating a form is to insert a Form object into your web page to hold all the form objects that will collect user input.

FIGURE 18.2
The Forms category in the Insert bar presents all the form objects you insert into your web page to collect user input.

To add a form, follow these steps:

1. Create a new web page and place the insertion point where you want to insert the form.
2. Select Insert, Form, Form or select the Form object in the Forms category of the Insert bar.
3. A message box might appear, as shown in Figure 18.3, telling you that you will not be able to see the form unless you view the invisible elements. Click OK and then, if necessary, select View, Visual Aids, Invisible Elements.

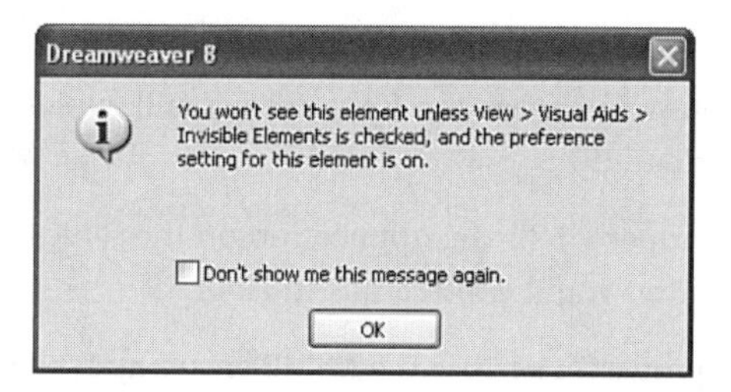

FIGURE 18.3 A message box might appear, telling you to view invisible elements to see the form you inserted into your web page.

4. A red, dashed-line box appears on the page, as shown in Figure 18.4. It represents the form.

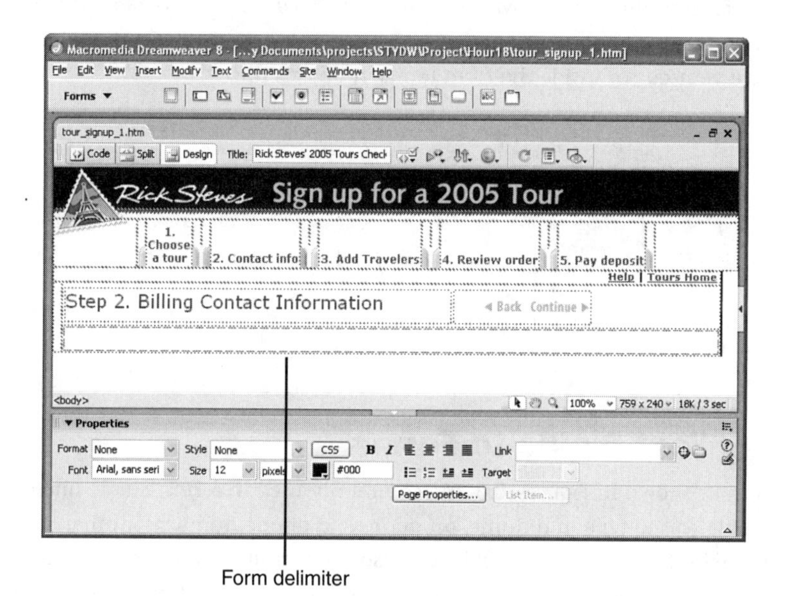

FIGURE 18.4 A form appears as a red, dashed-line box (a form delimiter) when invisible elements are turned on.

You can format the area within a form using tables, horizontal rules, text, and other items that would normally be in a web page. The only information that will be submitted, however, are the names of the form elements and the data the user enters into the form. The text and formatting objects you place within the form will not be submitted.

To select a form, click the edge of the form delimiter, or place the cursor within the form and select the `<form>` tag in the tag selector. The Property inspector shows the properties you can enter for a form:

- **Form Name**—This property is necessary if you plan to apply any behaviors (or your own custom scripts) to a form. It's a good idea to always name your forms. Dreamweaver puts a default form name in for you.

- **Action**—This property is a URL that points to an application, usually a script, on the server that will process the form data. You'll explore more about the form action in Hour 19.
- **Method**—This property tells the application on the server how the data should be processed. Again, you'll explore this in Hour 19.
- **Enctype**—This property specifies the MIME encoding type for the form data. If you don't set a value here, the default value is `application/x-www-form-urlencoded`.

Give your form a name, as shown in Figure 18.5. Because you'll explore the Action, Method, and Enctype properties in the next hour, you can just leave them blank for now. Place your cursor inside the form to insert objects into it.

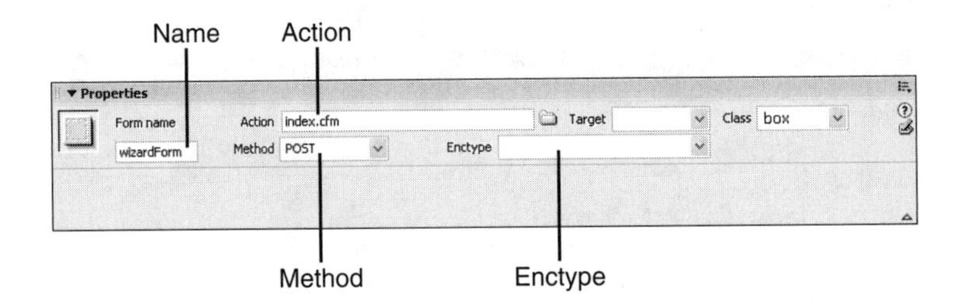

FIGURE 18.5 The Property inspector shows the attributes available to be set for a Form object.

Adding Text Fields to Forms

Text fields, as shown in Figure 18.6, are commonly used in forms. Single-line text fields enable you to type in a name, an address, a phone number, or other short pieces of text information. Text fields can also have multiple lines, called a **textarea** in Dreamweaver, suitable for comments or lengthy pieces of information. The example in Figure 18.6 was produced using one of the designs available in the New Document dialog box (File, New). Select the Page Designs category and the design called UI:Send Email B.

Now you'll continue creating your own form from scratch. Create a group of text fields designed to collect the user's first and last names, email address, and comments. Begin by inserting a single-line text field into your web page to collect the user's first name:

1. Make sure the insertion point is within the form. Type in **`Name:`** .
2. Add a Text Field object from the Forms category of the Insert bar, or select Insert, Form, Text Field. A text field appears in the form, as shown in Figure 18.7.

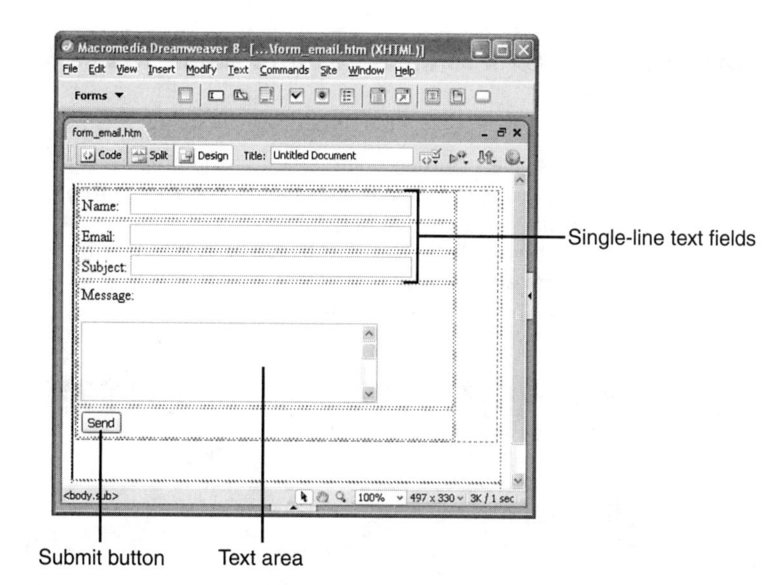

FIGURE 18.6
A group of text fields, a textarea, and a submit button are used to collect user information on an order form that is submitted to the server and then processed.

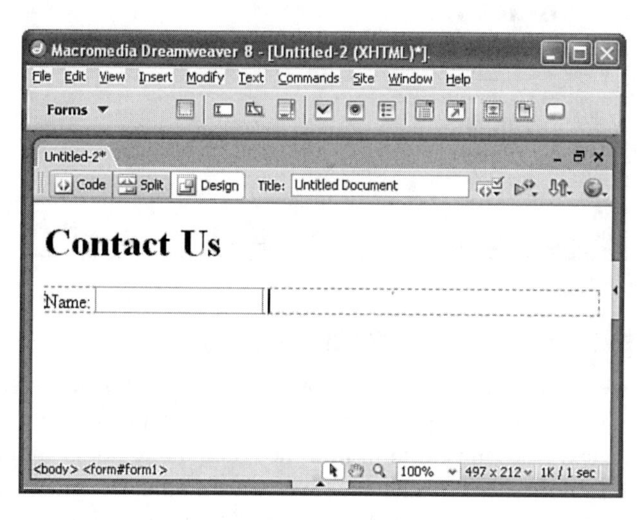

FIGURE 18.7
A text field is inserted within a form so a script or an application on the server can collect the data a user enters in the field on the web page.

3. Add a new line (Enter or Return key), type **`Email:`** , and then add another text field.

4. Add another new line (Enter or Return key), type **`Subject:`** , and then add another text field. The form should look as shown in Figure 18.8.

Did you Know?

Dreamweaver Asks to Insert a Form When You've Already Inserted One

If you get a dialog box asking you to insert a `<form>` tag but you thought you had already inserted one, the insertion point is not placed properly within the form. In this case, it's easiest to click No in the dialog box, delete the newly created object, and try again. If you are just beginning to create a form and forget to insert a Form object first, click Yes in the dialog box. Dreamweaver will insert a form around the form element you have just created.

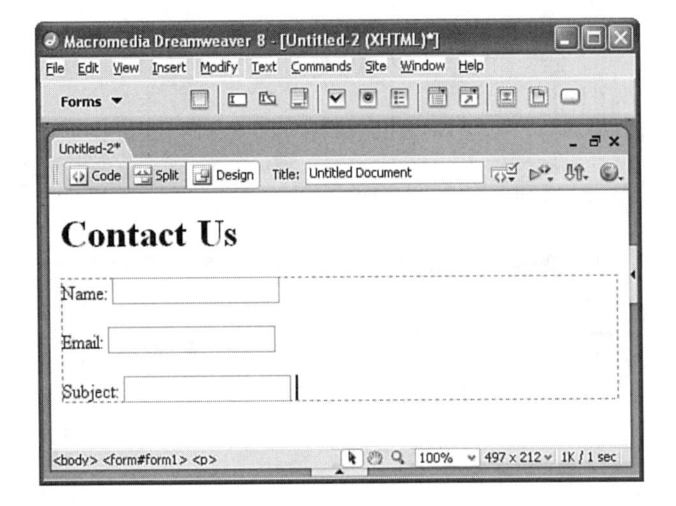

FIGURE 18.8 This form contains three text fields that you use to collect the user's first name, email address, and subject.

Applying Text Field Attributes

When you have a text field selected, the Property inspector presents the text field attributes, as shown in Figure 18.8. Dreamweaver fills in a unique default name. Rename all the text fields in your form with meaningful and unique names; possible names are `fullname`, `email`, and `subject`. As with other Dreamweaver objects, it is a good idea not to use spaces and punctuation in the names. Some scripts and applications are not designed to deal with form element names that contain spaces and punctuation.

Watch Out!

Don't Use *Name* as a Name

You need to name form objects carefully so users don't receive JavaScript error messages. You should never name an object on the page with any HTML attribute names. So, naming a text field *name* might be a logical choice, but it could cause JavaScript errors in some browsers because that is also the name of a tag attribute.

You can set both the size of the text field and the number of characters a user can enter into it. There are two width settings for a text field:

- **Char Width**—You use this setting to set the size of the text field and the number of characters visible in the field. If there are more characters in the text field than the width setting can accommodate, they will be submitted but simply won't be visible unless you scroll.
- **Max Chars**—You use this setting to limit the number of characters a user can enter into the text field. The user is not able to enter more characters than the value of Max Chars. Setting Max Chars might be useful when you know the absolute length of the data the user should enter, such as a Social Security number, and do not want the user to enter additional characters.

You can set three types of text fields in the Property inspector:

- **Single Line**—These text fields are useful for collecting small, discrete words, names, or phrases from the user.
- **Multi Line**—This type of text field presents an area with multiple lines that enables the user to enter larger blocks of text. This is the same as the Textarea object, which is available in the Forms category of the Insert bar.
- **Password**—These text fields are special single-line fields that mask what the user types into the field, using asterisks or bullets to shield the data from other people. This doesn't, however, encrypt the data that is submitted.

You can select any styles in the Class drop-down list to apply a CSS style to the text field. You learned about CSS styles in Hour 16, "Formatting Web Pages Using Cascading Style Sheets." You can set the font, background color, and other attributes of a text field by using CSS styles.

Did you Know?

Using One of the Built-in Style Sheets

You can select File, New and then select the CSS Style Sheets category to create one of the built-in style sheets that come with Dreamweaver. Select one of the Forms designs, such as Forms: Verdana, and click OK. Dreamweaver opens a style sheet file. Save this file with the .css extension and then attach the style sheet to the web page that contains the form. Using the Attach Style Sheet button at the bottom of the CSS Styles panel, select Link to link the style sheet you just created to the form you are creating. You should see the results immediately.

The first three fields in your form should remain single-line text fields. Type **`Message:`** on a new line and add a fourth field by creating a new paragraph and inserting a Textarea object from the Insert bar (or Insert, Form, Textarea). This object is exactly like the Text Field object, but it has the Multi Line property already applied.

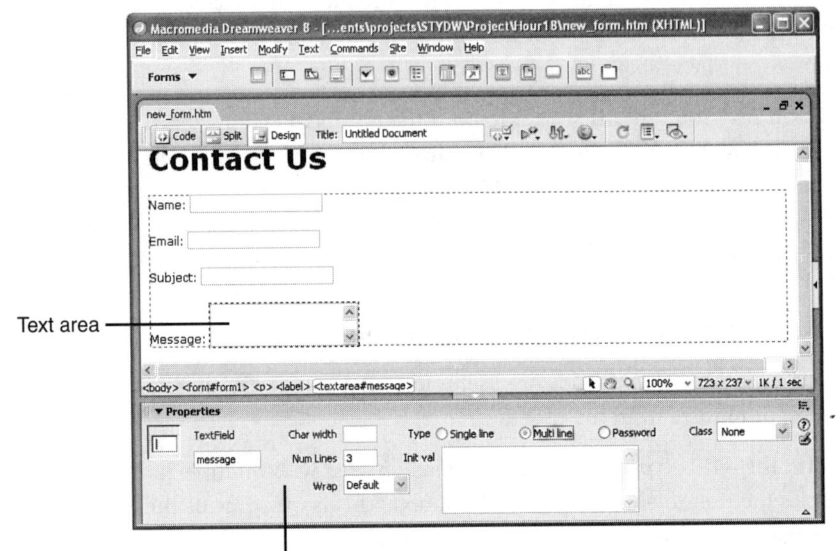

FIGURE 18.9
A textarea has Num Lines and Wrap attributes, which you can set in the Property inspector. Num Lines sets the number of lines, or height, of the textarea.

The Textarea object includes a property that enables you to enter the height of the object (the number of lines in the textarea). Enter a value into the Num Lines property to set the height. There is no Max Chars setting for a textarea; you can control only the number of lines visible on the screen.

By the Way

Change Char Width to Change the Size

You can't resize text fields by clicking and dragging their borders. You can only change the size by changing the Char Width property in the Property inspector.

The Wrap property is another property that is unique to textarea objects. The default setting is for the text in a textarea to wrap around to a new line when the user reaches the end of a line. You can turn wrapping off by choosing the Off command from the Wrap drop-down menu. There are two additional wrap settings: Physical and Virtual. With Physical set, the lines of text can wrap at the end of the box if you place a hard return (that is, a CRLF character) there. Virtual enables the lines of text to wrap at the end of the box, but no character is inserted.

You can add some text that appears in the text field when the user views the form. This could be instructions on what to enter into the field or a default value that the user could change if she wanted to. Enter text into the Init Val box in the Property inspector, as shown in Figure 18.10, so text is present when the user initially loads the form.

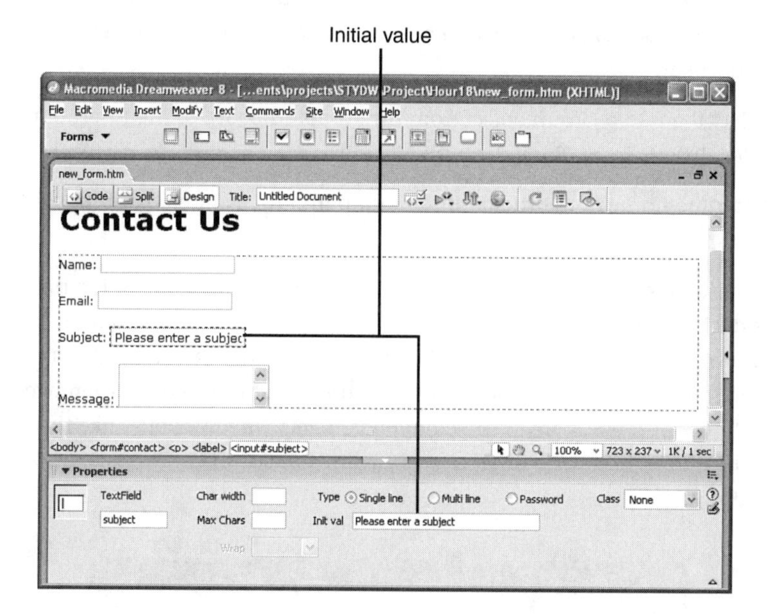

FIGURE 18.10 Enter text into the Init Val box in the Property inspector so it appears when the user initially loads the form.

Did you Know?

Using the Autoclear Snippet

Dreamweaver includes some form elements, along with other items, in the Snippets panel (Window, Snippets). You drag snippets from the panel and drop them on your web pages. A useful snippet for your form might be Text Field Autoclear; this snippet places a text field containing default text into a form. When the user clicks the text field, the default text automatically disappears. You'll explore snippets further in Hour 19 and Hour 22, "Customizing Dreamweaver."

Adding Radio Buttons and Check Boxes to Forms

Radio buttons are another type of form element you can use to collect user input. Radio buttons are grouped so the user can select only one button of the group at a time; when the user selects a different member of the group, the previously selected button is deselected. In order for radio buttons to be grouped, they all must have the same name.

To create a group of radio buttons, follow these steps:

1. Place the insertion point within a form where the radio buttons will be located. Type **`How did you hear about us?`** and press the Enter or the Return key.

2. Select the Radio Group object from the Forms category of the Insert bar or select Insert, Form, Radio Group.

3. Enter the name of the radio button group into the Name box of the Radio Group dialog box.

4. Enter a label name in the Label column and enter the value of the radio button when it is checked (called the *checked value*) in the Value column, as shown in Figure 18.11. The label is simply text that appears next to the button; it is not part of the form. Use the + and – buttons to add or remove radio buttons. At the bottom of the dialog box, select whether you'd like the buttons to be placed in a table or separated by line breaks. Click OK to save your settings.

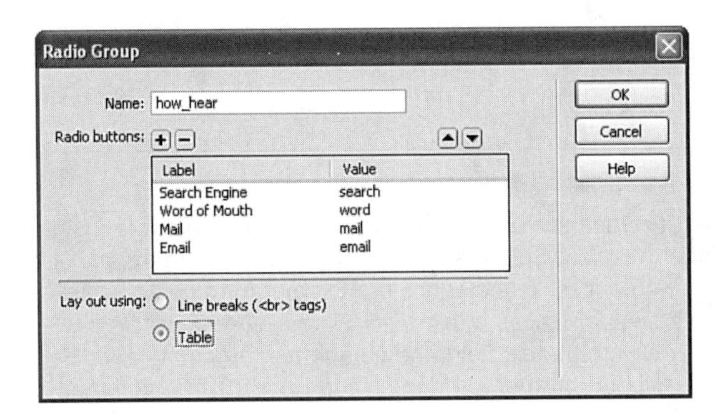

FIGURE 18.11
Add a radio button group. Each button has a label and a value.

5. When you select an individual radio button, its properties are displayed in the Property inspector. Choose whether the button will be checked or unchecked when the user first loads the form by selecting either the Checked or Unchecked options, which are located beside Initial State.

Check boxes collect user input when the user either checks or unchecks the box. They differ from radio buttons because they are not grouped; instead, they act independently. Radio buttons enable the user to select a single option, whereas check boxes enable the user to select any options that apply.

To add a check box to your form, follow these steps:

1. Place the insertion point within a form where the check box will be located. Type **`Receive Newsletter:`** .
2. Select the Check Box object from the Insert bar or select the Insert, Form, Check Box.
3. Enter a name for the check box into the box in the far left of the Property inspector.
4. Enter a checked value into the Checked Value box. If you do not specify a checked value, the value On is sent for the check box when the form is submitted. If there is an entry for the Checked Value setting, that value will be sent instead of simply On.
5. Choose whether the initial state of the check box is checked or unchecked in the Initial State setting.
6. Type a text label beside the check box. The settings should look as shown in Figure 18.12.

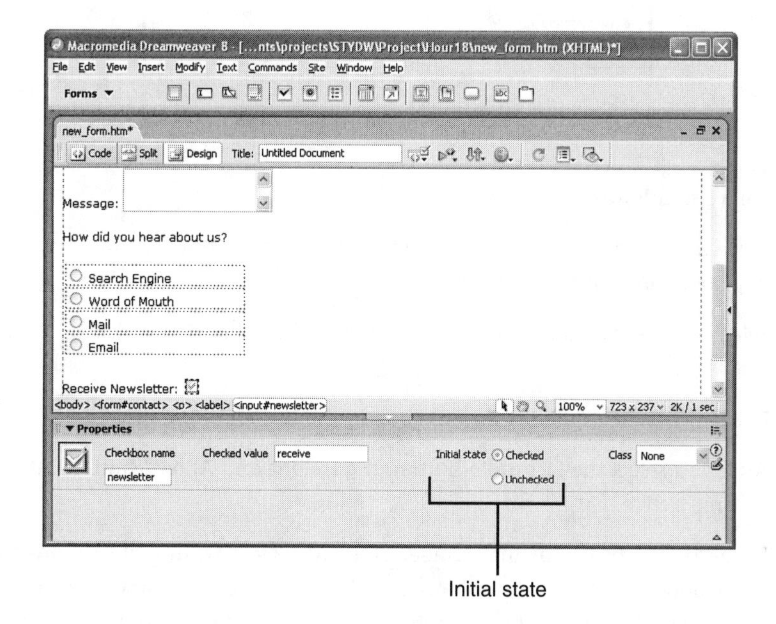

FIGURE 18.12
The check box settings are similar to the radio button settings. Check boxes cannot be grouped like radio buttons.

Adding Lists and Menus to Forms

Some form objects work better than others in certain situations (for example, selecting 1 of the 50 states for a U.S. address). If you allowed the user to enter a state in a text field, you might get some users entering the full name, like Washington; other users entering the correct postal abbreviation, like WA; and other users entering anything in between. Allowing the user to select from a drop-down menu helps you collect consistent data. In Dreamweaver, you add drop-down menus by using the List/Menu object.

The List/Menu object inserts a list of values. You create the List/Menu object as either a list, displaying a set number of lines, or a menu, a drop-down menu displaying all the list values. Figure 18.13 shows a list and a menu in a form displayed in a browser.

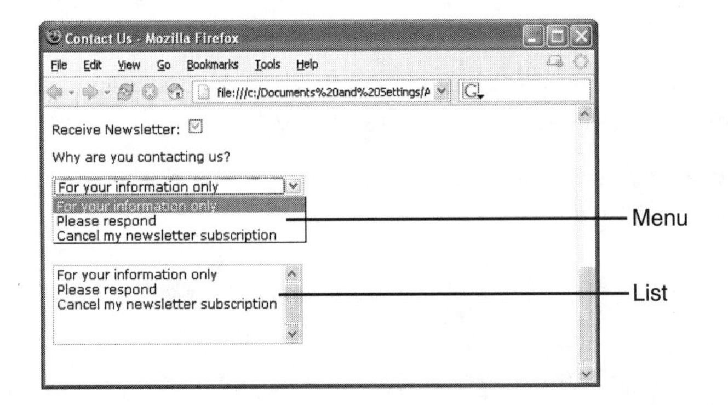

FIGURE 18.13
Lists display a certain number of values. A menu drops down when the user clicks it, allowing the user to select a value.

To create a list, follow these steps:

1. Place the insertion point within the form where the list will be located. Type **`Why are you contacting us?`**
2. Select the List/Menu object from the Insert bar or select Insert, Form, List/Menu.
3. Enter the name of the list into the box in the far left of the Property inspector.
4. After you select the List radio button, the Height and Allow Multiple attributes become active.
5. In the Height box, type the number of list items you want visible at one time (see Figure 18.14). If there are more list items than can be shown, scrollbars automatically appear. If the Height property isn't active, you have Menu selected instead of List.

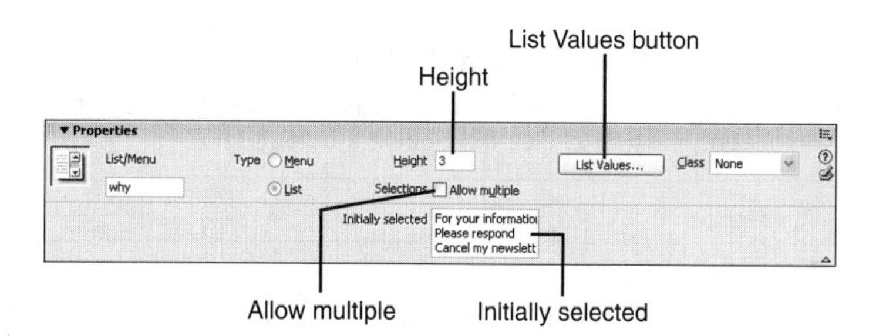

FIGURE 18.14
You set a list's height and other properties in the Property inspector.

6. Check the Allow Multiple check box if you want to allow the user to select multiple values in the list. You might want to add instructions that tell the user that he can select multiple entries by holding down the Ctrl key (or the Command key on the Macintosh) and clicking multiple selections.
7. Set up the list values by selecting the List Values button. The List Values dialog box appears, as shown in Figure 18.15.

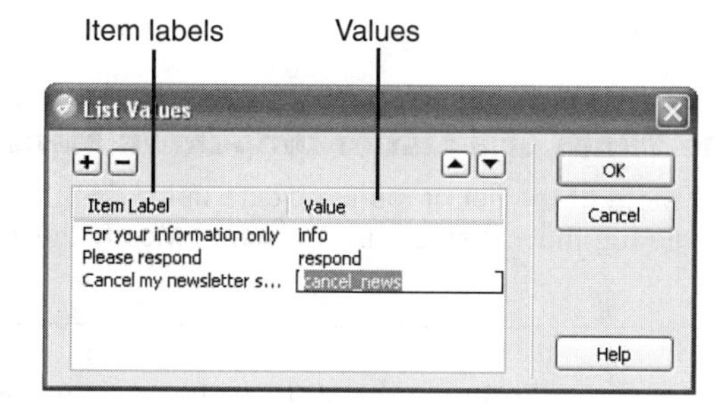

FIGURE 18.15
Select the + button in the List Values dialog box to add an item to the list.

8. Enter an item label and a value for each item in the list. The item label is what the user sees and selects. The value is what is sent back to a script on the server for processing. They can be the same, if appropriate. To add an item, click the + sign, enter the item label, tab to the Value field, and enter a value. You can tab forward and use Shift+Tab to go back if you want. Use the – button to delete entries, and use the arrow buttons to rearrange entries. When you are at the end of the list, pressing Tab creates a new item label and value pair.
9. Click OK in the List Values dialog box.
10. Select an item from the Initially Selected box if one of the items should be selected by default. Otherwise, the first item will appear.
11. Add a label beside the list.

Did you Know?

Make the First List Item a Blank Value

Some people like to create a blank name and value pair as the first item in a list or menu. This keeps the first choice from being a default choice.

Did you Know?

Select Objects

People who don't use Dreamweaver might call the list or menu objects **Select** objects. This is because the `<select>` tag is used to implement these objects in HTML.

Whereas a list can show a number of lines, a menu shows only one line until the user drops down the menu by clicking. Menus use less space than lists because a menu can drop down over other objects on the page when clicked, but it shrinks to only one line when it is inactive. You create a menu exactly the same way you create a list, except that you don't set the height and you cannot allow the user to select multiple entries. You can turn a list into a drop-down menu by selecting the Menu option as the type.

Did you Know?

Controlling the Width of a List or Drop-Down Menu

You can modify the width of the list or menu objects using CSS. Simply redefine the `<select>` tag, the tag that creates a list or menu. Modify the width property in the Box category.

For a quick and easy way to add standard menus, such as menus for years, numbers, or months, use the Snippets panel. The Forms section of the Snippets panel contains prebuilt menus and form elements you can simply drag and drop onto your web page.

Adding Push Buttons and Image Buttons to Forms

There are four types of buttons that you can add to forms:

- **Submit**—This type of button sends the data the user has entered into a form to a script or an application on the server. The submit button triggers the action that you've set in the form's Action box in the Property inspector.
- **Reset**—This type of button erases all the data the user has entered in the form. It also reloads any initial values.

- **None**—This type of generic button has no automatic function. You can add functionality to a generic button by applying a behavior to it.
- **Image**—This type of button acts like a submit button. All the data in the form is submitted, and the coordinates of where the user clicked are sent, too.

The first three buttons are push buttons you create by inserting Dreamweaver's Button object. They differ in the way they are configured in the Property inspector. The fourth button, the image button, is inserted using the Image Field object.

Adding Submit and Reset Buttons to Forms

In this section you'll add submit and reset buttons to your form. Usually, the submit button is on the left and the reset button is to the right of the submit button. To add a button to the form, follow these steps:

1. Position the insertion point and then select the Button object from the Insert bar or select Insert, Form, Button.
2. Select Submit Form as the action for this button.
3. Add another button to the right of the submit button.
4. Select Reset Form as the action for this button. The buttons should look like the buttons in Figure 18.16.

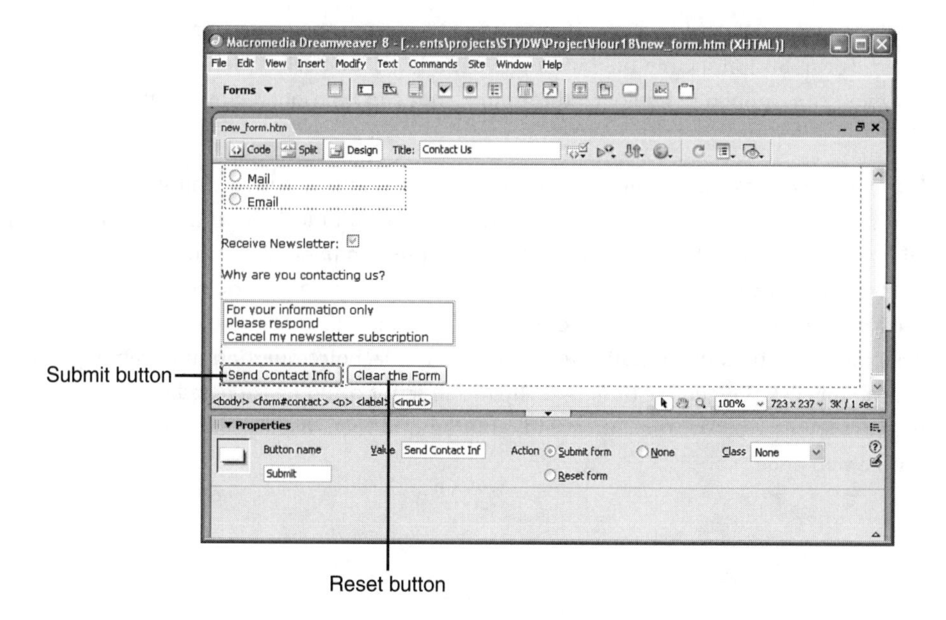

FIGURE 18.16
The submit button is usually placed on the left of the reset button. You need one submit button per form if you are sending this form to a script or to an application on a server.

You can accept the default labels that Dreamweaver gives the submit and reset buttons or you can give them new labels. You can change the label of either button; a button does not need to say Submit to function as a submit button.

Many web developers like to give a submit button a label that actually describes what the button does, such as Enter the Contest or Send Comment. Each form must have a submit button to send the form data. The reset button is optional. You should have only one submit button per form with multiple text fields.

Adding an Image Button to Forms

You can replace a submit button with an image button. When the user clicks the image, the form contents are submitted, and the coordinates of the location where the user clicked the image button are sent, too. Obviously, you do not need a submit button if you have an image button.

To add an image field to a form, first make sure the insertion point is inside the form. Add an image field by selecting the Image Field object from the Insert bar or selecting Insert, Form, Image Field. The Select Image Source dialog box appears, enabling you to navigate and select a standard web image file. The Property inspector displays the name, source, alt text, and alignment attributes for the field. You set these attributes as you would for any image.

Adding Generic Buttons to Forms

Add a generic button by selecting the Button object from the Insert bar or selecting Insert, Form, Button. Name the button, give it a label, and select None as the action. Now you can apply a behavior to this button that can be triggered by a button click.

You might want to use a generic button if your form isn't actually being submitted to a script on the server (the topic for the next hour). You may use what's called a client-side script, JavaScript that is contained in the web page that reacts to the form data. Submit buttons only work with server-side scripts but a generic button can be used, via Dreamweaver behaviors or custom JavaScript, to trigger a client-side script. An example of this functionality would be a multiplechoice question in a web page. When you click the generic button, a client-side script could be triggered to check whether the user picked the correct radio button and then display feedback for them on the web page.

Deleting a Form

Sometimes it is difficult to delete a form from the page. The easiest way to delete a form is to right-click (or Command+click on the Mac) the form delimiter to view the context menu. Then choose the Remove Tag <form> command. If the Remove Tag command does not say <form>, you have the wrong object selected. You could, of course, always select the `<form>` tag in the tag selector to delete the form.

Creating a Jump Menu to Navigate to Different URLs

A **jump menu** is a list of links that allows the viewer to jump to other websites or different web pages within the current site. Dreamweaver's Jump Menu object makes it easy to set up this type of jump menu. You can create a jump menu of email links, images, or any objects that can be displayed in a browser. The Jump Menu object uses JavaScript to redirect the browser.

Dreamweaver's Jump Menu object inserts a drop-down menu similar to the one you created a few minutes ago along with the JavaScript code contained in the Jump Menu behavior. You set up the list values in a special dialog box. The item labels appear in the drop-down menu, and the values contain the URLs to the web pages where the user will jump. If you need to edit the jump menu after you have created it in the special dialog box, you will need to brush up on the form skills you've learned in this hour and the behavior skills you've learned in previous hours.

To create a jump menu, follow these steps:

1. Place the insertion point on the page where you want the jump menu to appear. You don't need to insert a form because the Jump Menu object does that for you.

2. Either select the Jump Menu object from the Insert bar or select Insert, Form, Jump Menu. The Insert Jump Menu dialog box appears, as shown in Figure 18.17.

3. Type an item label for the first item in the jump menu in the Text box. The first item label is highlighted when you first open the Insert Jump Menu dialog box.

4. Enter a URL that will be launched when the item is selected. You can either type it in or use the Browse button to navigate to a local file.

5. Click the + button to add another item.

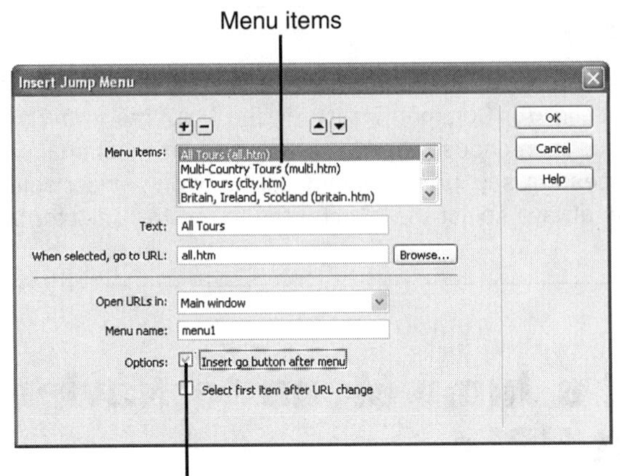

FIGURE 18.17 The Insert Jump Menu dialog box enables you to create a drop-down menu where the user can select an item to which to link.

6. Repeat steps 3–5 until you have entered all the items for the jump menu.
7. Select a target for the links in the Open URLs In drop-down menu. You will have target options only if your current web page is part of a frameset (Hour 14, "Using Frames to Display Multiple Web Pages") that is open in Dreamweaver.
8. Give the menu a unique name in the Menu Name box.
9. Select the appropriate Options check boxes. Click the Insert Go Button After Menu check box if you would like to have a button with the label Go that the user can press to jump. You can also choose the Select First Item After URL Change check box if you want the first item to be reselected after each jump selection.
10. When you are done making selections in the Insert Jump Menu dialog box, click OK. The jump menu within a form is inserted into your web page.

Did you Know?

Add an Initial Value

A common way to create a jump menu is to have the first item be the text Choose One... and do not give it a link. Because you never want the user to select this item, the inability to select the first item in the drop-down menu won't be a problem. Then select the check box that makes the first item always selected after you have jumped somewhere so the Choose One... selection reappears.

You can edit the jump menu by editing the Jump Menu behavior. Select the List/Menu object that the Jump Menu command creates and double-click the Jump

Menu behavior in the Behaviors panel. Add or remove list items by using the + and – buttons. Rearrange the list by using the up and down arrow buttons. You can turn on or off the Select First Item After URL Change setting.

You cannot add a Go button by editing the Jump Menu behavior. You can add one manually, though. Create a generic button by inserting a button into the form, giving it the label Go, and setting its action to None. Apply the Jump Menu Go behavior to the button triggered by the `onClick` event. Select the jump menu name from the drop-down menu, as shown in Figure 18.18.

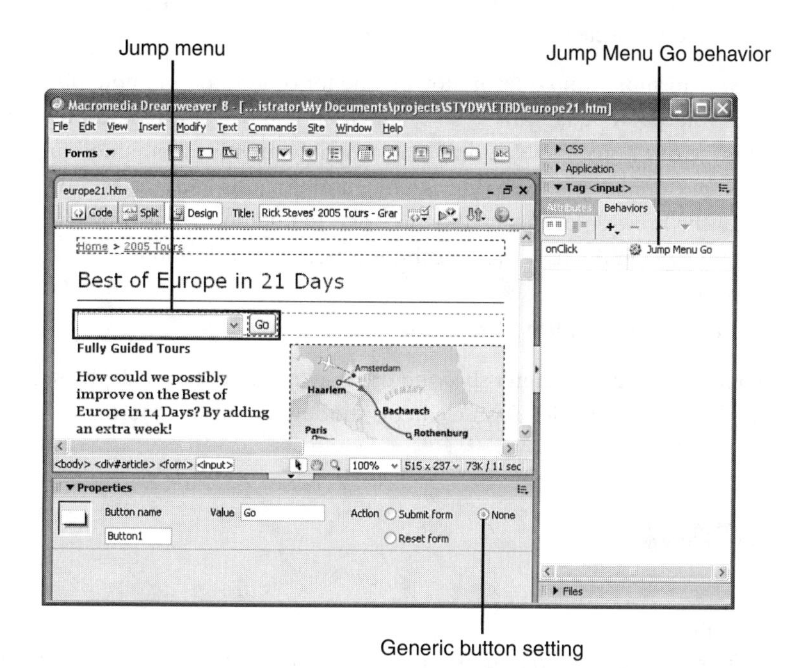

FIGURE 18.18 You can create your own Go button by inserting a generic button into a form and applying the Jump Menu Go behavior.

Summary

In this hour, you have learned how to insert and configure a form. You have learned how to add text fields, radio buttons, check boxes, lists, and menus to the form. You have learned how to add submit and reset buttons to the form and create a generic button. You have learned how to use Dreamweaver's Jump Menu object to create a menu that consists of a bunch of URLs to which the user can jump.

Q&A

Q. ***I just want to email my form contents. I know that in the next hour I'll learn about CGI and other scripting methods, but isn't there a quick-and-dirty way to do this?***

A. You can email form contents by using your email address as the action. Your email address needs to be prefaced with `mailto:` so it looks like this: `mailto:`*`you@yourdomain.com`*. In addition, you might need to type `"text/plain"` into the Enctype attribute in the Property inspector when the `<form>` tag is selected.

This way of submitting a form may be fine for collecting form data about where your co-workers want to go to lunch on Friday. They all know and trust you (at least I hope they do), and they probably all have their email programs set up in a similar fashion to yours. An email program must be set up properly with the browser for this method to work. In addition, some browsers put up a warning when the user tries to submit a form in this fashion.

Q. ***Why can't I see my form elements?***

A. If your form elements aren't showing up, they must not be inside the `<form>` tags. Some browsers hide form elements that are not inside a form.

Workshop

Quiz

1. What do you need to do to make a number of radio buttons act like they are a group?
2. How do you create a generic button?
3. What's the difference between a list and a menu?

Quiz Answers

1. All the radio buttons in a group must have the same name.
2. After you insert a button into a form, select None as the action. You can then attach Dreamweaver behaviors to the button if you like.

3. A list displays a configurable number of items and might allow the user to select more than one item to submit. A menu displays only one line and drops down when the user clicks it so an item can be selected. The user can select only one item at a time from a menu.

Exercises

1. Create a form to collect the user data of your choice. Format the form objects and labels with a table so they line up nicely. Place the submit and reset buttons in the bottom row of the table and merge the cells so the buttons are centered under the entire table.

2. Create a jump menu in a frame at the top of the page. Enter all your favorite URLs into the menu. Have the URLs load into a frame in the bottom of the page.

3. Experiment with using the form page designs and Snippets panel to quickly create forms. Create one of the built-in CSS Style Sheets that apply to forms and attach it to a forms page. Try modifying some of the styles in the style sheet.

HOUR 19

Introduction to Scripts: Sending and Reacting to Form Data

What You'll Learn in This Hour:

- How to use the Validate Form behavior
- How to set up a page to submit to a CGI script
- How to create secure web pages
- How Dreamweaver edits and displays ASP, ASP.NET, JSP, PHP, and CFML code

In Hour 18, "Creating a Form and Collecting Data," you learned how to create a form. In this hour, you'll decide what to do with the data that the user enters into your form. You need to send the data to a script on the server for processing. The script on the server can store data in a database, send it to an email address, send results back to the browser, or process it any way you want (depending on your scripting abilities!).

Client-Side Scripts

You can also have client-side scripts created in JavaScript to process form data, but those scripts do not have access to server resources and are not able to email data or insert it into a database.

Some of the types of information you might want to receive in a form can include orders, feedback, comments, guest book entries, polls, and even uploaded files. Creating the form and inserting form elements is usually the easy part. The difficult part is installing and configuring the scripts that process the data.

Validating a Form's Data by Using the Validate Form Behavior

Before you receive and process information from a form, you need to make sure the information is complete and in the right format. Dreamweaver has a Validate Form behavior thatc forces the user to enter data into a field, determines whether an email address has been entered, and makes sure the user enters numbers correctly.

The Validate Form behavior requires the user to enter the form data correctly before he can submit the data to a script or an application on the server. You can validate the form in two ways:

- Attach the Validate Form behavior to the submit button to validate the entire form when the submit button is clicked. The `onClick` event triggers the behavior.
- Attach the Validate Form behavior to individual text fields so the data entered is validated after the user leaves the field. The `onChange` event triggers the behavior when the user's focus leaves the field.

You must have a form with form objects in your web page before the Validate Form behavior is active in the + drop-down menu of the Behaviors panel. To validate a form, follow these steps:

1. Create a new form that has various text fields or open the form you created in Hour 18.
2. Select the submit button.
3. Open the Behaviors panel. Click the + button and select the Validate Form behavior.
4. The Validate Form dialog box appears. A list of all the text fields appears in the dialog box.
5. Set up validation settings for every text field that requires them.
6. Check the Required check box if an entry in the field must be filled in by the user.
7. Choose from among the four settings in the Accept category:
   - **Anything**—Select this setting if the user needs to enter data into the field but that data can be in any format. For instance, if you are asking for a phone number, you do not want to limit the user to entering only numbers because phone numbers are often formatted with other characters.

- **Number**—Select this setting if the user needs to enter data that is numeric.
- **Email Address**—Select this setting if the user needs to enter an email address. This setting checks for an @ symbol.
- **Number From**—Select this setting to check for a number within a range of specific numbers. Fill in both the low and high ends of the range.

8. Notice that your settings appear in parentheses beside the name of the text field in the Named Fields list (shown in Figure 19.1). Repeat steps 5–7 to validate all of the text fields.

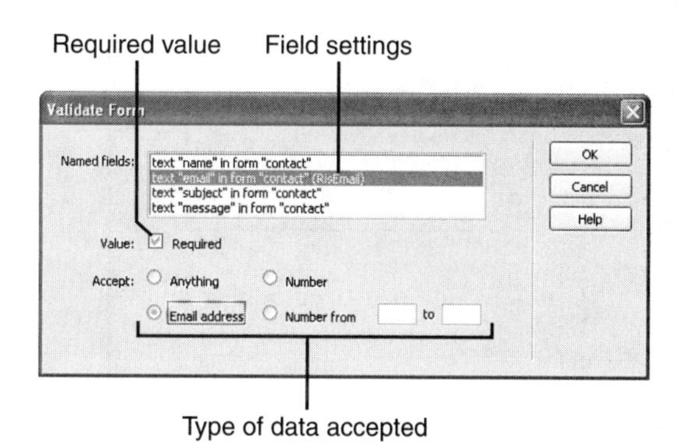

FIGURE 19.1
The validation settings appear in parentheses in the Named Fields list in the Validate Form dialog box.

9. When you are finished making changes in the Validate Form dialog box, click OK. Select the `onClick` event if the Validate Form behavior is attached to the submit button. Select the `onChange` event if the behavior is attached to an individual text field.

When the Validate Form behavior is triggered, the behavior checks the data in the form against the settings you have entered. You should make sure that the labels and instructions for your form clearly tell the user what type of data to enter and which fields are required. You should give the user the information to fill out the form properly so that she doesn't get frustrated with error messages.

Required Form Elements

A standard way to signal that a form element is required is to place an asterisk next to its label. It's becoming more common to use a bold label to signal that the form element is required. You should tell your users somewhere on the page what indicates that a form element is required.

If the user enters incorrect data, the message box shown in Figure 19.2 appears. This message tells the user that errors have occurred, lists the text fields' names, and explains why the data was rejected. This is another place where a meaningful name for a Dreamweaver object is important. If you are validating a form, it is a good idea to name a text field the same name as the label beside the field so the user can easily locate and change the field data.

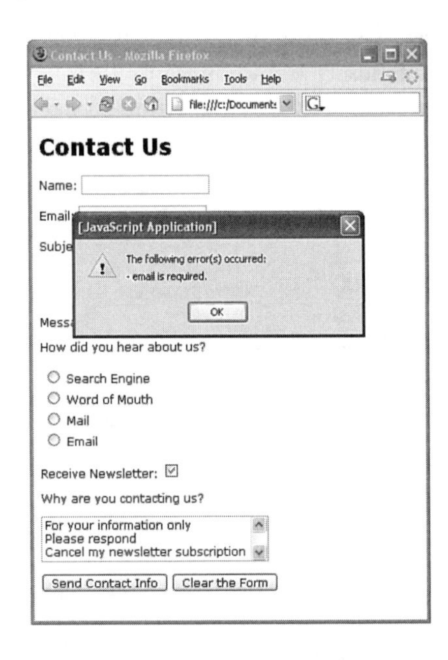

FIGURE 19.2 After running the validation script, a form that has errors or omissions displays this message, indicating which fields have either been omitted or filled out incorrectly.

Did you Know?

Better Form Validation

The Validate Form behavior offers rudimentary form validation. There are other validation behaviors that offer more choices—validating form objects other than just text fields, for instance—and that are available free on the Macromedia Exchange. Hour 22, "Customizing Dreamweaver," explains how you can download and install third-party extensions to Dreamweaver. One I particularly like is called Check Form, created by Jaro von Flocken (see www.yaromat.com/dw).

Receiving Information from a Form

The standard way to process a form is to have an application on the server that parses the data and performs an action on it. **Parsing** data is the act of dividing and interpreting the name-value pairs that are sent to the server.

Each name-value pair contains the name of the form element entered in Dreamweaver and the value that the user has entered or selected for that field. A text field has a name-value pair that contains the name of the text field and the value that was entered into the text field. A radio button group sends a name-value pair with the name of the radio button group and the value of the button that was selected when the user submitted the form. A list or a drop-down menu sends the name of the object and any items the user selected.

The name-value pairs are sent to a server via an **HTTP request** from the web browser. The request is passed by the web server software to the application server that handles the scripting language specified in the request, as shown in Figure 19.3. For instance, if the script is written in ColdFusion Markup Language (CFML), the ColdFusion application server handles the request. Depending on what is written in the script, the application server might request data from a database or send a request to an email server to send a specific email message. There are many ways scripts can be processed on the server. The application server usually returns some sort of output, usually HTML, that is sent by the web server back to the browser. This all takes place in milliseconds!

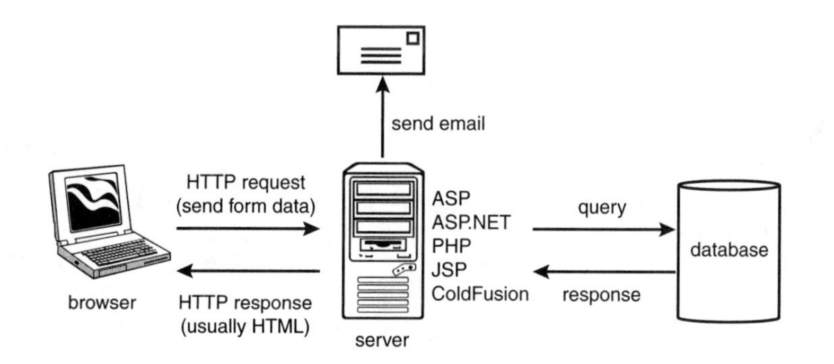

FIGURE 19.3
The browser sends a request to a script on the server and receives a response back. The script might control sending an email message or accessing and returning data from a database.

A popular way of processing forms on a server is by using a CGI script. Usually these scripts are written in Perl or other programming languages. Later in this hour, you will learn other ways of processing forms, with Active Server Pages (ASP), ASP.NET, JavaServer Pages (JSP), Hypertext Preprocessor (PHP), and CFML—proprietary processing systems that are powerful in creating web applications.

Luckily, there are a number of places on the Web to download already written CGI scripts. Because programming CGI scripts is beyond the scope of this book, the examples in this hour use an existing script that processes form data and sends it to a specific email address.

Did you Know?

Get Free Scripts on the Web

The Web is an incredibly generous place, and you can download all sorts of free scripts to use. If you don't know how to program CGI scripts and you are willing to process your forms generically, you'll find a number of great scripts available from Matt's Script Archive (www.scriptarchive.com) and Freescripts (www.freescripts.com).

CGI stands for **Common Gateway Interface**, and it is the definition of the standard method of communication between a script and the web server. The CGI script resides in a specific directory on the web server. It is common for access to this directory to be limited to webmasters for security reasons. You can contact your webmaster and ask whether a script is already available on your server to do what you want to do or whether the webmaster will install one for you. You might have a directory within your own web directory that can hold CGI scripts. Often this directory is called `cgi-bin` or has `cgi` in the directory name.

You should double-check that your hosting service, if you are using one, supports CGI scripts. Sometimes you can use only the scripts that the service has available; check that a form mail script is available. Carefully review the features of the type of account you are signing up for and ask questions, if necessary.

Did you Know?

Use a Form-Hosting Site

CGI scripts might expose a server to hackers on the Web, which is why access to the scripts directory is usually limited. If you don't have access to CGI scripts, you might want to use a form-hosting site (search for *free form hosting* on Yahoo! or any other search engine). The site www.formmail.com enables you to build and host forms without advertisements for less than a dollar per month.

These sites allow you to create forms that are processed at the form-hosting site. You simply link to the page with the form located on the hosting service's server. The disadvantage of using these services is that they usually display advertising on your form page.

Enter the URL to the CGI script in the Action text box in the Property inspector, as shown in Figure 19.4. The URL needs to be an absolute URL; it should not be relative, even if the script resides in a directory relative to your website. The documentation for the script will tell you whether the script expects the form name-value pairs to be submitted via either the `GET` or the `POST` method.

The `GET` and `POST` methods differ in the following ways:

- The `GET` method appends form data to the URL, a URL that can be saved as a bookmark in the browser. Data submitted via this method is limited to 1KB, you can't upload files, and sensitive data is displayed in the address field of the browser after submission.

- The POST method packages and sends the data invisibly to the user; the output doesn't appear in the URL. There are no limitations to the amount of data that can be sent, and the POST method allows uploading of files with forms.

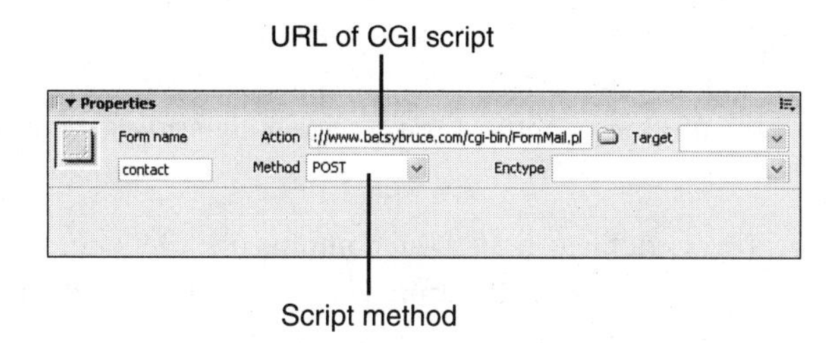

FIGURE 19.4 Enter the URL to the CGI script that will process your form in the Action text box of the Property inspector with the form selected.

Using the FormMail Script

Download Matt's FormMail script from www.scriptarchive.com/formmail.html to use with the rest of this hour. This script sends the contents of a form to an email address. The script can be configured a number of ways. If you are going to test the script, you need to install the script first. The script comes with a readme file that describes all the functions and parameters you can set in the script. The process to set up and call the FormMail script is similar to what you do to submit a form to any CGI script.

Watch Out!

Web Server Operating Systems

Web server applications reside on various operating systems. Unix and Windows NT are the most popular operating systems for servers. It's important that you know which operating system your web server uses. Scripts are written to run on certain operating systems. For instance, Matt's FormMail script is written to run on Unix. Other people have translated the script to other operating systems. Also, Unix filenames are case-sensitive, so you must be careful that you reference links and image files with the proper case.

To use the FormMail script., you must add to your form hidden fields containing parameters that tell the script what to do. Open the FormMail script in Dreamweaver or a text editor, such as Notepad, and you'll see instructions at the top of the file. The scripted processes are also contained in the file, so be careful what you change.

There are four variables that you need to configure at the top of the FormMail script before it is loaded onto the server:

- **`$mailprog`**—This variable needs to point to the Unix server's `sendmail` program. Leave it set at the default; if it doesn't work, your webmaster can give you the path. You do not need this variable if you are running the Windows NT version of the script. If your hosting company provided the FormMail script for you, it has probably modified this variable for you. A common path to the `sendmail` program is `usr/lib/sendmail`; you'll have to read your hosting service's documentation or contact the service to determine what address you need to use.
- **`@referers`**—This variable contains the domains (usually one) that are allowed access to the script. This setting keeps unauthorized domains from using the script and the resources on your server. My domain is www.betsybruce.com, so that's what I would enter into this variable. This prevents people with forms in domains other than mine from using my script to process their forms.
- **`@recipients`**—This variable defines the email addresses that can receive email from the form. This deters spammers from using the form to do their dirty deeds.
- **`@valid_ENV`**—This variable is configurable by the webmaster in order to define environment variables. You don't need to worry about this unless your webmaster gives you information on how to change it.

Adding a Hidden Field to a Form

Hidden fields are sent along with all the other form fields. The users cannot change the contents of these fields, nor can they see the fields unless they view your HTML source. You should create hidden fields for the recipient of the emailed form data, the subject that appears in the email subject field, and the URL to which the user is redirected after filling out the form. You can explore many other settings on your own.

Make sure that your form has the URL to the FormMail script on the server set the Action text box in the Property inspector. The FormMail script can accept either the `GET` method or the `POST` method for submitting the data. I suggest the `POST` method because it is more common and because you do not risk exceeding the amount of data that the `GET` method can handle.

To add hidden fields to your form, follow these steps:

1. Place the insertion point anywhere inside your form. It does not matter where the hidden fields are located.

2. Select the Hidden Field object from the Insert bar or select Insert, Form, Hidden Field.

3. Dreamweaver displays the Hidden Field symbol in your web page, as shown in Figure 19.5. You must have Invisible Elements checked (select View, Visual Aids, Invisible Elements); also, the Invisible Elements category in the Dreamweaver Preferences dialog box must have Hidden Form Fields checked.

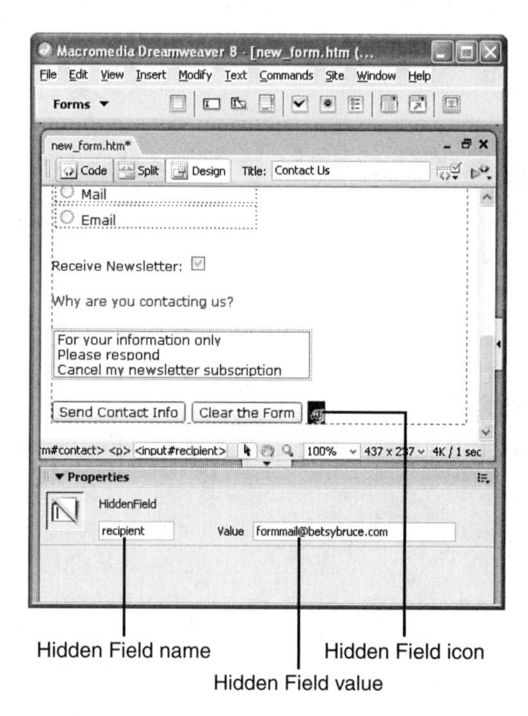

FIGURE 19.5 The Hidden Field symbol appears when you insert a hidden field into a form. The Property inspector shows a hidden field name-value pair.

4. Enter **`recipient`** in the text box on the left side of the Property inspector and your email address as the value, as shown in Figure 19.5. These name-value pairs are documented in the script documentation.

5. Optionally, add another hidden field to the form and enter the name **`redirect`**. Enter as the value of the field a URL that the user will be redirected to after submitting the form.

Type Carefully!

When you are naming your own objects in Dreamweaver, you can afford to occasionally make a typo or misspelling. Scripts and applications, however, are not forgiving of typos. Adding hidden fields requires you to enter the names exactly as they are listed in the documentation. It's often necessary that the letter case be exact as well because many servers are case-sensitive.

You can add a number of optional form fields to the FormMail script. See the documentation to read about them. When the user submits the form, the name-value pairs are sent to the email address specified in the hidden field named recipient. This is the simplest processing possible for a form. Other scripts can save data to databases, validate and process credit card information, and perform all sorts of other complex actions.

Exploring Submission Security

When your users submit form information, it travels in packets across the Internet, along with millions of other packets. **Packets** are electronic bundles of information that carry data to the server. These packets of information can be intercepted and read by people who understand how to intercept and reassemble data taken from the Web. After you've taken steps to secure sensitive data, don't forget to assure users that their transactions and data are indeed secure.

Again, this is a web server issue. The web server on which your site is located must have secure sockets enabled. Many ISPs offer this service. Ask your webmaster whether you have access to secure web pages.

A user accesses a secure URL exactly as he would a regular URL. The only difference is that the protocol portion of the URL changes from `http` to `https`. The user must have a browser that is capable of accessing secure pages. The browser displays a Lock icon in the status bar, as shown in Figure 19.6, when it is in secure mode.

You need to worry about secure submissions only when the user enters sensitive information, such as credit card numbers or other financial data. For polls, guest books, or feedback forms, you don't need to shield the information from potential thieves. Customers will expect you to protect only their sensitive data.

You need a server certificate to add security to your form submissions. A **certificate** is an electronic document that verifies that you are who you say you are. You might be able to use your web host's certificate, or you might need to purchase your own. One of the major certificate vendors is VeriSign, and you can learn more about certificates at VeriSign's website, www.verisign.com.

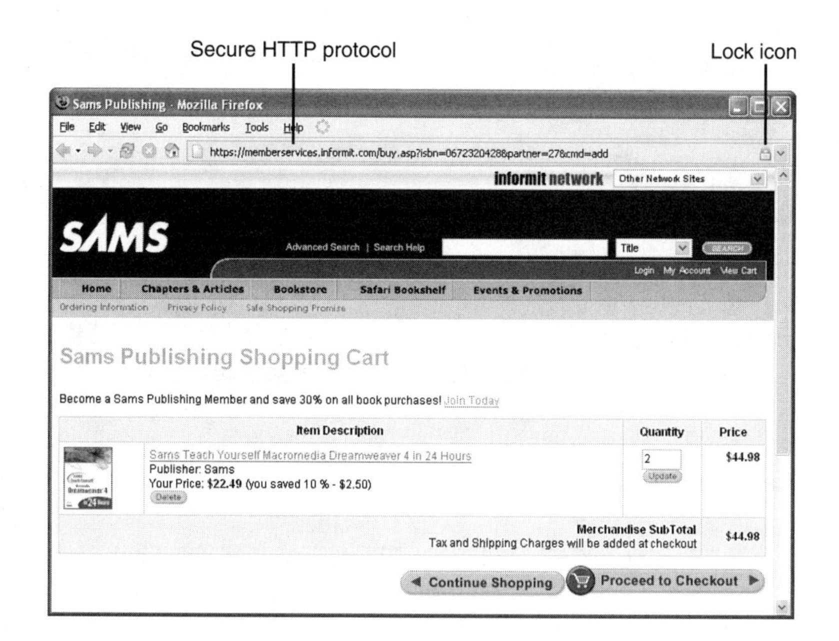

FIGURE 19.6
The browser displays a Lock icon in the status bar when the page is served via secure sockets.

Uploading a File from a Form

You might need to add a **file field** that enables users to upload files. You can collect images, homework assignments, or any types of files that you might need to have sent to you with a file field object. The user selects the Browse button, shown in Figure 19.7, to select a file from her local drive. When the user presses the Submit button, the file is sent to the server.

A file field has attributes similar to those of a text field, which you used in the last hour. You can set the size of the file field by putting a value in the Char Width box in the Property inspector. You can also set the Max Chars attribute and the Init Val attribute in the Property inspector. You need to give the file field a unique name.

The important question you need to answer before you use a file field is does your server allow anonymous file uploads? You also need to select `multipart/form-data` from the Enctype drop-down list for the `<form>` tag so the file is encoded correctly. Also, you should use the `POST` method to submit your form; the `GET` method does not work with file fields.

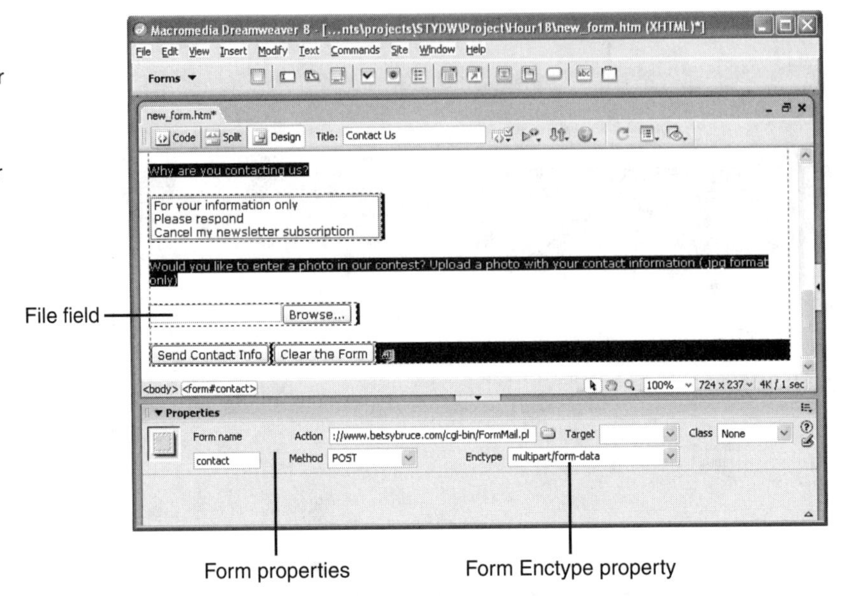

FIGURE 19.7 Use a file field to enable a user to upload a file to the server. However, make sure your server allows it before you create your form.

Preparing a Page to Interact with ASP, ASP.NET, JSP, PHP, or CFML

Besides using CGI scripts, there are other ways to process forms and create dynamic web applications. Like CGI scripting, these technologies interact with the web server to process web page information. Dreamweaver enables you to create dynamic web pages that incorporate server-side scripting. When you create a new web page, you create a dynamic page by selecting the Dynamic Page category in the New Document dialog box, as shown in Figure 19.8.

Dreamweaver supports these five major server-side scripting languages:

- **ASP**—Microsoft's ASP combines client-side scripting with processing on the server to create dynamic web pages. The capability to process ASP comes with Microsoft's Internet Information Server (IIS) 4+, which runs on Windows NT. (You can add the capability to process ASP to IIS 3.) Some third-party applications, such as ChiliSoft, can interpret ASP on Unix servers.
- **ASP.NET**—Microsoft's ASP.NET, released in 2002, is a server-side application platform that will eventually replace ASP. To run ASP.NET on your server, you need Microsoft IIS 5.0 or later, running on Windows 2000, Windows XP, or Windows Server 2003. You also need the .NET Framework Redistributable installed (available from http://msdn.microsoft.com/net and included automatically in Windows Server 2003).

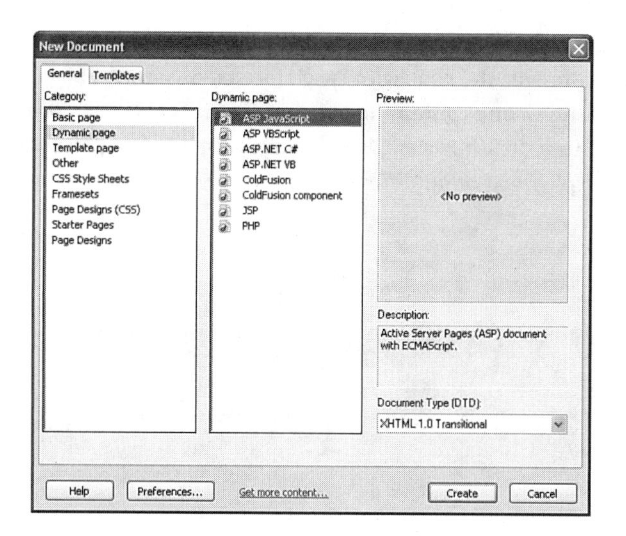

FIGURE 19.8
You can create ASP, ASP.NET, JSP, PHP, and CFML pages with Dreamweaver.

- **JSP**—JSP is a Java-based way to dynamically process web pages. JSP scripts interact with a JSP-enabled server. The popular Apache web server and the free Tomcat JSP application server are available. For Microsoft IIS, Macromedia JRun is a popular JSP application server.
- **PHP**—PHP is a free, open-source server-side scripting language that sends dynamic web pages to the user after interpreting PHP code. PHP is the open-source movement's answer to ASP.
- **CFML**—Macromedia's ColdFusion server interprets CFML to create dynamic web pages. The ColdFusion server application can run on many operating systems. CFML is slightly different from the other scripting languages described here because it is a tag-based language, like HTML.

All these scripting languages accomplish the same thing: enabling a client-side web page to interact with the server by accessing data, sending an email message, or processing input in some way. They all have advantages and disadvantages, and each uses a different syntax to add code to web pages.

Intrigued? Want to Learn More?

Sams Teach Yourself Macromedia Dreamweaver MX 2004 in 21 Days by John Ray picks up where this book leaves off, introducing you to dynamic websites and scripting. Also, check Appendix A, "Resources," for links to sites where you can learn more about these scripting methods.

You can embed ASP, ASP.NET, JSP, PHP, and CFML into your web pages, and Dreamweaver represents the code with special icons, as shown in Figure 19.9. When you define your site as one containing dynamic pages, your page looks slightly different from this. In a dynamic site, Dreamweaver displays a representation of the code; you can display actual data from the database by viewing the web page in Live Data view.

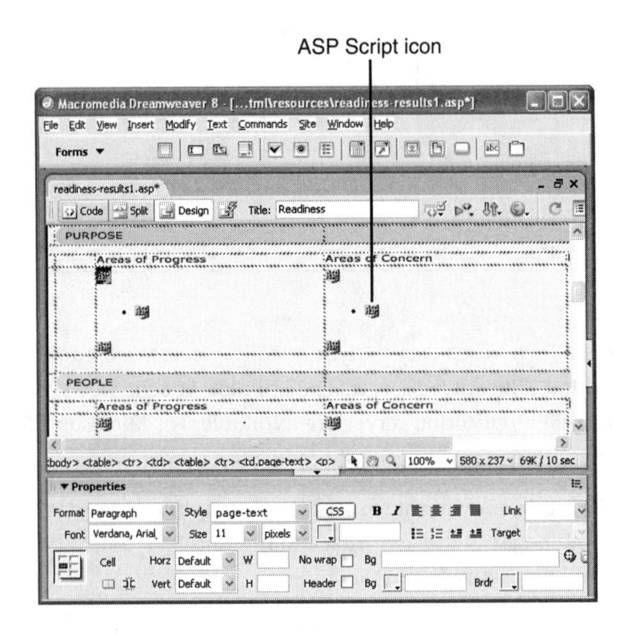

FIGURE 19.9
Special icons, in this case an ASP Script icon, appear when you're viewing invisible elements that represent code.

You can use ASP, ASP.NET, JSP, PHP, or CFML scripts contained in an external script file to process a form. Such a script acts like the CGI script you used earlier this hour. You reference the script's URL as the form's action in the Property inspector. Again, the script's directory must have the proper permission set in order for the script to execute. Figure 19.10 shows a form submitting its contents to an ASP script.

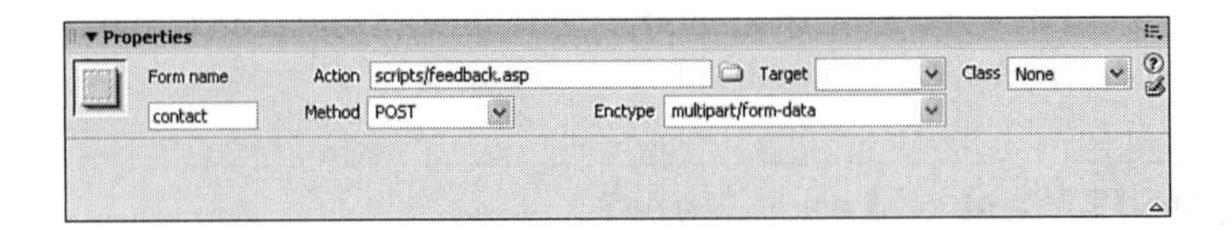

FIGURE 19.10
You enter the URL of an ASP script if the script will process your form when the user submits it.

When you define your site as a dynamic site, you can author dynamic web pages in Dreamweaver. Dreamweaver enables you to easily hook up your web content to databases. You can visually add ASP, ASP.NET, JSP, or CFML components.

Dreamweaver generates the code for you behind the scenes and displays the dynamic elements. You can even see how your web page will look with real data from the database right within Dreamweaver.

Did you Know?

Learn More with the Dreamweaver Tutorials

If you'd like to learn more about creating dynamic web pages, go through the tutorials that come with Dreamweaver.

Summary

In this hour, you have learned how CGI scripts work and how form data is submitted to them. You have learned how to use the Validate Form behavior to validate the data that the user enters into your form. You have inserted into a form hidden fields that contain a name-value pair. You have set the action for a form and learned the difference between the `GET` and `POST` methods for submitting data. You have learned about secure transactions. You have learned how to call ASP, ASP.NET, PHP, JSP, and CFML scripts.

Q&A

Q. ***I know an ASP programmer who will help me with my web pages. What do I need to tell her about my web pages so she can write a script to process them on the server?***

A. She needs to know what you have called the items in your form and how you want them processed. If she is sending the data to a database, she needs to know what you call the items in your form so she can parse the data into the correct place. She also needs to know if you need any validation or processing applied to the data. For instance, you might need to have individual prices added together as one total price.

Q. ***Should I learn Perl, ASP, ASP.NET, PHP, JSP, or CFML?***

A. It depends on what you want to do when you grow up! Do you have a knack for coding? If so, having skills in any of these technologies might be fun and look great on your résumé. Find out what technologies people at work are using. If you learn those technologies, your colleagues might be a good support system for your learning endeavor.

If you aren't very interested in coding but want to expand your web skill set, maybe it's a better idea to specialize in Dreamweaver—there's a lot to learn!

On the other hand, you can always learn more about databases. If you don't really enjoy coding, it can be a real chore. Dreamweaver offers objects and server behaviors that make it much easier than before to code dynamic web pages.

Workshop

Quiz

1. What pair of items is sent when a user submits a form?
2. What is a hidden text field?
3. What does it mean when a URL begins with `https`?

Quiz Answers

1. The name-value pair is sent when a user submits a form. This is the name of the form object and the value the user either entered or selected.
2. A hidden text field contains a name-value pair that the user cannot change. Generally, this data is required by the script to properly process the form.
3. A URL beginning with `https` signals that the URL is secure using the Secure HTTP protocol.

Exercises

1. Add a Google search box to a web page. You'll be adding a form that contacts the Google servers and returns results to the web page. You can find the code at www.google.com/searchcode.html; paste this code in Dreamweaver's Code view and then change to Design view to examine and edit it.
2. Experiment with the FormMail fields that you did not explore in this hour. The script also offers validation functionality that you could use instead of using the Dreamweaver Validate Form behavior. You can find the documentation online at www.scriptarchive.com/readme/formmail.html.
3. Find a form on a Web and look at it critically. Select the View Source command to see the HTML. Does the form have any hidden fields? Where is the form being submitted? You should look for the `<form>` and `</form>` tags that contain the code for the form.

PART VI

Organizing and Uploading a Project

HOUR 20

Uploading and Sharing a Project on the Web

What You'll Learn in This Hour:

- How to configure a remote site
- How to move your site onto a remote server
- How to import an existing site
- How to use Check In/Check Out

Finished websites reside on a web server where many people can access the web pages. While you are working on your websites, you want to move them onto the server for testing. At the end of the project, you need to move your web pages to a public server so other people can look at them. There are different ways to move the files onto a server and different methods for ensuring that the version of the files is correct and not accidentally overwritten.

Enabling Server Connection

When you defined a website in Dreamweaver, you defined a local site that exactly mirrors the final, public website. **Mirroring** means that the local site contains an exact copy of the files on the final site. Dreamweaver calls your final site the **remote site**. You work on the files in your local site and then upload them to the remote site by using Dreamweaver's file transfer commands.

When working in Dreamweaver, you don't need File Transfer Protocol (FTP) software or any other software to move your files onto the remote server. This capability is built right into Dreamweaver! It's more convenient to set up your remote site and transfer files while working in Dreamweaver than to jump out to another application.

Adding Your Remote Site

You define a remote site by editing the website definition (which you get to by selecting Site, Manage Sites). Select a site and click the Edit button to launch the Site Definition dialog box for the selected website. In the Basic tab, click the Next button until you reach the Sharing Files section of the Site Definition Wizard, as shown in Figure 20.1.

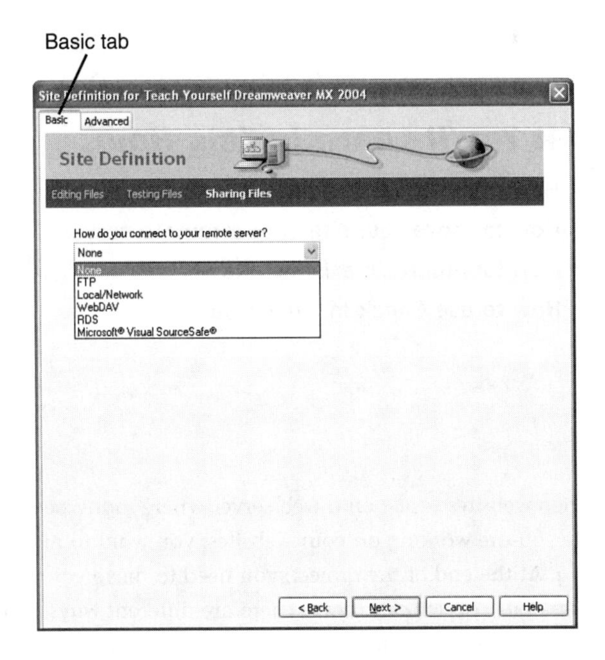

FIGURE 20.1 You set up the remote site definition in the Sharing Files section of the Site Definition Wizard.

You can choose five transfer methods from the drop-down menu:

- FTP
- Local/Network
- RDS
- SourceSafe Database
- WebDAV

The transfer method you select depends on where your remote site is located. The site might be on your company's intranet, and if so, you can transfer the local site up to the remote site by using a LAN, or Local/Network, connection. The site might be at your ISP, the folks who provide you with an Internet dial-up service or a web hosting service. In this case, you will probably connect to its servers by using FTP. SourceSafe, RDS, and WebDAV connections are less common than the others but are sometimes used in professional web development environments.

Setting FTP Information

You should select FTP access, as shown in Figure 20.2, if you need to transfer files over the Web to a remote server. The server could be physically located in your building, or it could be on the other side of the world. You need to enter the name of the FTP server into the What Is the Hostname or FTP Address of Your Web Server? text box. Often this is in the following format: `ftp.`*`domain`*`.com`.

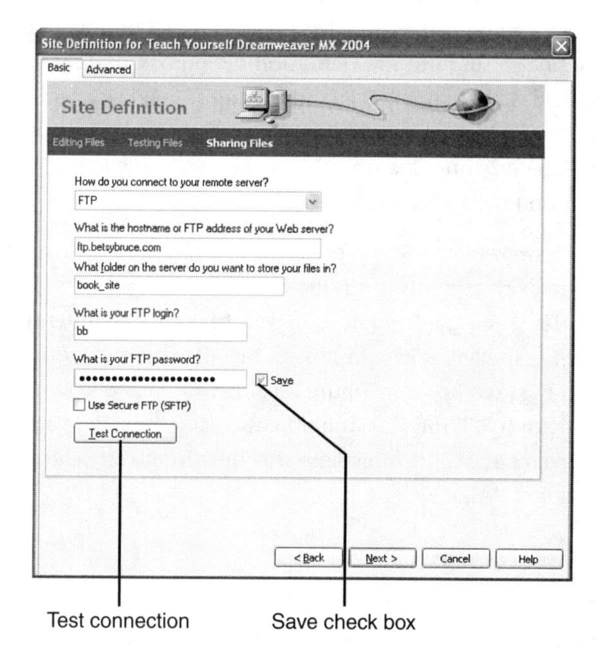

FIGURE 20.2 You need to set the FTP information, including the server address.

Watch Out!

No Protocol Necessary

Do not enter the server name preceded with the protocol, as you would in a browser (such as ftp://ftp.*domain*.com).

Enter the correct directory in the What Folder on the Server Do You Want to Store Your Files In? text box. You might need to get the path for this directory from your web or network administrator. If you are unsure what the root directory is on the remote site, try leaving the What Is the Hostname or FTP Address of Your Web

Server? box blank. The FTP server might put you directly in the correct directory because your account might be configured that way.

You need a login and a password to access the FTP server. The standard anonymous login, often used to download files over the Internet, will probably not work to upload files to a website. You need to log in as a user who has access and permission to get and put files in the directories that house your website. Dreamweaver saves your password by default. If other people have access to Dreamweaver on your computer and you don't want them to access your FTP account, deselect the Save check box.

Click the Test Connection button to make sure you've entered everything correctly and are successfully connecting to the FTP server. You can troubleshoot FTP connection problems by first closing the Site Definition dialog box and then selecting Window, Results and clicking the FTP Log tab. The FTP log lists the reason you didn't connect successfully. For instance, if the log states that the password was incorrect or the directory you are targeting doesn't exist, you can change these in the Site Definition Wizard and try again.

If you are behind a firewall or using a proxy server, you might have difficulties with FTP. Consult the network administrator about which settings you need to choose when setting up FTP. If you go through a firewall to access the Internet, you might need to configure the firewall port and host in the Site category of the Dreamweaver Preferences dialog box, as shown in Figure 20.3. If you have a slow connection to the Internet, the default FTP timeout might be too short, causing your FTP connection to time out too often. You can increase this time in the Site category of the Preferences dialog box.

Setting LAN Information

You should select Local/Network in the Site Definition Wizard, as shown in Figure 20.4, if the server is on a computer you can connect to directly by using a network. If you can access files on the server the same way you access your hard drive, moving files to and from it with ease, you have LAN access. You need to know the correct web-accessible directory; your web administrator should be able to give you that information.

Set up LAN access to the remote server by entering the path to the remote directory. Use the Browse icon to browse to the directory or type in the path. Checking the Refresh Remote File List Automatically might slow down Dreamweaver's performance a bit, but you will always have an up-to-date reflection of the remote site.

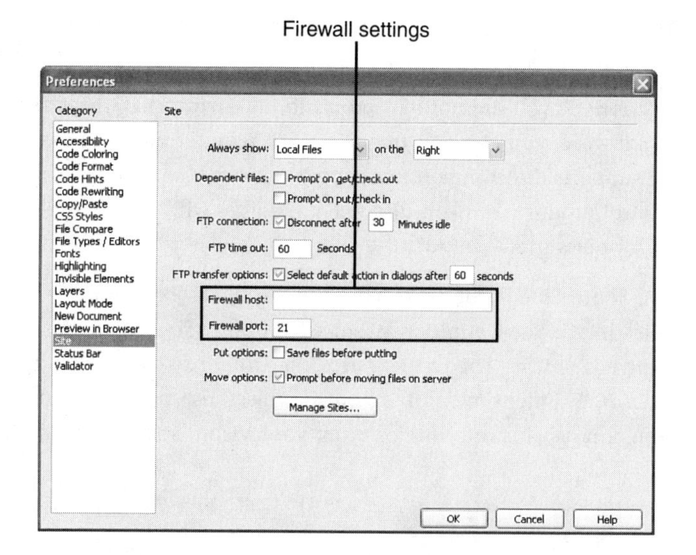

FIGURE 20.3 Configure firewall settings in the Dreamweaver Preferences dialog box if you have problems connecting to an FTP server behind a firewall.

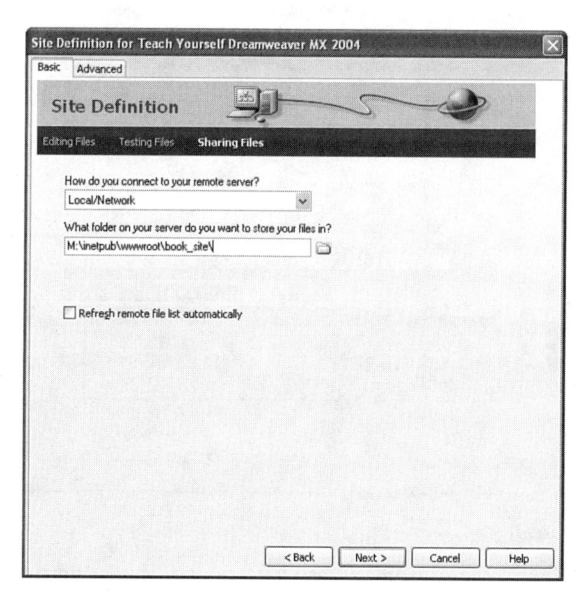

FIGURE 20.4 You select Local/Network when the remote directory resides within your LAN.

Setting RDS Access

You use the RDS setting only if your remote site is on a ColdFusion server. ColdFusion is one of the server-side scripting languages that Dreamweaver supports. As when you select FTP, you enter a hostname (the server address), a username, and a password to connect to this type of remote site.

Setting Source/Version-Control Application Information

You can connect directly from Dreamweaver to servers by using source- and version-control applications. If you are not in a professional environment that uses source-management software, you can skip this section or read it and file it away for later. Dreamweaver supports direct integration with Microsoft Visual SourceSafe, a popular version-control product. You can also exchange files with any source-control program that supports the WebDAV protocol.

Set up a Visual SourceSafe database as your remote site by selecting the SourceSafe Database choice in the Site Definition Wizard. Set up the SourceSafe database by clicking the Settings button. The Open SourceSafe Database dialog box appears as shown in Figure 20.5. Enter the database path, project, username, and password in this dialog. You can get this information from your Visual SourceSafe administrator.

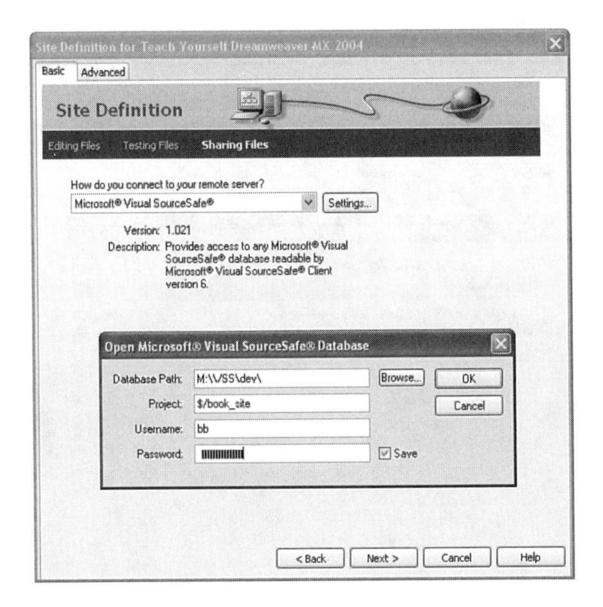

FIGURE 20.5 Enter the database, username, and password to connect to a SourceSafe database.

Another standard is WebDAV (sometimes just called DAV); the version-control information for WebDAV is set up similarly to a SourceSafe database. **WebDAV** stands for World Wide Web Distributed Authoring and Versioning, and it is a group of standards governing web collaboration that is an extension to HTTP. It's predicted that WebDAV access will eventually replace FTP access by extending HTTP to enable users to not only read from the Web but also to write to the Web.

Select WebDAV from the drop-down menu in the Site Definition Wizard, and then click the Settings button. The settings, shown in Figure 20.6, look different from the SourceSafe settings because you access this type of version-control application over the Web via a URL.

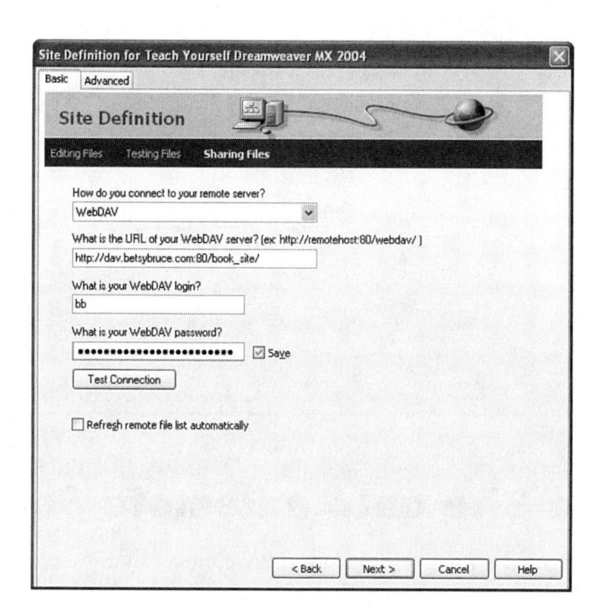

FIGURE 20.6
Enter a URL, username, and password to connect to a source-control application by using the WebDAV protocol.

Using the Remote Site Advanced Tab

Click the Advanced tab of the Site Definition dialog box to see a different view of your remote site's settings. The Remote Info category, shown in Figure 20.7, displays the login information, along with firewall and other settings. You can click back and forth between the Basic and Advanced tabs if you like.

Did you Know?

Passive FTP

If you are having problems connecting to the server when using FTP (you'll receive a message from Dreamweaver), you might want to select Use Passive FTP on the Advanced tab of the Site Definition dialog box. This often solves transfer problems, especially when you are transferring files from behind a firewall. Passive FTP is a more secure method of transferring data, where the client (Dreamweaver, in this case) controls the data going to and coming from the server.

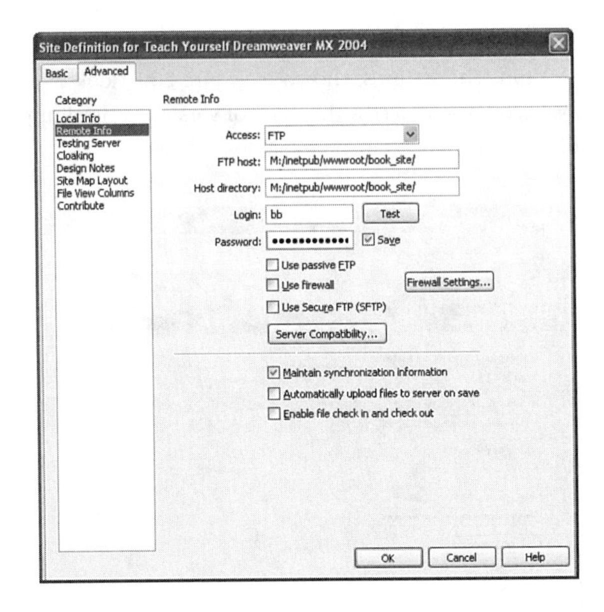

FIGURE 20.7
The Advanced tab shows all the remote site's settings.

Moving a Site onto a Remote Server

If your server is located on a LAN, you normally connect to the server when you log on to your computer, and you stay connected all day. If you access the remote server over the Internet by using FTP, you connect while getting and putting files onto the server, and then you disconnect. Even if you don't disconnect on your end, your connection will most likely time out on the server if you have been inactive for a period, and you will need to reconnect.

The Files panel contains buttons, as shown in Figure 20.8, that enable you to transfer files to and from the remote site. You can transfer files to your local site by selecting the Get button, and you can transfer files to the remote site by selecting the Put button. Later this hour, you'll learn about using the Synchronize command, which is a better way to transfer files. The Synchronize command detects whether a local file (or remote file) is newer and transfers it only if necessary, thus saving transfer time.

The buttons at the top of the Files panel are

- **Connect/Disconnect**—This button establishes a connection to an FTP server. The button has a little green light that is lit when you are connected to the FTP server. This button is always lit when you have LAN access to your remote site.
- **Refresh**—This button manually refreshes the list of files in the Files panel.

- **Get**—This button retrieves files from the remote site and moves them to your local site.
- **Put**—This button places files from your local site onto the remote site.
- **Expand/Collapse**—This button expands the Files panel into the Expanded Files panel.

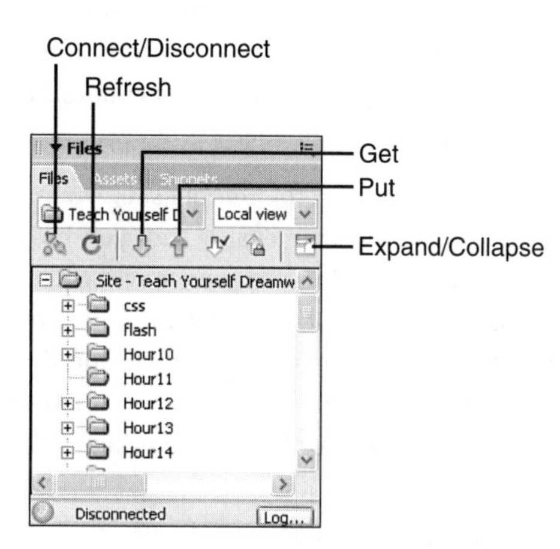

FIGURE 20.8
The buttons at the top of the Files panel help you transfer files between the local and remote sites.

Click the Expand/Collapse button on the far right of the Files panel to expand the panel, as shown in Figure 20.9. The expanded Files panel not only shows the local site, as does the collapsed Files panel, but it also shows the remote site. A list of the files on the remote site appears when you are connected. When you want to collapse the expanded Files panel, click the Expand/Collapse button again.

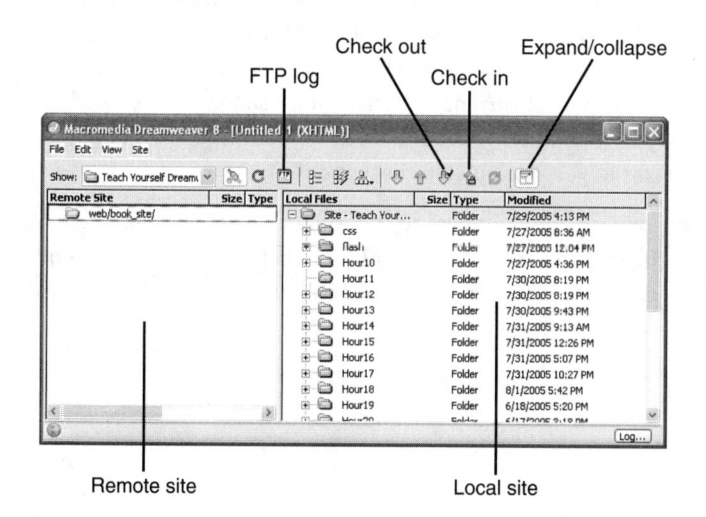

FIGURE 20.9
Use the Expand/ Collapse button to expand the Files panel.

Understanding Dreamweaver's Website Management Capabilities

Dreamweaver's file management system is useful if you are creating web pages along with other people. You use the Check In/Check Out tools in Dreamweaver to make sure that only one person is working on a file at a time. When you have a file checked out, no one else can check that file out until you check it back in, just like when you have a DVD or video checked out from the video store. Dreamweaver marks the file as checked out by you so your collaborators know who to bug if they also need to make changes to the file!

When you check out a file from the remote site, Dreamweaver retrieves a copy of that file from the remote server to ensure that you have the most up-to-date version of the file in your local site. When Dreamweaver gets the file, it overwrites the file that exists on your local drive. The checked-out file appears to Dreamweaver users with your name beside it on the remote server, signaling to your collaborators that you have checked it out. The file has a green check mark beside it in your local site, showing that you currently have that file checked out.

Enabling Check In/Check Out

After you define the remote site in the Site Definition Wizard and click Next, Dreamweaver asks if you'd like to enable Check In/Check Out. Because you overwrite files when you transfer them from the local site to the remote site, you need to be careful. You can use Check In/Check Out functionality so that you do not overwrite files that others have recently edited and uploaded to the remote site.

When you turn on Check In/Check Out on the Advanced tab of the Site Definition dialog box, options appear, as shown in Figure 20.10, that enable you to configure this feature. You choose whether you'd like to check out a file when you open a file in your local site that isn't currently checked out. I suggest you choose to view it as a read-only copy because then you can look at a file without checking it out; if you then need to edit it, you can quickly check it out.

Enter a name and an email address so that others accessing the remote site can see who has the file checked out. They'll be able to click your name and send you an email message about the file you have checked out.

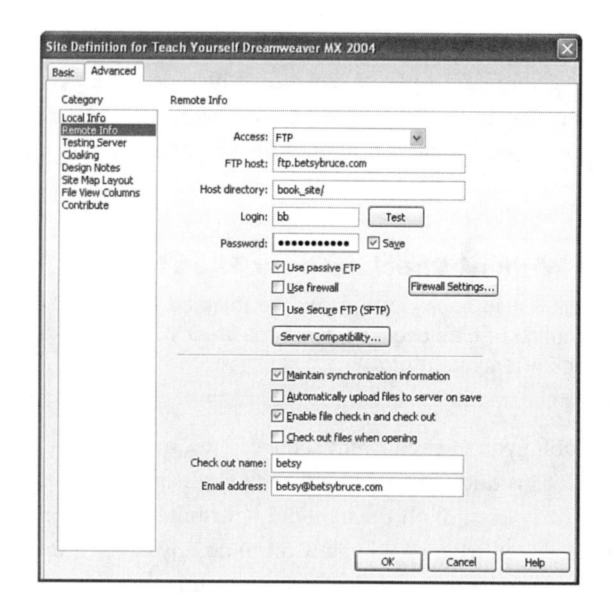

FIGURE 20.10 Enable Check In/Check Out so that you can control collaboration with others.

Transferring Files

When you check in a file to the remote site, Dreamweaver transfers the file back to the remote server to make it available for others to work on or view. Your name no longer appears beside the file name.

By the Way

Dreamweaver's Locking Mechanism

Dreamweaver creates a file on the remote server with the `.lck` (for lock) file extension. This file contains the name of the person who has checked out the file. You don't need to worry about creating these `.lck` files, but I mention them because you might get questions about these files from others who examine the remote site without Dreamweaver.

Watch Out!

Drag and Drop Might Be Dangerous

You can drag and drop files back and forth between the local and remote sites. However, you need to be careful where you drop the files. You might drop them in an incorrect directory. Dreamweaver automatically transfers files into the mirror image location when you select a file and use the buttons to transfer the file. This way, the file remains in its correct location.

Check In/Check Out is designed to help you manage a collaborative environment. The Check Out procedure forces you to download the most recent version of the file. While you have the file checked out, others cannot work on it. After you check the file back in, you can open the file but cannot save any changes because Dreamweaver marks it as read-only.

Did you Know?

Don't Leave Without Checking Your Files In!

Remember to check files back in when you are finished with them! Don't go on vacation with a bunch of files checked out if you want your co-workers to happily welcome you back when you return.

Dreamweaver enables you to circumvent some of the Check In/Check Out safeguards. You can, for instance, override somebody else's checked-out file and check it out yourself. You can also turn off the read-only attribute of a file and edit it without checking it out. However, why would you want to do any of these things? Dreamweaver's Check In/Check Out process is fine for a small environment where you don't expect mischief. If you need tighter security and version control, however, you should use one of the products on the market, such as Microsoft Visual SourceSafe, that enable very tight control.

Did you Know?

Everyone on the Team Needs to Use Check In/Check Out

Your project will work more smoothly if everyone who is collaborating on the project turns on the Check In/Check Out functionality for the site. Otherwise, it's too easy to overwrite a file that someone else has updated. Check In/Check Out works only if everyone on the team uses Dreamweaver and enables the Check In/Check Out functionality.

You can still use Get and Put when you have Check In/Check Out enabled. The Get command moves a file from the remote server and overwrites the local file. The file is read-only on your local machine because you won't have it checked out. If you try to put a file that someone has checked out onto the remote server, Dreamweaver warns you that changes to the remote copy of the file might be lost if you go ahead and transfer the file. You can choose to do the action anyway or cancel the action.

Did you Know?

The Synchronize Command

To get only the files that are more recent than the files on the local site onto the remote site, you use the Synchronize command, which is discussed in Hour 21, "Managing and Editing a Website."

To get or put files, first make sure the correct site is selected in the Site drop-down menu of the Files panel or the Site window. If you access your site via FTP, click the Connect button. If you are already connected or are accessing the files on a LAN, skip this step.

To get or check out files, follow these steps:

1. Select the files you want to transfer to your local site. You can also select an entire folder to transfer all of its contents.
2. Click the Get command, or click the Check Out command if you have Check In/Check Out enabled for this site.
3. Dreamweaver might display a dialog box, asking if you would also like to download dependent files. **Dependent files** are images and other assets that are linked to the files you are transferring. You can disable this dialog box by checking the Don't Ask Me Again check box. I prefer to transfer the asset files manually instead of having Dreamweaver do it automatically.

Did you Know?

Don't Transfer Dependent Files Multiple Times

Continually getting and putting dependent files slows down your transfers. Image files are usually much larger than HTML files and take longer to transfer. If the files haven't changed, you don't need to transfer them.

To put or check in files, follow these steps:

1. Select the files you want to transfer to the remote site.
2. Click the Put command, or click the Check In command if you have Check In/Check Out enabled for this site. If you transfer a file that is currently open, Dreamweaver prompts you to save the file before you put it on the remote site.
3. Dreamweaver might display a dialog box, asking if you would also like to upload dependent files. You can disable this dialog box by checking the Don't Ask Me Again check box.

Importing an Existing Website

When a website already exists at a remote site, you need to define the website in Dreamweaver, connect to the remote site, and download all the files in the site to work on it. Remember, you can edit only files that are located on your own machine. You can download and edit an existing site even if it wasn't created with Dreamweaver.

Downloading a site for the first time might take some time, depending on how you are accessing the site and what your network connection speed is. After you initially download all the files, however, you should need only to download any files that change.

To import an existing website, all you need to do is mirror the existing site on your local drive. There is no conversion process, and the files remain unchanged in Dreamweaver. To import an existing website, follow these steps:

1. Set up both your local and remote info in the Site Definition dialog box.
2. Connect to the remote site using the Connect/Disconnect button in the Files panel.
3. Select the top entry in the remote site of the Files panel, selecting the entire site. If you select a file instead, you get only that file and not the entire site.
4. Click the Get button to transfer all the files on the remote site to your local site.

You can also import and export a site definition, either to share with others or to back up your site definition. To do this, select the Export command from the Site menu in the Files panel. You can choose to either back up your site definition (saving your login, password, and local path information), or share the site definition with other users (without the personal information). Dreamweaver saves the file with the `.ste` extension. Select the Import command from the Site menu in the Files panel to import the site definition contained in the `.ste` file.

Summary

In this hour, you have learned how to connect to a remote site and transfer files. You have learned how to use the Advanced tab of the Site Definition dialog box and how to set up FTP, local/network, Visual SourceSafe, and WebDAV connections. You have also learned how to use Dreamweaver's internal version-control feature, Check In/Check Out.

Q&A

Q. ***When is it appropriate to use Check In/Check Out?***

A. There are two major uses for Check In/Check Out: for working in a small group and for working on a site from two computers. Check In/Check Out isn't designed for use by enterprise-type projects (those with many developers), but it is perfect for a small group of developers who are working on the same sites. I use it all the time when I work on a site with two computers (home and work computers, for instance). It helps me know whether I have uploaded my changes.

Q. ***Do you use the Site Definition Wizard or the Advanced tab of the Side Definition dialog box to define websites in Dreamweaver?***

A. I usually define a site initially by using the wizard because it's fast, but then I often tweak the site definition by using the Advanced tab.

Q. ***One of my co-workers left for a two-week vacation with a bunch of files checked out in his name. How can I work on these files while he is gone?***

A. When you attempt to check out the files, Dreamweaver warns you that someone else has them checked out. It then asks you to override your co-worker's checkout. If you click the Yes button, the files are checked out to you. Just hope that your co-worker hasn't made any changes to the files that he forgot to move onto the remote site.

Workshop

Quiz

1. When you're working in a collaborative environment and using FTP, it doesn't matter if everyone is using Dreamweaver's Check In/Check Out functionality. True or false?
2. Why do you need to define a remote site for a website?
3. What is Dreamweaver's most useful tool for troubleshooting a connection to a remote site via FTP?

Quiz Answers

1. False. It's too easy for one member of your group to overwrite the work of another member if not everyone is using the Check In/Check Out functionality. The only time you don't need to use this functionality when working with a group is when you are using a third-party program to manage version control.
2. In order to put website files on a public server or share files with a group, you need to define a remote site in Dreamweaver.

3. Dreamweaver's most useful tool in this situation is the FTP log. The FTP Log tab in the Results panel enables you to read the error messages sent back by the server. Or, select the View Site FTP Log button in the Expanded Files panel.

Exercises

1. Define a remote site connection, using either the FTP setting or the Local/Network setting. If you don't have access to a remote computer, create a directory on your hard drive and name it `remote`. Pretend that this is a directory on a LAN and define it as a remote site. Try transferring files back and forth between the local and remote sites.
2. Turn on Check In/Check Out functionality for a defined site and connect to the remote site. What changes in Dreamweaver?

HOUR 21

Managing and Editing a Website

What You'll Learn in This Hour:

- How to synchronize files on local and remote sites
- How to create a site map and manage links
- How to add design notes to document your project and share ideas with others
- How to generate reports about a website

Dreamweaver has a number of useful commands for managing an entire website. You can create (and even save) a site map that is a visual representation of the relationships of all the files in a website. There are commands to update links sitewide and to search and replace text in either the text or the HTML portions of a web page.

Managing the Local and Remote Sites

Dreamweaver has a number of useful commands that can help you make sitewide changes. In the next hour, you will use commands that are very powerful and can save you a lot of time. You should be careful when changing items sitewide in case you make a mistake. But of course, you could just fix such a mistake sitewide, too!

The commands that you apply to an entire site, such as the commands to transfer files, are available from the menus in the expanded Files panel. The expanded Files panel (showing both the local and remote sites) has File, Edit, View, and Site menus. When you don't have the Files panel expanded, these same menus and commands are available from the Files panel menu, shown in Figure 21.1.

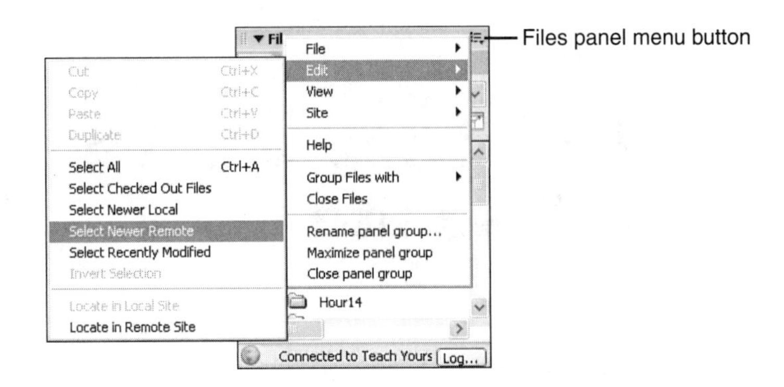

FIGURE 21.1 The Files panel menu gives you access to the same menus available when the Files panel is expanded.

Synchronizing Your Files on the Local and Remote Sites

You should synchronize your files on the local and remote sites so you are assured that you have the most up-to-date files in both places. Dreamweaver has three commands that are useful in determining which site has the newer files: Select Newer Local, Select Newer Remote, and Synchronize.

If you want to check whether new files reside on the local site or the remote site, use the Select Newer Local and Select Newer Remote commands, respectively, from the Edit menu in the Files panel.

To see which files are newer on the remote site, follow these steps:

1. Connect to the remote site by clicking the Connect (Connects to Remote Host) button at the top of the Files panel (F8) if you are using FTP to access the remote site.
2. Select either the root directory or a section of files in the local site.
3. Select Edit, Select Newer Remote in the Files panel.

Dreamweaver searches through the files on the remote site to see whether any are newer than the same files on the local site. The files that are newer on the remote site are all selected. If files that don't exist on the local site exist on the remote site, Dreamweaver selects those, too. With all the files selected, you simply get the files from the remote site to update your local files. To select files that are newer on the local site, you follow the same steps, except you use the Select Newer Local command in step 3.

You select the Synchronize command to automatically synchronize files between the local and the remote sites, bringing both sites up-to-date with the most recent files.

When you synchronize files, Dreamweaver analyzes the files on both the local and remote sites and gives you a report on which files need to be copied to synchronize the sites. You have total control over the process and can deselect any files you do not want transferred. Dreamweaver also tells you whether files are completely up-to-date and whether there is a need to synchronize.

In order to use the Synchronize command, you must have synchronization enabled in the site definition. Make sure that the Maintain Synchronization Information check box, shown in Figure 21.2, is checked in the Remote Info category of the Site Definition dialog box. Remember, that you can double-click the site name in the Site drop-down menu in the Files panel to quickly edit the site definition.

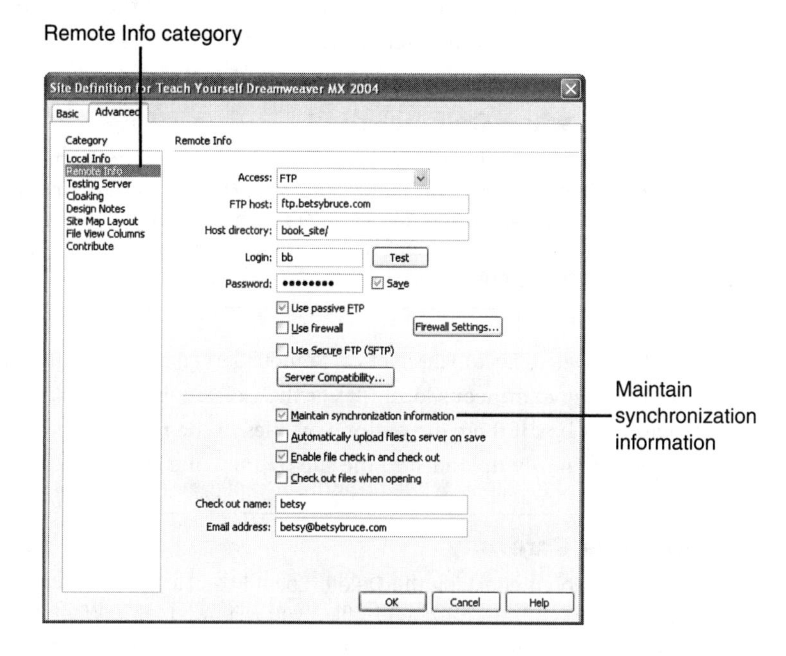

FIGURE 21.2
The Maintain Synchronization Information check box turns on synchronization functionality for the site.

To synchronize the files in the local and remote sites, follow these steps:

1. Make sure the site you want to synchronize is open in the Files panel. Select a different site from the Site drop-down menu if necessary.
2. If you want to synchronize only certain files or folders, select those files or folders.
3. Select Site, Synchronize from the Files panel menu. The Synchronize Files dialog box appears, as shown in Figure 21.3.

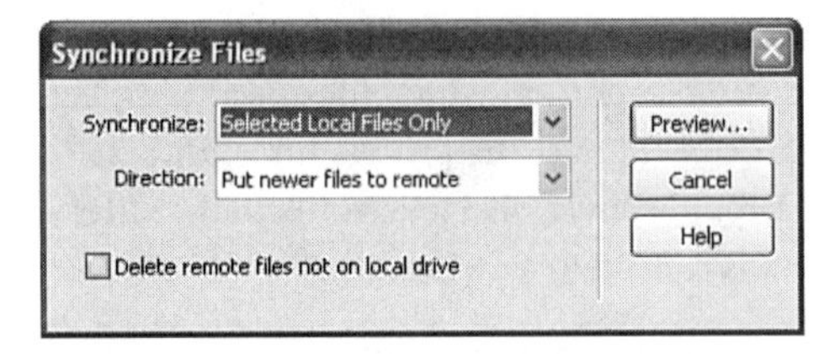

FIGURE 21.3
The Synchronize Files dialog box enables you to select which files to synchronize.

4. In the Synchronize drop-down menu, choose to synchronize the entire site or just the files you have selected.
5. Select how you want to transfer the files in the Direction drop-down menu. You can transfer the newer files to the remote site, get the newer files from the remote site, or get and put newer files in both directions.

By the Way

Synchronize when Collaborating

Because I often collaborate with groups of people on websites, I am usually interested in what files are newer on the remote site. Others on the team might have changed files and uploaded them while I was doing something else. I like to make sure I'm looking at the most recent files in the project by synchronizing to get the newer files from the remote site.

6. Check the Delete Local Files Not on Remote Server check box if you want to get rid of any extraneous local files or the Delete Remote Files Not on Local Drive check box if there are extraneous files in the remote site. Careful! Maybe the files are newly uploaded to the site by someone else.

Delete Files Carefully

Be very careful about checking the Delete Local Files Not on Remote Server check box because you don't want to delete files you will need later. When you select this check box, you are deleting the files from your hard drive. If the files do not exist anywhere else, you can't restore them. Checking this box is a quick way to clean your local site of files that are not being used.

7. Click the Preview button. If your files are up-to-date, you get a message saying no synchronization is necessary and asking if you'd like to view a list of files to manually synchronize. Dreamweaver displays the Synchronize dialog box, shown in Figure 21.4, if files need to be synchronized. The Synchronize dialog box lists all the files that must be transferred in order for the local and remote sites to be in sync.
8. When you are ready to transfer the files, click OK.

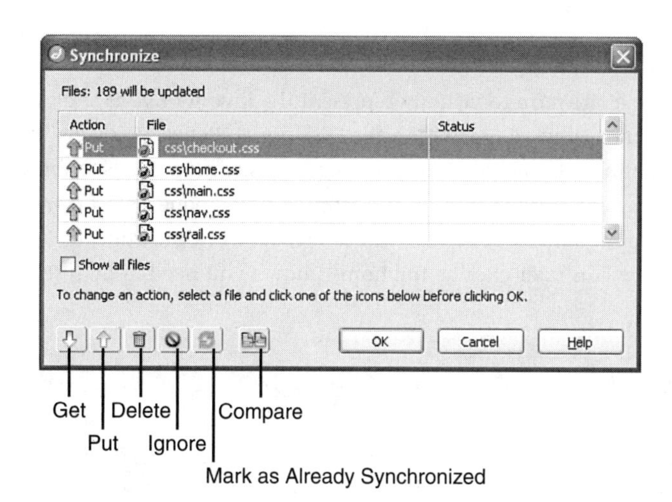

FIGURE 21.4 The Synchronize dialog box lists the files that need to be synchronized.

Several buttons at the bottom of the Synchronize dialog box enable you to modify the list of files to transfer. The following buttons help you fine-tune the synchronization process:

- **Get**—This command marks the file to be downloaded from the remote site to the local site.
- **Put**—This command marks the file to be uploaded from the local site to the remote site.
- **Delete**—This command marks the file to be deleted.
- **Ignore**—This command marks the file to be ignored by the synchronization process.
- **Mark as Already Synchronized**—This command marks the file as already synchronized.
- **Compare**—This command opens the file in a file comparison utility. You specify a file comparison software program in the File Compare category of Preferences (Edit, Preferences).

When you are updating and editing files on a live website, you will probably use the Synchronize command many times. It's a quick and mechanical method of deciding which files have been updated and need to be uploaded to the server. When you are collaborating with others, the Synchronize command is useful for helping you decide which files have been updated on the server and need to be updated on your local site. This saves you the trouble of downloading the entire site when only a few files have been updated.

Creating a Site Map

You can create a site map to visually represent the layout of your site. After you've defined a site map, you will view it in the Files panel. Before you view the site map, you need to define a home page for your site. The site map needs to know where "home" is in order to build the map. To define a home page, select a web page as the home page in your local site and select Site, Set as Home Page, as shown in Figure 21.5. You can later change the home page if you need to by reselecting this command.

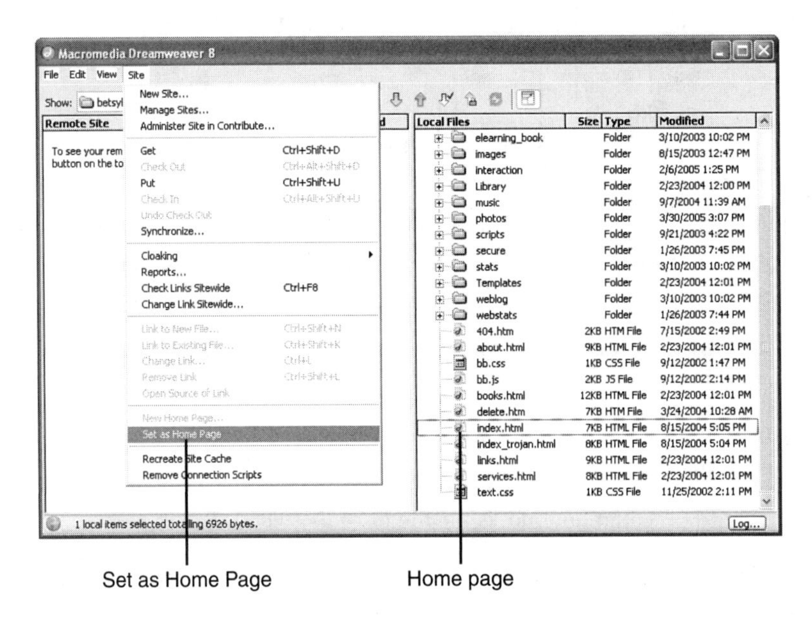

FIGURE 21.5
To use the Site Map feature, you first have to select a web page to be the home page in the site.

In the expanded Files Panel, select the Site Map button, shown in Figure 21.6, to display the site map. When you select this button, you can choose to display the map by itself (Map Only) or with the local files (Map and Files). Files appear as icons in the site map with lines drawn between related files to represent links. The following symbols appear next to the icons that describe the files:

- **Broken link**—A broken link appears as red text with a small picture of a broken link of chain.
- **Link**—A link appears as blue text with a small globe beside it.
- **File checked out by you**—A file that is checked out to you appears with a green check mark beside it.

- **File checked out by someone else**—A file that is checked out to someone else appears with a red check mark beside it.
- **Checked in or read-only file**—A file that is read-only appears with a lock beside it.

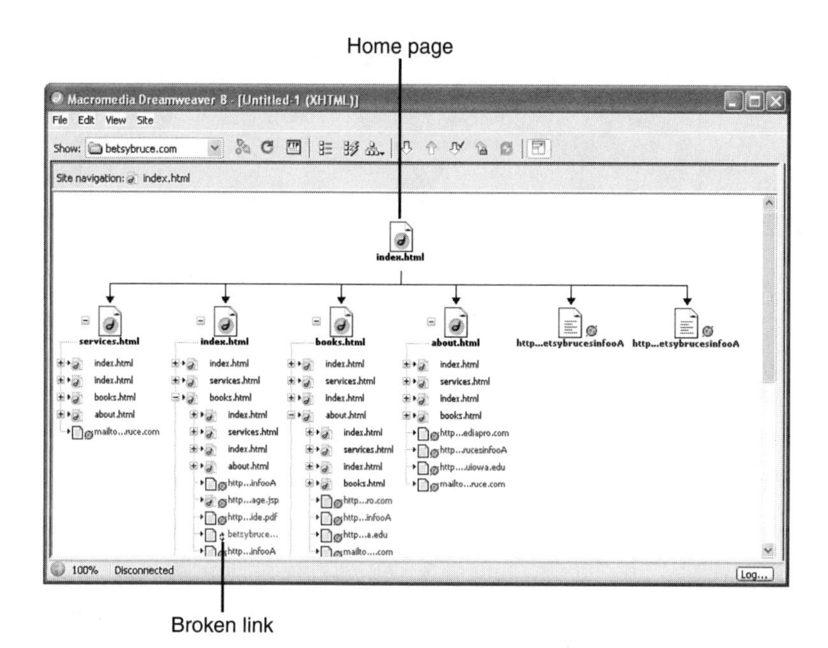

FIGURE 21.6
The site map shows the files in your site, along with icons that represent links, check-out information, and the read-only attribute.

> **Did you Know?**
>
> **Views in the Files Panel**
>
> You can view the site map in the collapsed Files panel instead of in the expanded Files panel. Select the Site Map command from the drop-down menu next to the Sites drop-down menu in the Files panel. It's more difficult to see all the files in the Files panel than in the expanded Files panel.

You can change the view in the site map by clicking any file and selecting View, View as Root. This places the icon you selected at the top of the site map. The files that are between the currently selected icon and the actual site root are displayed in the bar directly above the site map. You can click these files to jump to that level.

Select View, Site Map Options, Layout to modify the way the site map is displayed; this command opens the Site Definition dialog box to the Site Map Layout category, as shown in Figure 21.7. You must display the site map in the Files panel in order for this command to be active. You can set the number of columns (how many files are display horizontally in the site map) and the column width. You can also set when the site map displays each file's filename or page title under the icon in the site map.

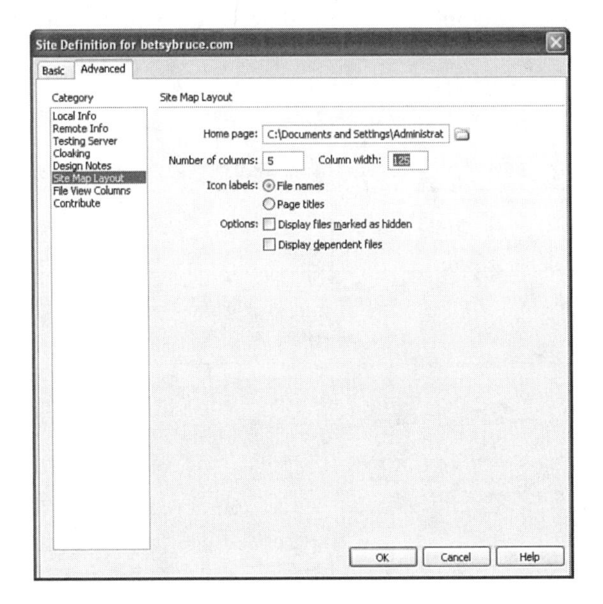

FIGURE 21.7 The Site Map Layout category of the Site Definition dialog box enables you to configure the number of columns and their width.

Save your site map as either a bitmap (.bmp) or a PNG (.png) file by selecting File, Save Site Map. You can embed a bitmap representation of your site map into a text document to send to a client or to save as documentation. You can also print the file as a reference or embed a PNG file in a web page.

Managing Your Links

Dreamweaver automatically updates links when you move or rename a file within the current website. Make sure when you define the website that you create a cache to speed up the update process. By default, the cache is turned on, and it's best that you do not turn it off in your site definition. When you move or rename web pages, Dreamweaver displays the Update Files dialog box. A list of linked files, as shown in Figure 21.8, is displayed in the dialog box. Click the Update button to update all the links or select individual files to update.

Use the Change Link Sitewide command to change the URL of a certain link throughout the site. For instance, if you displayed a link in your site for each day's menu in the cafeteria, you would need to change the link to a new web page every day. On Tuesday morning, you could select the Monday web page and then select Site, Change Link Sitewide. The Change Link Sitewide dialog box, shown in Figure 21.9, enables you to enter the old link and then select the path for the new link.

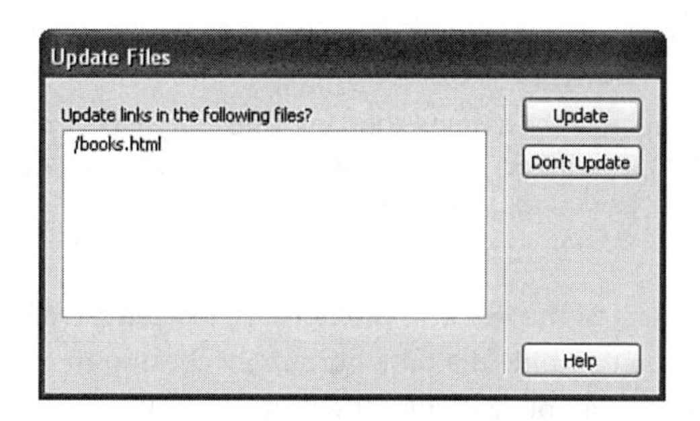

FIGURE 21.8
When you move or rename web pages, the Update Files dialog box appears, allowing you to update all the links to that file.

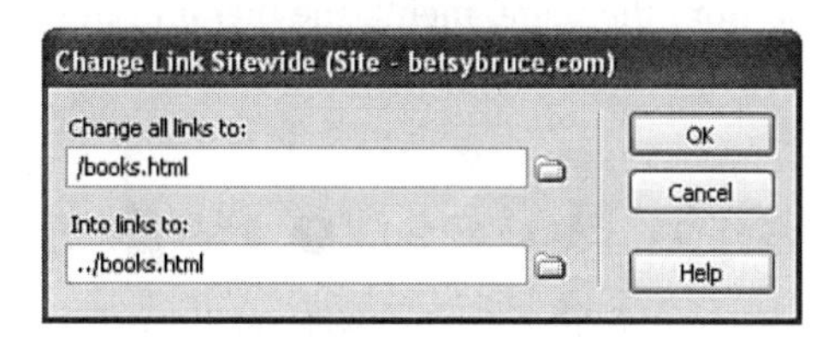

FIGURE 21.9
Use the Change Link Sitewide command to change all of the links to a certain web page.

You can use the Link Checker, shown in Figure 21.10, to check all the links in your site. To open the Link Checker, select Site, Check Links Sitewide command from the Files panel. The Link Checker displays three categories: broken links, external links, and orphaned files. External links are links that Dreamweaver cannot check. Orphaned files are files that do not have any files linking to them.

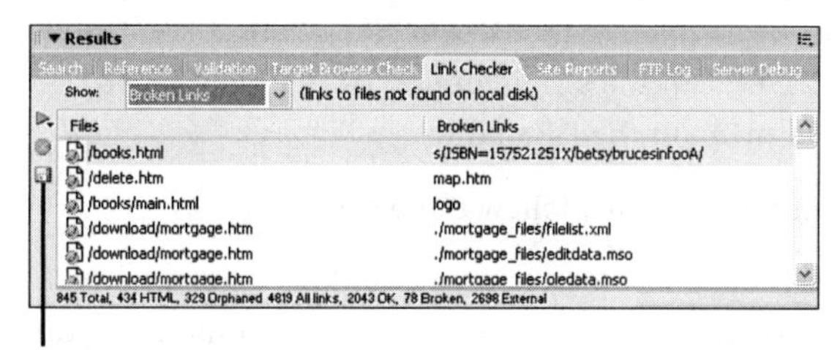

FIGURE 21.10
The Link Checker displays broken links, external links, and orphaned files.

Watch Out!

An Orphan Might Not Be an Orphan

Dreamweaver might say a file is an orphan even when that file is used in your site. The file might be referenced in a behavior, for instance, such as an image file used with the Swap Image behavior.

Broken links need to be fixed. Fortunately, Dreamweaver makes that easy. You just select the broken link displayed in the Results panel group, click the Browse icon, and navigate to the correct file to fix the link.

Save the Link Checker Report

You can save the report after running the Link Checker by clicking the Save Report button, the small floppy disk icon on the left side of the Results panel. Then you can easily refer to it as you fix any problems with your site.

The Link Checker opens in the Results panel group, located directly below the Property inspector. You can hide the panel group by clicking the arrow to the left of the panel title (Results), or you can close the panel group by selecting the Close Panel Group command from the panel menu, the menu in the upper-right corner of the panel.

Adding Design Notes to Pages

Design notes enable you to add notes to your web pages. You can use design notes to document your design process, share information with others, and keep any extra information that would be useful. Because design notes are not actually part of the web page, you can use them to record sensitive information you might not want people who view the web page to be able to read.

You can add a design note to any file in a website, including templates, images, and movies. You might want to add a design note to each image to list the name and location of the original image file. In order to add design notes to files in your site, design notes must be enabled in the Design Notes category of the Site Definition, as shown in Figure 21.11. Edit the site definition by double-clicking the site name in the Site drop-down menu of the Files panel.

To attach a design note to a file, follow these steps:

1. When a file is open in the Document window, select File, Design Notes. Or right-click (Command+click on the Mac) a file in the Files panel and select the Design Notes command.
2. The Design Notes dialog box appears, as shown in Figure 21.12. Select the type of design note you want from the Status drop-down menu.
3. Click the Date icon to insert today's date in the Notes field. Type a note in the field after the date.
4. Check the Show when File Is Opened check box if you want this design note to appear when someone opens the file next.

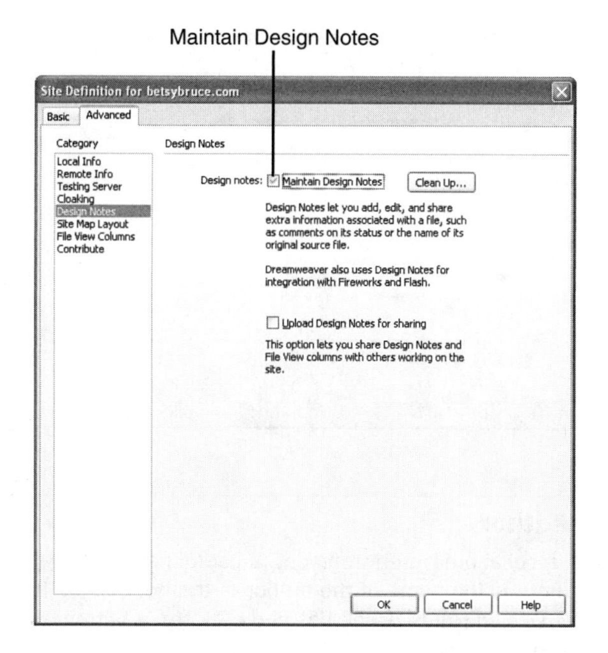

FIGURE 21.11
Enable Design Notes in the Design Notes category of the Site Definition dialog box.

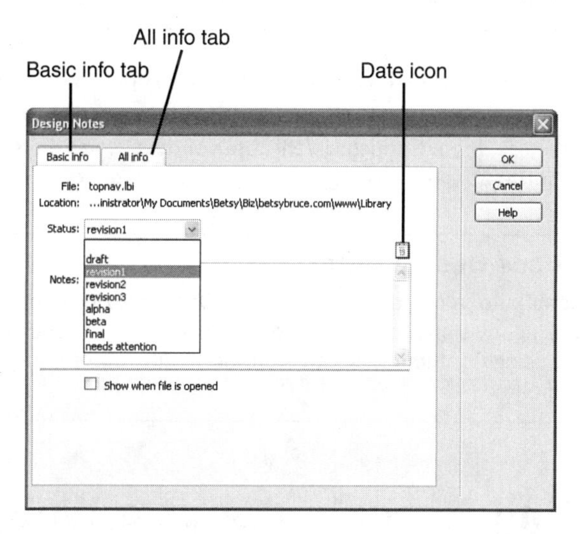

FIGURE 21.12
You select the type of design note you want from the Status drop-down menu.

5. Select the All Info tab in the Design Notes dialog box to see a list of the information in the current design note, as shown in Figure 21.13. Add a record to the list by clicking the + button, entering a name, and entering a value.
6. When you are done making changes in this dialog box, click OK.

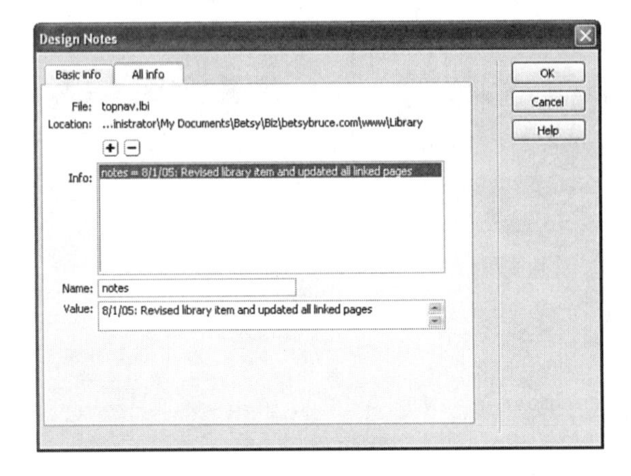

FIGURE 21.13 You can add additional data to design notes by selecting the All Info tab.

Did you Know?

Record the Author

When you are in a collaborative environment, a useful name and value data pair to add to a design note is the name of the author of the note. To do this, select the All Info tab in the Design Notes dialog box and click the + button. Name your new record Name and put your name in the Value field.

A design note remains associated with files even if it is copied, renamed, moved, or deleted. Dreamweaver saves your design notes in a directory called `notes` in your site root. This directory doesn't appear in the Site window. Notes are saved with the name of the file plus the `.mno` extension.

Watch Out!

Contribute Uses Design Notes

Macromedia Contribute, a companion product to Dreamweaver, uses design notes to facilitate tracking revisions to a file. If you are working in an environment where some users are using Contribute, don't delete or modify any of the design notes Contribute has created.

Generating Reports About a Website

The reports that come with Dreamweaver enable you to compile information about your site, such as when files were created or what errors you've found in your site. These reports are useful for examining, troubleshooting, and documenting your website. You can also save and print the results of the reports. The following reports are available in Dreamweaver:

- Checked Out By
- Design Notes
- Recently Modified
- Combinable Nested Font Tags
- Accessibility
- Missing Alt Text
- Redundant Nested Tags
- Removable Empty Tags
- Untitled Documents

To run a report, follow these steps:

1. Select Site, Reports (in either the Files panel or the menu bar). The Reports dialog box appears, as shown in Figure 21.14.

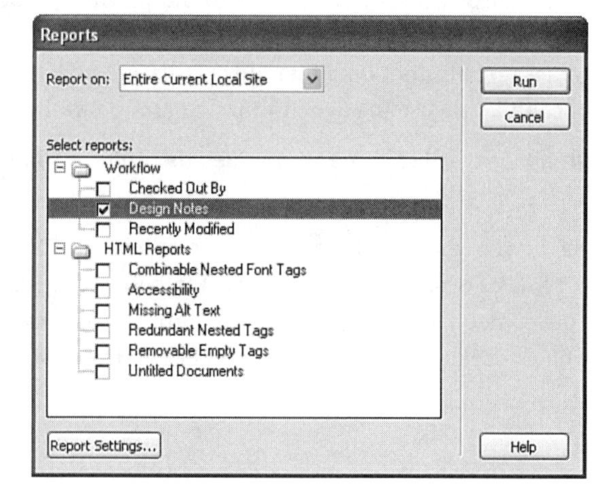

FIGURE 21.14 Many reports are available that give you information on either your current document or an entire site.

2. Select what you want to report on (the current document, the current site, selected files, or a certain folder).

3. Select one (or more) of the reports. Some reports have additional settings you can make in order to refine the search. If the Report Settings button is active at the bottom of the dialog box, additional settings are available for that report.

4. Click the Run button to run the report.

5. A Results panel group appears with a list of files. You can save this report as well as open the individual files that are referenced.

Summary

In this hour, you have learned how to synchronize files between local and remote sites and learned how to manage links in a website. You have also learned how to create site maps that visually represent the relationship between the files in a website. You learned how to add design notes to capture extra information about files in a website and how to run reports on a website. These skills are important when you need to manage websites and all the files they contain.

Q&A

Q. ***Am I really going to goof up my files if I use the Synchronize command?***

A. Using Synchronize can be a little scary. You might want to run the Select Newer Local and the Select Newer Remote commands first. Jot down the filenames that are selected. Then, when you run Synchronize, check to see if that command comes up with the same filenames. This will hopefully reassure you that you can confidently use the Synchronize command in the future!

Q. ***Why does Dreamweaver list some of my files as orphaned files when they really aren't?***

A. Dreamweaver checks whether files are linked to other files. The files that Dreamweaver lists as orphaned might be used in behaviors. For instance, you might have a web page loaded with the Open Browser Window behavior. Because the file is not actually linked to another file, Dreamweaver shows it as orphaned.

Workshop

Quiz

1. How can you tell which images in your entire site are missing the alt text?
2. Dreamweaver can attach a design note to any file, whether it's a web page or another type of file, in a website. True or false?
3. What image formats can a site map image be saved in?

Quiz Answers

1. Run the Missing Alt Text report on the entire site.
2. True. Dreamweaver can attach a design note to any file in a website.
3. Site map images can be saved as BMP or PNG files.

Exercises

1. Create a site map of a site you have set up and experiment by setting various pages as the root of the site. Try saving the map as a PNG file and inserting it into Dreamweaver. Try adding a new web page in the site map.
2. Run the Link Checker on a site you created or imported. Do you have any broken links? If so, fix them. Do you have any orphaned files? If you no longer need those files, delete them. If your site has external links, you should periodically check to see that they are still valid.

HOUR 22

Customizing Dreamweaver

What You'll Learn in This Hour:

- How to create and organize Dreamweaver snippets and custom snippets
- How to record custom commands and save history steps as commands
- How to use the Extension Manager to install third-party extensions to Dreamweaver
- How to modify Dreamweaver's keyboard shortcuts
- How to add your favorite objects to the Favorites category of the Insert bar
- How to use and save Dreamweaver searches

Some developers who are skilled in JavaScript create Dreamweaver behaviors, objects, and commands—extra functionality for Dreamweaver—that you can download free from the Web. Macromedia provides a site that collects these extensions—the Macromedia Exchange (www.macromedia.com/exchange)—where you can download extensions for not only Dreamweaver but also Flash, Fireworks, ColdFusion, and other Macromedia products. When Dreamweaver doesn't seem to have a behavior, an object, or a command for what you are trying to accomplish in your web page, search this website, and you might find just what you need.

There are also ways you can customize Dreamweaver yourself, creating reusable objects stored within Dreamweaver for easy access. This hour you'll explore how to create snippets and custom commands to help speed up the creation of web pages. You can also save searches to reuse or share with others.

Creating a Custom Snippet

Snippets are bits of code that are available from Dreamweaver's Snippets panel. You can use any of the multiple snippets available when you install Dreamweaver. You can also create custom snippets out of code that you use repetitively. This can speed up development of web pages as well as maintain consistency in your code.

By the Way

Shortcuts for Snippets

You can create keyboard shortcuts so you can insert your favorite snippets into a web page with just a couple of keystrokes. You'll learn how to add keyboard shortcuts to Dreamweaver and how to modify the existing shortcuts in the "Editing the Keyboard Shortcuts" section.

First, let's explore the existing snippets available in Dreamweaver. Some of these snippets might not interest you, but some might speed up your daily work in Dreamweaver. The lower half of the Snippets panel (Window, Snippets) displays categories of snippets, along with descriptions of what the snippets do (you might have to enlarge the Snippets panel to see the descriptions). The upper portion of the Snippets panel gives you a preview of the selected snippet. The default Snippets panel, shown in Figure 22.1, has the following categories:

- Accessible
- Comments
- Content Tables
- Footers
- Form Elements
- Headers
- JavaScript
- Meta
- Navigation
- Text
- Legacy

Watch Out!

Don't Use the Legacy Snippets

The Legacy Snippet folder contains snippets that use deprecated code—basically code that uses tags that are no longer part of HTML standard tags. You should avoid using these snippets.

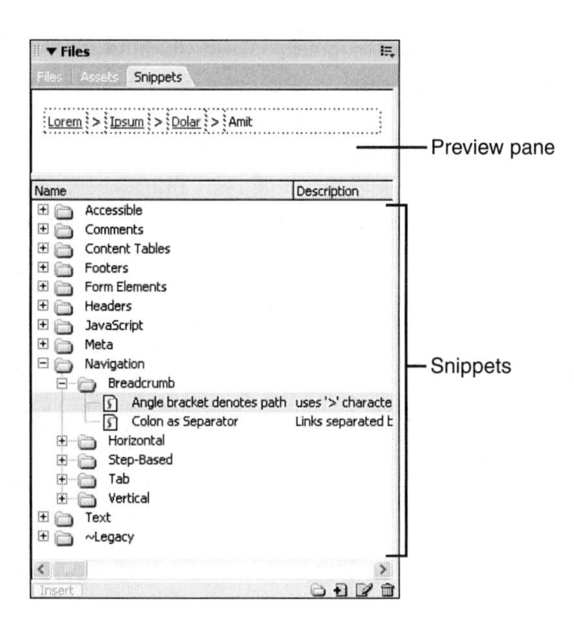

FIGURE 22.1
The Snippets panel has a number of snippets categories and displays a preview of the selected snippet.

You can create a new snippet out of an object or some code you use often. You can create a new snippet within an existing category, or you can create a new folder for your own personal snippets. To create a new snippets folder to hold your custom snippets, click the New Snippet Folder button (see Figure 22.2). Give your new folder a name. Now you can store new snippets in this folder or move existing snippets into the folder for easy access.

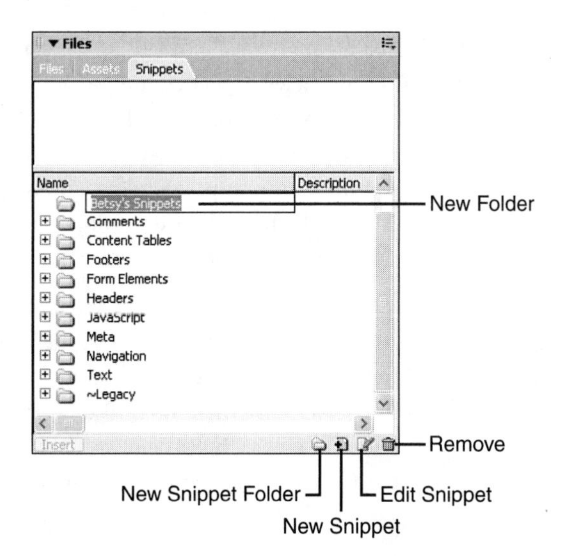

FIGURE 22.2
You can create a new snippet folder and new snippets in the Snippets panel.

Select the New Snippet button (refer to Figure 22.2) at the bottom of the Snippets panel to begin creating a snippet of code. In the Snippet dialog box that appears, as shown in Figure 22.3, you enter a name and a description for the snippet. You can select either the Wrap Selection radio button or the Insert Block radio button. The Wrap Selection setting divides the dialog box into two halves; the top half is inserted before the current selection, and the bottom half is inserted after. The Insert Block setting inserts the snippet as a block of code instead of wrapping it around other objects.

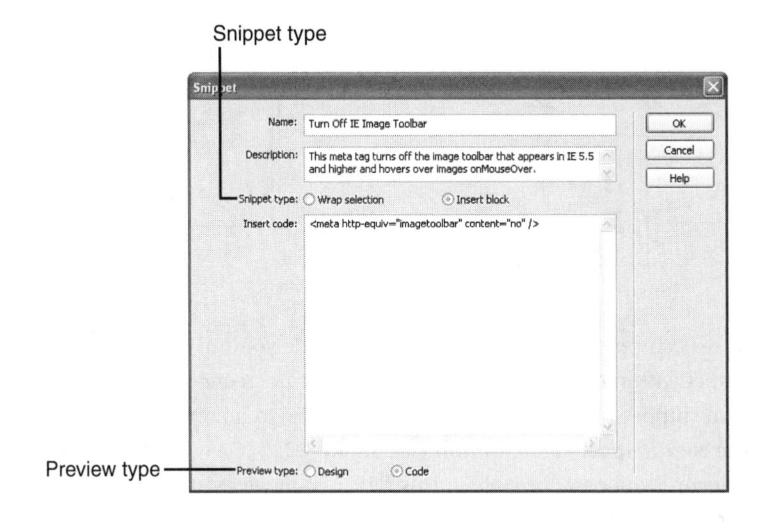

FIGURE 22.3 You can create a new snippet that either inserts a block of code (as shown) or wraps code around the current selection.

The snippet content goes into the Insert Code text box. The easiest way to insert code into a snippet is to first create the code in Dreamweaver, either in Design or Code view. When you select the New Snippet command with the code selected, Dreamweaver automatically places the code into the Insert Code text box. You can select how you'd like the snippet preview to appear in the Snippets panel by selecting either the Design radio button, which presents the snippet preview in Design view, or the Code radio button, which presents the snippet preview in Code view. These radio buttons are located at the bottom of the Snippet dialog box.

When you select the Wrap Selection radio button when creating a snippet, you enter code into two text boxes: the Insert Before text box and the Insert After text box. When you apply the snippet to an object on the page, the code in the Insert Before text box is added before the object, and the code in the Insert After text box is added after the object code. You need to create this type of snippet to package an object within the code you create in the snippet. For instance, if you want an object to be within a hyperlink, you need to add tags before and after the object, and you need to create a snippet with Wrap Selection selected to get the Insert Before and Insert After text boxes.

Editing the Keyboard Shortcuts

You can edit all the keyboard shortcuts in Dreamweaver by using the Keyboard Shortcuts dialog box, shown in Figure 22.4, which you can open by selecting Edit, Keyboard Shortcuts. Instead of modifying the existing set of keyboard shortcuts, you should create your own set. Drop down the Current Set drop-down menu to see the existing keyboard shortcut sets: Macromedia Standard, BBEdit, Dreamweaver 3, and Homesite. If you are used to the keyboard shortcuts of any of these other web editors, you can use those shortcut sets by selecting them in this menu.

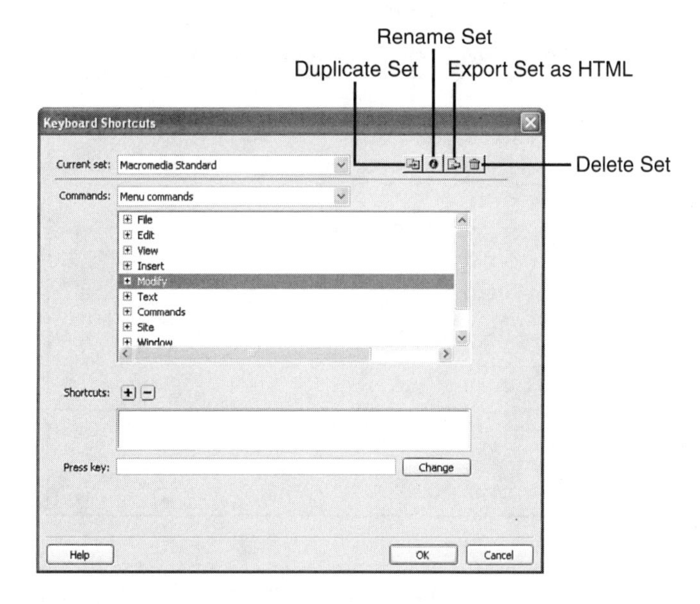

FIGURE 22.4 You can edit and access keyboard shortcut sets in the Keyboard Shortcuts dialog box.

You do not want to modify the Macromedia Standard keyboard shortcut set because you might need to revert to it later. Instead, you want to create your own version of that keyboard shortcut set by duplicating it; you do this by selecting the Duplicate Set button. Then you give your new set a name and make sure it is selected in the Current Set drop-down menu. Then you are ready to customize any of the keyboard shortcuts you want.

While editing keyboard shortcuts, you select commands from several categories in the Commands drop-down menu: Menu Commands, Site Panel, Code Editing,

Document Editing, Site Window, and Snippets. Select one of the categories and then select a command from the list. If the command already has a keyboard shortcut, it shows up in the Shortcuts list at the bottom of the dialog box. You can either modify the existing keyboard shortcut for that command or add an additional shortcut by clicking the + button.

To add or edit a keyboard shortcut, place the cursor in the Press Key text box at the bottom of the dialog box and press the key combination on your keyboard that you'd like to use for the keyboard shortcut. The keys are recorded in the Press Key text box, as shown in Figure 22.5. If that shortcut already exists for another command, you see an error message. You should press different keys until you come up with a unique keyboard shortcut for the command. Click the Change button to apply the shortcut to the command.

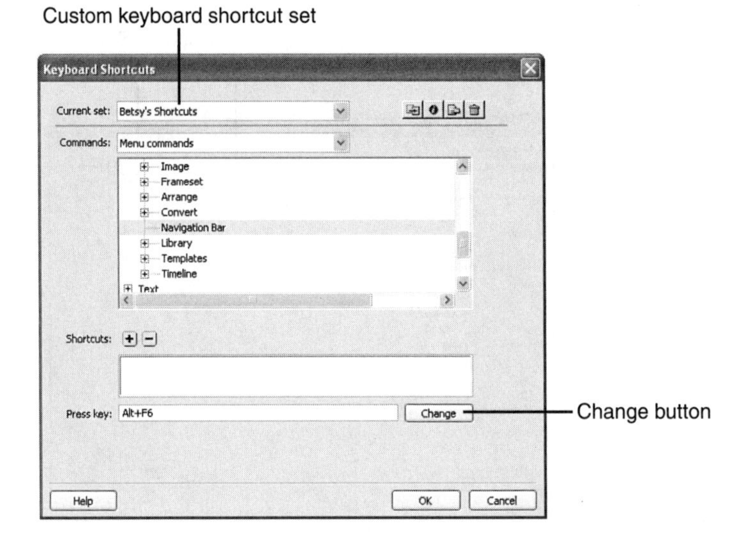

FIGURE 22.5 Press the keys on your keyboard to record a keyboard shortcut for a command.

Click OK to save your custom keyboard shortcuts. Make sure you test the shortcuts to ensure they work the way in which you want them. You can always open the Keyboard Shortcuts dialog box and edit your shortcuts later if needed.

By the way, did you notice you can give keyboard shortcuts to any of the custom snippets you created earlier this hour? Snippets is one of the command categories you can select to apply keyboard shortcuts. Select Snippets in the Commands drop-down menu and all the Snippets categories are displayed. Expand the categories until you find the name of the snippets you want to add a keyboard shortcut to, and then add the shortcut as you did earlier.

Print a List of Your Keyboard Shortcuts

When you make changes to the keyboard shortcuts available in Dreamweaver, you should document those changes to remind you while you are working. Click the Export Set as HTML button at the top of the Keyboard Shortcuts dialog box to create a web page listing all the commands and the corresponding keyboard shortcut. Give the web page a name in the Save as HTML File dialog box and save it to your hard drive. You can open this file in Dreamweaver and edit it if necessary. Preview this file in the browser and then print it out to have a paper copy of your shortcuts.

Making a Menu Command

Dreamweaver enables you to record and save a step or set of steps as a command. These recorded commands are like macros created in other applications, such as Word and Excel. **Commands** enable you to save a complicated set of steps to apply whenever you need to accomplish a repetitive task. There are two ways to accomplish this:

- Record a set of steps as you perform them and then play them back.
- Select a step or set of steps from the History panel and save them as a command.

Recording a Command

Dreamweaver enables you to record a set of steps and then play them back. Dreamweaver can record only a single set of steps in this way. When you record a new set of steps, the previous set is replaced. You can use a recorded set of steps again and again until you either record a new set of steps or close Dreamweaver. This functionality is useful when repeating the same set of steps over and over in Dreamweaver.

By the Way

Record Reproducible Steps

Dreamweaver keeps you from recording steps that are not reproducible by Dreamweaver. For instance, Dreamweaver cannot reproduce selecting text on the page, so you cannot save that as a step. Dreamweaver warns you if you cannot save a particular step.

To record a set of steps, first select the type of object to which you will apply your steps. If you've created a command that modifies text, you need to apply the command to text; it does not work if you apply it to a dissimilar object. You can't select objects while recording because Dreamweaver cannot record the selection step. After you've selected an appropriate object in the Document window, select Commands, Start Recording. The cursor changes into a little cassette icon. Perform the steps which you want to record and then select Commands, Stop Recording.

Apply the recorded command by selecting an object and then selecting Commands, Play Recorded Command. Dreamweaver performs the steps you previously recorded. You can continue to use this command until you either replace it with another command or close Dreamweaver.

You have to perform an additional step if you want to save the recorded command to use after you've shut down Dreamweaver. To save a command, select Commands, Play Recorded Command. A step called Run Command appears in the History panel (Window, History) list, as shown in Figure 22.6. Select the Run Command step and click the Save Selected Steps as a Command button. The Save as Command dialog box appears; now enter a name for the command.

FIGURE 22.6 The History panel displays the Run Command step that you can save and use during future Dreamweaver sessions.

Saving a Command from the History Panel

The History panel, shown in Figure 22.7, displays all the steps you've performed on the current document since you opened it. You can launch the History panel from the Window menu. The History panel enables you to undo certain steps, copy steps to the Clipboard and apply them to different web pages, and save a set of steps as a command.

Did you Know?

Change the Number of History Steps Recorded

You can set the number of steps Dreamweaver displays in the History panel in the General category of the Dreamweaver Preferences (Edit, Preferences) dialog box. The default setting for the Maximum Number of History Steps is 50.

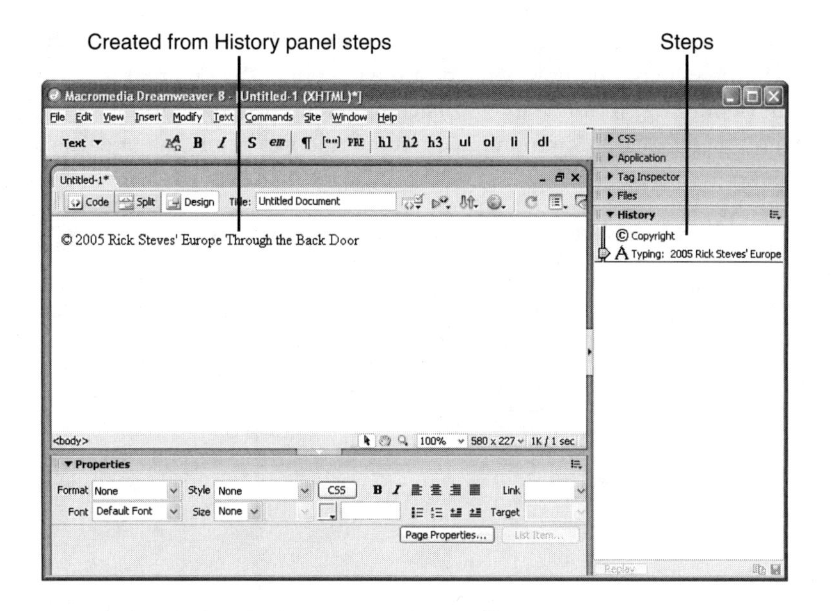

FIGURE 22.7 The History panel records and displays all the steps you've performed on the current web page.

Did you Know?

Clear the History Panel Steps

You can clear all the currently listed steps by selecting the Clear History command from the History panel drop-down menu.

The steps in the History panel are listed in the order in which you performed them, with the most recent step at the bottom of the list. You can undo steps by moving the slider up, as shown in Figure 22.8. Notice that the steps dim after they have been undone. To redo the steps, move the slider back down.

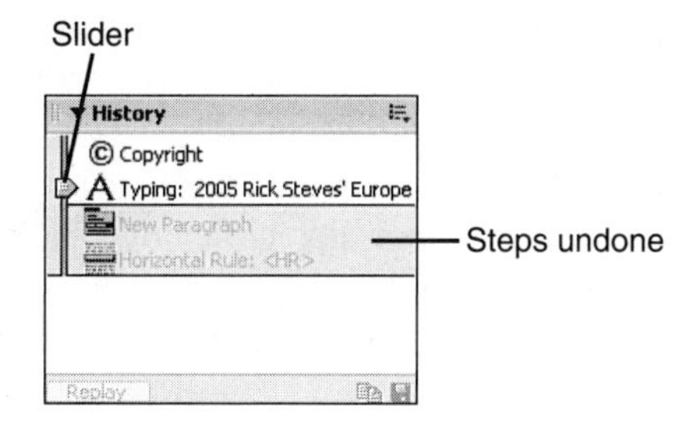

FIGURE 22.8 Move the slider up in the History panel to undo steps. The steps dim when they are undone. Move the slider back down to redo the steps.

You can save a set of steps from the History panel as a command. Select the steps in the panel by dragging the cursor over them. Click the Save Selected Steps as

Command button. When the Save as Command dialog box appears, name the command. This new command now appears at the bottom of the Commands menu, as shown in Figure 22.9. To run your custom commands, select them from the Commands menu. Select Commands, Edit Command List to rename or delete a command.

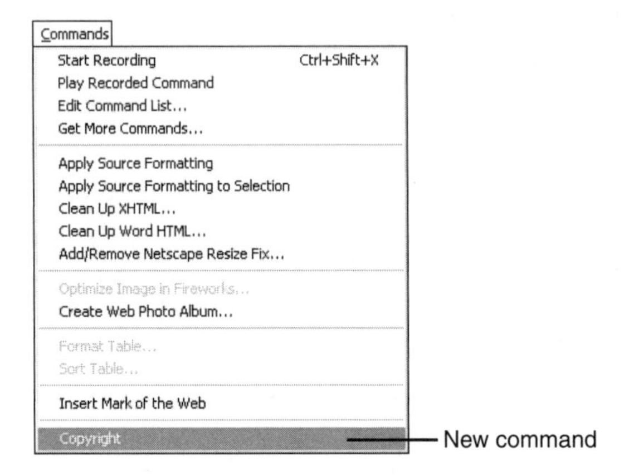

FIGURE 22.9 Custom commands that you create appear at the bottom of the Commands menu.

Adding Favorites to the Insert Bar

In Hour 2, "A Tour of Dreamweaver," you explored the Insert bar, but a single category was left for this hour: The **Favorites category** is the Insert bar category where you store your own custom group of Dreamweaver objects. You can add, group, and organize a list of specific objects to be displayed in the Favorites category.

To begin adding objects to your Favorites category, right-click (Control+click on the Mac) in the Insert bar with the Favorites category selected. A menu appears, listing the four Dreamweaver menus: Insert (Insert bar), Style Rendering, Document (the Document toolbar), and Standard (a menu that contains standard commands such as New Document and Copy but that isn't displayed by default when you install Dreamweaver). At the bottom of this drop-down menu is the Customize Favorites command, which enables you to add your favorite objects to the Favorites category. Right+click (Command+click on the Mac) to drop down the menu, shown in Figure 22.10, and then select the Customize Favorites command to display the Customize Favorite Objects dialog box.

Select objects from the Available Objects list on the left side of the dialog box, which shows all the objects listed in the Insert bar. Select an object in the Available Objects list and click the arrow button in the middle of the dialog box to move that object to the Favorites Objects list on the right side of the dialog box. Use the up- and down-arrow buttons to reorder the Favorites Objects list. Add a separator to the list, as shown in Figure 22.11, by clicking the Add Separator button; the separator is added below whatever you have selected in the Favorite Objects list.

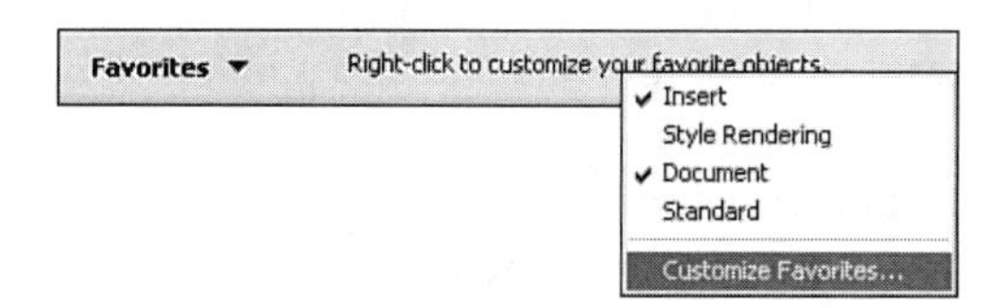

FIGURE 22.10 Select the Customize Favorites command by right-clicking on the Favorites category of the Insert bar.

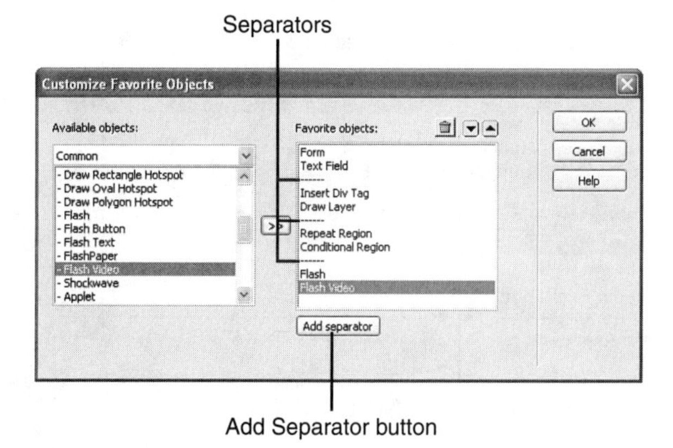

FIGURE 22.11 You can add a separator to your Favorites list to organize it.

After you click OK to save your list of favorites, those objects appear in the Favorites category of the Insert bar. The objects are not deleted from their original categories but are simply duplicated in the Favorites category so you can access them easily from a single category. You may modify your favorites from time to time, depending on the type of projects on which you are working.

Extending Dreamweaver by Using Third-Party Extensions

You can easily install third-party extensions to Dreamweaver by selecting Commands, Manage Extensions. This command launches the Macromedia Extension Manager, which enables you to automatically install and uninstall extensions that have been packaged in a standard Macromedia extensions format. Many extensions are available to extend Dreamweaver's functionality; check out the Macromedia Dreamweaver Exchange at www.macromedia.com/exchange.

Extensions can be commands, objects, suites, or behaviors. The Macromedia Exchange, shown in Figure 22.12, lists categories of extensions. You can also search for a certain type of extension at this site. When you select an extension from the list, you'll see a description of what it does and also a link to download the extension. Many extensions are free, but some of the extension developers charge a minor price for their work. Sometimes you can try the extension for a limited amount of time for free. Most of the extensions that carry a charge are well worth the money spent because they usually provide functionality you could not create, they speed up your development enormously, and they often have support documentation available.

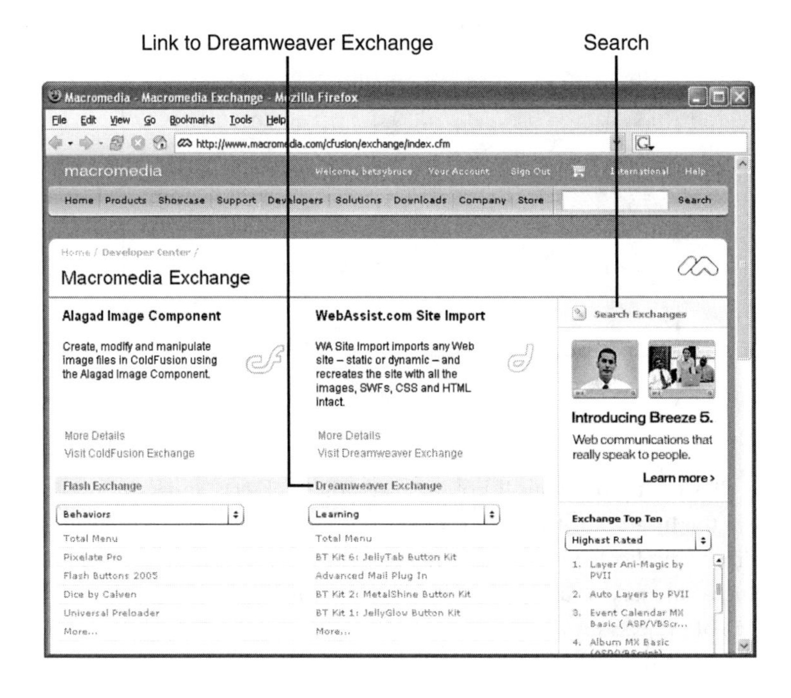

FIGURE 22.12 The Macromedia Exchange enables you to view and download extensions to Dreamweaver and other Macromedia projects. Select the link to the Dreamweaver Exchange to see only Dreamweaver extensions.

You'll need to create a free account in order to download extensions. After you download a Dreamweaver extension, you use the Extension Manager to install it to Dreamweaver. Extension Manager is installed automatically when you install Dreamweaver. It manages the extensions to all the Macromedia applications you have installed. You launch Extension Manager by selecting Help, Manage Extensions.

To use Extension Manager to install third-party extensions, follow these steps:

1. Download an extension file from the Dreamweaver Exchange website. An extension file has the `.mxp` file extension.

2. Launch Extension Manager, as shown in Figure 22.13.

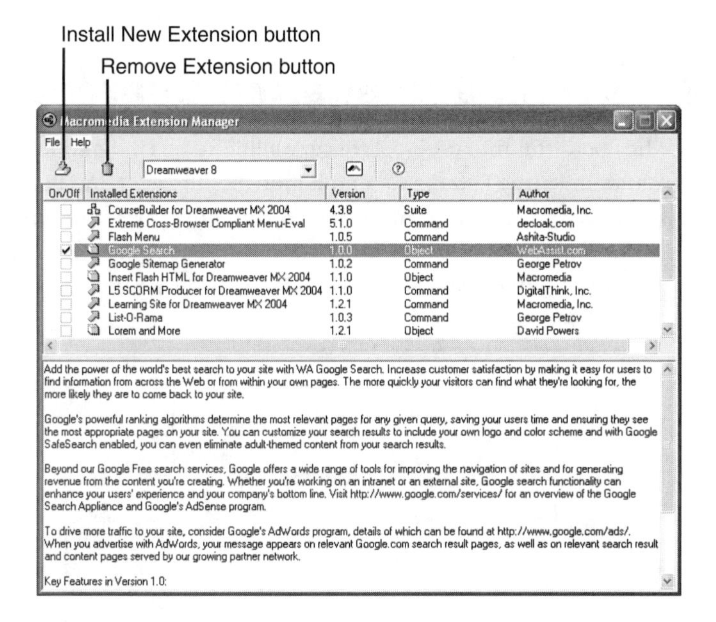

FIGURE 22.13
Extension Manager enables you to automatically install third-party extensions into Dreamweaver.

3. Click the Install New Extension button in Extension Manager. The Select Extension to Install dialog box appears.

4. Browse to the directory where you saved the file you downloaded. Select the file and click the Install button.

5. Accept the disclaimer by clicking the Accept button.

6. The extension is installed into Dreamweaver. The appropriate icons and commands are added automatically.

You can disable an extension by unchecking the check box next to the extension name under the On/Off column of Extension Manager. This does not delete the extension but simply makes it unavailable in Dreamweaver. To delete an extension, select the extension name and click the Remove Extension button in the Extension Manager.

By the Way

Extensions Available for All Studio Products

The Extension Manager not only manages extensions to Dreamweaver but also for Flash, Fireworks, Director, Authorware, and ColdFusion. If you use any of these other products, you can also download and install extensions for them via the Extension Manager.

Using, Saving, and Sharing Searches

Dreamweaver has powerful find and replace capabilities. The Find and Replace command is found under the Edit menu, and it launches the Find and Replace dialog box, shown in Figure 22.14. You can run a search on the current document, all open documents, a certain folder, or an entire current website. You can search the source code, search the text, or search for a specific tag by using the selections in the Search drop-down menu.

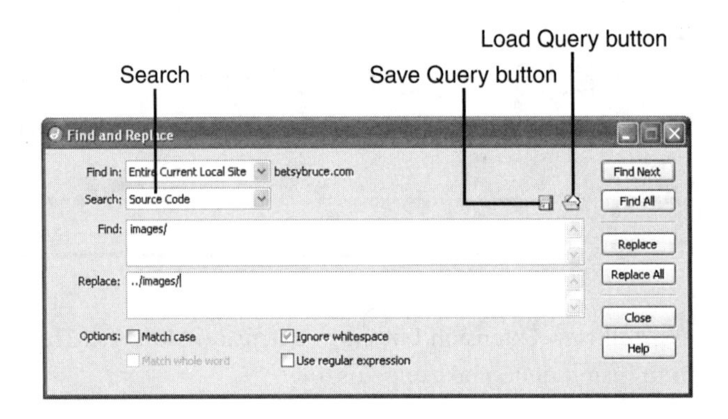

FIGURE 22.14
The Find and Replace dialog box enables you to search the source code, search the text, or search for a specific tag.

To conduct searches, you enter a pattern of text or code into the Find text box. Click the Find button to find the next instance of the pattern or click the Find All button to display a list of all instances of the pattern, as shown in Figure 22.15. The list is displayed in the Results panel group, beneath the Property inspector.

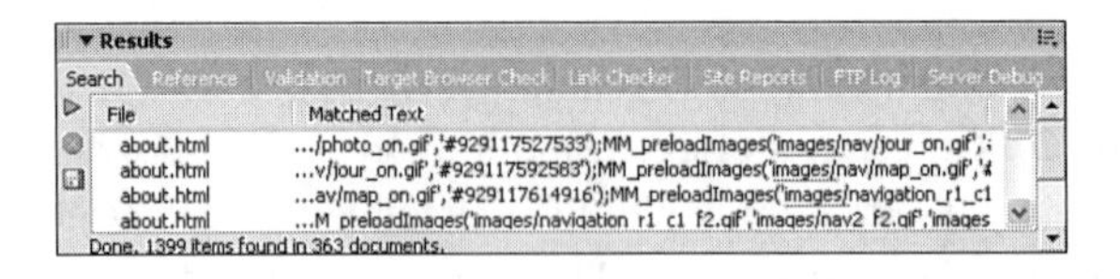

FIGURE 22.15
The results of a Find All search are displayed in the Search panel.

The Text and Source Code search categories are self-explanatory: You search for text within the web page by using a Text search, and you search for code within Dreamweaver's Code view using the Source Code search. The Specific Tag search is a little more complicated, however. You use the Specific Tag search to find HTML tags in your code and modify the tag, modify an attribute of a tag, or strip the tag out of the code completely.

For instance, you might want to search your website for font tags because these tags have been replaced by Cascading Style Sheets (CSS) styles, the more modern way of formatting page display. You can use a specific tag search to accomplish this:

1. In the Find and Replace dialog box, set the scope of your search in the Find In drop-down menu.
2. Select Specific Tag from the Search drop-down menu.
3. Select Font from the list of tags directly to the right of the Search drop-down menu.
4. If you are looking for font tags with a specific attribute, say the `face` attribute or the `size` attribute, enter the search characteristics in the Attributes section. Add or subtract attributes by using the + and – buttons. If your tag search has no attribute, click the – button to delete the initial attribute that is listed.
5. Set what will happen to the font tags by using the Action drop-down menu. To simply strip all the tags out of your site, use the Strip Tag action. To replace the font tags with a CSS style, use the Change Tag action and select Span from the drop-down menu to the right, as shown in Figure 22.16.

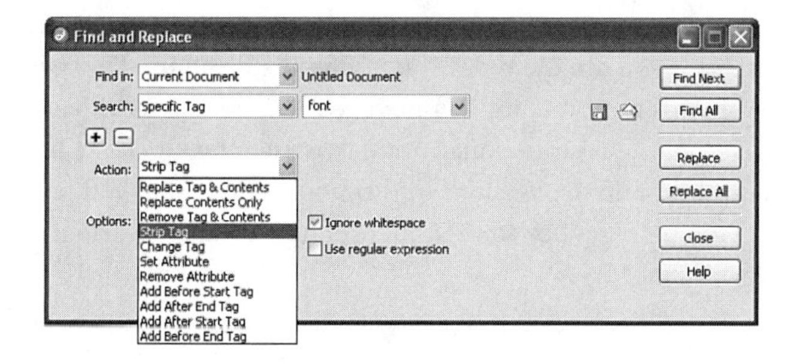

FIGURE 22.16 Select the replacement tag when doing a Specific Tag search.

6. Click the Find All button to display all the search findings.
7. Fine-tune your search by selecting the Find and Replace command again. Your search parameters are retained by Dreamweaver. If your search returns the correct findings, select the Replace command or the Replace All command.

Watch Out!

Find Before You Replace

Never click the Replace or Replace All buttons prior to confirming that your search returns the correct findings by using the Find or Find All buttons. You should confirm that the search returns the correct results, using the Find or Find All commands, before replacing everything.

8. In the Search panel, double-click each of the entries to apply a CSS style to the selection.

Did you Know?

Search for Text Within Tags

Use the Text (Advanced) Find and Replace commands to search for text within specific HTML tags.

If you've created a complicated search that you'd like to reuse later or share with others, you can save the search as a Dreamweaver query file. To do this, click the Save Query button to save the current query in the Find and Replace dialog box. Dreamweaver prompts you to browse to a location and then save a file with the `.dwr` file extension. To load this query, click the Load Query button (refer to Figure 22.14). You can share these `.dwr` files with others so they can run the query, too.

Summary

In this chapter, you have learned techniques and tips for customizing Dreamweaver the way you want it. You have learned how to use Dreamweaver snippets and create and organize your own snippets. You have also learned how to modify and create keyboard shortcuts if you are the type of user who prefers to use the keyboard rather than select commands from menus. You have learned how to record commands and save commands from the History panel. You have used the Macromedia Extension Manager to load third-party extensions into Dreamweaver. And you have learned how to use the Find and Replace command, and how to save a custom query to reuse or share with others.

Q&A

Q. ***What's the difference between snippets and Dreamweaver's library items?***

A. A snippet simply places objects or code into a web page, whereas a library item maintains a link to the library that enables you to update each instance of the item by updating the original. You'll learn about library items in Hour 23, "Using the Library: Reusing Elements of a Website."

Q. ***How can I remove items from the Favorites category of the Insert bar?***

A. Select the Customize Favorites command by right-clicking (Control+clicking on the Mac) the Insert bar. The Customize Favorites dialog box appears. Select the favorite you'd like to remove and then click the Remove button at the top of the dialog box (the small trash can).

Workshop

Quiz

1. What is the name of the application installed with Dreamweaver that facilitates loading third-party extensions into Dreamweaver?
2. Where do you change the number of steps maintained in the History panel?
3. What are the four searches you can do in the Find and Replace dialog box?

Quiz Answers

1. Macromedia Extension Manager is the application installed with Dreamweaver that facilitates loading third-party extensions into Dreamweaver.
2. You change the number of steps maintained in the History panel in the General category of the Dreamweaver Preferences dialog box.
3. You can do these searches in the Find and Replace dialog box: Source Code, Text, Text (Advanced), and Specific Tag.

Exercises

1. Use the Find and Replace command to search for a specific tag in your website. Click the Find All button to view the Search panel. Save the query to your hard drive.
2. Explore the Macromedia Exchange and identify an extension that you think is interesting. You will have to create a login before you can download an extension from the exchange. I like some of the extensions that will automatically create a calendar in your web page. If that interests you, use the search functionality to search for calendar extensions in the Dreamweaver exchange. Another interesting extension is the CourseBuilder extension that enables you to create quiz questions and various controls, such as sliders, in Dreamweaver.

HOUR 23

Using the Library: Reusing Elements of a Website

What You'll Learn in This Hour:

- How to create a library item either from existing content or from scratch
- How to add a library item to a web page
- How to edit an original library item and update linked library items
- How to use styles with library items

When designing web pages, you can create library items from objects you use often. If you update the original library item, it updates everywhere throughout your site. This is very handy!

Library items help you maintain consistency in a website. They also allow you to share design elements with other web developers. When you are in the design phase of a website, you should be thinking about common elements across all of the web pages in your site that would be appropriate to create as Dreamweaver library items.

You can turn all sorts of objects into library items. For instance, a navigation bar that is present in many of the pages in your website would be an excellent candidate for a library item. When you need to add a new button to the navigation bar, it is simple to add the button to the original library item and then update your entire site automatically with the change.

Creating a Library Item

You can create a library item, save it to the Library category of the Assets panel, and then apply it to any web page within your website. Anyone working on the same website can use the library item, and you can use library items created by others. You can include a library item in a web page multiple times. Library items can be created from any object contained in the body of the web page, such as forms, tables, text, Java applets, layers, and images.

You need to define a website before Dreamweaver can insert a library item. Dreamweaver creates a directory called `Library` in the root of your website where it stores all the library items. When you insert a library item into your web page, Dreamweaver inserts into the page a copy of everything contained in the library item.

By the Way

The Difference Between Library Items and Templates

Library items differ from Dreamweaver templates because **library items** are portions of a page, whereas a **template** is an entire page. Libraries and templates are similar, though, because both can automatically update all the linked items and pages. You'll learn about templates in Hour 24, "Creating Reusable Web Pages: Using Templates."

Using the Library Category of the Assets Panel

When you are creating and applying library items, you open the Library category of the Assets panel, shown in Figure 23.1. The Library category of the Assets panel shows all the library items that exist in the current website. Each website you create can have a different set of library items.

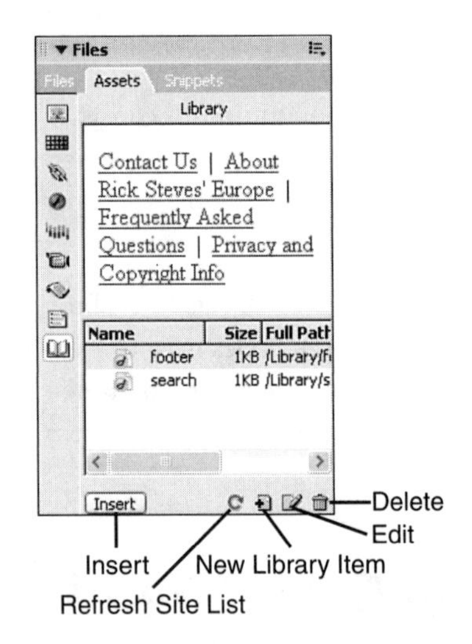

FIGURE 23.1 The Library category of the Assets panel displays all the library items in the current website. There are buttons at the bottom of the panel to insert, create, open, and delete library items.

The Library category of the Assets panel is divided into two halves. The bottom half lists the names of the library items in the website. The top half displays the contents of a library item you have selected in the bottom half. The buttons at the bottom of the panel include the following:

- **Insert**—You click this button to insert the currently selected library item at the location of the insertion point in the web page.
- **Refresh Site List**—You click this button to refresh the list in the Assets panel. This is useful for refreshing the list after you've added a new item.
- **New Library Item**—You click this button to create a new, blank library item.
- **Edit**—You click this button to open the library item in its own Dreamweaver Document window for editing.
- **Delete Library Item**—You click this button to remove the original library item from the library. This doesn't affect any instances of the library item (although the item can no longer be updated throughout the site).

Creating a Library Item

There are two ways to create library items:

- **From an existing object or group of objects**—After you decide to create a library item out of a group of objects on a web page, you select the objects and save them into the library.
- **From scratch, as a new, empty library item**—You can create a new library item, open it up, and add objects to it just as if it were a regular web page.

Creating a Library Item from Existing Content

You create a library item from an existing object or group of objects on your web page as follows:

1. Select an object or a group of objects. Select multiple objects either by dragging your cursor over them or by holding down the Shift key and clicking objects to add to the selection.
2. To add the selection to the library, drag and drop it onto the bottom half of the Library category of the Assets panel. Alternatively, select Modify, Library, Add Object to Library.
3. Give the library item a meaningful name. The Name field is selected immediately after you create the library item; at any time, you can reselect the name with a long single-click on the name field.

By the Way

Library Files

Dreamweaver creates an individual file for each library item. The file extension for library items is `.lbi`. If you look in the `Library` directory of your website, you will see one `.lbi` file for each library item you have in your website.

When you select a library item in the Assets panel, you see the contents of the library item in the top half of the Library category of the panel, as shown in Figure 23.2. The contents might look different from how they will look in the web page because the Library category of the Assets panel is small, and the objects wrap. Also, because the library item is only a portion of a web page, it appears with no page background color or applied CSS.

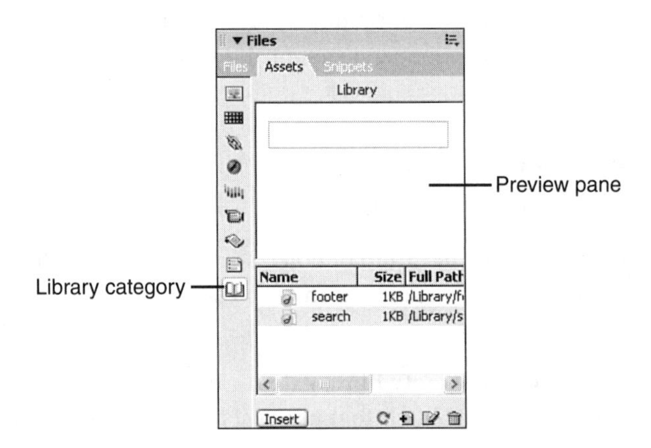

FIGURE 23.2 The Library category of the Assets panel displays a preview of a single library item in its top half and lists all the library items in the bottom half.

Creating a Library Item from Scratch

To create a library item from scratch, follow these steps:

1. Click the New Library Item button at the bottom of the Library category of the Assets panel. Dreamweaver creates a new, blank library item, as shown in Figure 23.3. A message telling you how to add content to the blank library item appears in the top half of the Library category of the Assets panel.

2. Give the library item a name. For example, create a copyright statement that will go at the bottom of each of your web pages. The name `Copyright` would be a good choice.

3. Double-click the library item in the Library category of the Assets panel. Dreamweaver opens the library item in a separate Document window. You can tell that you have a library item open because Dreamweaver displays

<<Library Item>> along with the name of the library item in the title bar, as shown in Figure 23.4.

4. Insert objects into the library item's Document window just as you would in any web page. Insert the copyright symbol (from the Text category in the Insert bar or by selecting Insert, HTML, Special Characters), a year, and a name.

5. Close the Document window and save the library item. Your changes are reflected in the Library category of the Assets panel.

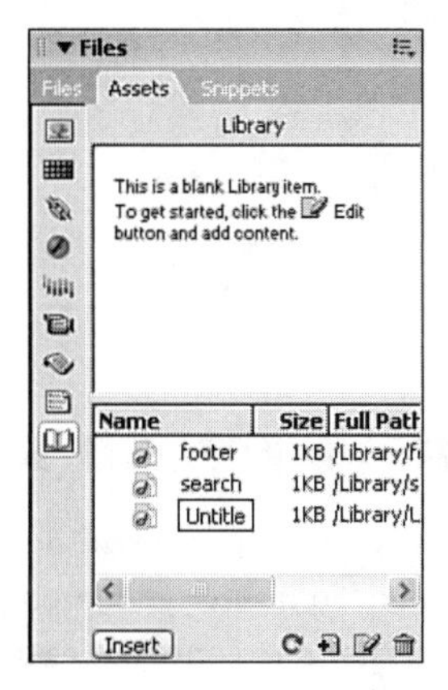

FIGURE 23.3 Create a new library item, open it, and add content.

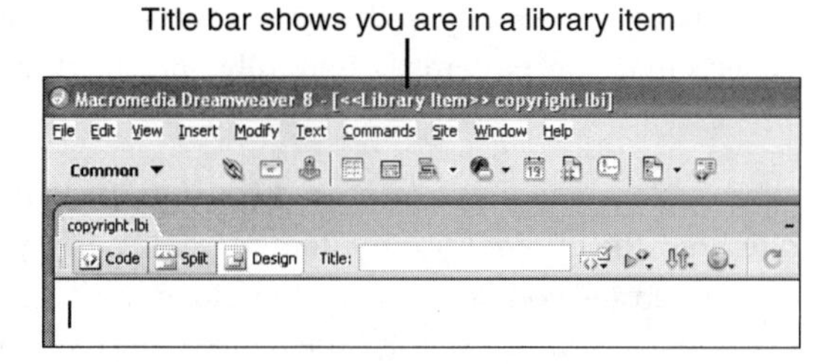

FIGURE 23.4 To add content to a library item, open it in a separate Dreamweaver Document window. The window shows <<Library Item>> in the title bar.

The Library category of the Assets panel has a pop-up menu containing useful commands, as shown in Figure 23.5. This same menu also pops up when you right-click (Control+click on the Mac) a library item in the Library category of the Assets panel. Using the New Library Item command is another way to create a library item.

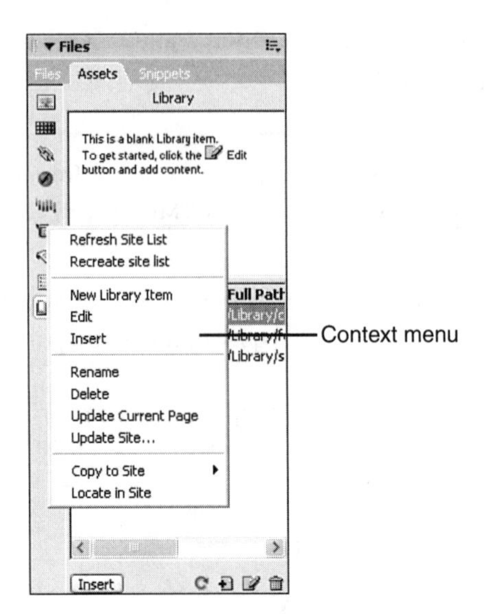

FIGURE 23.5 The Library category of the Assets panel pop-up menu has a number of commands to add, rename, open, and delete library items.

Adding a Library Item to a Page

After you have created a library item, you simply drag it from the list in the Library category of the Assets panel and drop it onto your web page, as shown in Figure 23.6. You can pick up the library item and move it to a different location in the Document window. You are not able to select individual objects contained in the inserted library item. When you click any of the objects, you select the entire library item; the group of objects in a library item is essentially one object in your web page.

When you insert a library item into a web page, a copy of its content is inserted. You no longer need to have the original library item present. When you upload your web page onto a remote website, you do not need to upload the `Library` directory. It is a good idea to keep the directory, though, in case you want to make changes to library items throughout the website.

Sharing Library Items on the Server

Consider uploading the library onto your server so others can use the library items, too. When collaborating with a group, you can share a library so everyone creates consistent web pages using the same library items.

The Property inspector, as shown in Figure 23.7, displays the library item attributes when a library item is selected in the Document window. The Src box displays the name of the library item (which you cannot change here). Three buttons in the Property inspector help you manage the library item:

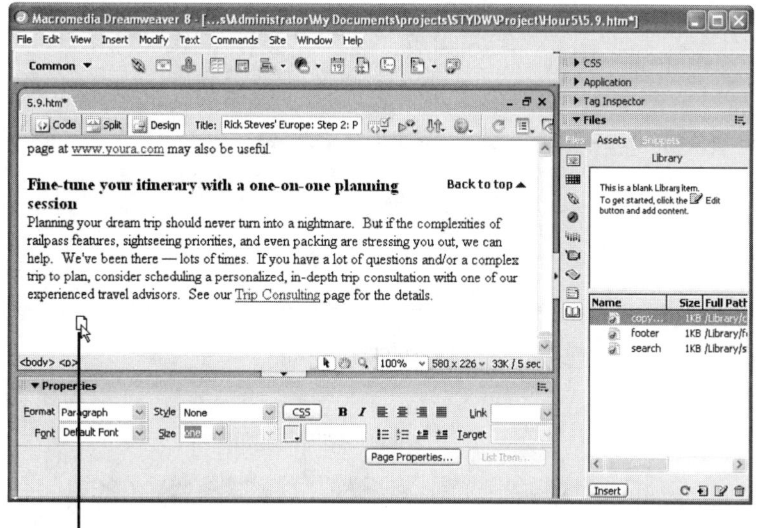

FIGURE 23.6
Drag a library item from the Library category of the Assets panel and drop it onto your web page.

- **Open**—This button opens the library item you wish to edit.
- **Detach from Original**—This button breaks the link between this instance of a library item and the original item. If the original library item is changed, a detached item is not updated. If you detach a library item from its original, the individual objects contained in the item are editable.
- **Recreate**—This button overwrites the original library item with the currently selected instance of the library item. This is useful if the original library item has been inadvertently edited or lost.

Dreamweaver applies a highlight to library items so they are easy to see in the Document window. The highlight appears only in Dreamweaver and not in the browser. In addition, the highlight appears only if Invisible Elements is selected (View, Visual Aids, Invisible Elements). You set the highlight color in the Highlighting category in the Dreamweaver Preferences dialog box, as shown in Figure 23.8.

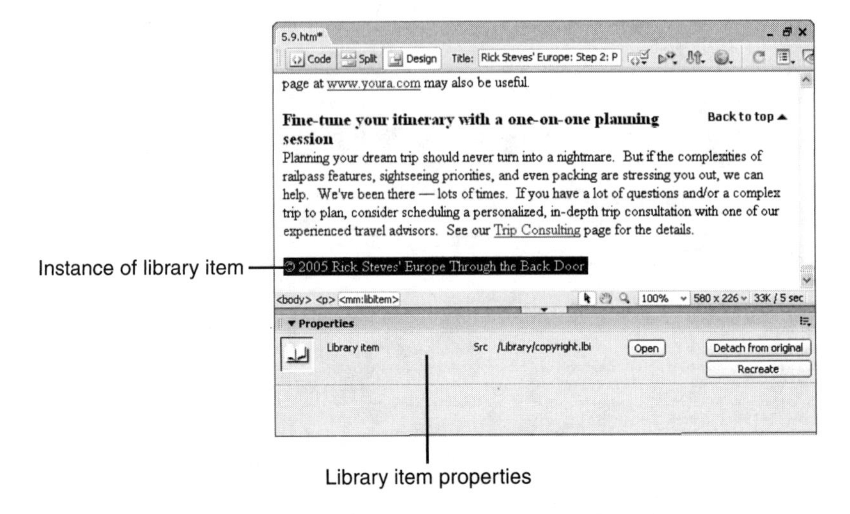

FIGURE 23.7 The Property inspector contains buttons to manage a library item. You can detach the item from its original or overwrite the item as the original.

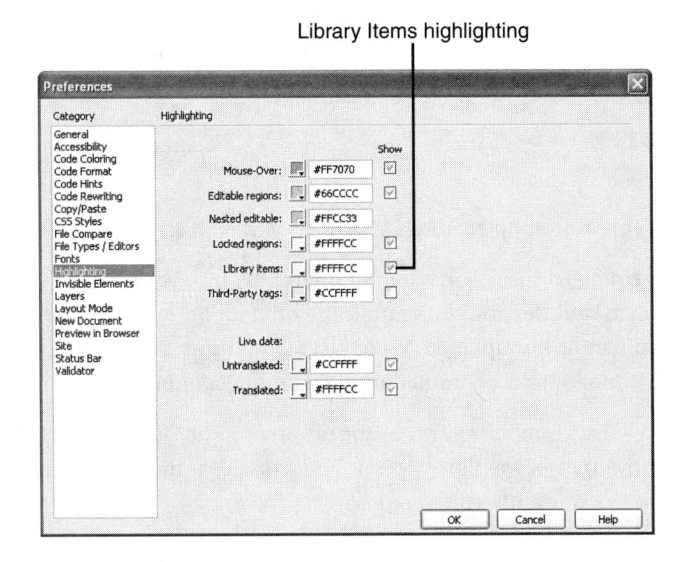

FIGURE 23.8 Set a highlight color for all library items in the Dreamweaver Preferences dialog box. The highlight appears only in Dreamweaver and not in the browser.

Making Changes to a Library Item

You edit a library item by opening the item to add or change objects in the Document window. Don't worry about the page background color when editing library items; the item appears on the background color of the page into which it is inserted. After you've inserted your previously created library item into a page, open the library item to edit it. Apply different formatting to some of the objects in the item.

After you are finished editing, save the library item (File, Save). Dreamweaver asks you whether you want to update all the documents in the website that contain the library item, as shown in Figure 23.9. Click Update to automatically update all linked library items.

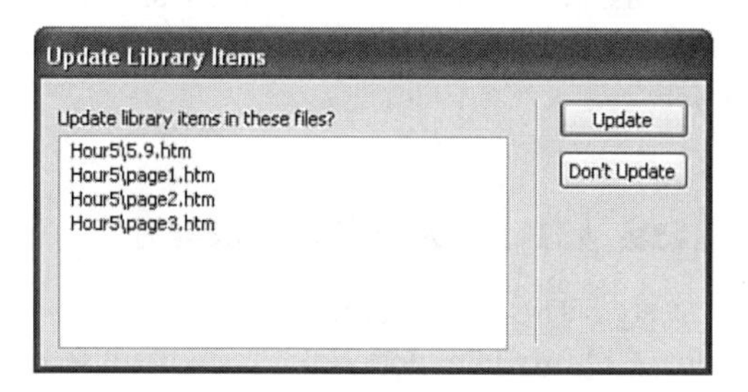

FIGURE 23.9 Click Update to begin updating all the library items in your entire website that are linked to the selected library item.

The Update Pages dialog box, shown in Figure 23.10, displays statistics on how many files were examined, how many were updated, and how many could not be updated. Check the Show Log check box if you want to see these statistics. Click Close to close the Update Pages dialog box.

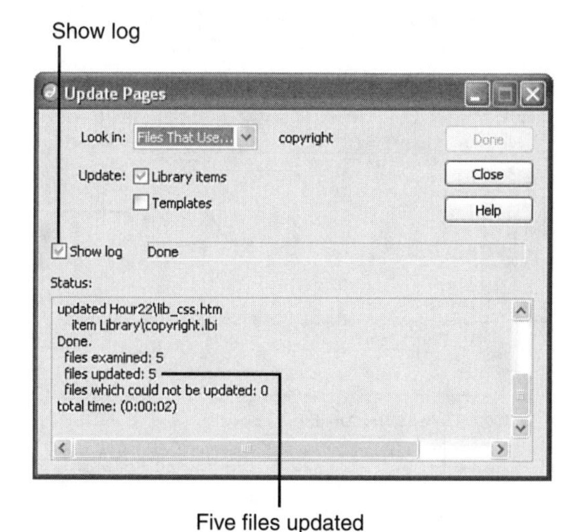

FIGURE 23.10 With Show Log checked, the Update Pages dialog box shows how many files were examined, how many were updated, and how many could not be updated.

Check Out Web Pages to Update

Watch Out!

Web pages containing library items might not be updated if you do not have those pages checked out because pages you don't have checked out are read-only, meaning you cannot make changes to them. Dreamweaver is not able to update any library items in files marked read-only. Make sure you have all the appropriate files checked out before you update a library item.

You can manually update linked library items at any time. Right-click on the library item in the Library category of the Assets panel and select either the Update Current Page command to update the current web page or the Update Site command to update the entire website. The Update Current Page command acts immediately, and no dialog box appears. When you issue the Update Site command, the Update Pages dialog box appears. Click the Start button to begin updating all the linked library items in the website.

Using Styles in Library Items

When you create a CSS style, Dreamweaver inserts the style definition into the head of the HTML document. A library item does not have a head section, as shown in Figure 23.11. You insert a library item into a web page, and the head of that web page could have styles defined in it. When you know the name of the class that you'd like to apply to the library item, you need to add <span> tags around the item, with the `class` attribute set to the name of the class, like this:

```
<span class="greenText">Library Item here</span>
```

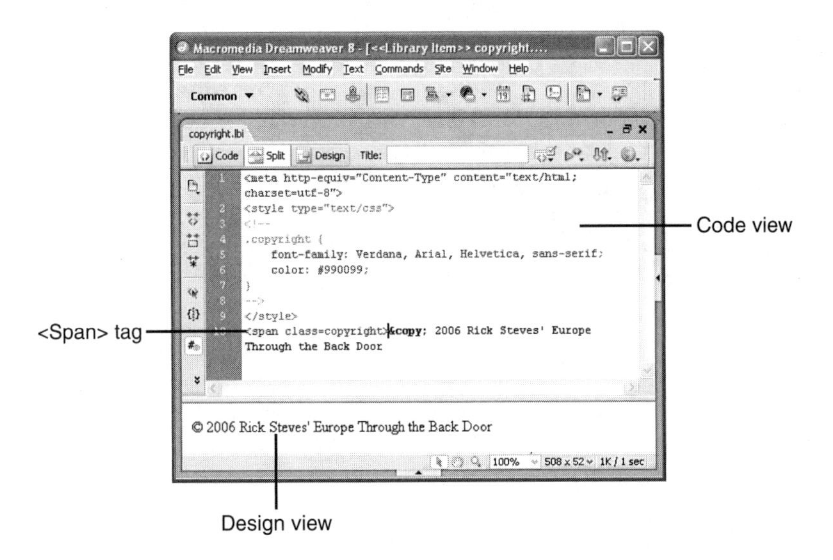

FIGURE 23.11 A library item doesn't include <head> or <body> tags.

You can apply styles to library items, but you need to link an external style sheet to the page. Make sure that every web page that includes the library item is linked to the style sheet containing the style definitions used in the library item. If you edit a style in the linked style sheet, all the library items reflect any changes to the style.

You can apply various types of CSS styles to library items but you have to remember to add the appropriate tags when creating the library items. The easiest way to format library items is to create CSS styles that are redefined HTML tags, such as defining the <H3> tag using CSS, and simply applying that tag to the text in the library item.

Summary

In this hour, you have learned how to create library items, both from existing content and from scratch. You have learned how to use the Library category of the Assets panel to manage, open, and edit library items. You have learned how Dreamweaver automatically updates all the linked library items in a website and how you can launch the process manually. You also learned how to add CSS to library items.

Q&A

Q. ***How can I apply edits I made to library items in only some of the linked files?***

A. I caution you to be careful if you are maintaining various pages, some with the newest version of the library item and some with an old version. You *can* select only the pages you want to update. But instead, why not open the library item, save it with a different name, apply your edits, and then replace it in the selected pages?

Q. ***What types of objects are appropriate to put in the library?***

A. Here are some examples of objects that you might want to put in the Dreamweaver library: a company logo, a group of layers that appear on each page as a background, a search box (small form), a frequently used button, a custom bullet image, and a placeholder for content that isn't finalized (you can detach it later). You will find plenty of uses for the library.

Workshop

Quiz

1. What is the file extension for library item files?
2. When you use library items, is it required to maintain the connection to the original item, reflecting updates to that item?
3. How do you unlink an instance of a library item from the original library item?

Quiz Answers

1. The file extension for library item files is `.lbi`.
2. No, library items may be detached from the original items so they do not reflect any changes to the original items when pages are updated.
3. Select the Detach from Original button from the Property inspector with the library item selected.

Exercise

Create a library item and add it to a page. Experiment with reopening the library item, editing it, and then updating the page to which it's connected. Try adding a CSS style to the library item and then insert the item into a web page that has that style already defined.

HOUR 24

Creating Reusable Web Pages: Using Templates

What You'll Learn in This Hour:

- How to create templates from existing content or from scratch
- How to apply a template to a web page
- How to edit an original template and update linked web pages
- How to mark a selection as editable or optional
- How to use behaviors and styles with templates

You create templates to provide a foundation for consistent, controlled web pages. **Templates** contain objects that you mark as editable; the rest of the template is locked. When you update an original template, the changes you make to it update throughout your site.

Creating a Template

You can create a template, save it to the Template category of the Assets panel, and then use it to create a new web page within a website. Anyone working on the same website can use the template, and you can use templates created by others.

You need to define a website before Dreamweaver can insert a template. Dreamweaver creates a directory called `Templates` in the root of your website where it stores the original template files. Dreamweaver keeps the code of a template in a file in the `Templates` directory and inserts a copy of the code when you insert a template in a web page.

By the Way

The Difference Between Templates and Library Items

A template differs from a library item in that a template is an entire web page, not just a portion of one. Also, templates can define certain regions as editable by the user whereas library items placed in web pages are not editable at all.

Using the Templates Category of the Assets Panel

To create and apply templates, open the Templates category of the Assets panel, as shown in Figure 24.1. The Templates category shows all the templates that exist in the current website. Each website you create can have a different set of templates.

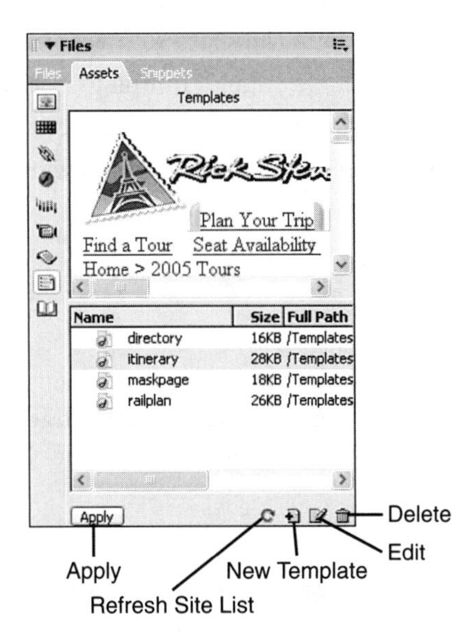

FIGURE 24.1 The Templates category of the Assets panel displays all the templates in the current website.

Did you Know?

Download Templates from the Web

Does the Templates category of the Assets panel look bare? Copy one or more of the sites available in the `Templates` directory from the Dreamweaver CD-ROM to your hard drive and set it up as a site in the Files panel. These templates are also available for download from the Macromedia website, at www.macromedia.com/software/dreamweaver/download/templates.

The Templates category of the Assets panel is divided into two halves. The top half displays the contents of the template, and the bottom half lists the names of the templates in the website. The buttons at the bottom of the panel include the following:

- **Apply**—You click this button to apply the currently selected template to the web page.
- **Refresh Site List**—You click this button to refresh the list in the Assets panel. This is useful for refreshing the list after you've added a new item.
- **New Template**—You click this button to create a new, blank template.
- **Edit**—You click this button to open the template in its own Dreamweaver Document window for editing.
- **Delete**—You click this button to remove the template from the `Templates` directory. This doesn't affect any instances of the templates except that the deleted template can no longer be updated throughout the site.

Creating a Template

There are two ways to create templates:

- **From an existing web page**—When you decide to create a template out of a web page, you can save the page as a template.
- **From scratch, as a new, empty template**—You can create a new template, open it, and then add objects to the template just as though it were a regular web page.

When you apply a template to a web page, a copy of all the content that the template contains is inserted into the page. You no longer need to have the original template present in order for the web page to display. When you upload your web page onto a remote website, you do not need to upload the `Templates` directory. You might want to upload the template onto your server so others can use the templates, too. You should keep the directory in case you want to make changes to templates throughout your website.

By the Way

Back Up Your Templates to the Server

Keeping the templates on the server ensures that you have a backup copy in case you accidentally change a template and need to restore the original.

Cloaking Affects Templates

Use Dreamweaver's Cloaking feature to prevent the `Templates` directory from being synchronized or uploaded when you are transferring files. You enable cloaking in the Site menu and then right-click (Control+click on the Mac) the `Templates` directory and select Cloaking, Cloak. The folder appears in the site with a red line through it.

Creating a Template from an Existing Web Page

To create a template from an existing web page, follow these steps:

1. Select File, Save as Template.
2. The Save As Template dialog box appears, as shown in Figure 24.2. Enter a meaningful name for the template. Click the Save button to save the template to the `Templates` directory.

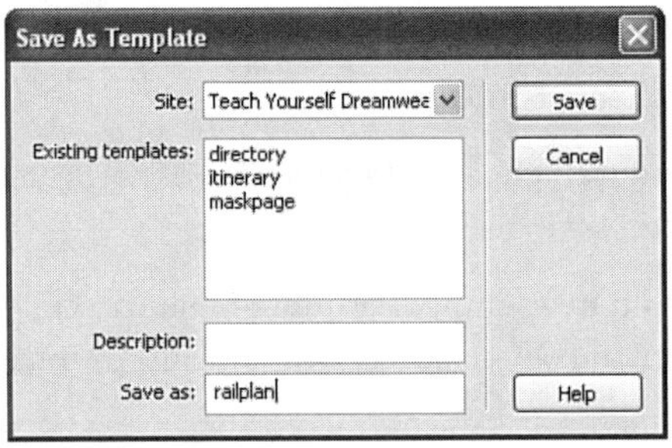

FIGURE 24.2
Give a new template a meaningful name in the Save as Template dialog box. This dialog box displays a list of existing templates in the current website.

3. A dialog box might appear, asking if you'd like to update links. Click the Yes button to agree. This tells Dreamweaver to make sure the document-relative links are correct when the template is saved to the `Templates` directory. If you plan on having all the linked objects, usually images, editable in the template, you do not need to worry about the path being correct for the linked objects.

By the Way

Template Files

Dreamweaver creates an individual file for each template. The file extension for templates is `.dwt`. In the `Templates` directory of your website, you see one `.dwt` file for each template you have in your website.

Creating a Template from Scratch

To create a new, empty template and then add objects to it, follow these steps:

1. Click the New Template button at the bottom of the Templates category of the Assets panel. Dreamweaver creates a new blank template, as shown in Figure 24.3. A message appears in the top half of the Templates category of the Assets panel, telling you how to add content to the blank template.

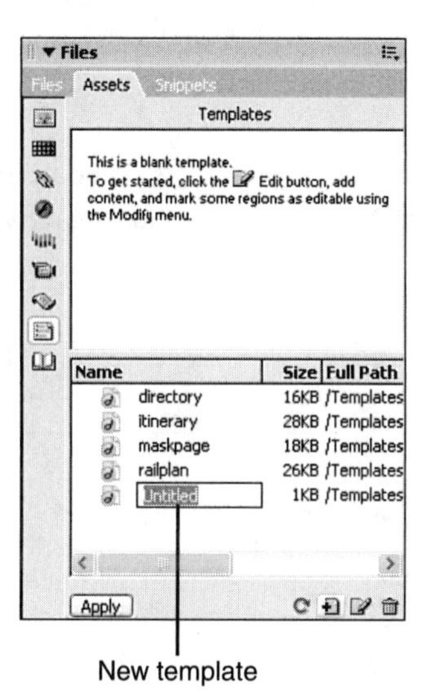

FIGURE 24.3
A message appears in the Templates category after you create a new blank template. The message tells you how to add content to the new template.

2. Give the template a name. For example, create a template for displaying your CD or book collection and call it `CD` or `book`.

3. Double-click the template in the Templates category of the Assets panel. Dreamweaver opens the template in a separate Document window. You can tell that you have a template open because Dreamweaver displays `<<Template>>` along with the name of the template in the title bar, as shown in Figure 24.4.

4. Insert objects into the template's Document window just as you would with any web page.

5. Close the Document window and save the template. Your changes are reflected in the Templates category of the Assets panel. Don't worry right now about the message you receive about your template not having any editable regions. You'll add some editable regions in a few minutes.

Shows you are in a template

FIGURE 24.4 To add content to a template, you open it in a separate Dreamweaver Document window. The window shows `<<Template>>` in the title bar.

The Templates category of the Assets panel has a pop-up menu that contains useful commands (see Figure 24.5). Different commands are available, depending on what is currently selected.

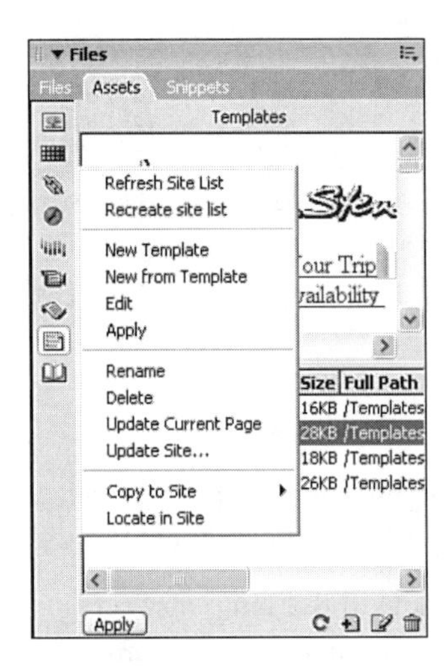

FIGURE 24.5 The Templates category of the Assets panel context menu has a number of commands to apply, rename, edit, and delete templates.

Making an Existing Region Editable

Before you apply a template to a web page, you need to mark regions of the template as **editable**. By default, all regions in the template are locked. Mark a region as editable if you will need to change, add, or update the content of this region in the pages you create based on this template.

You should leave locked all regions that do not need to be changed. If you need to make changes to a locked region, you can change the original template file and update all the web pages that are linked to that template. The commands for manipulating editable regions are located in the Templates submenu of the Modify menu, as shown in Figure 24.6.

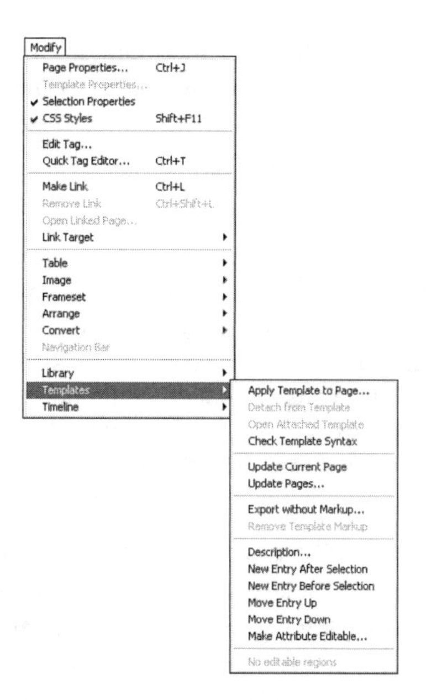

FIGURE 24.6
The Templates submenu of Dreamweaver's Modify menu contains the commands needed to manipulate editable regions.

Did you Know?

Placeholder Images

Use a placeholder image in your template to represent an image. You add a placeholder image to the page by selecting Insert, Image Objects, Image Placeholder.

To make an existing region editable, follow these steps:

1. Open a template and select the region that needs to be editable.
2. Select Insert, Template Objects, Editable Region. The New Editable Region dialog box appears, as shown in Figure 24.7.

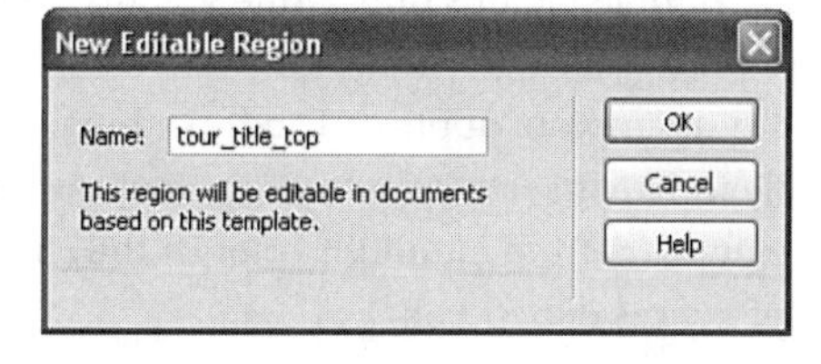

FIGURE 24.7
Name the new editable region in the New Editable Region dialog box.

3. Give the region a meaningful name.

After you create an editable region, the name of the region is listed at the bottom of the Templates submenu of the Modify menu while you are working on the template.

Select one of the region names in the menu to highlight that region in the Document window. Dreamweaver also automatically creates editable regions for the title of the document (called `doctitle`) and an empty region in the head of the document that is available for JavaScript code.

Did you Know?

Placeholder Text

I really like using David Powers' Lorem and More extension, available free at the Macromedia Exchange (www.macromedia.com/exchange). This extension gives you several types of placeholder text, including the classic lorem ipsum, extracts from a Cicero speech, a Shakespeare sonnet, and random corporate mumbo-jumbo words (my favorite). Review Hour 22, "Customizing Dreamweaver," for more information on downloading and installing extensions.

Dreamweaver gives you the ability to create editable regions on various objects in a template. For instance, you can make a layer editable. You can move the layer or change any of its properties after you apply the template to a web page. Or you can leave the layer locked and create an editable region within the layer. Then you can't move the layer or change the layer properties when you've applied the template, but you can put content within the layer.

By the Way

Import XML into Templates

You can import or export the editable regions of a Dreamweaver template as XML. To do so, use the commands under the Import and Export submenus of the File menu. This is a useful way to automate importing objects, especially text, into templates. The difficult part of this is creating the XML files, files marked up with custom tags, in the first place. If you already have a source of XML files that need to go into web pages, you should consider importing them into Dreamweaver templates.

Dreamweaver highlights editable regions only while you are editing the original template file so they are easy to pick out in the Document window. Just the opposite is true in a web page with a template applied: The locked regions are highlighted. The highlights are visible in Dreamweaver but not in the browser. To see highlights, select View, Invisible Elements. Set the highlight color in the Highlighting category in the Dreamweaver Preferences dialog box.

Making a New Editable Region

You can create an optional editable region in a template. To do so, select Insert, Template Objects, Optional Region. Then name the new region in the New Optional Region dialog box that appears. An optional editable region enables the web page author to decide whether content is needed in this region on the web page. If the region isn't necessary, the author can turn it off. An editable region appears with a rectangle around it and a tab showing its name, as shown in Figure 24.8.

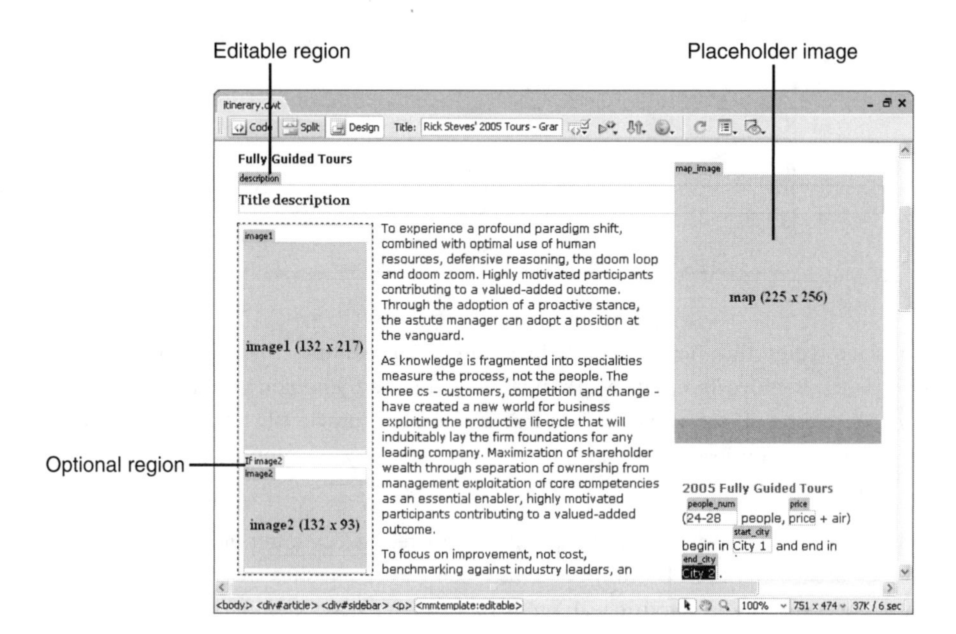

FIGURE 24.8
After you insert a new editable region into a template, it appears as a highlighted rectangular outline.

By the Way

You Can't Place an Editable Region Within an Editable Region

If Dreamweaver displays the message that the selection is already a part of an editable region, you need to move the selection. Examine the tag selector and look for the tag `<mmtemplate:editable>` or `<mmtemplate:if>`. If you see one of these tags, you need to modify your selection until that tag is no longer part of the selection.

Inserting an optional region (Insert, Template Objects, Optional Region) enables a person using the template to turn the region on or off in the page. Optional regions are not automatically editable. You must either nest an editable region inside an optional region or add an optional editable region (Insert, Templates Objects, Editable Optional Region) in order to edit the content in a web page based on the template. The New Optional Region dialog box, shown in Figure 24.9, prompts you to name the optional region.

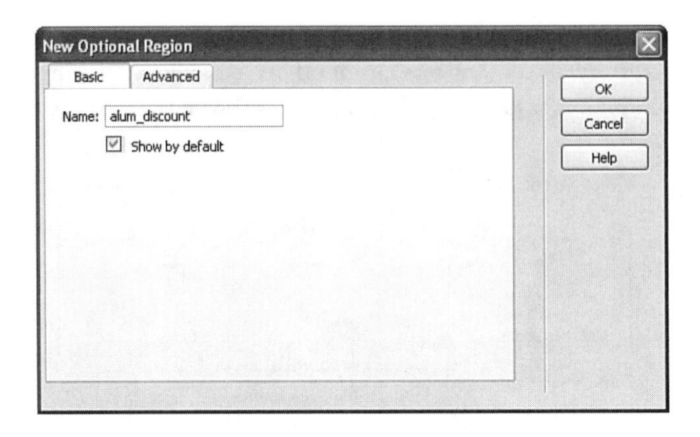

FIGURE 24.9
Add a new optional region or editable optional region.

To lock a region that has previously been marked as editable, select Modify, Templates, Remove Template Markup while you have the region you'd like to remove selected. If you have entered information into previously editable regions in web pages, you lose that information after you lock the region and update the web pages.

There are many other advanced capabilities of Dreamweaver templates. You can also create templates in Dreamweaver that can be used in sites created in Contribute, Macromedia's easy-to-use web publishing system. Web designers and developers work in Dreamweaver to create templates, CSS, and sometimes an initial version of a website they can hand over to people who are not web designers or developers. Using Contribute frees up web designers and developers to create complicated content and leaves small updates, changes, and routine tasks to others in a group environment. You can find out more about Contribute at www.macromedia.com/software/contribute.

Creating a Web Page from a Template

You can apply a template in three ways:

- Simply drag the template from the Templates category of the Assets panel and drop it onto a new web page.
- Select a template in the Templates category of the Assets panel and click the Apply button.

- Select the New command (File, New) and choose the Templates tab, as shown in Figure 24.10. Select the site on the left side of the dialog box and choose a template from the list in the middle of the dialog box. You can see a preview of the template on the right side of the dialog box.

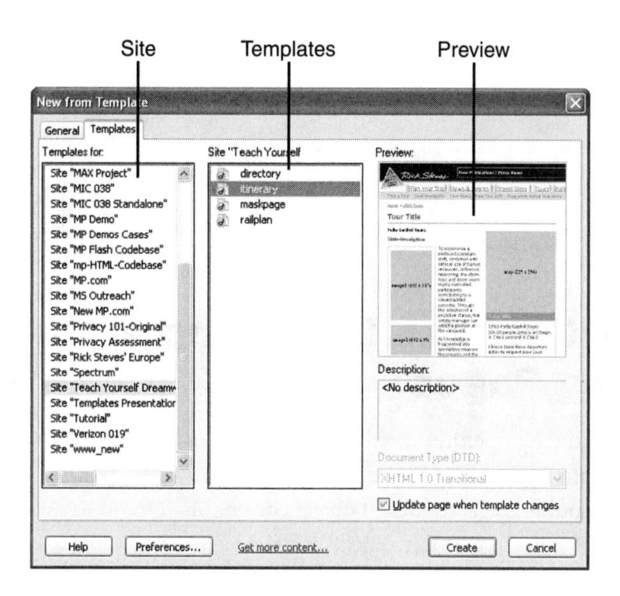

FIGURE 24.10
Create a new web page from a template by choosing the Templates tab from the New from Template dialog box.

Web pages based on templates allow you to edit content only in the editable regions. You can see these editable regions highlighted in the Document window (you need to have Invisible Elements turned on in the View menu and Highlighting turned on in the Preferences dialog box). The rest of the web page is blocked from editing. Simply remove any placeholder text or images within the editable region and add the final content to create a new web page.

When you create a web page based on a template with optional regions (either optional or editable optional), you need to set whether the optional content is turned on or off. Use Modify, Template Properties to open the Template Properties dialog box, as shown in Figure 24.11, to either turn on or turn off the optional region. The Template Properties command is available only when you are working on a page based on a Dreamweaver template; it isn't available while actually editing a template file.

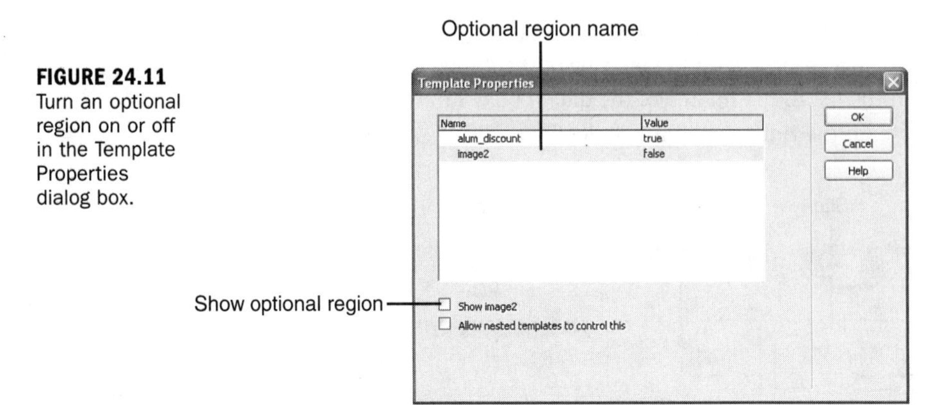

FIGURE 24.11 Turn an optional region on or off in the Template Properties dialog box.

Making Changes to a Template and Updating Pages

You edit a template by opening the template to add or change its contents. You can open the template from the Templates category of the Assets panel, or you can open it from the Files panel. Edits to locked objects are applied to all the web pages that use the template. Edits to editable objects have no effect on web pages that use the template.

After you edit and save a template, Dreamweaver asks you whether you want to update files. Select the files you want to update in the Update Template Files dialog box and then click Update to automatically update the linked files. The Update Pages dialog box displays statistics on how many files were examined, updated, and not able to be updated. Check the Show Log check box to see these statistics. Click the Close button to close the Update Pages dialog box.

Check Out Web Pages to Update

Certain files in a website might not be updated because you do not have those files checked out. When you have Check In/Check Out turned on in a website, files that are not checked out to you are marked as read-only. Dreamweaver is not able to update any files marked read-only.

You can also manually update files linked to templates. To do so, right-click the template in the Templates category of the Assets panel and select either the Update Current Page command (to update the current web page) or the Update Site command (to update the entire website). The Update Current Page command acts immediately and no dialog box appears. When you issue the Update Site command, the

Update Pages dialog box appears, as shown in Figure 24.12. Click the Start button to update all the linked templates in the website.

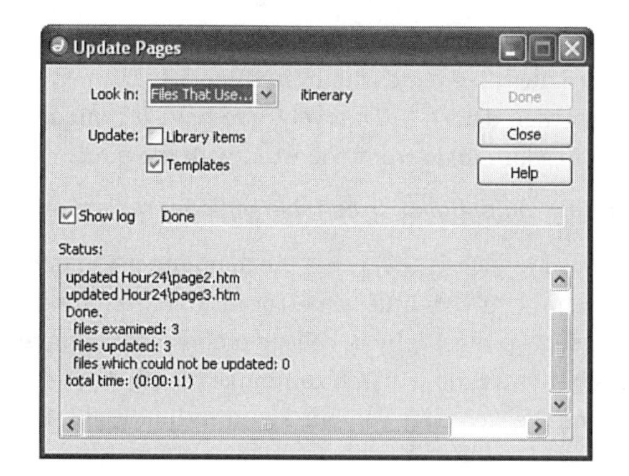

FIGURE 24.12
Update all the web pages that are based on templates (and library items, too) in a site.

Using Behaviors and Styles in Templates

You can use behaviors and styles in templates. Styles and JavaScript are applied to a web page based on the template. For you to be able to edit styles and behaviors in a web page, objects to which they are applied must be editable. Select an object that has a style or behavior and edit the style or behavior in the CSS Styles panel or the Behaviors panel.

Most web designers add links to external style sheets to their templates. That way the template content has access to all of the styles in the external style sheet. They will often place library items within templates, too. Even though Dreamweaver templates are designed to update the web pages that are created from them, it's not a good idea to do this all the time. Placing visual formatting in external style sheets enables you to update the look of the site without changing the template.

Summary

In this hour, you have learned how to create templates, both from existing content and from scratch. You have learned how to use the Templates category of the Assets panel to manage templates, and you have learned how to open and edit templates. You have learned how to make regions of a template editable regions and optional regions. You have learned how Dreamweaver automatically updates all the linked templates in a website and how you can launch that process manually.

Q&A

Q. *Is there any way I can use templates without having locked and editable regions?*

A. Yes. You can create a template with everything laid out perfectly, apply it to a web page, and then detach it. That way, you have a standard beginning point but have the freedom to do what you want with the page.

Q. *Why would I use an optional or editable optional region?*

A. This enables you to give people using the template the option to add or delete standard content with very little work. For instance, imagine you have a template that presents a biography of college professors and some biographies have photos but others do not. You can make the photo region optional so people creating the web page can quickly turn that off if it is unnecessary.

Workshop

Quiz

1. What is the file extension for template files?
2. Which regions, editable or locked, are highlighted when you are editing the original template file?
3. How do you turn an optional region on and off?

Quiz Answers

1. The file extension for template files is `.dwt`.
2. The editable regions are highlighted when you are editing the original template file. The locked regions are highlighted when you are in a web page based on a template.
3. In a web page based on a template that contains editable regions, select Modify, Template Properties, and turn on and off the properties in the list.

Exercises

1. Create a template and practice marking various objects as editable. Apply the template and see which objects can be marked as editable and which cannot. What properties can you edit?

2. Open a template you have already applied to a page, edit it, and practice updating the linked page. Open the page. Do you see the edits you made?

PART VII

Appendixes

Resources

You are in luck! You are learning about an information delivery medium—the World Wide Web—that contains a ton of information about itself. You as a web developer will find many helpful websites on topics that interest you. You might even be inspired to create your own website to share your knowledge with others.

Websites move and change quickly, so I apologize if some of these links are already out-of-date. Also, be aware that not all the information you get from the Web is accurate. It's a good idea to get information from trusted sources or to find sources to confirm the information you find from unknown sources.

Dreamweaver Development

- Dreamweaver FAQ (www.dwfaq.com)
- Macromedia's Dreamweaver Developer Center (www.macromedia.com/desdev/mx/dreamweaver)
- Macromedia's Dreamweaver Support Center (www.macromedia.com/support/dreamweaver)

General Web Development

- CNET Builder.com (builder.com.com)
- ProjectCool (www.devx.com/projectcool)
- SiteExperts (www.siteexperts.com)
- The Spot for Web Site Builders (thespot.i-depth.com)

- Web Developer's Virtual Library (www.wdvl.com)
- Webmonkey (webmonkey.wired.com/webmonkey/)
- World Wide Web Consortium (W3C) (www.w3.org)
- W3Schools HTML Tutorial (www.w3schools.com/html)

Dynamic HTML (DHTML)

- Dynamic Drive (www.dynamicdrive.com)
- The Dynamic Duo—Cross Browser DHTML (www.mark-itt.ru/docs/dynamic_duo)
- The Web Standards Project (www.webstandards.org/learn)

Dreamweaver Extensions

- Dreamweaver Depot (www.andrewwooldridge.com/dreamweaver)
- Dreamweaver Resources (www.arrakis.es/~andrewc/downloads/dream.htm)
- Dreamweaver Supply Bin (home.att.net/~JCB.BEI/Dreamweaver)
- Macromedia Exchange (www.macromedia.com/exchange/dreamweaver)
- Massimo's Corner (www.massimocorner.com)
- Rabi's Extensions (www.dreamweaver-extensions.com)
- Tom Muck's Dreamweaver Extension (www.tom-muck.com/extensions)
- Yaro's Yaromat (www.yaromat.com/dw)

Cascading Style Sheets

- Eric Meyer's Site (www.meyerweb.com)
- Deluxe CSS Dropdowns and Flyouts (www.positioniseverything.net/css-dropdowns.html)
- A List Apart (www.alistapart.com)
- Zen Garden (www.csszengarden.com)

Scripting Resources: CGI, JavaScript, and Server-Side Scripting

CGI

- Free Scripts (www.freescripts.com)
- Matt's Script Archive (www.scriptarchive.com)

JavaScript

- JavaScript Tricks (home.thezone.net/~rbennett/utility/javahead.htm)
- Webmonkey JavaScript Code Library (webmonkey.wired.com/webmonkey/reference/javascript_code_library)

Server-Side Scripting

- ASP101—Resources for Web Professionals (www.asp101.com)
- JSP Resource Index (www.jspin.com)
- Macromedia ColdFusion Developer's Center (www.macromedia.com/devnet/mx/coldfusion)
- PHP-Hypertext Preprocessor (www.php.net)

Accessibility

- Anybrowser.org Accessible Site Design (www.anybrowser.org/campaign/abdesign.shtml)
- Macromedia's Accessibility Center (www.macromedia.com/macromedia/accessibility)
- Web Accessibility Initiative (WAI) (www.w3.org/WAI)
- WebXACT free page analyzer (formerly Bobby) (webxact.watchfire.com)

Usability

- Advanced Common Sense (Steve Krug) (www.sensible.com)
- Microsoft Usability Research (www.microsoft.com/usability)
- useit.com—Jakob Nielsen's website (www.useit.com)

Downloads

- CNET Download.com (www.download.com)
- Chank Free Fonts (www.chank.com/freefonts.php)
- Color Cop (www.datastic.com/tools/colorcop)
- Free Layouts (www.freelayouts.com/templates/display/templates)
- Getty Images (creative.gettyimages.com)

Browsers

- Apple's Safari Browser (www.apple.com/macosx/features/safari)
- Microsoft Internet Explorer (www.microsoft.com/windows/ie)
- Mozilla Firefox (my favorite) (www.mozilla.org/products/firefox)
- Netscape Navigator (browser.netscape.com)
- Opera (www.opera.com)

Organizations

- Geek Cruises (Why not have some fun?!) (www.geekcruises.com)
- HTML Writer's Guild (www.hwg.org)
- Macromedia User Groups (www.macromedia.com/support/programs/usergroups)

Glossary

absolute path (or absolute URL) A type of path that contains all the information necessary to retrieve a file on the Internet, including the domain name.

accessibility The concept of creating websites so users with impairments are not prevented from finding resources and information, and that they enjoy content similar to what other visitors enjoy.

ActiveX Software components used in browsers (traditionally Internet Explorer, but also others) to display embedded web content. Most often, ActiveX controls are used to install additional functionality into the browser, such as the ability to play Flash or Shockwave content.

`.aiff` file An audio file format that is popular on the Mac. `.aiff` files are usually too large to be delivered over the Internet.

alt (alternative) text An attribute of an image or image map hotspots that contains a text description of a graphic that is useful for viewers with text-only browsers and visually impaired viewers using text readers.

antialias To blend the edges of text or an image with its background so it looks smoother.

API (Application Programming Interface) An interface between the user and an application that enables you, the developer, to change the user interface with scripting or another application.

applet A small application written in Java that is embedded in a web page and requires the user to have the plug-in control installed. An applet can perform calculations, display graphics, and do other simple tasks without accessing the server.

ASP (Active Server Pages) A web technology containing server-side scripts that run primarily on Microsoft web servers. These files end in `.asp` and contain HTML mixed with server-side VBScript or JScript (JavaScript) code.

ASP.NET The next generation of ASP available from Microsoft is used to write server-side web applications and web services. It creates dynamic web pages scripted in either Visual Basic.NET or C#.

asset One of a variety of files stored in a website, such as images, movies, and scripts. Assets can be viewed in Dreamweaver in the Assets panel.

Assets panel A Dreamweaver panel that displays all the images, URLs, colors, movies, scripts, templates, and library items in a site.

attribute A property or characteristic of an object or an HTML tag.

Authorware Web Player A player that enables a user to play Macromedia Authorware files in a web browser. Authorware is used to create training applications.

AutoPlay A setting that makes a Flash movie play automatically when the web page loads in the browser.

Autostretch A setting in Dreamweaver's Layout view that makes a table column stretch to fit the web browser window.

`.avi` file A sound and movie file format that requires a special player. `.avi` files are usually too large to be delivered over the Internet.

background image An attribute that specifies an image, usually repeated, to appear as the background in a web page, a table, a layer, or another object in a web page.

bandwidth The rate at which the current connection supports the transmission and reception of data.

behavior A combination of JavaScript code added to a web page and an event, such as a mouse click, that triggers the JavaScript. You add behaviors in Dreamweaver using the Behaviors panel.

body The part of a web page that contains all the visible content, such as images, text, tables, and other visual elements. The HTML tags for the body are `<body>` and `</body>`.

broadband An Internet connection that enables faster data transfer. DSL and cable TV are broadband services.

browser cache The directory on a user's hard drive where web pages and related files are stored to be viewed by the web browser.

browser events Signals from the browser that something has happened within a web page, either triggered by the user (such as the onClick event) or triggered by the page (such as the onLoad event).

bulleted list (or unordered list) A list of items preceded by bullet symbols. The HTML tags for an unordered list are `<ul>` and `</ul>`.

button down state The state of a button that is in the down position after it has been clicked by a user.

Button object An object that inserts a submit, reset, or generic button.

button over state A button state that appears when the cursor is rolled over the button.

button up state A button state that is in the up position.

C# An object-oriented programming language from Microsoft that is designed to work with Microsoft's .NET platform.

cable modem A technology for a high-bandwidth Internet connection over a cable TV line.

cell A single field in a table. The HTML tags for a cell are `<td>` and `</td>`.

cell padding The space between the cell content and the cell border.

cell spacing The space between adjoining table cells.

Center Align A setting that centers the selected text in the middle of a container such as a web page or table cell.

CFML (ColdFusion Markup Language) A technology from Macromedia for building websites that integrate with databases. These pages require that Macromedia ColdFusion Server be installed on the web server. This technology can be used on a variety of web servers.

CGI (Common Gateway Interface) script A standard way to process a user's request to a web server to receive data back or process the data (by sending it to an email address, for instance).

cgi-bin The directory where CGI scripts are kept on most servers.

check box A square box that can be checked on or off.

class selector A type of CSS style that can be applied to multiple elements on a page. The class selector name always begins with a period and is applied using the `class` attribute.

client-side image map An image map for which all the code is located within the web page, requiring no interaction with a server for the hyperlinks to work. This is the type of image map that Dreamweaver creates.

client-side script A script that resides within the web page and executes on the user's computer without contacting the server.

Code view A view in the Document window that displays the code of a web page.

Coder workspace The workspace that approximates the HomeSite workspace and that shows the panel groups on the left with the Code view initially shown.

Collapse button A button within the bar that separates the Document window and the panel groups that collapses all the panel groups and expands the Document window. An additional collapse button between the Document window and the Properties inspector functions the same way.

Color Cubes palette The default web-safe palette, which is arranged numerically.

column A vertical group of cells in a table.

comment Code that isn't displayed in a web page and that looks like this: <!— comment here—>. Using comments is a way of embedding information within the code of a web page without having it visible on the web page.

context menu A menu that contains commands applicable to the object that was selected when the menu was launched.

Continuous Tone palette A web-safe palette that is arranged by color tone.

CourseBuilder A free extension to Dreamweaver that creates interactions suitable for eLearning applications. Interaction categories include multiple choice, drag-and-drop, text entry, and explore questions, along with button, slider, and timer controls.

CSS (Cascading Style Sheets) A set of format definitions that determine how a given element appears in a web browser.

Date object An object that inserts the current date at the insertion point.

Design view A view in the Document window that displays the web page similarly to how it is displayed in a web browser.

Designer workspace The default WYSIWYG (what you see is what you get) workspace in Dreamweaver that enables you to design web pages within an environment that displays the pages similarly to how they appears in a web browser.

DHTML (Dynamic HTML) A collection of technologies that are used together to produce interactive web pages. The three main components of DHTML are layers, CSS, and JavaScript.

document-relative path A type of path that is relative to the location of the current document, allowing you to transfer the files to a server and have the links remain constantly relative.

Document window This is the part of the Dreamweaver interface that displays the web page, enabling you to build and edit it.

Draw Layout Cell object An object that draws a table cell while you're in Layout view.

Draw Layout Table object An object that draws a table while you're in Layout view.

DSL (digital subscriber line) A high-bandwidth Internet connection over a telephone line.

dynamic web pages Web pages that are built on the web server by inserting content drawn from databases and controlled by server-side scripts.

Email Link object An object that adds a hyperlink launching an empty email message window addressed to a specific email address when clicked.

expanded Files panel An expanded view of the Files panel that divides the window into two sides to display either the local and remote files or the site map.

Expander arrow The arrow in the upper-left corner of a panel group that expands and collapses the panel group.

extension One of a number of new features that can be installed into Dreamweaver by using the Extension Manager application.

fieldset A form object that groups related form fields together, drawing a box around them.

File field A form field that enables the user to upload a file.

Files panel The Dreamweaver panel that is used to plan, create, and manage the files and directories in a website.

firewall Hardware or software located on a network server or a personal computer that protects users on a private network from users on other networks.

Fireworks An image-editing program from Macromedia that excels at creating, slicing, and optimizing web graphics.

Fireworks HTML object HTML that has been exported from Macromedia Fireworks.

Flash A Macromedia program that creates vector-based animations that can be embedded into web pages and viewed in a browser with the Flash player.

Flash Button object One of a number of buttons that are configurable in Dreamweaver and that are Flash `.swf` files. These buttons include the standard button states and can use various fonts. Many of the Flash buttons include animation.

Flash object An object that places a Macromedia Flash movie at the insertion point.

Flash text One of a number of types of text that are configurable in Dreamweaver that are Flash `.swf` files. This text enables you to use various fonts in Dreamweaver without having those fonts available on the user's system.

font A set of text characters in a specific style and size.

form An object that enables the collection of information from website visitors via input elements such as text fields and radio buttons.

frame One of multiple, separately controlled web pages contained in a single web browser window.

frameset The web page that defines the size, orientation, and source web page for each of the individual frames it contains.

FTP (File Transfer Protocol) An Internet protocol that is used to exchange files among computers over the Internet.

GIF A standard web graphic format good for line art that contains large blocks of the same color. This format also enables image animation and transparency.

Grayscale palette A palette consisting of 256 tones of gray. It is not a web-safe palette.

gripper A dotted area in the upper-left corner of a panel group that enables you to drag the panel group in and out of its docked position.

H space The horizontal space to the left and the right of an image, measured in pixels.

head An element of a web page that's not visible in the browser but that contains information and code (JavaScript, styles, meta tags, and so on).

header The top row or left-most column, which describes the content of the column or row.

heading A type of text that is wrapped in one of six levels of HTML heading tags, `<h1></h1>` (largest) through `<h6></h6>` (smallest).

hexadecimal A base-16 numbering system used to describe RGB values of colors. Hexadecimal numbers contain the numerals 0–9 and the letters A–F.

hidden field A field that is not visible to the user and that contains information to be submitted with the other form elements.

home page The web page that is the entry point for the website.

horizontal rule A line across the page.

hotspot A region on an image map that has specific coordinates and contains a hyperlink.

`.htm` or `.html` file An HTML file that is viewable in a web browser.

HTML (Hypertext Markup Language) A language that consists of paired and individual markup tags and is used to create web pages.

Hyperlink object An object that inserts a hyperlink, including the text and the link location.

id selector A type of CSS style that can be applied to a single item in a web page. An id selector name always begins with # and is applied using the `id` attribute.

image A file that contains graphical information and is loaded into a web page by a web browser. The HTML tag for an image is the single `<img/>` tag.

Image field An image that acts as a submit button in a form.

image map An image that has regions defined as hyperlinks. These regions can be circular, rectangular, or polygonal.

Image object An object that places an image in a web format at the insertion point.

Image Placeholder object An image that inserts a placeholder for an image to be added to the web page later.

inline style A CSS style that is defined within the actual tag.

Insert bar A Dreamweaver interface component that contains buttons for inserting objects into web pages. The Insert bar contains all the same objects as the Insert menu.

insertion point A blinking cursor that marks the location where new content is inserted into a web page.

invisible element A visible representation in Dreamweaver of an object that is not visible in the web page, such as forms and named anchors.

Java A programming language developed by Sun Microsystems that can be used to program applications and create applets.

JavaScript An interpreted scripting language originally developed by Netscape that is used to add scripted functionality to web pages. Dreamweaver inserts JavaScript automatically by using behaviors. JavaScript is not related to the Java programming language.

JPEG (or JPG) A standard web graphic format good for photographs and images containing color gradients.

JSP (JavaServer Pages) A scripting language that is embedded in web pages and processed by servlets on the server. This technology can be used on a variety of web servers.

jump menu A drop-down menu within a form that enables viewers to navigate to multiple hyperlinks on the Web.

Justify Align A setting that distributes the selected text across a container, such as a web page or a table cell, so it forms a clean left and right margin.

keyframe A special frame in an animation (a timeline in Dreamweaver) where attributes of an object can be changed.

keyword A type of meta tag that contains keywords used by search engines to index the content on the page.

label A text description that is added to a form element that contributes to an accessible web page.

LAN (local area network) A group of computers connected together to share data, applications, and other resources.

layer A container that has positioning, visibility, and z-index attributes. Layers are elements of DHTML, and they are used in Dreamweaver timelines (animations). Most layers are created by using the HTML tags `<div>` and `</div>`.

layer object An object that turns the cursor into a marquee tool to draw a layer onto the Document window.

Layout view A view in Dreamweaver that enables you to draw cells and tables.

Layout View button A button in the Insert bar that enables you to display tables with selectable cells, with tables outlined in green and cells outlined in blue.

Left Align A setting that aligns the selected text with the left margin of a container such as a web page or a table cell.

Library An Assets panel category that stores web page objects, such as tables, images, or blocks of formatted text, to reuse throughout a website.

Line Numbers A setting that turns on line numbers to the left of the lines of code in Code view.

List/Menu object An object that inserts a list or a drop-down menu into a form using the `<select></select>` tag.

Live Data view A view that is used in dynamic websites to display live data from a database in the Document window.

local site The development computer on which website files are located.

loop To repeat playing an audio clip or a movie file.

MacOS palette A palette consisting of the 256 colors in the Macintosh OS palette. This is not a web-safe palette.

meta tag An HTML tag that encodes information about a web page that is usually used to index the page in Internet search engines.

MIDI (musical instrument digital interface) A compact sound format for recording and playing back music on digital synthesizers.

`.mov` file An Apple QuickTime sound and movie file format that requires a player capable of playing QuickTime files.

`.mp3` file An audio file format that can create small, high-quality files. It is a popular audio format on the Internet.

multimedia A combination of multiple media, such as images, text, sounds, and video.

named anchor An invisible element that is used to create hyperlinks within a web page.

Named Anchor object An object that places a named anchor at the insertion point.

Navigation Bar object An object that inserts a set of button images to be used for navigating throughout a website.

nested list A list within another list.

nested table A table within another table.

NoFrames content HTML that is displayed when the viewer does not have a frames-capable browser.

Noscript A command that inserts the `<noscript></noscript>` tags around HTML code displayed by browsers that do not support scripts.

numbered list (or ordered list) A list of items preceded by numbers or letters. The HTML tags for an ordered list are `<ol>` and `</ol>`.

Page layout The design and positioning of text and images on a web page.

palette A set of colors available in Dreamweaver from the color picker.

panel group A set of panels that are grouped together in the Dreamweaver interface.

PDF (Portable Document Format) A file format for encoding printable documents with fonts and navigation elements. These files are created with Adobe Acrobat and are viewed through Acrobat Reader.

PHP (Hypertext Preprocessor) A scripting language embedded in web pages and processed by the server. This technology is freely available open source and can be used on a variety of web servers.

playback head An indicator that shows the current frame in a Dreamweaver timeline.

player A third-party program, in the plug-in or ActiveX format, used to display nonstandard content in a web browser.

Plugin object An object that places any file requiring a browser plug-in at the insertion point.

plug-in A type of player used in Netscape and other browsers to display nonstandard web content.

PNG (portable network graphic) A standard web graphic format developed to replace the GIF format. Like the GIF format, the PNG format is good for line art containing large blocks of color and offers advanced transparency options.

pop-up message A JavaScript alert message created by the Popup Message behavior in Dreamweaver.

Property inspector A panel that enables you to set properties for the selected object. The Property inspector presents the properties of whatever object is currently selected in the Document window.

protocol A method of transferring information over the Internet. Examples are HTTP for web pages and FTP for file transfer.

Quick Tag Editor An editor that enables you to edit the content of a single tag.

QuickTime Player A player created by Apple for viewing QuickTime sounds and movies, along with many other formats.

radio button A circular button inserted as a group into a form.

radio button group A group of radio buttons that acts as a mutually exclusive group, enabling only one button in the group to be selected at one time.

RDS (Remote Directory Services) A method of exchanging files on a ColdFusion server with a local site.

RealMedia Multimedia content encoded with one of the methods available from RealNetworks and played with a RealPlayer application.

relative path A type of path that does not contain all the information necessary to get to the object but instead creates an address relative to the object's location. A relative path can be relative to a document's location (*see* document-relative path) or the website (*see* site-root relative path).

remote site The website located on a remote computer, usually a web server or staging area where groups can share project files.

Right Align A setting that aligns the selected text with the right margin of a container such as a web page or a table cell.

rollover An image effect in which one image is swapped with another image when the cursor rolls over it.

Rollover Image object An object that contains two images. One is the regular image and the other is the image that appears when the user puts his cursor over the image.

row A horizontal group of cells in a table.

rule (CSS Rule) The pairing of a property and a value to define a selector in CSS (an example is `h1 {color:red}`). CSS styles can have multiple rules.

screen resolution The number of pixels displayed on the horizontal and vertical axes of a monitor screen. Common screen resolutions are 800×600 and 1024×768.

script A block of coded instructions.

Section 508 Compliance Section 508 of the U.S. Government's Rehabilitation Act of 1973 mandates that government sites using technology must be accessible to those with disabilities. Compliance with this law is required for those delivering technology-based products, such as websites, to the U.S. Government.

selector The part of a CSS style that selects the part of the web page to which to apply the selector's rules. Simple selectors are usually applied to individual HTML tags, id selectors are applied to objects with a certain `id` attribute, and class selectors are applied to objects with a certain `class` attribute.

server-side image map An image map in which the code is located on the server. The web page makes contact with the server to resolve the hyperlink. In Dreamweaver-generated client-side image maps, the map instructions are located within the web page.

server-side script A script that resides on a web server and executes on the server.

servlet A small program that runs on the server and processes script commands.

`.shtml` file A file that contains a server-side include.

Shockwave Specially prepared Macromedia Director movies that play in web pages by using the Shockwave player.

Shockwave object An object that places a Shockwave movie at the insertion point.

site definition The description of the configuration, directory structure, and preferences for a particular website.

Site Definition Wizard A Dreamweaver wizard that guides you through the naming and configuration of a site definition.

site root-relative path A path to a file that is relative to the root of a website. This type of path works only on a properly configured web server.

snippet Stored content that can easily be inserted into web pages. Snippets are stored and accessed from the Snippets panel in Dreamweaver and are a handy place to store chunks of code that are used often.

SSI (server-side include) A variable that is inserted into a web page and processed by a web server. A common use of an SSI is to load a header or footer from a separate file into the page at request time.

Standard view The view in Dreamweaver in which tables are displayed as grids and cannot be drawn.

Standard View button A button that displays tables as grids of cells.

static web pages Web pages that can be displayed without any additional processing by the server.

status bar The bar at the bottom of the Dreamweaver window containing the tag selector, the window size drop-down menu, and the document size.

`.swf` file A Flash file that is viewable in the Flash player. A `.swf` file cannot be edited in Flash.

table A data structure that is made up of rows and cells and is used to organize information or a page layout.

Table object An object that creates a table at the insertion point.

Tabular Data object An object that creates a table at the insertion point and that is populated with data from an imported data file.

tag An HTML element descriptor that is either a single tag or a pair of tags surrounding content. HTML tags are contained in angle brackets (for example, `<table>` and `</table>`).

tag selector An element in the Dreamweaver interface, located in the status bar, that presents the hierarchy of tags, enabling you to select a tag and its contents.

targeting Creating a link that loads a web page into a specific frame in a frameset. There are four target reserve words: _top, _self, _parent, and _blank. The _blank target opens the web page in a new browser window.

template A special type of web page that is used in Dreamweaver to create locked and editable regions. Templates enable you to control the layout of content and are designed to ensure consistency and ease of updating multiple web pages at one time.

text field A single-line form field for collecting text in a form.

textarea A multiline form field for collecting text in a form.

tiling When an image repeats within a web page or a container. The image repeats both horizontally and vertically.

title The name of a web page that appears in the title bar of the browser and is saved as a favorite or bookmark. The HTML tags for title are `<title>` and `</title>` and they are held in the head of the web page.

title bar The bar at the top of the window that contains the filename and other window controls.

URL (uniform resource locator) The address of a file accessible on the Internet.

V space The vertical space on the top and bottom of an image, measured in pixels.

VB (Visual Basic) A programming environment from Microsoft that is used to create code written in BASIC.

VBScript An interpreted scripting language that is a subset of Microsoft's Visual Basic language. VBScript is commonly used when scripting ASP code.

visibility An attribute of layers that enables the content of a layer to be either visible or hidden on the web page.

Visual Basic .NET The next generation of Visual Basic, used to write Windows applications, ASP.NET web applications, and ASP.NET web services. The primary alternative .NET language to Visual Basic .NET is C#.

VSS (Visual SourceSafe) A version-control program from Microsoft that is used to share files in a group.

web server Computer hardware where web pages are stored and accessed by others using a web browser.

W3C (World Wide Web Consortium) Group that develops standards and specifications for web technologies. W3C is a forum for information, commerce, communication, and collective understanding. The website is located at www.w3c.org.

web-safe palette A group of 212 colors that can be displayed in both Internet Explorer and Netscape on both Windows and the Macintosh machines running in 256-color mode (8-bit color).

WebDAV A standard version-control system used to exchange files over the Internet.

Windows Media Player A player created by Microsoft to view many formats of audio and video files.

Windows OS palette A palette that consists of the 256 colors in the Windows palette. This is not a web-safe palette.

Word Wrap A setting that wraps the lines of HTML code in Code view.

workspace The Dreamweaver user interface. In Dreamweaver for Windows there are two workspace choices: an integrated interface and a floating interface. The workspace on the Mac uses the floating interface.

WYSIWYG (what you see is what you get) A graphical interface that presents a web page that is very close to what appears in the web browser. Pronounced "wiz-ee-wig."

XHTML (Extensible Hypertext Markup Language) A more structured version of HTML that applies the strict syntax rules of XML to HTML. XHTML supports user-created tags for storing and structuring data within web pages. The default document type definition in Dreamweaver uses transitional XHTML and Dreamweaver inserts XHTML tags into web pages by default.

XML (Extensible Markup Language) A structured, tag-based language for describing data. XML describes data but not the way the data is to be displayed.

z-index An attribute of layers that enables the content of a layer to be stacked above objects with z-index attributes lower in value.

Index

SYMBOLS

A

C

D

E

F

G

H

I

J – K

L

M

N

Q – R

U

V

W